GLEIM®

2021 Q3-Q4 EDITION

CPA REVIEW

BUSINESS ENVIRONMENT & CONCEPTS

by

Irvin N. Gleim, Ph.D., CPA, CIA, CMA, CFM

and

Garrett W. Gleim, CPA, CGMA

with the assistance of
Grady M. Irwin, J.D.

Gleim Publications, Inc.
PO Box 12848
Gainesville, Florida 32604
(800) 87-GLEIM or (800) 874-5346
(352) 375-0772
www.gleim.com/cpa
CPA@gleim.com

> For updates to this 2021 Q3-Q4 edition of
> *CPA Review: Business Environment and Concepts*
>
> **Go To:** www.gleim.com/CPAupdate
>
> **Or:** Email update@gleim.com with **CPA BEC 2021 Q3-Q4** in the subject line. You will receive our current update as a reply.
>
> Updates are available until the next edition is published.

ISSN: 1547-8084

ISBN: 978-1-61854-430-8 *CPA Review: Auditing and Attestation*
ISBN: 978-1-61854-431-5 *CPA Review: Business Environment and Concepts*
ISBN: 978-1-61854-432-2 *CPA Review: Financial Accounting and Reporting*
ISBN: 978-1-61854-433-9 *CPA Review: Regulation*
ISBN: 978-1-61854-394-3 *CPA Exam Guide: A System for Success*

This edition is copyright © 2021 by Gleim Publications, Inc. Portions of this manuscript are taken from previous editions copyright © 1994-2020 by Gleim Publications, Inc.

First Printing: April 2021

ALL RIGHTS RESERVED. No part of this material may be reproduced in any form whatsoever without express written permission from Gleim Publications, Inc. Reward is offered for information exposing violators. Contact copyright@gleim.com.

ACKNOWLEDGMENTS

Material from *Uniform CPA Examination, Selected Questions and Unofficial Answers*, Copyright © 1974-2021 by the American Institute of Certified Public Accountants, Inc., is reprinted and/or adapted with permission. Visit the AICPA's website at www.aicpa.org for more information.

The author is indebted to the Institute of Certified Management Accountants for permission to use problem materials from past CMA Examinations. Questions and unofficial answers from the Certified Management Accountant Examinations, copyright by the Institute of Certified Management Accountants, are reprinted and/or adapted with permission.

The author is grateful for permission to reproduce Certified Internal Auditor Examination Questions, Copyright © 1991-2021 by The Institute of Internal Auditors, Inc.

> **Environmental Statement** -- This book is printed on recycled paper sourced from suppliers certified using sustainable forestry management processes and is produced either TCF (Totally Chlorine-Free) or ECF (Elementally Chlorine-Free).

The publications and online services of Gleim Publications and Gleim Internet are designed to provide accurate and authoritative information with regard to the subject matter covered. They are sold with the understanding that Gleim Publications and Gleim Internet, and their respective licensors, are not engaged in rendering legal, accounting, tax, or other professional advice or services. If legal advice or other expert assistance is required, the services of a competent professional person should be sought.

You assume all responsibilities and obligations with respect to the selection of the particular publication or online services to achieve your intended results. You assume all responsibilities and obligations with respect to any decisions or advice made or given as a result of the use or application of your selected publication or online services or any content retrieved therefrom, including those to any third party, for the content, accuracy, and review of such results.

The events, persons, and locations depicted in this book are fictional and not intended to portray, resemble, or represent any actual events or places, or persons, living or dead. Any such resemblance or similarity is entirely coincidental.

ABOUT THE AUTHORS

Irvin N. Gleim is Professor Emeritus in the Fisher School of Accounting at the University of Florida and is a member of the American Accounting Association, Academy of Legal Studies in Business, American Institute of Certified Public Accountants, Association of Government Accountants, Florida Institute of Certified Public Accountants, The Institute of Internal Auditors, and the Institute of Management Accountants. He has had articles published in the *Journal of Accountancy*, *The Accounting Review*, and the *American Business Law Journal* and is author/coauthor of numerous accounting books, aviation books, and CPE courses.

Garrett W. Gleim, CPA, CGMA, leads production of the Gleim CPA, CMA, CIA, and EA exam review systems. He is a member of the American Institute of Certified Public Accountants and the Florida Institute of Certified Public Accountants and holds a Bachelor of Science in Economics with a Concentration in Accounting from The Wharton School, University of Pennsylvania. Mr. Gleim is coauthor of numerous accounting and aviation books and the inventor of multiple patents with educational applications. He is also an avid pilot who holds a commercial pilot rating and is a certified flight instructor. In addition, as an active supporter of the local business community, Mr. Gleim serves as an advisor to several start-ups.

A PERSONAL THANKS

This manual would not have been possible without the extraordinary effort and dedication of Jacob Bennett, Julie Cutlip, Ethan Good, Doug Green, Fernanda Martinez, Bree Rodriguez, Veronica Rodriguez, Teresa Soard, Justin Stephenson, Joanne Strong, Elmer Tucker, Candace Van Doren, and Ryan Van Tress, who typed the entire manuscript and all revisions and drafted and laid out the diagrams, illustrations, and cover for this book.

The authors also appreciate the production and editorial assistance of Sirene Dagher, Michaela Giampaolo, Jessica Hatker, Sonora Hospital-Medina, Katie Larson, Michael Lupi, Bryce Owen, Shane Rapp, Michael Tamayo, Alyssa Thomas, and Valerie Wendt.

The authors also appreciate the critical reading assistance of Ali Band, Corey Connell, Adrianna Cuevas, Kimberly Haft, Nicola Martens, Martin Salazar, and Maris Silvestri.

The authors also appreciate the video production expertise of Nancy Boyd, Gary Brook, Philip Brubaker, Matthew Church, Andrew Johnson, and Michaela Wallace, who helped produce and edit our Gleim Instruct Video Series.

Finally, we appreciate the encouragement, support, and tolerance of our families throughout this project.

REVIEWERS AND CONTRIBUTORS

Amy Ford, CPA, CMA, is a Senior Instructor of Accountancy at Western Illinois University, where she teaches principles of financial and managerial accounting courses as well as advanced managerial accounting and accounting for managers in the MBA program. Prior to teaching, she worked in public accounting for 4 years. Professor Ford is one of the CPA Gleim Instruct lecturers.

William A. Hillison, Ph.D., CPA, CMA, is a Professor Emeritus of Accounting at Florida State University. His primary teaching duties included graduate and undergraduate auditing and systems courses. Dr. Hillison provided substantial editorial assistance throughout the project.

Grady M. Irwin, J.D., is a graduate of the University of Florida College of Law, and he has taught in the University of Florida College of Business. Mr. Irwin provided substantial editorial assistance throughout the project.

Michael Kustanovich, M.A., CPA, is a Clinical Assistant Professor in the Department of Accountancy at the University of Illinois at Urbana-Champaign. He teaches advanced financial accounting courses at both the undergraduate and graduate levels, and he is the instructor of the CPA Exam Review Course there. Mr. Kustanovich provided substantial editorial assistance throughout the project.

Lung-Chih Lin, M.S. Acc., received a Master of Science in Accountancy with a concentration in Data Analytics from the University of Illinois at Urbana-Champaign. Mr. Lin provided editorial assistance throughout the project.

Mark S. Modas, M.S.T., CPA, holds a Bachelor of Arts in Accounting from Florida Atlantic University and a Master of Science in Taxation from Nova Southeastern University. Prior to joining Gleim, he worked in internal auditing, accounting and financial reporting, and corporate tax compliance in the public and private sectors. Mr. Modas provided substantial editorial assistance throughout the project.

J. Daniel Sinclair, M.S. Acc., CPA, received a Master of Science in Accountancy from the University of Florida and has 5 years of public accounting experience in risk consulting and tax advisory. Mr. Sinclair provided substantial editorial assistance throughout the project.

Chun Nam Wo, M.S. Acc., CPA, received a Master of Science in Accountancy with a concentration in Data Analytics from the University of Illinois at Urbana-Champaign. Mr. Wo provided substantial editorial assistance throughout the project.

Returns of books purchased from bookstores and other resellers should be made to the respective bookstore or reseller. For more information regarding the Gleim Return Policy, please contact our offices at (800) 874-5346 or visit www.gleim.com/returnpolicy.

ACCOUNTING TITLES FROM GLEIM PUBLICATIONS

Exam Questions and Explanations (EQE) Series:
- Auditing & Systems
- Business Law & Legal Studies
- Cost/Managerial Accounting
- Federal Tax
- Financial Accounting

CPA Review:
- Auditing & Attestation (AUD)
- Business Environment & Concepts (BEC)
- Financial Accounting & Reporting (FAR)
- Regulation (REG)

CMA Review:
- Part 1: Financial Planning, Performance, and Analytics
- Part 2: Strategic Financial Management

CIA Review:
- Part 1: Essentials of Internal Auditing
- Part 2: Practice of Internal Auditing
- Part 3: Business Knowledge for Internal Auditing

EA Review:
- Part 1: Individuals
- Part 2: Businesses
- Part 3: Representation, Practices and Procedures

Gleim Publications also publishes aviation training materials. Go to www.GleimAviation.com for a complete listing of our aviation titles.

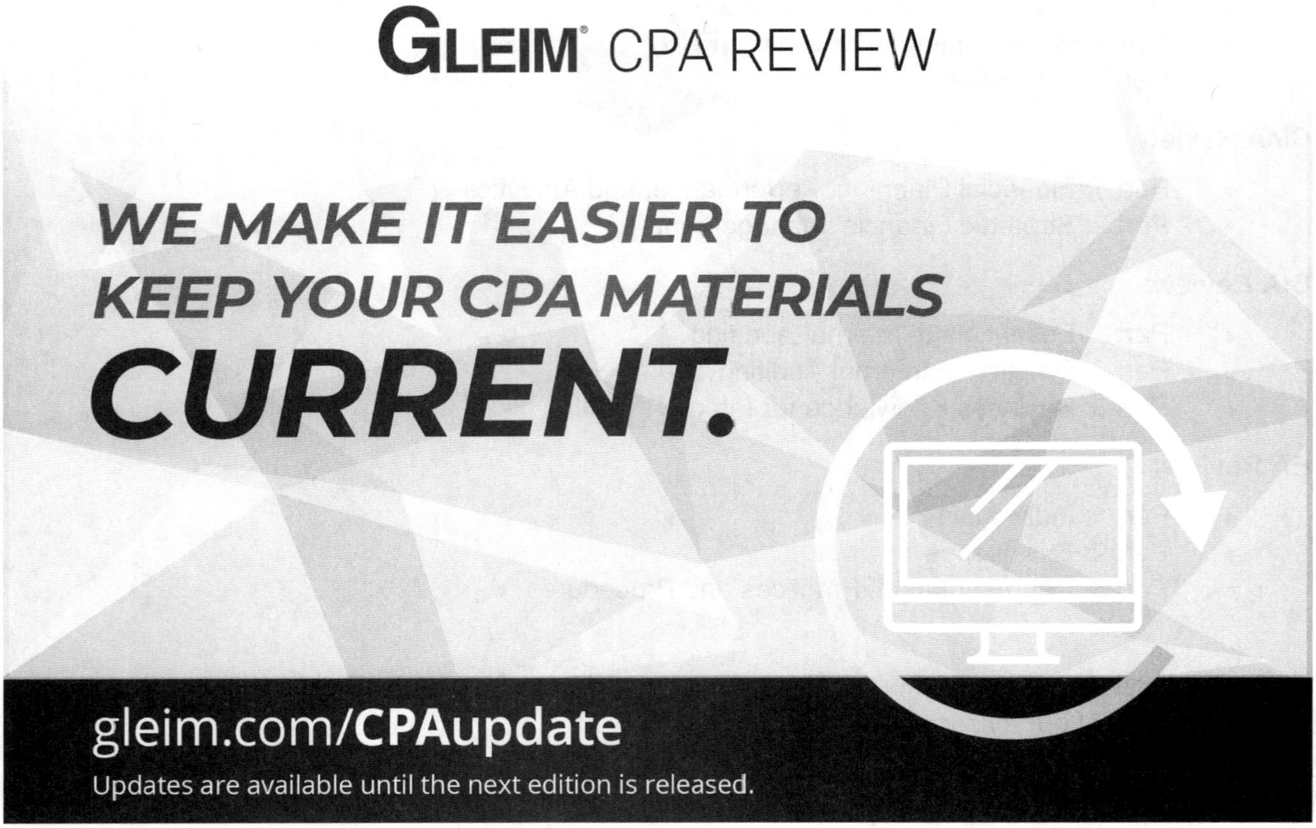
GLEIM® CPA REVIEW
WE MAKE IT EASIER TO
KEEP YOUR CPA MATERIALS
CURRENT.
gleim.com/CPAupdate
Updates are available until the next edition is released.

TABLE OF CONTENTS

	Page
Detailed Table of Contents	viii
A Message from Our Authors	x
Optimizing Your Business Environment and Concepts Score	1
Study Unit 1. Business Processes, Risks, and Internal Control	11
Study Unit 2. Accounting Cycles and Corporate Governance	41
Study Unit 3. COSO Enterprise Risk Management Framework	77
Study Unit 4. Microeconomics	105
Study Unit 5. Macroeconomics and Globalization	147
Study Unit 6. Foreign Exchange and Derivatives	181
Study Unit 7. Financial Risk Management	211
Study Unit 8. Corporate Capital Structure	239
Study Unit 9. Working Capital I: Cash and Receivables	271
Study Unit 10. Working Capital II: Inventory and Short-Term Financing	291
Study Unit 11. Capital Budgeting	313
Study Unit 12. IT Roles, Systems, and Processing	347
Study Unit 13. IT Software, Data, and Contingency Planning	381
Study Unit 14. IT Networks and Electronic Commerce	415
Study Unit 15. IT Security and Controls	435
Study Unit 16. Performance Measurement and Process Management	471
Study Unit 17. Costing Fundamentals	505
Study Unit 18. Costing Systems and Decision Making	531
Study Unit 19. Budgeting and Variance Analysis	567
Study Unit 20. Data Analytics	599
Appendix A: Acronyms	637
Appendix B: Optimizing Your Score on the Task-Based Simulations (TBSs) and Written Communications (WCs)	639
Appendix C: AICPA Uniform CPA Examination BEC Blueprint with Gleim Cross-References	669
Index	683

DETAILED TABLE OF CONTENTS

		Page
Study Unit 1.	Business Processes, Risks, and Internal Control	
1.1.	Business Processes	11
1.2.	Business Process Risks	15
1.3.	COSO Internal Control – Integrated Framework	18
1.4.	Internal Control and Fraud	31
Study Unit 2.	Accounting Cycles and Corporate Governance	
2.1.	Accounting Cycles and Transaction-Level Controls	42
2.2.	Corporate Governance Structure	56
2.3.	The Sarbanes-Oxley Act of 2002 (SOX)	61
2.4.	System and Organization Controls (SOC) for Service Organizations	65
Study Unit 3.	COSO Enterprise Risk Management Framework	
3.1.	Enterprise Risk Management (ERM)	78
3.2.	Applying the ERM Framework to Cyber Risk Management	94
Study Unit 4.	Microeconomics	
4.1.	Demand, Supply, and Equilibrium	105
4.2.	Elasticity	113
4.3.	Government Action in the Market and Wages	116
4.4.	Profits and Costs	119
4.5.	Marginal Analysis	121
4.6.	Market Structures -- Pure Competition	127
4.7.	Market Structures -- Monopoly	131
4.8.	Market Structures -- Monopolistic Competition	133
4.9.	Market Structures -- Oligopoly	134
Study Unit 5.	Macroeconomics and Globalization	
5.1.	Business Cycles	148
5.2.	Inflation	150
5.3.	Unemployment	153
5.4.	Demand Management through Fiscal Policy	155
5.5.	The Creation of Money	157
5.6.	Monetary Policy	161
5.7.	Globalization	163
5.8.	Protectionism	168
Study Unit 6.	Foreign Exchange and Derivatives	
6.1.	Currency Exchange Rates	181
6.2.	Derivatives	191
6.3.	Mitigating Exchange Rate Risk	198
Study Unit 7.	Financial Risk Management	
7.1.	Risk and Return	211
7.2.	Linear Regression and Correlation Analysis	216
7.3.	Quantifying Investment Risk	220
7.4.	Capital Asset Pricing Model (CAPM)	224
7.5.	Selecting the Forecasting Method	226

		Page
Study Unit 8.	Corporate Capital Structure	
8.1.	Bonds	240
8.2.	Equity	246
8.3.	Capital Structure and Solvency	250
8.4.	Component Costs of Capital	252
8.5.	Expected Value	255
8.6.	Weighted-Average Cost of Capital	257
Study Unit 9.	Working Capital I: Cash and Receivables	
9.1.	Working Capital Management	271
9.2.	Liquidity Ratios -- Calculation	275
9.3.	Liquidity Ratios -- Effects of Transactions	278
9.4.	Receivables Management	279
Study Unit 10.	Working Capital II: Inventory and Short-Term Financing	
10.1.	Inventory Management -- Methods	292
10.2.	Inventory Management -- Ratios	295
10.3.	The Operating Cycle and Cash Conversion Cycle	298
10.4.	Multiple Ratio Analysis	300
10.5.	Short-Term Financing	301
Study Unit 11.	Capital Budgeting	
11.1.	Capital Budgeting -- Basics	313
11.2.	Capital Budgeting -- Net Present Value (NPV)	319
11.3.	Capital Budgeting -- Internal Rate of Return (IRR)	327
11.4.	Capital Budgeting -- Payback Methods	329
11.5.	Ranking Capital Projects	331
11.6.	Comparison of Capital Budgeting Methods	333
Study Unit 12.	IT Roles, Systems, and Processing	
12.1.	Roles and Responsibilities within the IT Function	347
12.2.	Role of Information Systems in the Modern Organization	350
12.3.	IT Governance -- Vision and Strategy	353
12.4.	Transaction Processing	356
12.5.	Application Processing Phases	358
12.6.	Systems that Support Routine Processes	362
12.7.	Systems that Support Decision Making	366
Study Unit 13.	IT Software, Data, and Contingency Planning	
13.1.	Software	381
13.2.	Nature of Binary Data Storage	384
13.3.	Data Management	386
13.4.	Database Management Systems	391
13.5.	Application Development and Maintenance	393
13.6.	Business Resiliency	402
Study Unit 14.	IT Networks and Electronic Commerce	
14.1.	Networks and the Internet	415
14.2.	Electronic Commerce	420
14.3.	Electronic Data Interchange (EDI)	424

Detailed Table of Contents

	Page

Study Unit 15. IT Security and Controls
- 15.1. Risks Associated with Business Information Systems 435
- 15.2. COBIT -- A Framework for IT and Data Governance 438
- 15.3. Implementing the Cybersecurity Framework Using COBIT 2019 447
- 15.4. Electronic Transmission Security 450
- 15.5. Information Security 451
- 15.6. General Controls 455
- 15.7. Application Controls 459

Study Unit 16. Performance Measurement and Process Management
- 16.1. Responsibility Centers 471
- 16.2. Performance Measurement -- Financial and Nonfinancial Measures 475
- 16.3. Performance Measurement -- Balanced Scorecard 481
- 16.4. Process Management 484
- 16.5. Tools for Process Management 488
- 16.6. Costs of Quality 492
- 16.7. TQM and the ISO Framework 493

Study Unit 17. Costing Fundamentals
- 17.1. Cost Measurement Terminology 505
- 17.2. Basic Cost Calculations 507
- 17.3. Other Cost Measurement Concepts . . . 508
- 17.4. Absorption Costing and Variable Costing 511
- 17.5. Joint Product and By-Product Costing . . 520
- 17.6. Joint Cost Allocation Methods 522

Study Unit 18. Costing Systems and Decision Making
- 18.1. Job-Order Costing and Overhead Application 532
- 18.2. Process Costing 537
- 18.3. Activity-Based Costing (ABC) 543
- 18.4. Cost-Volume-Profit Analysis 548
- 18.5. Management Decision Making 553

Study Unit 19. Budgeting and Variance Analysis
- 19.1. Standard Costs 567
- 19.2. The Master Budget and Its Components 569
- 19.3. The Operating Budget 571
- 19.4. The Financial Budget 575
- 19.5. Flexible Budgeting and Variance Analysis 578
- 19.6. Variance Analysis -- Materials and Labor 581
- 19.7. Variance Analysis -- Overhead 584
- 19.8. Sales Variances 590

Study Unit 20. Data Analytics
- 20.1. Definitions: Data Analytics 599
- 20.2. Big Data and Data Analytics 600
- 20.3. Implementing Data Analytics 605
- 20.4. Data Visualization 608

A MESSAGE FROM OUR AUTHORS

Welcome to the 2021 Q3-Q4 Edition of Gleim CPA Review! The purpose of this book is to facilitate your preparation to pass the Business Environment and Concepts (BEC) section of the CPA Exam.

The CPA Exam is continuously changed in order to maintain its relevance and prestige in the world of accounting. As technology develops, accountants and auditors face new and increasingly complex challenges, which are reflected in the AICPA Blueprints. Our team of accounting experts ensures our materials are always up-to-date, so regardless of when you're preparing for the CPA Exam with Gleim, you have everything you need to succeed.

Our goal is to provide a comprehensive, effective, affordable, and easy-to-use study program. Our course

1. Explains how to maximize your score through learning strategies and exam-taking techniques.
2. Outlines all of the content topics described in the AICPA BEC Blueprint and tested on the BEC section of the exam in 20 easy-to-use study units.
3. Presents multiple-choice questions taken or modeled from CPA Examinations to prepare you for the types of questions you will find on your CPA Exam.
   a. In our book, the answer explanations are presented to the immediate right of each multiple-choice question for your convenience. Use a piece of paper to cover our detailed explanations as you answer the question and then review all answer choices to learn why the correct one is correct and why the other choices are incorrect.
   b. You also should practice answering these questions through our online platform, which mimics Prometric's user interface, so you are comfortable answering questions online like you will do on test day. Our adaptive course will focus and target your weak areas.
4. Contains an appendix explaining the different types of Task-Based Simulations (TBSs) and how to get the most points possible on the TBS testlets.

The outline format, spacing, and question and answer formats in this book are designed to increase readability, learning, understanding, and success on the CPA Exam. Our most successful candidates use the Gleim Premium CPA Review System, which includes Gleim Instruct videos; our Access Until You Pass Guarantee; our innovative SmartAdapt technology; expertly authored books; the largest test bank of multiple-choice questions and simulations; audio lectures; flashcards; and the support of our team of accounting experts.

Since the release of our first CPA Review book in 1974, Gleim has helped candidates pass more than 1 million CPA Exams with our study materials and recommended learning techniques. With our cutting-edge adaptive technology creating personalized learning paths, we will help candidates pass millions more. Candidates' success is based on the Gleim system of teaching not only the topics tested, but also what you can expect on exam day. We want you to feel confident and in control when you sit for the exam.

We want your feedback immediately after you take the exam and receive your exam score. Please go to www.gleim.com/feedbackBEC to share suggestions on how we can improve this edition. The CPA Exam is a **nondisclosed** exam, which means you must maintain the confidentiality of the exam by not divulging the nature or content of any CPA question or answer under any circumstances. We ask only for information about our materials and any improvements that can be made regarding topics that need to be added or expanded or need more emphasis. Our approach has AICPA approval.

Good Luck on the Exam,

– Dr. Irvin N. Gleim   – Garrett W. Gleim

April 2021

OPTIMIZING YOUR BUSINESS ENVIRONMENT AND CONCEPTS SCORE

Uniform CPA Examination	1
Gleim Premium CPA Review with SmartAdapt	2
Subject Matter for Business Environment and Concepts	3
Which Laws, Rules, and Pronouncements Are Tested?	4
AICPA's Nondisclosure Agreement	5
Gleim CPA Review Essentials	6
Time Budgeting and Question-Answering Techniques for BEC	7
How to Be in Control	9
Questions about Gleim Materials	9
Feedback	9

UNIFORM CPA EXAMINATION

CPA Exam Section	Auditing & Attestation	**Business Environment & Concepts**	Financial Accounting & Reporting	Regulation
Acronym	AUD	**BEC**	FAR	REG
Exam Length	4 hours	**4 hours**	4 hours	4 hours
Testlet 1: Multiple-Choice	36 questions	**31 questions**	33 questions	38 questions
Testlet 2: Multiple-Choice	36 questions	**31 questions**	33 questions	38 questions
Testlet 3: Task-Based Simulations	2 tasks	**2 tasks**	2 tasks	2 tasks
Standardized Break	Clock stops for 15 minutes			
Testlet 4: Task-Based Simulations	3 tasks	**2 tasks**	3 tasks	3 tasks
Testlet 5: Task-Based Simulations or Written Communications	3 tasks	**3 written communications**	3 tasks	3 tasks

Passing the CPA Exam is a serious undertaking. Begin by becoming an expert in the content, formatting, and functionality of the BEC exam before you take it. The objective is no surprises on exam day. Also, you will save time and money, decrease frustration, and increase your probability of success by learning all you can about how to prepare for and take BEC.

Review *CPA Exam Guide: A System for Success* at www.gleim.com/PassCPA for a complete explanation of how to prepare for and take each section of the CPA Exam. This free guide includes all of the basic information, test-taking techniques, and time management strategies you need.

More exam tactics and information, as well as breaking news and updates from the AICPA and NASBA, are available in our Resource Center at www.gleim.com/CPAresources and on our blog at www.gleim.com/CPAblog. Follow us on all your favorite social media networks for blog updates and other critical information.

CPA Exam Pass Rates

	Percentage of Candidates		
	2018	2019	2020
AUD	52	51	53
BEC	58	60	66
FAR	45	46	50
REG	53	56	62

The implication of these pass rates for you as a CPA candidate is that you have to be, on average, in the top 50% of all candidates to pass. The major difference between CPA candidates who pass and those who do not is their preparation program. You have access to the best CPA review material; it is up to you to use it. Even if you are enrolled in a review course that uses other materials, you will benefit with the Gleim Premium CPA Review System.

GLEIM PREMIUM CPA REVIEW WITH SMARTADAPT

Gleim Premium CPA Review features the most comprehensive coverage of exam content and employs the most efficient learning techniques to help you study smarter and more effectively. The Gleim Premium CPA Review System is powered by SmartAdapt technology, an innovative platform that continually zeros in on areas you should focus on when you move through the following steps for optimized CPA review:

Step 1:

Complete a diagnostic study session. Your results set a baseline that our SmartAdapt technology will use to create a custom learning track.

Step 2:

Solidify your knowledge by studying the suggested Knowledge Transfer Outline(s) or watching the suggested Gleim Instruct video(s).

Step 3:

Focus on weak areas and perfect your question-answering techniques by taking the adaptive quizzes and simulations that SmartAdapt directs you to.

Final Review:

After completing all study units, take the first Exam Rehearsal. Then, SmartAdapt will walk you through a Final Review based on your results. Finally, a few days before your exam date, take the second Exam Rehearsal so you feel confident that you are ready to pass.

To facilitate your studies, the Gleim Premium CPA Review System uses the most comprehensive test bank of exam-quality CPA questions on the market. Our system's content and presentation are the most realistic representation of the whole exam environment so you feel completely at ease on test day.

Learning from Your Mistakes

One of the main building blocks of the Gleim studying system is that learning from questions you answer incorrectly is very important. Each question you answer incorrectly is an **opportunity** to avoid missing actual test questions on your CPA Exam. Thus, you should carefully study the answer explanations provided so you understand why the original answer you chose is wrong as well as why the correct answer indicated is correct. This learning technique is the difference between passing and failing for many CPA candidates.

The Gleim Premium CPA Review System has built-in functionality for this step. After each quiz and simulation you complete, the Gleim system directs you to study why you answered questions incorrectly so you can learn how to avoid making the same errors in the future. Reasons for answering questions incorrectly include

1. Misreading the requirement (stem)
2. Not understanding what is required
3. Making a math error
4. Applying the wrong rule or concept
5. Being distracted by one or more of the answers
6. Incorrectly eliminating answers from consideration
7. Not having any knowledge of the topic tested
8. Using a poor educated-guessing strategy

SUBJECT MATTER FOR BUSINESS ENVIRONMENT AND CONCEPTS

Below, we have provided the AICPA's major content areas from the Blueprint for Business Environment and Concepts (BEC). The averaged percentage of coverage for each topic is indicated.

   I. (25%) Enterprise Risk Management, Internal Controls, and Business Processes
  II. (20%) Economics
 III. (15%) Financial Management
 IV. (20%) Information Technology
  V. (20%) Operations Management

Appendix C contains the Blueprint for BEC as well as cross-references to the study units in our materials where topics are covered. Remember that we have studied and restudied the Blueprint and explain the subject matter thoroughly in our CPA Review. Accordingly, you do not need to spend time with Appendix C. Rather, it should give you confidence that Gleim CPA Review is the best review available to help you PASS the CPA Exam.

The BEC section tests knowledge and skills necessary to demonstrate an understanding of the general business environment and business concepts in performing audit, attest, accounting, and review services; financial reporting; tax preparation; and other professional services.

To demonstrate the knowledge and skills associated with the business environment and concepts, the following general topics will be tested:

- Internal control frameworks and enterprise risk management frameworks:
    - Purpose and objectives and
    - Components and principles
- Key corporate governance provisions of the Sarbanes-Oxley Act of 2002
- Business processes, flows, and controls
- Market influences on the business environment
- Transactions:
    - Business reasons,
    - Underlying economic substance, and
    - Accounting implications
- Factors influencing a company's capital structure
- Calculation of metrics associated with the components of working capital
- Impact of business decisions on working capital
- Commonly used financial valuation and decision models
- Governance of information technology operations
- Information systems used to process and accumulate data and provide monitoring and financial reporting information
- Risks and controls over information technology
- Inherent risks in disaster recovery and business continuity plans
- Performance measurement and process management
- Cost accounting concepts and variance analysis techniques
- Budgeting and forecasting techniques

WHICH LAWS, RULES, AND PRONOUNCEMENTS ARE TESTED?

The following is the AICPA's pronouncement policy:

Changes in accounting and auditing pronouncements are eligible to be tested on the Uniform CPA Examination in the later of: (1) the first calendar quarter beginning after the pronouncement's earliest mandatory effective date, regardless of entity type* or (2) the first calendar quarter beginning six (6) months after the pronouncement's issuance date.

Changes in the Internal Revenue Code, and federal taxation regulations are eligible to be tested in the calendar quarter beginning six (6) months after the change's effective date or enactment date, whichever is later.

Changes in federal laws outside the area of federal taxation are eligible to be tested in the calendar quarter beginning six (6) months after their effective date.

Changes in uniform acts are eligible to be tested in the calendar quarter beginning one (1) year after their adoption by a simple majority of the jurisdictions.

For all other subjects covered in the Uniform CPA Examination, changes are eligible to be tested in the later of: (1) the first calendar quarter beginning after the earliest mandatory effective date, regardless of entity type* or (2) six (6) months after the issuance date.

Once a change becomes eligible for testing in the Uniform CPA Examination, previous content impacted by the change is removed. [This simply means that once a new pronouncement is testable, you will no longer be tested on the old pronouncement.]

* Note the following example: A pronouncement issued on February 1, 2020, is effective for public business entities for fiscal years beginning after December 15, 2020, and is effective for all other entities for fiscal years beginning after December 15, 2021. For purposes of the Uniform CPA Examination: (1) the pronouncement is eligible for testing on January 1, 2021 for all entity types and (2) the prior pronouncement is deemed superseded and no longer eligible for testing as of January 1, 2021.

AICPA's NONDISCLOSURE AGREEMENT

As part of the AICPA's nondisclosure policy and to prove each candidate's willingness to adhere to this policy, a confidentiality and break policy statement must be accepted by each candidate during the introductory screens at the beginning of each exam. Nonacceptance of this policy means the exam will be terminated and the test fees will be forfeited. This statement from the AICPA's Sample Test is reproduced here to remind all CPA candidates about the AICPA's strict policy of nondisclosure, which Gleim consistently supports and upholds.

"Policy Statement and Confidentiality Agreement

I hereby agree that I will maintain the confidentiality of the Uniform CPA Exam.
In addition, I agree that I will not:

- Divulge the nature or content of any Uniform CPA Exam question or answer under any circumstances
- Engage in any unauthorized communication during testing
- Refer to unauthorized materials or use unauthorized equipment during testing
- Remove or attempt to remove any Uniform CPA Exam materials, notes, or any other items from the exam room

I understand and agree that liability for test administration activities, including but not limited to the adequacy or accuracy of test materials and equipment, and the accuracy of scoring and score reporting, will be limited to score correction or test retake at no additional fee. I waive any and all right to all other claims. I further agree to report to the AICPA any exam question disclosures, or solicitations for disclosure, of which I become aware.

I affirm that I have had the opportunity to read the Candidate Bulletin and I agree to all of its terms and conditions.

I understand that breaks are only allowed between testlets. I understand that I will be asked to complete any open testlet before leaving the testing room for a break. In addition, I understand that failure to comply with this Policy statement and Confidentiality Agreement could result in the invalidation of my scores, disqualification from future exams, expulsion from the testing facility, and possibly civil or criminal penalties."

GLEIM CPA REVIEW ESSENTIALS

Gleim CPA Review has the following features to make studying easier:

1. **Backgrounds:** In certain instances, we have provided historical background or supplemental information. This information is intended to illuminate the topic under discussion and is set off in bordered boxes with shaded headings. This material does not need to be memorized for the exam.

BACKGROUND 12-1   ERP Packages

Because ERP software is costly and complex, it is usually installed only by the largest enterprises, although mid-size organizations are increasingly likely to buy ERP software. Major ERP packages include SAP ERP Central Component from SAP SE and Oracle e-Business Suite, PeopleSoft, and JD Edwards EnterpriseOne, all from Oracle Corp.

---

2. **Examples:** Illustrative examples, both hypothetical and those drawn from actual events, are set off in shaded, bordered boxes.

EXAMPLE 5-8   Reserve Ratio and Money Supply

If the Fed requires reserves of 4% on all deposits, a bank with $10 million on deposit can create $250 million of new money [$10,000,000 × (1.0 ÷ .04)].

---

3. **Gleim Success Tips:** These tips supplement the core exam material by suggesting how certain topics might be presented on the exam or how you should prepare for an issue.

> **SUCCESS TIP:** The AICPA frequently tests the inherent limitations of internal control. Be able to identify the basic limitations.

4. **Memory Aids:** These mnemonic devices are designed to assist you in memorizing important concepts.

    The following is a useful memory aid for the COSO categories of objectives:

    O = **O**perations
    R = **R**eporting
    C = **C**ompliance

5. **Detailed Table of Contents:** This information at the beginning of the book is a complete listing of all study units and subunits in the Gleim CPA BEC Review program. Use this list as a study aid to mark off your progress and to provide jumping-off points for review.

6. **Listing of Acronyms:** Appendix A contains a glossary of common BEC-related acronyms.

7. **Optimizing Your Score on the Task-Based Simulations (TBSs) and Written Communications (WCs):** Appendix B explains how to approach and allocate your time for the TBS and WC testlets. It also presents several example TBSs and WCs for your review.

8. **Blueprint with Gleim Cross-References:** Appendix C contains a reprint of the AICPA Blueprint for BEC along with cross-references to the corresponding Gleim study units.

9. **Core Concepts:** We have also provided additional study materials to supplement the Knowledge Transfer Outlines in the digital Gleim CPA Review Course. The Core Concepts, for example, are consolidated documents providing an overview of the key points of each subunit that serve as the foundation for learning. As part of your review, you should make sure that you understand each of them.

TIME BUDGETING AND QUESTION-ANSWERING TECHNIQUES FOR BEC

To begin the exam, you will enter your Launch Code on the Welcome screen. If you do not enter the correct code within 5 minutes of the screen appearing, the exam session will end.

Next, you will have an additional 5 minutes to view a brief exam introduction containing two screens: the nondisclosure policy and a section information screen. Accept the policy and then review the information screen, but be sure to click the Begin Exam button on the bottom right of the screen within the allotted 5 minutes. If you fail to do so, the exam will be terminated and you will not have the option to restart your exam.

These 10 minutes, along with the 5 minutes you may spend on a post-exam survey, are not included in the 240 minutes of exam time.

Once you complete the introductory screens and begin your exam, expect two testlets of 31 multiple-choice questions (MCQs) each, two testlets of Task-Based Simulations (each with 2 TBSs), and one testlet with 3 written communication (WC) tasks. You will have 240 minutes to complete the five testlets.

1. **Budget your time so you can finish before time expires.**

    a. Here is our suggested time allocation for BEC:

	Minutes	Start Time
Testlet 1 (MCQ)	38*	4 hours 00 minutes
Testlet 2 (MCQ)	38*	3 hours 22 minutes
Testlet 3 (TBS)	36	2 hour 44 minutes
Break	15	Clock stops
Testlet 4 (TBS)	36	2 hours 08 minutes
Testlet 5 (WC)	75	1 hour 32 minutes
**Extra time	17	0 hour 17 minutes

    *Rounded down

    b. Before beginning your first MCQ testlet, prepare a Gleim Time Management plan as recommended in *CPA Exam Guide: A System for Success*.

    c. As you work through the individual questions, monitor your time. In BEC, we suggest 38 minutes (1.25 minutes per question) for each testlet of 31 MCQs. If you answer five items in 6 minutes, you are fine, but if you spend 8 minutes on five items, you need to speed up. In the TBS testlets, spend no more than 18 minutes on each TBS. For more information on TBS time budgets, refer to Appendix B, "Optimizing Your Score on the Task-Based Simulations (TBSs) and Written Communications (WCs)." In the fifth testlet, spend 20 minutes or less on completing each WC, then 5 minutes or less reviewing each response.

    **BEC candidates may prefer to allocate more time to the TBSs and reduce the 17 minutes of extra review time after the WCs. In this case, we suggest 20 minutes per TBS, for a total time of 40 minutes in Testlet 3 and 40 minutes in Testlet 4, leaving 9 minutes of final review after the WCs.

    Remember to allocate your budgeted extra time, as needed, to each testlet.
    Your goal is to answer all of the items and achieve the maximum score possible. As you practice answering TBSs and WCs in the Gleim Premium CPA Review System, you will be practicing your time management.

2. **Answer the questions in consecutive order.**
   a. Do not agonize over any one question. **Stay within your time budget.**
   b. Never leave an MCQ unanswered. Your score is based on the number of correct responses. You will not be penalized for answering incorrectly. If you are unsure about a question,
      1) Make an educated guess.
      2) Flag it for review by clicking on the flag icon at the bottom of the screen.
      3) Return to it before you submit the testlet as time allows. Remember, once you have selected the Submit Testlet option, you will no longer be able to review or change any answers in the completed testlet.
3. **Read the question carefully to discover exactly what is being asked.**
   a. Ignore the answer choices so they do not affect your precise reading of the question.
   b. Focusing on what is required allows you to
      1) Reject extraneous information
      2) Concentrate on relevant facts
      3) Proceed directly to determining the best answer
   c. **Careful!** The requirement may be an exception that features negative words.
   d. Decide the correct answer before looking at the answer choices.
4. **Read the answer choices, paying attention to small details.**
   a. Even if an answer choice appears to be correct, do not skip the remaining choices. Each choice requires consideration because you are looking for the best answer provided.
   b. **Only one answer option is the best.** In the MCQs, four answer choices are presented, and you know one of them is correct. The remaining choices are distractors and are meant to appear correct at first glance. Eliminate them as quickly as you can.
   c. Treat each answer choice like a true/false question as you analyze it.
   d. In computational MCQs, the distractor answers are carefully calculated to be the result of common mistakes. Be careful, and double-check your computations if time permits.
      1) There will be a mix of conceptual and calculation questions. When you take the exam, it may appear that more of the questions are calculation-type because they take longer and are more difficult.
5. **Click on the best answer.**
   a. You have a 25% chance of answering correctly by guessing blindly, but you can improve your odds with an educated guess.
   b. For many MCQs, you can **eliminate two answer choices with minimal effort** and increase your educated guess to a 50/50 proposition.
      1) Rule out answers that you think are incorrect.
      2) Speculate what the AICPA is looking for and/or why the question is being asked.
      3) Select the best answer or guess between equally appealing answers. Your first guess is usually the most intuitive.

6. **Do not click the Submit Testlet button until you have consulted the question status list at the bottom of each MCQ screen.**
   a. Return to flagged questions to finalize your answer choices if you have time.
   b. Verify that you have answered every question.
   c. Stay on schedule because time management is critical to exam success.

Doing well on the **task-based simulations** and **written communications** requires you to be an expert on how to approach them both from a question-answering and a time-allocation perspective. Refer to Appendix B, "Optimizing Your Score on the Task-Based Simulations (TBSs) and Written Communications (WCs)," for a complete explanation of task-based simulations and how to optimize your score on each one.

HOW TO BE IN CONTROL

Remember, you must be in control to be successful during exam preparation and execution. Perhaps more importantly, control can also contribute greatly to your personal and other professional goals. Control is the process whereby you

1. Develop expectations, standards, budgets, and plans
2. Undertake activity, production, study, and learning
3. Measure the activity, production, output, and knowledge
4. Compare actual activity with expected and budgeted activity
5. Modify the activity, behavior, or study to better achieve the expected or desired outcome
6. Revise expectations and standards in light of actual experience
7. Continue the process or restart the process in the future

Exercising control will ultimately develop the confidence you need to outperform most other CPA candidates and PASS the CPA Exam!

QUESTIONS ABOUT GLEIM MATERIALS

Gleim has an efficient and effective way for candidates who have purchased the Gleim Premium CPA Review System to submit an inquiry and receive a response regarding Gleim materials **directly through their course**. This system also allows you to view your Q&A session online in your Gleim Personal Classroom.

Questions regarding the information in this **introduction and/or the Gleim *CPA Exam Guide*** (study suggestions, study plans, exam specifics) may be emailed to personalcounselor@gleim.com.

Questions concerning **orders, prices, shipments, or payments** should be sent via email to customerservice@gleim.com and will be promptly handled by our competent and courteous customer service staff.

For **technical support**, you may use our automated technical support service at www.gleim.com/support, email us at support@gleim.com, or call us at (800) 874-5346.

FEEDBACK

Please fill out our online feedback form (www.gleim.com/feedbackBEC) IMMEDIATELY after you take the CPA Business section so we can adapt our material based on where candidates say we need to increase or decrease coverage. Our approach has been approved by the AICPA.

10 *Notes*

STUDY UNIT ONE
BUSINESS PROCESSES, RISKS, AND INTERNAL CONTROL

(22 pages of outline)

1.1	Business Processes	11
1.2	Business Process Risks	15
1.3	COSO Internal Control – Integrated Framework	18
1.4	Internal Control and Fraud	31

Accountants, whether acting as an auditor during a walk-through or as a member of the controller's team, must first gain an understanding of the intricacies of the business. Business processes include the data, transactions, activities, and systems that are necessary for successful business operation. Accountants must understand business processes to ascertain the risks associated with those processes. They can then implement appropriate controls to minimize the identified risks.

1.1 BUSINESS PROCESSES

1. A **business process** is a set of related activities and tasks brought together to achieve a desired outcome. Typically, it is a series of tasks that culminate in a product, service, or business goal.

    a. Business processes can be broken into the following three types of business activities:

    1) Operating processes
    2) Projects
    3) Management and support processes

    b. It is important to note that business activities are not necessarily independent of each other. Corporate strategy may require overlap among types of activities.

2. **Operating processes** are the activities related to the business's core objectives.

    a. For service companies, operating processes are those activities that provide services to satisfy customers' needs.

    1) For example, the operating processes of an airline relate to customer transportation.

    b. For manufacturing companies, operating processes are those activities that produce and sell products to customers.

    1) For example, the operating processes of an aircraft manufacturer relate to the construction and sale of aircraft.

    c. Once operating processes are designed, they are typically continuous except for adjustments to improve efficiency or account for technological improvements.

3. **Projects** are related activities that either (a) are nonroutine or (b) contribute directly to achieving the business's core objectives but only happen over an extended period.

    a. A **nonroutine** project could be the activities related to a company's selection of a new vendor, for example, an airline choosing between a Boeing 737 and an Airbus A321.

    b. A project that **contributes directly to achieving core objectives over an extended period** could be an airline contracting chemists to produce a more efficient biofuel. This is outside the airline's normal operating processes for transporting customers but still contributes to its core objective of air travel.

4. **Management and support processes** are the activities that supervise and support the business. These processes are required for the success of the business, but they do not directly create value for the business's customers. Common examples of functions that provide management and support processes are human resources, accounting, and information technology departments. Often these departments provide the organizational governance and strategic direction of the business.

5. The **business model** consists of the business's objectives and how the business processes achieve these objectives. These objectives include the vision, mission, and high-level strategies. However, the business model is like an onion with multiple layers surrounding these high-level objectives, such as the annual goals and measures. Thus, once an objective is identified, the layers can be "peeled back" to determine the factors making up that objective.

6. Accountants can help improve a business's operations by first understanding the business model and then applying this knowledge to refine the business processes. The two main approaches to gaining an understanding of the business model are the top-down approach and the bottom-up approach.

    a. The **top-down approach** begins by determining the business's overarching objectives and then requires analysis of the key processes critical to achieving those objectives.

        1) A **key process** is a business process that would prevent the business from achieving one of its objectives if the business process were not performed.

        2) Once a key process is identified, the accountant must evaluate any subprocesses of the key process to determine whether they are required for the key process to be achieved. This continues until every process that makes up the key process is identified and the accountant has reached the activity level.

        3) The **activity level** is a basic activity conducted by either a person or an IT operation.

            a) Examples of activity levels performed by people include preparing a receiving report, operating a cash register for a transaction, or welding metal parts on a manufacturing line.

            b) Examples of activity levels performed by computer programs include automated scanning of barcodes to identify boxes arriving on a conveyor belt, completing a sale via an online store, or automated welding of metal on a manufacturing line.

        4) **Drawback.** The accountant performing this analysis is unlikely to have detailed knowledge of every facet of the business's activities. Therefore, there is the potential that some critical business subprocess may be overlooked and not identified.

b. The **bottom-up approach** begins by examining all the business processes at the activity level. The accountant works with each department or area of the business to identify and document their business processes. The benefit of the bottom-up approach versus the top-down approach is that the people responsible for the activities help identify and document them.

   1) Once an activity is identified, both the larger business process and related key business objective also must be identified. The following questions help with the identification process:

      a) How are employees expected to implement the activity or process?
      b) Why does the activity or process exist?
      c) How does the activity or process support the overarching strategy of the business?
      d) Does the activity or process achieve other indirect benefits for the business?

   2) After the business objectives are identified, the accountant needs to ascertain if there are inputs or other activities required to perform the activity or process. Often, departments have manuals that document related processes and activities.

   3) **Drawback.** This approach requires many staff members and is incredibly time intensive. The larger the business, the more difficult this approach is due to the sheer number of processes involved. Therefore, the smaller the business, the more likely an accountant would use the bottom-up approach.

7. **Key performance indicators (KPIs)** are used to provide management with an indication of how well employees are executing the processes and related activities. KPIs
   a. Are highly relevant to the business process or activity
   b. Are easily measurable and observable
   c. Have an acceptable or allowable range
   d. Are provided to employees so they can ascertain how well they are doing
   e. Are conducive to analyzing, tracking, and improving activities using data analytics

8. **Process Mapping**

    a. Once an accountant begins to understand the business processes and how they are integrated into the business model, visual depictions are helpful to identify potential improvements to the processes as well as document and confirm appropriate internal controls.

    b. **Process mapping** is a simple form of flowcharting used to depict a business process. Below is an example of a process map for invoice processing in the purchasing department.

    NOTE: PO means purchase order, and AP means accounts payable.

Process Map for Invoice Processing in Purchasing Department

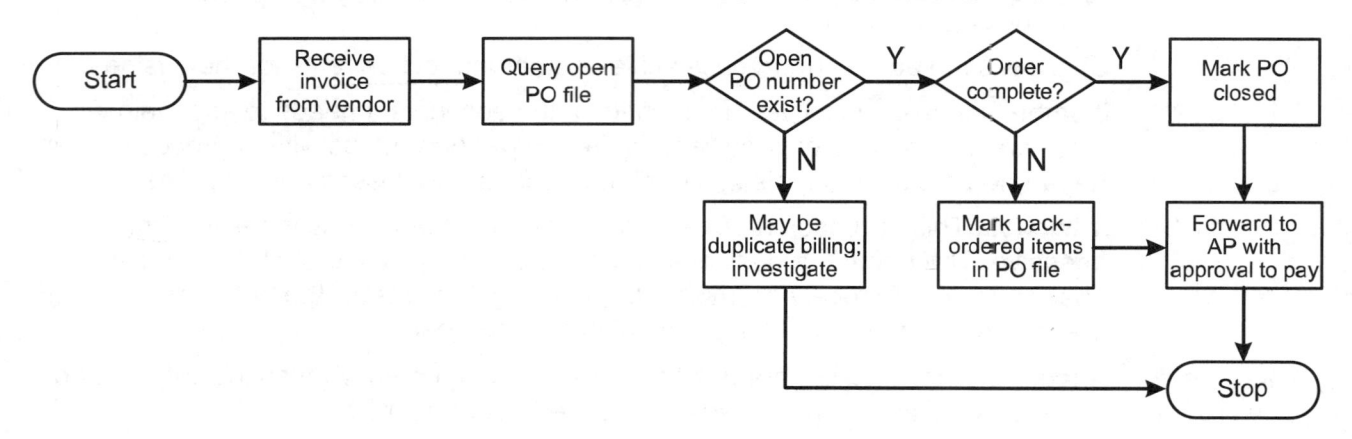

```
Start → Receive invoice from vendor → Query open PO file → Open PO number exist? --Y→ Order complete? --Y→ Mark PO closed
                                                            |N                  |N                         ↓
                                                            ↓                   ↓                   Forward to AP
                                                    May be duplicate    Mark back-ordered    with approval to pay
                                                    billing; investigate  items in PO file           ↓
                                                            └──────────────────────────────────────→ Stop
```

Figure 1-1

STOP & REVIEW

You have completed the outline for this subunit.
Study multiple-choice questions 1 through 4 beginning on page 33.

1.2 BUSINESS PROCESS RISKS

1. **Business Risks**
   a. After gaining an understanding of the overarching strategy and related business processes, accountants should develop a **risk profile** based on business risk.
   b. There are four general types of business risks: SCRO
      1) Strategic risks
      2) Compliance risks
      3) Reporting risks
      4) Operational risks
   c. Each of the risks above can be further organized into external and internal risks. The depiction below is a representation of some of the business risks businesses endure.

Strategic Risks		Compliance Risks	
External	**Internal**	**External**	**Internal**
Competitors	Customer satisfaction	Regulations	Policies
Reputation	Corporate governance	Licenses & permits	Ethics
Industry & market dynamics	Strategic focus	Litigation	Corruption
Economic			
Technology			

Reporting Risks		Operational Risks	
External	**Internal**	**External**	**Internal**
Financial statements	Internal control	Capitalization	Business process execution
Tax filings	Budgeting	Acts of God	Key employee continuity
Valuations	Performance measures (KPIs)	Supply chain	Cash management
			Employment levels
			Product development lapse

2. **Risk Management**
    a. **Risk** is the probability of an event occurring that will have an impact on the achievement of objectives.
        1) **Risk management** assesses and controls these risks to achieve an organization's goals.
            a) Management must focus on risks at all levels of the entity and take the necessary action to manage them.
            b) All risks that could affect achievement of objectives must be considered.
    b. **Risk Management Processes**
        1) **Contexts** within which risks should be managed must be identified before individual risks may be identified. Contexts include the following:
            a) Laws and regulations
            b) Capital projects
            c) Business processes
            d) Technology
            e) Market risk (e.g., interest rates, foreign exchange rates, equity investments)
            f) Organizations
        2) **Risk identification** should be performed at every level of the entity (entity-level, division, business unit) relevant to the identified context(s).
        3) The **risk assessment** process may be formal or informal. It involves (a) assessing the significance of an event, (b) assessing the event's likelihood, and (c) considering the means of managing the risk.
            a) The results of assessing the likelihood and impact of the risk events identified are used to prioritize risks and produce decision-making information.
        4) **Risk responses** are how an organization elects to manage individual risks.
            a) Each organization selects risk responses that align risks with the organization's **risk appetite** (the level of risk the organization is willing to accept).
        5) **Risk monitoring** (a) tracks identified risks, (b) evaluates current risk response plans, (c) monitors residual risks, and (d) identifies new risks.
    c. Risk is measured in terms of probability and impact.
        1) The **probability** that a risk will occur ranges from nearly 0% to nearly 100% certainty.
            a) An event with a 0% chance of occurring is impossible and is thus not a risk.
            b) A risk with a 100% chance of occurring is certain to occur and therefore can be fully anticipated.
        2) The magnitude of the **impact** varies in terms of monetary (financial loss) and nonmonetary (safety) values.

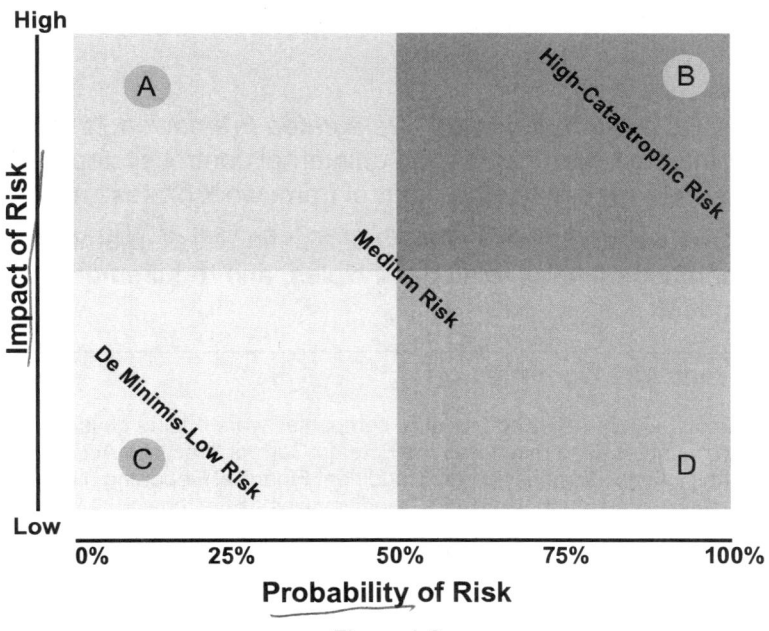

SU 1: Business Processes, Risks, and Internal Control   17

Figure 1-2

- **Low probability, low impact** – Risks in the proximity of **C** are low-level risks and can generally be ignored.
- **Low probability, high impact** – Risks in the proximity of **A** are of high significance if they materialize but are also highly unlikely to take place. Nevertheless, an action plan **should** be developed to combat the risks if the risks occur.
- **High probability, low impact** – Risks in the proximity of **D** are of low significance if they materialize, though they are likely to occur. Although the company can continue to function while dealing with the risks, an action plan **should** be developed to lower the chances that the risks occur.
- **High probability, high impact** – Risks in the proximity of **B** are of catastrophic significance and are top priority if they materialize. An action plan **must** be developed to combat the risks should the risks occur. Therefore, these risks should be constantly monitored and assessed.

d. Business risks can be mapped to the business processes using ERM as discussed in Study Unit 3.

e. Once a business risk is identified, the accountant must determine how to best respond. There are five basic responses to each risk:

1) Acceptance   AAPRT
2) Avoidance
3) Pursuit
4) Reduction
5) Transfer (e.g., insurance transfers risks from the business to the insurer)

STOP & REVIEW

You have completed the outline for this subunit.
Study multiple-choice questions 5 through 8 beginning on page 34.

1.3 COSO *INTERNAL CONTROL – INTEGRATED FRAMEWORK*

1. **Overview**

    a. Although the COSO *Internal Control – Integrated Framework* is widely accepted as the standard for the design and operation of internal control systems, regulatory or legal requirements may specify another control framework or design.

    b. The COSO framework consists primarily of a definition of internal control, categories of objectives, components and related principles, and requirements of an effective system of internal control.

> **BACKGROUND 1-1   Treadway Commission**
>
> The Watergate investigations of 1973-74 revealed that U.S. companies were bribing government officials, politicians, and political parties in foreign countries. The result was the Foreign Corrupt Practices Act of 1977. The private sector also responded by forming the National Commission on Fraudulent Financial Reporting (NCFFR) in 1985. The NCFFR is known as the Treadway Commission because James C. Treadway was its first chair.
>
> The Treadway Commission was originally sponsored and funded by five professional accounting organizations based in the United States. This group of five became known as the Committee of Sponsoring Organizations of the Treadway Commission (COSO). The Commission recommended that this group of five organizations cooperate in creating guidance for internal control. The result was *Internal Control – Integrated Framework*, published in 1992, which was modified in 1994 and again in 2013.
>
> The executive summary is available at www.coso.org/documents/990025P-Executive-Summary-final-may20.pdf.

2. **Definition of Internal Control**

    a. The COSO framework defines internal control as follows:

    Internal control is a process, effected by an entity's board of directors, management, and other personnel, designed to provide reasonable assurance regarding the achievement of objectives relating to operations, reporting, and compliance.

    b. Thus, internal control is

    1) Intended to **achieve** three classes of **objectives**
    2) An **ongoing process**
    3) Effected by **people** at **all** organizational **levels**, e.g., the board, management, and all other employees
    4) Able to provide **reasonable**, but not absolute, **assurance**
    5) **Adaptable** to an entity's structure

3. **Entity Objectives**

    a. Setting objectives is a prerequisite to internal control.

    b. Objectives should be specific, measurable or observable, attainable, relevant, and time-based.

    c. According to the definition of internal control, there are three categories of objectives: (1) operations, (2) reporting, and (3) compliance.

1) **Operations Objectives**
    a) Operations objectives relate to **achieving the entity's mission**.
        i) These objectives are based more on the entity's preferences and judgments, as opposed to laws, rules, regulations, or some other authority.
        ii) Entity-level objectives lead to related sub-objectives for operations within divisions. These objectives are directed at enhancing effectiveness and efficiency.
        iii) Appropriate objectives include improving
            - Financial performance,
            - Productivity,
            - Quality,
            - Innovation, and
            - Customer satisfaction.
    b) Operations objectives also include **safeguarding of assets**.
        i) Objectives related to protecting and preserving assets form the basis for assessing risk and developing controls to mitigate such risk.
        ii) Prevention of loss through waste, inefficiency, or bad business decisions relates to broader objectives than safeguarding of assets.
2) **Reporting Objectives**
    a) Reporting objectives relate to the entity's preparation of **financial** and **nonfinancial** reports for the organization (i.e., internal users) and stakeholders (i.e., external users).
        i) The primary purpose of reporting objectives is to provide reliable, timely, and transparent information to users of reports.
    b) There are two broad categories of reporting objectives: (1) **internal reporting** objectives and (2) **external reporting** objectives.
        i) Internal reporting objectives are influenced by the preferences and judgments of the entity's management and board.
        ii) External reporting objectives are influenced by externally established laws, rules, regulations, standards, and/or frameworks.
    c) There are four sub-categories of reporting objectives.
        i) **Internal financial** reporting objectives may relate to, for example, division-level financial reports.
        ii) **Internal nonfinancial** reporting objectives may relate to, for example, customer satisfaction measures.
        iii) **External financial** reporting objectives may relate to, for example, annual or interim financial statements.
        iv) **External nonfinancial** reporting objectives may relate to, for example, internal control reports.
    d) The COSO framework treats external reporting that does not conform to any externally established authority (i.e., a law, rule, regulation, standard, and/or framework) as **external communication**.

3) **Compliance Objectives**

   a) Compliance objectives relate to the entity's adherence to applicable laws, rules, and regulations.

      i) Examples include taxation, environmental protection, and employee relations.

   b) In contrast, compliance with **internal policies and procedures** relates to operational objectives.

4) The following is a useful memory aid for the COSO categories of objectives:

   O = **O**perations
   R = **R**eporting
   C = **C**ompliance

d. Overlap of Objectives

   1) An objective in one category may overlap or support an objective in another.

      a) An example is a policy to close the monthly books by the fifth working day of the following month.

         i) This objective applies to operations and reporting objectives.

e. Sub-Objectives

   1) Entity-level objectives are linked to more specific **sub-objectives** for the entity's subunits and functions (sales, production, marketing, IT, etc.).

   2) As conditions change, the sub-objectives must be altered to adapt to changes to the entity-level objectives.

4. **Components of Internal Control**

   a. Supporting the organization in its efforts to achieve objectives are the five components of internal control, which can be memorized using the memory aid "controls stop CRIME."

   C = **C**ontrol activities
   R = **R**isk assessment
   I = **I**nformation and communication
   M = **M**onitoring
   E = **C**ontrol **E**nvironment

NOTE: Each of these components is addressed on the following pages. However, the control environment is discussed first because it is considered the most crucial component. Risk assessment is discussed second followed by the other three components.

5. **Control Environment**

    a. The control environment is a set of standards, processes, and structures that pervasively affects the system of internal control. It is the foundation for the other four components. Five principles relate to the control environment:

    1) The organization demonstrates a commitment to **integrity** and **ethical values** by (a) communicating its attitude toward integrity and ethical values, (b) establishing standards of conduct, (c) evaluating performance based on the standards, and (d) correcting deviations in a timely and consistent manner.

        a) A written code of conduct is an element of a control environment that encourages teamwork in the pursuit of an entity's objectives.

    2) The board demonstrates **independence** from management and exercises **oversight** of internal control.

    3) With board oversight, management establishes **structures, reporting lines, and authorities and responsibilities**.

    4) The organization demonstrates a commitment to **attract, develop, and retain competent individuals** in alignment with objectives. Succession planning is included in this principle.

    5) The organization holds **individuals accountable** for their internal control responsibilities in pursuit of objectives. This includes performance evaluations, incentives, and disciplinary action.

    b. The most effective way to transmit ethical behavior throughout an organization is to set the example. This is referred to as "**tone at the top**."

6. **Risk Assessment**

    a. This component identifies and assesses risks to achieving the organization's objectives, which forms the basis for determining how risks should be managed. Four principles relate to risk assessment:

    1) The organization **specifies objectives** to enable the identification and assessment of risks.

        a) **Operations** objectives

            i) Reflect management's choices;
            ii) Consider **risk tolerances**, which are the acceptable levels of variation in performance relative to the achievement of objectives and are determined during the objective-setting process;
            iii) Include operations and financial performance goals; and
            iv) Form a basis for committing resources.

        b) **External financial reporting** objectives

            i) Must comply with applicable accounting standards,
            ii) Consider materiality, and
            iii) Reflect entity activities.

        c) **External nonfinancial reporting** objectives

            i) Must comply with externally established standards and frameworks,
            ii) Consider the required level of precision, and
            iii) Reflect entity activities.

d) **Internal reporting** objectives
   i) Reflect management choices,
   ii) Consider the required level of precision, and
   iii) Reflect entity activities.
e) **Compliance** objectives
   i) Reflect external laws and regulations and
   ii) Consider **risk tolerances**.

2) The organization **identifies risks** (internal and external) to the achievement of its objectives across the entity and **analyzes risks** to determine how the risks should be managed.

   a) Examples of internal risk factors at the entity level include interruptions of IT systems and the quality of personnel hired.
   b) Examples of external risk factors at the entity level include technological changes and changes in customer demand.
   c) Management should analyze risks.
      i) The analysis generally involves (a) estimating the significance of an event, (b) assessing its likelihood, and (c) considering the risk response in light of the organization's **risk tolerances**.
      ii) Inherent and residual risk (the post-response) must be considered. In general, the seriousness of a risk and its likelihood are inversely related.
   d) The **risk response** considers how each risk should be managed; whether to accept, avoid, reduce, or transfer the risk; and the design of controls.

3) The organization should consider the potential for fraud in **assessing fraud risks**. It not only must consider various types of fraud but also must assess the elements of fraud. The fraud triangle defines the three elements of fraud as

   a) Incentives and pressures,
   b) Opportunities, and
   c) Attitudes and rationalizations.

4) The organization **identifies and assesses changes** (internal and external) that could significantly affect the system of internal control and adopts appropriate controls. Examples of changes to be assessed include changes in the business model and changes in leadership.

   a) Risk frequently increases when
      i) The organization implements change and
      ii) Objectives differ from past performance.

7. **Control Activities**

    a. These policies and procedures help ensure that management directives to mitigate risks are carried out. Whether **automated** or **manual**, they are (1) applied at all levels of the entity, (2) within various stages of business processes, and (3) over the technology environment. They may be **preventive** or **detective**, and **segregation of duties** is usually present. Three principles relate to control activities:

        1) The organization **selects and develops control activities** that help mitigate risks to acceptable levels to ensure the achievement of objectives.

            a) Control activities are **integrated** with risk assessment.
            b) Management considers how **entity-specific** factors affect control activities.
            c) Management determines which **business processes** require control activities.
            d) The organization selects and develops a **mix of automated or manual control activities at different levels**.

        2) The organization selects and develops **general control activities over technology** to support the achievement of objectives.

        3) The organization **deploys control activities** through **policies** that establish what is expected and **procedures** that put policies into action.

    b. The three levels of control activities are entity-level, transaction-level, and process-level controls.

        1) **Entity-Level, Transaction-Level, and Process-Level Controls**

            a) **Entity-level controls** are designed to achieve organizational objectives and to address entity-wide risks. They include governance controls and management oversight controls.

                i) Entity-level **governance controls** are established by the board of directors at the highest level (governance level). They include organizational policies and procedures that define the entity's culture and communicate its expectations. Examples include IT policies, the code of conduct, oversight of controls, and setting the risk appetite.

                ii) Entity-level **management oversight controls** are implemented by management at the business unit level to achieve business unit objectives and address business unit risks. Examples include IT general controls and period-end controls.

b) **Transaction-level controls** (also called activity-level controls) are controls that affect a transaction or a group of transactions. Transaction-level controls are designed to achieve transaction objectives and to address risks specific to transactions. They include

   i) Authorizations and approvals that ensure that only valid transactions are initiated. For example, **biometric devices** are used to verify the identity of authorized users. Additionally, a bank's **positive pay** system compares the checks presented for payment with the list of issued checks provided by the payor before they are cashed.

   ii) Verifications of the existence and valuation of assets and liabilities.

   iii) Physical controls, including physical security of assets, authorization of access, and periodic counts.

   iv) Reconciliations that ensure two sets of records (e.g., bank balance and book balance) are in agreement, creating asset accountability.

   v) Controls over standing data, including periodically checking data stored in computers against manually held data.

   vi) Supervisory controls, such as using a centralized system to monitor and control groups of transactions.

   vii) Segregation of duties

c) **Process-level controls** are designed to achieve process objectives and to address process risks. Examples include physical inventory counts, performance assessment, and review of revenue center reports.

8. **Information and Communication**

   a. Information systems enable the organization to obtain, generate, use, and communicate information to (1) maintain accountability and (2) measure and review performance. Three principles relate to information and communication:

      1) The organization obtains or generates and uses **relevant, quality** information to support the functioning of internal control.

         a) Information can include both internal and external sources of data.
         b) Only high-quality information is appropriate.
         c) The cost and the benefit of obtaining the information are considered.

      2) The organization **internally communicates** information, including objectives and responsibilities for internal control, necessary to support the functioning of internal control.

         a) A process enables all personnel to perform their control responsibilities.
         b) Management and the board should communicate.
         c) Alternative internal (and external) communication lines, e.g., hotlines, are provided.
         d) The method of internal (and external) communication depends on the timing, audience, and nature of the information.

3) The organization **communicates with external parties** about matters affecting internal control.

   a) Relevant and timely information is communicated to shareholders, regulators, customers, etc.

   b) Input from external sources provides relevant information.

   c) External assessments are communicated to the board.

   d) Legal requirements are considered.

9. **Monitoring**

   a. Controls and their application change. Monitoring assesses the quality of internal control performance over time to ensure that controls continue to effectively manage existing risks. Two principles relate to monitoring:

      1) The organization selects, develops, and performs **ongoing or separate evaluations (or both)** to determine whether the components of internal control are present and functioning.

         a) **Ongoing** Evaluations

            i) Routine activities that are control-oriented include (a) the periodic reconciliation of operational division data with enterprise-wide financial data, (b) the presence or absence of customer complaints about billing, (c) the reports of internal and external auditors, and (d) training programs.

         b) **Separate** Evaluations

            i) The significance of risks determines the scope and frequency of separate evaluations of internal control.

            ii) In some environments, control self-assessment is appropriate. In others, the internal audit function should perform a thorough review.

            iii) The evaluator must understand how the system should work and its objectives and must test whether the system is working as designed.

      2) The organization **evaluates and communicates control deficiencies** in a timely manner.

         a) Whether deficiency is reportable depends on its effect on the entity's ability to achieve its objectives.

            i) Reporting should be to a level of the organization with sufficient authority to correct the deficiency.

b. An effective approach to monitoring consists of three phases: (1) establishing a foundation for monitoring, (2) designing and executing monitoring procedures, and (3) assessing and reporting results.

1) The **foundation for monitoring** phase consists of
   a) Tone at the top,
   b) Organizational structure, and
   c) Baseline understanding of internal control effectiveness.

2) The **design and execute** phase consists of
   a) Prioritizing risks,
   b) Identifying controls,
   c) Identifying persuasive information about controls, and
   d) Implementing monitoring procedures.

3) The **assess and report** phase consists of
   a) Prioritizing findings,
   b) Reporting results to the appropriate level, and
   c) Following up on corrective action.

c. **Monitoring for Change Continuum**

1) The causes of ineffective internal control systems include the following:
   a) They are **not** properly designed or implemented.
   b) They are properly designed and implemented but are not properly modified when **changes occur in the environment** (e.g., changes in risks, people, processes, or technology) in which they operate.
   c) They are properly designed and implemented, but **changes in their operation** cause them to be ineffective in managing or mitigating applicable risks.

2) A solution for managing the causes of ineffective internal control systems is the **monitoring for change continuum**. The continuum has four components:
   a) **The control baseline** is a **starting point** that includes an understanding of
      i) The internal control system's **design** and
      ii) Whether controls have been **implemented** to achieve the organization's internal control objectives.
   b) **Change identification** identifies, through ongoing monitoring and separate evaluations, changes in internal control.
   c) **Change management** evaluates the design and implementation of identified changes and establishes a **new baseline**.
   d) **Control revalidation/update** periodically revalidates the operation of internal control in the absence of changes.

10. Relationship of Objectives, Components, and Organizational Structure

a. The COSO model may be represented by a cube with rows, slices, and columns. (1) The rows are the five components, (2) the slices are the three objectives, and (3) the columns are an entity's organizational structure.

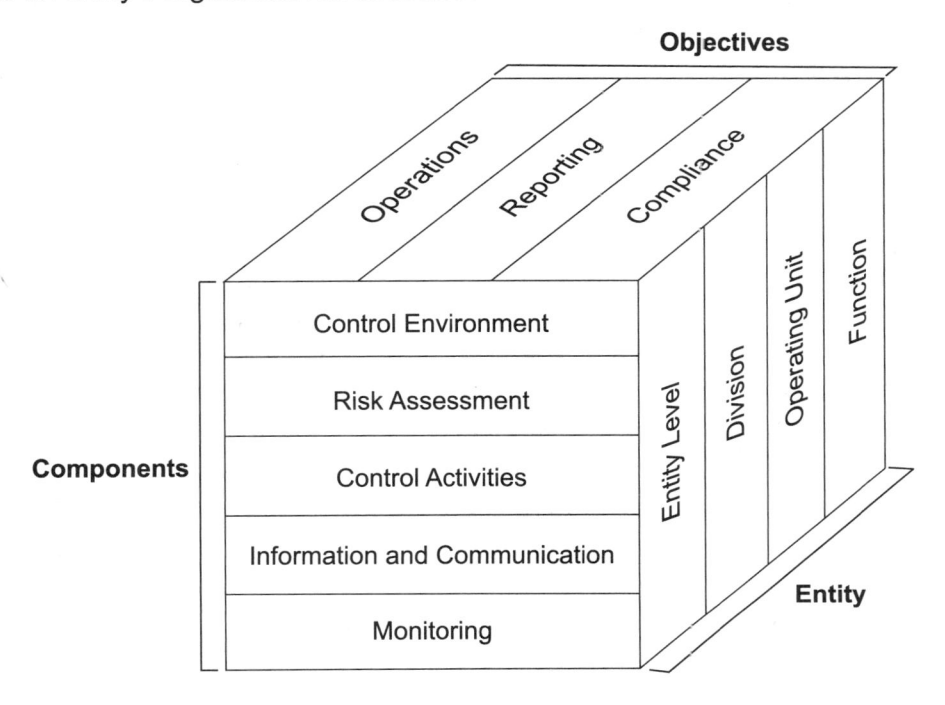

Figure 1-3

11. Requirements for Effective Internal Control

a. A system of internal control is effective if it provides **reasonable assurance** of achieving an entity's objectives relating to operations, reporting, and compliance. Such a system reduces the risk(s) of not achieving those objectives to an **acceptable level**.

b. An effective system of internal control requires that

1) Each of the five components of internal control and relevant principles is present and functioning.

   a) **Present** refers to whether the components and relevant principles exist in the design and implementation of the system of internal control.

   b) **Functioning** refers to whether the components and relevant principles continue to exist in the operation of the system of internal control.

2) The five components are operating together in an integrated manner.

   a) **Operating together** refers to whether all five components collectively reduce the risk of not achieving an objective to an acceptable level.

12. **Other Considerations**

    a. The use of **judgment** is required in designing, implementing, and conducting internal control and assessing its effectiveness.

    b. The use of **outsourced service providers** for certain business processes does not relieve the organization of its responsibility for the system of internal control.

    c. Although **technology innovation** creates opportunities and risks, the principles in the COSO framework do not change.

    d. The **organization's size** may affect how it implements internal control.

       1) Senior management of smaller organizations typically have a wider span of control and greater direct interaction with personnel than senior management of larger organizations. Larger organizations may need to rely on more formal mechanisms of control (e.g., written reports, formal meetings, or conference calls).

       2) Larger organizations have more resources than smaller organizations. Consequently, a smaller organization may have to outsource all, or parts, of its internal audit function or incur higher costs relative to larger organizations because of the lack of economies of scale.

13. **Roles and Responsibilities Regarding Internal Control**

    a. **Internal Parties**

       1) Board of Directors

          a) Responsible for **overseeing** the system of internal control.

          b) Defines expectations about integrity, ethical values, transparency, and accountability through its authority to select and terminate the CEO and other officers.

          c) Often performs certain duties through committees, which include the

             i) Audit Committee
             ii) Compensation Committee
             iii) Nomination/Governance Committee
             iv) Risk Committee
             v) Finance Committee

       2) Senior Management

          a) Sets the **tone at the top** and has primary responsibility for establishing proper ethical culture.

          b) Sets objectives.

          c) Has **overall responsibility** for designing, implementing, and operating an effective system of internal control.

             i) Maintains oversight and control over the entity's risks.

             ii) Guides the development and performance of control activities at the entity level.

             iii) Assigns responsibility for establishing more specific internal controls at the different levels of the entity.

             iv) Communicates expectations.

             v) Evaluates control deficiencies.

3) Operational Management
    a) Provides the **first line of defense** for effective management of risk and control.
    b) Develops and implements control and risk management processes.
4) Business-Enabling Functions
    a) Provide the **second line of defense** for effective management of risk and control.
    b) These functions support the entity through specialized skills and include various risk management and compliance functions.
    c) Additionally, these functions are typically responsible for the ongoing monitoring of control and risk.
5) Internal Auditors
    a) Provide the **third line of defense** for effective management of risk and control.
    b) Evaluate the adequacy and effectiveness of controls in responding to risks in the entity's oversight, operations, and information systems.
    c) To remain independent, the internal audit activity cannot be responsible for selecting and executing controls.
6) Other Entity Personnel
    a) Everyone in the organization is expected to (1) competently perform his or her appropriate control activities and (2) inform those higher in the organization about ineffective control.

b. **External Parties**
1) External Auditors
    a) Independent accountants are required to consider the auditee's system of internal control as part of their audit of the financial statements.
    b) The PCAOB also requires auditors of public companies to examine and report on internal control.
2) Legislators and Regulators
    a) The Foreign Corrupt Practices Act and the Sarbanes-Oxley Act set legal requirements regarding internal control.
3) Parties Interacting with the Entity
    a) Suppliers, customers, and others may interact with the entity's internal control.
4) Financial Analysts, Bond Rating Agencies, and the News Media
    a) The actions of these parties can inform an entity about how it is perceived by the world at large.
5) Outsourced Service Providers
    a) Some of an entity's business functions, e.g., IT, human resources, or internal audit, may be performed by external service providers.

14. **Limitations**

   a. Internal control only provides **reasonable assurance** of achieving objectives. It cannot provide absolute assurance because any system of internal control has the following **inherent limitations**:

      1) Established objectives must be **suitable** for internal control.

         a) For example, if an entity establishes unrealistic objectives, the system of internal controls will be ineffective.

      2) Human **judgment** is faulty, and controls may fail because of simple errors or mistakes.

      3) Controls may fail due to **breakdowns** (e.g., employee misunderstanding, carelessness, or fatigue).

      4) **Management** may inappropriately **override** internal controls, e.g., to fraudulently achieve revenue projections or hide liabilities.

      5) Manual or automated controls can be circumvented by **collusion**.

      6) **External events** are beyond an organization's control.

SUCCESS TIP

The AICPA frequently tests the inherent limitations of internal control. Be able to identify the basic limitations.

STOP & REVIEW

You have completed the outline for this subunit.
Study multiple-choice questions 9 through 16 beginning on page 36.

1.4 INTERNAL CONTROL AND FRAUD

1. **Types of Fraud**

   a. Fraudulent reporting occurs when an entity's reports are intentionally prepared with misstatements or omissions. According to the COSO internal control framework, organizations should consider the potential for fraud in the following areas:

      1) **Fraudulent external financial reporting.** This type of fraud involves an intentional act to deceive the users of the external financial reports.

      2) **Misappropriation of assets.** This type of fraud involves theft of the entity's assets.

      3) **Illegal acts.** These are violations of laws and regulations that could have a material direct or indirect impact on the external financial reports.

2. **Fraud Management Program**

   a. The components of an effective fraud management program include the following:

      1) Company ethics policy
      2) Fraud awareness
      3) Fraud risk assessment
      4) Ongoing reviews
      5) Prevention and detection
      6) Investigation

3. **Controls**

   a. Control is the principal means of managing fraud and ensuring the components of the fraud management program are present and functioning. (Control and types of control are covered in detail in Study Unit 2.)

   b. The **COSO internal control framework** (covered in detail in Subunit 1.3) can be applied in the fraud context to promote an environment in which fraud is effectively managed.

      1) The **control environment** includes such elements as a code of conduct, ethics policy, or fraud policy to set the appropriate tone at the top; hiring and promotion guidelines and practices; and board oversight.

      2) A **fraud risk assessment** generally includes the following:

         a) Identifying and prioritizing fraud risk factors and fraud schemes
         b) Determining whether existing controls apply to potential fraud schemes and identifying gaps
         c) Testing operating effectiveness of fraud prevention and detection controls
         d) Documenting and reporting the fraud risk assessment

      3) **Control activities** are policies and procedures for business processes that include authority limits and segregation of duties.

      4) Fraud-related **information and communication** practices promote the fraud risk management program and the organization's position on risk. The means used include fraud awareness training and confirming that employees comply with the organization's policies.

      5) **Monitoring** evaluates antifraud controls through independent evaluations of the fraud risk management program and use of it.

c. **Preventing fraud.** Essential elements in preventing fraud are setting the correct tone at the top and instilling a strong ethical culture.

1) **Safeguarding of assets** protects entities against the unauthorized use and disposal of assets. Examples include theft of assets and intellectual property.

d. **Detecting fraud.** An essential element in detecting fraud is employee feedback, as receiving fraud tips from employees is the most common way to detect fraud. Sources of employee feedback include a whistleblower hotline, exit interviews, and employee surveys.

4. **Management Responsibility for Controls**

   a. Management is primarily responsible for establishing and maintaining control. Management assesses fraud risk related to

      1) Safeguarding of assets
      2) Fraudulent reporting
      3) Corruption, such as illegal acts

   b. **Management override** takes place when management circumvents an entity's controls for an illegitimate purpose, such as personal gain or enhanced presentation of the entity's position.

      1) The following address these risks:

         a) Controls over significant, unusual transactions, particularly those that result in late or unusual journal entries
         b) Controls over journal entries and adjustments made in the period-end financial reporting process
         c) Controls over related party transactions
         d) Controls related to significant management estimates
         e) Controls that mitigate incentives for, and pressures on, management to falsify or inappropriately manage financial results

   c. Assessing the risk of management override is part of the assessment of fraud risk. The board of directors or audit committee oversees this assessment.

5. **Fraud Awareness**

   a. Fraud awareness is understanding the nature, causes, and characteristics of fraud.

      1) Fraud awareness is developed through periodic fraud risk assessments, training of employees, and communications between management and employees.

   b. Employee training about fraud should be tailored to each organization's fraud risks.

      1) Training typically covers the organization's values and code of conduct, types of fraud, and employee roles and responsibilities to report violations of ethical behavior.

STOP & REVIEW

You have completed the outline for this subunit.
Study multiple-choice questions 17 through 20 beginning on page 39.

QUESTIONS

1.1 Business Processes

1. Which of the following terms describes the type of business activity that indirectly creates value for the business's customers?

A. Operating processes.
B. Management and support processes.
C. Reporting processes.
D. Projects.

Answer (B) is correct.
   REQUIRED: The term describing a type of business activity.
   DISCUSSION: Management and support processes are the activities that supervise and support the business. These processes are required for the success of the business, but they do not directly create customer value.
   Answer (A) is incorrect. Operating processes are the activities related to the business's core objectives. They directly create value for customers. **Answer (C) is incorrect.** Reporting processes are not a type of business activity. **Answer (D) is incorrect.** Projects are related business activities that either (1) are nonroutine or (2) contribute directly to achieving core objectives but only over an extended period of time. Projects directly create value for customers.

2.

	Routine	Nonroutine
Directly relates to core objectives	I	II
Indirectly relates to core objectives	III	IV

Which of the above combinations describes an operating process as a type of business activity?

A. I.
B. II.
C. III.
D. IV.

Answer (A) is correct.
   REQUIRED: The combination of characteristics of operating processes.
   DISCUSSION: Routine activities that directly relate to the business's core objectives are operating processes.
   Answer (B) is incorrect. Projects are related business activities that either (1) are nonroutine or (2) contribute directly to achieving business core objectives but only over an extended period of time. Thus, nonroutine activities that directly relate to the business's core objectives are projects. **Answer (C) is incorrect.** Activities that indirectly relate to the business's core objectives, whether routine or nonroutine, are management and support processes. They are the activities that supervise and support the business. These processes are required for the success of the business, but they do not directly create value for customers. **Answer (D) is incorrect.** Management and support processes are activities that indirectly relate to the business's core objectives, whether routine or nonroutine. They are required for the success of the business, but they do not directly create value for customers.

3. When evaluating whether a key performance indicator (KPI) provides an indication of how well processes and related activities are executed, which of the following is **not** a criterion?

A. Relevance.
B. Invariance.
C. Measurability.
D. Clarity.

Answer (B) is correct.
   REQUIRED: The item not a criterion for a KPI.
   DISCUSSION: A KPI should have an acceptable or allowable range. An invariant KPI may lead to inflexibility in performance measurement.
   Answer (A) is incorrect. A KPI should be highly relevant to the business process or activity. **Answer (C) is incorrect.** A KPI should be easily measurable and observable. **Answer (D) is incorrect.** A KPI should be provided to employees so they can ascertain how well they are doing.

4. The bottom-up approach to understanding a business model

A. Begins by determining the business's objectives.
B. Is likely to overlook critical business processes.
C. Is more likely to be used by larger businesses.
D. Traces subprocesses to key processes.

Answer (D) is correct.
REQUIRED: The true statement about the bottom-up approach to understanding a business model.
DISCUSSION: The bottom-up approach begins by examining all business processes at the activity level. Once these subprocesses are identified, both the larger business processes (i.e., key processes) and related key business objectives are identified.
Answer (A) is incorrect. The top-down approach, not the bottom-up approach, begins by determining the business's objectives. **Answer (B) is incorrect.** The accountant performing a top-down analysis is unlikely to have detailed knowledge of every facet of the business's activities. This approach therefore has the potential to overlook some critical business processes. **Answer (C) is incorrect.** The larger the business, the greater the number of processes involved and the less likely that the business will use the bottom-up approach.

1.2 Business Process Risks

5. Which step in the risk management process assesses the actions to manage identified risks?

A. Risk context identification.
B. Risk assessment.
C. Risk response.
D. Risk monitoring.

Answer (D) is correct.
REQUIRED: The step in the risk management process that assesses risk management actions.
DISCUSSION: Risk monitoring is the last step in the risk management process. It involves (1) tracking identified risks, (2) evaluating current risk response plans (risk management actions), (3) monitoring residual risks, and (4) identifying new risks.
Answer (A) is incorrect. Risk context identification determines context (e.g., laws and regulations, capital projects, and business processes) within which risks should be managed before individual risks are identified. Assessment of risk mitigation actions is performed after risk context identification. **Answer (B) is incorrect.** Risk assessment (1) evaluates the significance of an event, (2) estimates the event's likelihood, and (3) considers the means of managing the risk. Assessment of risk management actions is performed after risk assessment. **Answer (C) is incorrect.** Implementing risk responses is the means by which an organization elects to manage individual risks in a manner that aligns with the risk appetite (the level of risk the organization is willing to accept). Risk management actions (risk responses) are assessed after this step.

6. Which of the following is a business risk?

A. Credit risk.
B. Liquidity risk.
C. Reporting risk.
D. Country risk.

Answer (C) is correct.
REQUIRED: The type of business risk.
DISCUSSION: The four general types of business risk are (1) strategic risks, (2) compliance risks, (3) reporting risks, and (4) operational risks. External reporting risks include those related to financial statements, tax filings, and valuations. Internal reporting risks include those related to internal control, budgeting, and key performance indicators (KPIs).
Answer (A) is incorrect. Credit risk is the risk that the borrower will default and not be able to repay principal or interest. It is an investment risk rather than a business risk. **Answer (B) is incorrect.** Liquidity risk is the risk that an investment security cannot be sold on short notice without a loss. It is an investment risk rather than a business risk. **Answer (D) is incorrect.** Country risk is the overall risk of investing in a foreign country. It is an investment risk rather than a business risk.

7. Risks are measured as the product of

A. Likelihood and duration.
B. Probability and impact.
C. Volatility and impact.
D. Volatility and duration.

Answer (B) is correct.
REQUIRED: The measurement of risks.
DISCUSSION: Risks are measured in terms of (1) the probability (risk) that an event will have an impact on the achievement of objectives and (2) the magnitude (impact) in terms of monetary (e.g., financial loss) and nonmonetary (e.g., safety) values.
Answer (A) is incorrect. Duration may be a measure of risks. But risks are not measured as the product of likelihood and duration. **Answer (C) is incorrect.** Volatility is a subset of the impact of risks. For example, impact encompasses the range and deviation of risks. Measuring risks as the product of volatility and impact double counts certain aspects of risks. **Answer (D) is incorrect.** Volatility and duration may be measures of risks. However, measuring risks as the product of volatility and duration is insufficient to quantify the risks.

8. When the risk identified involves a high probability of the occurrence of an adverse event and a low magnitude of loss, the business

A. Should develop action plans to manage the risk event if it occurs.
B. May ignore the risk.
C. Must develop action plans to constantly monitor, assess, and manage the risk.
D. Should develop action plans to lower the likelihood of loss.

Answer (D) is correct.
REQUIRED: The response to an identified risk.
DISCUSSION: Businesses can function in the presence of risks with low significance and a high probability of an adverse event. But action plans should be developed to lower the chances that an adverse event will occur.
Answer (A) is incorrect. The business should develop action plans to manage the risk event if it occurs but only if it has a low probability of occurrence and a high magnitude of loss. **Answer (B) is incorrect.** Ignoring the risk is indicated if the probability of occurrence and magnitude of loss are low. **Answer (C) is incorrect.** Developing action plans to constantly monitor, assess, and manage the risk is done when an adverse event has a high probability of occurrence and a high magnitude of loss.

1.3 COSO *Internal Control – Integrated Framework*

9. Which of the following factors are included in an entity's control environment?

A. Organizational structure, management philosophy, and monitoring.
B. Integrity and ethical values, assignment of authority, and human resource practices.
C. Competence of personnel, segregation of duties, and fraud risk assessment.
D. Risk assessment, assignment of responsibility, and human resource practices.

Answer (B) is correct.
REQUIRED: The factors in a control environment.
DISCUSSION: Five principles relate to the control environment. The principles are as follows: (1) the organization demonstrates a commitment to integrity and ethical values; (2) the board demonstrates independence from management and exercises oversight of internal control; (3) management establishes structures, reporting lines, and authorities and responsibilities; (4) the organization demonstrates a commitment to attract, develop, and retain competent individuals in alignment with objectives; and (5) the organization holds individuals accountable for their internal control responsibilities. Therefore, integrity and ethical values, assignment of authority, and human resource practices are factors considered in the control environment.
Answer (A) is incorrect. Monitoring is its own component of internal control. **Answer (C) is incorrect.** Segregation of duties and fraud risk assessment are factors in the control activities and risk assessment components, respectively, of internal control. **Answer (D) is incorrect.** Risk assessment is its own component of internal control.

10. Internal control is a process designed to provide reasonable assurance regarding the achievement of objectives related to

A. Reporting.
B. Operations.
C. Compliance.
D. All of the answers are correct.

Answer (D) is correct.
REQUIRED: The true statement regarding COSO's objectives in relation to internal control.
DISCUSSION: The COSO model for internal control establishes control objectives for operations, reporting, and compliance.
Answer (A) is incorrect. Operations and compliance also are control objectives. **Answer (B) is incorrect.** Reporting and compliance also are control objectives. **Answer (C) is incorrect.** Reporting and operations also are control objectives.

11. Which of the following is the control component that reflects the attitude and actions of the board and management regarding the significance of control within the organization?

A. Risk assessment.
B. Control activities.
C. Control environment.
D. Monitoring.

Answer (C) is correct.
REQUIRED: The control component that reflects the attitude and actions of the board and management regarding control.
DISCUSSION: According to the COSO model for internal control, the control environment reflects the attitude and actions of the board and management regarding the significance of control within the organization.
Answer (A) is incorrect. Risk assessment identifies and analyzes external or internal risks to achievement of the objectives at the activity level as well as the entity level. **Answer (B) is incorrect.** Control activities are the policies and procedures helping to ensure that management directives are executed and actions are taken to address risks to achievement of objectives. **Answer (D) is incorrect.** Monitoring is a process that assesses the quality of the system's performance over time.

12. An organization's directors, management, and internal auditors all have important roles in creating a proper control environment. Senior management is primarily responsible for

A. Establishing a proper ethical culture.
B. Designing and operating a control system that provides reasonable assurance that established objectives and goals will be achieved.
C. Ensuring that external and internal auditors adequately monitor the control environment.
D. Implementing and monitoring controls designed by the board of directors.

Answer (A) is correct.
REQUIRED: The best description of senior management's responsibility.
DISCUSSION: The COSO model treats internal control as a process, effected by an entity's board of directors, management, and other personnel, designed to provide reasonable assurance regarding the achievement of entity objectives. The control environment component of internal control reflects the attitude and actions of the board and management regarding the significance of control within the organization. It sets the organization's tone and influences the control consciousness of its personnel. Moreover, the control environment provides discipline and structure for the achievement of the primary objectives of internal control. The control environment includes, among other elements, integrity and ethical values. Thus, standards should be effectively communicated, e.g., by management example. Management also should remove incentives and temptations for dishonest or unethical acts.
Answer (B) is incorrect. Senior management has overall responsibility for designing, implementing, and operating an effective system of internal control. However, it is not primarily responsible for designing and operating a control system because senior management is not likely to be involved in the detailed design and day-to-day operations of a control system. **Answer (C) is incorrect.** Management administers risk and control processes. It cannot delegate this responsibility to the external or internal auditors. **Answer (D) is incorrect.** The board has oversight governance responsibilities but ordinarily does not become involved in the details of operations.

13. An adequate system of internal controls is most likely to detect a fraud perpetrated by a

A. Group of employees in collusion.
B. Single employee.
C. Group of managers in collusion.
D. Single manager.

Answer (B) is correct.
REQUIRED: The fraud most likely to be detected by an adequate system of internal controls.
DISCUSSION: Segregation of duties and other control processes serve to prevent or detect a fraud committed by an employee acting alone. One employee may not have the ability to engage in wrongdoing or may be subject to detection by other employees in the course of performing their assigned duties. However, collusion may circumvent controls. For example, comparison of recorded accountability for assets with the assets known to be held may fail to detect fraud if persons having custody of assets collude with record keepers.
Answer (A) is incorrect. A group has a better chance of successfully perpetrating a fraud than an individual employee. **Answer (C) is incorrect.** Management can override controls. **Answer (D) is incorrect.** Even a single manager may be able to override controls.

14. Which of the following most likely would **not** be considered an inherent limitation of the potential effectiveness of an entity's internal control?

A. Incompatible duties.
B. Management override.
C. Faulty judgment.
D. Collusion among employees.

Answer (A) is correct.
REQUIRED: The item not considered an inherent limitation of internal control.
DISCUSSION: Internal control has inherent limitations. The performance of incompatible duties, however, is a failure to assign different people the functions of authorization, recording, and asset custody, not an inherent limitation of internal control. Segregation of duties is a category of control activities.
Answer (B) is incorrect. Management establishes internal controls. Thus, it can override those controls.
Answer (C) is incorrect. Human judgment in decision making may be faulty. **Answer (D) is incorrect.** Controls, whether manual or automated, may be circumvented by collusion among two or more people.

15. Internal control can provide only reasonable assurance that the entity's objectives and goals will be met efficiently and effectively. One factor limiting the likelihood of achieving those objectives is that

A. The internal auditor's primary responsibility is the detection of fraud.
B. The audit committee is active and independent.
C. The cost of internal control should not exceed its benefits.
D. Management monitors performance.

Answer (C) is correct.
REQUIRED: The true statement about the limitation of internal control.
DISCUSSION: A limiting factor is that the cost of internal control should not exceed the benefits that are expected to be derived. Thus, the potential loss associated with any exposure or risk is weighed against the cost to control it. Although the cost-benefit relationship is a primary criterion that should be considered in designing and implementing internal control, the precise measurement of costs and benefits usually is not possible.
Answer (A) is incorrect. The internal audit activity's responsibility regarding controls is to evaluate effectiveness and efficiency and to promote continuous improvement. **Answer (B) is incorrect.** An effective governance function strengthens the control environment. **Answer (D) is incorrect.** Senior management's role is to oversee the establishment, administration, and assessment of the system of risk management and control processes. Among the responsibilities of the organization's line managers is the assessment of the control processes in their respective areas. Internal auditors provide varying degrees of assurance about the effectiveness of the risk management and control processes in select activities and functions of the organization.

16. Control activities do **not** encompass

A. Performance reviews.
B. Supervisory controls.
C. Physical controls.
D. Control revalidation.

Answer (D) is correct.
REQUIRED: The item not belonging to the control activities component.
DISCUSSION: The COSO model describes control activities as policies and procedures that help ensure that management directives are carried out. They are intended to ensure that necessary actions are taken to address risks to achieve the entity's objectives. Control activities have various objectives and are applied at various organizational and functional levels. However, control revalidation is part of the monitoring component.
Answer (A) is incorrect. Performance reviews is a category of control activities. **Answer (B) is incorrect.** Supervisory controls is a category of control activities. **Answer (C) is incorrect.** Physical controls is a category of control activities.

1.4 Internal Control and Fraud

17. Which of the following is a **false** statement comparing management override and management intervention?

A. Management override differs from management intervention in terms of legitimacy.
B. Management override and management intervention are departures from controls.
C. Only management intervention is documented and disclosed.
D. Neither management override nor management intervention is desirable for financial statement users.

Answer (D) is correct.
REQUIRED: The false statement comparing management override and management intervention.
DISCUSSION: Management override is management circumvention of an entity's controls for an illegitimate purpose, such as personal gain or profit manipulation. Management intervention departs from controls but is necessary to cope with special circumstances that otherwise may not be appropriately recorded. Thus, management intervention may increase the usefulness of financial statements to users.
Answer (A) is incorrect. Management override is for illegitimate purposes, but management intervention is for legitimate purposes. **Answer (B) is incorrect.** Management override and management intervention are departures from an entity's controls. **Answer (C) is incorrect.** Deviations resulting from management intervention are documented and disclosed. Management override, due to its illegitimate (or illegal) purposes, is not documented and disclosed.

18. Income smoothing is

A. A form of asset misappropriation.
B. A form of fraudulent financial reporting.
C. An illegal act.
D. Not a fraud.

Answer (B) is correct.
REQUIRED: The type of fraud represented by income smoothing.
DISCUSSION: Fraudulent financial reporting is an intentional act to deceive the users of the financial reports. Income smoothing uses accounting methods to shift revenues and expenditures among different periods to reduce variability in income. Thus, income smoothing is an intentional intercession in the financial reporting process.
Answer (A) is incorrect. Asset misappropriation is theft of an entity's assets (e.g., by embezzling cash or inventory). Income smoothing does not involve asset theft. **Answer (C) is incorrect.** Income smoothing uses accounting methods to shift revenues and expenditures among different periods to reduce variability in income. The use of acceptable accounting methods is not necessarily illegal. **Answer (D) is incorrect.** Income smoothing is intentional manipulation of income (e.g., to deceive users of financial statements).

19. Fraud management programs

A. Reduce the likelihood of misstatements, omissions, or errors.
B. Conclude by responding to frauds.
C. Have tangible and intangible components.
D. Involve only senior management of a business.

Answer (C) is correct.
REQUIRED: The true statement about fraud management programs.
DISCUSSION: An effective fraud management program includes tangible (e.g., company ethics policies and procedures) and intangible (e.g., fraud awareness) components.
Answer (A) is incorrect. Among other things, fraud management programs are intended to prevent or detect intentional misstatements or omissions in financial reports. Errors are unintentional. **Answer (B) is incorrect.** The final component in the COSO internal control framework is monitoring. It evaluates antifraud responses through independent assessments of the fraud management program and its use. **Answer (D) is incorrect.** Fraud management programs should apply at all levels of a business, from senior management to front-line employees.

20. Which of the following is **not** an example of management override?

A. Posting adjusting entries after year-end analyses have indicated changes in the overall economic environment.
B. Extending payment periods for certain vendors beyond those allowed by company policy.
C. Approving loans to clients with credit scores below those required by company policy.
D. Changing accounting estimates without following normal procedures.

Answer (A) is correct.
REQUIRED: The item not an example of management override.
DISCUSSION: Making adjustments based on new findings (e.g., changes in the overall economic environment) does not necessarily constitute management override. Rather, it may be an example of management intervention necessary to cope with special circumstances that otherwise may not be appropriately recorded.
Answer (B) is incorrect. Deferring payments contrary to company policy is an example of management override of a control. **Answer (C) is incorrect.** Approving loans to clients with unacceptable credit scores for the purpose of increasing revenue is management override of a control. **Answer (D) is incorrect.** Changing accounting estimates without following normal procedures is management override of a control.

Access the **Gleim CPA Premium Review System** featuring our SmartAdapt technology from your Gleim Personal Classroom to continue your studies. You will experience a personalized study environment with exam-emulating multiple-choice questions.

STUDY UNIT TWO
ACCOUNTING CYCLES AND CORPORATE GOVERNANCE

(27 pages of outline)

2.1	Accounting Cycles and Transaction-Level Controls	42
2.2	Corporate Governance Structure	56
2.3	The Sarbanes-Oxley Act of 2002 (SOX)	61
2.4	System and Organization Controls (SOC) for Service Organizations	65

This study unit includes four topics that are tested on the BEC section of the Exam. In the order of the topics presented in this study unit, the AICPA BEC Blueprint states that candidates should be able to (1) analyze the flow of transactions within key business processes, (2) describe the corporate governance structure within an organization, (3) identify and define key corporate governance provisions of the Sarbanes-Oxley Act of 2002, and (4) identify the appropriate System and Organization Controls (SOC) report to meet a user entity's needs.

2.1 ACCOUNTING CYCLES AND TRANSACTION-LEVEL CONTROLS

1. **Accounting Cycles and Controls**
   a. The key accounting processes can be described in terms of five cycles:
      1) Sales to customers on credit and recognition of receivables
      2) Collection of cash from customer receivables
      3) Purchases on credit and recognition of payables
      4) Payment (disbursement) of cash to satisfy payables
      5) Payment of employees for work performed and allocation of costs
   b. To describe these cycles in detail, flowcharts are used. Commonly used document flowchart symbols include the following:

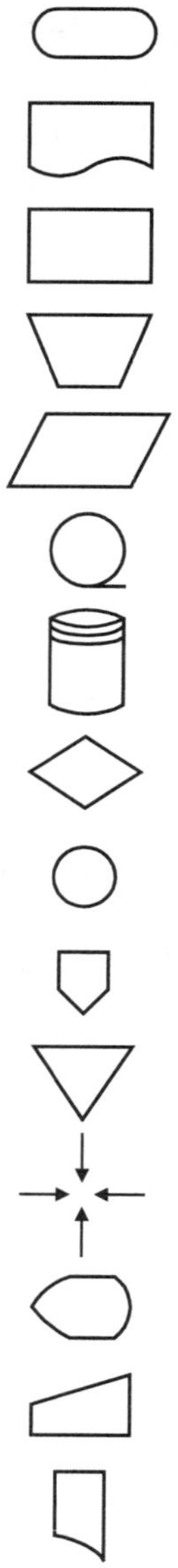

   - Starting or ending point or point of interruption
   - Input or output of a document or report
   - Computer operation or group of operations
   - Manual processing operation, e.g., prepare document
   - Generalized symbol for input or output used when the medium is not specified
   - Hard drive used for input or output
   - Hard drive or other digital media used for storage
   - Decision symbol indicating a branch in the flow
   - Connection between points on the same page
   - Connection between two pages of the flowchart
   - Storage (file) that is not immediately accessible by computer
   - Flow direction of data or processing
   - Display on a video terminal
   - Manual input into a terminal or other online device
   - Adding machine tape (batch control)

   Figure 2-1

c. On the following pages are five flowcharts and accompanying tables depicting the steps in the cycles and the controls in each step for an organization large enough to have an optimal segregation of duties.

1) Proper segregation of duties is (a) authorization of the transaction, (b) recording of the transaction, and (c) custody of assets related to the transaction.

2) In small- and medium-sized organizations, some duties must be combined. In this case, management or the auditor must assess whether organizational segregation of duties is adequate.

> **SUCCESS TIP**
>
> The flowcharts show the flow of documents through a typical system. The use of documents presents a visual picture of how each transaction is controlled. To simplify the presentation, the flowcharts do not show the disposition (filing) of documents. Also, text is added to clarify certain steps.
>
> In the diagrams that follow, documents that originate outside the organization are separated by a thick border.
>
> The following detailed explanations of the accounting cycles do **not** need to be memorized. However, you should be able to understand them. If you understand these cycles and their respective controls, you should be able to answer almost any type of question about accounting cycles and their controls on the CPA Exam.
>
> Please note that not all questions on the CPA Exam will follow the exact cycles described on the following pages.

2. **Sales-Receivables-Cash Receipts – Responsibilities of Personnel**

    a. The following are the responsibilities of personnel or departments in the sales-receivables-cash receipts cycle:

    1) **Sales** prepares sales orders based on customer orders.
    2) **Credit** reports to the treasurer, authorizes credit for all new customers, and initiates write-off of credit losses. Credit checks should be performed before credit approval.
    3) **Inventory Warehouse** maintains physical custody of products.
    4) **Inventory Control** maintains records of quantities of products in the Inventory Warehouse.
    5) **Shipping** prepares shipping documents and ships products based on authorized sales orders.
    6) **Billing** prepares customer invoices based on goods shipped.
    7) **Accounts Receivable** maintains the accounts receivable subsidiary ledger.
    8) **Mail Room** receives mail and prepares initial cash receipts records.
    9) **Cash Receipts** safeguards and promptly deposits cash receipts.
    10) **General Ledger** maintains the accounts receivable control account and records sales. Daily summaries of sales are recorded in a sales journal. Totals of details from the sales journal are usually posted monthly to the general ledger.
    11) **Receiving** prepares receiving reports and handles all receipts of goods or materials, including sales returns.

3. **Sales-Receivables Flowchart**

   a. Study the flowchart below. Understand and visualize the sales-receivables process and controls. The flowchart begins at "Start." Read the business activity and internal control descriptions in the table on the next page as needed.

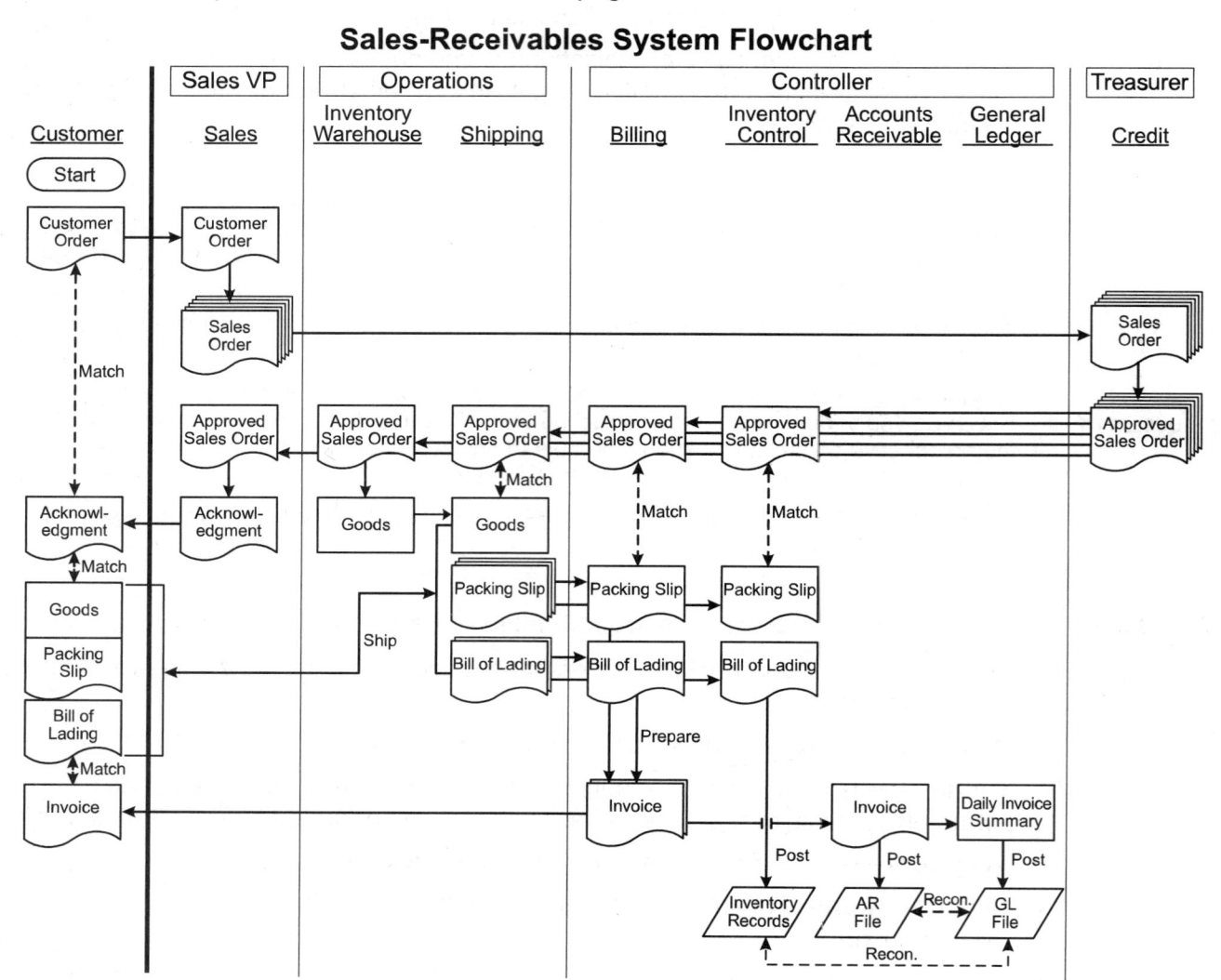

Figure 2-2

Sales-Receivables System Flowchart Table

Function	Authorization			Custody		Recording			
Department	Customer	Sales	Credit	Shipping	Inventory Warehouse	Billing	Inventory Control	Accounts Receivable	General Ledger

Step	Business Activity	Internal Control
1	Sales receives a **customer order** and prepares a multi-part **sales order** then forwards it to Credit.	Reconciling sequentially numbered sales orders helps ensure that orders are legitimate.
2	Credit performs a credit check. If the customer is creditworthy, Credit approves the **sales order**.	Ensures that goods are shipped only to actual customers and that the account is unlikely to become delinquent.
3	Credit sends copies of the **approved sales order** to Sales, Inventory Warehouse, Shipping, Billing, and Inventory Control.	Notifies these departments that a legitimate sale has been made.
4	Upon receipt of the **approved sales order**, Sales sends an **acknowledgment** to the customer.	The customer's expectation of receiving goods reduces the chances of misrouting or misappropriation.
5	Upon receipt of the **approved sales order**, the Inventory Warehouse pulls the goods and forwards them to Shipping.	Ensures that goods are removed from the Inventory Warehouse only as part of a legitimate sale.
6	Shipping verifies that the goods received from Inventory Warehouse match the **approved sales order**, prepares a **packing slip** and a **bill of lading**, and ships the goods to the customer.	Ensures that the correct goods are shipped.
7	Shipping forwards a copy of the **packing slip** and **bill of lading** to Inventory Control and Billing.	Notifies these departments that the goods have been shipped.
8	Upon receipt of the **packing slip** and **bill of lading**, Inventory Control matches them with the **approved sales order** and updates the inventory records.	Ensures that inventory records are updated once the goods have been shipped.
9	Upon receipt of the **packing slip** and **bill of lading**, Billing matches them with the **approved sales order**, prepares a multi-part **invoice**, and sends a copy to the customer. Typically, a **remittance advice** is included for use in the cash receipts cycle.	Ensures that customers are billed for all goods, and only those goods, that were actually shipped. Reconciling sequentially numbered invoices helps prevent misappropriation of goods.
10	Accounts Receivable receives an **invoice** copy from Billing and posts a journal entry to the AR file.	Ensures that customer accounts are kept current.
11	Accounts Receivable prepares a **daily invoice summary** for the day and forwards it to General Ledger for posting to the GL file.	Separation of the Accounts Receivable, Billing, and General Ledger helps assure integrity of recording.
12	General Ledger receives a **daily invoice summary** from AR to post to the GL file.	Updating inventory, AR, and GL files separately provides an additional accounting control when they are periodically reconciled.

46   SU 2: Accounting Cycles and Corporate Governance

4. **Cash Receipts Flowchart**

   a. Study the flowchart below. Understand and visualize the cash receipts process and controls. The flowchart begins at "Start." Read the business activity and internal control descriptions in the table on the next page as needed.

Cash Receipts System Flowchart

Customer	Treasurer		Controller		Bank
	Mail Room	Cash Receipts	Accounts Receivable	General Ledger	

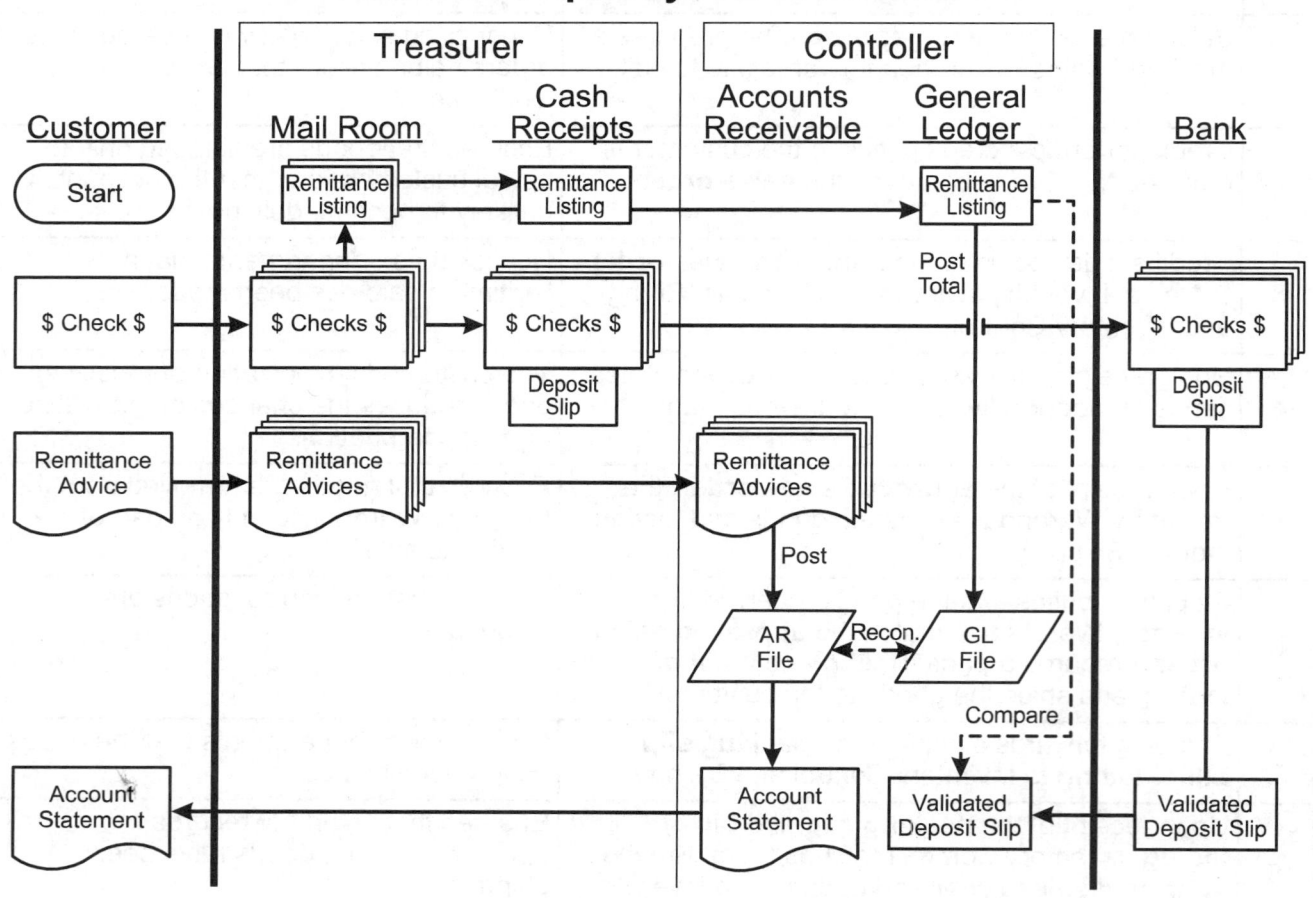

- Start
- $ Check $ → $ Checks $ (Mail Room) → $ Checks $ (Cash Receipts) → $ Checks $ (Bank)
- Remittance Listing (Mail Room) → Remittance Listing (Cash Receipts) → Remittance Listing (General Ledger) — Post Total
- Deposit Slip (Cash Receipts) ; Deposit Slip (Bank)
- Remittance Advice → Remittance Advices (Mail Room) → Remittance Advices (Accounts Receivable) → Post → AR File ←Recon.→ GL File
- Validated Deposit Slip (Bank) → Validated Deposit Slip (General Ledger) ; Compare with GL File
- Account Statement (Bank) → Account Statement (Accounts Receivable) → Account Statement (Customer)

Figure 2-3

Cash Receipts System Flowchart Table

Function	Authorization		Custody		Recording	
Department	Customer	Bank	Mail Room	Cash Receipts	Accounts Receivable	General Ledger

Step	Business Activity	Internal Control
1	Mail Room opens customer mail with two clerks always present. Customer **checks** are immediately endorsed "For Deposit Only into Account XXX." **Remittance advices** are separated (one is prepared if not included in the payment).	Reduces risk of misappropriation by a single employee. Checks stamped "For Deposit Only into Account XXX" cannot be diverted.
2	Mail Room prepares a **remittance listing** of all **checks** received during the day and forwards it with the checks to Cash Receipts.	Remittance listing provides a control total for later reconciliation.
3	Cash Receipts prepares a **deposit slip** and deposits checks in Bank. Bank validates the **deposit slip**.	Bank provides independent evidence that the full amount was deposited.
4	Mail Room sends **remittance advices** to Accounts Receivable for updating of customer accounts in the AR file.	Ensures that customer accounts are kept current.
5	Mail Room also sends a copy of the **remittance listing** to General Ledger for posting of the total to the GL file.	Updating AR and GL files separately provides an additional accounting control when they are periodically reconciled.
6	**Validated deposit slip** is returned to General Ledger to compare with **remittance listing**.	Ensures that all cash listed on the remittance listing from the Mail Room was deposited.
7	Accounts Receivable periodically sends an **account statement** to customers showing all sales and payment activity.	Customers will complain about mistaken billings or missing payments.

    b. A lockbox system (not depicted in the preceding flowchart) can ensure that cash receipts are not stolen by mail clerks or other employees. This system provides for customer payments to be sent to a post office box and collected directly by the bank. The bank forwards customer remittance information to the entity for recording purposes.

5. **Purchases-Payables-Cash Disbursements – Responsibilities of Personnel**
    a. Responsibilities of personnel and departments in the purchases-payables-cash disbursements cycle include the following:
        1) **Inventory Control** provides authorization for the purchase of goods and performs an accountability function (e.g., Inventory Control is responsible for maintaining perpetual records for inventory quantities and costs).
        2) **Purchasing** issues purchase orders for required goods.
        3) **Receiving** accepts goods for approved purchases, counts and inspects the goods, and prepares the receiving report.
        4) **Inventory Warehouse** provides physical control over the goods.
        5) **Accounts Payable** (vouchers payable) assembles the proper documentation to support a payment voucher (and disbursement) and records the account payable.
        6) **Cash Disbursements** evaluates the documentation to support a payment voucher and signs and mails the check.
            a) This department cancels the documentation to prevent duplicate payment.
        7) **General Ledger** maintains the accounts payable control account and other related general ledger accounts.

SU 2: Accounting Cycles and Corporate Governance 49

b. Study the flowchart below. Understand and visualize the purchases-payables process and controls. The flowchart begins at "Start." Read the business activity and internal control descriptions in the table on the next page as needed.

Purchases-Payables System Flowchart

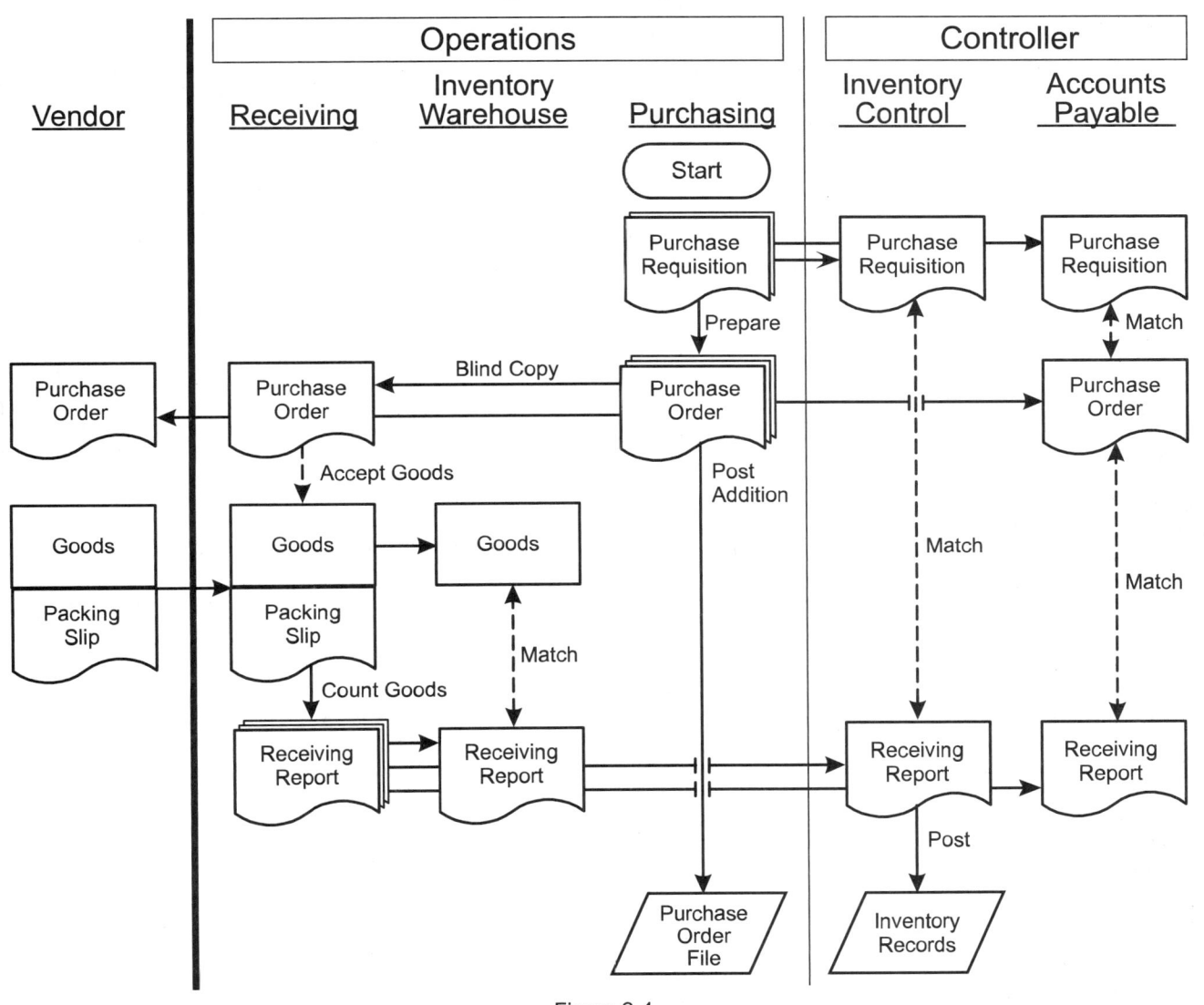

Figure 2-4

NOTE: Nothing is recorded in the general ledger for issuing a purchase order. A liability is not created until the goods and invoice are received (see the Cash Disbursements System Flowchart in Figure 2-5).

Purchases-Payables System Flowchart Table

Function	Authorization		Custody			Recording	
Department	Inventory Control	Purchasing	Vendor	Receiving	Inventory Warehouse	Accounts Payable	General Ledger

Step	Business Activity	Internal Control
1	Inventory Control prepares a **purchase requisition** when inventory reaches the reorder point due to sales and sends it to Purchasing and Accounts Payable.	Predetermined inventory levels trigger authorization to initiate a purchase transaction.
2	Purchasing locates the authorized vendor in the vendor file, prepares a **purchase order**, and updates the purchase order file.	• Purchasing ensures that goods are bought only from vendors who have been preapproved for reliability. • Reconciling sequentially numbered purchase orders helps ensure that orders are legitimate.
3	Purchasing sends the **purchase order** to Vendor, Receiving, and Accounts Payable. Receiving's copy has blank quantities.	• Receiving is put on notice to expect shipment. • Accounts Payable is put on notice that liability to this vendor will increase when goods arrive.
4	When goods arrive, Receiving accepts goods based on the file copy of the **purchase order**, prepares a **receiving report**, and forwards the **receiving report** with the goods to the Inventory Warehouse.	Because quantities are blank on Receiving's copy of the purchase order, employees must count items to prepare the receiving report.
5	The Inventory Warehouse verifies that goods received match those listed on the **receiving report**.	Detects any loss or damage between Receiving and the Inventory Warehouse. Inventory Warehouse accepts responsibility for safeguarding receipted goods.
6	Receiving sends the **receiving report** to Inventory Control for matching with the **purchase requisition** and updating of inventory records.	Ensures that inventory records are current.
7	Receiving also sends a copy of the **receiving report** to Accounts Payable for matching with the **purchase order** and **purchase requisition**.	Accounts Payable ensures that all documents reconcile and will await the arrival of the vendor invoice to record the payable transaction (as shown in the Cash Disbursements System Flowchart on the next page).

c. Study the flowchart below. Understand and visualize the cash disbursements process and controls. The flowchart begins at "Start." Read the business activity and internal control descriptions in the table on the next page as needed.

Cash Disbursements System Flowchart

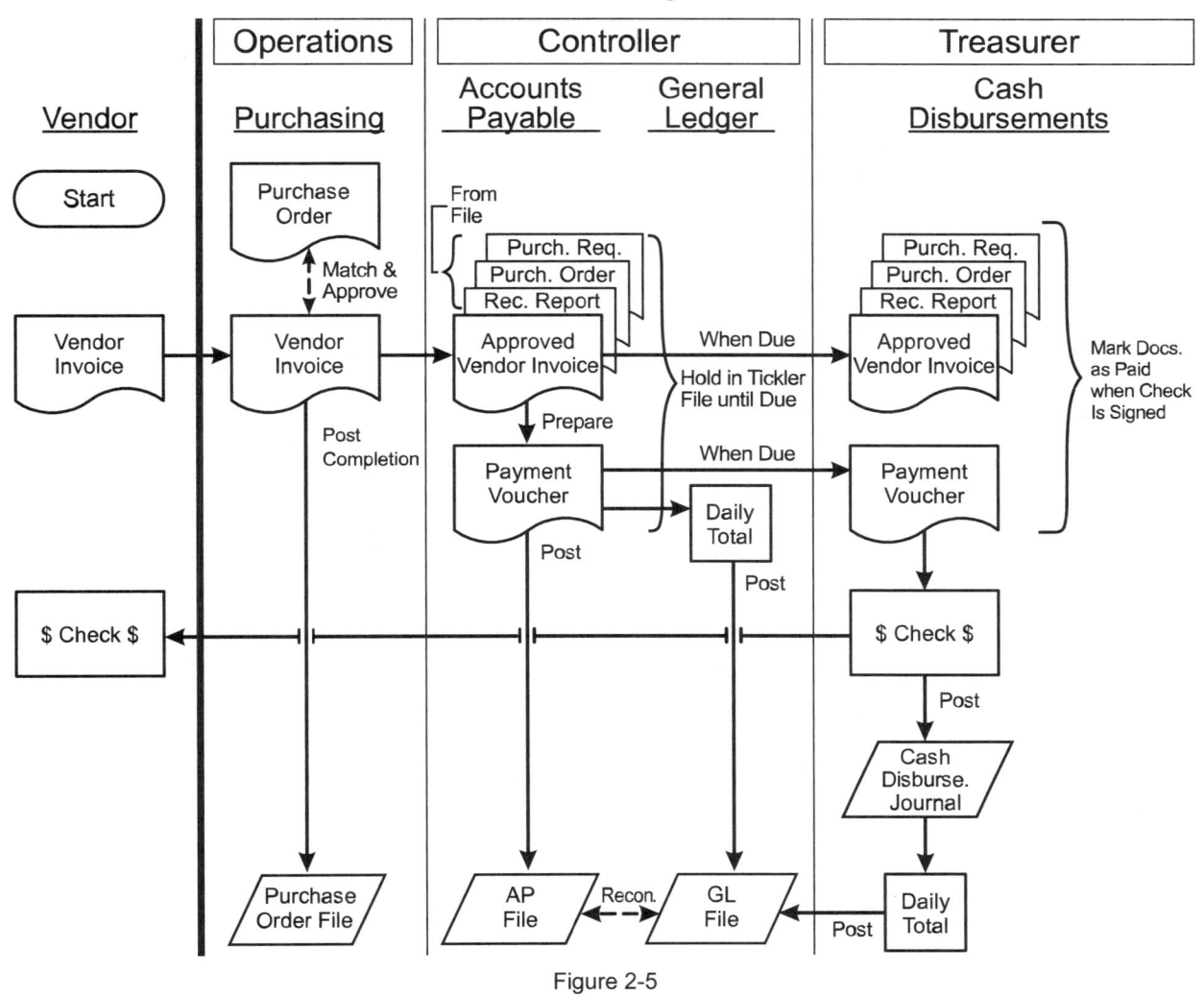

Figure 2-5

NOTE: A tickler file is a set of date-labeled file folders organized in a way that allows time-sensitive documents to be filed according to the future date on which each document needs action.

Cash Disbursements System Flowchart Table

Function	Authorization		Custody	Recording	
Department	Vendor	Purchasing	Cash Disbursements	Accounts Payable	General Ledger

Step	Business Activity	Internal Control
1	Purchasing receives a **vendor invoice**. The **vendor invoice** is matched with the **purchase order** and approved for payment. The **purchase order** is marked as closed in the purchase order file if completed, and the **approved vendor invoice** is forwarded to Accounts Payable.	• Purchasing ensures the vendor invoiced for the proper amount and the terms are as agreed. • Purchasing can follow up on partially filled orders.
2	Accounts Payable matches the **approved vendor invoice** with the file copies of the **purchase requisition, purchase order**, and **receiving report** and prepares a **payment voucher**. The **payment voucher** is recorded in the accounts payable file.	• Matching all documents provides assurance that only goods that were appropriately ordered, received, and invoiced are recorded as a liability. • Periodic reconciliation with the payment vouchers in the tickler file (maintained by due date) with the accounts payable file (maintained by vendor) ensures proper recording.
3	The **payment voucher**, with the attached documents, is filed in a tickler file by due date. The **daily total** of all payment vouchers is sent to the General Ledger to record the purchase (inventory) and liability (accounts payable).	Filing by due date ensures that payment will be made on a timely basis (e.g., to obtain discounts or avoid default).
4	On the due date, the **payment voucher** and attached documents are removed from the tickler file sent to Cash Disbursements for **check** preparation, signing, and mailing. The **check** is recorded in the cash disbursements journal.	• Cash Disbursements cannot issue a check without an approved payment voucher. • Large payments may require two signatures on the check to provide additional oversight.
5	The **payment voucher** and attached documents are stamped "Paid," and the **check** is mailed to the vendor.	Stamping the documents "Paid" prevents them from supporting a second, illicit payment voucher.
6	The **daily total** of all checks written and mailed for the day is sent to General Ledger to record the reduction in accounts payable and cash.	Periodic reconciliation of the accounts payable and general ledger ensures proper recording.

d. Other Payment Authorizations

1) This voucher disbursement system is applicable to virtually all required payments by the entity, not just purchases of inventory as described previously. The following are additional considerations:

   a) The authorizations may come from other departments based on a budget or policy (e.g., a utility bill might need authorization by the plant manager).
   b) Accounts Payable requires different document(s) (e.g., a utility bill with the signature of the plant manager) to support the preparation of the payment voucher and check.
   c) A debit other than inventory (e.g., utilities expense) is entered on the payment voucher and recorded in the general ledger. Accounts payable is still credited.
   d) The use of the tickler file and the functions of Cash Disbursements do not change when other types of payments are made.

6. **Payroll – Responsibilities of Personnel**

   a. The following are the responsibilities of organizational subunits in the payroll cycle:

   1) **Human Resources** provides an authorized list of employees and associated pay rates, deductions, and exemptions.
   2) **Payroll** is an accounting function responsible for calculating the payroll (i.e., preparing the payroll register) based on authorizations from Human Resources and the authorized time records from Timekeeping.
   3) **Timekeeping** is an accounting function that oversees the employees' recording of hours on clock cards (using the time clock) and that receives and reconciles the job time tickets from Production.
   4) **Production** manufactures the products.
   5) **Cost Accounting** is an accounting function that accumulates direct materials, direct labor, and overhead costs on job order cost sheets to determine the costs of production.
   6) **Accounts Payable** prepares the payment voucher based on the payroll register prepared by Payroll.
   7) **Cash Disbursements** signs and deposits a check based on the payment voucher into a separate payroll account, prepares individual employee paychecks, and distributes paychecks.
   8) **General Ledger** records the payroll.

b. Study the flowchart below. Understand and visualize the payroll process and controls. The flowchart begins at "Start." Read the business activity and internal control descriptions in the table on the next page as needed.

Payroll System Flowchart

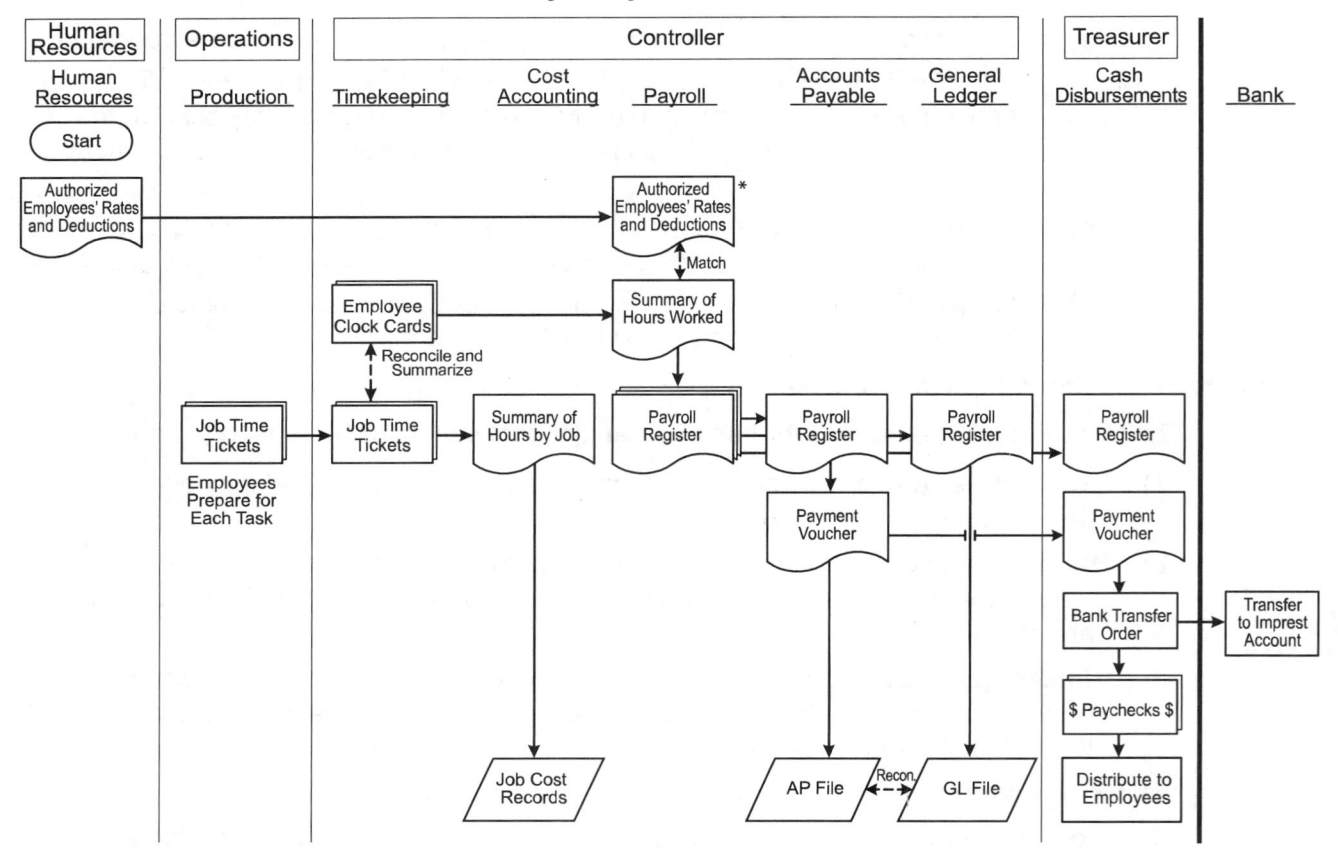

Figure 2-6

*Payroll receives only a list of authorized employees' rates and deductions and does not have authority to change those rates.

> **SUCCESS TIP**
>
> In subsequent study units, discussion of traditional document-based systems is adapted to address the use of electronic-based systems. For example, Study Unit 14, Subunits 2 and 3, consider how the document flow represented in the flowcharts can be replaced by information flow in an electronic system. The need for control is unchanged, but the specific controls used are different. Study Unit 14 contains a reminder to reconsider the flowcharts in this subunit if you need a refresher.

Payroll System Flowchart Table

Function	Authorization		Custody		Recording				
Department	Human Resources	Production	Cash Disbursements	Bank	Timekeeping	Cost Accounting	Payroll	Accounts Payable	General Ledger

Step	Business Activity	Internal Control
1	Human Resources sends an **authorized employees' rates and deductions** list to Payroll.	Ensures that only actual employees are included on the payroll and that rates of pay and withholding amounts are accurate.
2	Employees record the start and end times of their workdays on **employee clock cards** held in Timekeeping.	The recording process mechanically or electronically captures employee work hours.
3	Production employees record time worked on various tasks on **job time tickets**.	Allows accumulation of labor costs by job as well as tracking of direct and indirect labor.
4	At the end of each day, a production supervisor approves the **job time tickets** and forwards them to Timekeeping, where they are reconciled with the **employee clock cards**.	Ensures that employees worked only authorized hours. Reconciles the time allocated to direct and indirect labor with total time worked.
5	Timekeeping prepares a **summary of hours worked** by employee and forwards it to Payroll. Payroll matches it with the **authorized employees' rates and deductions** list and prepares a **payroll register**.	Ensures that employees are paid the proper amount.
6	Timekeeping prepares a **summary of hours worked by job** and forwards it to Cost Accounting for updating of the job cost records.	Ensures that direct labor costs are appropriately assigned to jobs.
7	Accounts Payable receives the **payroll register** from Payroll, prepares a **payment voucher**, and forwards it along with the **payroll register** to Cash Disbursements.	Ensures that a payable is accrued. Authorizes the transfer of cash to the payroll imprest account.
8	Payroll also forwards the **payroll register** to General Ledger for posting of the total to the GL file.	Updating AP and GL files separately provides an additional accounting control when they are periodically reconciled.
9	Cash Disbursements compares the **payment voucher** with the **payroll register** total and initiates the bank transfer to the payroll imprest fund.	Ensures that the correct amount is transferred to the payroll imprest account (and governmental authorities).
10	**Paychecks** are distributed to employees by the Treasurer function.	Treasurer has custody responsibility but no recording or authorization responsibility. This ensures that Payroll or supervisory personnel cannot perpetrate fraud by creating fictitious employees.

STOP & REVIEW

You have completed the outline for this subunit.
Study multiple-choice questions 1 through 4 beginning on page 68.

2.2 CORPORATE GOVERNANCE STRUCTURE

1. **Definition of Corporate Governance**

    a. **Governance** is a combination of people, policies, procedures, and processes (including internal control). It helps ensure that an entity effectively and efficiently directs its activities toward meeting the objectives of its stakeholders.

    1) **Stakeholders** are persons or other entities who are affected by the activities of the entity.

        a) Examples are shareholders, employees, suppliers, customers, neighbors of the entity's facilities, and government regulators.

    b. Corporate governance can be influenced by **internal or external** sources.

    1) Corporate charters and bylaws, boards of directors, codes of ethics, and internal audit functions are internal sources.

    2) The requirements of the Securities Act of 1933 and the Securities Exchange Act of 1934 administered by the Securities and Exchange Commission (SEC) are external sources.

2. **Code of Ethics**

    a. The primary purpose of a code of ethics is to promote an ethical culture within the corporation. An ethical culture is best promoted by senior management setting the example.

    b. Additional purposes of a code of ethics include

    1) Communicating acceptable values to employees,

    2) Establishing objective standards against which employees can evaluate their conduct,

    3) Providing guidance on what to do if employees encounter unacceptable behavior, and

    4) Communicating the corporation's values to outsiders.

    c. To be effective, the code should be periodically acknowledged by all employees and provide for disciplinary action for violators.

3. **Board of Directors**
    a. All **major corporate decisions** are made or approved by the board.
        1) Directly managing the day-to-day operations of the entity is management's responsibility. The board has an **oversight role**.
    b. The board has the following **duties**:
        1) Selection and removal of officers
        2) Decisions about capital structure (mix of debt and equity, consideration to be received for shares, etc.)
        3) Adding, amending, or repealing bylaws (unless this authority is reserved to the shareholders)
        4) Initiation of fundamental changes (mergers, acquisitions, etc.)
        5) Decisions to declare and distribute dividends
        6) Setting of management compensation (sometimes performed by a subcommittee called the compensation committee)
        7) Coordinating audit activities (most often performed by a subcommittee called the audit committee)
        8) Evaluating and managing risk (sometimes performed by a subcommittee called the risk committee)
    c. If permitted by the articles or bylaws, the board may delegate authority to **committees** composed of its members or corporate officers.
        1) Committees may exercise broad powers consistent with the limits of the resolutions by which they were established.
        2) Every public corporation (i.e., issuer) must have an **audit committee** consisting of independent directors.

4. **Officers**
    a. The corporation's officers (i.e., executive management) are responsible for carrying out the entity's **day-to-day operations**.
    b. The **chief executive officer (CEO)** is directly selected by, and reports to, the board of directors.
    c. The CEO in turn usually selects other executives such as the chief financial officer (CFO, also termed the treasurer) and chief information officer (CIO). These executives oversee the various functional areas of the entity.
    d. Officers are **agents of the corporation** and as such may enter the corporation into legally binding contracts.

5. **Fiduciary Duties**
   a. Directors and officers owe a **fiduciary duty** to the corporation to (1) act in its best interests, (2) be loyal, (3) use due diligence in discharging responsibilities, (4) be informed about information relevant to the corporation, and (5) disclose conflicts of interest. **Controlling or majority shareholders** owe similar duties.
      1) The fiduciary duty of directors and officers is generally divided into the **duty of care** and the **duty of loyalty**.
   b. The **duty of care** requires directors and officers to discharge their duties
      1) In good faith,
      2) In a manner (s)he reasonably believes to be in the best interests of the corporation, and
      3) With the care that a person in a similar position would reasonably believe appropriate under similar circumstances.
      4) **Reliance on others.** In exercising reasonable care, directors and officers may rely on information, reports, opinions, and statements prepared or presented by persons (an appropriate officer, employee, or specialist) whom the director **reasonably believes** to be competent in the matters presented.
         a) Directors and officers also may rely on the specialized knowledge of lawyers, accountants, investment bankers, and board committees.
      5) Directors and officers are expected to be **informed** about pertinent corporate information when giving advice. To exercise the required care, directors and officers should
         a) Attend relevant meetings
         b) Analyze corporate financial statements
         c) Review pertinent legal opinions
         d) Become knowledgeable about the available relevant information
   c. The **duty of loyalty** requires directors and officers to take certain steps when they are involved in a conflicting-interest transaction or are presented with a corporate opportunity.
      1) **Conflicting-interest transactions.** To protect the corporation against self-dealing, directors and officers are required to make **full disclosure** of any financial interest they may have in any transaction to which they and the corporation may be a party. Directors and officers must not make a secret profit.
         a) A transaction is **not** improper merely on the grounds of a director's or officer's conflict of interest.
            i) If the transaction (a) is **fair** to the corporation or (b) has been **approved** by a majority of informed, disinterested directors or shareholders, it is not voidable and does not result in sanctions even if the director or officer makes a profit.

2) Directors and officers may not usurp any **corporate opportunity**. They must give the corporation the right of first refusal.

EXAMPLE 2-1   Usurpation of a Corporate Opportunity

Skip, a director of The Fishing Corp., learns in his corporate capacity that a state-of-the-art, deep-sea hydroplane fishing vessel is available for a bargain price. The purchase of this unique hydroplane may be a business opportunity from which the corporation could benefit. If Skip purchases the hydroplane for himself without giving the corporation the right of first refusal, he is usurping a corporate opportunity.

---

6. **Internal Auditors**

    a. Internal auditing is an independent, objective assurance and consulting activity designed to add value and improve an organization's operations.

    b. The internal audit function should assess and make appropriate recommendations to improve the organization's governance processes for

    1) Making strategic and operational decisions
    2) Overseeing risk management and control
    3) Promoting appropriate ethics and values within the organization
    4) Ensuring effective organizational performance management and accountability
    5) Communicating risk and control information to appropriate areas of the organization
    6) Coordinating the activities of, and communicating information among, the board, external and internal auditors, other assurance providers, and management

7. **Corporate Governance Structure**

    a. The appropriateness of an entity's organizational structure depends in part on the nature of its activities.

    1) Accordingly, a highly structured organization with formal reporting lines may be appropriate regardless of entity size.

    b. An entity's organizational structure may be characterized as centralized or decentralized.

    1) In a **centralized** organization, decision-making authority is retained by senior management.
    2) In a **decentralized** organization, decision-making authority is granted to lower management.

    c. The degree of centralization or decentralization affects the entity's **ethical climate**.

    1) An entity that is highly centralized (decentralized) will have a more uniform (diverse) ethical culture than an entity that is decentralized (centralized).
    2) A decentralized environment may increase the risk that unethical decisions could be made by lower management because the ethical standards of unit managers may be inconsistent with those of the entity as a whole.

8. **Financial Reporting**
    a. A publicly held corporation's annual report to its shareholders must contain audited financial statements and other specified information.
    b. The **board of directors** is responsible for hiring, setting the compensation for, and overseeing the work of the independent auditor. In large corporations, a group of directors forms an **audit committee** to perform these functions.
        1) The audit committee also must
            a) Address complaints about accounting and auditing matters and
            b) Receive reports about
                i) All critical accounting policies and practices to be used,
                ii) All material alternative treatments of financial information within GAAP discussed with management,
                iii) Effects of the use of alternative disclosures and treatments, and
                iv) The treatments preferred by the external auditors.
        NOTE: Subunit 2.3 states other key corporate governance requirements of the Sarbanes-Oxley Act of 2002 related to audit committees.
    c. **Management** is responsible for the
        1) Preparation and fair presentation of the financial statements and
        2) Design, implementation, and maintenance of internal control relevant to their preparation and fair presentation.
    d. The **independent auditor's** responsibility is to express an opinion on whether the financial statements are fairly presented in accordance with GAAP.
        1) If the corporation is **publicly held** (i.e., an issuer), the auditor also must report on the effectiveness of **internal control** over financial reporting.

STOP & REVIEW

You have completed the outline for this subunit.
Study multiple-choice questions 5 through 9 beginning on page 69.

2.3 THE SARBANES-OXLEY ACT OF 2002 (SOX)

> **BACKGROUND 2-1 Context of Enactment of SOX**
>
> In late 2001 and 2002, massive accounting scandals were reported in the media. They involved such large firms as Enron (hid debt of over $1 billion in improper off-the-books partnerships), Global Crossing (inflated revenues; shredded accounting-related documents), and WorldCom (booked operating expenses as capital assets; made large off-the-books payments to founder). In response to these and many other fraudulent practices, Congress passed the Sarbanes-Oxley Act of 2002, named for its sponsors, Democratic Senator Paul Sarbanes of Maryland and Republican Representative Mike Oxley of Ohio.

SUCCESS TIP: The scope of SOX coverage on the BEC exam is limited to the key "corporate governance" provisions. In particular, the provisions on audit committees are frequently tested on the BEC exam. Therefore, candidates are encouraged to have an intimate knowledge of audit committees. The key SOX provisions affecting "public accounting firms" are tested in AUD. However, some of those provisions are covered below and on the following pages to provide greater context on the implications of SOX.

1. SOX applies to public companies who report to the SEC. While not legally applicable to private companies, private companies may enact similar guidelines to follow.
2. **Audit Committees**
    a. Each member of the issuer's **audit committee** shall be an **independent member** of the board of directors.
        1) To be independent, a member of the audit committee must not be affiliated with the issuer or receive any compensation (other than for service on the committee, board, or any other board committee) from the issuer.
            a) The audit committee must be comprised of **at least three** independent members.
    b. It is best business practice to have at least **one** member of the audit committee qualify as an **audit committee financial expert** (not a requirement).
        1) An issuer must **disclose** whether its audit committee has at least one audit committee financial expert, the name of the expert, and whether the expert is independent of management.
            a) If the audit committee lacks an audit committee financial expert, the issuer must disclose the reason(s).
        2) To be considered an audit committee financial expert, the director must have
            a) An understanding of generally accepted accounting principles (GAAP) and financial statements;
            b) Experience in
                i) The preparation or audit of financial statements of generally comparable issuers and
                ii) The application of GAAP in connection with the accounting for estimates, accruals, and reserves;
            c) Experience with internal accounting controls; and
            d) An understanding of audit committee functions.

c. The audit committee must be **directly responsible** for appointing, compensating, and overseeing the work of the independent auditor.

   1) The independent auditor must report directly to the audit committee, not to management.

d. The audit committee must also **establish procedures** for

   1) The receipt, retention, and treatment of complaints received regarding accounting, internal control, or auditing matters, and
   2) The confidential, anonymous submission of employees' concerns regarding questionable accounting or auditing matters.

> **SUCCESS TIP**
> Candidates should be able to identify failures to meet SOX requirements within the entity in the BEC section of the CPA Exam.

3. **Public Company Accounting Oversight Board (PCAOB)**

   a. The PCAOB was established to oversee the audits of public companies.
   b. The PCAOB
      1) Issues auditing and related standards for public companies;
      2) Inspects and investigates accounting firms; and
      3) Enforces compliance with its rules, professional standards, SOX, and relevant securities laws.

4. **Public Accounting Firms**

   a. Public accounting firms that act as independent auditors must register with the PCAOB.
   b. A public accounting firm is **prohibited** from performing certain **nonaudit services** for an audit client.
   c. The prohibited nonaudit services consist of the following:
      1) Bookkeeping
      2) Financial information systems design and implementation
      3) Appraisal or valuation services, fairness opinions, or contribution-in-kind reports
      4) Actuarial services
      5) Internal audit outsourcing services
      6) Management functions or human resources
      7) Broker-dealer, investment advisor, or investment banking services
      8) Legal services and expert services unrelated to the audit
   d. A public accounting firm may perform **permitted services** (e.g., tax services and statutory audits) for an audit client if those services are **preapproved by the audit committee**.

5. **Reporting -- CEO and CFO Certification (Section 302)**
    a. In every **annual (Form 10-K) or quarterly (Form 10-Q)** filing with the SEC, the CEO and CFO must certify the following:
        1) They have reviewed the report.
        2) To the best of their knowledge, the report and financial statements are free of material misstatements.
        3) They are responsible for the system of internal control and have evaluated its effectiveness.
        4) They have informed the audit committee and the independent auditors of all significant control deficiencies and any fraud, whether or not material.
        5) Significant changes were (or were not) made in internal controls, including corrective actions.

6. **Reporting -- Management's Assessment of Internal Controls (Section 404)**
    a. The **annual** report must contain the following:
        1) A statement that management has taken responsibility for establishing and maintaining an adequate system of internal control over financial reporting
        2) The name of the internal control model, if any, used to design and assess the effectiveness of the internal control system (COSO's *Internal Control – Integrated Framework* is the most widely used model in the United States)
        3) An assessment of whether internal control over financial reporting is effective
        4) A statement that an independent public accounting firm that is registered with the PCAOB also has assessed the system

7. **Loans to Directors and Executive Officers**
    a. Although certain exceptions apply (e.g., home improvement loans and consumer credit), issuers are generally prohibited from extending **personal loans** to any director or executive officer.

8. **Code of Ethics**

    a. Issuers are required to disclose whether or not they have adopted a code of ethics for **senior financial officers**.

        1) If they have **not** adopted a code of ethics for senior financial officers, then they must also disclose the reason(s) why.

9. **Penalties**

    a. Knowingly altering, destroying, covering up, falsifying, or making a false entry in any record with the intent to impede an investigation by a U.S. agency could result in a fine, imprisonment of up to 20 years, or both.

    b. **Retaliating against informants** (e.g., whistleblowers) could result in a fine, imprisonment of up to 10 years, or both.

    c. Separate penalties are provided for unknowingly and knowingly **certifying noncomplying filings**.

        1) **Unknowingly** certifying filings that do not meet the requirements of SOX can result in fines of up to $1,000,000 or up to 10 years imprisonment.

        2) **Knowingly** certifying filings that do not meet the requirements of SOX can result in fines of up to $5,000,000 or up to 20 years imprisonment.

    d. If an issuer is required to prepare an **accounting restatement** because of **misconduct**, the issuer's CEO and CFO must forfeit

        1) Any bonus or other incentive-based compensation received from the issuer during the previous 12 months and

        2) Any profits received from the sale of stock of the issuer during the previous 12 months.

    e. For certain violations, the SEC has the authority to prohibit persons from serving as a director or officer of any issuer.

STOP & REVIEW

You have completed the outline for this subunit.
Study multiple-choice questions 10 through 19 beginning on page 71.

2.4 SYSTEM AND ORGANIZATION CONTROLS (SOC) FOR SERVICE ORGANIZATIONS

> **BACKGROUND 2-2   SOC Reports**
>
> A service auditor's reports on a service organization's internal control are known as **SOC 1** reports (System and Organization Controls reports). SOC 2 and 3 reports that address nonfinancial reporting controls (e.g., security and privacy) may also be issued by service auditors. SOC 1 reports are addressed in the following outline, and the three types of reports are compared at the end of the subunit.

1. Some of an entity's business processes or functions, e.g., IT, human resources, payroll, or internal audit, may be performed by an external service organization.

    a. The service organization's services and controls over financial reporting are part of the user entity's business processes. Accordingly, the user entity (and the entity's independent auditor, termed the user auditor) must understand the activities and controls related to the outsourced services and how the service organization's internal control system affects the entity's system of internal control.

2. **Determining If an Outsourced Function Qualifies as a Service Organization**

    a. A service organization's services and controls are part of the client's information system relevant to financial reporting if they have an effect on

       1) The significant classes of transactions in the user entity's operations;

       2) The systems, both IT and manual, that initiate, authorize, record, process, correct, and report the user entity's transactions;

       3) How the user entity's information system captures significant events and conditions, other than transactions; or

       4) The process used to prepare statements, including significant estimates and disclosures.

3. **Definitions**

    a. The **user entity** uses a service organization. The user entity's financial statements are being audited.

    b. The **user auditor** audits and reports on the financial statements of the user entity.

    c. The **service organization** provides services to users that are relevant to their internal control over financial reporting.

    d. The **service auditor** reports on controls at a service organization in one of the following:

       1) A report on management's description of a service organization's system and the suitability of the design of controls (a **SOC 1 type 1 report**)

       2) A report on management's description of a service organization's system, the suitability of the design of the controls, and **operating effectiveness** of controls (a **SOC 1 type 2 report**)

    e. A **subservice organization** is used by another service organization to perform some of the services provided to user entities that are relevant to their internal control over financial reporting.

- f. **Complementary user entity controls (CUEC)** are those the service organization builds into the design of its own controls structure and will be implemented by user entities to achieve the control objectives of both the service organization and the user. Therefore, CUECs are the responsibility of the user entity.
    1) For example, a service organization provider of computer cloud storage requires users to transfer data in accordance with prescribed data encryption protocols, ensure virus protection software is up to date, and require passwords that are periodically changed so that only authorized personnel are permitted to access the system. Therefore, the service organization's control objectives are met when the user implements all of the controls.
- g. **Tests of controls** are designed to evaluate the operating effectiveness of controls in achieving the control objectives stated in management's description of the service organization's system.

4. **Objectives of the User Auditor**
    - a. The user auditor should
        1) Obtain an understanding of the nature and significance of the services provided by the service organization and their effect on the user entity's internal control relevant to the audit. The understanding should be sufficient to identify and assess the risks of material misstatement.
        2) Design and perform audit procedures responsive to those risks.
    - b. The understanding can be supported by the System and Organization Controls report **(SOC 1 report)** prepared by the auditor of the service organization (service auditor) and is intended to be used by the auditor of the user organization (user auditor).

5. The service auditor reports on controls at a service organization in one of the following:
    - a. A **SOC 1 type 1 report** expresses an opinion on the fair presentation of management's description of the service organization's system and whether the controls are suitably designed at the specified date.
        1) Suitable design means the controls can attain the control objectives if they operate effectively
    - b. A **SOC 1 type 2 report** expresses not only the type 1 opinions but also an opinion on whether the controls were **operating effectively** (meeting the control objectives).
        1) Type 2 reports relate to design and effectiveness throughout the period rather than at a specific date.

6. SOC 2 reports and SOC 3 reports are the same as SOC 1 reports except for the following differences:
    - a. SOC 2 and SOC 3 reports relate to the controls at the service organization over **security, availability, processing integrity, confidentiality, or privacy**.
    - b. SOC 2 reports are intended to be used by the parties stated in the report.
    - c. SOC 3 reports are intended to be used by anyone.

7. All reports should have a title with the word "independent," a date, and the name and address of the service auditor.

Issue	SOC 1 Reports	SOC 2 Reports	SOC 3 Reports
Relevant Subject Matter	Controls at the service organization over financial reporting	Controls at the service organization over security, availability, processing integrity, confidentiality, or privacy	Controls at the service organization over security, availability, processing integrity, confidentiality, or privacy
Purpose of Report	Opinion on management's description of the organization's system and the suitability of the design of controls (SOC 1 type 1 report) Or Opinion on management's description of the organization's system, the suitability of the design of the controls, and operating effectiveness of controls (SOC 1 type 2 report)	Opinion on management's description of the organization's system and the suitability of the design of controls (SOC 2 type 1 report) Or Opinion on management's description of the organization's system, the suitability of the design of the controls, and operating effectiveness of controls (SOC 2 type 2 report)	Opinion on management's description of the organization's system and the suitability of the design of controls (SOC 3 type 1 report) Or Opinion on management's description of the organization's system, the suitability of the design of the controls, and operating effectiveness of controls (SOC 3 type 2 report)
Users	User auditor	Limited to parties stated in the report	Anyone

STOP & REVIEW

You have completed the outline for this subunit.
Study multiple-choice questions 20 and 21 on page 76.

QUESTIONS

2.1 Accounting Cycles and Transaction-Level Controls

1. For effective internal control, the accounts payable department ordinarily should

A. Obliterate the quantity ordered on the receiving department copy of the purchase order.
B. Establish the agreement of the vendor's invoice with the receiving report and purchase order.
C. Stamp, perforate, or otherwise cancel supporting documentation after payment is mailed.
D. Ascertain that each requisition is approved as to price, quantity, and quality by an authorized employee.

Answer (B) is correct.
REQUIRED: The procedure performed by the accounts payable department.
DISCUSSION: The accounts payable department is responsible for matching the vendor's invoice against the corresponding purchase order and receiving report. This procedure provides assurance that a valid transaction has occurred and that the parties have agreed on the terms, such as price and quantity.
Answer (A) is incorrect. The purchasing department is responsible for sending copies of the purchase order to the different departments. **Answer (C) is incorrect.** The cash disbursements department is responsible for canceling supporting documentation when checks are signed. **Answer (D) is incorrect.** The purchasing department is responsible for approving each requisition.

2. Sound internal control principles dictate that, immediately upon receiving checks from customers by mail, a responsible employee should

A. Add the checks to the daily cash summary.
B. Verify that each check is supported by a prenumbered sales invoice.
C. Prepare a duplicate listing of checks received.
D. Record the checks in the cash receipts journal.

Answer (C) is correct.
REQUIRED: The procedure performed by the employee opening the mail.
DISCUSSION: The mail room receives all customer receipts, opens the mail, separates the checks from the remittance advices, and prepares a daily listing of checks received. This daily remittance list ordinarily is prepared in duplicate.
Answer (A) is incorrect. The checks are combined with the other receipts by the cashier. **Answer (B) is incorrect.** Each check should be supported by a remittance advice. **Answer (D) is incorrect.** The person opening the mail should not have access to the accounting records.

3. Which of the following are **not** directly involved in the revenue cycle?

A. Sales manager and the credit manager.
B. Treasurer and controller.
C. Billing clerk.
D. Receiving department clerk.

Answer (D) is correct.
REQUIRED: The person(s) not directly involved in the revenue cycle.
DISCUSSION: The receiving department clerk is involved in the purchases-payables cycle. The clerk counts the goods and prepares receiving reports that provide partial authorization for invoice payment.
Answer (A) is incorrect. The sales manager is responsible for executing sales transactions, and the credit manager authorizes sales. **Answer (B) is incorrect.** The treasurer has custody of cash receipts from sales, and the controller maintains records for the sales and billing cycle. **Answer (C) is incorrect.** The billing clerk is responsible for the preparation of invoices and the billing process.

4. Which of the following activities performed by a payroll clerk is a control weakness rather than a control strength?

A. Has custody of the check signature stamp machine.
B. Prepares the payroll register.
C. Forwards the payroll register to the chief accountant for approval.
D. Draws the paychecks on a separate payroll checking account.

Answer (A) is correct.
REQUIRED: The activity by a payroll clerk that is a control weakness.
DISCUSSION: Payroll checks should be signed by someone who is not involved in timekeeping, recordkeeping, or payroll preparation. The payroll clerk performs a recordkeeping function.
Answer (B) is incorrect. Preparing the payroll register is one of the recordkeeping tasks of the payroll clerk. **Answer (C) is incorrect.** The payroll register should be approved by an officer of the organization. This control is a strength. **Answer (D) is incorrect.** Paychecks should be drawn on a separate payroll checking account. This control is a strength.

2.2 Corporate Governance Structure

5. Davis, a director of Active Corp., is entitled to

A. Serve on the board of a competing business.
B. Take sole advantage of a business opportunity that would benefit Active.
C. Rely on information provided by a corporate officer.
D. Unilaterally grant a corporate loan to one of Active's shareholders.

Answer (C) is correct.
REQUIRED: The action not a breach of a director's duties.
DISCUSSION: In the course of exercising good business judgment and reasonable care, a director is entitled to rely on information provided by an officer (or professional specialist) if the director reasonably believes the officer has competence in the relevant area.
Answer (A) is incorrect. Serving as a director of a competing business is a conflict of interest. **Answer (B) is incorrect.** Usurping a business opportunity of the corporation is a breach of the director's fiduciary duty of loyalty. **Answer (D) is incorrect.** A director is not an agent of the corporation, and directors authorize corporate transactions by approving resolutions as a board.

6. Which of the following provisions must a for-profit corporation include in its articles of incorporation to obtain a corporate charter?

I. Provision for the issuance of voting stock
II. Name of the corporation

A. I only.
B. II only.
C. Both I and II.
D. Neither I nor II.

Answer (C) is correct.
REQUIRED: The provisions a for-profit corporation must include in its articles of incorporation.
DISCUSSION: A corporation comes into being when the articles of incorporation are filed with the secretary of state of the relevant state. Among the items that the articles ordinarily must include are the corporation's name and the number of authorized shares of stock. Because the articles must include the number of authorized shares of stock, the provision for issuance of voting stock is an implicit requirement.
Answer (A) is incorrect. The name of the corporation must be included in the articles. **Answer (B) is incorrect.** The articles must include the number of shares authorized to be issued. Thus, provision for issuance of voting stock is an implicit requirement. **Answer (D) is incorrect.** Both the name of the corporation and the provision for issuance of voting stock must be included in the articles.

7. In general, which of the following must be contained in articles of incorporation?

A. Names of states in which the corporation will be doing business.
B. Name of the state in which the corporation will maintain its principal place of business.
C. Names of the initial officers and their terms of office.
D. Number of shares of stock authorized to be issued by the corporation.

Answer (D) is correct.
  REQUIRED: The information required in articles of incorporation.
  DISCUSSION: Articles of incorporation must contain the name of the corporation, the number of authorized shares, the address of the initial registered office of the corporation, the name of its first registered agent at that address, and the names and addresses of the incorporators. The articles may also include names and addresses of the initial directors, purpose and duration of the corporation, and any provision that may be set forth in the bylaws.
  Answer (A) is incorrect. The names of states in which the corporation will be doing business need not be included in the articles. **Answer (B) is incorrect.** The name of the state in which the corporation will maintain its principal place of business need not be included in the articles. **Answer (C) is incorrect.** The names of initial officers and their terms of office need not be included in the articles.

8. The board of directors performs all of the following duties **except**

A. Managing day-to-day operations.
B. Selection and removal of officers.
C. Adding or repealing bylaws.
D. Initiation of fundamental changes.

Answer (A) is correct.
  REQUIRED: The duty not performed by the board of directors.
  DISCUSSION: The board of directors guides management. It does not directly manage day-to-day operations of the entity. That is management's responsibility, with the board having an oversight role. All major corporate decisions are made or approved by the board.
  Answer (B) is incorrect. The board has the duty of selection and removal of officers. **Answer (C) is incorrect.** Adding, amending, or repealing bylaws is a duty of the board. **Answer (D) is incorrect.** Initiation of fundamental changes, such as mergers or acquisitions, is a duty of the board.

9. A corporate director commits a breach of duty if

A. The director's exercise of care and skill is minimal.
B. A contract is awarded by the company to an organization owned by the director.
C. An interest in property is acquired by the director without prior approval of the board.
D. The director's action, prompted by confidential information, results in an abuse of corporate opportunity.

Answer (D) is correct.
  REQUIRED: The breach of a corporate director's duty.
  DISCUSSION: Corporate directors have a fiduciary duty to provide the corporation with business opportunities that come to them in their positions as directors of the corporation. A director who personally takes such a business opportunity has breached his or her duty of loyalty.
  Answer (A) is incorrect. A director is under a duty to use good business judgment, but (s)he is not responsible for the highest standard of care and skill. Moreover, a director may reasonably rely on information from competent officers, employees, and experts. **Answer (B) is incorrect.** A director is not prohibited from entering into a conflicting interest transaction if it is (1) fair to the corporation or (2) approved after required disclosure by a majority of disinterested directors or of shares voted by disinterested parties. **Answer (C) is incorrect.** A director has no duty to report personal property investments unless they relate to corporate business.

2.3 The Sarbanes-Oxley Act of 2002 (SOX)

10. The Sarbanes-Oxley Act of 2002 limits the nonaudit services that an audit firm can provide to public company audit clients. Which of the following is most likely to be a service that an auditor may provide to a public client?

A. Internal audit outsourcing.
B. Legal services.
C. Bookkeeping services.
D. Tax compliance services.

Answer (D) is correct.
REQUIRED: The type of service that an audit firm may provide to an audit client.
DISCUSSION: The Sarbanes-Oxley Act prohibits audit firms from providing bookkeeping, legal, and internal auditing services, among others, to public audit clients. Audit firms may, however, provide conventional tax planning and certain other nonaudit services to public audit clients if they are preapproved by the audit committee.
Answer (A) is incorrect. Internal audit outsourcing is a service that may not be provided to public audit clients. **Answer (B) is incorrect.** Legal and other expert services may not be provided to public audit clients if they do not pertain to the audit. **Answer (C) is incorrect.** Bookkeeping services may not be provided to public audit clients.

11. Which of the following is most likely a violation of the rules of the Public Company Accounting Oversight Board (PCAOB)?

A. An issuer's independent auditor also performs consulting work for the issuer on the design and operation of its internal controls.
B. An issuer offers its common shares and preferred shares on different stock exchanges.
C. An issuer's management is not independent of its board of directors.
D. An issuer uses the same independent auditor in 2 consecutive years.

Answer (A) is correct.
REQUIRED: The action prohibited by SOX.
DISCUSSION: The PCAOB prohibits a public accounting firm from performing internal auditing services for an audit client.
Answer (B) is incorrect. The PCAOB regulates public accounting firms, not stock offerings. **Answer (C) is incorrect.** The PCAOB cannot dictate terms of internal corporate governance. **Answer (D) is incorrect.** The PCAOB's rules do not prohibit issuers from using the same independent auditor in 2 consecutive years.

12. When Congress passed the Sarbanes-Oxley Act of 2002, it imposed greater regulation on public companies and their auditors and required increased accountability. Which of the following is **not** a provision of the act?

A. Certain executives must certify the fair presentation of the financial statements.
B. Management must establish and document internal control procedures.
C. The act created the Public Company Accounting Oversight Board (PCAOB).
D. One of the company's officers may serve on the audit committee.

Answer (D) is correct.
REQUIRED: The choice that is not a provision of the Sarbanes-Oxley Act of 2002.
DISCUSSION: The act requires that all members of the audit committee be independent of the corporation, meaning they can receive no compensation other than what they receive for serving on the board. Thus, no officers or employees of the corporation may serve on the audit committee.
Answer (A) is incorrect. The CEO and CFO of a public company must provide a statement to accompany the audit report. This statement certifies the fair presentation of the financial statements and disclosures. However, a violation of this requirement must be knowing and intentional. **Answer (B) is incorrect.** Section 404 of the act requires management to establish and document internal control procedures, and to include in annual reports a report on the entity's internal control over financial reporting. **Answer (C) is incorrect.** The PCAOB was created by the act as a private sector, nonprofit corporation to oversee the conduct of accounting firms in the performance of financial statement audits of issuers.

13. Section 302 of the Sarbanes-Oxley Act of 2002 requires the CEO and CFO, in every annual or quarterly filing with the SEC, to certify all of the following **except**

A. That they have taken every practical step to correct significant control deficiencies identified in the previous audit.
B. That they have evaluated the effectiveness of the system of internal control.
C. That they have taken responsibility for the system of internal control.
D. That to the best of their knowledge, the financial statements are free of material misstatements.

Answer (A) is correct.
REQUIRED: The required certification in SEC filings by the CEO and CFO.
DISCUSSION: Whether the issuer has taken sufficient steps to correct significant control deficiencies is a matter of the auditor's professional judgment.

14. Under the reporting requirements of Section 404 of the Sarbanes-Oxley Act of 2002, the CEO and CFO must include a statement in the annual report to the effect that

    A. The system of internal control has been assessed by an independent public accounting firm that is registered with the PCAOB.

    B. The system of internal control has been assessed by an independent public accounting firm that is not currently the subject of any PCAOB investigation.

    C. The board of directors has taken responsibility for establishing and maintaining an adequate system of internal control over financial reporting.

    D. The issuer has used the COSO model to design and assess the effectiveness of its system of internal control.

Answer (A) is correct.
    REQUIRED: The statement required by the Sarbanes-Oxley Act of 2002.
    DISCUSSION: The CEO and CFO must include a statement in the annual report to the effect that the system of internal control has been assessed by an independent public accounting firm that is registered with the PCAOB.
    Answer (B) is incorrect. Section 404 of SOX does not require that the independent auditor not be under investigation by the PCAOB. **Answer (C) is incorrect.** Section 404 of SOX requires the CEO and CFO to state that they, not the board, have taken responsibility for internal controls. **Answer (D) is incorrect.** Section 404 of SOX requires that if the issuer used an internal control model, it must be named; it does not have to be the COSO model.

15. An issuer's audit committee consists of its CEO and three outside board members. The issuer compensates the outside board members for their service on the board. Under the Sarbanes-Oxley Act of 2002, which of the following is a deficiency in the issuer's audit committee?

    A. Not enough audit committee members.

    B. The CEO is an audit committee member.

    C. All audit committee members are not officers in the corporation.

    D. The outside board members receive compensation for their service on the board.

Answer (B) is correct.
    REQUIRED: The violation of the Sarbanes-Oxley Act of 2002.
    DISCUSSION: Under the Sarbanes-Oxley Act of 2002, audit committee members must be independent. To be independent, members may not receive compensation from the corporation other than for their service on the board. A CEO receives compensation for services other than those performed as a board member and therefore violates the independence requirement for audit committee members.
    Answer (A) is incorrect. Under the Sarbanes-Oxley Act of 2002, the audit committee is only required to be comprised of at least three independent members. **Answer (C) is incorrect.** Under the Sarbanes-Oxley Act of 2002, audit committee members are not required to be officers of the issuing corporation. **Answer (D) is incorrect.** Under the Sarbanes-Oxley Act of 2002, audit committee members may receive compensation for their service on the board.

16. Which of the following represents a violation of the Sarbanes-Oxley Act of 2002?

I. An issuer's audit committee decides auditor compensation without board approval.
II. An issuer's audit committee selects the independent auditor without board approval.
III. An issuer's audit committee delegates to management the responsibility to oversee the work of the independent auditor.

A. I and II only.
B. II only.
C. III only.
D. None of the answers are correct.

Answer (C) is correct.
REQUIRED: The violation of the Sarbanes-Oxley Act of 2002.
DISCUSSION: Under the Sarbanes-Oxley Act of 2002, the audit committee is directly responsible for selecting, compensating, and overseeing the work of the independent auditor.
Answer (A) is incorrect. Under the Sarbanes-Oxley Act of 2002, the audit committee is directly responsible for selecting and compensating the independent auditor. Thus, board approval is not required. **Answer (B) is incorrect.** Under the Sarbanes-Oxley Act of 2002, the audit committee is directly responsible for selecting the independent auditor. Thus, board approval is not required. **Answer (D) is incorrect.** Under the Sarbanes-Oxley Act of 2002, the audit committee is directly responsible for overseeing the work of the independent auditor and therefore cannot delegate that responsibility to management.

17. An issuer's CEO and CFO certified the company's annual filing for Year 1 pursuant to the Sarbanes-Oxley Act of 2002. However, only the CEO certified the issuer's first quarterly filing for Year 2. The issuer has

A. Violated SOX because the CFO did not certify the quarterly filing.
B. Complied with SOX because only the CEO is required to certify quarterly filings.
C. Complied with SOX because the CEO and CFO are only required to certify annual filings.
D. Violated SOX because the issuer's Chief Audit Executive did not certify the annual filing.

Answer (A) is correct.
REQUIRED: The certification requirement of the Sarbanes-Oxley Act of 2002.
DISCUSSION: Pursuant to the Sarbanes-Oxley Act of 2002, an issuer's CEO and CFO must certify quarterly and annual filings.
Answer (B) is incorrect. Pursuant to the Sarbanes-Oxley Act of 2002, an issuer's CFO must also certify quarterly filings. **Answer (C) is incorrect.** Pursuant to the Sarbanes-Oxley Act of 2002, an issuer's CEO and CFO must also certify quarterly filings. **Answer (D) is incorrect.** No provision of the Sarbanes-Oxley Act of 2002 requires an issuer's Chief Audit Executive to certify filings.

18. A public accounting firm performs both audit and nonaudit services for an issuer. A violation of the Sarbanes-Oxley Act of 2002 occurs if

I. The issuer's audit committee preapproves the nonaudit services.
II. The issuer's audit committee preapproves the audit services.
III. The issuer's board preapproves the nonaudit services.
IV. The issuer's board preapproves the audit services.

A. I only.
B. II only.
C. III only.
D. III and IV only.

Answer (D) is correct.
REQUIRED: The violation of the Sarbanes-Oxley Act of 2002.
DISCUSSION: Under the Sarbanes-Oxley Act of 2002, an issuer's audit committee must preapprove audit services and nonaudit services performed by its independent auditor.
Answer (A) is incorrect. Under the Sarbanes-Oxley Act of 2002, an issuer's audit committee must preapprove nonaudit services performed by its independent auditor. Answer (B) is incorrect. Under the Sarbanes-Oxley Act of 2002, an issuer's audit committee must preapprove audit services. Answer (C) is incorrect. Although it is a violation of the Sarbanes-Oxley Act of 2002 (SOX) for an issuer's board to preapprove nonaudit services performed by its independent auditor, it is also a violation of SOX for an issuer's board to preapprove audit services.

19. Which of the following will most likely call into question the expertise of an audit committee financial expert?

A. Lack of understanding of generally accepted auditing standards.
B. Lack of understanding of fraud examination techniques.
C. Lack of experience with internal accounting controls.
D. Lack of experience with performing business valuations.

Answer (C) is correct.
REQUIRED: The lack of skill that would call into question the expertise of an audit committee financial expert.
DISCUSSION: Under the Sarbanes-Oxley Act of 2002, an audit committee financial expert must have—among other qualifications—experience with internal accounting controls.
Answer (A) is incorrect. Under the Sarbanes-Oxley Act of 2002, an audit committee financial expert is not required to have an understanding of generally accepted auditing standards. However, such person must have an understanding of generally accepted accounting principles. Answer (B) is incorrect. The Sarbanes-Oxley Act of 2002 does not require an audit committee financial expert to have an understanding of fraud examination techniques. Answer (D) is incorrect. The Sarbanes-Oxley Act of 2002 does not require an audit committee financial expert to have experience with performing business valuations.

2.4 System and Organization Controls (SOC) for Service Organizations

20. The activities of the user entity and the service organization have a high degree of interaction. The user auditor

A. Is not required to evaluate the service organization's controls.
B. Should obtain absolute assurance that the service organization's internal control will prevent or detect fraud or error.
C. Should not consider weaknesses in the service organization's internal control to be weaknesses in the user entity's system.
D. Need not test the service organization's internal control if the user entity has effective controls related to service organization processing.

Answer (D) is correct.
REQUIRED: The true statement about the interaction of controls at the service and user organizations.
DISCUSSION: The significance of controls at the service organization depends on the degree of interaction between its activities and those of the user entity. The degree of interaction is the extent to which the user entity can, and chooses to, implement effective controls over service organization processing. In these circumstances, the user auditor may be able to obtain an understanding from the user entity of the service organization's services that suffices to assess the RMMs. Accordingly, the user auditor need not obtain a type 1 or type 2 report.
Answer (A) is incorrect. When controls of both the user and the service organization interact, the service organization's controls should be evaluated in conjunction with the user's. **Answer (B) is incorrect.** Reasonable, not absolute, assurance should be obtained that the service organization's controls will prevent or detect fraud or error. **Answer (C) is incorrect.** The user auditor should consider the combination of controls at the user entity and service organization.

21. A service auditor's report on internal control may be issued on management's description of a service organization system and the suitability of the design of controls or management's description of a service organization system and the suitability and operating effectiveness of controls. Which of the following is true about a type 1 report?

A. It should state that the auditor did not test the effectiveness of the controls.
B. It should include an opinion about the design of internal control as well as conclusions about tests of controls.
C. It will include a list of all fraud and error discovered.
D. It need not be restricted in its use and may be made available to any third party.

Answer (A) is correct.
REQUIRED: The true statement about a service auditor's report.
DISCUSSION: A service auditor's type 1 report should contain a statement that the auditor did not test the effectiveness of the controls.
The AICPA has issued additional guidance on service auditor reports. The term System and Organization Controls (SOC) report is used in this guidance. The reports obtained by the user auditor in an audit are called SOC 1 reports (type 1 or type 2). Service auditors also may prepare SOC 2 and SOC 3 reports to provide assurance on more than internal controls over financial reporting (e.g., security, availability, processing integrity, confidentiality, or privacy). SOC 2 reports are to be used by those identified in the report, and SOC 3 reports may be used by any user.
Answer (B) is incorrect. A type 2 report states whether the controls described by management operated effectively. **Answer (C) is incorrect.** A type 2 report includes the number and nature of control deviations. **Answer (D) is incorrect.** A service auditor's report is intended solely for the use of service organization management, user organizations, and the independent auditors of user organizations.

Access the **Gleim CPA Premium Review System** featuring our SmartAdapt technology from your Gleim Personal Classroom to continue your studies. You will experience a personalized study environment with exam-emulating multiple-choice questions.

STUDY UNIT THREE
COSO ENTERPRISE RISK MANAGEMENT FRAMEWORK

(22 pages of outline)

3.1	Enterprise Risk Management (ERM)	78
3.2	Applying the ERM Framework to Cyber Risk Management	94

The Committee of Sponsoring Organizations of the Treadway Commission (COSO) has established a widely accepted framework for enterprise risk management (ERM).

This study unit covers enterprise risk management and applying the framework to cyber risk management.

3.1 ENTERPRISE RISK MANAGEMENT (ERM)

ERM Overview

1. **COSO Enterprise Risk Management Framework**

   a. *Enterprise Risk Management – Integrating with Strategy and Performance* (COSO ERM framework) is a framework designed to enhance awareness and oversight of enterprise risk management to allow organizations to improve their approach to managing risk.

   b. The COSO ERM framework provides a basis for coordinating and integrating all of an organization's risk management activities. Effective integration

      1) Improves **decision making** and
      2) Enhances **performance**.

   c. Effective enterprise risk management can

      1) Increase the range of opportunities
      2) Identify and manage risk entity-wide
      3) Increase positive outcomes
      4) Reduce performance variability
      5) Improve resource deployment
      6) Enhance enterprise resilience

2. **ERM Definition and Concepts**

   a. ERM is based on the premise that every organization exists to provide **value** for its stakeholders. Accordingly, ERM is defined as

      The culture, capabilities, and practices, integrated with strategy-setting and its performance, that organizations rely on to **manage risk** *in creating, preserving, and realizing* **value**. [emphasis added]

   b. Key Concepts and Phrases

      1) **Culture** consists of "[t]he attitudes, behaviors, and understanding **about risk**, both positive and negative, that influence the decisions of management and personnel and reflect the mission, vision, and core values of the organization." [emphasis added]

         a) **Mission** is the entity's core purpose, which establishes what it wants to accomplish and why it exists.
         b) **Vision** is the entity's aspirations for what it intends to achieve over time.
         c) **Core values** are the entity's essential beliefs about what is acceptable or unacceptable.

      2) **Capabilities** are the skills needed to carry out the entity's mission and vision.
      3) **Practices** are the collective methods used to manage risk.

4) **Integrating strategy setting and performance.**
   a) Risk must be considered in setting strategy, business objectives, performance targets, and tolerance.
      i) **Strategy** communicates how the organization will (a) achieve its mission and vision and (b) apply its core values. ERM enhances strategy selection.
      ii) **Business objectives** are the measurable steps taken to achieve the strategy.
      iii) **Tolerance** is the range of acceptable variation in performance results. (This term is identical to "risk tolerance" in the COSO internal control framework, which is covered in detail in Study Unit 1, Subunit 3.)
   b) The organization considers the effect of strategy on its risk profile and portfolio view.
      i) **Risk profile** is a composite view of the types, severity, and interdependencies of **risks** related to a specific strategy or business objective and their effects on **performance**. A risk profile may be created at any level (e.g., entity, division, operating unit, or function) or aspect (e.g., product, service, or geography) of the organization.
      ii) **Portfolio view** is similar to a risk profile. The difference is that it is a composite view of the risks related to **entity-wide** strategy and business objectives and their effects on **entity** performance.

5) **Managing risk.**
   a) **Risk** is "the possibility that events will occur and affect the achievement of strategy and business objectives."
   b) **Opportunity** is any action or potential action that creates or alters goals or approaches for the creation, preservation, or realization of value.
   c) **Reasonable expectation** (not absolute assurance) that the risk assumed is appropriate is provided by effective ERM practices.
   d) **Risk inventory** consists of all identified risks that could affect strategy and business objectives.
   e) **Risk capacity** is the maximum amount of risk the entity can assume.
   f) **Risk appetite** consists of the amount and types of risk the organization is willing to accept in pursuit of value.
   g) **Inherent risk** is the risk in the absence of management actions to alter its severity.
   h) **Risk response** is an action taken to bring identified risks within the organization's risk appetite.
      i) A **residual risk profile** includes risk responses.
   i) **Target residual risk** is the risk the entity prefers to assume knowing that management has acted or will act to alter its severity.
   j) **Actual residual risk** is the risk remaining after taking management actions to alter its severity. Actual residual risk should be equal to or less than target residual risk.

6) **Value** is
   a) **Created** when the benefits obtained from the resources used exceed their costs.
      i) For example, a new product is successfully launched and has a positive profit margin.
   b) **Preserved** when the value of resources used is sustained.
      i) An example is delivery of superior products.
   c) **Realized** when benefits are transferred to stakeholders.
   d) **Eroded** when management's strategy does not produce expected results or management does not perform day-to-day tasks.
      i) For example, resources are consumed to develop a new product that is never launched.

3. **ERM Roles and Responsibilities**
   a. The **board** provides risk **oversight** of ERM culture, capabilities, and practices. ERM can enhance enterprise resilience (the ability to anticipate and respond to change), and it provides a framework for boards to assess risk and embrace a mindset of resilience. Certain board committees may be formed for this purpose. Examples are
      1) An **audit** committee (often required by regulators),
      2) A **risk** committee that directly oversees ERM,
      3) An **executive compensation** committee, and
      4) A **nomination or governance** committee that oversees selection of directors and executives.
   b. **Management** has **overall responsibility** for ERM and is generally responsible for the **day-to-day** managing of risk, including the implementation and development of the COSO ERM framework.
      1) Through the ERM process, management will gain a better understanding of how explicit consideration of risk may impact the choice of strategy.
      2) Within management, the **CEO** has **ultimate responsibility** for ERM and achievement of strategy and business objectives.
   c. An organization may designate a **risk officer** as a centralized coordinating point to facilitate risk management across the entire enterprise.
   d. **Three lines of management accountability:**
      1) The first line consists of the principal **owners** of risk. They manage performance and risks taken to achieve strategy and objectives.
      2) The second line consists of the **supporting (business-enabling) functions** (e.g., risk officer) that (a) provide guidance on performance and ERM requirements, (b) evaluate adherence to standards, and (c) challenge the first line to take prudent risks.
      3) The third line consists of **assurance functions** (e.g., the internal audit function) that (a) perform audits (reviews) of ERM, (b) identify issues and improvements, (c) make recommendations, and (d) inform the board and executives of matters needing resolution.

ERM Components

4. **ERM Components**

    a. The COSO ERM framework consists of **five interrelated components**. The five components are supported by a set of principles.

    1) The **supporting aspect** components are

        a) Governance and culture and
        b) Information, communication, and reporting.

    2) The **common process** components are

        a) Strategy and objective-setting,
        b) Performance, and
        c) Review and revision.

5. **Governance and Culture**

    a. Governance sets the organization's tone and establishes responsibilities for ERM. Culture relates to the desired behaviors, values, and overall understanding about risk held by personnel within the organization. **Five principles** relate to governance and culture:

    1) The **board** exercises risk **oversight**.

        a) The full board ordinarily is responsible for risk oversight. However, the board may delegate risk oversight to a board committee, such as a **risk committee**.
        b) The board's oversight role may include, but is not limited to,

            i) Reviewing and challenging decisions related to strategy, risk appetite, and significant business decisions (e.g., mergers and acquisitions).
            ii) Approving management compensation.
            iii) Participating in stakeholder relations.

        c) Risk oversight is most effective when the board

            i) Has the necessary **skills, experience,** and **business knowledge** to (a) understand the organization's strategy and industry and (b) maintain this understanding as the business context changes.
            ii) Is **independent** of the organization.
            iii) Determines whether ERM capabilities and practices enhance value.
            iv) Understands the **organizational biases** (e.g., overreliance on quantitative data) influencing decision making and challenges management to minimize them.

    2) The organization establishes **operating structures**.

        a) They describe how the entity is organized and carries out its day-to-day operations.
        b) They generally are aligned with the entity's legal structure and management structure.

            i) The **legal structure** determines how the entity operates (e.g., as a single legal entity or as multiple, distinct legal entities).
            ii) The **management structure** establishes reporting lines (e.g., direct reporting versus secondary reporting), roles, and responsibilities. Management is responsible for clearly defining roles and responsibilities.

c) Factors to consider when establishing and evaluating operating structures include the entity's
   i) Strategy and business objectives, including related risks;
   ii) Nature, size, and geographic distribution;
   iii) Risks related to the entity's strategy and business objectives;
   iv) Assignment of authority, accountability, and responsibility at all levels;
   v) Types of reporting lines and communication channels; and
   vi) Reporting requirements (e.g., financial, tax, regulatory, and contractual).

3) The organization defines the desired **culture**.
   a) The board and management are responsible for defining culture.
   b) Culture is shaped by internal and external factors.
      i) **Internal** factors include (a) the level of judgment and autonomy provided to personnel, (b) standards and rules, (c) physical layout of the workplace, and (d) the reward system in place.
      ii) **External** factors include (a) legal requirements and (b) expectations of stakeholders (e.g., customers and investors).
   c) The organization's definition of culture determines its placement on the **culture spectrum**, which ranges from risk averse to risk aggressive.
   d) Judgment has a significant role in defining the desired culture and management of risk. Judgment is a function of personal experiences, risk appetite, capabilities and the level of information available, and organization bias.
   e) Culture is not static and will change over time.

4) The organization demonstrates commitment to **core values**.
   a) The organization's core values should be reflected in all its actions and decisions.
   b) The **tone of the organization** is the manner in which core values are communicated across the organization.
   c) When risk-aware culture and tone are aligned, stakeholders have confidence that the organization is abiding by its core values.
   d) Leadership helps establish and enforce accountability and a common purpose.

5) The organization **attracts**, **develops**, and **retains** capable individuals.
   a) Management is responsible for defining the human capital necessary (the needed competencies) to achieve strategy and business objectives.
   b) The **human resources function** assists management in developing competency requirements through processes that attract, train, mentor, evaluate, reward, and retain competent individuals.
   c) **Contingency plans** should be developed to prepare for succession. Such plans train selected personnel to assume responsibilities vital to ERM. An example is training a risk manager to assume the position of risk officer.

6. **Strategy and Objective Setting**
    a. Strategy must support the organization's mission, vision, and core values. The integration of ERM with strategy setting helps to understand the risk profile related to strategy and business objectives. **Four principles** relate to strategy and objective setting:
        1) The organization analyzes **business context** and its effect on the risk profile.
            a) Business context pertains to the relationships, events, trends, and other factors that influence the organization's current and future strategy and business objectives. Accordingly, business context includes the organization's internal and external environments.
                i) The **internal environment** consists of factors related to (a) capital (e.g., assets), (b) people (e.g., skills and attitudes), (c) processes (e.g., tasks, policies, and procedures), and (d) technology (e.g., new, amended, and/or adopted technology).
                ii) The **external environment** consists of factors related to **PESTLE** analysis: (a) political (government intervention and influence), (b) economic (e.g., interest rates and availability of credit), (c) social (e.g., consumer preferences and demographics), (d) technological (e.g., R&D activity), (e) legal (laws, regulations, and industry standards), and (f) environmental (e.g., climate change).
            b) Business context may be
                i) **Dynamic.** New, emerging, and changing risks can appear at any time (e.g., low barriers of entry allow new competitors to emerge).
                ii) **Complex.** Many interdependencies and interconnections exist (e.g., a transnational company has several operating units around the world, each with unique external environmental factors).
                iii) **Unpredictable.** Change occurs rapidly and in unanticipated ways (e.g., currency fluctuations).
            c) The effect of business context on the risk profile may be analyzed based on past, present, and future performance.
        2) The organization defines **risk appetite** (the amount of risk it is willing to accept in pursuit of value).
            a) The organization considers its mission, vision, culture, prior strategies, and risk capacity (the maximum risk it can assume) to set its risk appetite.
            b) In setting risk appetite, the entity seeks the optimal balance of opportunity and risk.
                i) Risk appetite is rarely set above risk capacity.
            c) Risk appetite may be expressed **qualitatively** (e.g., low, moderate, high) or **quantitatively** (e.g., as a percentage of a financial amount). It should reflect how risk assessment results are expressed.
            d) Entities may express risk appetite using the terms targets, ranges, ceilings, or floors.
            e) The board approves the risk appetite, and management communicates it throughout the organization.

3) The organization evaluates **alternative strategies** and their effects on the risk profile.
   a) Approaches to evaluating strategy include SWOT (Strengths-Weaknesses-Opportunities-Threats) analysis, competitor analysis, and scenario analysis.
   b) The organization must evaluate
      i) The strategy's alignment with its mission, vision, core values, and risk appetite and
      ii) The implications of the chosen strategy (its risks, opportunities, and effects on the risk profile).
   c) Strategy should be changed if it fails to create, realize, or preserve value.
4) The organization establishes **business objectives** that align with and support strategy.
   a) Business objectives are (1) specific, (2) measurable or observable, (3) obtainable, and (4) relevant.
   b) Business objectives may relate to, among others, financial performance, operational excellence, or compliance obligations.
   c) Performance measures, targets, and **tolerances** (the range of acceptable variation in performance) are established to evaluate the achievement of objectives.

7. **Performance**
   a. Performance relates to ERM practices that support the organization's decisions in pursuit of value. Those practices consist of identifying, assessing, prioritizing, responding to, and developing a portfolio view of risk. **Five principles** relate to performance:
      1) The organization **identifies risks** that affect the performance of strategy and business objectives.
         a) The organization should identify risks that disrupt operations and affect the **reasonable expectation** of achieving strategy and business objectives.
         b) **New**, **emerging**, and **changing** risks are identified. Examples are risks resulting from changes in business objectives or the business context.
            i) **Opportunities** (actions or potential actions that create or alter goals or approaches for the creation, preservation, or realization of value) also are identified. They differ from **positive events**, occurrences in which performance exceeds the original target.
         c) Risk identification **methods** and **approaches** include (1) day-to-day activities (e.g., budgeting, business planning, or reviewing customer complaints), (2) simple questionnaires, (3) facilitated workshops, (4) interviews, or (5) data tracking.
         d) The **risk inventory** consists of all risks that could affect the entity.
         e) Risk and opportunity identification should be comprehensive across all levels and functions of the entity.

2) The organization **assesses** the **severity of risk**. Severity is a measure of such considerations as impact, likelihood, and the time to recover from events.

   a) Common measures of severity include combinations of impact and likelihood.

      i) **Impact** is the result or effect of the risk. It may be positive or negative.

      ii) **Likelihood** is the possibility that an event will occur. Likelihood may be expressed qualitatively (e.g., a remote probability), quantitatively (e.g., a 75% probability), or in terms of frequency (e.g., once every 6 months).

   b) The **time horizon** to assess risk should be identical to that of the related strategy and business objective. For example, the risk affecting a strategy that takes 2 years to achieve should be assessed over the same period.

   c) **Uncertainty** refers to the inability of an entity to know in advance the likelihood or impact of future events on the achievement of objectives. Management must assess both the risk and opportunity of the uncertainty.

   d) Risk is assessed at **multiple levels** (e.g., entity, division, operating unit, and function) of the organization and linked to the related strategy and business objective.

      i) The severity of a risk may vary across levels. For example, a risk with high severity at the operating unit level may have low or moderate severity at the entity level.

   e) Qualitative and quantitative methods may be used to assess risk.

      i) **Qualitative** methods are more efficient and less costly than quantitative methods. Examples are interviews, surveys, and benchmarking.

      ii) **Quantitative** methods are more precise than qualitative methods. Examples are decision trees, modeling (probabilistic and nonprobabilistic), and Monte Carlo simulation.

   f) The organization should **reassess severity** whenever triggering events occur, such as changes in business context and risk appetite.

   g) The risk assessment should consider inherent risk, target residual risk, and actual residual risk.

   h) Assessment results may be presented using a **heat map**, which highlights the relative severity of each risk. The warmer the color, the more severe the risk.

Business Objective Heat Map

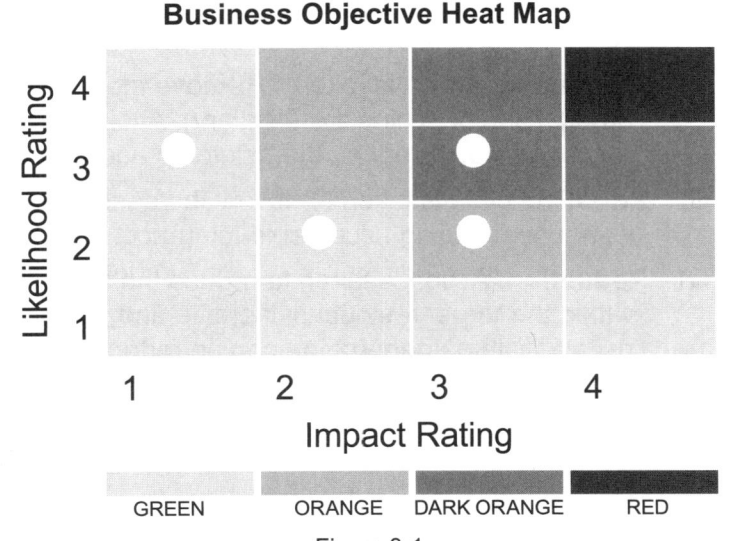

Figure 3-1

3) The organization **prioritizes risks** at all levels.

   a) Risk prioritization enables the organization to optimize the allocation of its limited resources.

   b) In addition to severity (e.g., impact and likelihood), the following factors are considered when prioritizing risks:

      i) Agreed-upon criteria,
      ii) Risk appetite,
      iii) The importance of the affected business objective(s), and
      iv) The organizational level(s) affected.

   c) **Agreed-upon criteria** are used to evaluate the characteristics of risks and to determine the entity's capacity to respond appropriately. Higher priority is given to risks that most affect the criteria. Example criteria include the following:

      i) **Complexity** is the nature and scope of a risk, e.g., interdependence of risks. An example is the risk of product obsolescence to a company's objective of being a market leader in technology.
      ii) **Velocity** is the speed at which a risk affects the entity.
      iii) **Persistence** is how long a risk affects the entity, including the time it takes the entity to recover.
      iv) **Adaptability** is the entity's capacity to adjust and respond to risks.
      v) **Recovery** is the entity's capacity (not the time) to return to tolerance, e.g., returning to normal operations after a natural disaster.

   d) Higher priority also is assigned to risks that

      i) Approach or exceed risk appetite,
      ii) Cause performance levels to approach the outer limits of tolerance, or
      iii) Affect the entire entity or occur at the entity level.

4) The organization identifies and selects **risk responses**, recognizing that risk may be managed but not eliminated. Risks should be managed within the business context and objectives, performance targets, and risk appetite.

   a) The following are the five categories of risk responses:

      i) **Acceptance.** No action is taken to alter the severity of the risk. Acceptance is appropriate when the risk is within the risk appetite.
      ii) **Avoidance.** Action is taken to remove the risk (e.g., discontinuing a product line or selling a subsidiary). Avoidance typically suggests no response would reduce the risk to an acceptable level.
      iii) **Pursuit.** Action is taken to accept increased risk to improve performance without exceeding acceptable tolerance.
      iv) **Reduction.** Action is taken to reduce the severity of the risk so that it is within the target residual risk profile and risk appetite. For example, the risk of systems penetration can be reduced by maintaining an effective information security function within the entity.
      v) **Sharing.** Action is taken to reduce the severity of the risk by transferring a portion of the risk to another party. Examples are insurance, hedging, joint ventures, and outsourcing.

SU 3: COSO Enterprise Risk Management Framework

    b) The following are the **factors** considered in selecting and implementing risk responses:
        i) They should be chosen for, or adapted to, the **business context**.
        ii) **Costs and benefits** should be proportionate to the severity of the risk and its priority.
        iii) They should further **compliance** with obligations (e.g., industry standards) and achievement of **expectations** (e.g., mission, vision, and stakeholder expectations).
        iv) They should bring risk within **risk appetite** and result in performance outcomes within **tolerance**.
        v) Risk response should reflect risk severity.
    c) **Control activities** are designed and implemented to ensure risk responses are carried out. (COSO guidance for control activities is outlined in item 7. in Study Unit 1, Subunit 3.)

5) The organization develops and evaluates its **portfolio view of risk** (entity-wide perspective).
    a) The culmination of risk identification, assessment, prioritization, and response is the full portfolio view of risk.
    b) The following four risk views have different levels of risk integration:
        i) **Risk view (minimal integration).** Risks are identified and assessed. Emphasis is on the event, not the business objective. An example is the risk of a breach impacting the entity's compliance with local regulations.
        ii) **Risk category view (limited integration).** Identified and assessed risks are categorized, e.g., based on operating structures. For example, the accounting department will have responsibilities for helping the organization manage its risks related to potential accounting rule changes.
        iii) **Risk profile view (partial integration).** Risks are linked to the business objectives they affect, and any dependencies between objectives are identified and assessed. For example, an objective of increased sales may depend on an objective to introduce a new product line.
        iv) **Portfolio view (full integration).** This composite view of risks relates to **entity-wide** strategy and business objectives and their effect on **entity** performance. At the top level, greater emphasis is on strategy. Thus, responsibility for business objectives and specific risks **cascades** through the entity.
    c) Using a portfolio view of risk, management determines whether the entity's **residual risk profile** (risk profile inclusive of risk responses) aligns with overall **risk appetite**.
    d) Qualitative and quantitative methods may be used to evaluate how changes in risk may affect the portfolio view of risk.
        i) **Qualitative** methods include benchmarking, scenario analysis, and stress testing.
        ii) **Quantitative** methods include statistical analysis.

8. **Review and Revision**

    a. The organization reviews and revises its current ERM capabilities and practices based on changes in strategy and business objectives. **Three principles** relate to review and revision:

    1) The organization identifies and assesses **changes** that may substantially affect strategy and business objectives.

        a) Changes in the organization's **business context and culture** are most likely to substantially affect strategy and business objectives.
        b) Such changes may result from changes in the organization's internal or external environment.
            i) Substantial changes in the **internal environment** include those due to rapid growth, innovation, and turnover of key personnel.
            ii) Substantial changes in the **external environment** include those in the economy or regulations.

    2) The organization reviews **entity performance** results and considers **risk**.

        a) Performance results that deviate from target performance or tolerance may indicate
            i) Unidentified risks,
            ii) Improperly assessed risks,
            iii) New risks,
            iv) Opportunities to accept more risk, or
            v) The need to revise target performance or tolerance.
        b) In reviewing performance, the organization seeks to answer questions such as
            i) Has the entity performed as expected and achieved its target?
            ii) What risks are occurring that may be affecting performance?
            iii) Was the entity taking enough risk to attain its target?
            iv) Was the estimate of the amount of risk accurate?

    3) The organization pursues **improvement** of ERM.

        a) The organization must continually improve ERM at all levels, even if actual performance aligns with target performance or tolerance.
        b) Methods of identifying areas for improvement include **continual** or **separate evaluations** and peer comparisons (reviews of industry peers). (COSO guidance for monitoring activities is outlined in Study Unit 1, Subunit 3, item 9.)

9. **Information, Communication, and Reporting**

    a. The organization must capture, process, manage (organize and store), and communicate timely and relevant information to **identify risks** that could affect strategy and business objectives. **Three principles** relate to information, communication, and reporting:

    1) The organization leverages its **information systems** to support ERM.

        a) Information is relevant if it helps the organization be more agile in decision making, giving it a competitive advantage.
        b) Organizations should consider what information is available, what information systems and technology are in use for capturing that information, and what the costs are of obtaining that information.
        c) Information must be available to decision makers when it is needed.

- d) Data may be **structured** or **unstructured** and obtained from internal (e.g., board meetings, emails, customer satisfaction surveys, or due diligence activities) or outside (e.g., external websites or news reports) sources.
    - i) Structured data are generally well organized and easily searchable (e.g., spreadsheets, public indexes, or database files).
    - ii) Unstructured data are unorganized or lack a predefined pattern (e.g., word processing documents, videos, photos, or email messages).
- e) Organizations classify information using risk categories or risk taxonomy.
- f) **Data management** practices help ensure that risk information is useful, timely, relevant, and of high quality. The following are the elements of effective data management:
    - i) **Data and information governance.** Standards are established for the delivery, quality, timeliness, security, and architecture of data. Roles and responsibilities also are defined for risk information owners and data owners.
    - ii) **Processes and controls.** Activities are implemented to ensure established data standards are reinforced and corrections are made as necessary.
    - iii) **Data management architecture.** Information technology is designed that determines what data are collected and how the data are used.
- g) Information systems must be **adaptable to change**. As the organization adapts its strategy and business objectives in response to changes in the business context, its information systems also must change.

2) The organization uses **communication channels** to support ERM.
   - a) Communications about risk.
       - i) Management communicates the organization's strategy and business objectives to internal (e.g., personnel and the board) and external (e.g., shareholders) stakeholders.
       - ii) Communications between management and the board should include continual discussions about **risk appetite** and adjust strategy and business objectives accordingly.
   - b) Channels and methods.
       - i) Organizations should adopt **open communication channels** to allow risk information to be sent and received both ways (e.g., to and from personnel or suppliers).
       - ii) Communication **methods** include written documents (e.g., policies and procedures), electronic messages (e.g., email), public events or forums (e.g., town hall meetings), and informal or spoken communications (e.g., one-on-one discussions).
       - iii) The board may hold **formal** quarterly meetings or call **extraordinary** meetings (special meetings to discuss urgent matters).

3) The organization **reports** on risk, culture, and performance at multiple levels and across the entity.

   a) The purpose of reporting is to **support** personnel in their
      i) Understanding of the relationships among risk, culture, and performance.
      ii) Decision making related to (a) setting strategy and objectives, (b) governance, and (c) day-to-day operations.
   b) Reporting combines qualitative and quantitative risk information, with greater emphasis on information that supports **forward-looking** decisions.
   c) **Management** is responsible for implementing **controls** to ensure reports are accurate, complete, and clear.
   d) The **frequency of reporting** is based on the severity and priority of the risk.
   e) Reports on **culture** may be communicated, among other means, in surveys and lessons-learned analyses.
   f) **Key indicators of risk** should be reported with key performance indicators (KPIs) to emphasize the relationship of risk and performance.

ERM Assessment and Implementation

10. **Assessing ERM**

    a. The COSO ERM framework provides criteria for assessing whether the organization's ERM culture, capabilities, and practices together effectively manage risks to strategy and business objectives.

    b. When the **components**, **principles**, and supporting **controls** are present and functioning, ERM is **reasonably expected** to manage risks effectively and to help create, preserve, and realize **value**.

       1) **Present** means the components, principles, and controls exist in the design and implementation of ERM to achieve objectives.
       2) **Functioning** means the components, principles, and controls continue to operate to achieve objectives.

11. **ERM Limitations**

    a. Limitations of ERM result from the possibility of
       1) Faulty human judgment,
       2) Cost-benefit considerations,
       3) Simple errors or mistakes,
       4) Collusion, and
       5) Management override of ERM practices.

12. **Applying ERM to Environmental, Social, and Governance (ESG) Risks**

    a. The COSO and the World Business Council for Sustainable Development (WBCSD) have collaborated on guidance for risk management and sustainability practitioners who apply ERM to ESG-related risks and opportunities. These risks also are known as sustainability, nonfinancial, or extra-financial risks.

       1) Environmental issues may include climate change, scarce natural resources, waste, pollution, emissions, and decarbonizing.
       2) Social issues may relate to human rights, labor standards, stakeholder opposition, and integration with local communities.
       3) Governance issues may include rights, responsibilities, and expectations of stakeholders and their effects on corporate governance and behavior.

b. The guidance for coping with **ESG-related risks** includes **actions** that may help to manage current risks and to develop the resilience to adapt to future **megatrends** (large, transformative global forces).

1) **Governance and culture**
    a) Define mandatory or voluntary requirements
    b) Consider embedding ESG in culture and core values
    c) Increase board awareness of risks
    d) Define operating structures, risk owners, reporting lines, and end-to-end ERM and strategic planning to improve oversight and collaboration
    e) Create opportunities for entity-wide collaboration
    f) Embed ESG-related skills, capabilities, and knowledge when hiring and managing employees to promote integration

2) **Strategy and objective-setting**
    a) Examine the value creation process and business model to understand the effects and dependencies on all sources of capital (financial, social, human, manufactured, natural, and intellectual) from the short to the long term. The following are useful tools:
        i) Megatrend analysis to understand the effects of emerging issues in the external environment
        ii) Strengths, weaknesses, opportunities, and threats (SWOT) analysis
        iii) Defining the effects and dependencies for all types of capital
        iv) Materiality assessment to describe significant issues
        v) Engagement with all stakeholders to understand emerging trends
        vi) Analysis using ESG-specific resources
    b) Align risk management with strategy, objectives, and risk appetite
    c) Consider the ESG-related risks that affect strategy or objectives

3) **Performance -- risk identification**
    a) Examine the risk inventory to determine which ESG risks have been identified
    b) Involve risk owners and sustainability practitioners in the process to exploit their expertise
    c) Meet with risk management and sustainability practitioners to understand risks
    d) Identify the risks that may affect strategic and operational plans
    e) Define the effects of risks precisely
    f) Use root-cause analysis to understand drivers of risks

4) **Performance -- risk assessment and priorities**
    a) Understand the output of the risk assessment (effects on strategy and business objectives)
    b) Understand the criteria for prioritizing risks
    c) Understand the measures of risk (quantitative or qualitative)
    d) Choose assessment approaches to measure risk severity
    e) Choose and document data, parameters, and assumptions
    f) Exploit expertise to prioritize risks
    g) Identify and challenge organizational bias against ESG issues

5) **Performance -- risk responses**

   a) Choose responses based on entity-specific factors (costs, benefits, and risk appetite)
   b) Draft the business case for responses and obtain agreement
   c) Implement responses
   d) Evaluate responses at the entity level to understand their overall effects on the risk profile

6) **Review and revision**

   a) Assess internal and external changes that may substantively affect the strategy or objectives
   b) Review ERM activities for revisions of ERM processes and capabilities
   c) Improve how ESG risks are managed by ERM

7) **Information, communication, and reporting**

   a) Identify channels for internal and external communication and reporting of relevant information
   b) Communicate and report relevant risk information internally to decision-makers and externally to regulators and stakeholders
   c) Seek continuous improvement of the quality of data

13. **ERM Implementation Steps**

    a. The COSO "ERM – Creating and Protecting Value" framework outlines an eight-step approach for the implementation of an effective ERM program.

        1) Step 1: Seek board and senior management involvement and oversight.

            a) **Agenda items** for the discussion of ERM are set. These include, for example, high-level objectives and expectations regarding a risk management initiative, a high-level approach, resources, and target dates for ERM efforts.

        2) Step 2: Identify and position a leader to drive the ERM initiative.

            a) The **risk management leader** (e.g., an existing member of senior management or a new officer such as the Chief Risk Officer) should have in-depth knowledge of the organization's overall strategic objectives and be delegated appropriate authority and allocated appropriate resources.
            b) The leader should have direct access to the executive management team.

        3) Step 3: Establish a management working group.

            a) The **management working group** consists of management from different levels (e.g., executive management, business unit management, strategic planning heads, etc.) and supports the risk management leader across the whole organization.
            b) The group usually evolves into a risk committee.
            c) Responsibilities of the group include building the ERM program, defining criteria for performance measurement, and establishing processes for reporting.

4) Step 4: Inventory the existing risk management practices of the organization.

   a) **Gaps and opportunities** can be identified to assist with developing action steps for the integration of strategies and risk practices.

5) Step 5: Conduct an initial assessment of key strategies and related strategic risks.

   a) Events or risks that impair success of the **key strategies** are identified.

6) Step 6: Develop a consolidated action plan and communicate to board and management.

   a) The action steps discussed in Step 4 are expanded into action plans that prioritize actions and allocate resources that require assignment of responsibilities and monitoring.

   b) **Communication plans** for existing risks and responses are also generally developed.

7) Step 7: Develop and/or enhance risk reporting.

   a) Risk reporting may be integrated with performance reporting.

   b) To enhance the reporting of risks, new reporting formats (e.g., dashboards, strategic maps, or a combination of graphs and colors) may be used and revised as appropriate.

8) Step 8: Develop the next phase of action plans and ongoing communications.

   a) After critically assessing the successes of the working group (e.g., levels of integration, benefits, or impacts on company culture), the next risk management processes in need of enhancement are identified to capture new opportunities or address new risks.

STOP & REVIEW

You have completed the outline for this subunit.
Study multiple-choice questions 1 through 14 beginning on page 99.

3.2 APPLYING THE ERM FRAMEWORK TO CYBER RISK MANAGEMENT

1. **Cyber Risk Definition and Concepts**
   a. Cyber risk, as defined by the U.S. National Institute of Standards and Technology (NIST), refers to the risk of financial loss, operational disruption, and reputational damage from the failure of digital technology.
   b. The causes of cyber risk include but are not limited to the following:
      1) Poor information system design
      2) Unintentional security breaches
      3) Intentional security breaches
   c. Cyber threat actors can be classified into the following categories based on the objectives of their attacks:
      1) **Nation-states** (foreign nations) and **spies** seek out national security secrets and valuable **intellectual property (IP)**, such as military communications.
      2) **Organized criminals** steal an entity's private information for personal or financial gain, e.g., stealing credit card information for identity theft. The information stolen is usually **personally identifiable information (PII)**, such as Social Security and bank account numbers.
      3) **Terrorists** attack critical facilities, infrastructure, or institutions, such as security exchanges or banks, via electronic means.
      4) **Hacktivists** fulfill social or political purposes using the private information of an entity, such as stealing and publishing information of companies that have caused environmental damage.
      5) **Company insiders** use, share, or sell private information from within an organization for personal gain, such as an employee using unpublished information for insider trading.
   d. As the impact, frequency, and complexity of cyber attacks continue to increase, cyber risk management must be incorporated into the risk management programs of all organizations.

2. **COSO ERM Framework and Cyber Risk Management**
   a. In 2019, COSO released *Managing Cyber Risk in a Digital Age*, which addresses how companies can apply the COSO ERM framework to cyber risks. The fundamental cyber risk management techniques provided in this guidance can be mapped to the interrelated components and principles under the COSO ERM framework to develop a cyber risk management program.
   b. Cyber risk management requires understanding how the COSO ERM framework can be utilized to manage cyber risks.
   c. Parties responsible for an entity's cyber risk management include but are not limited to an entity's
      1) Board of directors
      2) Audit committee
      3) Executives
      4) Cyber practitioners (e.g., third-party IT service providers)

3. **Component 1 – Governance and Culture**

    a. The following are the fundamental cyber risk management techniques related to the five principles of governance and culture.

    1) The **board** exercises cyber risk **oversight**.

        a) The board should possess or increase their competencies in understanding and evaluating cyber risks. If the board lacks the necessary knowledge and experience, an independent advisor may be used.

    2) The organization establishes **operating structures**.

        a) A **cyber risk management team** should be created to manage **entity-level** cyber risks.

            i) The team is generally led by the **chief information officer (CIO)** or the **chief information security officer (CISO)**. In addition, the team should be composed of **cross-departmental** and **cross-functional** parties.

            ii) The team should report to the board of directors regarding the impact of cyber risks and the initiatives to manage such risks.

            iii) The chief audit executive should be part of this team or an independent advisor to the team.

    3) The organization defines the desired **culture**.

        a) The organization embeds cybersecurity vigilance and awareness in the organizational culture and reward systems.

    4) The organization demonstrates commitment to **core values**.

        a) Commitment can be demonstrated by a **cyber risk management program** that is consistent with the core values and supports the core values through policies, standards, and communications.

    5) The organization **attracts, develops,** and **retains** capable individuals by

        a) Continuous employee training about cybersecurity, such as email alerts and training on how to detect phishing emails and other threats.

        b) Developing **qualified** cyber risk professionals internally or supplementing with outside service providers who are tasked with assessing cyber risks and implementing and monitoring the cyber risk management program.

        c) Training employees how and where to report potential cyber issues.

4. **Component 2 – Strategy and Objective Setting**

    a. The following are the fundamental cyber risk management techniques related to the four principles of strategy and objective setting.

    1) The organization analyzes the **business context** and its effects on the risk profile.

        a) The IT-related factors that influence the organization's strategy and business objectives, **both in the present and future**, must be considered.

        b) Due to constant changes in the operating environment of the organization, cybersecurity must be considered as the business context evolves.

            i) For example, a retailer should consider the transaction system used in its physical stores and the IT-related factors (such as information security) of an online platform if it plans to open an online store.

2) The organization defines its **risk appetite**.
   a) Risk appetite should be set to **balance** opportunity and risk, such as the benefits of adopting new technologies and the associated costs.
   b) The organization's risk appetite must be continually adjusted as both cyber risks and the business context constantly evolve.
   c) Organizations should inventory critical assets, identify risk, and assess where cyber-related risks exist.

3) The organization evaluates **alternative strategies** and their effects on the risk profile.
   a) Approaches to evaluating the strategies, or **security models**, help establish and assess the cyber risk management program.
   b) Cybersecurity control frameworks, such as the Control Objectives for Information and Related Technology (COBIT), are helpful in evaluating the effectiveness of security models.

4) Cyber risk management should align with the organization's strategies and **business objectives**.
   a) Performance targets (e.g., eliminating the risk of opening phishing emails by training employees) and tolerances (e.g., accepting cyber risks that do not affect day-to-day business operations) are established to evaluate the achievement of objectives.

5. **Component 3 – Performance**
   a. The following are the fundamental cyber risk management techniques related to the five principles of performance.
      1) The organization **identifies risks** that affect the performance of strategies and business objectives.
         a) The organization should identify what information, technology, and systems are **valuable** to the achievement of strategies and business objectives.
            i) Value depends on the specific conditions of each organization. For example, system downtime may be tolerable for some industries but is disastrous for others.
         b) Emerging cyber risks (i.e., due to technological advancement) should also be identified.
      2) The organization **assesses** the **severity of risk**.
         a) Severity is a combination of
            i) Impact (e.g., increased cyber attacks after opening an online store) and
            ii) Likelihood (e.g., the online store is targeted by a cyber attack once every 2 months).
         b) Assessment of cyber risks should be **industry specific** and based on the likely objectives of cyber threat actors. For example, organized criminals may have different objectives than hacktivists. (The different types and objectives of threat actors are detailed in item 1.c. on page 94.)
      3) Assigning values to information, technology, and systems is the foundation of **risk prioritization**.
         a) Time, budget, and resources should first be allocated to the most valuable information, technology, and systems.

4) Compared to traditional risks, cyber risks may come from more entry points, both internal and external to the entity. Control activities that ensure that the **risk responses** are carried out should therefore focus on (a) using preventive controls to limit access to the system (e.g., user authentication) and (b) using detective and corrective controls to identify and prevent similar breaches in the future as soon as possible (e.g., immediately detecting access by unauthorized users and blocking the loophole).

   a) The constantly evolving nature of cyber risks makes cyber risk avoidance ineffective or impossible. Other risk responses discussed in Subunit 3.1 may, however, be used in managing cyber risks.

5) The **portfolio view of cyber risks**, including risk identification, assessment, prioritization, and response, should be continually adjusted because of the constantly evolving business context.

6. **Component 4 – Review and Revision**

   a. The following are the fundamental cyber risk management techniques related to the three principles of review and revision.

      1) Technological **changes** are common sources of opportunities. However, they also create vulnerabilities. Thus, significant changes must be **iteratively** identified and assessed. The organization should evaluate each change and determine how to best manage the cyber risk.

         a) Significant changes may come from either

            i) The internal environment (e.g., the failure of a risk response) or
            ii) The external environment (e.g., evolution of a technology used in operation).

      2) **Performance** results that deviate from a target or tolerance may indicate

         a) Unidentified cyber risks (e.g., an unidentified loophole in the system)
         b) Improperly assessed risks (e.g., inappropriate value assigned to a system)
         c) New risks (e.g., risks from new types of cyber attacks)
         d) Opportunities to accept more risk (e.g., emerging technology)
         e) The need to revise a target performance or tolerance

      3) **Improvements** help factor in unidentified or emerging cyber risks.

         a) Opportunities from technological advancement can also be captured.

7. **Component 5 – Information, Communication, and Reporting**

   a. The following are the fundamental cyber risk management techniques related to the three principles of information, communication, and reporting.

      1) **Information systems** support cyber risk management by

         a) Providing complete, accurate, and relevant data input for decision making
         b) Increasing the speed at which information is provided, thereby facilitating real-time decision making
         c) Easing reporting of cyber risks (e.g., automated or event-driven reporting)
         d) Enabling the use of third-party service providers (e.g., by easing the information flows between the parties)

2) **Communication channels** should exist at every level of the entity and direct information internally and externally.
    a) The following are examples of existing communication channels.
        i) Emails sent to each employee informing them of any attempted cyber attack
        ii) Activity reports of employees sent to management for risk identification and assessment
        iii) Periodic information interchange (e.g., management meetings) with outside parties
    b) The channels chosen should be based on the specific needs of the communication, such as
        i) Nature (e.g., phone calls may not be effective for contract negotiation)
        ii) Urgency (e.g., emails may not be effective if immediate feedback is required)
        iii) Sensitivity (e.g., unsecured channels should not be used to share private and sensitive information)
3) The organization **reports** on risk, culture, and performance at multiple levels and across the entity.
    a) The organization should review the related federal and state laws and regulations for reporting or disclosure requirements.
    b) Reporting should be tailored to various levels of the organization and different audiences based on the facts and level of detail required.
    c) The level of reporting depends on the impact and severity of the issue.
        i) Minor issues are reported to the **cyber risk management team** or the **information security team** with a detailed description of the issues.
        ii) Major issues are reported to **executive management**.
        iii) In certain circumstances, such as cybersecurity breaches by executive management, issues are reported to the **board of directors**.

STOP & REVIEW

You have completed the outline for this subunit.
Study multiple-choice questions 15 through 18 beginning on page 103.

SU 3: COSO Enterprise Risk Management Framework

QUESTIONS

3.1 Enterprise Risk Management (ERM)

1. According to COSO, the benefits of enterprise risk management (ERM) include all of the following **except**

   A. Decreased performance variability.
   B. Elimination of all risks.
   C. Improved resource allocation.
   D. Improved risk identification and management.

Answer (B) is correct.
   REQUIRED: The item not a benefit of ERM.
   DISCUSSION: ERM helps to manage risks, but it does not eliminate risks.
   Answer (A) is incorrect. ERM helps management decrease performance variability by setting performance tolerances that align with strategy, business objectives, and risk appetite. **Answer (C) is incorrect.** ERM helps to improve resource allocation by deploying resources based on the severity and priority of risks. **Answer (D) is incorrect.** ERM helps improve risk identification and management by integrating ERM practices throughout the entire organization, starting with strategy selection through performance results.

2. Management considers risk appetite for all of the following reasons **except**

   A. Aligning with development of strategy.
   B. Aligning with business objectives.
   C. Implementing risk responses.
   D. Setting risk capacity.

Answer (D) is correct.
   REQUIRED: The item not a reason for considering risk appetite.
   DISCUSSION: Risk appetite consists of the types and amount of risk the entity is willing to accept in pursuit of value. Among other things, risk appetite should be considered in

   1. Aligning with development of strategy.
   2. Aligning with business objectives.
   3. Prioritizing risks.
   4. Implementing risk responses.

   Risk capacity is the maximum amount of risk an entity is able to assume. Management considers risk capacity in setting risk appetite.
   Answer (A) is incorrect. Management considers risk appetite when evaluating strategic options. **Answer (B) is incorrect.** Management considers risk appetite when setting objectives. **Answer (C) is incorrect.** Management considers risk appetite when implementing risk responses.

3. Which risk response reflects a change from acceptance to sharing?

A. An insurance policy on a manufacturing plant was not renewed.
B. Management purchased insurance on previously uninsured property.
C. Management sold a manufacturing plant.
D. After employees stole numerous inventory items, management implemented mandatory background checks on all employees.

Answer (B) is correct.
REQUIRED: The risk response reflecting a change from acceptance to sharing.
DISCUSSION: The categories of risk responses under the COSO ERM model are avoidance, acceptance, reduction, pursuit, and sharing. If management does not insure a building, the response is acceptance. Acceptance is appropriate when the risk to strategy and business objectives is within the risk appetite. However, once management purchases insurance, the risk is shared with an outside party.
Answer (A) is incorrect. Not renewing insurance is a change from risk sharing to risk acceptance. **Answer (C) is incorrect.** Selling property avoids all the risks of ownership. **Answer (D) is incorrect.** Management originally accepted the risk of employee theft by not implementing pre-hire investigations. Conducting background checks on all employees reduces the risk of theft.

4. The components of enterprise risk management (ERM) should be present and functioning. What does "present" mean?

I. Components exist in the design of ERM.
II. Components exist in the implementation of ERM.
III. Components continue to operate to achieve strategy and business objectives.

A. I only.
B. II only.
C. I and II.
D. I, II, and III.

Answer (C) is correct.
REQUIRED: The meaning of "present" in the phrase "present and functioning."
DISCUSSION: The components and principles of ERM, and their related controls, should be present and functioning to help the entity achieve its strategy and business objective. "Present" means such components, principles, and controls exist in the design and implementation of ERM.
Answer (A) is incorrect. The components also should exist in the implementation of ERM. **Answer (B) is incorrect.** The components also should exist in the design of ERM. **Answer (D) is incorrect.** "Functioning" means the components, principles, and controls continue to operate to achieve strategy and business objectives.

5. An entity defines its risk appetite in which component of the COSO ERM framework?

A. Performance.
B. Strategy and objective-setting.
C. Governance and culture.
D. Control environment.

Answer (B) is correct.
REQUIRED: The component of the COSO ERM framework in which risk appetite is defined.
DISCUSSION: The entity defines risk appetite in the strategy and objective-setting component of ERM. In defining risk appetite, the entity considers its mission, vision, culture, prior strategies, and risk capacity.
Answer (A) is incorrect. Although the risk appetite concept is applied in the performance component, it is defined in the strategy and objective-setting component. **Answer (C) is incorrect.** The entity defines its risk appetite in the strategy and objective-setting component of ERM. The governance and culture component is the basis for all of the components. **Answer (D) is incorrect.** The control environment is a component of the COSO internal control framework, not the ERM framework.

6. Which of the following components are supporting aspects of the COSO ERM framework?

A. Governance and culture; review and revision.
B. Performance; review and revision.
C. Governance and culture; information, communication, and reporting.
D. Strategy and objective-setting; performance.

Answer (C) is correct.
REQUIRED: The components that are supporting aspects of the COSO ERM framework.
DISCUSSION: The supporting aspect components of the COSO ERM framework are (1) governance and culture and (2) information, communication, and reporting.
Answer (A) is incorrect. Review and revision is a common process component of the COSO ERM framework. **Answer (B) is incorrect.** Performance and review and revision are common process components of the COSO ERM framework. **Answer (D) is incorrect.** Strategy and objective-setting and performance are common process components of the COSO ERM framework.

7. Inherent risk is

A. A potential event that may affect the achievement of strategy and business objectives.
B. A risk response.
C. The risk after management takes action to alter its severity.
D. The risk when management has not taken action to reduce the impact or likelihood of an adverse event.

Answer (D) is correct.
REQUIRED: The definition of inherent risk.
DISCUSSION: Inherent risk is the risk when management does not act to alter its severity. Severity commonly is measured as a combination of impact and likelihood.
Answer (A) is incorrect. A risk event is a potential event that may affect the entity adversely. **Answer (B) is incorrect.** A risk response is an action taken to bring identified risks within the entity's risk appetite. **Answer (C) is incorrect.** The risk remaining after management takes action to alter its severity is actual residual risk.

8. An entity determined that its variable interest rate on borrowing will increase significantly in the near future. Consequently, the entity hedged its variable rate by locking in a fixed rate for the relevant period. According to COSO, this decision is which type of response to risk?

A. Reduction.
B. Acceptance.
C. Sharing.
D. Avoidance.

Answer (C) is correct.
REQUIRED: The type of risk response.
DISCUSSION: Sharing reduces the risk by transferring a portion of the risk to another party. By entering into a hedging transaction, the entity transferred a portion of the risk to the party that offered the fixed rate.
Answer (A) is incorrect. Reduction lowers the risk so that it is within the target residual risk profile and the risk appetite. **Answer (B) is incorrect.** Acceptance takes no action to alter the risk. **Answer (D) is incorrect.** Avoidance ends exposure to the risk. Not borrowing is the avoidance response.

9. Enterprise risk management

A. Guarantees achievement of organizational objectives.
B. Requires establishment of risk and control activities by internal auditors.
C. Involves the identification of events with negative impacts on organizational objectives.
D. Includes selection of the best risk response for the organization.

Answer (C) is correct.
REQUIRED: The definition of ERM.
DISCUSSION: Enterprise risk management (ERM) is defined as the culture, capabilities, and practices, integrated with strategy setting and performance, that organizations rely on to manage risk in creating, preserving, and realizing value.
Answer (A) is incorrect. Risk management processes cannot guarantee achievement of objectives. Answer (B) is incorrect. Involvement of internal auditors in establishing control activities impairs their independence and objectivity. Answer (D) is incorrect. ERM selects not the best risk response but the risk response within the organization's risk appetite and performance tolerance.

10. Limitations of ERM may arise from all of the following **except**

A. Faulty human judgment.
B. Cost-benefit considerations.
C. Collusion.
D. Failure to achieve objectives.

Answer (D) is correct.
REQUIRED: The limitations of ERM.
DISCUSSION: Limitations of ERM arise from the possibility of (1) faulty human judgment, (2) cost-benefit considerations, (3) simple errors or mistakes, (4) collusion, and (5) management override of ERM decisions. The failure to achieve objectives is a risk of poor enterprise risk management.

11. According to COSO's ERM framework, which view of risk is fully integrated?

A. Portfolio view.
B. Risk view.
C. Risk profile view.
D. Risk category view.

Answer (A) is correct.
REQUIRED: The fully integrated view of risk.
DISCUSSION: A portfolio view is fully integrated. It is a composite view of the risks related to entity-wide strategy and business objectives and their effect on entity performance.
Answer (B) is incorrect. A risk view is minimally integrated. Risks are identified and assessed. Answer (C) is incorrect. A risk profile view is partially integrated. It is a composite view of the types, severity, and interdependencies of risks related to a specific strategy or business objective and their effect on performance. Answer (D) is incorrect. A risk category results from limited integration. The risks assessed in the risk view (minimal integration) are categorized.

12. According to the COSO ERM framework, which of following best describes the difference between strategy and business objectives?

A. Strategy is the plan to achieve business objectives.
B. Business objectives are the steps to achieve strategy.
C. Strategy is the organization's core purpose, and business objectives are what the organization aspires to achieve over time.
D. Business objectives are broader in scope than strategy.

Answer (B) is correct.
REQUIRED: The difference between strategy and business objectives.
DISCUSSION: Strategy is the plan to achieve the entity's mission and vision and apply its core values. Business objectives are the measurable steps taken to achieve the entity's strategy.
Answer (A) is incorrect. Strategy is the plan to achieve the organization's mission and vision and apply its core values. Answer (C) is incorrect. Mission is the organization's core purpose, but vision is its aspirations for what it intends to achieve over time. Answer (D) is incorrect. Strategy is the overall plan to achieve the organization's mission and vision. It reflects a broader scope than business objectives.

13. The premise of enterprise resource management (ERM) is that an organization exists to provide value for its

A. Employees.
B. Customers.
C. Stakeholders.
D. Shareholders.

Answer (C) is correct.
REQUIRED: The premise of ERM.
DISCUSSION: ERM is based on the premise that every organization exists to provide value for its stakeholders. Accordingly, ERM is defined as the culture, capabilities, and practices, integrated with strategy-setting and performance, that organizations rely on to manage risk in creating, preserving, and realizing value.
Answer (A) is incorrect. Employees are a subset of stakeholders. **Answer (B) is incorrect.** Customers are a subset of stakeholders. **Answer (D) is incorrect.** Shareholders are a subset of stakeholders.

14. Which step in the COSO eight-step approach for implementing an effective enterprise risk management program involves identifying gaps and opportunities to integrate strategies and risk practices?

A. Step 3.
B. Step 4.
C. Step 5.
D. Step 6.

Answer (B) is correct.
REQUIRED: The correct step in the implementation of an enterprise risk management program.
DISCUSSION: Step 4 of the eight-step approach involves inventorying the existing risk management practices of the organization, identifying gaps and opportunities to integrate strategies and risk practices, and developing action steps to close the gaps or implement the opportunities.
Answer (A) is incorrect. Step 3 of the eight-step approach involves establishing a management working group to support the risk management leader across the whole organization. **Answer (C) is incorrect.** Step 5 of the eight-step approach involves conducting an initial assessment of key strategies and related strategic risk and identifying events or risks that impair success of the key strategies. **Answer (D) is incorrect.** Step 6 of the eight-step approach involves developing a consolidated action plan and communicating the plan to the board of directors and management.

3.2 Applying the ERM Framework to Cyber Risk Management

15. A chemical company was revealed to be involved in the illegal disposal of chemical waste after its private information was stolen in a cyber attack. Which of the following threat actors is most likely behind the cyber attack?

A. Company insiders.
B. Organized criminals.
C. Nation-states and spies.
D. Hacktivists.

Answer (D) is correct.
REQUIRED: The most likely cyber threat actor behind a cyber attack.
DISCUSSION: Hacktivists fulfill social or political purposes using the private information of an entity. Stealing and revealing information about the illegal act of a chemical company that is causing environmental damage is likely to be for social or political purposes.
Answer (A) is incorrect. Company insiders use, share, or sell private information from within an organization for personal gain, such as profiting from insider trading. Revealing the illegal act of an organization is unlikely to be for personal gain. **Answer (B) is incorrect.** Organized criminals steal private information for personal gain, e.g., stealing credit card information for identity theft or financial advantage. Revealing the illegal act of an organization is unlikely to be for personal gain. **Answer (C) is incorrect.** Nation-states and spies are interested in national security secrets and valuable intellectual property, such as military communications. Illegal waste disposal by a chemical company is unlikely to be related to national security or intellectual property.

16. The cyber risk management team is **not**

A. Responsible for managing cyber risks at all levels of the entity.
B. Led by chief information executives.
C. Responsible to report to the board of directors.
D. Composed of managers from different departments.

Answer (A) is correct.
REQUIRED: The false description of the cyber risk management team.
DISCUSSION: The cyber risk management team is responsible for managing cyber risks at the entity level, not at all levels of the entity. Department-level cyber risks are managed by departmental managers.
Answer (B) is incorrect. The cyber risk management team is generally led by the chief information executives, such as the chief information officer (CIO) or chief information security officer (CISO). **Answer (C) is incorrect.** The cyber risk management team should report to the board of directors regarding the impacts of cyber risks and the initiatives to manage such risks. **Answer (D) is incorrect.** The cyber risk management team should be composed of cross-departmental and cross-functional parties.

17. Which of the following risk responses is **not** effective in managing cyber risks?

A. Risk reduction.
B. Risk avoidance.
C. Risk sharing.
D. Risk acceptance.

Answer (B) is correct.
REQUIRED: The risk response that is not effective in managing cyber risks.
DISCUSSION: Since the business context of an organization and cyber risks are constantly evolving, responses that aim to avoid cyber risks are ineffective or nearly impossible to implement.
Answer (A) is incorrect. Cyber risks can be reduced. For example, the risk of unauthorized access can be reduced by using passwords. **Answer (C) is incorrect.** Risk sharing is an effective response to cyber risks. For example, insurance can be used to cover losses due to cyber risks. **Answer (D) is incorrect.** Risk acceptance, which involves taking no action to alter the severity of the risk, is appropriate when the cyber risk is within the risk appetite of the organization.

18. When choosing a communication channel to manage cyber risks, which of the following is **not** a factor considered?

A. Cost.
B. Nature.
C. Sensitivity.
D. Urgency.

Answer (A) is correct.
REQUIRED: The factors considered in choosing a communication channel.
DISCUSSION: While the cost of a communication channel is a constraint to choosing the channel, it is generally not a determinant factor.
Answer (B) is incorrect. When choosing a communication channel, the nature of the communication should be considered. For example, phone calls may not be effective for contract negotiation. **Answer (C) is incorrect.** The sensitivity of the information communicated affects the communication channel. For example, unsecured channels should not be used to share private or sensitive information. **Answer (D) is incorrect.** The urgency of the communication should be considered when choosing the communication channel. For example, emails may not be effective if immediate feedback is required.

STUDY UNIT FOUR

MICROECONOMICS

(31 pages of outline)

4.1	Demand, Supply, and Equilibrium	105
4.2	Elasticity	113
4.3	Government Action in the Market and Wages	116
4.4	Profits and Costs	119
4.5	Marginal Analysis	121
4.6	Market Structures -- Pure Competition	127
4.7	Market Structures -- Monopoly	131
4.8	Market Structures -- Monopolistic Competition	133
4.9	Market Structures -- Oligopoly	134

Microeconomics is the analysis of the behaviors of individual units within a larger economy. It specifically examines the factors that affect individuals' decisions about the efficient allocation of scarce resources among alternative uses. Economic theories assume the goal is to maximize profits for particular firms and satisfaction (or utility) for individuals.

4.1 DEMAND, SUPPLY, AND EQUILIBRIUM

1. **Demand -- the Buyer's Side of the Market**

   a. Demand vs. Quantity Demanded

      1) Demand is a schedule of the amounts of a good or service that consumers are willing and able to purchase at various prices during a period of time. Quantity demanded is the amount that will be purchased at a specific price during a period of time.

      Demand Schedule

Price per Unit	Quantity Demanded
$10	0
$9	1
$8	2
$7	3
$6	4
$5	5
$4	6
$3	7
$2	8
$1	9
$0	10

      2) A demand schedule can be graphically depicted as a relationship between the prices of a commodity (on the vertical axis) and the quantity demanded at the various prices (horizontal axis), if other determinants of demand are constant.

      3) A change in quantity demanded results from a change in price; a change in demand results from factors other than price.

b. **The Law of Demand**

1) If all other factors are constant, the price of a product and the quantity demanded are inversely related. The higher (lower) the price, the smaller (greater) the quantity demanded. The result is a movement **along** a demand curve.

   a) For example, as price decreases from P_1 to P_2, quantity demanded increases from Q_1 to Q_2.

Movement Along a Demand Curve

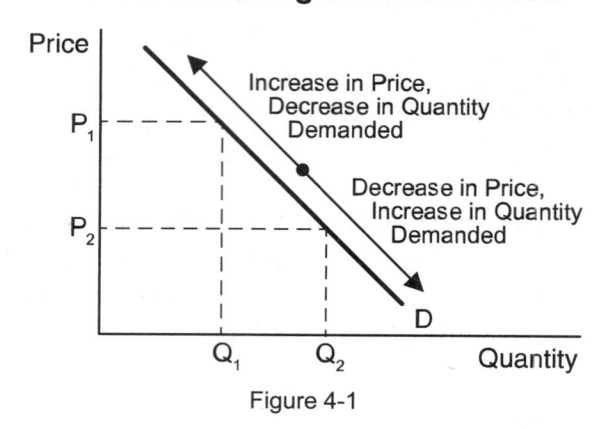

Figure 4-1

c. **Factors Other than Price**

1) A change in any of the determinants of demand (factors other than price) results in a **shift** of the demand curve.

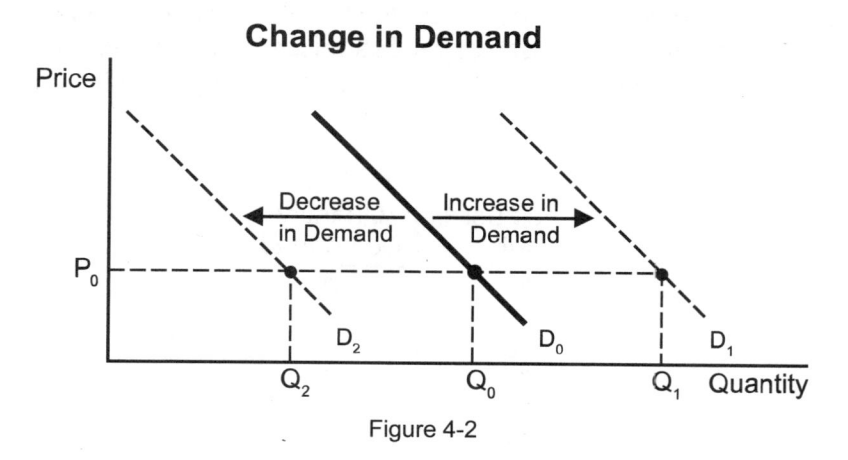

Change in Demand

Figure 4-2

   a) A shift to the right (D_0 to D_1) indicates that more goods ($Q_1 > Q_0$) will be sold at a given price (P_0). A shift to the left (D_0 to D_2) indicates that fewer goods ($Q_2 < Q_0$) will be sold at a given price (P_0).

2) The determinants of demand are
    a) Consumer incomes
        i) Most goods are **normal goods**, that is, commodities for which demand is positively (directly) related to income (e.g., steak, new clothes, and airline travel). Thus, demand for these goods shifts to the right as incomes rise. These goods are often referred to as "more is better."
        ii) However, a few goods are **inferior goods**, that is, commodities for which demand is negatively (inversely) related to income (e.g., potatoes, used clothing, and bus transportation). In this situation, demand shifts to the left as incomes rise. These goods are often referred to as "less is better."
        iii) For example, as income rises, a consumer would substitute new clothing (normal goods) for used clothes (inferior goods). The opposite is also true.
    b) Consumer taste and preference
        i) If a product becomes more (less) popular, the demand curve shifts to the right (left).
    c) Prices of related goods
        i) If a price increase in Product A results in an increase in demand for Product B, Products A and B are **substitutes**. For example, when beef prices rise, the demand for chicken increases because consumers switch to chicken as the more affordable option. Consumers substitute chicken for beef in their shopping.
        ii) If a price increase in Product A results in a decrease in demand for Product B, Products A and B are **complements**. For example, if the price of printers increases, the demand for printer ink cartridges decreases because consumers never use cartridges alone.
    d) Consumer expectations
        i) For example, as a hurricane approaches Florida, there is an increased demand for chainsaws and power generators (their demand curves shift to the right) due to the expectation of a natural disaster.
    e) Number of consumers
        i) An increase in the number of consumers shifts the demand curve to the right (increase in demand).
        ii) A decrease in the number of consumers shifts the demand curve to the left (decrease in demand).

2. Supply -- the Seller's Side of the Market

a. **Price vs. Quantity Supplied**

1) Supply is a schedule of the amounts of a good that producers are willing and able to offer to the market at various prices during a specified period. Quantity supplied is the amount that will be offered at a specific price during a period.

2) A supply schedule can be graphically depicted as a relationship between the prices of a commodity (on the vertical axis) and the quantity offered at the various prices (horizontal axis) if other determinants of supply are constant.

3) A change in quantity supplied results from a change in price; a change in supply results from factors other than price.

b. **The Law of Supply**

1) If all other factors are constant, the price of a product and the quantity supplied are directly related. The higher (lower) the price, the greater (lower) the quantity supplied. The result is a movement **along** a supply curve.

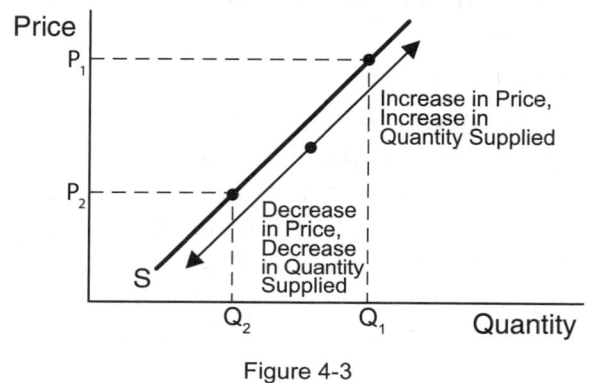

Movement Along a Supply Curve

Figure 4-3

a) Thus, as price increases from P_2 to P_1, quantity supplied increases from Q_2 to Q_1.

c. **Factors Other than Price**

1) A change in any of the determinants of supply (factors other than price) results in a **shift** of the supply curve.

Change in Supply

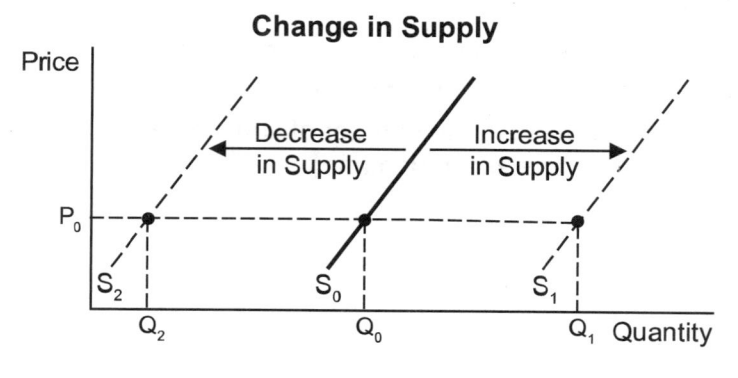

Figure 4-4

a) A shift to the right (S_0 to S_1) indicates that more goods ($Q_1 > Q_0$) will be supplied at a given price (P_0). A shift to the left (S_0 to S_2) indicates that fewer goods ($Q_2 < Q_1$) will be supplied at a given price (P_0).

2) The determinants of supply are
   a) Costs of inputs
      i) An increase in the costs of inputs, such as employees' wages and materials, decreases supply, shifting the supply curve to the left.
      ii) A decrease in the costs of inputs increases supply, shifting the supply curve to the right.
   b) A change in efficiency of the production process
      i) For example, better technology that improves the production process (e.g., automated manufacturing) increases supply, shifting the supply curve to the right.
   c) Expectations about price changes
      i) If a product's price is expected to decrease, firms will increase supply before the decrease in price to sell as much as possible at the higher price. The supply curve shifts to the right. Production is then decreased when prices fall (law of supply affects quantity supplied).
   d) Taxes and subsidies
      i) An increase in taxes or a decrease in subsidies decreases supply, shifting the supply curve to the left.
      ii) A decrease in taxes or an increase in subsidies increases supply, shifting the supply curve to the right.

3. **Market Equilibrium**
   a. Market demand is the sum of the individual demand curves of all buyers. Market supply is the sum of the individual supply curves of all sellers.
      1) Market equilibrium is the combination of price and quantity at which the market demand and market supply curves intersect.

Market Equilibrium

P_E = Equilibrium Price
Q_E = Equilibrium Quantity

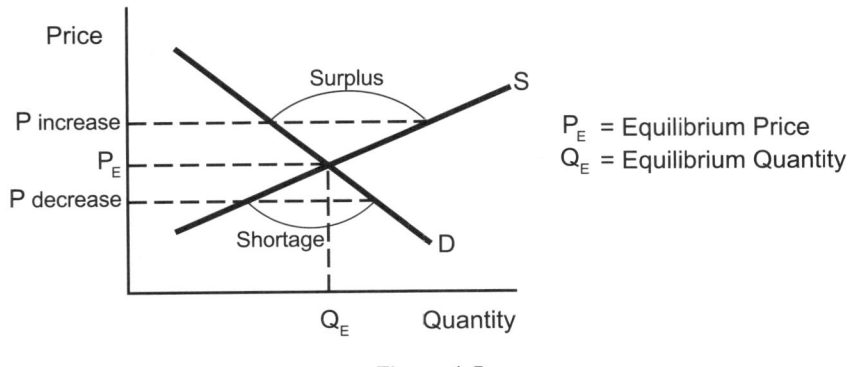

Figure 4-5

   b. At the intersection of the supply and demand curves, anyone wishing to purchase economic goods at the market price can do so. Anyone offering the goods can sell everything they bring to market.
      1) **Equilibrium** is at the **market-clearing price** and **the market-clearing quantity**.

c. The market forces of supply and demand create an automatic, efficient rationing system.

1) When the market price exceeds the equilibrium price, the quantity supplied exceeds the quantity demanded by consumers. A surplus results.

   a) The competition among sellers to eliminate excess inventories causes price cuts and lower production.
   b) As the price falls, more buyers enter the market. Eventually, the price settles at the equilibrium price, and the surplus is eliminated.
   c) Government intervention can create a market surplus. An example is a price floor for an agricultural commodity. If the price is above equilibrium, supply exceeds demand. We will discuss this further in Subunit 4.3, item 3.

2) When the market price is lower than the equilibrium price, the quantity demanded by consumers is greater than the quantity supplied. A shortage results.

   a) Consumers compete for scarce goods by bidding up prices.
   b) As the price rises, new suppliers enter the market. Eventually, the price settles at the equilibrium price, and the shortage is eliminated.
   c) Government intervention also can create shortages. An example is a price ceiling for apartment rents. If the price is below equilibrium, demand exceeds supply. We will discuss this further in Subunit 4.3, item 2.

d. The shift in the demand and supply curves results in various effects on equilibrium price and quantity.

1) Shift in demand curve only (Figure 4-6)

   a) When the demand curve shifts to the right (D_0 to D_1), the initial equilibrium price (P_0) and equilibrium quantity (Q_0) increase to P_1 and Q_1, respectively.
   b) When the demand curve shifts to the left (D_0 to D_2), equilibrium price (P_0) and equilibrium quantity (Q_0) decrease to P_2 and Q_2, respectively.

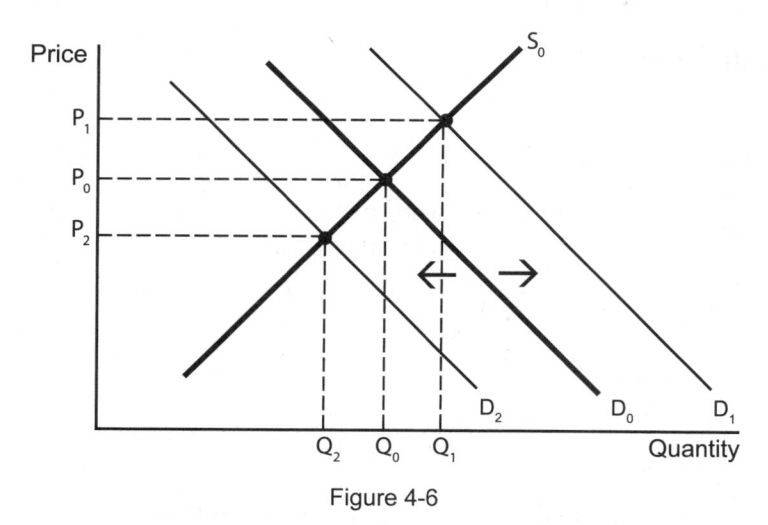

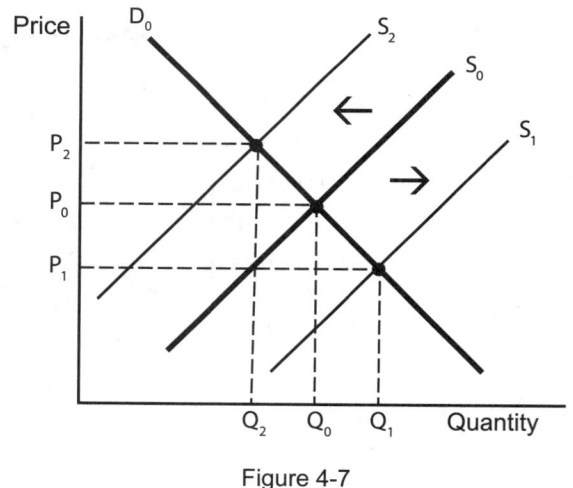

Figure 4-6

Figure 4-7

2) Shift in supply curve only (Figure 4-7)

   a) When the supply curve shifts to the right (S_0 to S_1), equilibrium price (P_0) decreases to P_1 and equilibrium quantity (Q_0) increases to Q_1.
   b) When the supply curve shifts to the left (S_0 to S_2), equilibrium price (P_0) increases to P_2 and equilibrium quantity (Q_0) decreases to Q_2.

3) Shift in both supply and demand curve towards the same direction (Figures 4-8 and 4-9)

   a) When the demand and supply curves both shift to the left (right) and the decrease (increase) in demand equals the decrease (increase) in supply, equilibrium price (P_0) remains the same.

      i) When both shift to the left, equilibrium quantity decreases from Q_0 to Q_1.
      ii) When both shift to the right, equilibrium quantity increases from Q_0 to Q_2.

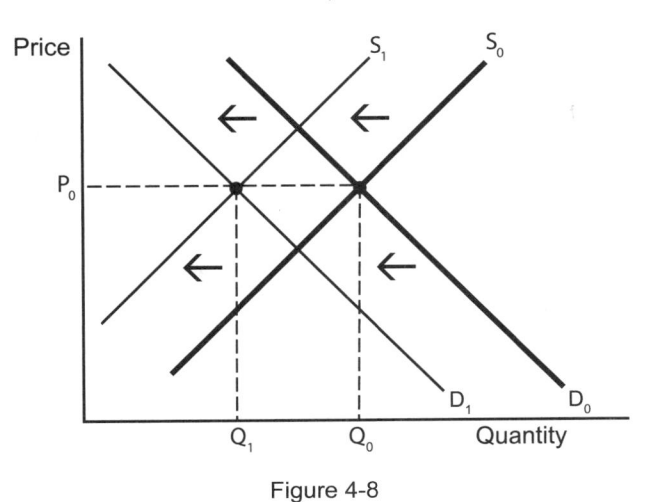

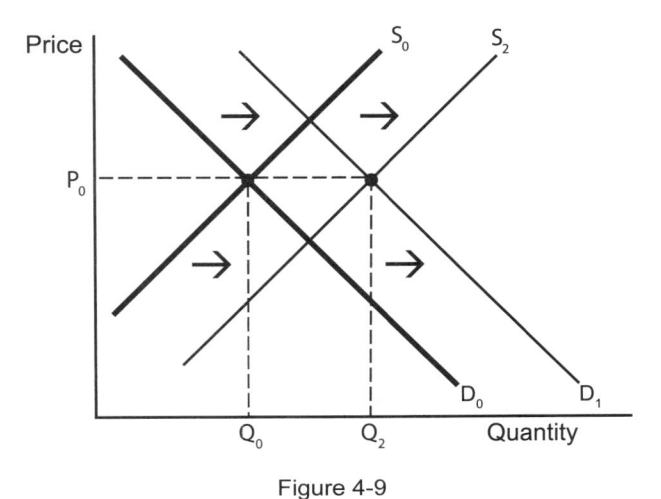

Figure 4-8

Figure 4-9

   b) Rightward shift in both demand and supply curve

      i) When the increase in demand is greater than the increase in supply, the equilibrium price (P_0) increases to P_1 and equilibrium quantity (Q_0) increases to Q_1 (Figure 4-10).

      ii) When the increase in demand is less than the increase in supply, the equilibrium price (P_0) decreases to P_2 and the equilibrium quantity (Q_0) increases to Q_2 (Figure 4-11).

Figure 4-10

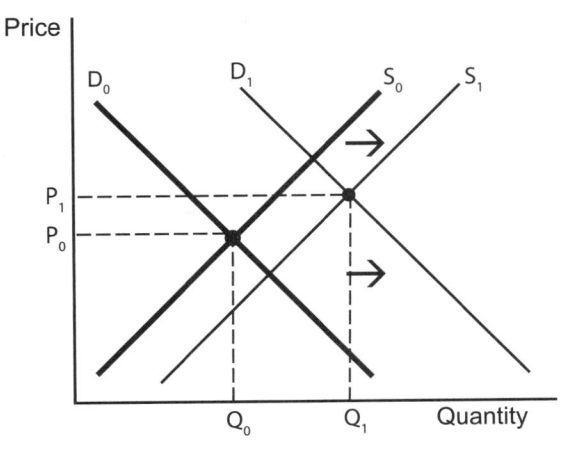

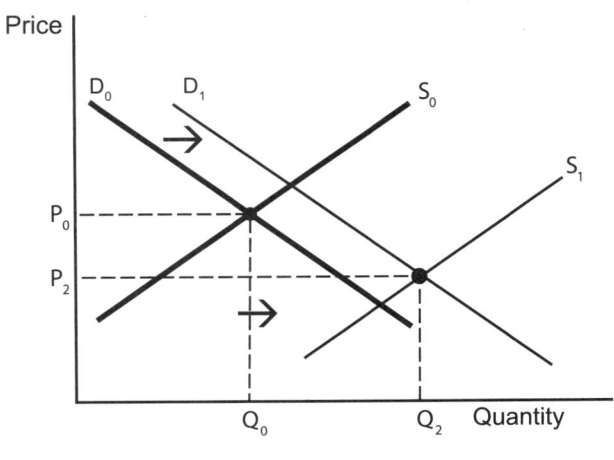

Figure 4-11

c) Leftward shift in both demand and supply curve

   i) When the decrease in demand is greater than the decrease in supply, the equilibrium price (P_0) decreases to P_1 and the equilibrium quantity (Q_0) decreases to Q_1 (Figure 4-12).

   ii) When the decrease in demand is less than the decrease in supply, the equilibrium price (P_0) increases to P_2 and the equilibrium quantity (Q_0) decreases to Q_2 (Figure 4-13).

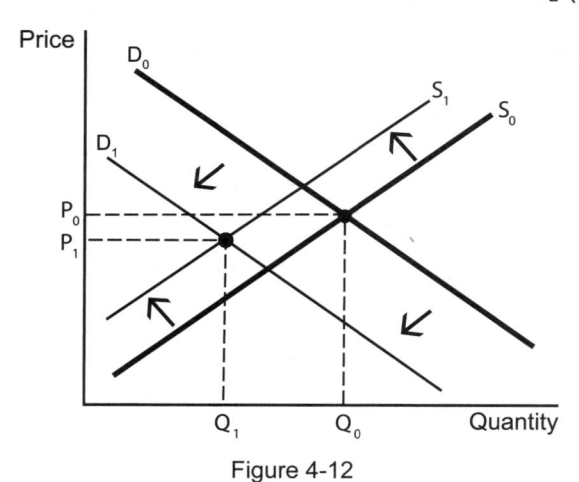

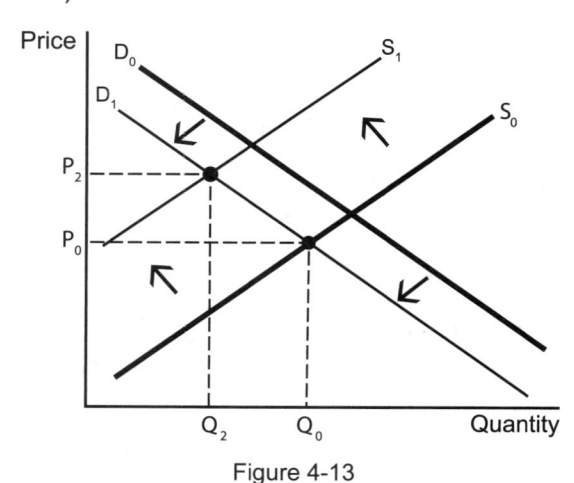

Figure 4-12

Figure 4-13

4) Shift in both supply and demand curve towards opposite directions are not illustrated in detail here, but the change in equilibrium quantity and price can be easily determined by drawing graphs.

e. The effects on equilibrium of **shifts** in the supply and demand schedules are summarized below:

	Demand increase (rightward shift)	**Demand constant**	**Demand decrease (leftward shift)**
Supply increase (rightward shift)	P_0 uncertain Q_0 increase	P_0 decrease Q_0 increase	P_0 decrease Q_0 uncertain
Supply constant	P_0 increase Q_0 increase	— —	P_0 decrease Q_0 decrease
Supply decrease (leftward shift)	P_0 increase Q_0 uncertain	P_0 increase Q_0 decrease	P_0 uncertain Q_0 decrease

SUCCESS TIP

Rather than memorize, the best way to understand demand, supply, and equilibrium is to solve related questions by drawing a graph.

STOP & REVIEW

You have completed the outline for this subunit.
Study multiple-choice questions 1 through 3 beginning on page 136.

4.2 ELASTICITY

1. **Elasticity of Demand**

    a. Price elasticity of demand (E_d) measures the sensitivity of the quantity demanded of a product to a change in its price.

        1) The two common methods to calculate the price elasticity of demand are the point method and the midpoint method.

    b. **Point Method**

        1) The point method measures the price elasticity of demand at a given point on the demand curve for a specific change in the product's price.

$$\%\Delta Q = \frac{\text{Quantity demanded \textbf{after} the change} - \text{Quantity demanded \textbf{before} the change}}{\text{Quantity demanded \textbf{before} the change}}$$

$$\%\Delta P = \frac{\text{Price \textbf{after} the change} - \text{Price \textbf{before} the change}}{\text{Price \textbf{before} the change}}$$

$$E_d = \frac{\text{Percentage change in quantity demanded}}{\text{Percentage change in price}} = \frac{\%\Delta Q}{\%\Delta P}$$

    c. **Midpoint Method (Arc Method)**

        1) The midpoint method measures the price elasticity of demand of a range for a specific change in the product's price. This method uses the midpoint of the quantities and prices to measure elasticity. The following is the algebraically simplified version of the formula:

$$E_d = \frac{\%\Delta Q}{\%\Delta P} = \frac{(Q_1 - Q_2) \div (Q_1 + Q_2)}{(P_1 - P_2) \div (P_1 + P_2)}$$

            a) **Absolute value** is used when calculating the coefficient of elasticity.

EXAMPLE 4-1   Point and Arc Methods

Roxy's Ice Cream Shoppe sells 100 quarts of chocolate a day at $6 each. If it lowers the price to $3 per quart, it will sell 300 quarts a day.

Point Method

$$\%\Delta Q = \frac{300 - 100}{100} = 2 = 200\%$$

$$\%\Delta P = \frac{\$3 - \$6}{\$6} = 0.5 = 50\%$$

$$E_d = \frac{\%\Delta Q}{\%\Delta P} = \frac{200\%}{50\%} = 4$$

The elasticity absolute value of 4 indicates that the specific change of the product's price by 50% (from $6 to $3) will increase the demand for the product by 200% (from Q = 100 to Q = 300).

Midpoint (Arc) Method

	Num.	Denom.		Num.	Denom.		Num.	Denom.	Elasticity
$E_d =$	$\frac{100-300}{100+300}$	$\div \frac{\$6-\$3}{\$6+\$3}$	$=$	$\frac{200}{400}$	$\div \frac{\$3}{\$9}$	$=$	0.500	$\div\ 0.333$	$=$ **1.50**

The elasticity absolute value of 1.5 indicates that the range on the demand curve between P = $6 and P = $3 is relatively elastic.

d. When the demand elasticity coefficient is

1) **Greater than one**, demand is in a **relatively elastic** range. The percentage change in the quantity demanded is higher than the percentage change in the price.

$$\%\Delta Q > \%\Delta P$$

a) For example, a 10% decline in the price of ice cream results in a 20% increase in ice cream demanded.

2) **Equal to one**, demand has **unitary elasticity** (usually a very limited range). The percentage change in the quantity demanded is equal to the percentage change in the price.

$$\%\Delta Q = \%\Delta P$$

3) **Less than one**, demand is in a **relatively inelastic** range. The percentage change in the quantity demanded is lower than the percentage change in the price.

$$\%\Delta Q < \%\Delta P$$

a) For example, a 20% decline in the price of ice cream results in a 10% increase in ice cream demanded.

4) **Infinite**, demand is **perfectly elastic** (depicted as a horizontal line).

a) In pure competition (discussed in Subunit 4.6), the number of firms is so great that one cannot influence the market price. The demand curve faced by a single seller in such a market is perfectly elastic (although the demand curve for the market as a whole has the normal downward slope).

EXAMPLE 4-2	Perfectly Elastic Demand

Consumers will buy a farmer's total output of soybeans at the market price but will buy none at a slightly higher price. Moreover, the farmer cannot sell below the market price without incurring losses.

5) **Equal to zero**, demand is **perfectly inelastic** (depicted as a vertical line).

a) Some consumers' need for a certain product is so high that they will pay whatever price the market sets. The number of these consumers is limited, and the amount they desire is relatively fixed.

EXAMPLE 4-3	Perfectly Inelastic Demand

Drug addiction tends to result in demand that is unresponsive to price changes. Existing buyers (addicts) are not driven out of the market by a rise in price, and no new buyers are induced to enter the market by a reduction in price.

e. The price elasticity of demand of a product can be affected by the availability of substitute products in the market.

1) As more substitute products become available, the demand for the product becomes more elastic. A small increase in the product's price causes a proportionally larger decrease in the quantity demanded because substitutes are available.

2) As fewer substitute products become available in the market, the demand for the product becomes more inelastic.

f. Price elasticity of demand is useful for determining how a change in the price of a product will affect total revenue (Quantity × Price).

1) If the product demand is price elastic, as price **increases**, the percentage decrease in the quantity demanded is greater than the percentage increase in price. Thus, total revenue decreases.

2) If the product demand is price unitary elastic, as price **increases**, the percentage decrease in the quantity demanded is equal to the percentage increase in price. Thus, total revenue stays the same.

3) If product demand is price inelastic, as price **increases**, the percentage decrease in the quantity demanded is less than the percentage increase in the price. Thus, total revenue increases.

Effect on Total Revenue

	Elastic Range	Unitary Elasticity	Inelastic Range
Price increase	Decrease	No change	Increase
Price decrease	Increase	No change	Decrease

2. **Elasticity of Supply**

   a. Price elasticity of supply (E_s) measures the sensitivity of the quantity supplied of a product to a change in its price.

   $$E_s = \frac{\text{Percentage change in quantity supplied}}{\text{Percentage change in price}}$$

   1) The same methods used in the calculation of price elasticity of demand are used to calculate the price elasticity of supply.

   2) When the supply elasticity coefficient is

      a) **Greater than one**, supply is in a **relatively elastic** range. The percentage change in the quantity supplied is higher than the percentage change in the price.

      $$\%\Delta Q > \%\Delta P$$

      b) **Equal to one**, supply has **unitary elasticity** (usually a very limited range). The percentage change in the quantity supplied is equal to the percentage change in the price.

      $$\%\Delta Q = \%\Delta P$$

      c) **Less than one**, supply is in a **relatively inelastic** range. The percentage change in the quantity supplied is lower than the percentage change in the price.

      $$\%\Delta Q < \%\Delta P$$

      d) **Infinite**, supply is **perfectly elastic** (depicted as a horizontal line).

e) **Equal to zero**, supply is **perfectly inelastic** (depicted as a vertical line).

   i) A perfectly inelastic supply curve indicates that, in the very short run, a seller cannot change the quantity supplied.

EXAMPLE 4-4   Perfectly Inelastic Supply

A farmer offering a perishable good with no means of storage must sell the entire crop regardless of the price buyers offer. The farmer cannot offer a larger quantity because the harvest has ended for the season.

STOP & REVIEW

You have completed the outline for this subunit.
Study multiple-choice questions 4 through 6 beginning on page 137.

4.3 GOVERNMENT ACTION IN THE MARKET AND WAGES

1. **Price Controls**

   a. Price controls are attempts by government to remedy perceived imbalances of power between economic actors, i.e., sellers and buyers in the marketplace.

2. **Price Ceilings**

   a. To keep essential goods and services affordable to all, sellers sometimes are forced to charge below the equilibrium price.

   b. Shortages result because the market is unwilling to supply all that is demanded at the (government-mandated) artificially low price.

Price Ceiling and Resulting Shortage

P_0 = Initial equilibrium price
Q_0 = Initial equilibrium quantity
P_1 = Artificial ceiling set by government (price not allowed to rise above this ceiling)
Q_S = Quantity supplied at P_1
Q_D = Quantity demanded at P_1
$Q_D - Q_S$ = Amount of shortage

Figure 4-14

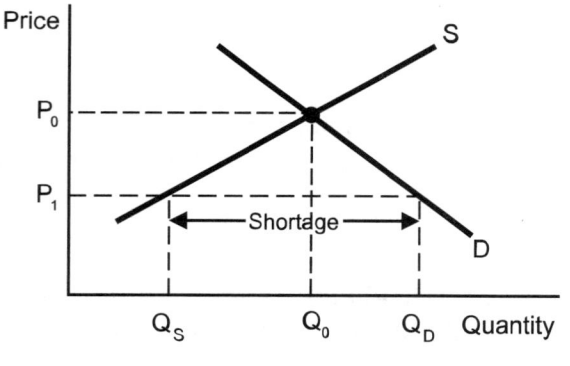

   c. Rent controls and usury laws are examples.

3. **Price Floors**

   a. To compensate certain suppliers perceived to be treated adversely by market forces, buyers sometimes are required to pay above the equilibrium price for certain products or services.

   b. Surpluses result because sellers are encouraged by the artificially high price to produce more than the market is willing to buy.

   Price Floor and Resulting Surplus

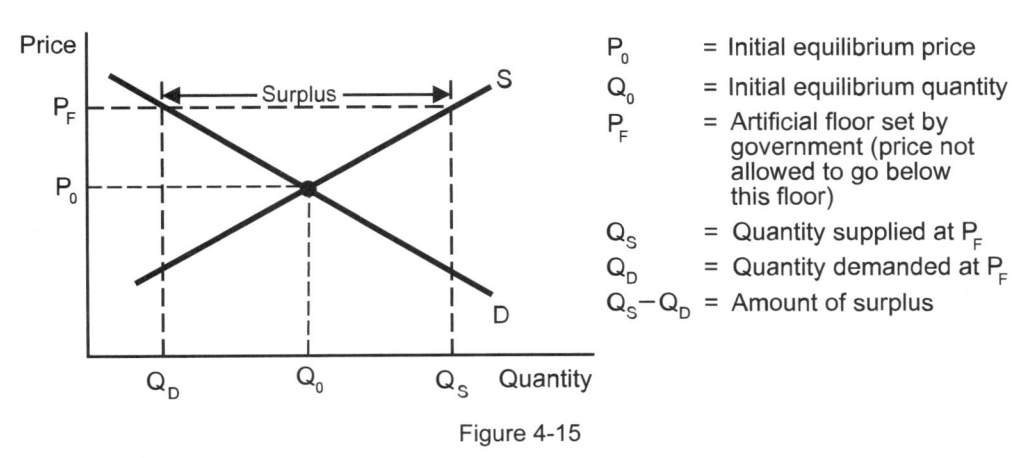

   P_0 = Initial equilibrium price
   Q_0 = Initial equilibrium quantity
   P_F = Artificial floor set by government (price not allowed to go below this floor)
   Q_S = Quantity supplied at P_F
   Q_D = Quantity demanded at P_F
   $Q_S - Q_D$ = Amount of surplus

   Figure 4-15

   c. Price supports for agricultural products and minimum wage legislation are examples.

4. **Wage Determination**

   a. A wage is the amount paid to the factor of production (labor) that includes the efforts of blue-collar and white-collar workers, professionals, and small business owners. The term "wage" customarily relates to amounts paid per unit of time.

   1) Many firms are competing for a large number of equally skilled workers who provide their services independently, so neither firms nor workers can affect the market rate for labor. Thus, both firms and workers are necessarily price takers.

   2) Market demand for labor is the total of the individual firms' demand curves, i.e., their marginal revenue product (MRP) curves.

   3) The market supply curve has a positive slope because, given little unemployment, firms must raise wages to hire additional workers.

      a) The upward slope reflects the need of firms to match the opportunity costs of workers, such as wages paid in employment alternatives or greater leisure.

   4) The wage rate and the level of employment in the market are determined by the intersection of the market labor demand curve and the market labor supply curve, i.e., labor market equilibrium.

   5) Each firm must accept the market wage rate as determined by the point of labor market equilibrium.

5. **Minimum Wage Laws**

   a. The minimum wage can be set by the government higher than the equilibrium wage (depicted as W_E). In this case, the quantity of labor demanded will be less than supplied. This can result in a higher unemployment rate.

   Market with Minimum Wage

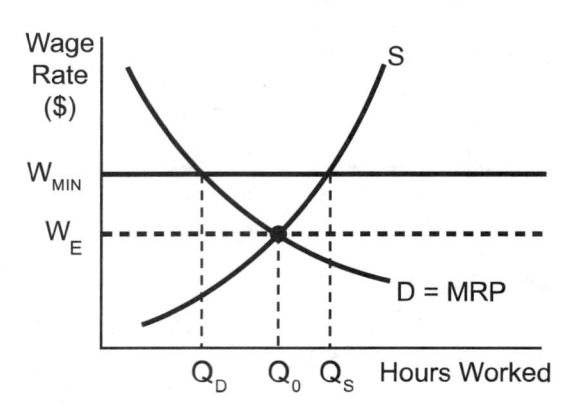

   Figure 4-16

   b. Arguments against the Minimum Wage

      1) Because a wage rate above equilibrium is established by law, unemployment is increased. It would be far better for people with marginal skills to have work at some level of pay than to be idle.

      2) The higher labor cost may drive some firms out of business.

   c. Arguments for the Minimum Wage

      1) Because many labor markets are monopsonies (markets with one buyer), minimum wage laws raise pay without increasing unemployment.

      2) The minimum wage may improve productivity.

         a) Because firms cannot pay a substandard wage no matter how menial the task, employers may be encouraged to move workers into productive activities.

         b) A minimum wage may reduce employee turnover, allowing the retention of experienced workers.

6. **Unions and Wages**

   a. Unions often negotiate higher rates of pay for their members. It can also be argued that unions can push the wage higher so the company employs fewer workers than it would without union intervention. In this case, workers who are not employed through the union have to find work outside union employment.

STOP & REVIEW

You have completed the outline for this subunit.
Study multiple-choice questions 7 through 10 beginning on page 138.

4.4 PROFITS AND COSTS

1. **Explicit vs. Implicit Costs**

   a. **Explicit costs** require actual cash payments. For this reason, they also are known as out-of-pocket or outlay costs.

      1) Explicit costs are **accounting costs**. They are recognized in formal accounting records.

EXAMPLE 4-5	Accounting Costs (Total Explicit Costs)
An entrepreneur opening a gift shop has to make certain cash payments to start the business.	
Inventory	$59,000
Rent	4,000
Utilities	1,000
Total explicit costs	**$64,000**

   b. **Implicit costs** are not recognized in formal accounting records.

      1) An implicit cost is an **opportunity cost**, i.e., the maximum benefit forgone by using a scarce resource for a given purpose instead of the next-best alternative.

      2) To measure the true economic success or failure of the venture, the entrepreneur in Example 4-5 must consider more than the explicit costs in the accounting records.

         a) The entrepreneur's opportunity costs often are important implicit costs. For example, (s)he could have worked for another firm rather than open the gift shop.

         b) Startup costs are resources that could have been invested in financial instruments.

         c) The **normal profit** is the income that the entrepreneur could have earned by applying his or her skills and resources in another venture. A normal profit is an implicit cost.

EXAMPLE 4-6	Normal Profit (Total Implicit Costs)
The gift shop entrepreneur's normal profit is	
Salary forgone	$35,000
Investment income forgone	3,600
Total implicit costs	**$38,600**

   c. **Economic costs** are total costs (explicit and implicit).

      1) The standard for an economic decision is whether the revenues from the venture cover all costs, both explicit and implicit.

EXAMPLE 4-7	Economic Costs
The gift shop entrepreneur's economic costs are	
Explicit costs	$ 64,000
Implicit costs	38,600
Total economic costs	**$102,600**

2. **Accounting vs. Economic Profit**

   a. **Accounting profits** are earned when the income of an organization exceeds its expenses.

EXAMPLE 4-8	Accounting Profit	
After the first year of operation, the gift shop owner made an accounting profit.		
	Sales revenue	$100,000
	Explicit costs	(64,000)
	Accounting profit	**$ 36,000**

   b. **Economic profits** are earned when the income of an organization exceeds its economic costs. They are not earned until the income exceeds not only costs recorded in the accounting records but also its implicit costs. Economic profit also is called **pure profit**.

EXAMPLE 4-9	Economic Loss	
After total costs are considered, the result is different.		
	Accounting profit	$ 36,000
	Implicit costs	(38,600)
	Economic loss	**$ (2,600)**

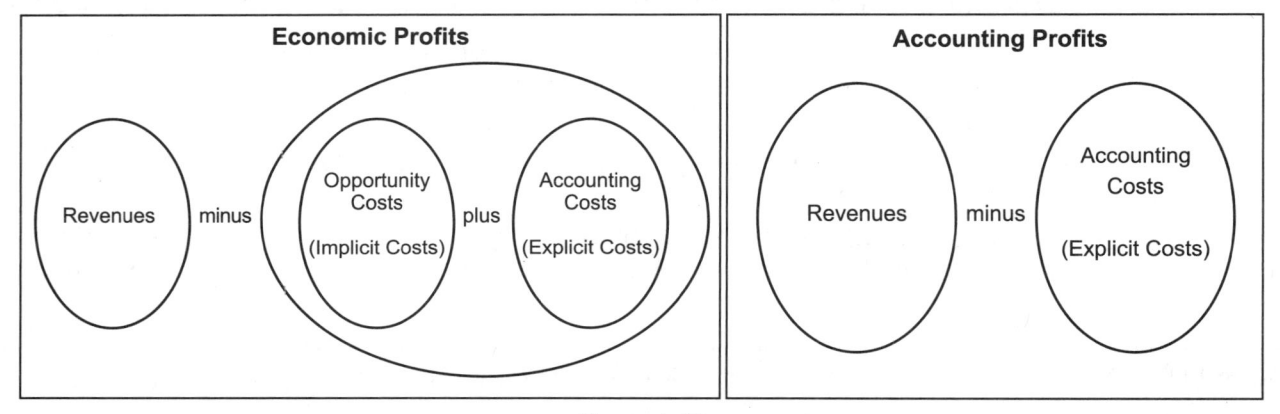

   Figure 4-17

   1) **Normal profit** occurs when total revenue equals total costs (explicit and implicit), that is, when economic profit equals zero.

3. **Short- vs. Long-Run Costs**

   a. The **short run** is a period so brief that a firm cannot vary its fixed costs. Thus, Short-run costs = Variable costs + Fixed costs.

   b. The **long run** is a period long enough that all inputs, including those incurred as fixed costs, can be varied. Thus, Long-run costs = Variable costs.

      1) Investment in new, more productive equipment results in higher total fixed costs but may result in lower total and per-unit variable costs.

STOP & REVIEW

You have completed the outline for this subunit.
Study multiple-choice questions 11 through 13 beginning on page 139.

4.5 MARGINAL ANALYSIS

1. **Marginal Analysis**

    a. Marginal analysis allows economic decisions to be made based on projecting the results of varying the levels of resource consumption and output production.

        1) **Total product** is the entire production of a good or service for a given period.
        2) **Marginal product** is the additional output obtained by adding one extra unit of input. It is calculated by dividing the change in total output at a given input by the change in inputs.

    b. As inputs are added to a process, each additional unit of input results in increased production. However, past the point of diminishing marginal returns, the increase is smaller with each unit. That is, the benefit of adding input units decreases.

        1) This principle is the **law of diminishing returns**.
        2) Eventually, so many inputs enter the process that it becomes inefficient, and total output actually decreases. This is the point of negative marginal returns.

            a) EXAMPLE: Too many cooks in the kitchen get in each other's way and slow production.

EXAMPLE 4-10   Diminishing Marginal Returns

The table below reflects the changes in total product and marginal product as additional units of input are added to the production process.

Units of Input	Total Product	Marginal Product
1	2	2
2	6	4
3	12	6
4	20	8
5	29	9
6	**39**	**10**
7	48	9
8	56	8
9	62	6
10	66	4
11	68	2
12	66	−2

At the sixth unit of input, marginal product peaks and then begins to decrease. This is the point of diminishing marginal returns. When the twelfth unit is added, the production process is receiving so much input that the efficiency of the process is actually decreased, and total output also decreases.

c. These relationships can be depicted graphically as follows:

Marginal Returns

Point of diminishing marginal returns (at input 6)

Point of negative marginal returns (at input 11)

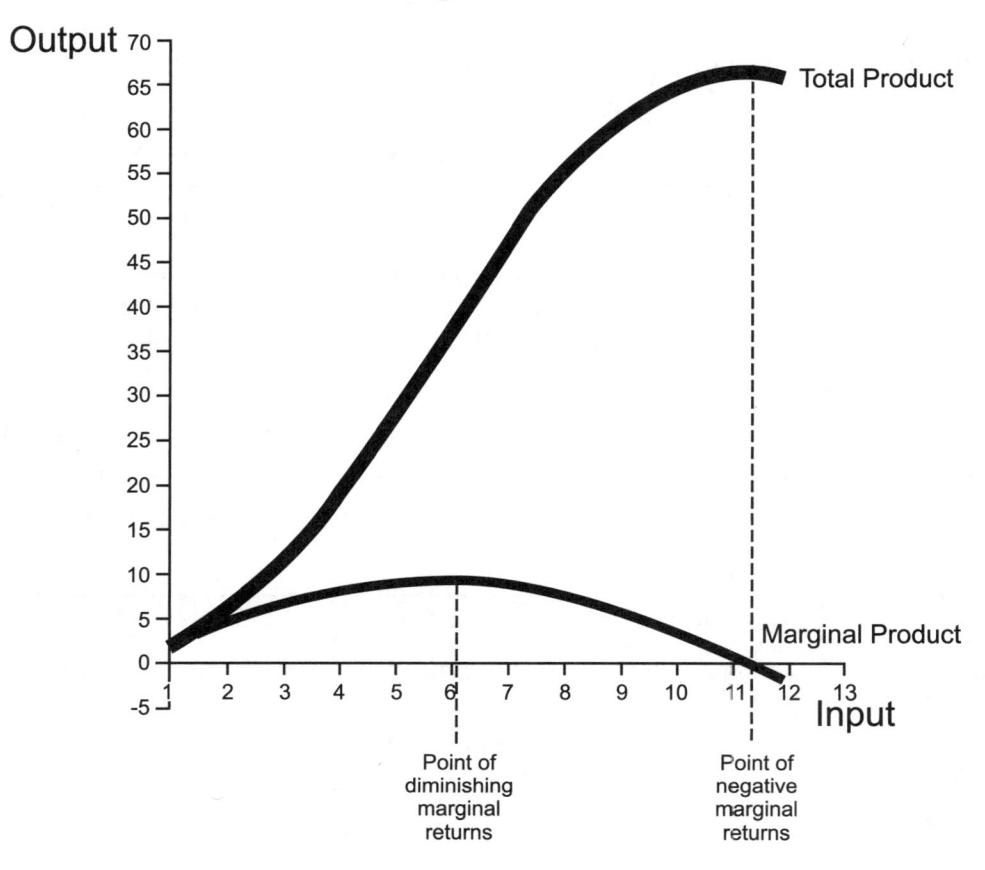

Figure 4-18

2. Marginal Revenue

a. Marginal revenue is the additional (incremental) revenue produced by generating one additional unit of output. It is the difference in total revenue at each level of output.

1) If the product is sold in a competitive market (the seller does not have monopoly power), the seller must reduce its price to sell additional units.
2) Thus, as total revenue increases with the sale of each additional unit, it increases by a smaller amount. The result is constantly decreasing marginal revenue.

EXAMPLE 4-11   Decreasing Marginal Revenue

A company has the following revenue data for one of its products:

Units of Output	Unit Price	Total Revenue	Marginal Revenue
1 ×	$580 =	$ 580	$580
2 ×	575 =	1,150	570
3 ×	570 =	1,710	560
4 ×	565 =	2,260	550
5 ×	560 =	2,800	540
6 ×	555 =	3,330	530
7 ×	550 =	3,850	520
8 ×	545 =	4,360	510
9 ×	540 =	4,860	500
10 ×	535 =	5,350	490
11 ×	530 =	5,830	480
12 ×	525 =	6,300	470

---

b. Revenue by itself cannot determine the proper level of output. Cost also must be considered.

3. Marginal Cost

a. Marginal cost is the additional (incremental) cost incurred by generating one additional unit of output. It is the difference in total cost at each level of output.

1) Unit cost tends to decrease as the process becomes more efficient. However, beyond a certain point, the process becomes less efficient, and unit cost increases.
2) Thus, total cost initially increases gradually, but eventually it increases at a higher rate. This is reflected in a decreasing, then increasing, of marginal cost.

EXAMPLE 4-12   Marginal Cost Behavior

The following are cost data for a product, assuming each unit of output requires exactly one unit of input:

Units of Output	Unit Cost	Total Cost	Marginal Cost
1 ×	$570.00 =	$ 570	$570
2 ×	405.00 =	810	240
3 ×	340.00 =	1,020	210
4 ×	**305.00** =	**1,220**	**200**
5 ×	287.00 =	1,435	215
6 ×	279.17 =	1,675	240
7 ×	279.29 =	1,955	280
8 ×	284.38 =	2,275	320
9 ×	295.00 =	2,655	380
10 ×	309.50 =	3,095	440
11 ×	326.82 =	3,595	500
12 ×	347.08 =	4,165	570

4. **Profit Maximization**

    a. The firm's goal is to maximize profits, not revenues. Thus, marginal revenue must be compared with marginal cost to determine the point of profit maximization.

        1) Profit maximization occurs at the output at which **marginal revenue equals marginal cost**. Beyond this point, increasing production results in costs so high that total profit is diminished.

EXAMPLE 4-13   Point of Profit Maximization

Comparing marginal revenue and marginal cost data allows determination of the point of profit maximization.

Units of Output	Marginal Revenue		Marginal Cost		Marginal Profit	Total Revenue		Total Cost		Total Profit
1	$580	−	$570	=	$ 10	$ 580	−	$ 570	=	$ 10
2	570	−	240	=	330	1,150	−	810	=	340
3	560	−	210	=	350	1,710	−	1,020	=	690
4	550	−	200	=	350	2,260	−	1,220	=	1,040
5	540	−	215	=	325	2,800	−	1,435	=	1,365
6	530	−	240	=	290	3,330	−	1,675	=	1,655
7	520	−	280	=	240	3,850	−	1,955	=	1,895
8	510	−	320	=	190	4,360	−	2,275	=	2,085
9	500	−	380	=	120	4,860	−	2,655	=	2,205
10	**490**	−	**440**	=	**50**	**5,350**	−	**3,095**	=	**2,255**
11	480	−	500	=	(20)	5,830	−	3,595	=	2,235
12	470	−	570	=	(100)	6,300	−	4,165	=	2,135

Beyond an output of 10 units, marginal profit is negative. By definition, this output is the point of highest total profit.

Marginal Analysis

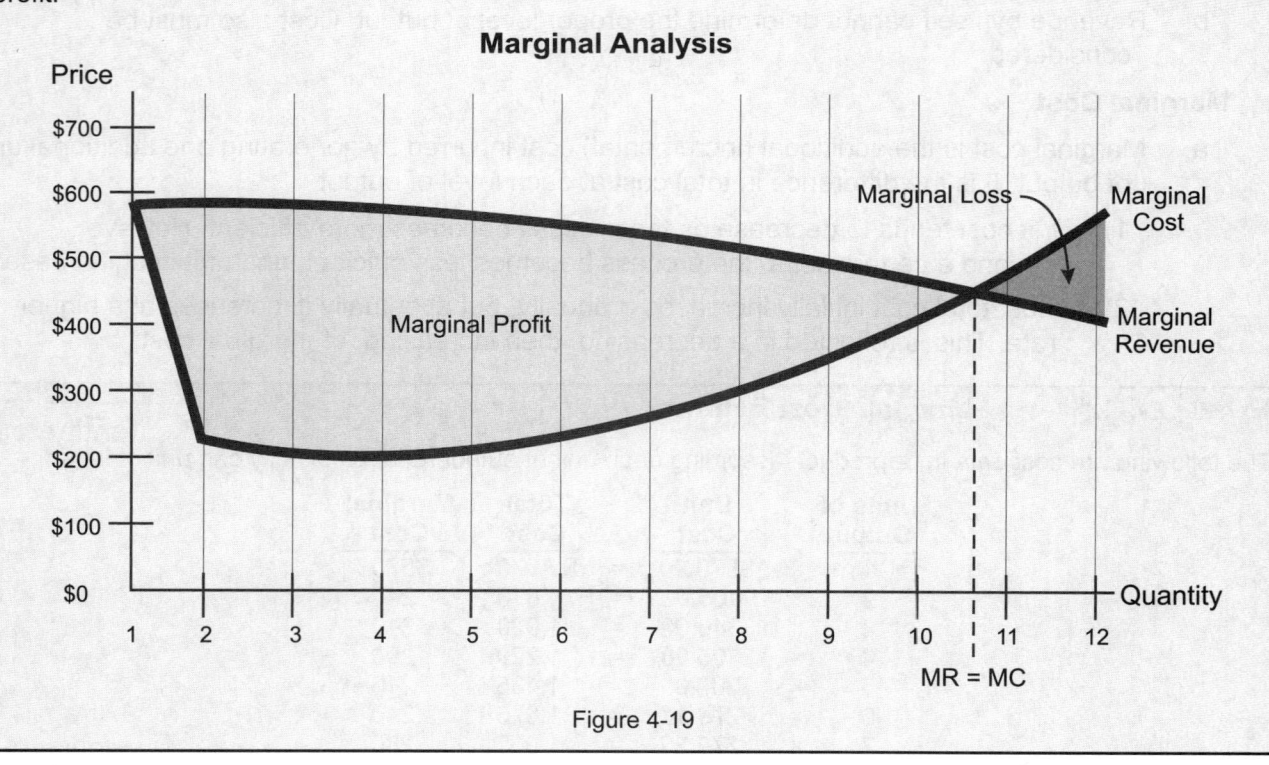

Figure 4-19

5. **Average Total Cost (ATC) and Marginal Cost (MC)**

   a. Total costs of production (TC) equals the sum of total fixed costs (FC) and total variable costs (VC).

   $$TC = FC + VC$$

   b. Average total cost (ATC = TC ÷ Q) equals the sum of average fixed costs (AFC = FC ÷ Q) and average variable costs (AVC = VC ÷ Q).

   c. An increase in fixed costs results in the following:

   1) An increase in AFC
   2) An increase in TC and ATC
   3) No effect on VC or AVC

   d. The marginal cost curve (MC = ΔTC ÷ ΔQ) always intersects the ATC curve and the AVC curve at their minimum points.

Cost Relationships in the Short Run

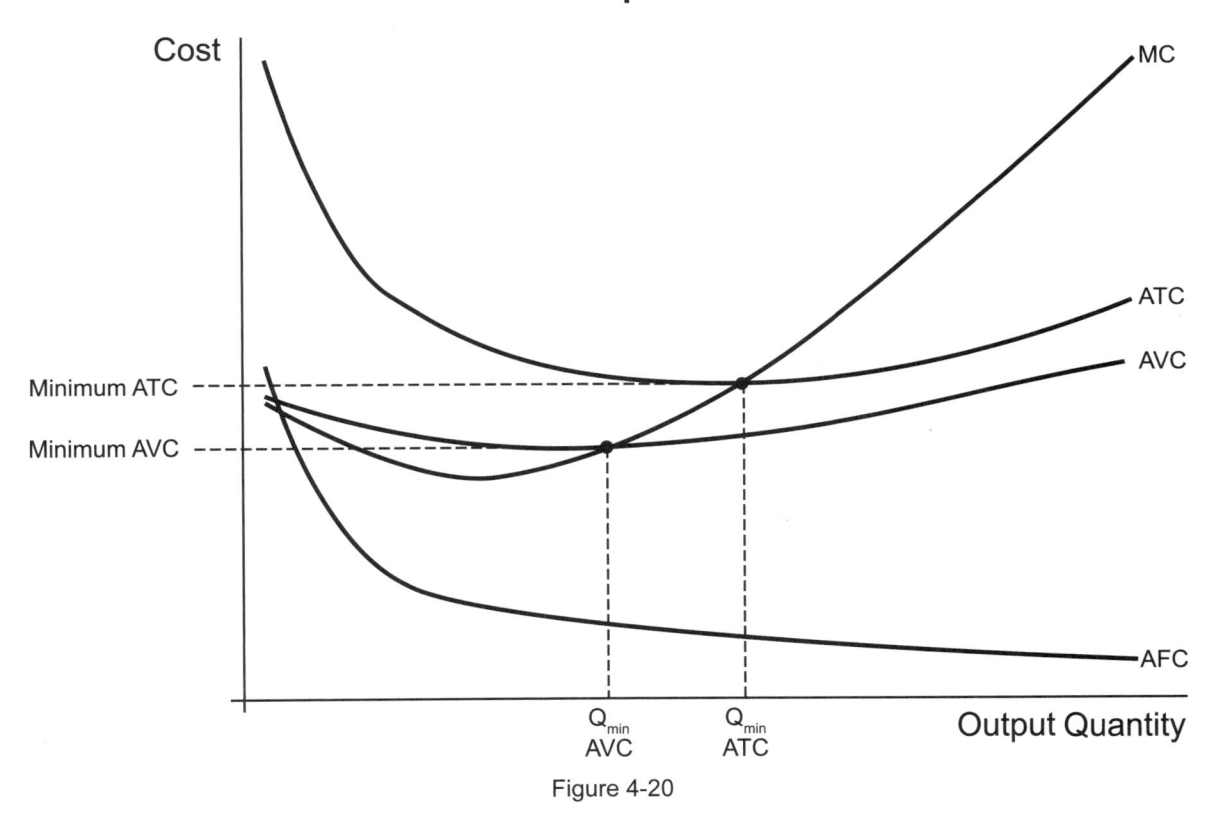

Figure 4-20

6. **Long-Run Cost Relationships**

   a. The shape and position of the short-run average total cost (SRATC) curve is determined by productivity.

   1) The number of SRATC curves equals the possible variations of production processes. The long-run average total cost (LRATC) curve therefore is extrapolated from all possible SRATC curves. It represents the lowest ATC for any output that can be produced.

LRATC Curve

Q_E = Maximum quantity for economies of scale

Q_D = Minimum quantity for diseconomies of scale

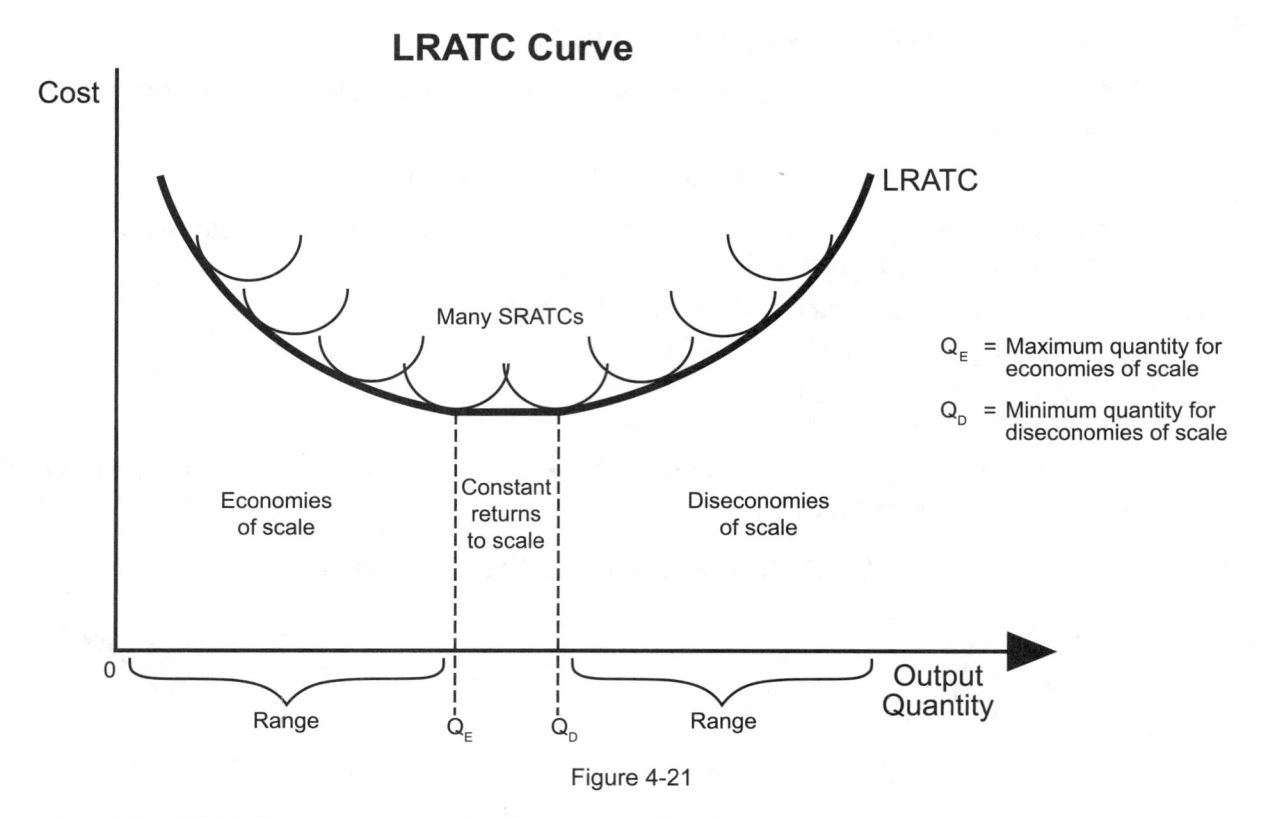

Figure 4-21

b. The LRATC curve derives its shape from the phenomenon of economies and diseconomies of scale.

1) **Economies of scale** (increasing returns to scale). Initially, as production increases, average costs of production tend to decline and the marginal cost of production tends to decrease. Some of the reasons are

   a) Increased specialization and division of labor,
   b) Better use and specialization of management, and
   c) Use of more efficient machinery and equipment.

2) **Constant returns to scale.** For a certain range of output, an increase in production results in no change in average costs and marginal cost of production does not change as output changes.

3) **Diseconomies of scale** (decreasing returns to scale). Eventually, as output continues to increase, the marginal cost of production tends to increase.

   a) The most frequent reason for diseconomies of scale is the difficulty of managing a large-scale entity.

STOP & REVIEW

You have completed the outline for this subunit.
Study multiple-choice questions 14 through 16 beginning on page 140.

4.6 MARKET STRUCTURES -- PURE COMPETITION

1. **Defining Characteristics**

    a. A very large number of buyers and sellers act independently. Examples are the stock market and agricultural markets.

    b. The product is homogeneous or standardized. Thus, the product of one seller is a perfect substitute for that of any other. The only basis for competition is price.

    c. Each seller produces an immaterial amount of the industry's total output and thus cannot influence the market price.

    d. No barriers to entry or exit from the market exist.

    e. Every seller or buyer has perfect information.

    　　1) Pure competition exists only in theory, but the model is useful for understanding basic economic concepts. It also provides a standard of comparison with real-world markets.

2. **Industry Demand and Firm Demand**

    a. The industry demand curve for a normal good in perfect competition is downward sloping.

    　　1) However, each seller can satisfy only a small part of the demand and must accept the equilibrium price of the market (P_0). Thus, the demand curve from the seller's perspective is perfectly elastic (horizontal). (Elasticity of demand was covered in Subunit 4.2.)

Pure Competition

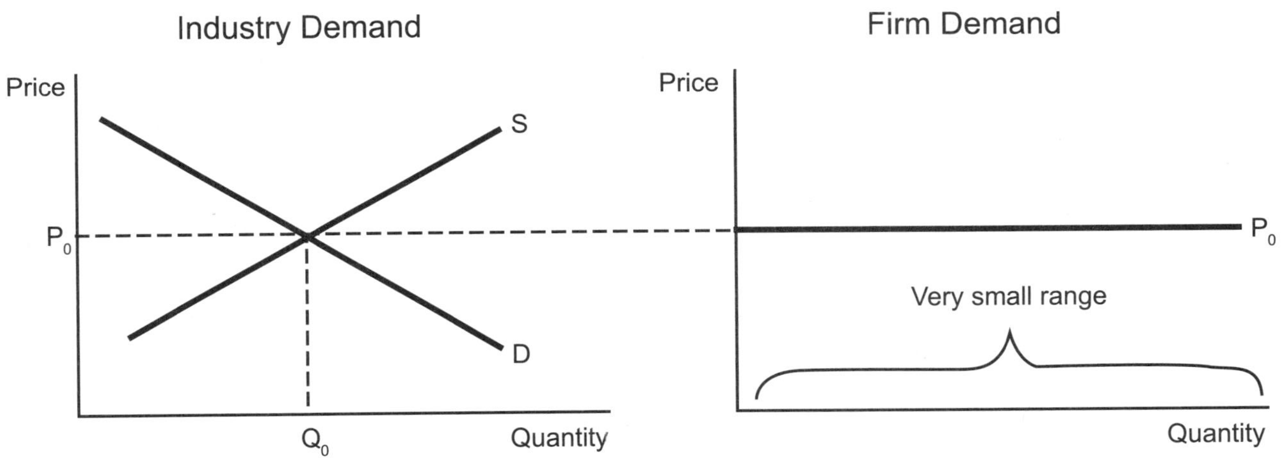

Figure 4-22

　　2) The small segment of the industry's demand curve occupied by each seller necessarily is at the point of market equilibrium.

　　3) Sellers in perfect competition therefore are price takers because they must sell at the market price.

EXAMPLE 4-14 — Effects of Perfectly Elastic Demand

The seller's perfectly elastic demand curve means that marginal revenue, average revenue, and market price are equal.

Units of Output		Unit Price (Average Revenue)		Total Revenue	Marginal Revenue
1	×	$960	=	$ 960	$960
2	×	960	=	1,920	960
3	×	960	=	2,880	960
4	×	960	=	3,840	960
5	×	960	=	4,800	960
6	×	960	=	5,760	960
7	×	960	=	6,720	960
8	×	960	=	7,680	960

3. **Short-Run Profit Maximization in Pure Competition**

   a. In the short run, a seller should produce (continue to operate) when it can earn a profit or incur a loss smaller than fixed costs. This is because short-run costs include both variable costs and fixed costs (costs incurred even if a firm closes). Thus, a firm could lose less money by continually operating instead of shutting down.

      1) If the revenue drops below the average variable cost, the seller should shut down instead of continually operating.

	Revenue	Variable cost	Fixed cost	Shut down Loss	Operating Loss
Scenario A	$10	($4)	($8)	($8)	**($2)**
Scenario B	$10	($10)	($2)	($2)	($2)
Scenario C	$10	($14)	($2)	**($2)**	($6)

   a) In scenario A, the revenue is above the variable cost. The seller would incur a loss of $8 if shut down and incur a loss of only $2 if (s)he chose to **continue operating**.

   b) In scenario B, the revenue is equal to variable cost. The seller would incur a loss of $2 whether (s)he chose to operate or shut down.

   c) In scenario C, the revenue is below the variable cost. The seller would incur a loss of $6 if (s)he chose to operate and incur a loss of only $2 if (s)he chose to **shut down**.

SU 4: Microeconomics

b. For all market structures, a seller that does not close should produce the output at which marginal revenue equals marginal cost **(MR = MC)**.

EXAMPLE 4-15   **Short-Run Profit Maximization in Pure Competition**

If the next unit of output adds more in revenue (MR) than in cost (MC), the seller increases total profit or decreases total losses. For a purely competitive seller, price equals MC is the same as MR equals MC. MR equals MC at an output of 7 units in the table below.

Units of Output	Revenue Total	Revenue Marginal	Cost Total	Cost Marginal	Profit Total	Profit Marginal
1	$ 960	$960	$1,800	$1,800	$(840)	$(840)
2	1,920	960	2,500	700	(580)	260
3	2,880	960	3,100	600	(220)	360
4	3,840	960	3,600	500	240	460
5	4,800	960	4,200	600	600	360
6	5,760	960	4,980	780	780	180
7	**6,720**	**960**	**5,940**	**960**	**780**	**0**
8	7,680	960	7,060	1,120	620	(160)

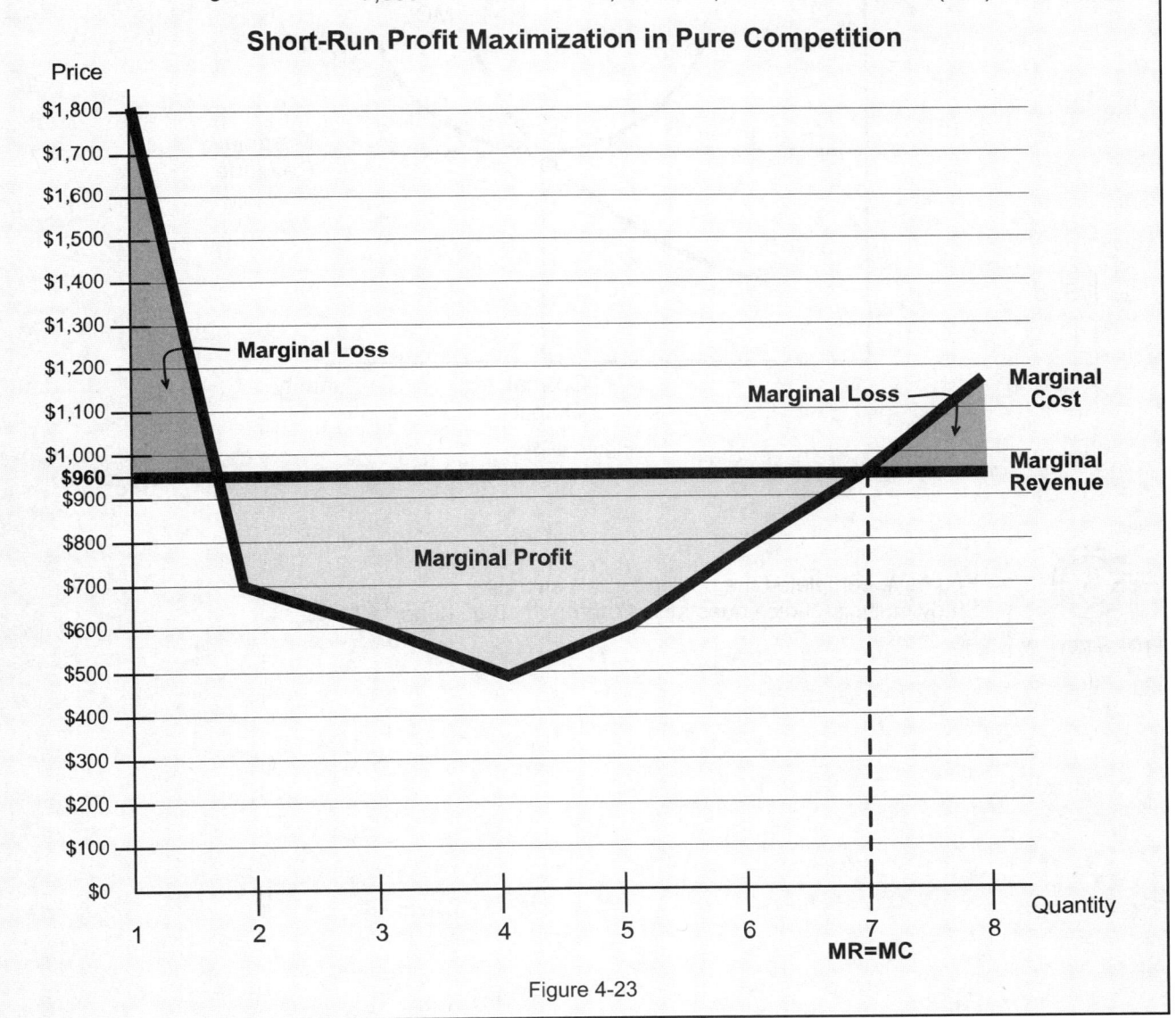

Short-Run Profit Maximization in Pure Competition

Figure 4-23

4. **Long-Run Equilibrium in Pure Competition**
    a. Because sellers are earning a normal profit (economic profit = 0), the industry attracts new entrants.
        1) New competitors shift the supply curve to the right, thus lowering the price.
        2) The lower price results in losses for sellers with high costs, and those sellers leave the market. The exit of the sellers shifts the supply curve to the left.
        3) The output generated by the industry returns to the previous level, and the price can rise again. Equilibrium is restored. Thus, in the long run, economic profit is zero.
    b. The surviving sellers have the lowest average total cost. Price and quantity are at the intersection of the MR and MC curves.

Long-Run Equilibrium for a Purely Competitive Firm

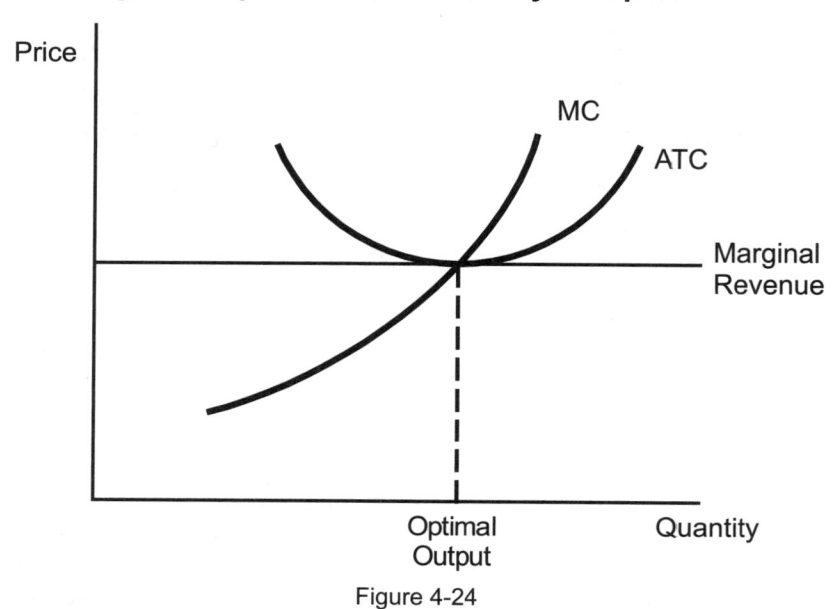

Figure 4-24

STOP & REVIEW

You have completed the outline for this subunit.
Study multiple-choice questions 17 through 19 on page 142.

4.7 MARKET STRUCTURES -- MONOPOLY

1. **Characteristics**
   a. The industry consists of one seller.
   b. The product has no close substitutes.
   c. The seller can strongly influence price because it is the sole supplier of the product.
   d. Entry by other sellers is completely blocked.

2. **Natural Monopolies**
   a. A natural monopoly exists when economic or technical conditions permit only one efficient supplier.
      1) Very large operations are needed to achieve low unit costs and prices (economies of scale are great). Thus, the long-term average cost of meeting demand is minimized when the industry has one seller. Examples are utilities, such as electricity and gas distribution.

3. **Pricing Power**
   a. Economists use two terms to describe a monopolist's pricing behavior:
      1) A **price maker** sets prices as high as it wants because it is not limited by competition.
      2) A **price searcher** does not set prices arbitrarily high but seeks the price that maximizes its profits.

4. **Demand**
   a. Unlike the horizontal firm demand curve in pure competition covered in Subunit 4.6, the demand curve is downward sloping because a monopolist can sell more units only by lowering price.
      1) Furthermore, the monopolist's demand curve is the industry's demand curve, not a small part as in pure competition.
      2) A monopolist's price decrease affects all the units sold, not just the additional unit(s). Thus, a monopolist's marginal revenue curve is below the demand curve.
      3) A monopolist's marginal revenue continuously decreases as output increases. Total revenue decreases if marginal revenue is less than $0.

EXAMPLE 4-16 Marginal Revenue in a Monopoly

Units of Output		Unit Price (Average Revenue)		Total Revenue	Marginal Revenue
1	×	$960	=	$ 960	$960
2	×	910	=	1,820	860
3	×	860	=	2,580	760
4	×	810	=	3,240	660
5	×	760	=	3,800	560
6	×	710	=	4,260	460
7	×	660	=	4,620	360
8	×	610	=	4,880	260

5. **Profit Maximization**
   a. Unlike a firm in pure competition, the monopolist can set output at the level at which profits are maximized **(MR = MC)**.
      1) The corresponding price is based on a downward-sloping demand curve.
         a) Monopoly does **not** result in the highest possible price, and the monopolist does **not** produce at the lowest average total cost.

EXAMPLE 4-17   Price Searching for a Monopolist

The monopolist produces 5 units and sells them at $760 each.

Units of Output	Selling Price per Unit	Revenue Total	Revenue Marginal	Cost Total	Cost Marginal	Profit Total	Profit Marginal
1	$960	$ 960	$960	$ 800	$ 800	$ 160	$ 160
2	910	1,820	860	1,480	680	340	180
3	860	2,580	760	1,980	500	600	260
4	810	3,240	660	2,320	340	920	320
5	760	3,800	560	2,800	480	1,000	80
6	710	4,260	460	3,480	680	780	(220)
7	660	4,620	360	4,420	940	200	(580)
8	610	4,880	260	5,720	1,300	(840)	(1,040)

6. **Economic Consequences**

   a. Given sufficiently low costs and adequate demand, a monopolist earns an economic profit in the long run. In the graph below, D_M is the industry demand curve, and MC is the industry supply curve. (The monopolist is the industry.)

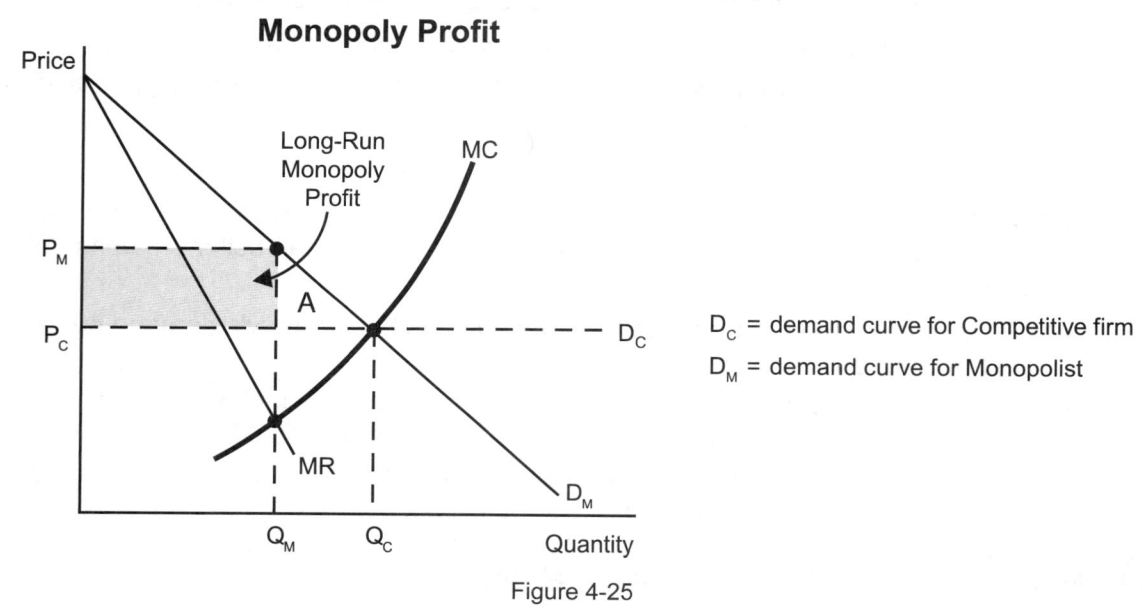

   Monopoly Profit

   D_C = demand curve for Competitive firm
   D_M = demand curve for Monopolist

   Figure 4-25

   b. In a purely competitive industry, the market price and quantity are P_C and Q_C, respectively.

      1) However, a monopolist restricts output to the profit-maximizing level (Q_M for MR = MC). The resulting price is therefore P_M. MR for the monopolist is less than price, and the MR curve is below the demand curve.

         a) Accordingly, output is lower ($Q_M < Q_C$), and prices are higher ($P_M > P_C$) than under pure competition.

   c. In a monopoly, allocation of resources is not as efficient as other market structures because it produces fewer outputs and charges higher prices than other market structures.

STOP & REVIEW

You have completed the outline for this subunit.
Study multiple-choice questions 20 and 21 on page 143.

SU 4: Microeconomics

4.8 MARKET STRUCTURES -- MONOPOLISTIC COMPETITION

1. **Characteristics**
    a. The industry has a large number of firms. The number is fewer than in pure competition, but it suffices to prevent firms from colluding to restrict output and fix prices.
    b. Products are differentiated. In pure competition, products are standardized, so price is the only basis for competition. In monopolistic competition, products can be differentiated on a basis other than price, such as quality, brands, and styles. Thus, advertising may be crucial.
    c. Few barriers to entry and exit exist. Because firms tend not to be large, great economies of scale do **not** exist. The cost of product differentiation is the most significant barrier to entry.

2. **Short-Run Profit Maximization**
    a. Profit is maximized when MR equals MC. The price is the point on the demand curve corresponding to this quantity.

    Short-Run Profits in Monopolistic Competition

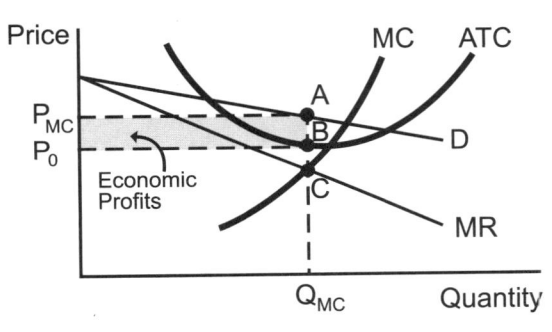

    A = profit-maximizing price and quantity
    B = lowest point on ATC curve
    C = profit-maximizing quantity (MR = MC)

    Figure 4-26

    1) If the profit-maximizing price (P_{MC}) is higher than the minimum average total cost, the firm earns an economic profit in the short run.
    2) If the profit-maximizing price (P_{MC}) is lower than the minimum average total cost, the firm incurs a loss in the short run and leaves the industry in the long run.

3. **Long-Run Equilibrium**
    a. In the long run, the economic profit of all firms is $0 because firms will enter a profitable industry and leave an unprofitable one.
        1) In a profitable monopolistically competitive industry, the possibility of earning economic profits attracts new entrants.
        2) The presence of new firms requires all firms to differentiate their products further, increasing average total costs.
        3) Higher costs eliminate the economic profits that attracted the new entrants. The firms least able to absorb the higher costs leave the market.
        4) The remaining firms now have higher costs and steady demand. The economic profits generated earlier are replaced with normal profits.

You have completed the outline for this subunit.
Study multiple-choice questions 22 and 23 on page 144.

STOP & REVIEW

4.9 MARKET STRUCTURES -- OLIGOPOLY

1. **Characteristics**
   a. The industry has few large firms. Firms operating in an oligopoly are mutually aware and mutually interdependent. Their decisions as to price, advertising, etc., are significantly dependent on the actions of the other firms.
   b. Products can be differentiated (e.g., autos) or standardized (e.g., steel).
   c. Each firm sets price and production level after considering mutual interdependence.
   d. Entry is difficult because of barriers that can be natural, e.g., an absolute cost advantage, or created, e.g., ongoing advertising or ownership of patents.

2. **Industry Demand**
   a. The price rigidity normally found in oligopolistic markets can be explained in part by the **kinked demand curve** theory. Its essence is that firms will follow a price decrease by a competitor but not a price increase. This is based on the assumption that a firm in an oligopoly strives to protect existing market shares.
      1) If price and quantity for the industry are at P_0 and Q_0 as shown in Figure 4-27, a firm that raises its price will move into the elastic portion of the demand curve (P_0 to P_1).
         a) A small increase in price in this portion of the curve leads to a large decline (Q_0 to Q_1) in quantity demanded. Competitors have little incentive to follow, so the price-raising firm loses market share.
      2) However, if the firm cuts its price (P_0 to P_2), it enters the inelastic portion of the demand curve. The distance between Q_0 and Q_2 is smaller than the difference between Q_0 and Q_1. A large price decrease is needed to generate even a modest increase in sales.
         a) More importantly, the discontinuous marginal revenue curve means that marginal revenue falls substantially after a small price cut. Competitors also must reduce their prices so that the first firm gains no market share.
      3) Price and quantity therefore tend to remain at point A on the demand curve.

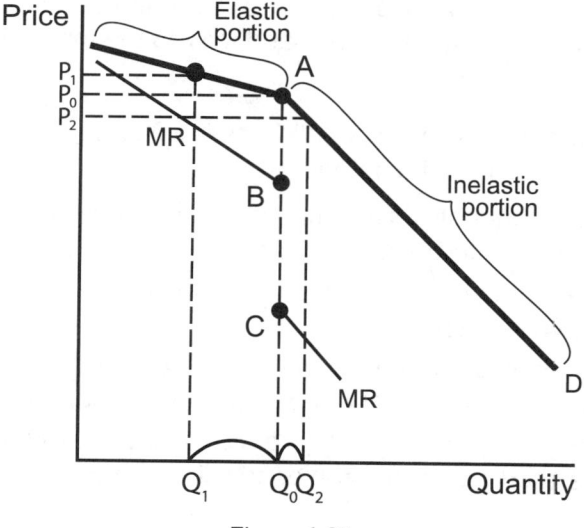

   Figure 4-27

   b. To avoid the hazards of the kinked demand curve, price leadership is typical in oligopolistic industries.
      1) Price changes are announced first by a major firm in the industry. After the industry leader has acted, other firms match its price.

3. **Cartels**

    a. A cartel is a group of oligopolistic firms that agree to set prices. This practice is illegal except in international markets.

       1) The economic effects are similar to those of a monopoly. Each firm restricts output, charges a higher price, and earns the maximum profit.

       2) Thus, each firm in effect becomes a monopolist, but only because it is colluding with other members of the cartel.

    b. Cohesion of the cartel is maintained only if the members maintain their agreed-upon prices and production quotas.

       1) A cartel fails if one member attempts either to increase profits by producing more or to increase market share by cutting prices.

4. **Boycotts**

    a. A boycott is a concerted effort to avoid doing business with a particular supplier, forcing a leftward shift in the demand curve for that supplier.

       1) Usually, the motivation is moral or ethical rather than purely economic.

5. **Game Theory**

    a. Game theory is an interactive decision tool used to study strategic behavior.

       1) For example, oligopolistic firms are mutually aware and interdependent. Many of their decisions, such as pricing, depend on the actions of competitor firms.

       2) Accordingly, game theory, with its analysis of rules, strategies, and payoffs, can be used to understand rivalries of many kinds, whether or not economic.

Characteristics of Different Market Structures

	Number of sellers	Barriers to entry and exit	Product nature	Sellers' control over price	Long-run profitability	Firm's elasticity of demand	Examples
Pure Competition	Many	No barrier	Homogeneous	Price taker	Zero	Perfectly elastic	Stock market
Monopoly	One	Completely blocked	Unique	Has control	Positive	Inelastic	Utilities
Monopolistic Competition	A large number of firms (but fewer than in pure competition)	Few barriers	Differentiated	Has control	Zero	Highly elastic	Restaurants, hotels
Oligopoly	Few large firms	High barriers	Differentiated or standardized	Has control (mutually interdependent)	Positive (less than monopoly)	Elastic portion and inelastic portion	Auto makers, steel

You have completed the outline for this subunit.
Study multiple-choice questions 24 and 25 on page 145.

STOP & REVIEW

QUESTIONS

4.1 Demand, Supply, and Equilibrium

1. The demand curve for a normal good is

A. Upward sloping because firms produce more at higher prices.
B. Upward sloping because higher-priced goods are of higher quality.
C. Vertical.
D. Downward sloping because of the income and substitution effects of price changes.

Answer (D) is correct.
REQUIRED: The true statement about the demand curve for a normal good.
DISCUSSION: The demand curve for a normal good is downward sloping to the right. At high prices, the amount demanded is relatively low. As prices decrease, the amount demanded increases. The substitution effect is the change in the cost of a good relative to others that will cause a cheaper good to be substituted for more expensive ones. The income effect is the change in purchasing power experienced by consumers as a result of a price change (real income increases or decreases). Both of these effects cause the price of a product and the quantity demanded to be inversely related.
Answer (A) is incorrect. An upward-sloping demand curve suggests that consumers purchase more of a product if its price is raised. **Answer (B) is incorrect.** An upward-sloping demand curve suggests that consumers purchase more of a product if its price is raised. **Answer (C) is incorrect.** A vertical demand curve signifies that the quantity demanded does not change with price.

2. If the average household income increases and there is relatively little change in the price of a normal good, then the

A. Supply curve will shift to the left.
B. Quantity demanded will move farther down the demand curve.
C. Demand will shift to the left.
D. Demand curve will shift to the right.

Answer (D) is correct.
REQUIRED: The result of an increase in income given little change in the price of a normal good.
DISCUSSION: The demand schedule is a relationship between the prices of a product and the quantity demanded at each price, holding other determinants of the quantity demanded constant. A movement along an existing demand curve occurs when the price is changed. A shift in the curve itself occurs when any of the determinants changes. Such shifts can be caused by a change in the tastes and preferences of consumers toward a product, for example, as a result of a successful advertising campaign, an increase in consumer income (if a product is a normal good), or changes in the prices of substitute or complementary products. An increase in consumer income would shift the demand curve to the right and result in greater consumption of the product at each price.
Answer (A) is incorrect. The increase in income shifts the demand, not the supply, curve. **Answer (B) is incorrect.** Moving down an existing demand curve is the effect of a lower price. The change in income shifts the economy to a new demand curve. **Answer (C) is incorrect.** A shift to the left means that consumers will buy fewer products at each price. This leftward shift in response to increased income is characteristic of an inferior good, not a normal good. The demand for inferior goods is inversely related to income. Hamburger is an inferior good, and steak is a normal good.

3. The situation depicted in the graph below could be caused by

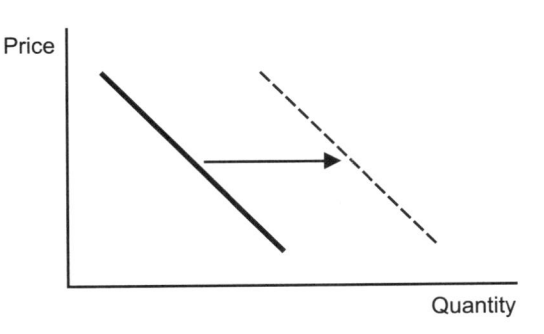

Price / Quantity graph showing a downward-sloping demand curve shifting rightward.

A. A price cut by all producers.
B. A price hike by all producers.
C. A rise in the country's population.
D. An improvement in manufacturers' productivity.

Answer (C) is correct.
   REQUIRED: The possible cause of a rightward demand curve shift.
   DISCUSSION: A downward-sloping curve relating price to quantity depicts the demand schedule for a normal good. When a country's population grows, producers can sell more of their products at every price level. This is depicted as a rightward shift in the demand curve.
   Answer (A) is incorrect. A price cut by all producers would be depicted as a downward movement along a fixed curve. **Answer (B) is incorrect.** A price hike by all producers would be depicted as an upward movement along a fixed curve. **Answer (D) is incorrect.** An improvement in manufacturers' productivity would be depicted by a shift in the (upward-sloping) supply curve, not the (downward-sloping) demand curve.

4.2 Elasticity

4. If the coefficient of elasticity is zero, then the consumer demand for the product is said to be

A. Perfectly inelastic.
B. Perfectly elastic.
C. Unit inelastic.
D. Unit elastic.

Answer (A) is correct.
   REQUIRED: The applicable term when the coefficient of elasticity is zero.
   DISCUSSION: When the coefficient of elasticity (Percentage change in quantity ÷ Percentage change in price) is less than one, demand is inelastic. When the coefficient is zero, demand is perfectly inelastic.
   Answer (B) is incorrect. Demand is perfectly elastic when the coefficient is infinite. **Answer (C) is incorrect.** "Unitary inelasticity" is not a meaningful term in this context. **Answer (D) is incorrect.** Unitary elasticity exists when the coefficient is exactly one.

5. As the price for a particular product changes, the quantity of the product demanded changes according to the following schedule.

Total Quantity Demanded	Price per Unit
100	$50
150	45
200	40
225	35
230	30
232	25

Using the arc method, the price elasticity of demand for this product when the price decreases from $50 to $45 is

A. 0.20
B. 10.00
C. 0.10
D. 3.80

Answer (D) is correct.
   REQUIRED: The price elasticity of demand using the arc method.
   DISCUSSION: A product's price elasticity of demand is measured as the percentage change in quantity demanded divided by the percentage change in price. When price falls from $50 to $45, the coefficient is 3.8, calculated as follows:

$$E_d = [(150 - 100) \div (150 + 100)] \div [(\$50 - \$45) \div (\$50 + \$45)]$$
$$= (50 \div 250) \div (\$5 \div \$95)$$
$$= 20.0\% \div 5.26\%$$
$$= 3.8$$

   Answer (A) is incorrect. The figure of 0.20 equals the 10% decline in price divided by the 50% change in quantity demanded. **Answer (B) is incorrect.** The figure of 10.00 assumes a 5% change in price. It also does not calculate the change over the sum of the endpoints of the range. **Answer (C) is incorrect.** The figure of 0.10 is the percentage change in price.

6. Last week, the quantity of apples demanded fell by 6%. If this was a result of a 10% price increase, what is the price elasticity of demand for apples?

A. 1.67
B. 1.06
C. 0.16
D. 0.60

Answer (D) is correct.
REQUIRED: The price elasticity of demand.
DISCUSSION: The price elasticity of demand is calculated by dividing the percentage change in quantity demanded by the percentage change in price. Thus, the change in quantity of 6% divided by the 10% price increase produces an elasticity of 0.6.
Answer (A) is incorrect. The inverse of the elasticity is 1.67. **Answer (B) is incorrect.** Adding the 6% quantity decline to 1 results in 1.06. **Answer (C) is incorrect.** The price elasticity of demand is found by dividing the 6% quantity decline by the 10% price increase, not by adding them.

4.3 Government Action in the Market and Wages

7. Government price regulations in competitive markets that set maximum or ceiling prices below the equilibrium price will in the short run

A. Cause demand to decrease.
B. Cause supply to increase.
C. Create shortages of that product.
D. Produce a surplus of the product.

Answer (C) is correct.
REQUIRED: The short-run effect of price ceilings that are below the equilibrium price.
DISCUSSION: A price ceiling lower than the equilibrium price causes shortages to develop. The artificially low price results in an amount supplied less than that at the equilibrium price. It also causes consumers to demand more of the commodity than at the equilibrium price.
Answer (A) is incorrect. The amount demanded will increase as a result of the artificially low price. **Answer (B) is incorrect.** The amount supplied will decline as a result of the artificially low price. **Answer (D) is incorrect.** Surpluses do not occur as a result of price ceilings regardless of whether they are above or below the equilibrium price.

8. A government price support program will

A. Lead to surpluses.
B. Lead to shortages.
C. Improve the rationing function of prices.
D. Encourage firms to leave the industry.

Answer (A) is correct.
REQUIRED: The effect of a government price support program.
DISCUSSION: A government price support program, which sets a price higher than the market price, will cause producers to supply more goods than can be absorbed by the market. The effect will be surpluses because the amount supplied will exceed the amount demanded. In these cases, the government must buy up the surplus and either destroy it or seek other distribution channels; both are highly inefficient outcomes.
Answer (B) is incorrect. No shortages will occur. Suppliers will be induced by the higher-than-equilibrium price to produce more than the amount demanded. **Answer (C) is incorrect.** No rationing would occur. Consumers will be able to buy all they desire because supply will exceed demand. **Answer (D) is incorrect.** Firms will be encouraged to enter the industry by the availability of greater revenue than that provided by consumer demand. In fact, price support programs are often designed with the intention of keeping marginal firms from leaving the industry.

SU 4: Microeconomics

9. If a rent control law in a competitive housing market establishes a maximum or ceiling rent that is above the market or equilibrium rent,

A. The law has no effect on the rental market.
B. A surplus of rental housing units will result.
C. Supply will decrease as price increases.
D. Demand will increase as price increases.

Answer (A) is correct.
REQUIRED: The effect of establishing a maximum price above the equilibrium price.
DISCUSSION: If the market equilibrium price is less than the maximum rent allowed, a rent control law will have no effect on the market.
Answer (B) is incorrect. If a minimum or floor rent that is above the market equilibrium rent is charged, consumers would demand less housing and a surplus would occur. **Answer (C) is incorrect.** Price is a determinant of quantity supplied, not supply. **Answer (D) is incorrect.** Price is a determinant of quantity demanded, not demand.

10. The amounts paid to laborers are

A. Real wages.
B. Nominal wages.
C. Productivity wages.
D. Minimum wages.

Answer (B) is correct.
REQUIRED: The term for wages actually paid to laborers.
DISCUSSION: Nominal wages are the amounts actually paid (and received), while real wages represent the purchasing power of goods and services that can be acquired by the nominal wages. The level of real wages is determined by the productivity of labor. As productivity increases, the demand for labor also increases.
Answer (A) is incorrect. Real wages represent the purchasing power of the wages paid. **Answer (C) is incorrect.** Productivity wages is a nonsense term. **Answer (D) is incorrect.** A minimum wage is established by law. It is a nominal wage, but all amounts paid to laborers are not minimum wages.

4.4 Profits and Costs

11. A corporation's net income as presented on its income statement is usually

A. More than its economic profits because opportunity costs are not considered in calculating net income.
B. More than its economic profits because economists do not consider interest payments to be costs.
C. Equal to its economic profits.
D. Less than its economic profits because accountants include labor costs, while economists exclude labor costs.

Answer (A) is correct.
REQUIRED: The true statement about a corporation's net income.
DISCUSSION: Economic (pure) profit equals total revenue minus economic costs. Economic costs are defined by economists as total costs, which are the sum of outlay costs, and opportunity costs, which are the values of productive resources in their best alternative uses. The return sufficient to induce the entrepreneur to remain in business (normal profit) is an implicit (opportunity) cost. Net income as computed under generally accepted accounting principles considers only explicit costs, not such implicit costs as normal profit and the opportunity costs associated with not using assets for alternative purposes. Thus, net income will be higher than economic profit because the former fails to include a deduction for opportunity costs, for example, the salary forgone by an entrepreneur who chooses to be self-employed.
Answer (B) is incorrect. Both economists and accountants treat interest as a cost. **Answer (C) is incorrect.** Economic profits will be less than net income. **Answer (D) is incorrect.** Economic profits will be less than net income.

12. A normal profit is

A. The same as an economic profit.
B. The same as the accountant's bottom line.
C. An explicit or out-of-pocket cost.
D. A cost of resources from an economic perspective.

Answer (D) is correct.
REQUIRED: The true statement about normal profit.
DISCUSSION: Normal profit is the level of profit necessary to induce entrepreneurs to enter and remain in the market. Economists view this profit as an implicit cost of economic activity.
Answer (A) is incorrect. Economic (pure) profit is the residual return in excess of normal profit. Economic profit equals accounting profit minus implicit costs. Normal profit occurs when total revenue equals total costs (explicit and implicit), that is, when economic profit equals zero. **Answer (B) is incorrect.** Accounting profit is the excess of total revenue over explicit costs (out-of-pocket payments to outsiders). **Answer (C) is incorrect.** A normal profit is an implicit cost.

13. In the economic theory of production and cost, the short run is defined to be a production process

A. That spans a time period of less than 1 year in length.
B. In which there is insufficient time to vary the amount of all inputs.
C. That is subject to economies of scale.
D. That always produces economic profits.

Answer (B) is correct.
REQUIRED: The short run in the economic theory of production and cost.
DISCUSSION: The short run is defined as a period so brief that a firm has insufficient time to vary the amount of all inputs. Thus, the quantity of one or more inputs is fixed. The long run is a period long enough that all inputs, including plant capacity, can be varied.
Answer (A) is incorrect. The short run can be more or less than a year depending upon a firm's ability to change its inputs. **Answer (C) is incorrect.** Economies of scale are associated with the long run. **Answer (D) is incorrect.** Economic profits may be earned, either in the long or short run, when a firm earns more than the profits needed for it to remain in operation.

4.5 Marginal Analysis

14. Because of economies of scale, as output from production expands,

A. The short-run average cost of production decreases.
B. The long-run average cost of production increases.
C. The long-run total cost decreases.
D. The slope of the demand curve increases.

Answer (A) is correct.
REQUIRED: The effect of economies of scale.
DISCUSSION: When a firm experiences economies of scale, the average unit cost of production decreases as production increases. This phenomenon is attributable to spreading fixed costs over a greater number of units of output. Both the short-run and long-run average costs are lower because of economies of scale.
Answer (B) is incorrect. Long-run unit production costs decline with economies of scale. **Answer (C) is incorrect.** Total costs increase with increased production; only the average cost per unit declines. **Answer (D) is incorrect.** Changes in the supply curve do not affect the demand curve.

15. When long-run average cost is declining over a range of increasing output, the firm is experiencing

A. Increasing fixed costs.
B. Technological efficiency.
C. Decreasing returns.
D. Economies of scale.

Answer (D) is correct.
REQUIRED: The condition experienced when long-run average cost declines over a range of increasing output.
DISCUSSION: When long-run average cost declines as output increases, the firm is experiencing economies of scale. Average cost falls when marginal cost is below it and rises when marginal cost is above it. Average cost reaches its minimum when it equals marginal cost. Some of the reasons for this phenomenon are increased specialization and division of labor, better use and specialization of management, and use of more efficient machinery and equipment.
Answer (A) is incorrect. An increase in fixed costs could cause average costs to increase. Also, by definition, all long-run costs are variable. **Answer (B) is incorrect.** Technological efficiency refers to the ratio of physical output of a given technology and the maximum output that is possible. An increase in technological efficiency is only one of the ways that economies of scale can occur. **Answer (C) is incorrect.** A decline in average cost means the firm is experiencing increasing returns, not decreasing returns.

16. Because of the existence of economies of scale, business firms may find that

A. Each additional unit of labor is less efficient than the previous unit.
B. As more labor is added to a factory, increases in output will diminish in the short run.
C. Increasing the size of a factory will result in lower average costs.
D. Increasing the size of a factory will result in lower total costs.

Answer (C) is correct.
REQUIRED: The true statement about economies of scale.
DISCUSSION: As most firms expand output, average costs of production initially tend to decline. The reasons for this include increased specialization and division of labor, better use and specialization of management, and use of more efficient machinery and equipment. Consequently, increasing the size of a factory often results in lower average costs.
Answer (A) is incorrect. Economies of scale refer to the savings in costs as production increases; less efficient labor would lead to higher costs. **Answer (B) is incorrect.** Output should increase, although average productivity may or may not change. **Answer (D) is incorrect.** Increasing factory size will normally increase total costs but result in lower average costs.

4.6 Market Structures -- Pure Competition

17. Which one of the following is **not** a key assumption of perfect competition?

A. Firms sell a homogeneous product.
B. Customers are indifferent about which firm they buy from.
C. The level of a firm's output is small relative to the industry's total output.
D. Each firm can price its product above the industry price.

Answer (D) is correct.
REQUIRED: The assumption not made about perfect competition.
DISCUSSION: Perfect competition is characterized by a market structure with many buyers and sellers acting independently, a homogeneous or standardized product, free entry into and exit from the market, perfect information, no control over the industry price, and the absence of nonprice competition. Moreover, customers are indifferent about which firm they buy from because price is the only difference between one seller and the next.
Answer (A) is incorrect. A homogeneous product is a key assumption of perfect competition. **Answer (B) is incorrect.** Customer indifference regarding choice of seller is a key assumption of perfect competition. **Answer (C) is incorrect.** Small firm output relative to the industry is a key assumption of perfect competition.

18. Mr. Smith is hired as a consultant to a firm in a perfectly competitive industry. At the current output level the price is $20, the average variable cost is $15, average total cost is $22, and marginal cost is $20. In order to maximize profits in the short-run, Mr. Smith will recommend that the firm should

A. Not change output.
B. Decrease production.
C. Increase production.
D. Shut down.

Answer (A) is correct.
REQUIRED: The action a firm should take when marginal cost equals selling price.
DISCUSSION: For profit maximization, a firm operating under pure competition should produce the level of output at which price is equal to marginal cost. Since price and marginal cost are both $20, the firm is already at its profit-maximizing position.
Answer (B) is incorrect. A firm should not decrease output when price is at least equal to marginal cost. **Answer (C) is incorrect.** There is no incentive to increase production when marginal cost is equal to selling price. **Answer (D) is incorrect.** A firm should not shut down as long as price exceeds variable cost; any excess of price over variable cost provides a contribution toward the coverage of fixed costs.

19. All of the following are true about perfect competition **except** that

A. There is free market entry without large capital costs for entry.
B. There are many firms participating in the market.
C. In the long run, an increase in profit will have no effect on the number of firms in the market.
D. Firms are price takers.

Answer (C) is correct.
REQUIRED: The false statement about perfect competition.
DISCUSSION: Perfect competition assumes a large number of buyers and sellers that act independently, a homogeneous or standardized product, free entry into and exit from the market, perfect information, no nonprice competition, no control over prices (sellers are price takers rather than price setters), and an equilibrium price equal to the average total cost. Given free entry into the market and perfect information, an increase in profits in the industry will attract new firms. This will have the long-run effect of reducing the price to the level at which no economic profits are earned.
Answer (A) is incorrect. An absence of barriers to entry is a characteristic of pure competition. **Answer (B) is incorrect.** A large number of firms is a characteristic of pure competition. **Answer (D) is incorrect.** Firms in pure competition must accept the market price.

4.7 Market Structures -- Monopoly

20. A characteristic of a monopoly is that

A. A monopoly will produce when marginal revenue is equal to marginal cost to maximize profits.
B. There is a unique relationship between the market price and the quantity supplied.
C. In optimizing profits, a monopoly will increase its supply curve to where the demand curve becomes inelastic.
D. There are multiple prices for the product to the consumer.

Answer (A) is correct.
REQUIRED: The characteristic of a monopoly.
DISCUSSION: A monopoly consists of a single firm with a unique product. Such a firm has significant price control. To maximize profits, it increases production until its marginal revenue equals its marginal cost. In a monopoly, price will be higher and output lower than in perfect competition.
Answer (B) is incorrect. The monopolist is in control of the quantity supplied. Thus, the supply can be limited to produce the profit-maximizing price. **Answer (C) is incorrect.** To optimize profits, a monopoly will produce at the point when its marginal revenue equals its marginal cost. **Answer (D) is incorrect.** There is only one price when a monopoly exists.

21. Any business firm that has the ability to control the price of the product it sells

A. Faces a downward-sloping demand curve.
B. Has a supply curve that is horizontal.
C. Has a demand curve that is horizontal.
D. Will sell all output produced.

Answer (A) is correct.
REQUIRED: The true statement about a business firm with the ability to control the price of its product.
DISCUSSION: A firm that can control the price of its product is a monopolist. In a monopoly, the industry demand curve is also the firm's demand curve. The demand curve is downward-sloping since the lower the price, the higher the demand for a product.
Answer (B) is incorrect. A horizontal supply curve implies that the company will produce any quantity of output at the constant price. The ability to control one's price implies a changing price level. **Answer (C) is incorrect.** A horizontal demand curve implies an unchanging price. **Answer (D) is incorrect.** The firm will not be able to sell all of its output if it sets the price higher than what consumers are willing to pay. Also, a monopolist's incentive is not to sell the maximum that can be produced, but to sell the amount that maximizes profits.

4.8 Market Structures -- Monopolistic Competition

22. All of the following are characteristics of monopolistic competition **except** that

A. The firms sell a homogeneous product.
B. The firms tend not to recognize the reaction of competitors when determining prices.
C. Individual firms have some control over the price of the product.
D. The consumer demand curve is highly elastic.

Answer (A) is correct.
REQUIRED: The item not a characteristic of monopolistic competition.
DISCUSSION: Monopolistic competition assumes a large number of firms with differentiated (heterogeneous) products and relatively easy entry into the market. Sellers have some price control because of product differentiation. Monopolistic competition is characterized by nonprice competition, such as advertising, service after the sale, and emphasis on trademark quality. In the short run, firms equate marginal revenue and marginal cost. In the long run, firms tend to earn normal (not economic) profits, and price exceeds marginal cost, resulting in an underallocation of resources. Firms produce less than the ideal output, and the industry is populated by too many firms that are too small in size. Price is higher and output less than in pure competition.
Answer (B) is incorrect. Responses to competitors' actions are unnecessary if products are sufficiently differentiated to make price competition meaningless. **Answer (C) is incorrect.** Product differentiation permits some price control. **Answer (D) is incorrect.** The availability of close substitutes makes the product demand curve elastic.

23. Entry into monopolistic competition is

A. Blocked.
B. Difficult, with significant obstacles.
C. Rare, as significant capital is required.
D. Relatively easy, with only a few obstacles.

Answer (D) is correct.
REQUIRED: The true statement about entry into monopolistic competition.
DISCUSSION: Monopolistic competition is characterized by the existence of a large number of firms, differentiated products, relative ease of entry, some control of price by the firms, and significant nonprice competition (e.g., by advertising). Entry into monopolistic competition is more difficult than entry into pure competition, but it is relatively easy compared with entry into a monopoly.
Answer (A) is incorrect. Entry is possible and relatively easy. Blocked entry is typical of monopoly. **Answer (B) is incorrect.** Difficult entry is typical of oligopoly. **Answer (C) is incorrect.** Given the large number of firms, most are likely to be small, with correspondingly low economies of scale and capital needs.

4.9 Market Structures -- Oligopoly

24. The distinguishing characteristic of oligopolistic markets is

A. A single seller of a homogeneous product with no close substitute.
B. A single seller of a heterogeneous product with no close substitute.
C. Lack of entry and exit barriers in the industry.
D. Mutual interdependence of firm pricing and output decisions.

Answer (D) is correct.
REQUIRED: The distinguishing characteristic of oligopolistic markets.
DISCUSSION: The oligopoly model is much less specific than the other market structures, but there are typically few firms in the industry. Thus, the decisions of rival firms do not go unnoticed. Products can be either differentiated or standardized. Prices tend to be rigid (sticky) because of the interdependence among firms. Entry is difficult because of either natural or created barriers. Price leadership is typical in oligopolistic industries. Under price leadership, price changes are announced first by a major firm. Once the industry leader has spoken, other firms in the industry match the price charged by the leader. The mutual interdependence of the firms influences both pricing and output decisions.
Answer (A) is incorrect. Oligopolies contain several firms; a single seller is characteristic of a monopoly.
Answer (B) is incorrect. Oligopolies contain several firms; a single seller is characteristic of a monopoly.
Answer (C) is incorrect. Oligopolies are typified by barriers to entry; that is the reason the industry has only a few firms.

25. An oligopolist faces a "kinked" demand curve. This terminology indicates that

A. When an oligopolist lowers its price, the other firms in the oligopoly will match the price reduction, but if the oligopolist raises its price, the other firms will ignore the price change.
B. An oligopolist faces a non-linear demand for its product, and price changes will have little effect on demand for that product.
C. An oligopolist can sell its product at any price but, after the "saturation point," another oligopolist will lower its price and therefore shift the demand curve to the left.
D. Consumers have no effect on the demand curve, and an oligopolist can shape the curve to optimize its own efficiency.

Answer (A) is correct.
REQUIRED: The meaning of an oligopolist's kinked demand curve.
DISCUSSION: An oligopoly consists of a few firms. Thus, the decisions of rivals do not go unnoticed. Prices tend to be rigid (sticky) because of the interdependence among firms. Because competitors respond only to certain price changes by one of the firms in an oligopolistic industry, the demand curve for an oligopolist tends to be kinked. Price decreases are usually matched by price decreases, but price increases are often not followed. If other firms do not match a lower price, a price decrease by an oligopolist would capture more of the market. If other firms match the price decrease, less of the market will be captured.
Answer (B) is incorrect. Price changes will have an effect on demand for an oligopolist's product. **Answer (C) is incorrect.** An oligopolist must essentially match the price of other firms in the industry. A change in price does not shift the demand curve. **Answer (D) is incorrect.** An oligopolist cannot shape its demand curve.

Access the **Gleim CPA Premium Review System** featuring our SmartAdapt technology from your Gleim Personal Classroom to continue your studies. You will experience a personalized study environment with exam-emulating multiple-choice questions.

GLEIM CPA REVIEW
#1 CPA EXAM PREP

KNOW WHAT TO STUDY. KNOW WHEN YOU'RE READY.

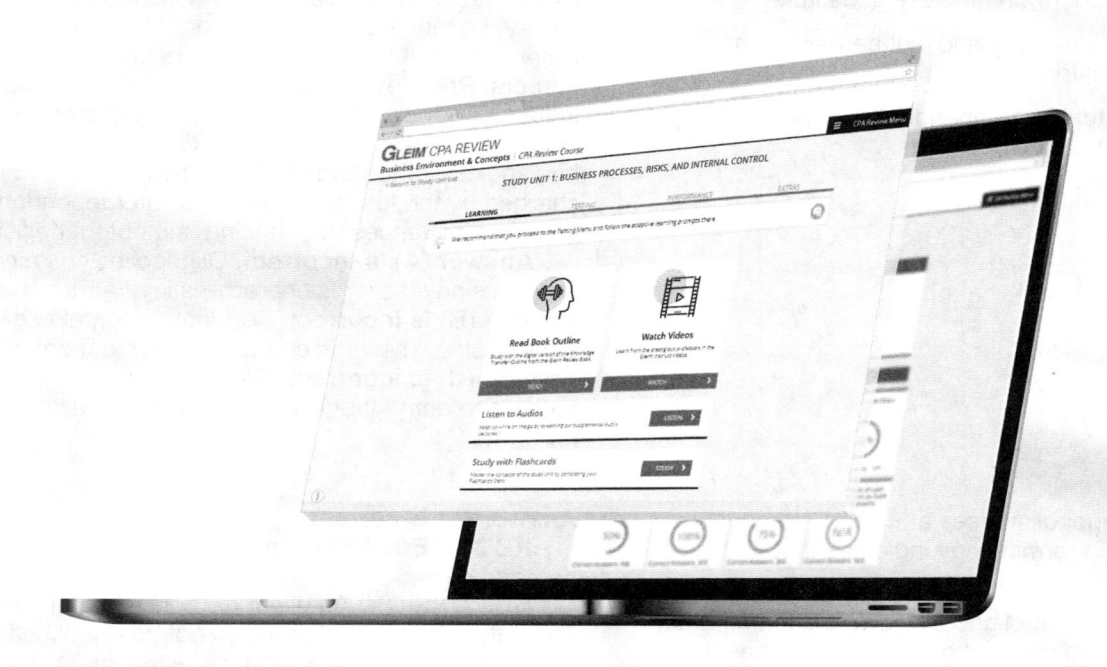

FEATURES OUR INNOVATIVE SMARTADAPT™ TECHNOLOGY

SmartAdapt identifies where you need to focus (and where you don't) throughout your studies.

Also featuring:

- Personalized support from our team of Exam Experts
- Comprehensive test bank of exam-emulating simulation and multiple-choice questions
- One-of-a-kind, no-hassle Access Until You Pass® guarantee
- Two Exam Rehearsals (full-length mock exams) to help you get exam-day ready

GleimCPA.com | 800.874.5346

STUDY UNIT FIVE
MACROECONOMICS AND GLOBALIZATION

(24 pages of outline)

5.1	Business Cycles	148
5.2	Inflation	150
5.3	Unemployment	153
5.4	Demand Management through Fiscal Policy	155
5.5	The Creation of Money	157
5.6	Monetary Policy	161
5.7	Globalization	163
5.8	Protectionism	168

Macroeconomics is the study of how the aggregate economy behaves as a whole. The focus is primarily on forecasting national income by examining predictable patterns and trends and their influence on each other. Gross domestic product, employment/unemployment, inflation, and other factors are the primary target variables for governments who use fiscal and monetary policy tools to achieve their goals of growth, full employment, and stable prices. Fiscal policies of spending and taxation are the primary tools of governmental bodies (Subunit 5.4). Monetary policy is the tool of the Federal Reserve (Subunits 5.5 and 5.6).

International economics describes the economic effects in productive resources and consumer preferences between nations. Due to these differences, the patterns and consequences of transactions affect trade, investment, and migration. Protectionism (i.e., the lack of free trade) concerns government policies that affect a business entity's industry as well as the overall economy.

5.1 BUSINESS CYCLES

1. **Overview**

   a. Over the very long run, economic growth in capitalistic economies has not been steady. The overall trend of growth is periodically interrupted by periods of instability. This tendency toward instability within the context of overall growth is the business cycle.

   The Business Cycle

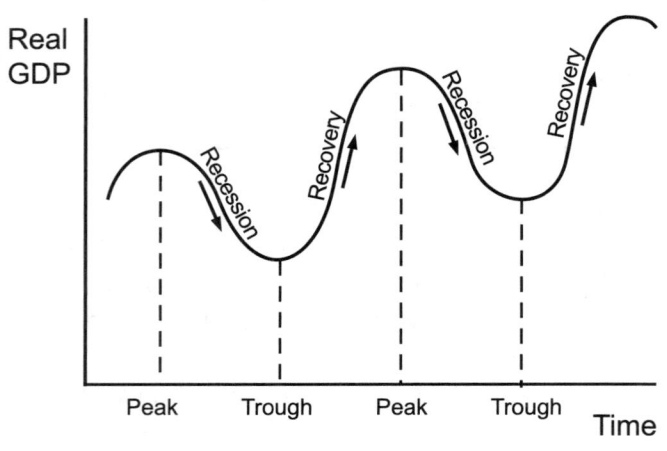

   [Figure 5-1: Graph showing Real GDP on y-axis and Time on x-axis, with alternating Recession and Recovery phases marked at Peak, Trough, Peak, Trough points.]

   Figure 5-1

   1) At a **peak**, the economy is
      a) At or near full employment and
      b) At or near maximum output for the current level of resources and technology.
   2) A **recession (contraction)** is a period during which real GDP falls and unemployment rises.
      a) If the recession is severe enough, prices fall and the phase is considered a **depression**.
   3) In a **trough**, economic activity reaches its lowest point.
   4) During a **recovery (expansion)**, output and employment rise. Eventually, the price level also rises.

   > **SUCCESS TIP:** In addition to identifying the phases of the business cycle, a candidate should be able to assess the business cycle's effects on an entity's operations and its industry.

   b. Possible Causes of Recessions or Troughs

      1) When consumer confidence declines, i.e., when consumers become pessimistic about the future, they spend less. Unsold inventory increases, and businesses respond by reducing production and laying off workers.
      2) A miscalculation in fiscal or monetary policy by the government may suffice to cause a recession or a trough.
      3) Often a major default triggers a cascade of confidences leading to reduced lending and consumption.

2. **Economic Indicators**

   a. Economists use economic indicators to forecast changes in economic activity. Economic indicators are variables that in the past have had a high correlation with the change in GDP.

      1) The best-known sets of economic indicators are those prepared by The Conference Board, a private research group.
      2) Indicators may lead, lag, or coincide with economic activity.
      3) These indicators in isolation are not meaningful. It is the composite index that has predictive uses. This index has historically been valuable but not infallible.

b. A **leading** economic indicator is a forecast of future economic trends.

   1) A change in any of the following leading economic indicators suggests a future change in real GDP in the same direction:

      a) The average workweek for production workers
      b) New orders for consumer goods and materials
      c) Stock prices
      d) New orders for nondefense capital goods
      e) Building permits for houses
      f) The money supply
      g) Index of consumer indications
      h) The spread between short-term and long-term interest rates

   2) A change in either of the following leading economic indicators suggests a future change in real GDP in the opposite direction:

      a) Initial claims for unemployment insurance (because more people out of work indicates slowing business activity)
      b) Vendor performance (because vendors have slack time and are carrying high levels of inventory)

c. A **lagging** indicator changes after the change in the economic activity has occurred.

   1) The following are lagging economic indicators:

      a) Average duration of unemployment
      b) Commercial and industrial loans outstanding
      c) Average prime rate charged by the banks
      d) Change in the consumer price index for services

d. A **coincident** indicator changes at the same time as the change in the economic activity.

   1) The following are coincident economic indicators:

      a) Industrial production
      b) Manufacturing and trade sales
      c) Personal income minus transfer payments

SUCCESS TIP

You do not need to memorize all of the economic indicators. If one of these economic indicators is in the stem of a multiple-choice question, you need to understand how it may affect future growth or contraction of the economy. A written communication question on economic indicators may be required, but your response should be acceptable if you can remember some of them. Most accounting majors should have acquired the necessary knowledge from course work and coverage of business news, e.g., stock prices (such as the S&P 500 and the Dow Jones Industrial Average), unemployment claims, and interest rates.

STOP & REVIEW

You have completed the outline for this subunit.
Study multiple-choice questions 1 through 3 beginning on page 171.

5.2 INFLATION

1. **Overview**

> **SUCCESS TIP**
>
> The AICPA has tested topics related to inflation on recent CPA Exams. Multiple-choice questions have asked how inflation is measured and inflation's effects on the economy.

   a. Inflation is a sustained increase in the general level of prices. The reported rate of inflation is therefore an average of the increase across all prices in the economy. But this definition does not sufficiently explain all the effects of inflation.

      1) The value of any unit of money (e.g., the U.S. dollar) is measured by the goods and services that can be acquired in exchange for it. This measure is money's purchasing power. Inflation decreases purchasing power.

   b. The percentage rate of inflation is calculated using a price index.

      1) A **price index** is a measure of the price of a market basket of goods and services in one year compared with the price in a designated base year. By definition, the index for the base year is 100.

         a) The rate of inflation is calculated by using the change in the index.

         $$\frac{\text{Current-year price index} - \text{Prior-year price index}}{\text{Prior-year price index}}$$

EXAMPLE 5-1   Rate of Inflation

If the price index of the market basket was 10% higher than the base year in Year 3 and was 15% higher in Year 4, the inflation rate for Year 4 is

$$\frac{115 - 110}{110} = 4.55\%$$

---

      2) The **Consumer Price Index (CPI)** is the most common price index for adjusting nominal GDP. It measures changes in the general price level by a pricing of items on a typical urban household shopping list.

         $$\text{CPI} = \frac{\text{Cost of market basket in current year}}{\text{Cost of market basket in base year}} \times 100$$

BACKGROUND 5-1   Consumer Price Index (CPI)

The CPI is computed monthly by the Bureau of Labor Statistics (an agency of the U.S. Department of Labor). According to the agency's website (www.bls.gov/cpi/), prices for the goods and services used to calculate the CPI are collected in 87 urban areas throughout the country and from about 23,000 retail and service establishments. Data on rents are collected from about 50,000 landlords or tenants. The base period for the CPI (i.e., the period for which the index equaled 100) is the period 1982-1984.

---

         a) The CPI also is a relevant tool in business analysis. For example, rising prices can reduce the purchasing power and profit of a business.

b) To compare two monetary amounts in constant dollars, they must be deflated using the appropriate price index. The difference then must be divided by the prior period's amount.

EXAMPLE 5-2   CPI Adjustment to Constant Dollars

A law firm is analyzing its revenue history. This year's billings were $1,080,000, and last year's were $950,000. This year's CPI is 115, and last year's was 107.

	Nominal Dollars		CPI (in hundredths)		Constant Dollars
This year's billings:	$1,080,000	÷	1.15	=	$939,130
Last year's billings:	950,000	÷	1.07	=	887,850
Difference	$ 130,000				$ 51,280

Thus, nominal billings increased by 13.7% ($130,000 ÷ $950,000). But after adjusting for inflation, they increased by only 5.8% ($51,280 ÷ $887,850).

---

2. **Real Income vs. Nominal Income**

   a. Nominal income is the money received by a consumer as wages, interest, rent, and profits. For example, a worker might have an annual salary, and therefore a nominal income, of $64,000.

   b. Real income is the purchasing power of the income received. It is nominal income adjusted for inflation. Purchasing power relates directly to the consumer's standard of living.

   c. Real income decreases when the rate of increase in nominal income is less than the inflation rate.

3. **Macroeconomic Effects of Inflation**

   a. Unexpected inflation can cause economic chaos.
   b. The efficiency of economic relationships relies on stable pricing.

4. **Effects on Financial Reporting**

   a. In financial reporting, the principal effects of inflation are on inventory, cost of goods sold, and equipment and depreciation.

      1) In a last-in, first-out (LIFO) inventory accounting system, the most recently purchased goods are expensed first. In a period of rapidly rising prices, LIFO increases cost of goods sold and decreases operating income, thereby decreasing income tax liability.

         a) If the entity uses first-in, first-out (FIFO) inventory accounting, cost of goods sold consists of lower inventory costs, thereby increasing operating income.

      2) The depreciable base of a long-lived asset is its historical cost. During a period of rising prices, depreciation expense is lower at historical cost than if it were stated in terms of replacement cost. Reported operating income is higher in the current period, but replacing such assets as they are retired is more expensive.

5. **Two Types of Inflation**

    a. **Demand-pull inflation** is caused by an excess of demand over supply.

EXAMPLE 5-3	Demand-Pull Inflation

    The economy of Spain during the Age of Exploration was almost wrecked by the influx of gold and silver from the Western Hemisphere. The sudden infusion of wealth allowed consumers the ability to buy more goods and demand-pull inflation resulted. The effect was to increase the prices of existing goods. This historical example demonstrates the principle that the value of money is derived from the wealth that underlies it.

    b. **Cost-push inflation** is caused by increased per-unit production costs that are passed on to consumers as higher prices.

    1) Increases in materials costs are the principal cause, particularly when they occur suddenly in the form of a **supply shock**.

EXAMPLE 5-4	Supply Shock

    The fourth war between the Arab nations and Israel began in October 1973. While the Soviet Union supplied aid to the Arab countries, the United States aided the Israelis. In retaliation, the Organization of Petroleum Exporting Countries (OPEC) declared an embargo of oil shipments to the U.S.

    The price of petroleum products skyrocketed, and the quantity available plummeted. U.S. automobile drivers sometimes waited in line for hours to buy gasoline at much higher prices than they were accustomed to. Because the U.S. economy is dependent on petroleum products, the increase in production costs for practically everything had a severe effect on the country.

    OPEC ended the embargo in March 1974, but the economic effects were felt in the U.S. for years afterward.

6. **Deflation**

    a. Deflation is a sustained decrease in the general price level. It is caused by conditions that are the opposite of those causing demand-pull and cost-push inflation.

    1) A decrease in demand not accompanied by a decrease in supply causes a leftward shift of the aggregate demand curve. Firms sell inventory even if they incur losses. Prices and output fall.

    2) An increase in output not accompanied by an increase in demand causes a rightward shift of the aggregate supply curve. Prices fall.

STOP & REVIEW

You have completed the outline for this subunit.
Study multiple-choice questions 4 through 6 beginning on page 172.

5.3 UNEMPLOYMENT

1. **Overview**

    a. Unemployment is the failure of an economy to employ fully its labor force. The **unemployment rate** is stated in percentage terms.

    $$\frac{\text{Number of unemployed}}{\text{Size of labor force}} \times 100$$

    > **BACKGROUND 5-2   Unemployment Rate**
    >
    > The unemployment rate is based on the Current Population Survey, a monthly survey of households conducted by the U.S. Census Bureau on behalf of the Bureau of Labor Statistics (www.bls.gov/cps).

    b. The **labor force** (the equation's denominator) includes all individuals **except** those who are (1) under the age of 16; (2) incarcerated or institutionalized; (3) homemakers, full-time students, and retirees; and (4) discouraged workers (who are unemployed and able to work but are not actively seeking work).

    1) Among those included in the labor force, no distinction is made between full- and part-time workers. They are considered equally employed.

    c. The number of unemployed (the equation's numerator) consists of those who are willing and able to work and are seeking employment.

    d. The official statistics can be distorted by

    1) Workers who falsely claim to be seeking work or
    2) Those unemployed in the underground economy (e.g., cash-only basis workers).

2. **Three Types of Unemployment**

    a. **Frictional unemployment** is the amount of unemployment caused by the normal workings of the labor market.

    1) This group can include those

        a) Moving to another location,
        b) Stopping work temporarily to obtain further education and training, and
        c) Who are between jobs.

    2) This definition acknowledges that normal unemployment exists at any given time in a dynamic economy.

    b. **Structural unemployment** results when

    1) The composition of the workforce does not match the need. It can be a result of changes in consumer demand or technology.

        a) The computer revolution has drastically changed the skills required for many jobs and completely eliminated others.

    2) The available jobs are not in the location where unemployed workers live.

    c. **Cyclical unemployment** is directly related to the level of an economy's output. It is likely to occur in the recession phase of the business cycle. For this reason, it is sometimes called **deficient-demand unemployment**.

    1) As consumers spend less, firms reduce production and lay off workers.
    2) The Great Depression of the 1930's was a period of low prices, low demand, and extremely low industrial output. During the worst of this period, as much as 25% of the American labor force was unemployed.

3. **Full Employment**

    a. The **natural rate of unemployment** consists of frictional and structural unemployment combined (cyclical unemployment is omitted).

        1) Economists consider the economy to be at **full employment** when the economy is at the natural rate of unemployment. Thus, full employment is **not** "100% employment."
        2) The rate varies over time because of demographic and institutional changes in the economy.

    b. The economy's potential output is the real (i.e., inflation-adjusted) domestic output, or potential national income, that could be achieved if the economy sustained full employment.

4. **Macroeconomic Effects of Unemployment**

    a. Lost value to the economy is the primary economic cost of unemployment. The goods not produced and services not provided by idle workers can never be regained.

    b. Unemployment has social costs, including loss of skills, personal and family stress, violence and other crime, and social upheaval.

5. **Inflation and Unemployment**

    a. The inverse relationship between inflation and unemployment can be described using the Phillips Curve.

    b. When the unemployment rate is low, firms have to pay higher wages to attract workers, thereby increasing labor costs and product prices. Thus, the lower (higher) the unemployment rate, the higher (lower) the inflation.

    Short-Term Phillips Curve

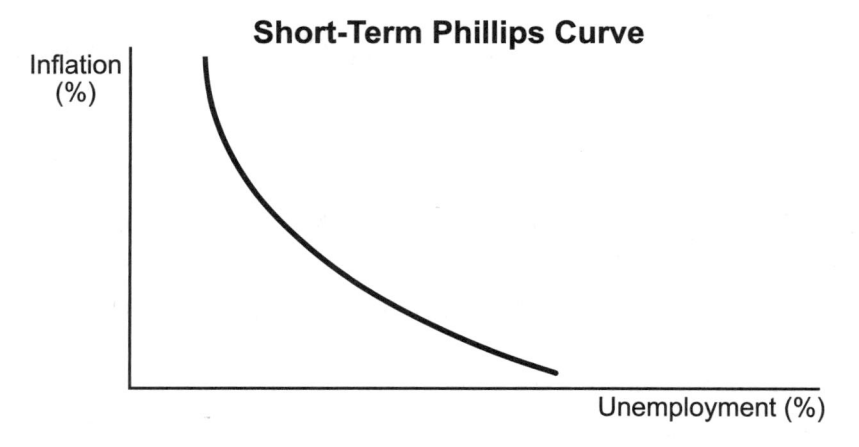

    Figure 5-2

        1) The Phillips curve applies only in the short-term.
        2) In the long-term, inflationary policies do not decrease unemployment.

STOP & REVIEW

You have completed the outline for this subunit.
Study multiple-choice questions 7 through 9 beginning on page 173.

5.4 DEMAND MANAGEMENT THROUGH FISCAL POLICY

1. **Overview**

    a. Government affects the economy through its fiscal and monetary policies.

    1) Fiscal policy is the use of taxation and expenditures to reach macroeconomic objectives, taking in revenues (taxes) and making purchases (the annual expenditures).

    2) Monetary policy is covered in Subunit 5.6.

    b. Fiscal policies can be discretionary or nondiscretionary.

    1) **Discretionary** fiscal policy involves spending that is under the control of individuals within the government, such as contracting for new weapons systems.

    2) **Nondiscretionary** fiscal policy is enacted in law. Certain outlays, e.g., Social Security, must be made regardless of their consequences or source of funding because Congress has made them a legal requirement. No individual bureaucrat or group can choose to withhold (or increase) these expenditures.

    c. The following tools of fiscal policy are used by the government:

    1) Tax policy
    2) Government spending (highway maintenance, military buildup, etc.)
    3) Transfer payments (welfare, food stamps, unemployment compensation, etc.)

2. **Using Fiscal Policy**

    a. A reduction in consumer expectations leads to a decrease in consumption.

    b. Recession and unemployment follow as a result of real GDP decreasing.

    c. To promote growth and reduce unemployment, the federal government may increase its spending.

    1) Because of the multiplier effect, an increase in government spending increases real GDP.

    2) The **multiplier effect** occurs because each dollar spent by a consumer in the economy becomes another consumer's income, and so forth. The increase in the consumption for every additional dollar consumers receive in income is the **marginal propensity to consume (MPC)**. The remainder that was not spent is saved.

        a) Spending has a cumulative effect on the economy, greater than the initial amount.

3. **Issues in Fiscal Policy**

   a. **Keynesian theory** calls for expansionary fiscal policy during times of recession (to stimulate aggregate demand) and contractionary policy during an expansion (to prevent inflation).

   b. If a recessionary gap exists, the government adopts **expansionary policies**.

      1) Taxes can be decreased and transfer payments increased, giving consumers more disposable income.
      2) Government can increase its spending, increasing demand for goods and services from the private sector.
      3) Federal deficit increases under expansionary policies.

   c. An **inflationary gap** is the amount by which the economy's aggregate expenditures at the full-employment GDP exceed those necessary to achieve full-employment GDP.

   d. If an inflationary gap exists, the government adopts **contractionary policies** to reduce aggregate demand.

      1) Taxes can be increased and transfer payments decreased, giving consumers less disposable income.
      2) Government can decrease its spending, reducing demand for goods and services from the private sector.
      3) Federal deficit decreases under contractionary policies.

You have completed the outline for this subunit.
Study multiple-choice questions 10 through 12 on page 175.

STOP & REVIEW

5.5 THE CREATION OF MONEY

1. **Three Uses of Money**

   a. Medium of exchange. The existence of money greatly facilitates the free exchange of goods and services by providing a common means of valuation. Without money, all goods and services would have to be bartered, creating extraordinary inefficiencies.

   b. Unit of account. Money also provides a convenient basis for bookkeeping. Anything stated in terms of money can be easily compared.

   c. Store of value. Any society using the barter basis is subject to great inefficiencies. Many objects of great value, such as perishable food, spoil, making them worthless. The value of a unit of money is determined by the quantity of goods and services it can be exchanged for, not by its inherent characteristics.

2. **Interest Rates**

   a. When money is borrowed, the debtor pays the lender an amount in addition to the sum that was borrowed (interest).

      1) The two major determinants of the interest rate on a loan are

         a) Overall economic conditions as reflected in the prime rate, which is the rate to the most credit-worthy customers, and

         b) The creditworthiness of the borrower.

   b. Economists distinguish between real and nominal interest rates.

      1) The **nominal interest rate** is the stated rate on a loan.

      2) The **real interest rate** equals the nominal rate minus the rate of inflation that the lender expects over the life of the loan.

         a) The lender must charge this inflation premium to compensate for the purchasing power lost while the loan is at the borrower's disposal.

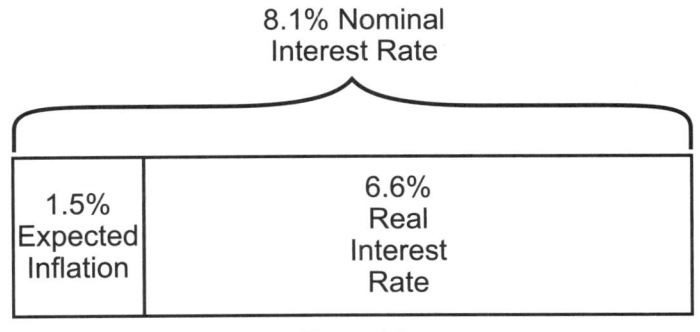

```
                    8.1% Nominal
                    Interest Rate
        ┌─────────────────────────────────┐
        │  1.5%    │      6.6%            │
        │ Expected │      Real            │
        │ Inflation│    Interest          │
        │          │      Rate            │
        └──────────┴──────────────────────┘
```

Figure 5-3

   c. Misunderstandings over the difference between real and nominal interest rates can lead to distortions in the economy.

      1) For example, a loan bearing 10% interest may seem excessive to a borrower. But if inflation is 8%, the borrower is paying a real rate of only 2%.

      2) For example, a loan bearing 6% interest may seem to be a bargain. But if inflation is 1%, the borrower is actually paying 5% real interest.

3. **The Supply of Money**

   a. The U.S. Federal Reserve System tracks and reports the amount of money in circulation.

      1) The metrics used by the Fed are called M1 and M2. M1 includes only the most liquid forms of money. M2 includes M1 and less-liquid forms of money.

EXAMPLE 5-5   Money Supply

The following is a hypothetical money supply calculation for an economy the approximate size of the U.S.:

	In Billions
Currency (Paper money + Coins)	$ 600
Checking accounts	700
M1 money supply	**$1,300**
Savings accounts, including money market accounts	2,900
Small time deposits (< $100,000)	1,400
Money market mutual funds	800
M2 money supply	**$6,400**

BACKGROUND 5-3   Money Stock Measures

Although they need not be memorized for the CPA Exam, the Federal Reserve's latest Money Stock Measures are at www.federalreserve.gov/releases/h6/current/default.htm.

---

   b. The **velocity of money (V)** is the number of times each unit of currency is used to purchase a final product in a given period.

$$V = \frac{\text{Nominal GDP}}{\text{Money Supply}}$$

EXAMPLE 5-6   Velocity of Money

Assume nominal GDP is $8,320 billion. Using the amounts from Example 5-5, the velocities of money can be calculated as follows:

V_{M1} = $8,320 billion ÷ $1,300 billion = 6.4 times

V_{M2} = $8,320 billion ÷ $6,400 billion = 1.3 times

In the M1 money supply, each dollar is used 6.4 times to purchase a final product in a given period. In the M2 money supply, each dollar is used 1.3 times to purchase a final product in a given period.

4. **Banks and the Creation of Money**

   a. The example M1 money supply calculation illustrates that paper money and coins (currency) are less than half the total.

      1) The money in the economy greatly exceeds the currency in circulation because of the creation of money by banks.

EXAMPLE 5-7	Creation of Money

A bank customer deposits $1,000, and the bank then lends $800. The depositor's statement shows that (s)he has a claim to $1,000 of cash, and the borrower has $800 of cash. Thus, $1,800 exists when only $1,000 existed previously. The bank has created $800.

BACKGROUND 5-4	Federal Reserve System

From its founding, the United States tended to view a central bank as an anti-democratic institution. Thus, instead of having a single central bank like many other countries, the United States has 12 regional Federal Reserve Banks. The Federal Reserve, established in 1913, is independent of the rest of the federal government. This independence, and the long terms of its members, protect the Fed's decisions from political pressures. The Board of Governors is responsible for overseeing the operations of the Federal Reserve System. The Federal Open Market Committee (FOMC) is responsible for administering monetary policy.

SUCCESS TIP

In today's world, the actions taken by the Federal Reserve receive extensive media coverage. Be prepared to answer questions about policies pursued of the Federal Reserve for different economic situations.

5. **Bank Reserves**
    a. Fractional reserve banking is the practice of prohibiting banks from lending all the money they receive on deposit.
    b. The required **reserve ratio** is the percentage of each dollar deposited that a bank is required to either (1) keep in its vault or (2) deposit with the Federal Reserve Bank in its district.
        1) The minimum that must be held by law is required reserves.

BACKGROUND 5-5   Required Reserve Ratio

For example, the Fed recently required medium-sized banks to keep 3% in reserve (in the vault or on deposit with the district Fed). An explanation and a complete table of the current reserve requirements are at www.federalreserve.gov/monetarypolicy/reservereq.htm.

---

            a) The amount of customer deposits that exceeds required reserves is **excess reserves**. It is from excess reserves that the bank makes loans.
        2) Fractional reserves obviously do not suffice to prevent a bank's collapse in the event customers withdraw excessive amounts. The Federal Deposit Insurance Corporation provides depositors with insurance on their deposits and examines banks for safety.
            a) The Fed has the sole authority to set minimum reserve requirements for all depository institutions, which influences the money supply.
    c. The amount of money banks potentially can create is approximated using the monetary multiplier.

$$\text{Monetary multiplier} = \frac{1}{\text{Required reserve ratio}}$$

        1) The money supply decreases as required reserves are raised.

EXAMPLE 5-8   Reserve Ratio and Money Supply

If the Fed requires reserves of 4% on all deposits, a bank with $10 million on deposit can create $250 million of new money [$10,000,000 × (1.0 ÷ .04)].

STOP & REVIEW

You have completed the outline for this subunit.
Study multiple-choice questions 13 through 15 on page 176.

5.6 MONETARY POLICY

1. **Goals and Tools of Monetary Policy**

   a. The Fed balances the goals of gradual, steady economic growth and price stability (manageable inflation).

      1) The Fed has three tools of monetary policy:

         a) Open-market operations
         b) The required reserve ratio
         c) The discount rate (equals the rate charged by the Fed on loans to member banks)

      2) Fiscal and monetary policy can be combined to influence aggregate demand.

   b. **Open-market operations** are the Fed's strongest tool. It can choose potential effects that are immediate and range from large to small.

      1) U.S. Treasury securities are traded on the open market. The Fed can either purchase them from, or sell them to, commercial banks.

         a) When the Fed wishes to increase the money supply, it purchases Treasury securities. It removes securities from the market and injects money.
         b) When the Fed wishes to decrease the money supply, it sells Treasury securities. It removes money from the economy and injects securities.

      2) The **federal funds rate** is the rate banks charge each other for overnight loans.

         a) A bank's excess reserves do not have to be idle. They can be lent on a short-term basis to other banks with deficient reserves.
         b) When the Fed buys Treasury securities, the money supply increases and the federal funds rate falls. When the Fed sells Treasury securities, the money supply decreases and the federal funds rate rises.

      3) The following table summarizes the effects of changes in the money supply resulting from open-market operations:

Increase Money Supply	Decrease Money Supply
1. The Fed expects a **recession**.	1. The Fed expects higher **inflation**.
2. The Fed **buys securities** on the open market.	2. The Fed **sells securities** on the open market.
3. The Fed **credits cash to reserve accounts** of banks selling securities. • The increase in cash **creates excess reserves**. Banks are more willing to lend. • Greater availability of cash for overnight loans decreases the **federal funds rate.**	3. The Fed **decreases cash in reserve accounts** of banks buying securities. • The decrease in cash **reduces excess reserves**. Banks are less able to lend. • Lower availability of cash for overnight loans **increases the federal funds rate.**
4. Lower interest rates stimulate investment spending by businesses.	4. Higher interest rates discourage investment spending by businesses.
5. Greater investment spending increases real GDP and decreases unemployment.	5. Lower investment spending decreases inflation.

c. Changes in the required **reserve ratio** are used less frequently. Requiring banks to retain more funds in reserve accounts reduces profits.

   1) Lowering the reserve ratio increases the money supply.

      a) If reserves decrease, banks have more money to lend.

   2) Raising the reserve ratio decreases the money supply.

      a) If reserves increase, banks have less money to lend.

d. The **discount rate** is the rate Federal Reserve banks charge for short-term loans directly to commercial banks.

   1) Increasing the discount rate reduces borrowing and the money supply.

      a) Banks are most likely to borrow from the Fed because of temporary shortages of reserves. If such loans are more expensive, banks are more likely to increase reserves to ensure that borrowing is unnecessary.

   2) Decreasing the discount rate increases borrowing and the money supply.

BACKGROUND 5-6   The Fed and the 2008 Market Crisis

The widely-held belief is that (1) the Fed is a lender of last resort and (2) borrowing from the Fed is a sign of financial weakness. Thus, banks tend to do so only in emergencies and prefer that the Fed maintain their anonymity.

The direct provision of cash by the Federal Reserve is not publicized. As reported in *Bloomberg Businessweek* on August 22, 2011, the Fed quietly lent $669 billion to the 10 largest U.S. banks during the market crisis of late 2008, an amount that far exceeded the widely discussed $160 billion bailout by the U.S. Treasury. The magazine could only report this information after "compilation of data obtained through Freedom of Information Act requests, months of litigation, and an act of Congress." Including both U.S. and foreign banks (e.g., Royal Bank of Scotland and UBS AG), the Fed had $1.2 trillion in loans outstanding on December 5, 2008.

---

e. There are also alternative methods that the Federal Reserve can use to control the money supply. The **margin requirements** are the required amount of deposits investors must put into a brokerage account before purchasing securities.

   1) Increasing the margin requirements reduces the stock that can be purchased and the money supply.

   2) Decreasing the margin requirements increases the stock that can be purchased and the money supply.

f. The Fed adopts **expansionary monetary policy** to increase the money supply and adopts **contractionary monetary policy** to reduce the money supply.

Summary of Monetary Policy Tools

Monetary policy tools	Expansionary monetary policy	Contractionary monetary policy
Open-market operations	Purchase U.S. Treasury securities	Sell U.S. Treasury securities
The required reserve ratio	Lower the required reserve ratio	Raise the required reserve ratio
The discount rate	Decrease the discount rate	Increase the discount rate

---

STOP & REVIEW

You have completed the outline for this subunit.
Study multiple-choice questions 16 through 18 on page 177.

5.7 GLOBALIZATION

1. **Impact of Globalization on the Business Environment**

    a. The business environment and decision making become increasingly complex as globalization brings capital flows, international competition, technological innovation, migration of labor and work, environmental concerns, etc.

    1) Globalization significantly increases business risks ranging from exchange rate and interest rate fluctuation to piracy in the global supply chain.

    2) Globalization increases cross-border investments and international competition. Cross-border investments face regulatory obstacles that impact trade, such as protectionism, taxation, and environmental laws.

    3) Managing a global workforce is difficult because the operations are further separated on a global scale. A related challenge is reconciling cultural and religious differences while maintaining a diverse workforce to empower global and local success.

    4) Globalization of the financial market leads to increasing mergers and acquisitions in the financial service industry. Capital flows more freely across the globe as a result.

    5) Cross-border restructuring happens more frequently as companies seek to obtain global capital, increase economies of scale, improve market share, increase geographical diversification, etc.

2. **Resource Planning in Globalization**

    a. Resource planning is essential because profit maximization requires production of the optimal output at the least cost. The resources used in production (e.g., labor and materials) are acquired in markets. Firms often seek resources in other countries.

    b. **Derived** demand is the demand for the **inputs** to production (factors), e.g., lumber, derived from the demand for the **outputs** (final goods), e.g., a house.

3. **Factors Affecting Demand for Resources**

    a. Demand for the final product that the resource produces. An increase (decrease) in the demand for the final output will also increase (decrease) the demand for resources.

    b. Productivity of the resource. As the productivity of an input increases, input price decreases, thereby demand for it increases. Productivity increases when

    1) The makeup or components of goods change such that the final good is produced more efficiently.

    2) Technical improvements are made in those combining resources.

    3) Technical improvements are made in the resource itself.

    c. Prices of other resources.

    1) If the price of a resource that can substitute for another resource decreases, the demand for the second resource decreases. This result is the **substitution** effect.

        a) For example, as the price of ridesharing services decreases, ridesharing is substituted for cars, and the demand curve for cars shifts to the left.

    2) If two resources are **complements**, a decrease in the price of one causes an increase in the demand for the other.

        a) For example, as the price of computers decreases, the demand curve for computer technicians shifts to the right.

4. **Elasticity of Resource Demand**

   a. The elasticity of resource demand applies to movements along, not the shift of, a demand curve. The elasticity of demand for a resource is directly related to the

   1) Elasticity of demand for the final product. Thus, if the demand for t-shirts becomes more elastic, the demand for cotton becomes more elastic.

   2) Availability of resource substitutes. For example, as more rayon becomes available, the demand for cotton becomes more elastic.

   3) Proportion of total production cost represented by the resource. For example, if cotton is a large proportion of the total cost of blended fabric, an increase in the price of cotton significantly increases the total cost. Accordingly, the firm's demand for cotton becomes more elastic. In this instance, the blend of the fabric would shift to have more lower-cost material and less higher-cost material.

5. **Illegal Pricing**

   a. Some countries (and industries within countries) attempt to gain advantage in the market for their benefit through tactics such as illegal pricing. The following are examples of pricing tactics that are generally considered illegal.

   1) **Predatory pricing** is pricing products below cost to harm competitors.

      a) The U.S. Supreme Court has held that a price is predatory if (1) it is below an appropriate measure of costs, and (2) the seller has a reasonable prospect of recovering its losses in the future through higher prices or greater market share.

   2) **Price discrimination** among customers is illegal if it has the effect of lessening competition, although price discrimination may be permissible if the competitive situation requires it and if costs of serving some customers are lower.

   3) **Collusive pricing** involves conspiracies to restrict output and set artificially high prices which violates antitrust laws.

   4) **Dumping** is selling below cost in foreign countries and may trigger retaliatory tariffs or other sanctions.

6. **Restructuring in a Global Context**

   a. Forms of Business **Restructuring**

   1) A **merger** is the combination of two companies to form a new company (Company A + Company B = Company C).

   2) An **acquisition** is a business combination that involves the purchase of one company by another in which no new company is formed (Company A + Company B = Company A).

   3) In a **joint venture**, two or more entities agree to pool their resources to achieve specific objectives. Unlike mergers or acquisitions, a joint venture forms a temporary partnership. After the specific objective is achieved, the joint venture will be dissolved or sold.

   4) A **divestiture** is the partial or full disposal of a business unit through sale, exchange, closure, or bankruptcy.

b. Business Purposes of **Mergers and Acquisitions**

1) Fluctuation in exchange rates can influence cross-border mergers and acquisitions. Companies in countries where the currency is stronger are more likely to acquire the company in countries where the currency is weaker. (Currency exchange rates are discussed in Study Unit 6, Subunit 1.)
2) When a company buys out a supplier or a distributor, the company saves supply costs or shipping costs that would have been spent if the supplier or the distributor were independent from the company. This is **vertical integration**.
3) Many companies acquire or merge with competitors to gain market share and eliminate competition. This is **horizontal integration**.
4) Firms diversify through mergers and acquisitions to grow, improve profitability, and manage risk.
    a) **Concentric diversification** results from developing or acquiring related businesses that do not have products, services, or customers in common with current businesses. However, they offer internal synergies, e.g., through common use of brands, R&D, plant facilities, or marketing expertise.
    b) **Horizontal diversification** is the acquisition of businesses making products unrelated to current offerings but that might be demanded by the firm's current customers.
    c) **Conglomerate diversification** is the acquisition of wholly unrelated businesses. The objectives of such an acquisition are financial, not operational, because of the absence of common products, customers, facilities, expertise, or other synergies.

c. Business Purposes for a **Joint Venture**

1) A joint venture enables businesses to share assets, costs, expertise, and business risks.
2) The flexibility of a joint venture helps businesses avoid costly mergers, acquisitions, and transfer of ownership. Entities have the freedom to choose alliances with multiple firms and not be tied to an alliance with one firm (e.g., in the case of a merger). Ultimately, joint ventures allow open-ended and new business opportunities.
3) Like mergers and acquisitions, a joint venture helps businesses gain access to market share, obtain capital, and achieve diversification.

d. Business Purposes for **Divestiture**

   1) Companies divest when part of the business is not performing well to prevent further loss.
   2) Regulators might require companies to divest for antitrust concerns.
   3) Divestiture could be a part of the bankruptcy process when a healthier company arises from the bankruptcy.
   4) Companies could obtain funds by divesting part of the business to solve financial difficulties and provide much-needed liquidity.
   5) Companies sometimes divest so they can focus on their prominent operations and improve core competency.
   6) Companies could also divest when they believe two separate entities would be more profitable than a consolidated entity.
   7) As the exchange rate for a domestic currency falls, a foreign company might purchase a subsidiary from the domestic country. Once the exchange rate in the domestic country rises, the foreign company sells the subsidiary to gain the difference between the purchase and selling price.

e. **Culture Change in Mergers and Acquisitions**

   1) Organizational culture undergoes significant changes after a merger or acquisition. Four modes of acculturation can be triggered.

      a) **Integration** refers to incorporating external individuals into a workplace as equals. The members of the acquired company try to maintain their culture to a certain degree; however, they are willing to integrate into the acquirer's culture simultaneously.
      b) **Assimilation** is the abandonment of one culture in favor of another when becoming part of a new workplace. The members of the acquired company gradually abandon their culture and willingly adopt the acquiring company's culture.
      c) **Separation** occurs when the two entities distance themselves from one another culturally. The members of the acquired company try to maintain their own culture and resist adopting the acquiring company's culture.
      d) **Deculturation** refers to the loss or desertion of cultural characteristics in the workplace. The employees in the acquired company do not value their previous workplace culture, and they refuse to assimilate into the acquirer's culture.

7. **Business Process Outsourcing**
    a. Business process outsourcing is the transfer of some of an organization's business processes to an outside provider to improve service quality while achieving
        1) Cost savings,
        2) Operating effectiveness, or
        3) Operating efficiency.
    b. Such processes as human resources, payroll, and information services may not be core competencies of some organizations. To streamline operations and reduce costs, they outsource processes.
        1) By contracting with outside service providers who specialize in these functions, the organization also may avoid the problem of knowledge loss when key employees leave.
    c. **Advantages** of outsourcing include the following:
        1) Access to expertise
        2) Superior service quality
        3) Avoidance of changes in the organization's infrastructure
        4) Cost predictability
        5) Use of human and financial capital
        6) Avoidance of fixed costs
    d. The potential **disadvantages** include the following:
        1) Inflexibility of the relationship
        2) Loss of core knowledge
        3) Loss of control over the outsourced function
        4) Unexpected costs
        5) Vulnerability of important information
        6) Need for contract management
        7) Dependence on a single vendor

STOP & REVIEW

You have completed the outline for this subunit.
Study multiple-choice questions 19 through 21 on page 178.

5.8 PROTECTIONISM

1. **Overview**

   a. Even though individuals generally are benefited by free trade, governments often establish policies designed to impact the workings of the marketplace. **Protectionism** is any measure taken by a government to protect domestic producers.

2. **Forms of Protectionism**

   a. **Tariffs** are taxes imposed on imported goods.

      1) Tariffs can discourage consumption of foreign goods, raise revenue, or both.
      2) To achieve both goals, the government must set the tariff rate very carefully. The effect of tariffs also depends on the elasticity of demand and how market participants react to the tariff. If the rate is set too high, demand for the good is decreased and revenue declines.

   > **BACKGROUND 5-7   U.S. Revenue before Enactment of Income Tax**
   >
   > Until the income tax was enacted in 1913, the U.S. government raised most of its revenue from tariffs.

   b. **Import quotas** set limits on the quantity of different products that can be imported.

      1) In the short run, import quotas improve a country's balance of payments by decreasing foreign outflow payments. But the prices of domestic products increase.

         a) A country's **balance of payments** is the sum of all transactions between domestic and foreign individuals, firms, and governments.

      2) An **embargo** is a total ban on some kinds of imports. It is an extreme form of import quota.
      3) As a result of import quotas and tariffs, domestic consumers pay higher prices and consume fewer goods. However, the domestic producers are able to sell more goods. Thus, domestic consumers pay a subsidy to domestic producers.

   c. **Domestic content rules** require that at least a portion of any imported product be constructed from parts manufactured in the importing nation.

      1) This rule is sometimes used by capital-intensive nations (e.g., United States). Parts can be produced using idle capacity and then sent to a labor-intensive country (e.g., Philippines) for final assembly.

   d. A **trigger price** mechanism automatically imposes a tariff barrier against unfairly cheap imports by levying a duty (tariff) on all imports below a particular reference price.

   e. **Antidumping** rules prevent foreign producers from selling excess goods on the domestic market at less than cost to squeeze out competitors and gain control of the market. This is a form of predatory pricing.

f. **Repatriation** is the process of transferring money earned in a foreign location back to the domestic location.
   1) Exchange controls by the foreign country limit foreign currency transactions and set exchange rates. The purpose is to limit the ability of a firm selling in a country to repatriate its earnings to its home country.
   2) Tax policy can impose additional costs on earnings that are repatriated. For example, the U.S. has a worldwide corporate taxation system that taxes foreign earnings only when they are repatriated. Thus, many companies choose to keep their capital offshore to avoid high tax rates in the U.S.

g. **Export subsidies** are payments by the government to producers in certain industries in an attempt to increase exports.
   1) A government may impose **countervailing duties** on imported goods if those goods were produced in a foreign country with the aid of a governmental subsidy. The purpose is to protect domestic producers by offsetting subsidies made by foreign governments to foreign producers.

h. Certain exports may require **licenses**, especially if these sales are potentially not in the interest of national security. For example, sales of technology with military applications are limited by many nations that are members of the Wassenaar Arrangement. The related U.S. legislation is the Export Administration Act of 1979.

i. The Export Trading Company Act of 1982 provides an alternative to reduce the trade deficit by encouraging American exports to foreign markets. The act permits competitors to form export trading companies without regard to U.S. antitrust legislation.

3. **Economic Effects of Tariffs and Quotas**
   a. Workers are shifted from relatively efficient export industries into less efficient protected industries. Real wages decline as prices rise, as does total world output.
   b. Under a tariff, the excess paid by the customer for an imported good is government revenue that can be spent for domestic purposes.
      1) Under a quota, prices also are increased (by the induced shortage), but the excess is paid to the exporter in the foreign country.
   c. A tariff is imposed on all importers equally. Thus, the more efficient firms can still charge lower prices.
      1) But an import quota does not affect foreign importers equally because import licenses can be granted based on political favoritism.

4. **Arguments Regarding Protectionism**

   a. Reducing imports protects domestic jobs.

      1) This argument is compelling because the costs of cheaper imports are obvious, direct, and concentrated. People lose jobs and firms go out of business. The benefits of unrestricted trade are less noticeable. Lower prices, higher wages, and more jobs in export industries are future effects.

      2) An argument against protectionism is that many of the ill effects of job loss can be mitigated by government programs to help in displaced-worker transition. Such measures are not protectionist.

   b. Certain industries are essential to national security.

      1) This argument is sound for some firms. But firms only peripherally related to national defense can claim that they are crucial to national security.

      2) The national security concern also may result in the opposite of protectionism. For example, the U.S. government forbids exports of nuclear technology and certain weapons to countries such as Cuba, Iran, and North Korea. Thus, domestic exporters are hurt by government policies.

   c. Infant industries need protection in the early stages of development.

      1) An extension of the infant-industry argument is the strategic trade policy argument. It states that a government should use trade barriers strategically to reduce the risk of product development by domestic firms, particularly for products involving advanced technology.

      2) Two counterarguments are usually offered. One is that, if the firm is promising, venture capitalists will provide financing until the entity becomes profitable. Also, some firms dependent on special government protections never become self-sufficient.

5. **Global Capital Flow**

   a. The rise of high-speed electronic communications makes the flow of capital much faster than in earlier eras.

   b. Emerging-market countries can attract capital with much greater ease than before, thereby exploiting their particular **comparative advantages**. The economic balance of power can shift rapidly back and forth between developed and developing nations.

6. **Sustainability**

   a. The sustainability movement is built upon the goal of creating a higher standard of living for the present and the future, with a focus on reducing waste, energy use, and distribution costs while protecting the environment.

   b. As the sustainability movement has become more important to consumers, major brands are attempting to provide their products and services in a more sustainable manner and to advertise that practice to consumers.

STOP & REVIEW

You have completed the outline for this subunit.
Study multiple-choice questions 22 through 24 on page 179.

QUESTIONS

5.1 Business Cycles

1. Which of the following options describes the phases of business cycle, in order of occurrence?

A. Recession, recovery, trough, peak.
B. Peak, recession, trough, recovery.
C. Peak, recovery, trough, recession.
D. Trough, recession, recovery, peak.

Answer (B) is correct.
  REQUIRED: The chronological order of business cycle phases.
  DISCUSSION: The peak phase represents an economy that is at or near full employment, and at or near the maximum output for the current level of resources and technology. However, the peak cannot last indefinitely and is ended by a contraction in the economy, known as the recession phase. As the economy continues to contract, it will eventually reach its lowest point in terms of productivity. The low point is known as the trough phase. Similar to the peak, the trough cannot last indefinitely. Eventually, the economy will enter the recovery phase. Therefore, the correct order of the business cycle phases is peak, recession, trough, and recovery.
  Answer (A) is incorrect. The peak phase occurs before the recession phase. Additionally, the recovery phase occurs after the trough phase. **Answer (C) is incorrect.** The recession phase occurs before the trough phase. Additionally, the recovery phase occurs after the trough phase. **Answer (D) is incorrect.** The peak phase occurs before the recession phase. Additionally, the trough phase occurs between the recession phase and the recovery phase.

2. Which of the following may provide a leading indicator of a future increase in gross domestic product?

A. A reduction in the money supply.
B. A decrease in the issuance of building permits.
C. An increase in the timeliness of delivery by vendors.
D. An increase in the average hours worked per week of production workers.

Answer (D) is correct.
  REQUIRED: The leading indicator of an increase in GDP.
  DISCUSSION: An economic indicator is highly correlated with changes in aggregate economic activity. A leading indicator changes prior to a change in the direction of the business cycle. The leading indicators included in the Conference Board's index are (1) average weekly hours worked by manufacturing workers, (2) unemployment claims, (3) consumer goods orders, (4) stock prices, (5) orders for fixed assets, (6) building permits, (7) timeliness of deliveries, (8) money supply, (9) consumer confidence, and (10) the spread between the yield on 10-year Treasury bonds and the federal funds rate. An increase in weekly hours worked by production workers is favorable for economic growth.
  Answer (A) is incorrect. A falling money supply is associated with falling GDP. **Answer (B) is incorrect.** A decline in the issuance of building permits signals lower expected building activity and a falling GDP. **Answer (C) is incorrect.** An increase in the timeliness of delivery by vendors indicates slacking business demand and a potentially falling GDP.

3. Diana has noticed that many of her coworkers at Bubble, Inc., have been laid off over the past year due to low profits. Also, prices were lowered recently due to economic conditions. Even though Diana is worried about her future at Bubble, she has noticed that employment has risen over the past month and that prices are slowly increasing. Because other companies have had the same experience, what phase of the business cycle is the economy currently in?

A. Peak.
B. Recession.
C. Trough.
D. Recovery.

Answer (D) is correct.
  REQUIRED: The phases of the business cycle.
  DISCUSSION: During a recovery, employment rises. The price level eventually also rises. Employment has been increasing in many companies, and the price level is slowly recovering.
  Answer (A) is incorrect. At a peak, the economy is at or near full employment. **Answer (B) is incorrect.** A recession is a period during which unemployment rises. **Answer (C) is incorrect.** In a trough, employment reaches its lowest point.

5.2 Inflation

4. The value of money varies

A. Directly with the tax rates.
B. Directly with government spending.
C. Directly with investment.
D. Inversely with the general level of prices.

Answer (D) is correct.
  REQUIRED: The correct statement about the value of money.
  DISCUSSION: Part of the value of money comes from its usefulness as a store of value or wealth. As prices rise, the purchasing power of a stock of money held diminishes. Accordingly, the value of money and the general level of prices must be inversely related.
  Answer (A) is incorrect. Tax rates do not directly influence the value of money. Tax rates might indirectly affect the value of money through their possible influence on the general level of prices. **Answer (B) is incorrect.** Government spending does not directly influence the value of money. Government spending may indirectly affect the value of money by influencing the general level of prices. **Answer (C) is incorrect.** Investment does not directly influence the value of money. Investment might indirectly affect the value of money through its possible influence on the general level of prices.

5. Demand-pull inflation occurs when

   A. Incomes rise suddenly.
   B. There are excessive wage increases.
   C. There are rapid increases in raw materials prices.
   D. There are substantial changes in energy prices.

Answer (A) is correct.
REQUIRED: The cause of demand-pull inflation.
DISCUSSION: When incomes rise suddenly, consumers demand more of everything, driving up the price level.
Answer (B) is incorrect. Excessive wage increases result in cost-push inflation. **Answer (C) is incorrect.** A rapid increase in materials prices is a supply shock. It may be the cause of stagflation but not of demand-pull inflation. **Answer (D) is incorrect.** Changes in the prices of an important input can be increases or decreases. Thus, they do not necessarily predict inflation.

6. Assume that real gross domestic product (GDP), measured in Year 1 dollars, rose from $3,000 billion in Year 1 to $4,500 billion in Year 10. Assume also that the price index rose from 100 to 200 during the same period. The GDP for Year 1 expressed in terms of Year 10 prices is

   A. $1,500 billion.
   B. $3,000 billion.
   C. $4,500 billion.
   D. $6,000 billion.

Answer (D) is correct.
REQUIRED: The GDP for Year 1 adjusted for inflation.
DISCUSSION: Between Year 1 and Year 10, the price index doubled (from 100 to 200). Thus, the nominal value of Year 1 GDP ($3,000 billion) also must be doubled when restated in Year 10 terms. The Year 1 GDP in Year 10 prices is $6,000 billion.
Answer (A) is incorrect. The amount of $1,500 billion assumes deflation rather than inflation from Year 1 to Year 10. **Answer (B) is incorrect.** The amount of $3,000 billion is the nominal value of the Year 1 GDP. **Answer (C) is incorrect.** The amount of $4,500 billion is the actual Year 10 GDP. The question asks about the restated Year 1 GDP.

5.3 Unemployment

7. Which of the following types of unemployment typically results from technological advances?

   A. Cyclical.
   B. Frictional.
   C. Structural.
   D. Short-term.

Answer (C) is correct.
REQUIRED: The type of unemployment that typically results from technological advances.
DISCUSSION: Structural unemployment results when the composition of the workforce does not match the need. It is the result of changes in consumer demand, technology, and geographical location.
Answer (A) is incorrect. Cyclical unemployment is directly related to the level of an economy's output. **Answer (B) is incorrect.** Frictional unemployment is the amount of unemployment caused by the normal workings of the labor market. **Answer (D) is incorrect.** Unemployment that results from technological advances is more likely to be long-term.

8. The rate of unemployment caused by changes in the composition of employment opportunities over time is referred to as the

A. Frictional unemployment rate.
B. Cyclical unemployment rate.
C. Structural unemployment rate.
D. Full employment unemployment rate.

Answer (C) is correct.
REQUIRED: The rate of unemployment caused by changes in the composition of employment opportunities over time.
DISCUSSION: Economists define full employment as occurring when cyclical unemployment is zero. Thus, the natural rate of unemployment (the full employment unemployment rate) equals the sum of structural and frictional unemployment. Cyclical unemployment is caused by insufficient aggregate demand. Frictional unemployment occurs when both jobs and the workers qualified to fill them are available. This definition acknowledges that workers change jobs, are laid off, abandon paid work temporarily, etc. Structural unemployment exists when aggregate demand is sufficient to provide full employment, but the distribution of the demand does not correspond precisely to the composition of the labor force. This form of unemployment results when the required job skills or the geographic distribution of jobs change.
Answer (A) is incorrect. Frictional unemployment results from imperfections in the labor market.
Answer (B) is incorrect. Cyclical unemployment is caused by a deficiency of aggregate spending.
Answer (D) is incorrect. The full employment unemployment rate is the sum of frictional and structural unemployment.

9. Unemployment that is caused by a mismatch between the composition of the labor force (in terms of skills, occupation, industries, or geographic location) and the makeup of the demand for labor is called

A. Real wage unemployment.
B. Deficient-demand unemployment.
C. Frictional unemployment.
D. Structural unemployment.

Answer (D) is correct.
REQUIRED: The term for unemployment caused by a mismatch between the composition of the labor force and the makeup of the demand for labor.
DISCUSSION: Structural unemployment exists when aggregate demand is sufficient to provide full employment, but the distribution of the demand does not correspond precisely to the composition of the labor force in terms of skills, industries, etc.
Answer (A) is incorrect. Real wage unemployment is not a meaningful term in this context. **Answer (B) is incorrect.** Deficient-demand unemployment (cyclical unemployment) is directly related to the level of an economy's output. It is likely to occur in the recession phase of the business cycle. **Answer (C) is incorrect.** Frictional unemployment is defined as the amount of unemployment caused by the normal workings of the labor market. It includes, for example, unemployment resulting from time lost in changing jobs.

5.4 Demand Management through Fiscal Policy

10. What is the amount needed to close the recessionary gap if the economy's full-employment real gross domestic product (GDP) is $1.2 trillion and its equilibrium real GDP is $1.0 trillion?

A. $200 billion.
B. $200 billion divided by the multiplier.
C. $200 billion multiplied by the multiplier.
D. $200 billion times the reciprocal of the marginal propensity to consume (MPC).

Answer (B) is correct.
REQUIRED: The amount of the recessionary gap.
DISCUSSION: The $200 billion difference between full-employment GDP and equilibrium GDP can be eliminated by additional consumption, government spending, or exports. Because of the multiplier effect, the amount of the increase can be less than $200 billion. The amount of additional activity necessary to close the gap is ($200 billion ÷ Multiplier).
Answer (A) is incorrect. The amount of $200 billion ignores the effect of the multiplier. **Answer (C) is incorrect.** The amount of $200 billion should be divided by the multiplier. **Answer (D) is incorrect.** The multiplier is based on the reciprocal of the marginal propensity to save (MPS), not the MPC.

11. If a government were to use only fiscal policy to stimulate the economy from a recession, it would

A. Raise consumer taxes and increase government spending.
B. Lower business taxes and government spending.
C. Increase the money supply and increase government spending.
D. Lower consumer taxes and increase government spending.

Answer (D) is correct.
REQUIRED: The actions taken if a government were to use only fiscal policy to stimulate the economy.
DISCUSSION: According to Keynesian economics, fiscal policy should be expansionary when the economy is in recession. Increases in government spending, decreases in taxation, or both have a stimulative effect. To achieve this effect, the increase in spending should not be matched by a tax increase, the effect of which is contractionary. Thus, deficit spending is the result of an expansionary fiscal policy.
Answer (A) is incorrect. Raising consumer taxes is contractionary. **Answer (B) is incorrect.** Lower government spending is contractionary. **Answer (C) is incorrect.** Increasing the supply of money involves monetary, not fiscal, policy.

12. The full-employment gross domestic product (GDP) is $1.3 trillion, and the actual gross domestic product is $1.2 trillion. The marginal propensity to consume (MPC) is 0.8. When inflation is ignored, what increase in government expenditures is necessary to produce full employment?

A. $100 billion.
B. $80 billion.
C. $20 billion.
D. $10 billion.

Answer (C) is correct.
REQUIRED: The effect of marginal propensity to consume when government expenditures are increased.
DISCUSSION: The gap between full-employment GDP and actual GDP is $100 billion ($1.3 trillion – $1.2 trillion). Using the multiplier effect, the government can spend an amount less than this to achieve an ultimate increase of $100 billion. This lower amount can be found by dividing the desired increase by the multiplier. The multiplier equals 1 divided by the marginal propensity to save (MPS), which is 1 minus the marginal propensity to consume (MPC). Since the MPS is .20 (1.0 – .80 MPC), the multiplier is 5 (1.0 ÷ .20 MPS). Therefore, the government only needs to increase expenditures by $20 billion ($100 billion total needed ÷ 5 multiplier) to achieve the desired effect.
Answer (A) is incorrect. An increase of $100 billion is the required total increase in government expenditures; i.e., it results from failing to take the multiplier effect into account. **Answer (B) is incorrect.** An increase of $80 billion results from incorrectly using the MPC rather than the multiplier. **Answer (D) is incorrect.** An increase of $10 billion results from incorrectly using a multiplier of 10.

5.5 The Creation of Money

13. The Federal Reserve System's reserve ratio is the

A. Specified percentage of a commercial bank's deposit liabilities that must be deposited in the central bank or kept on hand.
B. Rate that the central bank charges for loans granted to commercial banks.
C. Ratio of excess reserves to legal reserves that are deposited in the central bank.
D. Specified percentage of a commercial bank's excess reserves to total liabilities.

Answer (A) is correct.
REQUIRED: The definition of the reserve ratio.
DISCUSSION: The reserve ratio is the percentage of the customer deposits that banks must keep on hand or deposit with the Fed. These deposits are required by law to ensure the soundness of the bank and also serve as a tool for monetary policy. Accordingly, changes in the reserve ratio affect the money supply.
Answer (B) is incorrect. The discount rate is the rate the Fed charges for loans to commercial banks.
Answer (C) is incorrect. Excess reserves are amounts in excess of the reserve requirement.
Answer (D) is incorrect. The reserve ratio is the percentage of the customer deposits that banks must keep on hand or deposit with the Fed.

14. A bank with a reserve ratio of 20% and deposits of $1,000,000 can create how much new money?

A. $5,000,000
B. $1,000,000
C. $800,000
D. $200,000

Answer (A) is correct.
REQUIRED: The amount by which a bank can create new money given the reserve ratio and the amount of deposits.
DISCUSSION: The amount of new money a bank can create equals actual bank deposits times the monetary multiplier (or divided by the required reserve ratio). This bank therefore can create $5,000,000 of new money ($1,000,000 ÷ 0.2).
Answer (B) is incorrect. Reserves need to be only 20% of deposits. Accordingly, bank deposits of $1,000,000 with a reserve ratio of 20% support a 500% increase in money supply.
Answer (C) is incorrect. The amount of $800,000 equals the increase in net lendable funds, assuming a $1,000,000 increase in deposits.
Answer (D) is incorrect. The reserve is 20% of deposits, not the reverse.

15. The money supply in a nation's economy will decrease following

A. Open-market purchases by the nation's central bank.
B. A decrease in the discount rate.
C. An increase in the reserve ratio.
D. A decrease in the margin requirement.

Answer (C) is correct.
REQUIRED: The item that causes a decrease in the money supply.
DISCUSSION: The reserve ratio is the minimum percentage of its deposits that a bank must keep on deposit with the Federal Reserve or in its vault. When the reserve ratio increases, banks must maintain larger reserves, and less money is available for lending and investment. Consequently, the money supply decreases.
Answer (A) is incorrect. Open-market purchases by the central bank increase the money supply by increasing commercial banks' reserves.
Answer (B) is incorrect. A decrease in the rate charged to member banks for loans by the Federal Reserve (the discount rate) increases the money supply by increasing bank reserves.
Answer (D) is incorrect. A decrease in the margin requirement decreases the minimum down payment that purchasers of stock must make. This credit control affects the stock market and has no direct impact on the money supply.

5.6 Monetary Policy

16. All of the following actions are valid tools that the Federal Reserve Bank uses to control the supply of money **except**

A. Buying government securities.
B. Selling government securities.
C. Changing the reserve ratio.
D. Printing money when the level of M1 appears low.

Answer (D) is correct.
REQUIRED: The item that is not a valid tool of the Fed in controlling the money supply.
DISCUSSION: The amount of money to print is a decision for the Department of the Treasury (an executive branch agency), not the Federal Reserve (an independent agency). Moreover, paper currency and coins make up only about half of the M1 money supply. The Fed has other, more complex tools for implementing monetary policy.
Answer (A) is incorrect. Buying government securities is one method the Fed uses to control the money supply. **Answer (B) is incorrect.** Selling government securities is one method the Fed uses to control the money supply. **Answer (C) is incorrect.** Changing the reserve ratio is one method the Fed uses to control the money supply.

17. The primary mechanism of monetary control of the Federal Reserve System is

A. Changing the discount rate.
B. Conducting open market operations.
C. Changing reserve requirements.
D. Using moral persuasion.

Answer (B) is correct.
REQUIRED: The primary mechanism of monetary control used by the Fed.
DISCUSSION: Open market operations (buying and selling government securities) are the primary means used by the Fed to control the money supply. Fed purchases are expansionary. They increase bank reserves and the money supply. Fed sales are contractional. If money is paid into the Federal Reserve, bank reserves are reduced, and the money supply decreases.
Answer (A) is incorrect. Changing the discount rate is a less important tool of monetary policy. **Answer (C) is incorrect.** Changing reserve requirements is a less important tool of monetary policy. **Answer (D) is incorrect.** Moral persuasion is not a means of controlling the money supply.

18. Which of the following results could be expected from an open market operation of the Federal Reserve?

A. A sale of securities would lower interest rates.
B. A purchase of securities would raise interest rates.
C. A purchase of securities would lower security prices.
D. A sale of securities would raise interest rates.

Answer (D) is correct.
REQUIRED: The expected result from the given open market operation.
DISCUSSION: A sale of securities removes money from the economy and reduces bank reserves. Thus, banks cannot lend as much as previously, and higher interest rates follow. Money supply and interest rates are inversely related.
Answer (A) is incorrect. A sale increases interest rates. **Answer (B) is incorrect.** A purchase of securities increases reserves, allows banks to make more loans, and results in lower interest rates. **Answer (C) is incorrect.** A purchase of securities removes securities from the economy, increasing securities prices.

5.7 Globalization

19. Derived demand can best be described as

- A. The demand derived purely from the market structure of a particular industry.
- B. The demand for a final product generated by the demand for a complementary good.
- C. The demand for an input generated by the demand for the final product.
- D. The demand for a final product generated by an abundant supply of inputs.

Answer (C) is correct.
REQUIRED: The definition of derived demand.
DISCUSSION: Derived demand is the demand for the inputs to the production process (sometimes called factors) derived from the demand for the outputs of the process (i.e., final goods).
Answer (A) is incorrect. Derived demand is the demand for an input generated by the demand for the final product. **Answer (B) is incorrect.** The demand for complementary goods is not properly referred to as derived demand. **Answer (D) is incorrect.** Demand for a final product based on the supply of its inputs is not a meaningful economic concept.

20. Which of the following pricing policies results in establishment of a price to external customers higher than the competitive price for a given industry?

- A. Collusive pricing.
- B. Dual pricing.
- C. Predatory pricing.
- D. Transfer pricing.

Answer (A) is correct.
REQUIRED: The pricing policy that results in a higher overall price in the market.
DISCUSSION: Collusion involves competitive businesses working together to gain advantage in the market. Inflating the price of a good or service higher than the competitive price to realize higher profits is indicative of collusive behavior.
Answer (B) is incorrect. Dual pricing is the process of setting different prices based on the currency in which the good or service is being purchased. **Answer (C) is incorrect.** Predatory pricing is the practice of offering goods or services at an extremely low price designed to force competitors out of the market. **Answer (D) is incorrect.** Transfer pricing is the price that different divisions of the same company charge each other for supplies and labor.

21. Price discrimination is accomplished most effectively in markets with which of the following characteristics?

- A. Fairly distinct segments of customers.
- B. High competition that generates many price changes.
- C. Advanced technology capabilities that determine optimal pricing.
- D. Excess capacity that meets high demand at different price levels.

Answer (A) is correct.
REQUIRED: The market in which price discrimination will be the most effective.
DISCUSSION: Discriminatory pricing adjusts for differences among customers. Because it is easier to differentiate customers who fall into fairly distinct segments, discriminatory policies can be more effectively applied.
Answer (B) is incorrect. High competition that generates many price changes facilitates the implementation of a target or optimal pricing strategy. **Answer (C) is incorrect.** Advanced technological capabilities that determine optimal pricing facilitates more effective pricing of a company's goods based on real-time supply and demand, not discriminatory reasons. **Answer (D) is incorrect.** A market where excess capacity meets high demand at different price levels facilitates implementation of a target or optimal pricing strategy.

5.8 Protectionism

22. The appropriate remedy for the dumping of products by a foreign firm in the U.S. market would be to

A. Pass "buy American" laws.
B. Impose restrictions on U.S. exports to the offending country.
C. Impose countervailing duties or tariffs.
D. Deny "most favored nation" treatment to exporters of the offending country.

Answer (C) is correct.
REQUIRED: The appropriate remedy for the dumping of products by a foreign firm in the U.S. market.
DISCUSSION: Dumping is the practice of supporting exports by selling products at a lower price in foreign markets than in the domestic market. The result is that foreign goods can be purchased in the U.S. at a price much lower than would be charged by a U.S. manufacturer. Because dumping lowers the price of foreign goods, the appropriate remedy is for the importing nation to impose a tariff that reduces the price differential.
Answer (A) is incorrect. The passing of laws requiring domestic sourcing could result in a decline in overall domestic consumption, higher prices, and retaliatory foreign action. **Answer (B) is incorrect.** A country does not benefit from restricting its exports. **Answer (D) is incorrect.** Denying most favored nation treatment makes trade with a country more difficult and is a more extreme remedy than necessary.

23. Domestic content rules

A. Tend to be imposed by capital-intensive countries.
B. Tend to be imposed by labor-intensive countries.
C. Exclude products not made domestically.
D. Restrict demand for affected products.

Answer (A) is correct.
REQUIRED: The description of domestic content rules.
DISCUSSION: Domestic content rules require that at least a portion of any imported product be constructed from parts manufactured in the importing nation. This rule sometimes is used by capital-intensive nations. Parts can be produced using idle capacity and then sent to a labor-intensive country for final assembly.
Answer (B) is incorrect. Labor-intensive exporters are more likely to assemble final products. **Answer (C) is incorrect.** Domestic content rules place limits on, but do not exclude, imports. **Answer (D) is incorrect.** Supply is restricted.

24. What is the most likely economic effect of tariffs and quotas?

A. Workers are shifted into more efficient export industries.
B. Tariffs but not quotas affect all importers of the affected goods equally.
C. Total world output increases.
D. The price increase is received by exporters in foreign countries.

Answer (B) is correct.
REQUIRED: The effect of tariffs and quotas.
DISCUSSION: A tariff has an equal effect on all goods on which it is applied. Import licenses, however, may be awarded based on political favoritism.
Answer (A) is incorrect. The effect is to shift workers into relatively inefficient domestic protected industries. **Answer (C) is incorrect.** Total world output decreases. **Answer (D) is incorrect.** A tariff increases the domestic government's general tax revenues.

Access the **Gleim CPA Premium Review System** featuring our SmartAdapt technology from your Gleim Personal Classroom to continue your studies. You will experience a personalized study environment with exam-emulating multiple-choice questions.

Notes

STUDY UNIT SIX
FOREIGN EXCHANGE AND DERIVATIVES

(21 pages of outline)

6.1	Currency Exchange Rates	181
6.2	Derivatives	191
6.3	Mitigating Exchange Rate Risk	198

The ability of countries to trade affects the value of their currencies. In our global economy, the value of a nation's currency can have dramatic effects on the nation's economy as well as the business conditions for business entities operating in the respective nation. CPAs employ derivatives as a way to mitigate financial risk. Because firms today operate in a global economy, the AICPA usually tests candidates on how to mitigate financial risk associated with currency exchange.

6.1 CURRENCY EXCHANGE RATES

SUCCESS TIP

The AICPA has tested the topic of currency exchange rates on recent CPA Exams. CPA candidates should have a solid understanding of currency exchange rates and the effects of globalization on the business environment.

1. **The Market for Foreign Currency**

    a. When an entity buys merchandise, a capital asset, or a financial instrument from another country, the seller wants to be paid in his or her domestic currency.

    1) Thus, in general, when the demand for a country's merchandise, capital assets, and financial instruments rises, demand for its currency rises.

    b. For international exchanges to occur, the two currencies involved must be easily converted at some prevailing exchange rate.

    1) The exchange rate is the price of one country's currency in terms of another country's currency.

EXAMPLE 6-1   Currency as a Commodity

Conceptually, a currency can be considered to be a commodity. The exchange rate is essentially the price of a currency. An exchange rate of 0.9 euro per USD can be understood as "each USD costs 0.9 euro," similar to "each apple costs 0.9 euro."

The exchange rate changing from 0.9 euro to 1.0 euro per USD is equivalent to that same apple now costing 1 euro. Therefore, as each USD "costs" more, the USD gains value in relation to the euro.

This can also be used in exchange rate conversion. An exchange rate of 0.9 euro/USD, equivalent to "an apple costs 0.9 euro," can be converted to 1.11 USD/euro. An apple costs 0.9 euro; therefore, each euro can buy 1.11 apples (1 apple ÷ 0.9 euro).

Exchange rates can be calculated using the following formula:

$$\text{Currency A} \div \text{Currency B} = \frac{1}{\text{Currency B} \div \text{Currency A}}$$

c. The exchange rate between two currencies is not always available (e.g., when a market for exchanging the two currencies does not exist). To determine the exchange rate, the **cross rate** can be used.

1) The cross rate is the product or quotient of the exchange rates of each currency with a common currency that effectively cancels out the common currency and rearranges the remaining currencies. The desired currencies are thus valued proportionally to one another.

2) The cross rate can be calculated using the following formulas depending on which exchange rates are available (whether the common currency is in the numerator or the denominator). For instance, if the exchange rate between Currency A and Currency C is needed, the following are two ways to determine the exchange rate given different cross rates:

$$\frac{\text{Currency A}}{\text{Currency B}} \times \frac{\text{Currency B}}{\text{Currency C}} = \frac{\text{Currency A}}{\text{Currency C}}$$

a) If the exchange rate known is in the form of Currency C divided by Currency B, then division is necessary to rearrange the calculation and determine Currency A divided by Currency C.

$$\frac{\text{Currency A}}{\text{Currency B}} \div \frac{\text{Currency C}}{\text{Currency B}} = \frac{\text{Currency A}}{\text{Currency B}} \times \frac{\text{Currency B}}{\text{Currency C}} = \frac{\text{Currency A}}{\text{Currency C}}$$

EXAMPLE 6-2	Cross Currency Rate

A British company needs to purchase materials from a company in Switzerland. In order to pay the Swiss company, the British company must purchase Swiss francs. The British company must determine the exchange rate of Swiss francs per British pound, which in this example is not hypothetically available. However, the exchange rate of U.S. dollars to each currency is available, which can be used to determine the cross rate.

The U.S. dollar to British pound exchange rate is $1.23/£, and the U.S. dollar to Swiss franc exchange rate is $1.03/F. The Swiss franc per British pound cross rate is the quotient of the two rates. By dividing the dollar-to-pound exchange rate by the dollar-to-franc exchange rate, (1) the common U.S. dollar currency unit is canceled out and (2) the quotient is expressed as the ratio between the Swiss franc and the British pound (F1.23/£1.03). Therefore, the Swiss franc per British pound cross rate is F1.19/£.

$$\frac{\$1.23}{£1} \div \frac{\$1.03}{F1} = \frac{\$1.23}{£1} \times \frac{F1}{\$1.03} = \frac{F1.23}{£1.03} = F1.19/£$$

2. **Exchange Rate Systems**

    a. **Fixed Exchange Rate System**

    1) In a fixed exchange rate system, the value of a country's currency in relation to another country's currency is either fixed or allowed to fluctuate only within a very narrow range. For example, the Bahamian dollar is pegged to the U.S. dollar at a 1:1 ratio.

    2) The one significant advantage of a fixed exchange rate is that it provides predictability in international trade by eliminating uncertainty about gains and losses on exchange rate fluctuations.

EXAMPLE 6-3	Advantage of Fixed Exchange Rates

    Since July 1986, the Saudi government has allowed its currency to trade within an extremely narrow band surrounding the ratio of 3.75 riyals to 1 U.S. dollar. Because the U.S. buys large amounts of petroleum from Saudi Arabia, this system has the advantage of adding stability to the U.S. oil market.

    3) A disadvantage is that a government can manipulate the value of its currency.

EXAMPLE 6-4	Disadvantage of Fixed Exchange Rates

    One of the complaints of authorities in the U.S. about the enormous trade deficit with China is the belief that the Chinese government has held the value of the yuan in an artificially low range to make its exports more affordable. (After years of urging by the U.S. government, China allowed its currency to rise almost 18% between 2005 and 2008. After further negotiations, China agreed in April 2012 to allow the value of the yuan to fluctuate by as much as 1.0% against the value of the dollar on any given day. This doubled the size of the previous trading band of 0.5%.)

    b. **Freely Floating Exchange Rate System**

    1) In this system, exchange rates are determined entirely by supply and demand.

        a) The advantage is that the system tends to automatically correct any disequilibrium in the balance of payments.

        b) The disadvantage is that a freely floating system makes a country vulnerable to economic conditions in other countries.

    c. **Managed Float Exchange Rate System**

    1) Under a managed float, market forces determine exchange rates until they move too far in one direction or another. The government then intervenes to maintain the currency within the broad range considered appropriate.

        a) The advantage of managed float is that it has the market-response nature of a freely floating system while allowing for government intervention when necessary.

    2) The dominant exchange rate system in use among the world's largest economies is the managed float system.

3. **Exchange Rates and Purchasing Power**

   a. The graph below depicts the relationship between the supply of, and demand for, a foreign currency by consumers and investors who use a given domestic currency.

   Exchange Rate Equilibrium

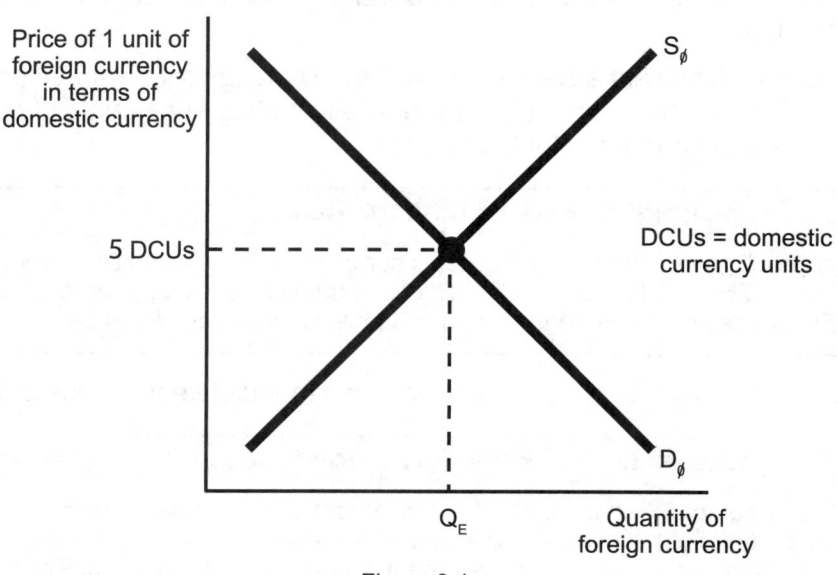

   Figure 6-1

   1) The demand curve for the foreign currency is downward sloping. When that currency becomes cheaper, goods and services denominated in that currency are more affordable and domestic consumers need more of it.

   2) The supply curve for the foreign currency is upward sloping. When that currency becomes more expensive, goods and services denominated in the domestic currency become more affordable to users of the foreign currency. Thus, they inject more of their currency into the domestic market.

b. When one currency can be exchanged for more units of another currency, the first currency **appreciates** in relation to the second currency. The second currency **depreciates** in relation to the first.

1) This phenomenon has definite implications for international trade. The currency that appreciates has greater purchasing power. Any financial instrument denominated in that currency is more valuable (expensive).

2) The appreciation or depreciation affects the business strategies of firms. When a firm's domestic currency depreciates, the demand for their product increases, so the firm is likely to expand operations. The opposite can also be true.

EXAMPLE 6-5	Exchange Rate Fluctuations

A U.S. company buys merchandise from an EU company for €1,000,000, due in 60 days. On the day of the sale, $0.795 is required to buy a single euro. By the 60th day, $0.812 is required to buy a euro. The dollar has therefore depreciated in relation to the euro, and the euro has appreciated in relation to the dollar. Accordingly, the dollar has lost purchasing power in relation to the euro. The U.S. firm needed $795,000 to pay a €1,000,000 debt on the date of sale. On the due date, it must pay $812,000, resulting in a loss of $17,000.

3) Other factors being constant, as the domestic currency depreciates, export prices decrease and import prices increase. Domestic goods become cheaper than foreign goods. Thus, export quantities increase and import quantities decrease. The opposite effects occur when the domestic currency appreciates.

c. The five factors that affect currency exchange rates can be classified as three trade-related factors and two financial factors.

1) Trade-related factors

a) Relative inflation rates
b) Relative income levels
c) Government intervention

2) Financial factors

a) Relative interest rates
b) Ease of capital flow

4. **Trade-Related Factors that Affect Exchange Rates**
   a. **Relative Inflation Rates**
      1) Recall from Study Unit 5 that the nominal interest rate consists of the real interest rate plus the expected inflation rate.
      2) When the rate of inflation in a foreign country rises relative to the rate of inflation in a domestic country, the products of that foreign country become relatively expensive and the demand for that country's currency falls.
         a) This leftward shift of the demand curve results from the reduced purchasing power of that currency.
      3) As investors sell this currency, more of it is available, which is reflected in a rightward shift of the supply curve.
      4) A new equilibrium point is at a lower price in terms of investors' domestic currencies.
         a) As a result of the higher inflation in a foreign country, the domestic currency has appreciated in relation to that foreign currency.

Changes in Supply of and Demand for the Currency of a Foreign Country with Higher Relative Inflation

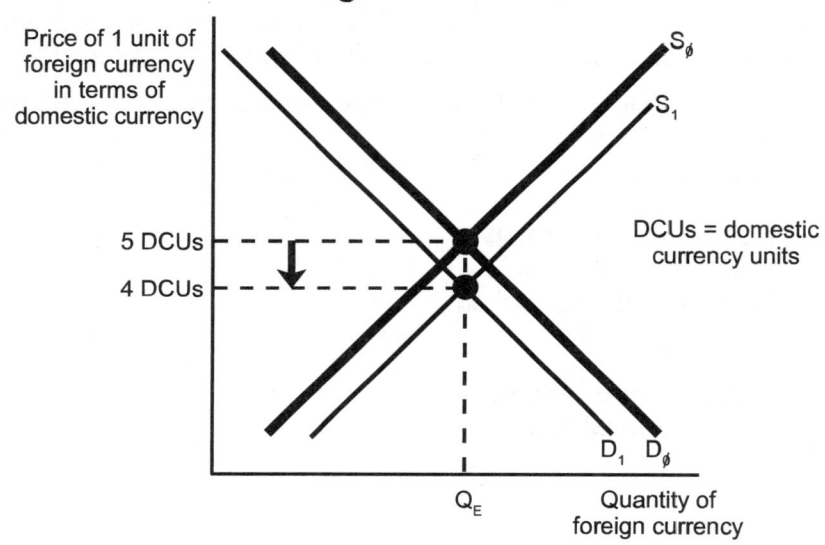

Figure 6-2

   b) The difference between the countries' inflation rates approximately equals the change in the currency exchange rate between the two countries.
      i) For example, X has a 3% nominal inflation rate and Y has a 7% nominal rate. Because of the difference in nominal inflation rates, X's currency appreciates against Y's currency by approximately 4% (7% − 3%). This example assumes the real interest rate is constant between nations.

b. **Relative Income Levels**

1) Persons with higher incomes look for new consumption opportunities in other countries, increasing the demand for those currencies and shifting the demand curve to the right.

    a) As domestic incomes rise, the prices of foreign currencies also rise and the local currency depreciates.

Changes in Supply of and Demand for the Currency of a Foreign Country When Domestic Incomes Rise

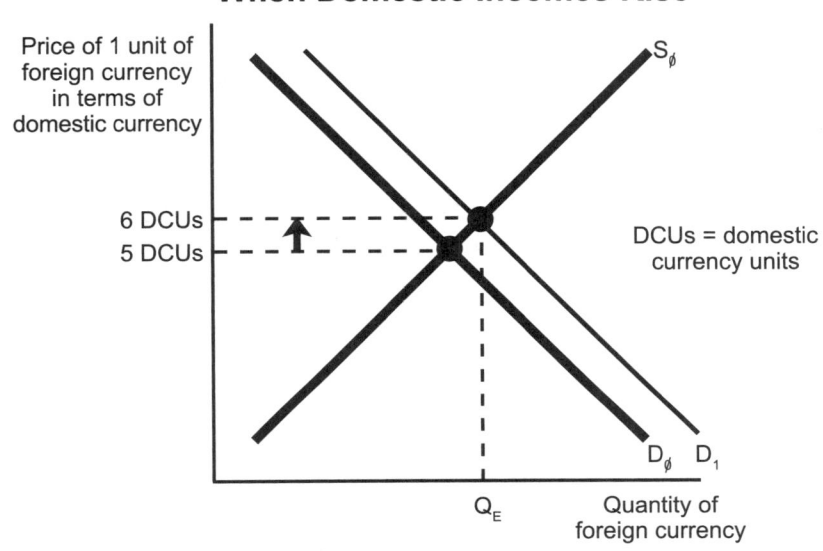

Figure 6-3

c. **Government Intervention**

1) Actions by national governments, such as trade barriers and currency restrictions, complicate the process of exchange rate determination.

    a) **Trade barriers** decrease imports of foreign goods and increase demand for domestic goods. Thus, the domestic currency appreciates without hurting domestic producers.

        i) However, trade barriers hurt consumers because consumers pay more for goods and ultimately have access to less diverse goods.

    b) **Currency controls** limit exchange rate volatility by restricting the use of foreign currency or using a fixed exchange rate. As more people purchase the domestic currency, it appreciates against the foreign currency.

    c) When the effects are not fully anticipated, an expansionary **monetary policy** (increase in money supply) reduces the exchange rate. A restrictive monetary policy (decrease in money supply) increases the exchange rate.

    d) When the effects are not fully anticipated, **fiscal policy** tends to have conflicting effects on the exchange rate. However, an expansionary fiscal policy generally is more likely to lead to currency appreciation, but a restrictive fiscal policy generally is more likely to lead to currency depreciation.

5. Financial Factors that Affect Exchange Rates

a. **Relative Interest Rates**

1) When the interest rates in a foreign country rise relative to those of a domestic country, more investors are willing to buy the foreign country's currency to make investments and the demand for the foreign currency rises.

   a) This rightward shift of the demand curve results because holders of other currencies seek the higher returns available in the foreign country.

2) As more investors buy the high-interest country's currency to make investments, less of it is available, which is reflected in a leftward shift of the supply curve.

3) A new equilibrium point is at a higher price in terms of investors' domestic currencies.

   a) An investor's domestic currency has depreciated against the currency of a foreign country with higher interest rates.

Changes in Supply of and Demand for the Currency of a Foreign Country with Rising Interest Rates

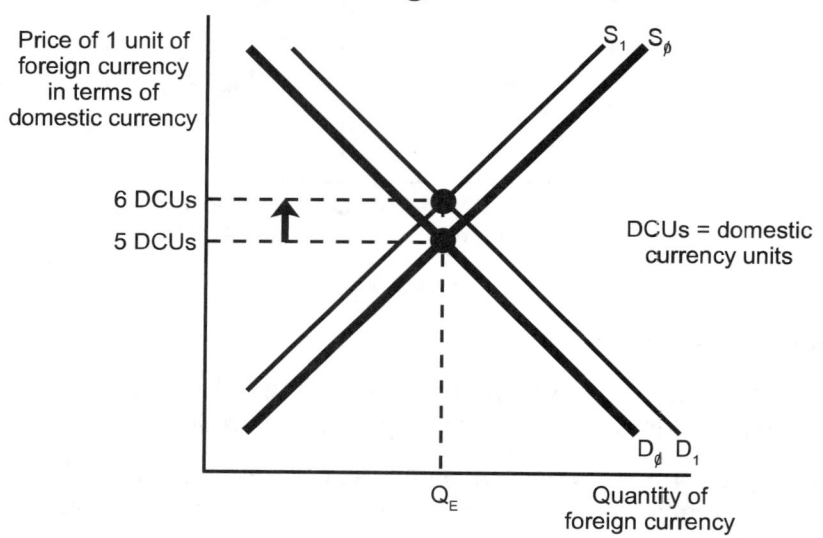

Figure 6-4

b. **Ease of Capital Flow**

1) If a country with high real interest rates removes restrictions on the cross-border movement of capital, the demand for the currency and the currency's value rises as investors seek higher returns.

2) This factor has become by far the most important of those listed.

   a) The speed with which capital can be moved electronically and the huge amounts involved in the global economy are more significant than the effects of the trade-related factors.

6. Graphical Depiction

Exchange Rate Determination

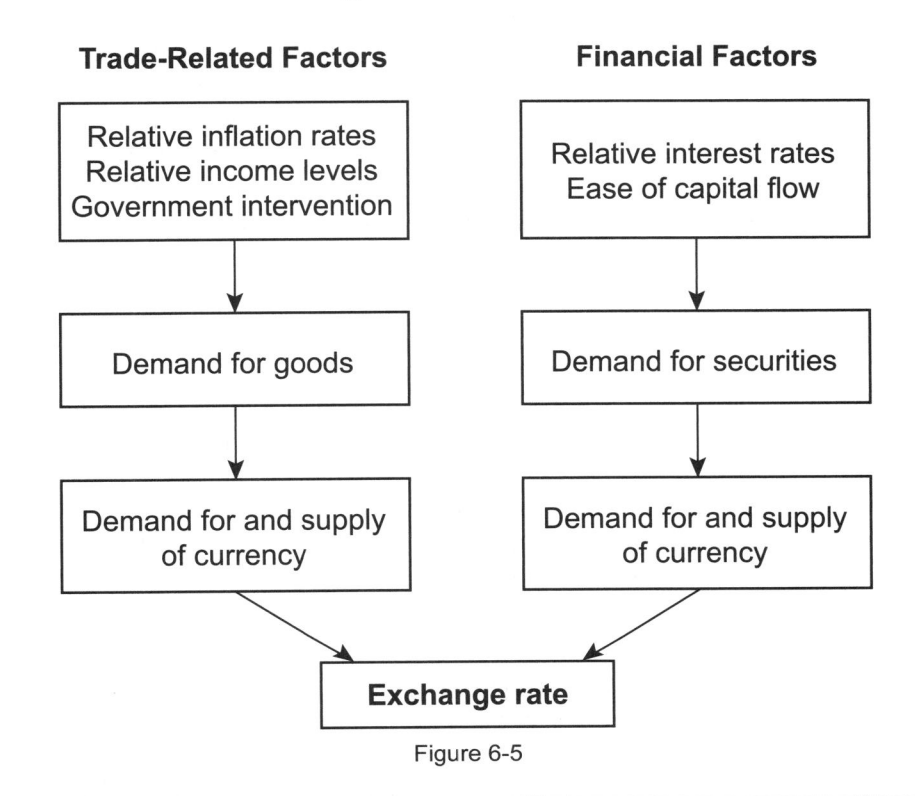

Trade-Related Factors

Relative inflation rates
Relative income levels
Government intervention

↓

Demand for goods

↓

Demand for and supply of currency

Financial Factors

Relative interest rates
Ease of capital flow

↓

Demand for securities

↓

Demand for and supply of currency

↓

Exchange rate

Figure 6-5

SUCCESS TIP

Candidates who can understand the relationship between the value of currency and financial or trade-related factors should be able to handle a variety of CPA questions. For example, when the real interest rate increases, the currency value appreciates. Also, when the real interest rate decreases, the currency value depreciates. Therefore, the real interest rate and the currency value have a direct relationship.

Trade-Related Factors that Occur in Domestic Economy	Domestic Currency Value	Foreign Currency Value*
Real interest rate	Direct	Indirect
Inflation rate	Indirect	Direct
Relative income level	Indirect	Direct
Demand for goods (or securities)	Direct	Indirect
Demand for currency	Direct	Indirect
Supply of currency	Indirect	Direct

*Assumes the foreign economy's trade-related factors are constant, i.e., are not changing.

7. **Exchange Rates**

   a. The **spot rate** is the number of units of a foreign currency that can be received today ("on the spot") in exchange for a single unit of the domestic currency.

   > **EXAMPLE 6-6   Spot Rate**
   >
   > A currency trader is willing to give 1.6 Swiss francs today in exchange for one British pound. Today's spot rate for the pound is therefore 1.6 Swiss francs, and today's spot rate for the franc is £0.625 (1 ÷ ₣1.6).

   b. The **forward rate** is the number of units of a foreign currency that can be received in exchange for a single unit of the domestic currency at some definite date in the future.

   > **EXAMPLE 6-7   Forward Rate**
   >
   > The currency trader contracts to provide 1.8 Swiss francs in exchange for one British pound 30 days from now. Today's 30-day forward rate for the pound is therefore 1.8 Swiss francs, and the 30-day forward rate for the franc is £0.555 (1 ÷ ₣1.8).

   c. If the exchange rate for the domestic currency is higher in relation to a foreign currency in the forward market than in the spot market, the domestic currency is trading at a **forward premium** in relation to the foreign currency.

   > **EXAMPLE 6-8   Forward Premium**
   >
   > The pound is currently trading at a forward premium in relation to the Swiss franc (₣1.8 > ₣1.6). The market believes that the pound is going to appreciate in relation to the Swiss franc.

   d. If the exchange rate for the domestic currency is lower in relation to a foreign currency in the forward market than in the spot market, the domestic currency is trading at a **forward discount** in relation to the foreign currency.

   > **EXAMPLE 6-9   Forward Discount**
   >
   > The Swiss franc is currently trading at a forward discount in relation to the pound (£0.555 < £0.625). The market believes that the Swiss franc is going to depreciate in relation to the pound.

   e. The implications of these relationships can be generalized as follows:

If the domestic currency is trading at a forward	Then it is expected to
Premium	Gain purchasing power
Discount	Lose purchasing power

STOP & REVIEW

You have completed the outline for this subunit.
Study multiple-choice questions 1 through 8 beginning on page 202.

6.2 DERIVATIVES

1. **Terminology**

    a. An entity has a **long position** in an asset whenever the entity benefits from a rise in the asset's value.

    > **EXAMPLE 6-10   Long Position**
    >
    > An investor buys 100 shares of Collerup Corporation stock. The investor now has a long position in Collerup Corporation. In financial market terminology, it is called "long Collerup."

    b. An entity has a **short position** in an asset when the entity benefits from a value decline. Entities take short positions when they believe the value of the asset will fall.

      1) Typically, the entity with the short position must borrow the asset from an entity that owns it before the "short sale" occurs.

    > **EXAMPLE 6-11   Short Position**
    >
    > Money Management Fund A believes that the share price of Collerup Corporation will decrease (perhaps due to a future poor earnings announcement). Fund A therefore borrows a block of Collerup shares from Fund B, which Fund A then sells on the appropriate stock exchange. Fund A is selling short because the fund can replace the borrowed shares later when the share value falls.
    >
    > - If the price of Collerup decreases, Fund A can repurchase the shares at the lower price and return them to Fund B, making a profit.
    > - If Fund A guessed wrong and the share price of Collerup remains the same or increases, then, to fulfill its obligation to return the borrowed shares to Fund B, Fund A must purchase the shares on the stock exchange (at the higher price), incurring a loss.

2. **Overview**

    a. A **derivative instrument** is an investment whose value is based on another asset's value, such as an option to buy shares (call option).

      1) For example, in a free and open exchange market (e.g., Stubhub), season tickets to a favorite sports team are based on the entertainment value (i.e., how well the team will perform) of the respective sports team. If the team does well, the individual tickets for future games can be sold for more money than if the team does not do well.

         a) Thus, the value of tickets (a derivative instrument) are based on the value of the team's performance (the underlying).

    b. The financial definition of a derivative instrument is a transaction in which each party's gain or loss is derived from some other economic event, for example, (1) the price of a given stock, (2) a foreign currency exchange rate, or (3) the price of a certain commodity.

      1) One party enters into the transaction to speculate (incur risk) and the other enters into it to hedge (avoid risk). Alternatively, two parties with opposite investments may work together to hedge each other.

    c. Derivatives are often used to hedge (or insure against) financial risks.

    d. Derivatives are a type of financial instrument, along with cash, accounts receivable, notes receivable, bonds, preferred shares, etc.

3. **Hedging**

   a. To hedge an investment, the entity takes a position in a financial instrument (usually a derivative) that is almost perfectly correlated with the original asset (the underlying) but in the opposite direction. By taking an opposite position in the derivative, the entity is able to effectively negate any changes in value to its original investment.

   b. Hedging uses offsetting commitments to minimize or avoid the effect of adverse price movements. For example, if the original investment would require the entity to make a $100 payment, the derivative investment (being used as a hedge) would pay the entity $100. Thus, the entity is effectively made whole by the derivative investment.

   1) Of course, this is how a hedge works in theory. In practice, the derivative instrument is not perfectly correlated. In a more realistic example, the entity may need to pay $102 and the derivative instrument would pay the entity $99.

   c. The overall goal of hedging is to minimize changes in total value and have the hedge act as insurance against price (or value) fluctuations.

   d. Consider this simple example of a hedge transaction: Your favorite sports team is playing against its rival, and you bet on the rival. If your favorite team wins, you are happy it beat its rival. If your favorite team loses, your sorrows are negated by the happiness of winning the bet.

4. **Options**

   a. A party who buys an option has bought the right to demand that the counterparty (the seller or writer of the option) buy or sell an underlying asset on or before a specified future date. The buyer holds all of the rights, and the seller has all of the obligations. The buyer pays a fee (option premium) to be able to determine whether the seller buys (sells) the underlying asset from (to) the buyer.

   > **SUCCESS TIP**
   >
   > Many CPA candidates become intimidated when studying options. A listed option is merely a standardized legal contract that requires two parties to comply with its terms. These contracts are no more complicated than the legal contract a person has with his or her cell phone carrier. Individuals pay the cell phone company money, and in return the cell phone provider is obligated to supply the individual with telephone service when the individual wants to make a phone call. Furthermore, some cell phone carriers charge on the basis of pay-as-you-go, while others charge a fixed amount for a fixed amount of minutes. There are many terms associated with cell phone providers and, similar to cell phones, options have their own terminology. The terms below are useful for people in finance because they indicate how a contract is standardized, allowing people to communicate quickly and succinctly when discussing options.

   1) A **call option** gives the buyer (holder) the right to purchase (the right to call for) the underlying asset (stock, currency, commodity, etc.) at a fixed price on or before the expiration date.

   2) A **put option** gives the buyer (holder) the right to sell (the right to put onto the market) the underlying asset (stock, currency, commodity, etc.) at a fixed price on or before the expiration date.

   3) The asset that is subject to being bought or sold under the terms of the option is the **underlying**.

   4) The party buying an option is the **holder**. The seller is the **writer**.

   5) The exercise of an option is always at the discretion of the option holder (the buyer) who has, in effect, bought the right to exercise the option or not. The seller of an option has no choice. (S)he must perform if the holder chooses to exercise.

   6) An option has an expiration date after which it can no longer be exercised.

5. **Valuing an Option**

    a. **Option premium** is the price or value of the option. Holders pay the option premium to acquire the right.

    b. The two best-known models for valuing options are the Black-Scholes formula for call options and the binomial method. The equations are beyond the scope of this text, but some general statements can be made about the factors that affect the outcomes.

    1) **Exercise price.** The exercise price (also called "strike price") is the price at which the holder can purchase (call option) or sell (put option) the underlying asset in the option contract.

        a) Thus, an increase in the exercise price of an option results in a decrease in the value of a call option and an increase in the value of a put option.

    2) **Price of the underlying.** As the price of the underlying increases, the value of a call option also increases.

        a) The value of a put option decreases as the price of the underlying increases. Selling at the exercise price, which is at a lower-than-market price, is not advantageous.

    3) **Interest rates.** Buying a call option is similar to buying the underlying on credit. Buying the right to purchase the underlying asset (call option) is much cheaper than buying the underlying asset directly due to the cost to carry the underlying asset.

        a) The holder of the call option may invest the difference between the option premium and the price of the underlying in a savings account and receive interest income. Thus, a rise in interest rates makes call options more attractive to buyers and increases their value.

            i) Instead of receiving interest income from selling the underlying asset and investing the proceeds in a saving account, the holder of a put option needs to hold the underlying asset to deliver it under the put option.

            ii) Thus, a rise in interest rates makes the put options less attractive to buyers (holders) and decreases the value of the put options.

    4) **Time until expiration.** The longer the term of an option, the greater the chance that the underlying price will change and the option will be **in-the-money**. A call option is "in-the-money" if, for example, the price of the underlying is $20 and the strike price is less than $20 (e.g., $15 or $19).

        a) Thus, when comparing two options that are similar except for time until expiration, an increase in the term of an option (both calls and puts) will result in an increase in the value of the option.

    5) **Volatility of price of the underlying.** Because the holder's loss on an option is limited to the option premium (amount paid for the option), the holder prefers greater volatility of the price of the underlying. The more volatile the price of the underlying, the greater the chance that it will change and the option will be in-the-money.

        a) An increase in the volatility of the price of the underlying results in an increase in the value of the option (both calls and puts).

c. These factors and their effects are summarized as follows:

Increase in	Value of call option	Value of put option
Exercise price of option	Decrease	Increase
Price of underlying	Increase	Decrease
Interest rates	Increase	Decrease
Time until expiration	Increase	Increase
Volatility of price of underlying	Increase	Increase

d. Intrinsic value is the value of the option today if it is exercised today. If the intrinsic value of an option is zero, it does not mean the market value of the option is zero because the value of an option includes the time value of money, interest rates, and market volatility in addition to the intrinsic value. Often, options trade at prices above their intrinsic value.

NOTE: Intrinsic value cannot be negative.

1) The **intrinsic value of a call option** is the amount by which the exercise price is less than the current price of the underlying.

    a) If an option has a positive intrinsic value, it is in-the-money.

EXAMPLE 6-12   Intrinsic Value of a Call Option

An investor holds call options for 200 shares of Locksley Corporation with an exercise price of $48 per share. Locksley stock is currently trading at $50 per share. The investor's options have an intrinsic value of $2 each ($50 − $48).

---

    b) If an option has an intrinsic value of $0, it is out-of-the-money.

EXAMPLE 6-13   Out-of-the-Money Call Options

An investor holds call options for 200 shares of Locksley Corporation with an exercise price of $48 per share. Locksley stock is currently trading at $45 per share. The investor's options are out-of-the-money. They have no intrinsic value.

Call Contract Position

Price of Underlying
Strike price $100
Price of call $10

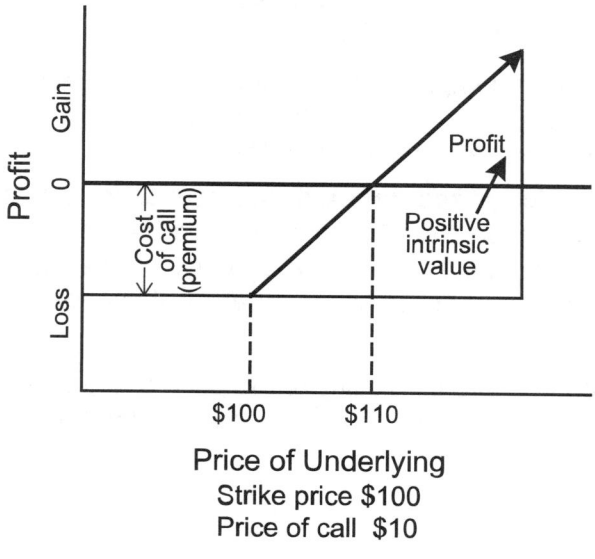

Figure 6-6

SU 6: Foreign Exchange and Derivatives 195

2) The **intrinsic value of a put option** is the amount by which the exercise price is greater than the current price of the underlying.

   a) If an option has a positive intrinsic value, it is in-the-money.

EXAMPLE 6-14   Intrinsic Value of a Put Option

An investor holds put options for 200 shares of Locksley Corporation with an exercise price of $48 per share. Locksley stock is currently trading at $45 per share. The investor's options have an intrinsic value of $3 each ($48 − $45).

---

   b) If an option has an intrinsic value of $0, it is out-of-the-money.

EXAMPLE 6-15   Out-of-the-Money Put Options

An investor holds put options for 200 shares of Locksley Corporation with an exercise price of $48 per share. Locksley stock is currently trading at $50 per share. The investor's options are out-of-the-money. They have no intrinsic value.

Put Contract Position

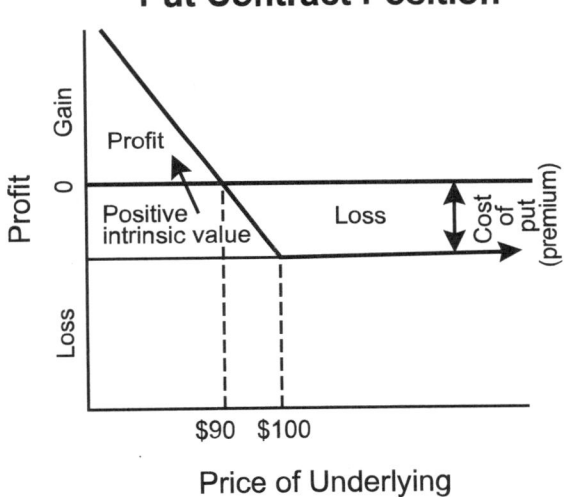

Price of Underlying
Strike price $100
Price of put $10

Figure 6-7

6. **Forward Contracts**

    a. One method of mitigating risk is the simple forward contract. These are not standardized contracts. The two parties agree that, at a set future date, one of them will perform and the other will pay a specified amount for the performance.

        1) A common example is that of a retailer and a wholesaler who agree in September on the prices and quantities of merchandise to be shipped to the retailer's stores in time for the winter holiday season. The retailer has locked in a price and a source of supply, and the wholesaler has locked in a price and a customer.

    b. The significant difference between a forward contract and a listed option is that a forward contract imposes obligations to fulfill the contractual obligations (e.g., delivering bushels of wheat or foreign currency). Both parties must meet those obligations, i.e., to deliver merchandise and to pay. On the other hand, listed options do not typically require fulfilling obligations, such as delivering wheat, and they are settled based on the net closing positions. Neither forward contracts nor listed options allow nonperformance.

        1) Forward contracts are frequently used in transactions to exchange foreign currencies.

7. **Futures Contracts**

    a. A futures contract is a commitment to buy or sell an asset at a fixed price during a specific future period. In contrast with a forward contract, the counterparty to a futures contract is unknown. In contrast with an options contract, a futures contract is a commitment, not a choice.

    b. Futures contracts are standardized forward contracts with predetermined quantities and dates. These standardized contracts are traded actively on futures exchanges.

        1) Forward contracts are negotiated individually between the parties on a one-by-one basis. In contrast, futures contracts are essentially commodities that are traded on an exchange, making them available to more parties.

            a) The clearinghouse matches sellers who will deliver during a given period with buyers who are seeking delivery during the same period. The clearinghouse also underwrites the contract, removing the risk of nonperformance by either party.

        2) Futures contracts are available only for standard amounts (e.g., 62,500 British pounds, 100,000 Brazilian reals, or 12,500,000 Japanese yen) and with specific settlement dates (typically the third Wednesday in March, June, September, and December).

            a) This rigidity makes them less flexible than forward contracts because forward contracts are customized for the parties.

BACKGROUND 6-1 Market for Trading Currency Futures

The largest market in the world for trading currency futures is the Chicago Mercantile Exchange.

- c. Because futures contracts are actively traded, the result is a **liquid market** in futures that permits buyers and sellers to net their positions. In contrast, forward contracts are not liquid because they are customized to meet the needs of each party and are not standardized.
- d. Another distinguishing feature of futures contracts is that the market price is posted and netted to each person's account at the close of every business day. In other words, each party's gains or losses are tallied in its brokerage account. If significant losses are incurred in the brokerage account, the broker requires funds be added to the brokerage account. This practice is called **mark-to-market**.
    1) A mark-to-market provision minimizes a futures contract's chance of default because profits and losses on the contracts must be received or paid each day through a clearinghouse.

EXAMPLE 6-16   Hedge of a Futures Contract

On August 1, Year 1, a firm wishes to hedge 120,000 Brazilian reals that it is contractually due to receive on November 7, Year 1. The spot rate on August 1, Year 1, is 3 USD/BRL. The firm sells a 100,000 December Year 1 Brazilian real futures contract at 2.8 USD/BRL. On November 1, Year 1, the company buys a 100,000 December Year 1 Brazilian real futures contract at 2.9 USD/BRL. The company then translates 120,000 real into U.S. dollars by selling 120,000 real on the spot market, which is trading at 2.92 USD/BRL.

$$(2.8 \text{ USD/BRL} - 2.9 \text{ USD/BRL}) \times 100{,}000 \text{ BRL} = \$(10{,}000)$$
$$120{,}000 \text{ BRL} \times 2.92 \text{ USD/BRL} = \$350{,}400$$
$$\text{Net proceeds} = \$340{,}400$$
$$\text{Effective exchange rate} = 340{,}400 \text{ USD} \div 120{,}000 \text{ BRL} = 2.84$$

---

8. **Margin Requirements**
    a. A **margin account** is a brokerage account in which the investor borrows money (obtains credit) from a broker to purchase securities, such as derivative instruments. The broker charges interest on the credit provided.
    b. A **margin requirement** (set by the Federal Reserve Board's Regulation T) is the minimum down payment that the purchasers of securities must deposit in the margin account.
        1) When the margin account falls below the margin requirement, the broker informs the investor to add funds to the account. This is called a **margin call**.

STOP & REVIEW

You have completed the outline for this subunit.
Study multiple-choice questions 9 through 15 beginning on page 205.

6.3 MITIGATING EXCHANGE RATE RISK

SUCCESS TIP: Currency exchange is one of the biggest financial risks firms face in the global economy. The AICPA tests this area heavily on the CPA Exam.

1. **Exchange Rate Fluctuations**
   a. Fluctuations in currency exchange rates can significantly affect a firm's profits.
   b. The settlement date is the future date when the transaction will occur. The settlement amount is the agreed-upon amount of the transaction.
   c. Currencies are exchanged at the spot market price. When a party wires money internationally, the currency is exchanged on the spot market.
   d. A firm with a **payable** denominated in a **foreign** currency wants the foreign currency to depreciate by the settlement date so that fewer units of its domestic currency are required to pay the debt.
      1) A firm with a **payable** denominated in the **domestic** currency is indifferent to fluctuations in the exchange rate for the two currencies. The settlement amount is fixed in terms of its domestic currency.
   e. A firm with a **receivable** denominated in a **foreign** currency wants the foreign currency to appreciate by the settlement date. When the firm converts the foreign currency into its domestic currency, the conversion results in more units of the domestic currency.
      1) A firm with a **receivable** denominated in its **domestic** currency is indifferent to fluctuations in the exchange rate for the two currencies. The settlement amount is fixed in terms of its domestic currency.
   f. These effects can be summarized in the following table:

| | A Domestic Firm with Foreign Currency ||
As of the Settlement Date	Net Inflows	Net Outflows
	Will Experience a	
If the domestic currency has appreciated and the foreign currency has depreciated	(Loss)	Gain
If the domestic currency has depreciated and the foreign currency has appreciated	Gain	(Loss)

2. **Exposures to Exchange Rate Risk**
   a. **Transaction exposure** is the exposure to fluctuations in exchange rates between the date a transaction is entered into and the settlement date.
   b. **Economic exposure** is the exposure to fluctuations in exchange rates resulting from overall economic conditions.
   c. **Translation exposure** is the exposure to fluctuations in exchange rates between the date a transaction is entered into and the date that financial statements denominated in another currency must be reported.

3. **Transaction Exposure**
   a. Multinational corporations enter into numerous individual cross-border transactions during a year. Each transaction is subject to exchange rate variations between the transaction date and the settlement date.
   b. To address transaction exposure, a firm must
      1) Estimate its net cash flows in each currency for affected transactions
         a) If inflows and outflows in a given currency are nearly equal, transaction exposure is minimal, even if the currency itself is volatile.
      2) Measure the potential effect of exposure in each currency
         a) A range of possible rates for each currency must be estimated, reflecting that currency's volatility.
      3) Use hedging methods to mitigate exposure to exchange rate fluctuations

4. **Hedging in Response to Transaction Exposure**
   a. Hedging and Uncertainty
      1) When hedging, some amount of possible gain is forgone to protect against potential loss.
   b. Basic Hedging Principles
      1) When a debtor is to pay a foreign currency amount at some time in the future, the risk is that the foreign currency will appreciate. If the foreign currency appreciates, more domestic currency is required to pay the debt.
      2) The hedge is to purchase the foreign currency forward to fix a definite price.

EXAMPLE 6-17   Hedge of a Foreign Currency Liability

A U.S. firm knows that it will need 100,000 Canadian dollars in 60 days to pay an invoice. The firm hedges by purchasing 100,000 Canadian dollars 60 days forward. The firm is buying a guarantee that it will have C $100,000 available for use in 60 days. The 60-day forward rate for a Canadian dollar is US $0.99. Thus, for the privilege of having a guaranteed receipt of 100,000 Canadian dollars, the firm commits now to paying $99,000 in 60 days.

The counterparty to the hedge (the seller of Canadian dollars) also might be hedging, but it could be speculating or simply making a market in the instrument. The two parties are indifferent to each other's goals.

---

      3) When a creditor is to receive a foreign currency amount at some time in the future, the risk is that the foreign currency will depreciate. If the foreign currency depreciates, the creditor receives less domestic currency in the conversion.
      4) The hedge is to sell the foreign currency forward to fix a definite price.

EXAMPLE 6-18   Hedge of a Foreign Currency Receivable

A U.S. firm knows that it will be receiving 5,000,000 pesos in 30 days from the sale of some equipment at one of its facilities in Mexico. The spot rate for a peso is $0.77, and the 30-day forward rate is $0.80. The firm wants to be certain that it can sell the pesos it will receive in 30 days for $0.80 each. The firm hedges by selling 5,000,000 pesos 30 days forward. The firm is buying a guarantee that it can sell 5,000,000 pesos in 30 days and receive $4,000,000 (5,000,000 × $0.80) in return.

The spot rate on day 30 is $0.82. Thus, the U.S. firm could have made more money by forgoing the hedge and simply waiting to convert the pesos on day 30. However, this possibility was not worth the risk that the peso might have fallen below $0.80.

The counterparty to the hedge (the buyer of pesos) also might be hedging, but it could be speculating or simply making a market in the instrument. The two parties are indifferent to each other's goals.

c. The following are the most common methods for addressing transaction exposure:

1) **Money Market Hedges**

   a) The least complex method for hedging exchange rate risk is the money market hedge.

   b) A firm with a payable denominated in a foreign currency can buy a money market instrument denominated in that currency that is timed to mature when the payable is due. Exchange rate fluctuations between the transaction date and the settlement date are avoided.

   c) A firm with a receivable denominated in a foreign currency can borrow the amount and convert it to its domestic currency now, then pay the foreign loan when the receivable is collected.

2) **Forward Contracts**

   a) Large corporations that have close relationships with major banks can enter into contracts for individual transactions in large amounts.

   b) The bank guarantees that it will make available to the firm a given quantity of a certain currency at a definite rate at some time in the future. The price charged by the bank for this guarantee is the premium.

EXAMPLE 6-19   Foreign Currency Forward Contracts

A large U.S. firm purchases equipment from a Korean manufacturer for 222,000,000 won, due in 90 days. The exchange rate on the date of sale is $1 to 1,110 won. The U.S. firm suspects that the won may appreciate over the next 90 days and wants to fix a forward rate of 1-to-1,110. The firm negotiates a contract in which its bank promises to deliver 222,000,000 won to the firm in 90 days for $200,000. In return for this guarantee, the firm pays the bank a 2% premium ($200,000 × 2% = $4,000).

---

   c) The use of any mitigation strategy has an opportunity cost. The firm in the example above must execute its part of the contract whether or not the exchange rate with the won has fluctuated.

   i) If the won falls in value or rises less than the 2% premium in relation to the dollar, the firm has incurred an economic loss on the transaction.

3) **Futures Contracts** (discussed on page 196 in the previous subunit)

4) **Currency Options** (discussed on pages 192 through 195 in the previous subunit)

5. **Economic Exposure**

   a. Economic exposure is the exposure to fluctuations in exchange rates resulting from overall economic conditions.

EXAMPLE 6-20   Effects of Economic Conditions on Exchange Rates

An exporter may require all of its customers to pay their invoices in the exporter's domestic currency. Thus, customers bear all the transaction risk of exchange rate variation. If the exporter's currency appreciates beyond a certain exchange rate, the exporter's products no longer will be price-competitive, and the customers will buy from local firms, reducing the exporter's cash inflows.

A manufacturer establishes operations in a low-wage country. As that country's economy strengthens, its currency appreciates and real wages increase. The manufacturer's cash outflows therefore have increased, eliminating the original cost advantage.

b. Estimating Economic Exposure

1) The degree of exposure can be estimated using either of two approaches:

a) Sensitivity of earnings. The entity prepares a pro forma income statement for operations in each country.

b) Sensitivity of cash flows. The entity performs a regression analysis, weighting each net cash flow by the amount of that currency in the firm's portfolio.

2) Next, the entity constructs multiple scenarios (performs a sensitivity analysis) using various estimated exchange rates and determines the ultimate effect of each scenario on accrual-basis earnings or cash flows.

c. Mitigating Economic Exposure

1) A high level of economic exposure may require restructuring the entity's operations using the following guidelines:

Reliance on	Actions to Be Taken when Foreign Currency	
	Inflows Are Greater	Outflows Are Greater
Sales to foreign customers	Reduce foreign sales	Increase foreign sales
Purchases from foreign suppliers	Increase foreign orders	Reduce foreign orders

6. **Translation Exposure**

a. Translation exposure is the risk that a foreign subsidiary's balance sheet items and results of operations, denominated in a currency different from the parent's, will change as a result of exchange rate fluctuations.

b. The degree of a firm's exposure to translation risk is determined by three factors:

1) Proportion of Total Business Conducted by Foreign Subsidiaries

a) A firm with half of its revenues derived from overseas subsidiaries has a high degree of exposure to translation risk. A 100% domestic firm has none.

b) A 100% domestic firm with foreign customers or suppliers still has transaction and economic risk.

2) Locations of Foreign Subsidiaries

a) A firm with a subsidiary in a country with a volatile currency has more translation risk than a firm with a subsidiary in a country with a stable currency.

3) Applicable Accounting Method

a) This can be either a cash flow hedge or fair value.

STOP & REVIEW

You have completed the outline for this subunit.
Study multiple-choice questions 16 through 22 beginning on page 208.

QUESTIONS

6.1 Currency Exchange Rates

1. If the value of the U.S. dollar in foreign currency markets changes from $1 = .75 euros to $1 = .70 euros,

A. The euro has depreciated against the dollar.
B. Products imported from Europe to the U.S. will become more expensive.
C. U.S. tourists in Europe will find their dollars will buy more European products.
D. U.S. exports to Europe should decrease.

Answer (B) is correct.
REQUIRED: The effect of a depreciation in the value of the dollar.
DISCUSSION: The dollar has declined in value relative to the euro. If an American had previously wished to purchase a European product that was priced at 10 euros, the price would have been about $13.33. After the dollar's decline in value, the price of the item has increased to about $14.29. Thus, imports from Europe should decrease and exports should increase.
Answer (A) is incorrect. The euro has appreciated (increased in value) relative to the dollar. **Answer (C) is incorrect.** Dollars will buy fewer European products. **Answer (D) is incorrect.** U.S. exports should increase because the euro has appreciated with respect to the dollar.

2. If the U.S. dollar-peso exchange rate is $1 for 9 pesos, a product priced at 45 pesos will cost a U.S. consumer

A. $0.20
B. $5
C. $45
D. $405

Answer (B) is correct.
REQUIRED: The price in dollars of a product for which the price is quoted in pesos.
DISCUSSION: At a 1-for-9 rate, the price in U.S. dollars is $5, calculated by dividing 45 pesos by 9.
Answer (A) is incorrect. The amount of $0.20 is based on an inversion of the numerator and denominator in the calculation. **Answer (C) is incorrect.** The amount of $45 is the price in pesos, not dollars. **Answer (D) is incorrect.** The amount of $405 is based on multiplying 45 and 9.

3. If the central bank of a country raises interest rates sharply, the country's currency will likely

A. Increase in relative value.
B. Remain unchanged in value.
C. Decrease in relative value.
D. Decrease sharply in value at first and then return to its initial value.

Answer (A) is correct.
REQUIRED: The effect on a country's currency if its central bank raises interest rates sharply.
DISCUSSION: Exchange rates fluctuate depending upon the demand for each country's currency. If a country raises its interest rates, its currency will appreciate. The demand for investment at the higher interest rates will shift the demand curve for the currency to the right. The reverse holds true for a decrease in interest rates.

SU 6: Foreign Exchange and Derivatives

4. The U.S. dollar has a freely floating exchange rate. When the dollar has fallen considerably in relation to other currencies, the

A. Trade account in the U.S. balance of payments is neither in a deficit nor in a surplus because of the floating exchange rates.

B. Capital account in the U.S. balance of payments is neither in a deficit nor in a surplus because of the floating exchange rates.

C. Fall in the dollar's value cannot be expected to have any effect on the U.S. trade balance.

D. Cheaper dollar helps U.S. exporters of domestically produced goods.

Answer (D) is correct.
  REQUIRED: The true statement about the fall in the price of the dollar relative to other currencies.
  DISCUSSION: A decline in the value of the dollar relative to other currencies lowers the price of U.S. goods to foreign consumers. Thus, exporters of domestically produced goods benefit. A low value of the dollar also decreases imports by making foreign goods more expensive.
  Answer (A) is incorrect. Net exports increase as a result of dollar depreciation. **Answer (B) is incorrect.** The capital account benefits from the cheaper dollar. Foreigners can buy more dollars with fewer yen, euros, etc. Moreover, foreign capital inflow increases because of the federal government's budget deficits. Thus, the U.S. has a net capital inflow. **Answer (C) is incorrect.** The fall in the dollar has a positive effect on the nation's trade deficit. Exports increase and imports decrease.

5. The spot rate for one Australian dollar is $0.92685 and the 60-day forward rate is $0.93005. Which one of the following statements is consistent with these facts?

A. The U.S. dollar is trading at a forward discount with respect to the Australian dollar.

B. The U.S. dollar is trading at a forward premium with respect to the Australian dollar.

C. The U.S. dollar has lost purchasing power with respect to the Australian dollar.

D. The U.S. dollar has gained purchasing power with respect to the Australian dollar.

Answer (A) is correct.
  REQUIRED: The conclusion about a forward exchange rate.
  DISCUSSION: The exchange rate for the Australian dollar is higher in the forward market than the spot market. The Australian dollar is therefore trading at a forward premium. Accordingly, the U.S. dollar is trading at a forward discount.
  Answer (B) is incorrect. The U.S. dollar is trading at a forward discount in relation to the Australian dollar. **Answer (C) is incorrect.** No conclusion about purchasing power changes can be drawn without information about past exchange rates. **Answer (D) is incorrect.** No conclusion about purchasing power changes can be drawn without information about past exchange rates.

6. A shift of the demand curve for a country's currency to the right could be caused by which of the following?

A. A foreign government placing restrictions on the importation of the country's goods.

B. A fall in the country's interest rates.

C. Domestic inflation worsens.

D. A rise in consumer incomes in another country.

Answer (D) is correct.
  REQUIRED: The condition that could cause a rise in demand for a country's currency.
  DISCUSSION: Citizens with higher incomes look for new consumption opportunities in other countries, driving up the demand for those currencies. Thus, as incomes rise in one country, the prices of foreign currencies rise as well.
  Answer (A) is incorrect. A shift to the right is caused by a foreign government's removal of restrictions on the importation of the country's goods. **Answer (B) is incorrect.** A shift to the right is caused by a rise, not a fall, in the country's interest rates. **Answer (C) is incorrect.** As a country's inflation rate rises, its currency loses purchasing power and investors move their capital elsewhere, reducing demand for the country's currency.

7. The accompanying graph depicts the supply of and demand for U.S. dollars in terms of euros at a moment in time. Currently, the equilibrium exchange rate is $1 to 0.65 €. If inflation of the dollar exceeds that of the euro, the new equilibrium exchange rate would most likely settle at

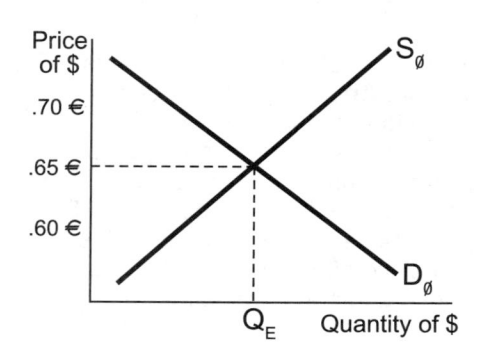

	Quantity	Price
A.	Indeterminate	0.70 €
B.	Lower than Q_E	0.70 €
C.	Higher than Q_E	0.60 €
D.	Indeterminate	0.60 €

Answer (D) is correct.
REQUIRED: The graphic depiction of inflation of a base currency against a foreign currency.
DISCUSSION: The graph depicts the supply of and demand for the U.S. dollar by holders of euros. When the U.S. dollar inflates faster than the euro, the U.S. dollar loses purchasing power. As the weakening U.S. dollar becomes less attractive, the demand for it falls (its demand curve shifts to the left) and the supply for it increases (its supply curve shifts to the right). A new equilibrium point is at a lower price. However, a new equilibrium quantity cannot be determined. If the supply curve shift is greater (lesser) than the demand curve shift, the new equilibrium quantity will be higher (lower); if the supply curve shift is equal to the demand curve shift, the equilibrium quantity will remain the same.
Answer (A) is incorrect. The new equilibrium price will be lower. **Answer (B) is incorrect.** The new equilibrium quantity cannot be determined, and the new equilibrium price will be lower. **Answer (C) is incorrect.** The new equilibrium quantity cannot be determined.

8. Which one of the following statements supports the conclusion that the U.S. dollar has gained purchasing power against the Japanese yen?

A. Inflation has recently been higher in the U.S. than in Japan.

B. The dollar is currently trading at a premium in the forward market with respect to the yen.

C. The yen's spot rate with respect to the dollar has just fallen.

D. Studies recently published in the financial press have shed doubt on the interest rate parity (IRP) theory.

Answer (C) is correct.
REQUIRED: The statement that supports the conclusion that the U.S. dollar has gained purchasing power against the Japanese yen.
DISCUSSION: If the yen's spot rate has just fallen, more yen are required to buy a single dollar. The yen has therefore depreciated, i.e., lost purchasing power. At the same time, the dollar has gained purchasing power.
Answer (A) is incorrect. Higher inflation in the U.S. than in Japan reflects a loss, not a gain, of the dollar's purchasing power. **Answer (B) is incorrect.** No conclusion can be drawn about changes in purchasing power simply from a statement about forward rates. **Answer (D) is incorrect.** No conclusion can be drawn about changes in purchasing power simply from evidence for or against the interest rate parity (IRP) theory.

6.2 Derivatives

9. The use of derivatives to either hedge or speculate results in

- A. Increased risk regardless of motive.
- B. Decreased risk regardless of motive.
- C. Offsetting risk when hedging and increased risk when speculating.
- D. Offsetting risk when speculating and increased risk when hedging.

Answer (C) is correct.
REQUIRED: The effects on risk of hedging and speculating.
DISCUSSION: Derivatives, including options and futures, are contracts. Unlike stocks and bonds, they are not claims on business assets. A futures contract is entered into as either a speculation or a hedge. Speculation involves the assumption of risk in the hope of gaining from price movements. Hedging is the process of using offsetting commitments to minimize or avoid the effect of adverse price movements.
Answer (A) is incorrect. Hedging decreases risk by using offsetting commitments that avoid the impact of adverse price movements. **Answer (B) is incorrect.** Speculation involves the assumption of risk in the hope of gaining from price movements. **Answer (D) is incorrect.** Speculating increases risk, while hedging offsets risk.

10. A put is an option that gives its owner the right to do which of the following?

- A. Sell a specific security at fixed conditions of price and time.
- B. Sell a specific security at a fixed price for an indefinite time period.
- C. Buy a specific security at fixed conditions of price and time.
- D. Buy a specific security at a fixed price for an indefinite time period.

Answer (A) is correct.
REQUIRED: The right of the owner of a put option.
DISCUSSION: A put option gives the buyer the right to sell the underlying asset at a fixed price. An option has an expiration date after which it can no longer be exercised.
Answer (B) is incorrect. An option has an expiration date after which it can no longer be exercised. **Answer (C) is incorrect.** A call option gives the buyer the right to buy the underlying asset. **Answer (D) is incorrect.** A call option gives the buyer the right to buy the underlying asset. An option can no longer be exercised after the expiration date.

11. Each of the following financial instruments is a derivative **except**

- A. A fixed interest, 5-year note payable.
- B. Interest rate futures.
- C. An agreement to buy a piece of equipment in 6 months at a price determined today.
- D. A contract to purchase a commodity in 6 months at a price determined today.

Answer (A) is correct.
REQUIRED: The financial instrument that is not a derivative.
DISCUSSION: A derivative instrument is an investment transaction (financial contract) in which the parties' gain or loss is derived from some other economic event, for example, the price of a given stock, a foreign currency exchange rate, or the price of a certain commodity. A fixed interest note payable is not considered a derivative as its value is not derived from some other underlying asset or economic event.
Answer (B) is incorrect. A futures contract is a commitment to buy or sell an asset at a fixed price during a specific future period. Since the price of (gain or loss on) interest rate futures is derived from the underlying interest bearing asset, futures are a type of derivative. **Answer (C) is incorrect.** This is an example of a forward contract. A forward contract is a derivative, since the gain or loss from the contract is derived from the difference between the price of the equipment today and the price 6 months from today. **Answer (D) is incorrect.** This is an example of a forward contract. A forward contract is a derivative, since the gain or loss from the contract is derived from the difference between the price of the commodity today and the price 6 months from today.

12. An accountant using the Black-Scholes model to value stock options has input the exercise price of the options, the time to expiration for the options, and an interest rate. Which of the following variables also is required for the model?

A. Common stock price.
B. Put market price.
C. Call market price.
D. Discount rate.

Answer (A) is correct.
REQUIRED: The variable required for the Black-Scholes model.
DISCUSSION: The Black-Scholes formula is a model for valuing options. The variables required for the model include exercise price, price of the underlying, interest rates, and time until expiration. Because the accountant has already input the exercise price of the options, the time to expiration for the options, and an interest rate, the other variable required is the price of the underlying. The asset that is subject to being bought or sold under the terms of the option is the underlying. Because the accountant uses the model to value stock options, stock is the underlying, and common stock price is required for the model.
Answer (B) is incorrect. The Black-Scholes formula requires the following inputs: exercise price, price of the underlying, applicable interest rates, and the time until expiration. Therefore, the price of the underlying is still required. The underlying security for options is generally common stock. As such, the put market price is not required. Answer (C) is incorrect. The Black-Scholes method requires the following inputs: exercise price, price of the underlying, applicable interest rates, and the time until expiration. According to the facts of the question, the price of the underlying is still required. The underlying security for options is generally common stock. As such, the call market price is not required. Answer (D) is incorrect. The Black-Scholes method requires the following inputs: exercise price, price of the underlying, applicable interest rates, and the time until expiration. Therefore, a discount rate is not required.

13. Which of the following options is (are) worth exercising?

	Exercise Price	Price of Underlying Asset
Put Option A	$30	$27
Call Option B	$29	$26
Put Option C	$25	$25
Call Option D	$20	$24

A. Options A, B, and C.
B. Options A and B.
C. Options A and D.
D. Option D only.

Answer (C) is correct.
REQUIRED: The option(s) that is(are) worth exercising.
DISCUSSION: An option is worth exercising if its intrinsic value is positive. A call option gives the holder the right to purchase (i.e., call for) the underlying asset at a fixed price, called the exercise or strike price. The intrinsic value of a call option is the amount by which the exercise price is less than the market price of the underlying asset. Thus, the intrinsic value of call option D is positive ($24 − $20 = $4). A put option gives the holder the right to sell (i.e., put onto the market) the underlying asset at a fixed price. The intrinsic value of a put option is the amount by which the exercise price is greater than the price of the underlying asset. Thus, the intrinsic value of put option A is positive ($30 − $27 = $3).
Answer (A) is incorrect. Because their intrinsic values are $0, options B and C are not worth exercising. Answer (B) is incorrect. The intrinsic value of call option B is $0. The holder of this option will prefer to buy the underlying asset at its market price of $26 rather than to exercise the option to buy this asset for $29. Answer (D) is incorrect. Option A is also worth exercising. Its intrinsic value ($30 − $27 = $3) is positive.

14. A forward contract involves a commitment today to purchase a product

A. On a specific future date at a price to be determined some time in the future.
B. At some time during the current day at its present price.
C. On a specific future date at a price determined today.
D. Only when its price increases above its current exercise price.

Answer (C) is correct.
   REQUIRED: The terms of a forward contract.
   DISCUSSION: A forward contract is an executory contract in which the parties involved agree to the terms of a purchase and a sale, but performance is deferred. Accordingly, a forward contract involves a commitment today to purchase a product on a specific future date at a price determined today.
   Answer (A) is incorrect. The price of a forward contract is determined on the day of commitment, not some time in the future. **Answer (B) is incorrect.** Performance is deferred in a forward contract, and the price of the product is not necessarily its present price. The price can be any price determined on the day of commitment. **Answer (D) is incorrect.** A forward contract is a firm commitment to purchase a product. It is not based on a contingency. Also, a forward contract does not involve an exercise price. (An exercise price is an element of an option contract.)

15. A distinguishing feature of a futures contract is that

A. Performance is delayed.
B. It is a hedge, not a speculation.
C. The parties know each other.
D. The price is marked to market each day.

Answer (D) is correct.
   REQUIRED: The distinguishing feature of a futures contract.
   DISCUSSION: A characteristic of futures contracts is that their prices are marked to market every day at the close of the day. Thus, the market price is posted at the close of business each day. A mark-to-market provision minimizes a futures contract's chance of default because profits and losses on the contracts must be received or paid each day through a clearinghouse.
   Answer (A) is incorrect. Both a forward contract and a futures contract are executory. **Answer (B) is incorrect.** A futures contract may be speculative. **Answer (C) is incorrect.** In a forward contract, the parties know each other. In a future contract, the counterparty is unknown.

6.3 Mitigating Exchange Rate Risk

16. An American importer of English clothing has contracted to pay an amount fixed in British pounds 3 months from now. If the importer worries that the U.S. dollar may depreciate sharply against the British pound in the interim, it would be well advised to

A. Buy pounds in the forward exchange market.
B. Sell pounds in the forward exchange market.
C. Buy dollars in the futures market.
D. Sell dollars in the futures market.

Answer (A) is correct.
REQUIRED: The action to hedge a liability denominated in a foreign currency.
DISCUSSION: The American importer should buy pounds now. If the dollar depreciates against the pound in the next 90 days, the gain on the forward exchange contract offsets the loss from having to pay more dollars to satisfy the liability.
Answer (B) is incorrect. Selling pounds increases the risk of loss for someone who has incurred a liability. However, it is an appropriate hedge of a receivable denominated in pounds. **Answer (C) is incorrect.** The importer needs pounds, not dollars. **Answer (D) is incorrect.** Although buying pounds might be equivalent to selling dollars for pounds, this is not the best answer. This choice does not state what is received for the dollars.

17. An American importer expects to pay a British supplier 500,000 British pounds in 3 months. Which of the following hedges is best for the importer to fix the price in dollars?

A. Buying British pound call options.
B. Buying British pound put options.
C. Selling British pound put options.
D. Selling British pound call options.

Answer (A) is correct.
REQUIRED: The best hedge of an expected payment in British pounds.
DISCUSSION: The importer wants to hedge the risk that the fixed amount of foreign currency it must pay in 3 months will gain purchasing power during that time. Buying a call option gives the importer the right to buy (call for) the foreign currency in 3 months at a fixed price, regardless of exchange rate fluctuations in the meantime.
Answer (B) is incorrect. A put option gives the owner the right to sell the underlying asset for a fixed price. It represents a short position because the owner benefits from a price decrease. Accordingly, buying British pound put options serves to hedge a future receipt (not payment) of pounds. **Answer (C) is incorrect.** Selling British pound put options allows the buyer to hedge the risk of holding pounds. **Answer (D) is incorrect.** Selling British pound call options allows the buyer to hedge the risk of an expected purchase of pounds.

18. An importing partnership has experienced a dramatic surge in its exporting business and is looking for ways to minimize its risks from foreign currency fluctuations. The partnership's imports and exports to European Union countries are at similar levels. Which of the following methods most effectively minimizes risk?

A. Purchase futures of the currency in which the payables will be paid.
B. Hold payables and receivables due in the same currency and amount.
C. Enter into an interest rate swap to mitigate the effects of exchange rate fluctuations.
D. Conduct all foreign transactions in U.S. dollars.

Answer (B) is correct.
REQUIRED: The most effective method of mitigating exchange rate risk.
DISCUSSION: By holding payables and receivables in the same currency and amount, any currency fluctuations will simultaneously cause the same gains and losses, eliminating the effects of the currency fluctuation. With imports and exports at similar levels, this is a realistic strategy to pursue.
Answer (A) is incorrect. Purchasing futures of the currency in which payables will be paid only mitigates exchange risk from foreign currency imports and does not mitigate the risks associated with foreign currency exports. **Answer (C) is incorrect.** An interest rate swap mitigates risk related to variable interest rates, not currency. **Answer (D) is incorrect.** It is impractical, and likely impossible, to perform all foreign transactions in U.S. dollars. The prices of products in European Union countries are not generally nominated in U.S. dollars.

19. A U.S. manufacturer sold a piece of equipment to an engineering firm in New Zealand. The New Zealand firm must pay the invoice in U.S. dollars in 30 days and would like to mitigate the risk that the New Zealand dollar will depreciate against the U.S. dollar in the meantime. The type of exchange rate risk contemplated by the New Zealand firm is known as

A. Transition exposure.
B. Economic exposure.
C. Transaction exposure.
D. Translation exposure.

Answer (C) is correct.
REQUIRED: The type of exchange rate exposure embodied in a sale transaction.
DISCUSSION: Transaction exposure is the exposure to fluctuations in exchange rates between the date a transaction is entered into and the settlement date.
Answer (A) is incorrect. Transition exposure is not a meaningful term. **Answer (B) is incorrect.** Economic exposure is the exposure to fluctuations in exchange rates resulting from overall economic conditions. **Answer (D) is incorrect.** Translation exposure is the risk that a foreign subsidiary's balance sheet items and the results of operations denominated in a currency different from the parent's currency will change in value as a result of exchange rate changes.

20. A company based in West Palm Beach, Florida, is building a resort in Jamaica. The Jamaican property owners must make a progress payment of US $1 million in 30 days. The spot rate for the U.S. dollar is 88 Jamaican dollars (J $), and the 30-day forward rate is J $90. The most likely hedge in response to the transaction exposure inherent in this situation is

A. The contractor will purchase J $88,000,000 in the spot market.
B. The contractor will sell J $90,000,000 in the 30-day forward market.
C. The property owners will purchase US $1,000,000 in the 30-day forward market.
D. The property owners will sell US $1,000,000 in the 30-day forward market.

Answer (C) is correct.
REQUIRED: The most likely hedging transaction in response to a receivable/payable.
DISCUSSION: This receivable or payable is denominated in the currency of the creditor. Thus, the creditor has no incentive to hedge. The debtors (the property owners) want to hedge against the possibility that their domestic currency will depreciate against the U.S. dollar in the next 30 days. The typical mitigation strategy is to purchase the amount needed to pay the debt so that funds are available when needed.
Answer (A) is incorrect. The party on the receivable side of this transaction has no need to hedge. The debt is denominated in its domestic currency. **Answer (B) is incorrect.** The party on the receivable side of this transaction has no need to hedge. The debt is denominated in its domestic currency. **Answer (D) is incorrect.** The debtors need US $1,000,000 in 30 days to pay the invoice. Thus, they will purchase, not sell, the U.S. dollar in the forward market.

21. A company headquartered in Vancouver, British Columbia, is building a pipeline for a company in Russia. The invoice amount is due in 90 days and is denominated at 28 million rubles. The Canadian dollar is trading for 28 rubles currently and 29 rubles 90 days forward. Which of the following strategies will the Canadian firm most likely pursue in the 90-day forward market to hedge the transaction exposure inherent in this situation?

A. Sell 29,000,000 rubles.
B. Purchase 28,000,000 rubles.
C. Purchase 29,000,000 rubles.
D. Sell 28,000,000 rubles.

Answer (D) is correct.
REQUIRED: The most likely hedging transaction in response to a foreign-denominated receivable.
DISCUSSION: The Canadian company knows that it will be receiving 28,000,000 rubles in 90 days. The firm wants to ensure that it will be able to sell these rubles at that time for a certain number of Canadian dollars. The Canadian firm therefore hedges by selling 28,000,000 rubles in the 90-day forward market. The company is buying a guarantee that it will be able to sell a definite number of rubles in 90 days and receive a definite number of Canadian dollars in return, regardless of fluctuations in the exchange rate in the meantime.
Answer (A) is incorrect. The creditor firm will receive only 28 million rubles. **Answer (B) is incorrect.** The creditor firm wants to sell, not purchase, forward rubles. **Answer (C) is incorrect.** The creditor firm wants to sell, not purchase, forward rubles. Also, the firm will receive only 28 million rubles.

22. A company with significant sales in a particular foreign country has recently been subjected to extreme variations in the exchange rate with that country's currency. These variations are expected to continue. To mitigate the resulting economic exposure, a likely strategy for the company to implement would be to

A. Reduce sales to that country.
B. Increase sales to that country.
C. Reduce orders from suppliers in other foreign countries.
D. Increase orders from suppliers in other foreign countries.

Answer (A) is correct.
REQUIRED: The most likely strategy to mitigate economic exposure to exchange rate variation.
DISCUSSION: When cash inflows from a country with a volatile currency exceed cash outflows to that country, the appropriate strategy to mitigate economic exposure is to decrease sales to that country.
Answer (B) is incorrect. The appropriate strategy to mitigate this economic exposure is to decrease, not increase, sales to that country. **Answer (C) is incorrect.** Reducing orders from suppliers in other foreign countries will not address this economic exposure. **Answer (D) is incorrect.** Increasing orders from suppliers in other foreign countries will not address this economic exposure.

STUDY UNIT SEVEN
FINANCIAL RISK MANAGEMENT

(17 pages of outline)

7.1	Risk and Return	211
7.2	Linear Regression and Correlation Analysis	216
7.3	Quantifying Investment Risk	220
7.4	Capital Asset Pricing Model (CAPM)	224
7.5	Selecting the Forecasting Method	226

The complex modern organization regularly confronts financial risk. A CPA is expected to understand how to mitigate this risk through **financial risk management**. Study Unit 6 discusses the mitigation of exchange rate risk through the use of derivatives. This study unit reviews the basics of risk and return, as well as how to quantify risks through the capital asset pricing model (CAPM), linear regression, and correlation analysis.

Every investment has an expectation of a return and some amount of risk. An investing entity can receive an adequate return on its investments while minimizing risk by quantifying and understanding the principles of risk and return.

7.1 RISK AND RETURN

1. **Types of Investment Risk**

    a. **Credit default risk** is the risk that the borrower will default and not be able to repay principal or interest. This risk is estimated by credit-rating agencies.

    b. **Liquidity risk** is the risk that a security cannot be sold on short notice without a loss.

    c. **Maturity risk**, also called **interest rate risk**, is the risk that an investment security will fluctuate in value between the time it was issued and its maturity date. The longer the time until maturity, the greater the degree of maturity risk. It may also be paid back before maturity.

    d. **Inflation risk** is the risk that purchasing power of the currency will decline. (Study Unit 5, Subunit 2, describes the causes and effects of inflation.)

    e. **Political risk** is the probability of loss from actions of governments, such as changes in tax laws or environmental regulations or expropriation of assets.

    f. **Exchange rate risk** is the risk of loss because of fluctuation in the relative value of a foreign currency in which the investment is payable.

    g. **Business risk** (or **operations risk**) is the risk of fluctuations in earnings before interest and taxes or in operating income when the firm uses no debt, which causes cash flows to be inadequate to pay interest and principal on time.

        1) It is the risk inherent in operations that excludes **financial risk**, the risk to the shareholders of financial leverage.

        2) Business risk depends on factors such as

            a) Demand variability,
            b) Sales price variability,
            c) Input price variability, and
            d) The amount of operating leverage.

    h. **Country risk** is the overall risk of investing in a foreign country.

    i. **Principal risk** (default risk) is the risk of losing the principal invested.

2. **Two Basic Types of Investment Risk**
   a. Based on statistical analysis of stock market data, risk can be categorized as systematic or unsystematic.
   b. All firms have **systematic risk**, also called **market risk**. Changes in the economy as a whole, such as inflation or the business cycle, affect all players in the market. Systematic risk is unavoidable.
      1) For this reason, systematic risk sometimes is called **undiversifiable risk**. Because all investments are affected, it cannot be reduced by diversification.
   c. **Unsystematic risk**, also called idiosyncratic risk or company risk, is the risk inherent in a particular investment. Thus, it is the risk of a specific firm. This type of risk is determined by the firm's industry, products, customer loyalty, degree of leverage, management competence, etc.
      1) Unsystematic risk sometimes is called **diversifiable risk**. Because individual investments are affected by the particular strengths and weaknesses of the firm, this risk can be reduced by diversification. (Item 4. in Subunit 7.3 explains diversification.)

3. **Relationship between Risk and Return**
   a. Whether the expected return on an investment suffices to attract an investor depends on (1) its risk, (2) the risks and returns of alternative investments, (3) the investor's attitude toward risk, and (4) the investor's portfolio of investments.
      1) Most investors (and people in general) are **risk-averse**. For them, the utility of a gain is less than the disutility of a loss of the same amount. For instance, the pain of losing $1,000 is worse than the happiness gained from earning $1,000.

EXAMPLE 7-1   Risk Aversion

Risk aversion is reflected by actions of people in a casino. Many are willing to bet $1 on one of the numbers on a roulette table because the chance of a gain of multiple dollars versus the loss of $1 is acceptable. However, as the minimum amount of a bet increases (from $1 to $100 to $1,000), the number of willing casual gamblers decreases because the chance for earning hundreds or thousands of dollars versus the probability of losing $100 or $1,000 is not acceptable. Thus, risk aversion keeps many people from gambling as the minimum bet increases.

---

   a) Because of risk aversion, risky securities must have higher expected returns. These returns induce investors to accept additional risk. In Example 7-1 above, if a casino were to provide better odds (i.e., a higher expected return) for higher bet amounts, more casual gamblers may be induced to place higher minimum bets.
   b) In financial and economic models, all investors are assumed to be risk averse.

2) A **risk-neutral** investor adopts an expected value approach. (S)he regards the utility of a gain as equal to the disutility of a loss of the same amount.

   a) In the case of a casino gambler, a risk-neutral person is as willing to gamble for a high amount as a low amount (assuming the odds are commensurate with the expected value).

3) A **risk-seeking** investor has an optimistic attitude toward risk. (S)he regards the utility of a gain as exceeding the disutility of a loss of the same amount.

   a) In the case of a casino gambler, a risk-seeking person is more willing to play roulette than craps, baccarat, or poker due to the greater risk.

   b) Some seek risk as the reward, such as sky divers.

b. The greater the risk of the investment, the higher the rate of return required by the investor. For each type of investment risk, the investor requires an additional risk premium that compensates him or her for bearing that risk.

1) The **risk premium** is the excess of an investment's expected rate of return over the risk-free interest rate.

2) The **risk-free rate** is the interest rate on the safest investment. In practice, the stated interest rate on U.S. Treasury bills is considered to be the risk-free interest rate.

   a) A holder of U.S. Treasury bills generally is exposed only to inflation risk. Thus, the market rate of interest on U.S. Treasury bills equals the risk-free rate of interest plus the inflation premium.

3) The **required rate of return** considers all investment risks that relate to a specific security.

EXAMPLE 7-2	Required Rate of Return	
	Real risk-free rate	3%
	Inflation premium	1%
	Risk-free rate	4%
	Liquidity risk premium	1%
	Default risk premium	2%
	Maturity risk premium	1%
	Required rate of return	8%

4. **Investment Securities**

    a. Financial managers may select from a wide range of financial instruments to raise capital or invest.

        1) The safety of an investment and its potential return have an inverse relationship. The following is a short list of widely available investment securities:

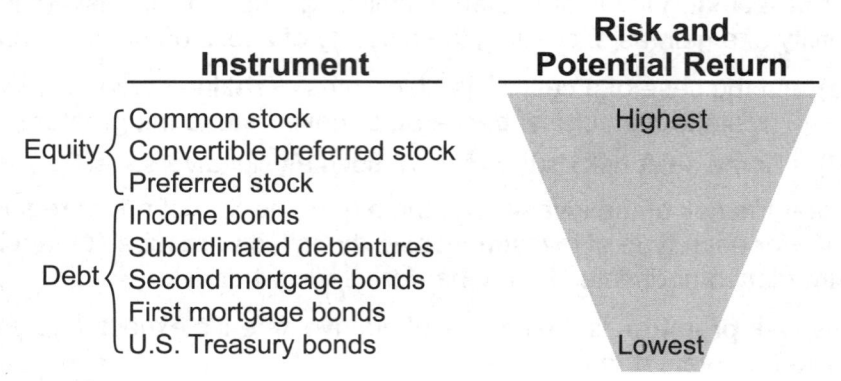

	Instrument	Risk and Potential Return
Equity	Common stock Convertible preferred stock Preferred stock	Highest
Debt	Income bonds Subordinated debentures Second mortgage bonds First mortgage bonds U.S. Treasury bonds	↓ Lowest

Figure 7-1

    b. The reasons for the varying risks and potential returns of these securities can be summarized as follows:

        1) Equity securities are considered riskier than debt because an entity's owners are not legally guaranteed a return.

            a) Common shareholders are the residual owners of a corporation. They are last in order of priority during liquidation, but they have the right to receive distributions of excess profits. Thus, the equity investments have a higher upside (or reward) than debt investments.

            b) Preferred shareholders usually have a higher priority than common shareholders in liquidation, but their potential returns are limited by the board of directors. They may participate in extra dividends or their shares may be converted into common stock.

        2) Issuers of debt securities are legally obligated to redeem them. Because these returns are guaranteed, their risks and returns are lower than those for equity investments.

            a) Income bonds pay a return only if the issuer is profitable.
            b) Debentures are unsecured debt securities, which means they are not collateralized.
            c) Mortgage bonds are secured (or collateralized) by real property.
            d) U.S. Treasury bonds are backed by the full faith and credit of the United States government.

        3) Precious metals (also called commodities) normally are considered a risky investment because their prices are highly volatile. During periods of high inflation, however, currency loses purchasing power rapidly, and precious metals, such as gold, may be a safe investment.

5. **Rate of Return**

   a. A return is the amount received by an investor as compensation for accepting the risk of the investment.

   $$\text{Return} = \text{Amount received} - \text{Amount invested}$$

   > **EXAMPLE 7-3 Investor's Return**
   >
   > An investor paid $100,000 for an investment that returned $112,000. The investor's return is $12,000 ($112,000 − $100,000).

   b. The rate of return is a percentage of the amount invested.

   $$\text{Rate of return} = \frac{\text{Return}}{\text{Amount invested}}$$

   > **EXAMPLE 7-4 Rate of Return**
   >
   > The investor's rate of return in Example 7-3 is 12% ($12,000 ÷ $100,000).

SUCCESS TIP: Note that the return formula presented above differs from the return on investment (ROI) formula presented in Study Unit 16, Subunit 2. The rate of return (above) is a finance formula that reflects a specific investment's profitability relative to the amount invested. But the ROI formula (discussed in Study Unit 16, Subunit 2) indicates how well a business is using its resources to generate operating income.

STOP & REVIEW: You have completed the outline for this subunit. Study multiple-choice questions 1 through 5 beginning on page 228.

7.2 LINEAR REGRESSION AND CORRELATION ANALYSIS

1. **Simple Regression**

    a. Regression analysis is the process of deriving a linear equation that describes the relationship between two variables.

        1) Simple regression is used for one independent variable. Multiple regression is used for more than one.

    b. The simple regression equation is the algebraic formula for a straight line.

    $$y = a + bx$$

    If: y = the dependent variable
    a = the y intercept
    b = the slope of the regression line
    x = the independent variable

        1) The best straight line that fits a set of data points is derived using calculus.

    c. Regression analysis is particularly valuable for quantifying risk in financial risk management as well as for budgeting and cost accounting purposes.

        1) One extremely common application of simple regression in a business setting is the estimation of a mixed cost function, one with a fixed component and a variable component.

        2) The y-axis intercept is the fixed portion, and the slope of the regression line is the variable portion.

EXAMPLE 7-5   Linear Regression Analysis of Manufacturing Costs

A firm has performed a linear regression analysis and determined that total manufacturing costs (y) consist of fixed costs of $420,000 and variable costs of $32 per unit of output. This relationship can be stated mathematically as follows:

$$y = \$420,000 + \$32x$$

If the firm is planning to produce 12,000 units of output, its forecast for total manufacturing costs is $804,000 ($420,000 + $32 × 12,000).

EXAMPLE 7-6   Simple Regression

The firm has collected the following observations on units of output (independent variable) and total manufacturing costs (dependent variable) to support its linear regression analysis:

	Units of Output (000s)	Actual Total Manufacturing Costs ($000s)
A	5	$ 620
B	8	640
C	14	850
D	17	1,010

-- Continued on next page --

EXAMPLE 7-6 -- Continued

The observations are graphed as follows:

Simple Regression

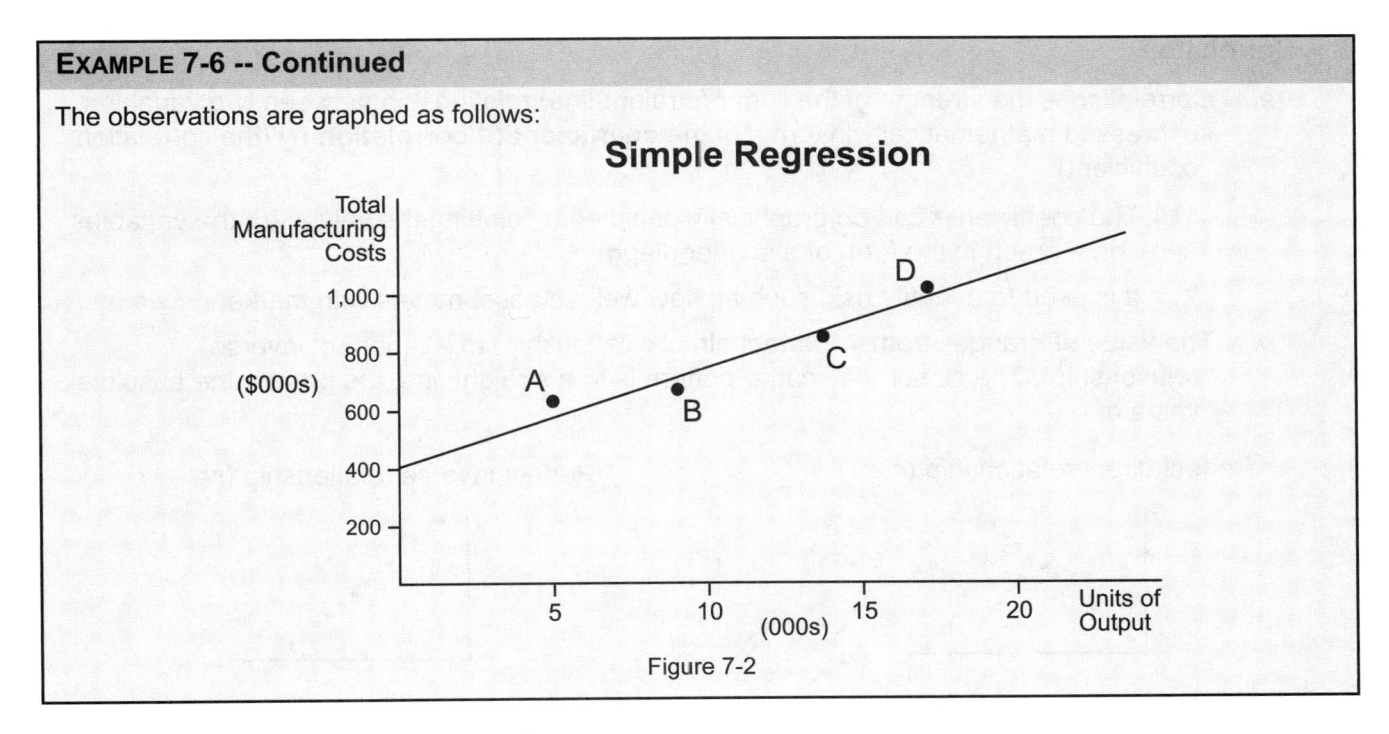

Figure 7-2

2. **Aspects of Regression Analysis**

   a. The linear relationship established for x and y is valid only across the relevant range, the range from the highest to the smallest measures in the data set. The user must identify the relevant range and ensure that projections lie within it.

      1) If a known data set of output is between 5,000 and 20,000, a manager should understand the same equation may be inaccurate at a production level of 200 or 100,000.

   b. Regression analysis assumes that past relationships are a basis for valid projections.

   c. Regression does not determine causality.

      1) Although x and y move together, the apparent relationship may be caused by some other factor. For example, car wash sales volume and sunny weather are strongly correlated, but car wash sales do not cause sunny weather.

3. **Correlation**

   a. Correlation is the strength of the linear (straight-line) relationship between two variables, expressed mathematically in terms of the **coefficient of correlation** *(r)* (the correlation coefficient).

      1) The coefficient *r* can be graphically depicted by plotting the values for the variables on a graph in the form of a scatter diagram.
      2) It is used to quantify risk, such as how well an asset moves with market prices.

   b. The value of *r* ranges from 1 (perfect direct relationship) to –1 (perfect inverse relationship). The closer the scatter pattern is to a straight line, the greater the absolute value of *r*.

   Perfect direct relationship (*r* = 1)

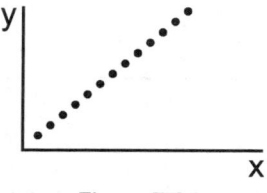

   Figure 7-3

   Perfect inverse relationship (*r* = –1)

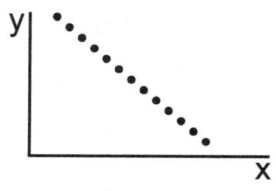

   Figure 7-4

   Strong direct relationship (*r* = 0.7)

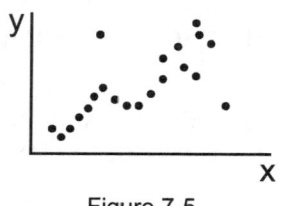

   Figure 7-5

   No linear relationship (*r* = 0)

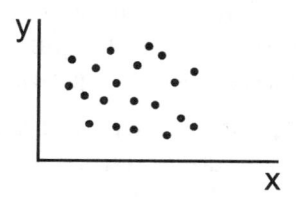

   Figure 7-6

      1) A coefficient of correlation of zero does not mean that the two variables are unrelated, only that any relationship cannot be expressed as a linear equation.

   c. Correlation is not causation. We only know that two variables move together, not what causes them to move.

4. **Standard Error**

   a. The standard error measures how well the linear equation represents the data. It is the vertical distance between the data points in a scatter diagram and the regression line.

      1) The closer the data points to the regression line, the lower the standard error.

5. **High-Low Method**

   a. The high-low method generates a regression line using only the highest and lowest of a series of observations.

EXAMPLE 7-7   High-Low Method

A regression equation for electricity costs can be based on the high-cost month and the low-cost month. If the lowest costs were $400 in April when production was 800 machine hours and the highest costs were $600 in September when production was 1,300 hours, the equation is determined as follows:

High month	$600 for	1,300 hours
Low month	400 for	800 hours
Increase	$200	500 hours

Because costs increased $200 for 500 additional hours, the variable cost is $.40 per machine hour ($200 ÷ 500 hours). For the low month, the total variable portion of that monthly cost is $320 ($.40 × 800 hours). Given that the total cost is $400 and $320 is variable, the remaining $80 must be a fixed cost. The regression equation is y = 80 + .4x.

---

   1) The major criticism of the high-low method is that the high and low points may be abnormalities not representative of normal events.

STOP & REVIEW

You have completed the outline for this subunit.
Study multiple-choice questions 6 through 11 beginning on page 230.

7.3 QUANTIFYING INVESTMENT RISK

1. This subunit covers the methodologies to quantify risks associated with business entities.

   a. These methodologies could be used to quantify risks involving equity prices, exchange rates (i.e., the price of a type of currency versus another type of currency), and interest rates (i.e., the price to borrow money).

2. **Probability and Standard Deviation**

   a. Probability provides a method for mathematically expressing the likelihood of possible outcomes.

   b. A **probability distribution** is the set of all possible outcomes of a decision, with a probability assigned to each outcome. For example, a simple probability distribution might be defined for the possible returns on a stock investment. A different return could be estimated for each of a limited number of possible states of the economy, and a probability could be determined for each state. Such a distribution is **discrete** because the outcomes are limited.

3. **Measures of Risk – Standard Deviation and Variance**

   a. The **expected rate of return ($\bar{R}$)** on an investment is determined using an expected value calculation. It is an average of the possible outcomes weighted according to their probabilities.

   $$\text{Expected rate of return } (\bar{R}) = \sum (\text{Possible rate of return} \times \text{Probability})$$

EXAMPLE 7-8   Expected Rate of Return

A company is considering investing in the common stock of one of two firms, Xatalan Corp. and Yarmouth Co. The expected rates of return on the two securities based on the weighted averages of their probable outcomes are calculated as follows:

Xatalan Corporation Stock					Yarmouth Company Stock				
Rate of Return %		Probability %		Weighted Average	Rate of Return %		Probability %		Weighted Average
80 %	×	60%	=	48 %	30 %	×	70%	=	21 %
(50)%	×	40%	=	(20)%	(10)%	×	30%	=	(3)%
Expected rate of return ($\bar{R}$)				**28 %**	**Expected rate of return ($\bar{R}$)**				**18 %**

The expected rate of return on Xatalan stock is higher, but the risk of each investment also should be measured.

b. Risk is the probability that the actual return on an investment will differ from the expected return. One measure of risk is the standard deviation (variance's square root) of the distribution of an investment's return.

$$\text{Standard deviation }(\sigma) = \sqrt{\sum[(R_i - \overline{R})^2 \times \text{Probability}]} = \sqrt{\text{Variance}}$$

If: R_i = Possible rate of return
$\overline{R}$ = Expected rate of return

1) The **standard deviation** measures the tightness of the distribution and the riskiness of the investment. In practice, the standard deviation is often annualized by multiplying weekly/monthly/quarterly returns by the square root of the time ratio. For example, for monthly returns, the annualized standard deviation equals the standard deviation of monthly returns multiplied by the square root of 12.

   a) A large standard deviation reflects a broadly dispersed probability distribution, meaning the range of possible returns is wide. But, the smaller the standard deviation, the tighter the probability distribution and the lower the risk.

   b) Thus, the greater the standard deviation, the riskier the investment.

Small Standard Deviation   **Large Standard Deviation**

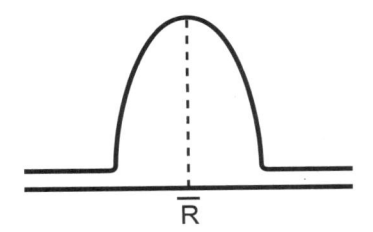

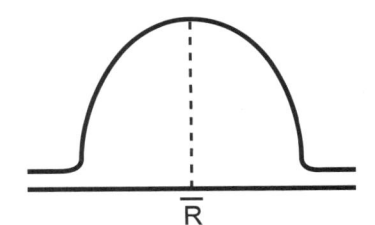

Figure 7-7

EXAMPLE 7-9   Standard Deviation

The following are the standard deviations of the returns on the investments from Example 7-8:

Xatalan Corporation Stock

Standard deviation $(\sigma) = \sqrt{[(80\% - 28\%)^2 \times 60\%] + [(-50\% - 28\%)^2 \times 40\%]} = \sqrt{40.56\%} = \mathbf{63.69\%}$

Yarmouth Company Stock

Standard deviation $(\sigma) = \sqrt{[(30\% - 18\%)^2 \times 70\%] + [(-10\% - 18\%)^2 \times 30\%]} = \sqrt{3.306\%} = \mathbf{18.33\%}$

The investment in Xatalan stock has a higher expected return than the investment in Yarmouth stock (28% > 18%). It also is riskier because its standard deviation is greater (63.69% > 18.33%). Accordingly, to determine which investment has the preferable risk-return tradeoff, the coefficient of variation (CV) of the expected returns on the two investments is measured (in Example 7-10 on the next page).

c. The **coefficient of variation (CV)** is useful when the rates of return and standard deviations of two investments differ. It measures the **risk per unit of return**.

$$\text{Coefficient of variation} = \frac{\text{Standard deviation}}{\text{Expected rate of return}}$$

$$CV = (\sigma) \div \overline{R}$$

1) The lower the ratio, the better the risk-return tradeoff.

EXAMPLE 7-10   **Coefficient of Variation**

The coefficients of variation for the expected return of the two potential investments from Examples 7-8 and 7-9 are calculated as follows:

		Coefficient of Variation
Xatalan Corporation Stock:	$\sigma \div \overline{R} = 63.69\% \div 28\%$ =	**2.275**
Yarmouth Company Stock:	$\sigma \div \overline{R} = 18.33\% \div 18\%$ =	**1.018**

The investment in Yarmouth has a better risk-return tradeoff. Its coefficient of variation is lower than that of the investment in Xatalan (1.018 < 2.275).

---

4. **Diversification**

   a. The measures presented above and on the previous pages relate to the risk and return for individual securities. However, few investors hold only one security.

      1) The goal of portfolio management is to hold a group of securities that provides a reasonable rate of return without the risks associated with one security.

         a) Expected portfolio **return** is the weighted average of the returns on the individual securities.

         b) Portfolio **risk** is usually less than a simple average of the standard deviations of the component securities. This is one benefit of diversification.

   b. **Idiosyncratic risk** (also called diversifiable risk or unsystematic risk) is associated with one investment security. Specific risk potentially can be minimized by diversification.

      1) Diversification reduces aggregate volatility.

         a) Some stocks move in the same direction as other stocks in the portfolio but by a smaller amount. Some stocks move in the opposite direction from other stocks.

         b) Thus, by combining imperfectly correlated securities into a portfolio, the risk of the group as a whole is less than the average of their standard deviations.

      2) In theory, diversifiable risk should continue to decrease as the number of different securities held increases.

         a) But, in practice, the benefits of diversification become extremely small when more than about 20 to 30 different securities are held. Moreover, commissions and other transaction costs increase with greater diversification.

c. **Market risk** (also called undiversifiable risk or systematic risk) is the risk of the stock market as a whole. For an ideal, well-diversified portfolio, it is the only risk.

d. The **coefficient of correlation** *(r)* measures the degree to which any two variables, e.g., the prices of two stocks, are related.

   1) In practice, the coefficient of correlation can be used to determine how (a) a security performs against its benchmarks or (b) securities behave against other securities within a portfolio.

   2) Investment risks can be diversified by adding negatively correlated securities to the existing portfolio.

   3) The coefficient of correlation has a range from 1.0 to −1.0. (Subunit 7.2, fully covers correlation.)

      a) Perfect positive correlation (1.0) means that the two variables always move together.

      b) Perfect negative correlation (−1.0) means that the two variables always move in opposite directions.

      c) If a pair of securities has a coefficient of correlation of 1.0, the risk of the two together is the same as the risk of each security by itself. If a pair of securities has a coefficient of correlation of −1.0, all specific (unsystematic) risk has been eliminated.

   4) The ideal portfolio consists of securities with a wide enough variety of coefficients of correlation that only market risk remains.

STOP & REVIEW

You have completed the outline for this subunit.
Study multiple-choice questions 12 through 16 beginning on page 232.

7.4 CAPITAL ASSET PRICING MODEL (CAPM)

1. Investors want to reduce their risk and take advantage of diversification by holding a portfolio of securities. To measure how a particular security contributes to the risk and return of a diversified portfolio, investors can use the **capital asset pricing model (CAPM)**.
2. The CAPM quantifies the required return on an equity security by relating the security's level of risk to the average return available in the market.
3. The CAPM formula is based on the idea that the investor must be compensated for an investment in two ways: time value of money and risk.

CAPM Formula
Required rate of return = $R_F + \beta(R_M - R_F)$

If: R_F = Risk-free rate
 R_M = Market return
 β = Measure of the systematic risk or volatility of the individual security in comparison with the market (diversified portfolio)

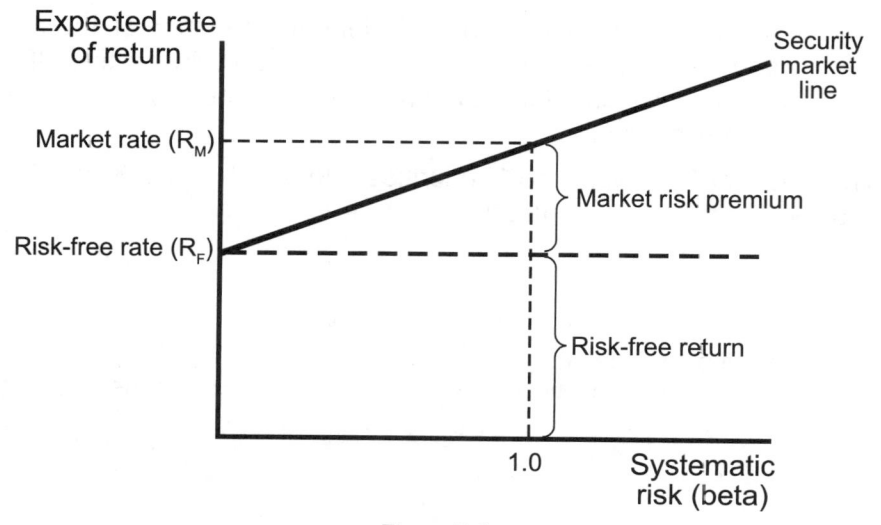

Figure 7-8

a. The time value component is the **risk-free rate** (denoted R_F in the formula). It is the return provided by the safest investments, e.g., U.S. Treasury securities.

b. The risk component consists of

 1) The **market risk premium** (denoted $R_M - R_F$), the return provided by the market above the risk-free rate, weighted by

 2) A measure of the security's market risk, called **beta** (β).

 a) The effect of an individual security on the volatility of a portfolio is measured by its sensitivity to movements by the overall market. This sensitivity is stated in terms of a stock's beta coefficient (β).

 b) Thus, the beta of the market portfolio equals 1, and the beta of U.S. Treasury securities is 0.

3) A β of 1.5 indicates the security will return 150% of the market return (in terms of risk premium). If the market returns 10%, the security returns 15%. If the market loses 10%, the security loses 15%.

4) A β of .8 indicates the security will return 80% of the market return (in terms of risk premium). If the market returns 10%, the security returns 8%. If the market loses 10%, the security loses 8%.

5) The **security risk premium** is $\beta(R_M - R_F)$. Thus, the required rate of return of the security is the risk-free rate of return (R_F) plus the security risk premium.

   a) In practice, the security risk premium of a stock is found by subtracting the U.S. Treasury interest rate from the stock's annual return (or appreciation).

   b) For example, if a stock appreciated by 10% year over year and the 3-month treasury bill rate is 3%, the security risk premium is 7%.

6) The **security market line (SML)** is the graphical representation of the relationship between the expected rate of return and market, or systematic (beta) risk.

EXAMPLE 7-11   CAPM

An investor is considering the purchase of a stock with a beta of 1.2. Treasury bills currently are paying 8.6%, and the average return on the market is 10.1%. (U.S. Treasuries are considered to be as close to risk-free as possible.) To be induced to buy this stock, the return that the investor must receive is calculated as follows:

$$\begin{aligned} \text{Required rate of return} &= R_F + \beta(R_M - R_F) \\ &= 8.6\% + 1.2(10.1\% - 8.6\%) \\ &= 8.6\% + 1.8\% \\ &= 10.4\% \end{aligned}$$

STOP & REVIEW

You have completed the outline for this subunit.
Study multiple-choice questions 17 through 22 beginning on page 234.

7.5 SELECTING THE FORECASTING METHOD

1. **Various Approaches to Quantify or Understand Risk**
    a. **Sensitivity Analysis**
        1) Sensitivity analysis uses trial-and-error to determine the effects of changes in variables or assumptions on final results. It is useful in deciding whether expending additional resources to obtain better forecasts is justified.
        2) The trial-and-error method inherent in sensitivity analysis is greatly facilitated by the use of computer software. A major use of sensitivity analysis is in capital budgeting. Small changes in interest rates or payoffs can make a significant difference in the profitability of a project.
        3) For example, a sensitivity analysis can be performed to predict the changes in price of a bond if the interest rate decreases by 0.5%.
    b. **Simulation**
        1) This method is a sophisticated refinement of probability theory and sensitivity analysis. The computer is used to generate many examples of results based upon various assumptions.
        2) Project simulation is frequently expensive. Unless a project is exceptionally large and expensive, full-scale simulation is usually not worthwhile.
    c. **Monte Carlo Simulation**
        1) This method often is used in simulation to generate the individual values for a random variable. The performance of a quantitative model under uncertainty may be investigated by randomly selecting values for each of the variables in the model (based on the probability distribution of each variable) and then calculating the value of the solution.
        2) Performing the process many times produces the distribution of results from the model.
        3) For example, the profit of a product depends on factors including product quality, price, units sold, marketing expenses, customer service, etc. The factors also affect each other. A Monte Carlo simulation can be used to generate random values for these variables based on the probabilities related to the factors to help determine optimal parameters for the profit.
    d. **Delphi Approach**
        1) The Delphi approach solicits opinions from experts, summarizes the opinions, and feeds the summaries back to the experts (without revealing participants to each other). The process is repeated until the opinions converge on an optimal solution.
        2) EXAMPLE: Management sends questionnaires to experts asking about the possible leading cause of a new product having low sales. Management then summarizes the opinions collected from the experts, chooses the most likely leading cause, and sends another questionnaire to experts asking for the best way to solve the problem based on the identified leading cause.
    e. **Time Series Analysis**
        1) Time series analysis (also called trend analysis) is the process of projecting future trends based on past experience. It is a regression model in which the independent variable is time.
        2) For example, a time series can be used to show the rises and falls of revenue with the changes of seasons or stock price changes over a specified period.

f. **Risk Assessment Tools**

1) **Market value at risk (VAR)** determines the potential decline in market value of a portfolio at a given level of confidence over a specified time period.

    a) For example, if the 1-month VAR on a portfolio is $250 million with a confidence level of 98%, there is a 2% chance that the market value of the portfolio will drop more than $250 million over a 1-month period.

    b) **Back testing** is a technique used to determine a value at risk model's accuracy in predicting loss. It compares the losses forecasted using a value at risk model and actual losses.

2) **Earnings at risk (EAR)** determines the potential decline in earnings due to interest rate changes at a given level of confidence over a specified time period.

    a) For example, if the 1-week EAR is $200 million with a confidence level of 95%, there is a 5% chance that the deviation from expected earnings due to interest rate changes will be more than $200 million over a 1-week period.

3) **Cash flow at risk (CFAR)** determines the potential decline in cash flows at a given level of confidence over a specified time period.

    a) For example, if the 1-year CFAR is $220 million with a confidence level of 90%, there is a 10% chance that the deviation from expected cash flows will be more than $220 million over a 1-year period.

> **SUCCESS TIP**
> Some of the forecasting-related questions on the CPA Exam require the candidate to read about a forecasting situation and then choose the appropriate method. Thus, candidates should be as comfortable recognizing when to use the different forecasting methods as they are in working through the details of applying them.

2. Accounting estimates often incorporate approaches that quantify risks and unknowns.

    a. Management is responsible for the process that prepares accounting estimates. It must

        1) Identify circumstances requiring accounting estimates;
        2) Understand factors affecting the accounting estimate;
        3) Accumulate relevant, sufficient, and reliable data;
        4) Predict the most likely circumstances and factors;
        5) Determine the estimate based on these predictions and other relevant factors; and
        6) Present the estimate per correct accounting principles with adequate disclosure.

    b. Management judgment includes

        1) Experience and knowledge covering events (past and current).
        2) Assumptions about expected conditions, events, etc., and changes therein.

STOP & REVIEW
You have completed the outline for this subunit.
Study multiple-choice questions 23 and 24 on page 237.

QUESTIONS

7.1 Risk and Return

1. A company is evaluating its experience with five recent investments. The following data are available:

Investment	Cost of Investment	Amount Received
A	$ 8,500	$ 8,390
B	4,200	4,610
C	12,100	12,400
D	7,900	8,220
E	11,000	11,400

Rank the investments in order from highest rate of return to lowest.

A. C, E, A, D, B.
B. B, D, E, C, A.
C. B, E, D, C, A.
D. A, C, E, D, B.

Answer (B) is correct.
REQUIRED: The order of investments from highest rate of return to lowest.
DISCUSSION: Rate of return is equal to the return on an investment (the amount received minus the amount invested) divided by the amount invested. The calculation for these five investments can be performed as follows:

Investment	Cost of Investment	Amount Received	Return	Rate of Return
A	$ 8,500	$ 8,390	$(110)	(1.3%)
B	4,200	4,610	410	9.8%
C	12,100	12,400	300	2.5%
D	7,900	8,220	320	4.1%
E	11,000	11,400	400	3.6%

Answer (A) is incorrect. The ranking C, E, A, D, B is in order by amount received, not rate of return. Answer (C) is incorrect. The ranking B, E, D, C, A is in order by return, not rate of return. **Answer (D) is incorrect.** The ranking A, C, E, D, B is from lowest rate of return to highest.

2. Dr. G paid $10,000 for an investment that returned $400. What is the investor's rate of return?

A. Cannot be determined without additional information.
B. 4.0%
C. 2.5%
D. 8.0%

Answer (B) is correct.
REQUIRED: The investor's rate of return.
DISCUSSION: A return is the amount received by an investor as compensation for taking on the risk of the investment. The rate of return is the return stated as a percentage of the amount invested. In this case, it is 4% ($400 ÷ $10,000).
Answer (A) is incorrect. The rate of return can be calculated. **Answer (C) is incorrect.** Reversing the numerator and denominator, and dividing the result by 1,000, results in a rate of 2.5%. **Answer (D) is incorrect.** The rate of 8.0% results from incorrectly multiplying the investor's rate of return by 2.

3. Catherine & Co. has extra cash at the end of the year and is analyzing the best way to invest the funds. The company should invest in a project only if the

A. Expected return on the project exceeds the return on investments of comparable risk.
B. Return on investments of comparable risk exceeds the expected return on the project.
C. Expected return on the project is equal to the return on investments of comparable risk.
D. Return on investments of comparable risk equals the expected return on the project.

Answer (A) is correct.
REQUIRED: The rule for deciding whether to invest in a project.
DISCUSSION: Investment risk is analyzed in terms of the probability that the actual return on an investment will be lower than the expected return. Comparing a project's expected return with the return on an asset of similar risk helps determine whether the project is worth investing in. If the expected return on a project exceeds the return on an asset of comparable risk, the project should be pursued.

SU 7: Financial Risk Management

4. The risk of loss because of fluctuations in the relative value of foreign currencies is called

A. Expropriation risk.
B. Multinational beta.
C. Exchange rate risk.
D. Undiversifiable risk.

Answer (C) is correct.
REQUIRED: The risk of loss because of fluctuations in the relative value of foreign currencies.
DISCUSSION: When amounts to be paid or received are denominated in a foreign currency, exchange rate fluctuations may result in exchange gains or losses. For example, if a U.S. firm has a receivable fixed in terms of units of a foreign currency, a decline in the value of that currency relative to the U.S. dollar results in a foreign exchange loss.
Answer (A) is incorrect. Expropriation risk is the risk that the sovereign country in which the assets backing an investment are located will seize the assets without adequate compensation. **Answer (B) is incorrect.** The beta value in the capital asset pricing model for a multinational firm is the systematic risk of a given multinational firm relative to that of the market as a whole. **Answer (D) is incorrect.** Undiversifiable risk is risk that cannot be offset through diversification.

5. Beginning January 2, Year 1, a company deposited $50,000 in a savings account for 2 years. The account earns 10% interest, compounded annually. What amount of interest did the company earn during the 2-year period?

A. $10,500
B. $10,000
C. $5,500
D. $5,000

Answer (A) is correct.
REQUIRED: The amount of compound interest earned during the 2-year period.
DISCUSSION: Compounding interest is the practice of adding interest to the carrying amount of the principal rather than paying it in cash. The amount of interest earned in Year 1 ($50,000 × 10% = $5,000) was added to the principal, which was then used to calculate the amount of interest earned in Year 2 [($50,000 + $5,000) × 10% = $5,500]. The total amount of interest earned during the 2-year period was thus $10,500 ($5,000 Year 1 + $5,500 Year 2). This amount also can be calculated as follows: [($50,000 × 1.1 × 1.1) − $50,000].
Answer (B) is incorrect. The amount of $10,000 is interest that would have been earned using simple, not compound, interest. **Answer (C) is incorrect.** The amount of $5,500 is the interest earned in the second year. **Answer (D) is incorrect.** The amount of $5,000 is the interest earned in the first year.

7.2 Linear Regression and Correlation Analysis

6. Correlation is a term frequently used in conjunction with regression analysis and is measured by the value of the coefficient of correlation, r. The best explanation of the value r is that it

    A. Is always positive.

    B. Interprets variances in terms of the independent variable.

    C. Ranges in size from negative infinity to positive infinity.

    D. Is a measure of the relative relationship between two variables.

Answer (D) is correct.
    REQUIRED: The best explanation of the coefficient of correlation (r).
    DISCUSSION: The coefficient of correlation (r) measures the strength of the linear relationship between the dependent and independent variables. The magnitude of r is independent of the scales of measurement of x and y. The coefficient lies between –1.0 and +1.0. A value of zero indicates no linear relationship between the x and y variables. A value of +1.0 indicates a perfectly direct relationship, and a value of –1.0 indicates a perfectly inverse relationship.
    Answer (A) is incorrect. The coefficient is negative if the relationship between the variables is inverse. **Answer (B) is incorrect.** The coefficient relates the two variables to each other. **Answer (C) is incorrect.** The size of the coefficient varies between –1.0 and +1.0.

7. The coefficient of correlation that indicates the weakest linear association between two variables is

    A. –0.73

    B. –0.11

    C. 0.12

    D. 0.35

Answer (B) is correct.
    REQUIRED: The correlation coefficient that indicates the weakest linear association between two variables.
    DISCUSSION: The coefficient of correlation can vary from –1 to +1. A –1 coefficient indicates a perfect negative correlation, and a +1 coefficient indicates a perfect positive correlation. A zero coefficient of correlation indicates no linear association between the variables. Thus, the coefficient of correlation that is nearest to zero indicates the weakest linear association. Of the options given in the question, the correlation coefficient that is nearest to zero is –0.11.
    Answer (A) is incorrect. The coefficient of –0.73 signifies a strong negative correlation. **Answer (C) is incorrect.** The coefficient of 0.12 is a slightly stronger correlation. **Answer (D) is incorrect.** The coefficient of 0.35 is a considerably stronger correlation.

8. In regression analysis, which of the following coefficients of correlation represents the strongest linear relationship between the independent and dependent variables?

    A. 1.03

    B. –0.02

    C. –0.89

    D. 0.75

Answer (C) is correct.
    REQUIRED: The correlation coefficient with the strongest relationship between independent and dependent variables.
    DISCUSSION: A coefficient of –1.0 signifies a perfect inverse relationship, and a coefficient of 1.0 signifies a perfect direct relationship. Thus, the higher the absolute value of the coefficient of correlation, the stronger the linear relationship. A coefficient of –0.89 suggests a very strong inverse relationship between the independent and dependent variables.
    Answer (A) is incorrect. A coefficient of 1.03 is impossible. **Answer (B) is incorrect.** A coefficient of –0.02 is very weak. **Answer (D) is incorrect.** A coefficient of 0.75 is 0.25 from the maximum, whereas –0.89 is only 0.11 from the minimum.

SU 7: Financial Risk Management

Questions 9 and 10 are based on the following information. Jackson Co. has the following information for the first 4 months of this year:

	Machine Hours	Cleaning Expense
January	2,100	$ 900
February	2,600	1,200
March	1,600	800
April	2,000	1,000

9. Using the high-low method, what is Jackson's variable cost of cleaning per machine hour?

A. $.40
B. $.48
C. $2.00
D. $2.50

Answer (A) is correct.
   REQUIRED: The variable cost in the high-low method.
   DISCUSSION: The high-low method is used to generate a regression line by basing the equation on only the highest and lowest of a series of observations. In this problem, March was the lowest and February the highest.

February	$1,200	for	2,600	hours
March	(800)	for	(1,600)	hours
Increase	$ 400	for	1,000	hours

Thus, it costs $400 for 1,000 hours, or $.40 for an hour.
   Answer (B) is incorrect. The average of the cleaning expense per machine hour for the high and low months is $.48. **Answer (C) is incorrect.** The March machine hours divided by the March cost is $2.00. **Answer (D) is incorrect.** The increase in hours divided by the increase in cost is $2.50.

10. Jackson's management expects machine hours for the month of May to be 1,400 hours. What is their expected total cost for the month of May using the high-low method?

A. $560
B. $650
C. $720
D. $760

Answer (C) is correct.
   REQUIRED: The expected total cost using the high-low method.
   DISCUSSION: The expected total cost, using the high-low method, can be found as follows:

First, calculate the variable cost per machine hour.

($1,200 − $800) ÷ (2,600 hours − 1,600 hours) = $.40

Then, using the data from February (or March), calculate the expected fixed costs.

Total cost	$1,200
Minus: Variable cost (2,600 hours × $.40)	(1,040)
Fixed cost	$ 160

Finally, calculate the expected total cost.

Expected total cost = Expected fixed cost + Expected variable cost
= $160 + (1,400 hours × $.40 per hour)
= $160 + $560
= $720

Answer (A) is incorrect. The variable cost is $560, not the total cost. **Answer (B) is incorrect.** The expected total cost for May is not $650. **Answer (D) is incorrect.** The expected total cost for May is not $760.

11. In the standard regression equation y = a + bx, the letter b is best described as a(n)

A. Independent variable.
B. Dependent variable.
C. Y intercept.
D. Slope of the regression line.

Answer (D) is correct.
REQUIRED: The meaning of the letter b in the standard regression equation.
DISCUSSION: In the standard regression equation, b represents the slope of the regression line. For example, in a cost determination regression, y equals total costs, b is the variable cost per unit, x is the number of units produced, and a is fixed cost.
Answer (A) is incorrect. The independent variable is x. **Answer (B) is incorrect.** The dependent variable is y. **Answer (C) is incorrect.** The y intercept is a.

7.3 Quantifying Investment Risk

12. City Development, Inc., is considering a new investment project that will involve building a large office block in Frankfurt-am-Main. The firm's financial analysis department has estimated that the proposed investment has the following estimated rate of return distributions:

Rate of Return	Probability
(5%)	30%
10%	50%
20%	20%

Calculate the expected rate of return.

A. 5.5%
B. 7.5%
C. 10.5%
D. 11.7%

Answer (B) is correct.
REQUIRED: The expected rate of return for an investment project.
DISCUSSION: The expected rate of return on an investment can be calculated by weighting each potential rate of return by its probability of occurrence and summing the results. City Development's expected rate of return for this development is:

Rate of Return	Probability	Expected Rate of Return
(5.0)%	30.0%	(1.5)%
10.0%	50.0%	5.0%
20.0%	20.0%	4.0%
		7.5%

Answer (A) is incorrect. The rate of 5.5% is a nonsense result. **Answer (C) is incorrect.** The rate of 10.5% results from improperly treating the negative 5% return as a positive number. **Answer (D) is incorrect.** The rate of 11.7% results from treating the negative return as a positive number and weighting the three possible results equally.

13. If two projects are completely and positively linearly dependent (or positively related), the measure of correlation between them is

A. 0
B. +.5
C. +1
D. −1

Answer (C) is correct.
REQUIRED: The measure of correlation when two projects are positively linearly dependent.
DISCUSSION: The measure of correlation when two projects are linearly dependent in a positive way is +1.
Answer (A) is incorrect. A zero correlation indicates no linear relationship. **Answer (B) is incorrect.** The measure +.5 does not indicate linearity. **Answer (D) is incorrect.** A measure of −1 would indicate a negative correlation.

14. Russell, Inc., is evaluating four independent investment proposals. The expected returns and standard deviations for each of these proposals are presented below.

Investment Proposal	Expected Returns	Standard Deviation
I	16%	10%
II	14%	10%
III	20%	11%
IV	22%	15%

Which one of the investment proposals has the **least** risk per unit of return?

A. Investment I.
B. Investment II.
C. Investment III.
D. Investment IV.

Answer (C) is correct.
REQUIRED: The investment proposal with the least risk per unit of return.
DISCUSSION: The coefficient of variation (CV) measures the risk per unit of return by dividing the standard deviation (σ) by the expected return. The investment with the lowest CV has the best risk-return tradeoff. The CVs of Russell's four investment proposals can thus be calculated as follows:

	Standard Deviation		Expected Returns		Coefficient of Variation
Investment I	10%	÷	16%	=	62.5%
Investment II	10%	÷	14%	=	71.4%
Investment III	11%	÷	20%	=	55.0%
Investment IV	15%	÷	22%	=	68.2%

Answer (A) is incorrect. The coefficient of variation for Investment I is 0.625 (10% ÷ 16%), which is not the lowest coefficient of the four. **Answer (B) is incorrect.** Investment II has the highest relative level of risk with a coefficient of variation of 0.714 (10% ÷ 14%). **Answer (D) is incorrect.** The coefficient of variation for Investment IV is 0.682 (15% ÷ 22%), which is not the lowest coefficient of the four.

15. The risk of a single stock is

A. Interest rate risk.
B. Unsystematic risk.
C. Portfolio risk.
D. Market risk.

Answer (B) is correct.
REQUIRED: The risk of a single stock.
DISCUSSION: Unsystematic risk is the risk of a single stock, but portfolio risk is the net risk of holding a portfolio of diversified securities. Portfolio risk therefore includes systematic and unsystematic risk.
Answer (A) is incorrect. Interest rate risk is the risk of changes in interest rates. **Answer (C) is incorrect.** Portfolio risk is the net risk of multiple securities. **Answer (D) is incorrect.** Market risk is systematic risk.

16. The expected rate of return for the stock of Cornhusker Enterprises is 20%, with a standard deviation of 15%. The expected rate of return for the stock of Mustang Associates is 10%, with a standard deviation of 9%. The stock with the worse risk/return relationship is

A. Cornhusker because the return is higher.
B. Cornhusker because the standard deviation is higher.
C. Mustang because the standard deviation is higher.
D. Mustang because the coefficient of variation is higher.

Answer (D) is correct.
REQUIRED: The stock with the worse risk/return relationship.
DISCUSSION: The coefficient of variation is useful when the rates of return and standard deviations of two investments differ. It measures the risk per unit of return by dividing the standard deviation by the expected return. The coefficient of variation is higher for Mustang (.09 ÷ .10 = .90) than for Cornhusker (.15 ÷ .20 = .75).
Answer (A) is incorrect. The existence of a higher return is not necessarily indicative of high risk. **Answer (B) is incorrect.** The level of standard deviation by itself is not enough for determining the stock's risk-return relationship. **Answer (C) is incorrect.** Mustang does not have the higher standard deviation.

7.4 Capital Asset Pricing Model (CAPM)

17. If Dexter Industries has a beta value of 1.0, then its

A. Return should equal the risk-free rate.
B. Price is relatively stable.
C. Expected return should approximate the overall market.
D. Volatility is low.

Answer (C) is correct.
REQUIRED: The result when the beta value is 1.0.
DISCUSSION: The effect of an individual security on the volatility of a portfolio is measured by its sensitivity to movements by the overall market. This sensitivity is stated in terms of a stock's beta coefficient. If the beta coefficient is 1.0, the price of that stock tends to move in the same direction and to the same degree as the overall market. The expected return can be calculated from the CAPM model formula.

$$\text{Expected return} = R_F + \beta(R_M - R_F)$$
$$R_F = \text{Risk-free rate}$$
$$R_M = \text{Market return}$$

When $\beta = 1$, expected return is equal to the market return.
Answer (A) is incorrect. Return is equal to the risk-free rate when $\beta = 0$. **Answer (B) is incorrect.** A beta value of 1.0 only means the price of the stock moves in concert with that of the overall market; if the market is not stable, the stock price will not be either. **Answer (D) is incorrect.** A beta value of 1.0 only means the price of the stock moves with that of the overall market. If the market is volatile, the stock price also will be.

18. If the return on the market portfolio is 10% and the risk-free rate is 5%, what is the effect on a company's required rate of return on its stock of an increase in the beta coefficient from 1.2 to 1.5?

A. 3% increase.
B. 1.5% increase.
C. No change.
D. 1.5% decrease.

Answer (B) is correct.
REQUIRED: The effect on a company's required rate of return on its stock of an increase in the beta coefficient.
DISCUSSION: The required rate of return on equity capital can be estimated with the capital asset pricing model (CAPM). CAPM consists of adding the risk-free rate (i.e., the return on government securities, denoted R_F) to the product of the beta coefficient (a measure of the issuer's risk) and the difference between the market return and the risk-free rate (denoted $R_M - R_F$, referred to as the risk premium). Below is the basic equilibrium equation for the CAPM:

$$\text{Required rate of return} = R_F + \beta(R_M - R_F)$$

In this situation, the risk premium is 5% (10% − 5%). Thus, the required rate of return when the beta coefficient is 1.2 is 11% [5% + (1.2 × 5%)], and the required rate when the beta coefficient is 1.5 is 12.5% [5% + (1.5 × 5%)]. This is an increase of 1.5% (12.5% − 11%).

19. The betas and expected returns for three investments being considered by Sky, Inc., are given below.

Investment	Beta	Expected Return
A	1.4	12%
B	0.8	11%
C	1.5	13%

The return on the market is 11% and the risk-free rate is 6%. If the capital asset pricing model (CAPM) is used for calculating the required rate of return, which investments should the management of Sky make?

A. B only.
B. A and C only.
C. B and C only.
D. A, B, and C.

Answer (A) is correct.
REQUIRED: The investment(s) that should be made based on the CAPM.
DISCUSSION: The required rate of return on equity capital can be estimated with the capital asset pricing model (CAPM). CAPM consists of adding the risk-free rate (i.e., the return on government securities, denoted R_F) to the product of the beta coefficient (a measure of the issuer's risk) and the difference between the market return and the risk-free rate (denoted $R_M - R_F$, referred to as the risk premium). Below is the basic equilibrium equation for the CAPM:

$$\text{Required rate of return} = R_F + \beta(R_M - R_F)$$

The risk premium is 5% (11% − 6%).

The CAPM can be thus applied to each of the three investments as follows:

Investment A: 6% + (1.4 × 5%) = 13.0%
Investment B: 6% + (0.8 × 5%) = 10.0%
Investment C: 6% + (1.5 × 5%) = 13.5%

These required rates of return can be compared with the expected rates to evaluate which investments should be accepted and which should be rejected.

	Required Rate		Expected Rate	Decision
Investment A:	13.0%	>	12%	Reject
Investment B:	10.0%	<	11%	Accept
Investment C:	13.5%	>	13%	Reject

Answer (B) is incorrect. The required rates of return for Investment A and Investment C exceed their expected returns. Answer (C) is incorrect. The required rate of return for Investment C exceeds its expected return. Answer (D) is incorrect. The required rates of return for Investment A and Investment C exceed their expected returns.

20. An analyst covering Guilderland Mining Co. common stock estimates the following information for next year:

Expected return on the market portfolio	12%
Expected return on Treasury securities	5%
Expected beta of Guilderland	2.2

Using the CAPM, the analyst's estimate of next year's risk premium for Guilderland's stock is closest to

A. 7.0%
B. 10.4%
C. 15.4%
D. 21.4%

Answer (C) is correct.
REQUIRED: The expected risk-adjusted premium of a stock based on the capital asset pricing model.
DISCUSSION: According to the capital asset pricing model, the risk premium of a particular stock is the excess of the market rate of return over the risk-free rate weighted by the stock's beta coefficient. For Guilderland Mining, this calculation is

Stock's risk premium = 2.2 × (12% − 5%)
= 2.2 × 7%
= 15.4%

Answer (A) is incorrect. The percentage of 7.0% is the difference between the overall market rate of return and the risk-free rate. Answer (B) is incorrect. The percentage of 10.4% results from improperly subtracting the risk-free rate from the stock's risk premium. Answer (D) is incorrect. The percentage of 21.4% results from multiplying beta by market rate of return, then subtracting risk-free rate from it.

21. The common stock of Wisconsin's Finest Cheese has a beta coefficient of 1.7. The following information about overall market conditions is available:

Expected return on U.S. Treasury bonds   6%
Expected return on the market portfolio   8.5%

Using the capital asset pricing model (CAPM), what is the risk premium on the market?

  A. 10.3%
  B. 4.3%
  C. 2.5%
  D. 1.7%

Answer (C) is correct.
   REQUIRED: The risk premium on the market using CAPM.
   DISCUSSION: The risk premium on the market is the return on the market portfolio (8.5%) minus the risk-free return as measured by the return on U.S. Treasury securities (6%), or 2.5%.
   Answer (A) is incorrect. The rate of 10.3% is the expected return on the stock. **Answer (B) is incorrect.** The rate of 4.3% is the risk premium on the stock, not the market. **Answer (D) is incorrect.** The stock's beta coefficient and the risk premium on the market are not the same in this case.

22. Using the capital asset pricing model (CAPM), the required rate of return for a firm with a beta of 1.5 when the market return is 10% and the risk-free rate is 8% is

  A. 5%
  B. 8%
  C. 10%
  D. 11%

Answer (D) is correct.
   REQUIRED: The required rate of return using the capital asset pricing model.
   DISCUSSION: The CAPM quantifies the required rate of return on a security by relating the security's level of risk to the average return available in the market. The required rate of return is calculated as follows:

$$\text{Required rate of return} = R_F + \beta(R_M - R_F)$$
$$= 8\% + [1.5 \times (10\% - 8\%)]$$
$$= 8\% + (1.5 \times 2\%)$$
$$= 11\%$$

   Answer (A) is incorrect. The required rate of return cannot be lower than the risk-free rate. **Answer (B) is incorrect.** The required rate of return for the safest investments (U.S. Treasury securities) is the risk-free rate of 8%. **Answer (C) is incorrect.** The market return, not the required rate of return, is 10%.

7.5 Selecting the Forecasting Method

23. Through the use of decision models, managers thoroughly analyze many alternatives and decide on the best alternative for the company. Often the actual results achieved from a particular decision are not what was expected when the decision was made. In addition, an alternative that was not selected would have actually been the best decision for the company. The appropriate technique to analyze the alternatives by using expected inputs and altering them before a decision is made is

A. Expected value analysis.
B. Linear programming.
C. Program evaluation review technique (PERT).
D. Sensitivity analysis.

Answer (D) is correct.
REQUIRED: The technique that involves altering expected inputs during the decision process.
DISCUSSION: After a problem has been formulated into any mathematical model, it may be subjected to sensitivity analysis. Sensitivity analysis examines how the model's outcomes change as the parameters change.
Answer (A) is incorrect. Expected value analysis is used to determine an anticipated return or cost based upon probabilities of events and their related outcomes. **Answer (B) is incorrect.** Linear programming optimizes a function given certain constraints. **Answer (C) is incorrect.** PERT is a network method used to plan and control large projects.

24. A widely used approach that managers use to recognize uncertainty about individual items and to obtain an immediate financial estimate of the consequences of possible prediction errors is

A. Expected value analysis.
B. Learning curve analysis.
C. Sensitivity analysis.
D. Regression analysis.

Answer (C) is correct.
REQUIRED: The approach that gives an immediate financial estimate of the consequences of possible prediction errors.
DISCUSSION: After a problem has been formulated into any mathematical model, it may be subjected to sensitivity analysis. Sensitivity analysis examines how the model's outcomes change as the parameters change.
Answer (A) is incorrect. Expected value is the probabilistically weighted average of the outcomes of an action. **Answer (B) is incorrect.** Learning curve analysis quantifies how labor costs decline as employees learn their jobs through repetition. **Answer (D) is incorrect.** Regression, or least squares, analysis determines the average change in the dependent variable given a unit change in one or more independent variables.

GLEIM
GO TO ONLINE COURSE

Access the **Gleim CPA Premium Review System** featuring our SmartAdapt technology from your Gleim Personal Classroom to continue your studies. You will experience a personalized study environment with exam-emulating multiple-choice questions.

STUDY UNIT EIGHT
CORPORATE CAPITAL STRUCTURE

(21 pages of outline)

8.1	Bonds	240
8.2	Equity	246
8.3	Capital Structure and Solvency	250
8.4	Component Costs of Capital	252
8.5	Expected Value	255
8.6	Weighted-Average Cost of Capital	257

The balance sheet of a corporation reports the firm's resources and capital structure. Resources consist of the assets used to earn a return. The capital structure consists of the amounts contributed by creditors (Subunit 8.1) and owners (Subunit 8.2). A firm's ability to remain in business in the long run is solvency (Subunit 8.3).

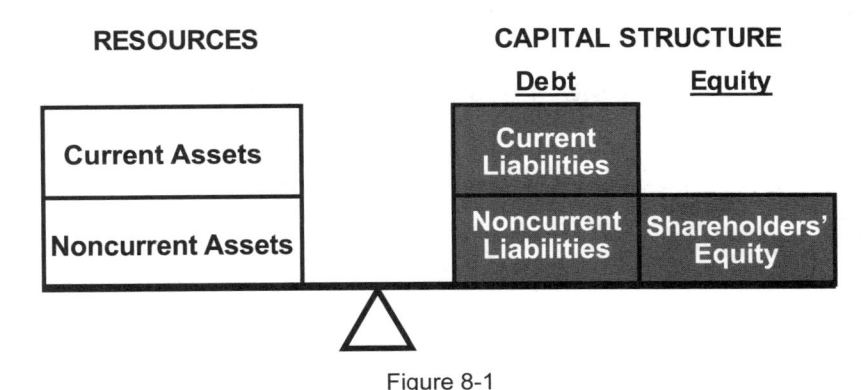

Figure 8-1

Every corporation must determine the appropriate mix of debt and equity in the capital structure. Each component has a cost that changes as economic conditions vary, and as more or less of a component is used. Finding the right mix is the subject of Subunits 8.4 and 8.6.

BACKGROUND 8-1	Corporate Capital Terminology
Many terms are used in business to describe who is borrowing money and who is lending money.	

Borrower	Lender
Debtor	Debtee
Payer	Payee
Issuer	Investor
	Creditor
	Holder

8.1 BONDS

1. **Overview**

    a. Bonds are the main form of long-term debt financing for corporations and governments.

       1) A bond is a formal contract to pay an amount of money (par value, maturity amount, or face amount) to the holder at a certain date (maturity date). Also, most bonds provide for a series of cash interest payments based on a specified percentage (stated rate or coupon rate) of the face amount at specified intervals.

          a) The agreement is included in a legal document called an **indenture**.

    b. Issuing bonds requires legal and accounting work. The expense is rarely justified for bonds with maturities of less than 5 years.

       1) In general, the longer the term of a bond, the higher the return (yield) demanded by investors to compensate for increased risk, such as the time value of money, interest rate risk, inflation, cyclical economic risk, etc.

          a) This relationship is the **term structure of interest rates**. It is depicted by the yield curve.

    Positive (Normal) Yield Curve

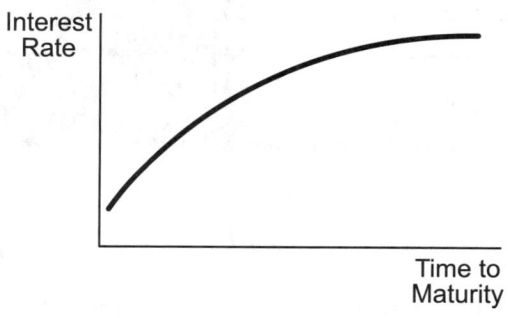

    Figure 8-2

    c. The indenture may require the issuer to maintain a **bond sinking fund**. The objective of the fund is to accumulate sufficient assets to pay the bond principal at maturity.

       1) The amounts transferred into this account earn revenues over time. Thus, the bond sinking fund accumulates money to provide the necessary funds to repay the bonds in the future.

    d. **Advantages of Bonds to the Issuer**

       1) Interest paid on debt is tax deductible (referred to as a tax shield).
       2) Control of the firm is not shared with debtholders.

e. **Disadvantages of Bonds to the Issuer**

1) Unlike returns on equity investments, the payment of interest and principal on debt is a legal obligation. If cash flow is insufficient, the firm could become insolvent.
2) The legal requirement to pay interest and principal increases a firm's risk and reduces its retained earnings. Since shareholders demand increased retained earnings, they are less likely to invest in the firm, thus decreasing the share price.
3) Bonds may require collateral, which is specific property pledged to a lender in case of default.
4) The amount of debt financing available to the individual firm is limited. Generally accepted standards of the investment community usually require a certain debt-to-equity ratio. Beyond this limit, the cost of debt may rise rapidly, or debt may not be available. (The debt-to-equity ratio is covered in Subunit 8.3.)

2. **Types of Bonds**
   a. Maturity Pattern
      1) A **term bond** has a single maturity date at the end of its term.
      2) A **serial bond** matures in stated amounts at regular intervals.
   b. Valuation
      1) **Variable (or floating) rate bonds** pay interest that is dependent on market conditions. In other words, the interest rate of the bonds changes (or floats).
      2) **Zero-coupon or deep-discount bonds** have no stated rate of interest and require no periodic cash payments. The interest component consists entirely of the bond's discount.
      3) **Commodity-backed bonds** are payable at prices related to a commodity such as gold.
   c. Redemption Provisions
      1) **Callable bonds** may be repurchased by the issuer at a specified price before maturity. When interest rates are declining, the issuer can replace high-interest debt with low-interest debt.
         a) Call provisions allow the issuer to repurchase and retire the bonds (or other fixed-income instruments) early. They typically specify when the bond may be called and the price to be paid. Callable bonds have higher interest rates than comparable noncallable bonds.
         b) If the sum of the interest payments avoided exceeds the premium paid to retire the debt, it is an advantage to issuers and a disadvantage to investors to call the bond.
      2) **Convertible bonds** may be converted into equity securities of the issuer at the option of the holder under certain conditions. The ability to become equity holders is an incentive to potential investors.

d. Securitization
   1) **Mortgage bonds** are backed by specific assets, usually real estate.
   2) **Debentures** are backed by the issuer's credit, not specific assets.
e. Ownership
   1) **Registered bonds** are issued in the name of the holder. Only the registered holder may receive interest and principal payments.
   2) **Bearer bonds** are not individually registered. Interest and principal are paid to whoever presents the bond.
f. Priority
   1) **Subordinated debentures** and second mortgage bonds are junior securities with claims inferior to those of senior bonds.
g. Repayment Provisions
   1) **Income bonds** pay interest contingent on the issuer's profitability.
   2) **Revenue bonds** are issued by governmental units and are payable from specific revenue sources.

3. **Bond Ratings**
   a. Credit-rating agencies judge the creditworthiness of bonds. The higher the rating, the more likely the firm will pay the interest and principal.
   b. The three largest firms are Moody's, Standard & Poor's, and Fitch.
      1) **Investment-grade bonds** are safe investments and have the lowest yields. The highest rating assigned is AAA, and the lowest investment-grade bond is BBB–. Some fiduciary organizations (such as banks and insurers) are allowed to invest only in investment-grade bonds.
      2) **Noninvestment-grade bonds**, also called speculative-grade, high-yield, or junk bonds, have high risk. The ratings range from BB+ to DDD.

4. **Bond Valuation**
   a. A bond issuer's main concern is the cash received from investors.
      1) This amount equals the **present value** of the cash flows from the bonds (principal at maturity and periodic interest) discounted at the market (effective) interest rate.
      2) Use of the **effective rate** ensures that the bonds' yield to maturity (ultimate rate of return to the investor) equals the rate of return in the market at the time of sale.
   b. Cash proceeds may be equal to, less than, or greater than the face amount of the bonds, depending on the relationship of the bonds' stated rate of interest to the market rate.
      1) Bonds are sold **at par** if the stated rate equals the market rate at the time of sale (Present value = Face amount).
      2) If the bonds' **stated rate is lower than the market rate**, periodic interest payments are lower than those currently available. Thus, the bonds are sold for less than par value (at a **discount**) so that the effective interest rate equals the market rate.

SU 8: Corporate Capital Structure

EXAMPLE 8-1   **Issuance of Bonds at a Discount**

On January 1, Year 1, a firm issues 100 bonds at 6% annual interest with a face amount of $1,000 maturing in 5 years. At issuance, the market rate is 8%. The proceeds are calculated as follows:

Using PV/FV Tables

Face amount:
Present value of a single payment of
$100,000 discounted at 8% for 5 years $100,000 × .68058 = $68,058

Interest payments:
Present value of an ordinary annuity of
$6,000 discounted at 8% for 5 years $6,000 × 3.99271 = 23,956
Total proceeds $92,014

Using Formula

Face amount:

$$PV = \frac{Amount}{(1+i)^n}$$

$$\frac{\$100,000}{(1+.08)^5} = \$68,058$$

Interest payments:

$$PV = \frac{Amount_1}{(1+r)^1} + \frac{Amount_2}{(1+r)^2} + \ldots + \frac{Amount_n}{(1+r)^n}$$

$$\frac{\$6,000}{1.08^1} + \frac{\$6,000}{1.08^2} + \frac{\$6,000}{1.08^3} + \frac{\$6,000}{1.08^4} + \frac{\$6,000}{1.08^5} = \$23,956$$

The issuer receives cash of $92,014 and records a discount on bonds payable of $7,986 ($100,000 − $92,014).

---

3) If the bonds' **stated rate is higher than the market rate**, periodic interest payments are higher than those currently available. Thus, the bonds are sold for more than par value (at a **premium**) so that the effective interest rate equals the market rate.

EXAMPLE 8-2   **Issuance of Bonds at a Premium**

On January 1, Year 1, a firm issues bonds with the same terms as those in Example 8-1, except that the stated rate is 8% and the effective rate is 6%. The present value of the face amount is $74,726 ($100,000 × .74726) and the present value of the interest payments is $33,699 ($8,000 × 4.21236). The issuer therefore receives cash of $108,425 ($74,726 + $33,699) and records a premium on bonds payable of $8,425.

---

c. The amortization of discount or premium over the term of the bonds results in a carrying amount at maturity equal to their face amount.

1) The bond discount or premium must be amortized using the effective interest method (unless the results of another method, such as the straight-line method, are not materially different).

d. When bonds are traded among investors in the secondary market, the issuer is not a party to the transaction and receives no cash.

1) The price of the resold bonds is determined by a risk assessment of the issuer and the market rate of interest at the time of the trade. Accordingly, the bonds are priced to achieve a new yield.

5. **Leverage**
    a. Leverage is the relative amount of fixed cost in a firm's cost structure. In other words, leverage is the amount of debt a firm has. Leverage creates risk because fixed costs must be paid, regardless of sales.
        1) A firm's total leverage consists of operating leverage and financial leverage.
    b. **Operating leverage** is the extent to which a firm's costs of operating are fixed. A firm's **degree of operating leverage (DOL)** is a ratio that measures the effect that given fixed operating costs have on earnings.

    $$DOL = \frac{\%\text{ change in earnings before interest and taxes (EBIT)}}{\%\text{ change in sales}}$$

    1) For example, if the firm's EBIT increases by 24% as a result of an increase in sales of 12%, the firm's DOL is 2 (24% ÷ 12%).
    2) The DOL helps the firm determine the operating leverage that maximizes the firm's EBIT.
    3) A firm with a high percentage of fixed costs is riskier than a firm in the same industry that relies more on variable costs. It generates more earnings by increasing sales.

    c. **Financial leverage** is the degree of debt (fixed financial costs) in the firm's financial structure. A firm's **degree of financial leverage (DFL)** is a ratio that measures the effect that an amount of fixed financing costs has on earnings per share (EPS).

    $$EPS = \frac{\text{Net income available to common shareholders}}{\text{Weighted-average common shares outstanding}}$$

    $$DFL = \frac{\%\text{ change in earnings per share (EPS)}}{\%\text{ change in earnings before interest and taxes (EBIT)}}$$

    1) Net income available to common shareholders is net income minus preferred dividends.
    2) For example, if the firm's EPS increases by 12% as a result of an increase in EBIT of 6%, the firm's DFL is 2 (12% ÷ 6%).
    3) When a firm has a high percentage of fixed financial costs, it must accept more risk to increase its EPS.

d. **The degree of total (combined) leverage (DTL)** is the product of the degrees of operating and financial leverage.

$$DTL = DOL \times DFL = \frac{\% \text{ change in EBIT}}{\% \text{ change in sales}} \times \frac{\% \text{ change in EPS}}{\% \text{ change in EBIT}} = \frac{\% \text{ change in EPS}}{\% \text{ change in sales}}$$

1) For example, if the firm's EPS increases by 10% as a result of an increase in sales of 2%, the firm's DTL is 5 (10% ÷ 2%).
2) A firm with a higher DTL provides a higher return to investors, but it is also more risky. The risk is due to a higher likelihood of default.

e. The value of a levered firm is the value of an unlevered firm plus the present value (PV) of the interest tax savings.

$$\text{Interest tax savings} = T_c \times (r_{debt} \times D)$$
$$\text{PV of the interest tax savings} = T_c \times (r_{debt} \times D) \div r_{debt}, \text{ assuming the debt is permanent}$$

T_c = Corporate tax rate
r_{debt} = Rate of interest on the debt
D = Amount of debt

6. **Debt Covenants**

    a. Debt covenants are restrictions imposed on a borrower by the creditor in a formal debt agreement (indenture).
    b. The following are examples of debt covenants:

        1) Limitations on issuing additional long-term or short-term debt
        2) Limitations on dividend payments
        3) Maintenance of certain financial ratios
        4) Maintenance of specific collateral that secures the debt

    c. The more restrictive the debt covenants, the lower the risk the borrower will not pay. The less risky the investment, the lower the interest rate on the debt (the risk premium is lower).
    d. If the debtor violates a covenant, the debt becomes due immediately.

You have completed the outline for this subunit.
Study multiple-choice questions 1 through 4 beginning on page 260.

STOP & REVIEW

8.2 EQUITY

1. **Common Stock**

    a. Common shareholders are the owners of the corporation. Common shareholder rights, although reasonably uniform throughout the U.S., depend on the laws of the state of incorporation.

        1) Equity ownership involves risk because holders of common stock are not guaranteed a return and are last in priority in a liquidation. Shareholders' capital is a source of funds for payment of creditors if losses occur on liquidation.

    b. Common shareholders ordinarily have a **preemptive right** to purchase additional stock issues in proportion to their current ownership percentages.

    c. Common shareholders have voting rights. They select the board of directors and vote on resolutions.

    d. **Market capitalization** (market cap) refers to the market value of a company's outstanding shares. It is equal to the shares of common stock outstanding times the fair market value per share.

    e. **Advantages to the Corporation**

        1) Common stock does not require a fixed dividend. Dividends are paid from profits when available.

        2) Common stock has no fixed maturity date for repayment of capital.

        3) The sale of common stock increases the creditworthiness of the firm by providing more capital (or money) for the corporation to use.

    f. **Disadvantages to the Corporation**

        1) Cash dividends on common stock are not tax-deductible and are paid from after-tax profits. This means common stockholders are double taxed: once on the corporate income and once individually on their personal dividend income. It also means that paying dividends does not decrease a corporation's net income.

        2) New common stock sales dilute EPS available to current shareholders.

        3) Underwriting costs (e.g., fees to issue new common stock) typically are higher for common stock than debt.

        4) Too much equity may raise the average cost of capital of the firm above its optimal level.

g. **Common stock valuation** based on dividend payout models

1) When the dividend per share of common stock is constant and expected to be paid continuously, the price per share is calculated as follows:

$$P_0 = D \div r$$

P_0 = Current price per share
D = Dividend per share (constant)
r = Required rate of return

2) The **dividend growth model** assumes that dividends per share and price per share increase at the same constant rate (which can be positive or negative). The price per share can be calculated as follows:

$$P_0 = \frac{D_0(1+g)}{r-g} = \frac{D_1}{r-g}$$

P_0 = Current stock price per share
D_0 = Current dividends per share
D_1 = Dividends per share expected next year
r = Required rate of return (discount rate)
g = Growth rate (constant)

EXAMPLE 8-3   Dividend Growth Model

A firm currently pays dividends of $10 per common share. The dividends are expected to increase at a constant rate of 5% per year. If investors' required rate of return is 8%, the current market value of a common share is $350.

$$P_0 = \frac{D_0(1+g)}{r-g} = \frac{\$10(1+5\%)}{8\%-5\%} = \$350$$

---

a) The required rate of return (the cost of common stock) can be derived from the dividend growth model.

$$r = \frac{D_1}{P_0} + g$$

b) Disadvantages of the dividend growth model include that it

i) Assumes the dividend growth rate is constant and is always less than the required rate of return.

ii) Cannot be used to value stock price if a company does not pay dividends.

3) The **dividend discount model** can also be used to calculate stock price.

$$P_0 = [D_1 \div (1+r)^1] + [D_2 \div (1+r)^2] + [D_3 \div (1+r)^3] + \ldots + [D_t \div (1+r)^t]$$

P_0 = Current stock price per share
D = Dividends per share
r = Discount rate
t = Final period

2. **Preferred Stock**

    a. Preferred stock is a hybrid of debt and equity.

        1) Preferred stock dividends are generally established in terms of issuance as a percentage of par value, making preferred stock dividends fixed payments.
        2) Preferred stock has priority over common stock in terms of dividend payment (preferred stock dividends must be paid before common stock dividends can be paid), but preferred stock dividends are not required payments.
        3) Also, preferred shareholders have priority over common shareholders in bankruptcy.

    b. **Advantages to the Corporation**

        1) Preferred stock is equity and increases the creditworthiness of the firm.
        2) Control is still held by common shareholders. (Preferred stock rarely has voting rights.)
        3) Superior earnings of the firm are usually still reserved for the common shareholders.
        4) Preferred stock does not require periodic payments. Thus, nonpayment of dividends does not lead to bankruptcy.

    c. **Disadvantages to the Corporation**

        1) Cash dividends on preferred stock are not tax-deductible and are paid from after-tax profits. The result is a substantially greater cost relative to bonds because preferred stockholders also enjoy the value of ownership, but bondholders do not.
        2) In periods of economic difficulty, accumulated unpaid dividends (**dividends in arrears**) may create managerial and financial problems for the firm.

    d. **Typical Preferred Stock Provisions**

        1) Priority in assets and earnings. If the firm is bankrupt, the preferred shareholders have priority over common shareholders.
        2) Accumulation of dividends. If preferred dividends are cumulative, dividends in arrears must be paid before any common dividends can be paid.
        3) Convertibility. Preferred stock issues may be convertible into common stock at the option of the shareholder.
        4) Participation. Preferred stock may participate with common stock in excess earnings of the firm. In other words, preferred stockholders not only receive their preferred dividend, but also receive common shareholder dividends on a pro-rata basis. For example, 8% participating preferred stock might pay a preferred dividend each year of 8% and, when the corporation is extremely profitable, receives an ordinary dividend equal to what the common shareholders receive.

            a) But **nonparticipating preferred stock** receives no further dividends than are required.

        5) Par value. Par value is the liquidation value, and a percentage of par equals the preferred dividend.

e. **Preferred stock valuation** applies the same method used to value a bond that is described in Subunit 8.1.

1) Future cash flows associated with the security are discounted at an investor's required rate of return (market rate) used to value preferred stock.

2) The future cash flows from bonds consist of principal at maturity and periodic interest. Future cash flows from preferred stock are assumed to consist only of the estimated future annual dividends (D_p).

$$D_p = \text{Par value of preferred stock} \times \text{Preferred dividend rate}$$

3) Unlike a bond, which has a specific maturity date, preferred stock is assumed to be outstanding in perpetuity. The discount rate used is the investor's required rate of return (r).

$$\text{Preferred stock price } (P_p) = \frac{D_p}{r}$$

a) For example, the value of a share of preferred stock with a par value of $100 and a dividend rate of 5% to an investor with a required rate of return of 10% is $50 [($100 × 5%) ÷ 10%].

3. **Other Market-Based Measures**

a. Increasing shareholder wealth is the fundamental goal of any corporation. Two common ratios measure the degree of success toward this goal.

b. The **dividend payout ratio** measures what portion of accrual-basis earnings was actually paid out to common shareholders in the form of dividends.

$$\text{Dividend payout ratio} = \frac{\text{Dividend paid per share}}{\text{Earnings per share}} = \frac{\text{Cash dividend}}{\text{Net income}}$$

c. The **dividend yield ratio** measures how much a company distributes to shareholders relative to its price per share.

$$\text{Dividend yield} = \frac{\text{Dividend per share}}{\text{Market price per share}}$$

d. **Shareholder return** measures the return on a purchase of stock.

$$\text{Shareholder return} = \frac{\text{Ending stock price} - \text{Beginning stock price} + \text{Annual dividends per share}}{\text{Beginning stock price}}$$

You have completed the outline for this subunit.
Study multiple-choice questions 5 through 8 beginning on page 262.

STOP & REVIEW

8.3 CAPITAL STRUCTURE AND SOLVENCY

1. **Capital Structure**

    a. A firm's capital structure includes its sources of financing, both long- and short-term. These sources are debt (external sources) and equity (internal sources).

    b. **Debt** is the creditor interest in the firm.

        1) The firm is contractually obligated to repay debtholders. The terms of repayment (timing of interest and principal) are specified in the debt agreement.

        2) If the return on debt exceeds the interest paid, debt financing is advantageous. The return is increased because interest payments on debt are tax-deductible.

        3) The disadvantage of debt is that it increases the firm's risk. Debt must be paid regardless of whether the firm is profitable.

    c. **Equity** is the ownership interest in the firm.

        1) Equity is permanent capital contributed by the firm's owners to earn a return.

        2) However, a return on equity is uncertain. Equity is a residual interest in the firm's assets. It is residual because it is a claim only to assets remaining after all debt has been paid.

        3) Periodic returns to owners of excess earnings are dividends. The firm may be contractually obligated to pay dividends to preferred shareholders but not common shareholders.

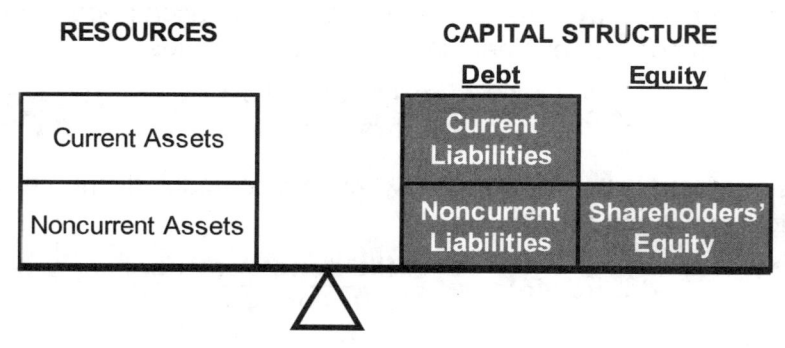

Figure 8-3

    d. Capital structure decisions affect the risk of a firm. For example, a firm with a higher percentage of debt capital is riskier than a firm with a higher percentage of equity capital.

        1) Thus, when the relative amount of debt is high, equity investors demand a higher rate of return on their investments to compensate for the additional risk of financial leverage.

        2) But a firm with a relatively larger proportion of equity capital may be able to borrow at lower rates. Debt holders accept lower interest rates in exchange for lower risk.

2. **Solvency**

    a. Solvency is a firm's ability to pay its noncurrent obligations as they come due and to remain in business in the long run.

       1) The ability to service debt from current earnings is part of the effective use of leverage.

    $$\text{Times-interest-earned ratio} = \frac{\text{Earnings before interest and taxes (EBIT) or income before interest expense and taxes}}{\text{Interest expense}}$$

    b. The key elements of solvency are the firm's capital structure and degree of leverage. (The degree of leverage is defined in item 5. in Subunit 8.1.)

3. **Capital Structure Ratios**

    a. Capital structure ratios report the relative proportions of debt and equity in a firm's capital structure.

    b. The **total debt ratio** (also called the debt to total assets ratio) reports the total debt burden carried by a firm per dollar of assets.

    $$\text{Total debt ratio} = \frac{\text{Total debt}}{\text{Total assets}}$$

EXAMPLE 8-4   **Total Debt Ratio**

The following are a firm's ratios for the current and prior years:

	Debt		Asset		Ratio
Current year:	$1,000,000	÷	$1,800,000	=	0.556
Prior year:	$950,000	÷	$1,600,000	=	0.594

Although total debt increased in absolute terms, this ratio improved because total assets increased even more.

---

   c. The **total-debt-to-total-capital ratio** measures the percentage of the firm's capital provided by creditors. Total capital includes equity and interest-bearing debt.

    $$\text{Total debt to total capital} = \frac{\text{Total debt}}{\text{Total capital}}$$

EXAMPLE 8-5   **Total-Debt-to-Total-Capital Ratio**

	Debt		Capital		Ratio
Current year:	$1,000,000	÷	$1,700,000	=	0.588
Prior year:	$950,000	÷	$1,500,000	=	0.633

The firm became slightly less reliant on debt during the current year. Although total debt increased, equity increased by a greater percentage. The firm is therefore less leveraged than before.

---

   1) When total debt to total capital is low, more of the firm's capital is supplied by the shareholders. Thus, creditors prefer this ratio to be low to provide a cushion against losses.

d. The **debt-to-equity ratio** is a direct comparison of the firm's debt with its equity.

$$\text{Debt to equity} = \frac{\text{Total debt}}{\text{Shareholders' equity}}$$

EXAMPLE 8-6   **Debt-to-Equity Ratio**

	Debt		Shareholders' Equity		Ratio
Current year:	$1,000,000	÷	$800,000	=	1.25
Prior year:	$950,000	÷	$650,000	=	1.46

The amount by which the firm's debt exceeds its equity declined in the current year.

---

1) Like the previous ratio, the debt-to-equity ratio reflects long-term debt-payment ability. Again, a low ratio means a lower relative debt and less risk for creditors.

e. The **long-term-debt-to-total-equity ratio** reports long-term debt per dollar of equity.

$$\text{Long-term debt to total equity} = \frac{\text{Long-term debt}}{\text{Shareholder's equity}}$$

EXAMPLE 8-7   **Long-Term-Debt-to-Total-Equity Ratio**

	Debt		Shareholders' Equity		Ratio
Current year:	$610,000	÷	$800,000	=	0.763
Prior year:	$675,000	÷	$650,000	=	1.038

The firm has reduced its long-term debt. It now has less than one dollar of long-term debt for every dollar of equity.

---

1) A firm with a low ratio has a better chance of obtaining new debt financing at a favorable rate.

STOP & REVIEW

You have completed the outline for this subunit.
Study multiple-choice questions 9 and 10 on page 264.

8.4 COMPONENT COSTS OF CAPITAL

1. **Overview**

    a. Investors provide funds to corporations with the understanding that management will deploy those funds in such a way that the investor will ultimately receive a return.

    1) If management does not provide the required rate of return, investors sell their stock on the secondary market, causing the market value of the stock to drop. Creditors then demand higher rates on the firm's debt.

    2) For this reason, investors' required rate of return (also called their opportunity cost of capital) becomes the firm's cost of capital.

SU 8: Corporate Capital Structure   253

    b.   Equity holders demand higher returns than debt holders.

        1)   Providers of equity capital are exposed to more risk than are lenders because

            a)   The firm is not legally obligated to pay them a return, and
            b)   In case of liquidation, creditors have priority.

        2)   To compensate for this higher risk, equity investors demand a higher return, making equity financing more expensive than debt.

    c.   A firm's cost of capital is used to discount the future cash flows of long-term projects the firm is considering. Potential investments with a rate of return higher than the cost of capital will increase the value of the firm and shareholders' wealth. On the other hand, potential investments with a rate of return lower than the cost of capital will decrease the value of the firm and shareholders' wealth.

2. **Component Costs of Capital**

    a.   A firm's cost of capital is the required rate of return by investors on the firm's debt and equity (both preferred and common).

    b.   Component cost of capital includes (1) cost of long-term debt, (2) cost of preferred stock, and (3) cost of common equity (retained earnings).

        1)   The component cost of **long-term debt** is the after-tax interest rate on the debt because interest payments are tax-deductible.

$$\text{Effective rate} \times (1.0 - \text{Marginal tax rate})$$

            a)   If debt is issued at face value, the effective rate equals the coupon rate.
            b)   If debt is issued at a premium or discount, the effective rate equals the coupon payment divided by the issue price.

                i)   For example, if the coupon rate is 10% and the bonds are issued at a premium price of $105, then the calculation is

$$(\$10 \div \$105) \times (1.0 - \text{Marginal tax rate})$$

                ii)   If the coupon rate is 15% and the bonds are issued at a discount price of $95, then the calculation is

$$(\$15 \div \$95) \times (1.0 - \text{Marginal tax rate})$$

        2)   The component cost of **preferred stock** is calculated using the dividend yield ratio.

$$R_{\text{preferred stock (old)}} = \frac{\text{Cash dividend on preferred stock}}{\text{Market price of preferred stock}}$$

            a)   The market price of preferred stock upon issuance equals the net proceeds (Gross proceeds – Flotation costs). Flotation (issuance) costs reduce the net proceeds received, raising the cost of capital.

                i)   Thus, the component cost of preferred stock also can be derived by using the following formula:

$$R_{\text{preferred stock (new)}} = \frac{\text{Cash dividend on preferred stock}}{\text{Preferred stock market price} - \text{Flotation costs}}$$

3) The costs of debt and preferred stock reflect the requirements of creditors and prospective purchasers of preferred shares, respectively. However, **retained earnings** (internal equity capital) already belong to the common shareholders. These earnings would be distributed to them as dividends if not retained. Accordingly, the component cost of retained earnings is the rate of return required by common shareholders.

   a) If the firm cannot use retained earnings profitably, it should be distributed to the common shareholders as dividends so they can make their own investments.

   b) The following is the traditional formula for cost of **common equity**:

   $$R_{\text{common equity (basic)}} = \frac{\text{Next dividend per share}}{\text{Share price}}$$

   c) An advanced formula combines the basic formula above with the dividend growth model described in Subunit 8.2:

   $$R_{\text{common equity (advanced)}} = \frac{\text{Next dividend per share}}{\text{Share price}} + \text{Dividend growth rate}$$

   d) The methods of calculating the cost of common equity also include the **capital asset pricing model (CAPM)** described in Study Unit 7, Subunit 4. It quantifies the required return on an equity security by relating the security's level of risk to the average return available in the market (portfolio). The CAPM may be used to calculate the cost of common equity as

   $$R_{\text{common equity}} = R_F + \beta(R_M - R_F)$$

   If: R_F = Risk-free return
   R_M = Market return
   β = Measure of the systematic risk or volatility of the individual security in comparison to the market (diversified portfolio)

EXAMPLE 8-8   Component Costs of Capital

A firm has outstanding bonds with a coupon rate of 7% and an effective rate of 5%. Its 9%, $60 par-value preferred stock currently is trading at $67.50 per share. The firm's $1 par-value common stock trades at $1.40 per share and pays a 14% dividend with 5% growth rate. The applicable tax rate is 35%.

The component costs of capital are calculated as follows:

Long-Term Debt	Preferred Equity	Common Equity
Cost = Effective rate × (1.0 − Tax rate) = 5% × (1.0 − .35) = 5% × .65 = 3.25%	Cost = Cash dividend ÷ Market price = ($60 × 9%) ÷ $67.50 = $5.40 ÷ $67.50 = 8%	Cost = (Next dividend ÷ Market price) + Growth rate = {[$1 × 14% × (1 + 5%)] ÷ $1.40} + 5% = ($.147 ÷ $1.40) + 5% = 15.5%

You have completed the outline for this subunit.
Study multiple-choice questions 11 through 14 beginning on page 264.

STOP & REVIEW

8.5 EXPECTED VALUE

1. Expected value is a means of associating a dollar amount with each possible outcome of a probability distribution. The outcome yielding the highest expected value (which may or may not be the most likely one) is the optimal alternative.

   a. The decision is under the manager's control.

   b. The state of nature is the future event whose outcome the manager is attempting to predict.

   c. The payoff is the financial result of the combination of the manager's decision and the actual state of nature.

2. The expected value is calculated by multiplying the probability of each outcome by its payoff and adding the products. This calculation often is called a payoff table.

EXAMPLE 8-9   Expected Value

An investor is considering the purchase of two identically priced properties. Their value will change if a road is built.

The following are estimates that road construction will occur:

Future State of Nature (SN)	Event	Probability
SN 1	No road is ever built.	.10 = 10%
SN 2	A road is built this year.	.20 = 20%
SN 3	A road is built more than 1 year from now.	.70 = 70%
		100%

The following are estimates of the values of the properties (payoffs) for each event:

Property	SN 1	SN 2	SN 3
Bivens Tract	$10,000	$40,000	$35,000
Newnan Tract	$20,000	$50,000	$30,000

The expected value of each property is determined by multiplying the probability of each state of nature (outcome) by its payoff and adding all of the products.

		Expected Value
Bivens Tract:	.1($10,000) + .2($40,000) + .7($35,000) =	$33,500
Newnan Tract:	.1($20,000) + .2($50,000) + .7($30,000) =	$33,000

Thus, the Bivens Tract is the better investment.

3. A **criticism** is that expected value is based on repetitive trials, but many business decisions ultimately involve only one event.

EXAMPLE 8-10	Expected Value and a Nonrepetitive Event

A company wishes to launch a communications satellite. The probability of launch failure is .2, and the payoff is $0. The probability of a successful launch is .8, and the payoff is $25,000,000. The expected value is

.2($0) + .8($25,000,000) = $20,000,000

But $20,000,000 is not a possible payoff. Either the satellite orbits for $25,000,000, or it crashes for $0.

4. The difficulty of constructing a payoff table is the determination of all possible outcomes of decisions and their probabilities. Thus, a probability distribution must be established.

    a. The assigned probabilities may reflect prior experience with similar decisions, the results of research, or subjective estimates.

EXAMPLE 8-11	Expected Value Absent Risk Neutrality

A dealer in yachts may order 0, 1, or 2 yachts for inventory.

The dealer projects demand as follows:

Demand	Probability
0 yachts	.10 = 10%
1 yacht	.50 = 50%
2 yachts	.40 = 40%
	100%

The cost of carrying an excess yacht is $50,000, and the gain for each yacht sold is $200,000. The profit or loss resulting from each combination of decision and outcome is as follows:

			Expected Value		
Decision	State of Nature		Stock 0 Yachts	Stock 1 Yacht	Stock 2 Yachts
	Demand = 0				
Stock 0 yachts	$ 0 × 10%	=	$0		
Stock 1 yacht	(50,000) × 10%	=		$ (5,000)	
Stock 2 yachts	(100,000) × 10%	=			$ (10,000)
	Demand = 1				
Stock 0 yachts	$ 0 × 50%	=	$0		
Stock 1 yacht	200,000 × 50%	=		$100,000	
Stock 2 yachts	150,000 × 50%	=			$ 75,000
	Demand = 2				
Stock 0 yachts	$ 0 × 40%	=	$0		
Stock 1 yacht	200,000 × 40%	=		$ 80,000	
Stock 2 yachts	400,000 × 40%	=			$160,000
All expected values			**$0**	**$175,000**	**$225,000**

In this example, a risk-averse decision maker may not wish to accept the risk of losing $100,000 by ordering two yachts, even though that decision has the highest expected value.

SU 8: Corporate Capital Structure

5. Although exact probabilities may not be known, the use of expected value analysis forces managers to evaluate decisions logically. At the least, managers are forced to consider all outcomes of each decision.

SUCCESS TIP

Expected value calculations and analysis may appear difficult. However, you are simply multiplying the probability of each outcome by its payoff and summing the products. In the calculation of the net expected value or expected incremental profit from an investment, do not forget to subtract the amount of the initial investment.

STOP & REVIEW

You have completed the outline for this subunit.
Study multiple-choice questions 15 through 18 beginning on page 266.

8.6 WEIGHTED-AVERAGE COST OF CAPITAL

SUCCESS TIP

The weighted-average cost of capital has been tested recently using general conceptual questions and calculation questions.

1. **Weighted-Average Cost of Capital (WACC)**

   a. Corporate management usually designates a target capital structure, i.e., the proportion of each component of capital: long-term debt, preferred equity, and common equity.

   b. A firm's WACC combines the three components of capital into one composite rate of return on the combined components of capital. The weights are based on the target capital structure, which is effectively expected-value analysis (discussed in Subunit 8.5).

EXAMPLE 8-12   Weighted-Average Cost of Capital

The firm has a target capital structure of 20% long-term debt, 30% preferred equity, and 50% common equity. The weighted-average cost of capital is calculated as follows:

	Target Weight		Cost of Capital		Weighted Cost
Long-term debt	20%	×	3.25%	=	0.65%
Preferred equity	30%	×	8.00%	=	2.40%
Common equity	50%	×	15.50%	=	7.75%
					10.80%

258 SU 8: Corporate Capital Structure

c. A formula to calculate the WACC given no preferred equity is

$$WACC = \left[\left(\frac{Value_{Debt}}{Value_{Equity} + Value_{Debt}}\right) \times R_{Debt} \times (1 - R_{Tax})\right] + \left[\left(\frac{Value_{Equity}}{Value_{Equity} + Value_{Debt}}\right) \times R_{Equity}\right]$$

|———————— Debt Component ————————|———— Equity Component ————|

R_{Equity} = Cost of equity
R_{Debt} = Cost of debt
$Value_{Equity}$ = Market value of the firm's equity
$Value_{Debt}$ = Market value of the firm's debt
R_{Tax} = Corporate tax rate

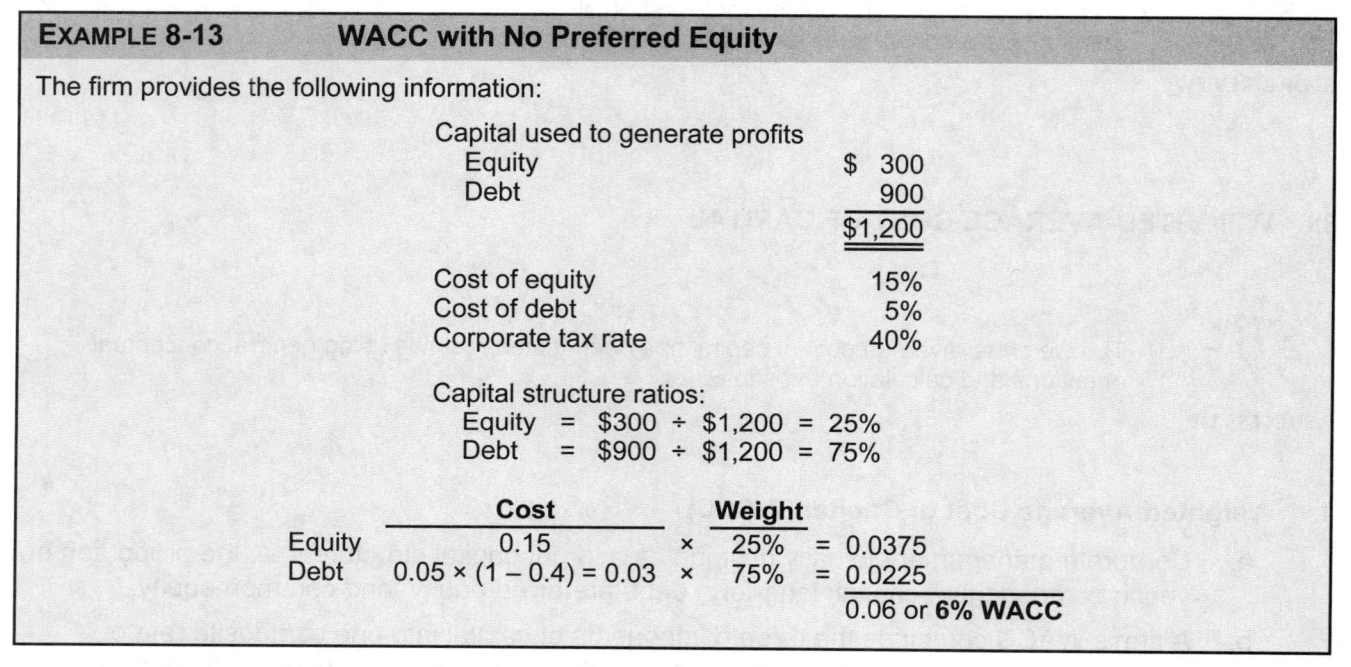

EXAMPLE 8-13   WACC with No Preferred Equity

The firm provides the following information:

```
Capital used to generate profits
    Equity                              $   300
    Debt                                    900
                                        $ 1,200

Cost of equity                              15%
Cost of debt                                 5%
Corporate tax rate                          40%

Capital structure ratios:
    Equity = $300 ÷ $1,200 = 25%
    Debt   = $900 ÷ $1,200 = 75%
```

	Cost		Weight	
Equity	0.15	×	25%	= 0.0375
Debt	0.05 × (1 − 0.4) = 0.03	×	75%	= 0.0225
				0.06 or **6% WACC**

---

d. A formula to calculate WACC with preferred equity is

$$WACC = \frac{D}{V} \times R_d \times (1 - T) + \frac{E}{V} \times R_e + \frac{P}{V} \times R_p$$

|——— Debt Component ———|— Common Equity Component —|— Preferred Equity Component —|

R_e = Cost of common equity (required return on common equity)
R_d = Cost of debt (required return on debt)
R_p = Cost of preferred equity (required return on preferred equity)
E = Market value of the firm's common equity
D = Market value of the firm's debt
P = Market value of the firm's preferred equity
T = Corporate tax rate
$V = E + D + P$ = Capital used to generate profits

SU 8: Corporate Capital Structure

1) The market values of the firm's debt, common equity, and preferred equity should reflect the targeted capital structure rather than the current capital structure.

2) Although the WACC formula includes the market value of debt, the carrying amount may be used as a proxy. However, if the firm is in financial distress, the market value and carrying amount may differ greatly.

3) The debt component is multiplied by (1 – T) to incorporate the tax benefit of interest expense.

EXAMPLE 8-14 — **Weighted-Average Cost of Capital**

The following excerpt is from a firm's most recent balance sheet:

Component	Carrying Amount	Proportions
11.4% Bonds Payable	$ 2,200,000	10.00%
11.5% Preferred Stock	4,600,000	20.91%
Common Stock	14,000,000	63.64%
Retained Earnings	1,200,000	5.45%
Totals	**$22,000,000**	**100.00%**

In order to calculate its WACC, the firm must first determine the component costs of long-term debt and preferred equity. The company has historically provided a 16% return on common equity. The firm is in a 35% marginal tax bracket. Assume that the market price of the preferred stock is the same as the book value.

Component cost of long-term debt = Effective rate × (1.0 – Marginal tax rate)
= 11.4% × (1.0 – .35)
= 7.41%

Component cost of preferred equity = Cash dividend ÷ Market price of stock
= ($4,600,000 × 11.5%) ÷ $4,600,000
= 11.5%

The firm can now determine its WACC by multiplying the cost of each component of capital by the proportion of total market value represented by that component.

Component	(1) Market Value	(2) Weight		(3) Component Cost		(2) × (3) Weighted Cost
11.4% Bonds Payable	$ 2,200,000	10.00%	×	7.41%	=	0.7410%
11.5% Preferred Stock	4,600,000	20.91%	×	11.5%	=	2.4047%
Common Stock	14,000,000	63.64%	×	16.0%	=	10.1824%
Retained Earnings	1,200,000	5.45%	×	16.0%	=	0.8720%
Totals	**$22,000,000**	**100.00%**				**14.2001%**

Generally, the component cost of retained earnings is considered to be the same as that for common stock.

The firm will invest in projects that have an expected return that is greater than 14.2001% (firm's WACC). These projects will generate additional free cash flow and will create positive net present value for the shareholders.

STOP & REVIEW

You have completed the outline for this subunit.
Study multiple-choice questions 19 through 21 beginning on page 268.

QUESTIONS

8.1 Bonds

1. This year, Nelson Industries increased earnings before interest and taxes (EBIT) by 17%. During the same period, earnings per share increased by 42%. The degree of financial leverage that existed during the year is

- A. 1.70
- B. 4.20
- C. 2.47
- D. 5.90

Answer (C) is correct.
   REQUIRED: The degree of financial leverage.
   DISCUSSION: If earnings before interest and taxes increased by 17%, and earnings per share income was up 42%, the firm is using leverage effectively. The degree of financial leverage is the percentage change in earnings per share divided by the percentage change in EBIT. Accordingly, Nelson's degree of financial leverage is 2.47 (.42 ÷ .17).

2. If Brewer Corporation's bonds are currently yielding 8% in the marketplace, why is the firm's cost of debt lower?

- A. Market interest rates have increased.
- B. Additional debt can be issued more cheaply than the original debt.
- C. There should be no difference; cost of debt is the same as the bonds' market yield.
- D. Interest is deductible for tax purposes.

Answer (D) is correct.
   REQUIRED: The reason a firm's cost of debt is lower than its current market yield.
   DISCUSSION: Because interest is deductible for tax purposes, the actual cost of debt capital is the net effect of the interest payment and the offsetting tax deduction. The actual cost of debt equals the interest rate times the difference of 1 minus the marginal tax rate. Thus, if a firm with an 8% market rate is in a 40% tax bracket, the net cost of the debt capital is 4.8% [8% × (1.0 − .40)].
   Answer (A) is incorrect. The tax deduction always causes the market yield rate to be higher than the cost of debt capital. **Answer (B) is incorrect.** Additional debt may or may not be issued more cheaply than earlier debt, depending upon the interest rates in the marketplace. **Answer (C) is incorrect.** The cost of debt is less than the yield rate given that bond interest is tax deductible.

SU 8: Corporate Capital Structure

3.

Interest Rate %

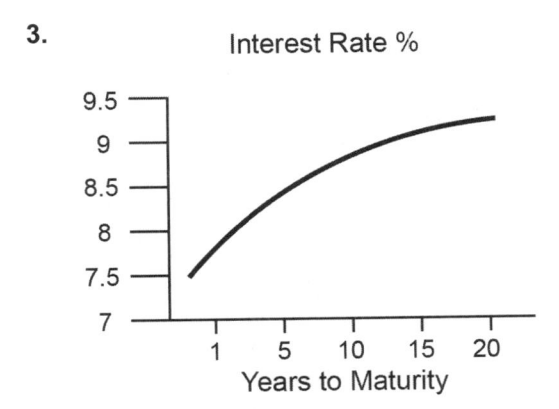

[Graph showing yield curve rising from about 7.5% at 1 year to about 9.3% at 20 years]
Years to Maturity

The yield curve shown implies that the

A. Credit risk premium of corporate bonds has increased.
B. Credit risk premium of municipal bonds has increased.
C. Long-term interest rates have a higher annualized yield than short-term rates.
D. Short-term interest rates have a higher annualized yield than long-term rates.

Answer (C) is correct.
REQUIRED: The implication of the yield curve.
DISCUSSION: The term structure of interest rates is the relationship between yield to maturity and time to maturity. This relationship is depicted by a yield curve. Assuming the long-term interest rate is an average of expected future short-term rates, the curve will be upward sloping when future short-term interest rates are expected to rise. Furthermore, the normal expectation is for long-term investments to pay higher rates because of their higher risk. Thus, long-term interest rates have a higher annualized yield than short-term rates.
Answer (A) is incorrect. The yield curve does not reflect the credit risk premium of bonds. **Answer (B) is incorrect.** The yield curve does not reflect the credit risk premium of bonds. **Answer (D) is incorrect.** Long-term interest rates should be higher than short-term rates.

4. If a $1,000 bond sells for $1,125, which of the following statements are true?

I. The market rate of interest is greater than the coupon rate on the bond.
II. The coupon rate on the bond is greater than the market rate of interest.
III. The bond sells at a premium.
IV. The bond sells at a discount.

A. I and III.
B. I and IV.
C. II and III.
D. II and IV.

Answer (C) is correct.
REQUIRED: The true statements about a bond that sells at more than its face value.
DISCUSSION: The excess of the price over the face value is a premium. A premium is paid because the coupon rate on the bond is greater than the market rate of interest. Thus, because the bond is paying a higher rate than other similar bonds, its price is bid up by investors.
Answer (A) is incorrect. If a bond sells at a premium, the market rate of interest is less than the coupon rate. **Answer (B) is incorrect.** A bond sells at a discount when the price is less than the face amount. **Answer (D) is incorrect.** A bond sells at a discount when the price is less than the face amount.

8.2 Equity

5. Each share of nonparticipating, 8%, cumulative preferred stock in a company that meets its dividend obligations has all of the following characteristics **except**

A. Voting rights in corporate elections.
B. Dividend payments that are not tax deductible by the company.
C. No principal repayments.
D. A superior claim to common stock equity in the case of liquidation.

Answer (A) is correct.
   REQUIRED: The item not characteristic of nonparticipating, cumulative preferred stock.
   DISCUSSION: Dividends on cumulative preferred stock accrue until declared. That is, the carrying amount of the preferred stock increases by the amount of any undeclared dividends. Participating preferred stock participates with common shareholders in excess earnings of the firm. Accordingly, 8% participating preferred stock might pay a dividend each year greater than 8% when the corporation is extremely profitable. Thus, nonparticipating preferred stock will receive no more than what is stated on the face of the stock. Preferred shareholders rarely have voting rights. Voting rights are exchanged for preferences regarding dividends and liquidation of assets.
   Answer (B) is incorrect. A corporation does not receive a tax deduction for making dividend payments on any type of stock. **Answer (C) is incorrect.** Preferred stock normally need not be redeemed as long as the corporation remains in business. **Answer (D) is incorrect.** Preferred shareholders do have priority over common shareholders in a liquidation.

6. In general, it is more expensive for a company to finance with equity capital than with debt capital because

A. Long-term bonds have a maturity date and must therefore be repaid in the future.
B. Investors are exposed to greater risk with equity capital.
C. Equity capital is in greater demand than debt capital.
D. Dividends fluctuate to a greater extent than interest rates.

Answer (B) is correct.
   REQUIRED: The reason equity financing is more expensive than debt financing.
   DISCUSSION: Providers of equity capital are exposed to more risk than are lenders because the firm is not obligated to pay them a return. Also, in case of liquidation, creditors are paid before equity investors. Thus, equity financing is more expensive than debt because equity investors require a higher return to compensate for the greater risk assumed.
   Answer (A) is incorrect. The obligation to repay at a specific maturity date reduces the risk to investors and thus the required return. **Answer (C) is incorrect.** The demand for equity capital is directly related to its greater cost to the issuer. **Answer (D) is incorrect.** Dividends are based on managerial discretion and may rarely change; interest rates, however, fluctuate daily based upon market conditions.

SU 8: Corporate Capital Structure

7. Preferred and common stock differ in that

A. Failure to pay dividends on common stock will not force the firm into bankruptcy, while failure to pay dividends on preferred stock will force the firm into bankruptcy.
B. Common stock dividends are a fixed amount, while preferred stock dividends are not.
C. Preferred stock has a higher priority than common stock with regard to earnings and assets in the event of bankruptcy.
D. Preferred stock dividends are deductible as an expense for tax purposes, while common stock dividends are not.

Answer (C) is correct.
REQUIRED: The difference between preferred and common stock.
DISCUSSION: In the event of bankruptcy, the claims of preferred shareholders must be satisfied before common shareholders receive anything. The interests of common shareholders are secondary to those of all other claimants.
Answer (A) is incorrect. Failure to pay dividends will not force the firm into bankruptcy, whether the dividends are for common or preferred stock. Only failure to pay interest will force the firm into bankruptcy. **Answer (B) is incorrect.** Preferred dividends are fixed. **Answer (D) is incorrect.** Neither common nor preferred dividends are tax deductible.

8. Unless the shares are specifically restricted, a holder of common stock with a preemptive right may share proportionately in all of the following **except**

A. The vote for directors.
B. Corporate assets upon liquidation.
C. Cumulative dividends.
D. New issues of stock of the same class.

Answer (C) is correct.
REQUIRED: The item not a right of common shareholders.
DISCUSSION: Common stock does not have the right to accumulate unpaid dividends. This right often is attached to preferred stock.
Answer (A) is incorrect. Common shareholders have the right to vote (although different classes of shares may have different privileges). **Answer (B) is incorrect.** Common shareholders have the right to share proportionately in corporate assets upon liquidation (but only after other claims have been satisfied). **Answer (D) is incorrect.** Common shareholders have the right to share proportionately in any new issues of stock of the same class (the preemptive right).

8.3 Capital Structure and Solvency

9. The relationship of the total debt to the total equity of a corporation is a measure of

A. Liquidity.
B. Profitability.
C. Creditor risk.
D. Break even.

Answer (C) is correct.
REQUIRED: The characteristic measured by the relationship of total debt to total equity.
DISCUSSION: The debt-to-equity ratio is a measure of risk to creditors. It indicates how much equity is available to absorb losses before the interests of debt holders are impaired. The less leveraged the firm, the safer the creditors' interests.
Answer (A) is incorrect. Liquidity relates to how quickly cash can be made available to pay debts as they come due. Answer (B) is incorrect. The debt-to-equity ratio evaluates a firm's capital structure and is not oriented toward the balance sheet. It does not measure the use (profits) made of assets. Answer (D) is incorrect. Breakeven relates to profitability, not financing.

10. If the ratio of total liabilities to equity increases, a ratio that must also increase is

A. Times interest earned.
B. Total liabilities to total assets.
C. Return on equity.
D. The current ratio.

Answer (B) is correct.
REQUIRED: The ratio that increases if the ratio of total liabilities to equity increases.
DISCUSSION: Because total assets equal the sum of liabilities and equity, a factor that increases the liabilities-to-equity ratio also increases the liabilities-to-assets ratio.
Answer (A) is incorrect. No determination can be made of the effect on interest coverage without knowing the amounts of income and interest expense. Answer (C) is incorrect. The return on equity may be increased or decreased as a result of a factor that increases in the liabilities-to-equity ratio. Answer (D) is incorrect. The current ratio equals current assets divided by current liabilities, and additional information is necessary to determine whether it is affected. For example, an increase in current liabilities from short-term borrowing increases the liabilities-to-equity ratio but decrease the current ratio.

8.4 Component Costs of Capital

11. Global Company Press has $150 par-value preferred stock with a market price of $120 a share. The organization pays a $15 per share annual dividend. Global's current marginal tax rate is 40%. Looking to the future, the company anticipates maintaining its current capital structure. What is the component cost of preferred stock to Global?

A. 4%
B. 5%
C. 10%
D. 12.5%

Answer (D) is correct.
REQUIRED: The cost of preferred stock.
DISCUSSION: The component cost of preferred stock is the dividend divided by the market price (also called the dividend yield). No tax adjustment is necessary because dividends are not deductible. Given that the market price is $120 when the dividend is $15, the component cost of preferred capital is 12.5% ($15 ÷ $120).
Answer (A) is incorrect. The preferred stock dividend is not deductible for tax purposes. Answer (B) is incorrect. The preferred stock dividend is not deductible for tax purposes. Answer (C) is incorrect. The denominator is the market price, not the par value.

12. Maloney, Inc.'s $1,000 par-value preferred stock paid its $100 per share annual dividend on April 4 of the current year. The preferred stock's current market price is $960 a share on the date of the dividend distribution. Maloney's marginal tax rate (combined federal and state) is 40%, and the firm plans to maintain its current capital structure. The component cost of preferred stock to Maloney would be closest to

A. 6%
B. 6.25%
C. 10%
D. 10.4%

Answer (D) is correct.
REQUIRED: The component cost of preferred stock in the firm's capital structure.
DISCUSSION: The component cost of preferred stock is equal to the dividend yield, i.e., the cash dividend divided by the market price of the stock. (Dividends on preferred stock are not deductible for tax purposes; therefore, there is no adjustment for tax savings.) The annual dividend on preferred stock is $100 when the price of the stock is $960. The result is a cost of capital of about 10.4% ($100 ÷ $960).
Answer (A) is incorrect. Preferred dividends are not tax deductible. **Answer (B) is incorrect.** Preferred dividends are not tax deductible. **Answer (C) is incorrect.** The denominator is the current market price, not the par value.

13. What is the after-tax cost of preferred stock that sells for $5 per share and offers a $0.75 dividend when the tax rate is 35%?

A. 5.25%
B. 9.75%
C. 10.50%
D. 15%

Answer (D) is correct.
REQUIRED: The cost of preferred stock.
DISCUSSION: The component cost of preferred stock is the dividend yield, i.e., the cash dividend divided by the market price of the stock ($.75 ÷ $5.00 = 15%). Preferred dividends are not deductible for tax purposes.
Answer (A) is incorrect. The figure of 5.25% results from incorrectly multiplying the cost by the tax rate. **Answer (B) is incorrect.** The figure of 9.75% results from incorrectly multiplying the cost by the tax rate, which is not appropriate. Preferred dividends are not deductible for tax purposes. **Answer (C) is incorrect.** The figure of 10.50% is based on the assumption of a 30% tax rate and deductibility of dividends.

14. Cox Company has sold 1,000 shares of $100 par, 8% preferred stock at an issue price of $92 per share. Stock issue costs were $5 per share. Cox pays taxes at the rate of 40%. What is Cox's cost of preferred stock capital?

A. 8.00%
B. 8.25%
C. 8.70%
D. 9.20%

Answer (D) is correct.
REQUIRED: The cost of preferred equity.
DISCUSSION: Because the dividends on preferred stock are not deductible for tax purposes, the effect of income taxes is ignored. Thus, the relevant calculation is to divide the $8 annual dividend by the quantity of funds received from the issuance. In this case, the funds received equal $87 ($92 proceeds − $5 issue costs). Thus, the cost of capital is 9.2% ($8 ÷ $87).
Answer (A) is incorrect. The figure of 8.00% results from using the par value rather than the selling price and failing to subtract the issue costs. **Answer (B) is incorrect.** The figure of 8.25% results from adding the issue costs rather than subtracting them. **Answer (C) is incorrect.** The figure of 8.70% results from failing to subtract the issue costs.

8.5 Expected Value

15. Philip Enterprises, distributor of video discs, is developing its budgeted cost of goods sold for next year. Philip has developed the following range of sales estimates and associated probabilities for the year:

Sales Estimate	Probability
$ 60,000	25%
85,000	40
100,000	35

Philip's cost of goods sold averages 80% of sales. What is the expected value of Philip's budgeted cost of goods sold?

A. $85,000
B. $84,000
C. $68,000
D. $67,200

Answer (D) is correct.
REQUIRED: The expected value of cost of goods sold.
DISCUSSION: The expected value is calculated by weighting each sales estimate by the probability of its occurrence. Consequently, the expected value of sales is $84,000 [($60,000 × .25) + ($85,000 × .40) + ($100,000 × .35)]. Cost of goods sold is therefore $67,200 ($84,000 × .80).
Answer (A) is incorrect. The amount of $85,000 is the sales estimate with the highest probability.
Answer (B) is incorrect. The amount of $84,000 is the expected value of sales. **Answer (C) is incorrect.** The amount of $68,000 is 80% of the sales estimate with the highest probability.

16. During the past few years, Wilder Company has experienced the following average number of power outages:

Number per Month	Number of Months
0	3
1	2
2	4
3	3
	12

Each power outage results in out-of-pocket costs of $800. For $1,000 per month, Wilder can lease a generator to provide power during outages. If Wilder leases a generator in the coming year, the estimated savings (or additional expense) for the year will be

A. $(15,200)
B. $(1,267)
C. $3,200
D. $7,200

Answer (C) is correct.
REQUIRED: The estimated savings or additional expense from leasing the generator, given expected levels of occurrence.
DISCUSSION: Each outage costs $800, but this expense can be avoided by paying $1,000 per month ($12,000 for the year). The expected-value approach uses the probability distribution derived from past experience to determine the average expected outages per month.

$$3 \div 12 \times 0 = 0.0$$
$$2 \div 12 \times 1 = 0.16667$$
$$4 \div 12 \times 2 = 0.66667$$
$$3 \div 12 \times 3 = \underline{0.75000}$$
$$1.58334$$

The company can expect to have, on average, 1.58334 outages per month. At $800 per outage, the expected cost is $1,266.67. Thus, paying $1,000 to avoid an expense of $1,266.67 saves $266.67 per month, or $3,200 per year.
Answer (A) is incorrect. The annual amount the company will lose without a generator is $(15,200).
Answer (B) is incorrect. The monthly amount the company will lose without a generator is $(1,267).
Answer (D) is incorrect. The amount saved if two outages occur per month is $7,200.

SU 8: Corporate Capital Structure

17. Pongo Company's managers are attempting to value a piece of land they own. One potential occurrence is that the old road bordering the land gets paved. Another possibility is that the road does not get paved. A third outcome is that the road might be destroyed and completely replaced by a new road. Based on the following future states of nature, their probabilities, and subsequent values of the land, what is the expected value of the land?

Future States of Nature (SN)	Probability
SN 1: Current road gets paved	.5
SN 2: Road does not get paved	.4
SN 3: Current road destroyed and replaced with new road	.1

Estimates of land value under each possible future state of nature:

Value if SN 1: $200,000
Value if SN 2: $100,000
Value if SN 3: $550,000

A. $133,333
B. $195,000
C. $225,000
D. $283,333

Answer (B) is correct.
 REQUIRED: The expected value of the land.
 DISCUSSION: The expected value of the land is determined by multiplying the probability of each state of nature (outcome) by its payoff and adding all of the products. Thus, the land's expected value is (0.5)($200,000) + (0.4)($100,000) + (0.1)($550,000) = $195,000.
 Answer (A) is incorrect. The amount of $133,333 places too much weight on the second option.
 Answer (C) is incorrect. The amount of $225,000 gives too much weight to the third option. **Answer (D) is incorrect.** The amount of $283,333 uses a simple unweighted average of the returns from the three options.

18. A beverage stand can sell either soft drinks or coffee on any given day. If the stand sells soft drinks and the weather is hot, it will make $2,500; if the weather is cold, the profit will be $1,000. If the stand sells coffee and the weather is hot, it will make $1,900; if the weather is cold, the profit will be $2,000. The probability of cold weather on a given day at this time is 60%. The expected payoff for selling coffee is

A. $1,360
B. $2,200
C. $3,900
D. $1,960

Answer (D) is correct.
 REQUIRED: The expected payoff for selling coffee.
 DISCUSSION: The expected payoff calculation for coffee is

Expected payoff = Prob. hot (Payoff hot) + Prob. cold (Payoff cold)
 = .4($1,900) + .6($2,000)
 = $1,960

Answer (A) is incorrect. The least the company can make by selling coffee is $1,900. **Answer (B) is incorrect.** The most the company can make by selling coffee is $2,000. **Answer (C) is incorrect.** The most the company can make by selling coffee is $2,000.

8.6 Weighted-Average Cost of Capital

19. An accountant for Stability, Inc., must calculate the weighted-average cost of capital of the corporation using the following information.

		Component Cost
Accounts payable	$35,000,000	-0-
Long-term debt	10,000,000	8%
Common stock	10,000,000	15%
Retained earnings	5,000,000	18%

What is the weighted average cost of capital of Stability?

A. 6.88%
B. 8.00%
C. 10.25%
D. 12.80%

Answer (D) is correct.
REQUIRED: The weighted-average cost of capital.
DISCUSSION: Because the effect of income taxes is ignored in this situation, the stated rate on the firm's long-term debt is considered to be its effective rate. The weighted-average cost of capital (WACC) can thus be calculated as follows:

	Carrying Amount	Weight	Cost of Capital	Weighted Cost
Long-term debt	$10,000,000	40% ×	8% =	3.2%
Common stock	10,000,000	40% ×	15% =	6.0%
Retained earnings	5,000,000	20% ×	18% =	3.6%
Totals	$25,000,000	100%		12.8%

Answer (A) is incorrect. The figure of 6.88% results from improperly ignoring the weighted cost of common stock. Answer (B) is incorrect. The figure of 8.00% is the component cost of debt. Answer (C) is incorrect. The figure of 10.25% results from improperly performing a simple average on the four balance sheet items listed.

20. Scrunchy-Tech, Inc., has determined that it can minimize its weighted-average cost of capital (WACC) by using a debt-equity ratio of 2/3. If the firm's cost of debt is 9% before taxes, the cost of equity is estimated to be 12% before taxes, and the tax rate is 40%, what is the firm's WACC?

A. 6.48%
B. 7.92%
C. 9.36%
D. 10.80%

Answer (C) is correct.
REQUIRED: The firm's weighted-average cost of capital.
DISCUSSION: A firm's weighted-average cost of capital (WACC) is derived by weighting the (after-tax) cost of debt of 5.4% [9% × (1 – 40%)] and cost of equity of 12%. The tax rate does not affect the cost of equity. Scrunchy-Tech's WACC can be calculated as follows:

Component	Weight	Component Cost		Totals
Debt	40% ×	5.4%	=	2.16%
Equity	60% ×	12.0%	=	7.20%
	100%			9.36%

Answer (A) is incorrect. Improperly subtracting the effect of taxes from the cost of equity results in 6.48%. Answer (B) is incorrect. Improperly subtracting the effect of taxes from equity, but not from debt, results in 7.92%. Answer (D) is incorrect. Improperly using the before-tax cost of debt results in 10.80%.

SU 8: Corporate Capital Structure

21. Osgood Products has announced that it plans to finance future investments so that the firm will achieve an optimum capital structure. Which one of the following corporate objectives is consistent with this announcement?

A. Maximize earnings per share.
B. Minimize the cost of debt.
C. Maximize the net worth of the firm.
D. Minimize the cost of equity.

Answer (C) is correct.
REQUIRED: The consistent corporate objective.
DISCUSSION: Financial structure is the composition of the financing sources of the assets of a firm. Traditionally, the financial structure consists of current liabilities, long-term debt, retained earnings, and stock. For most firms, the optimum structure includes a combination of debt and equity. Debt is cheaper than equity, but excessive use of debt increases the firm's risk and drives up the weighted-average cost of capital.
Answer (A) is incorrect. The maximization of EPS may not always suggest the best capital structure. **Answer (B) is incorrect.** The minimization of debt cost may not be optimal; as long as the firm can earn more on debt capital than it pays in interest, debt financing may be indicated. **Answer (D) is incorrect.** Minimizing the cost of equity may signify overly conservative management.

Access the **Gleim CPA Premium Review System** featuring our SmartAdapt technology from your Gleim Personal Classroom to continue your studies. You will experience a personalized study environment with exam-emulating multiple-choice questions.

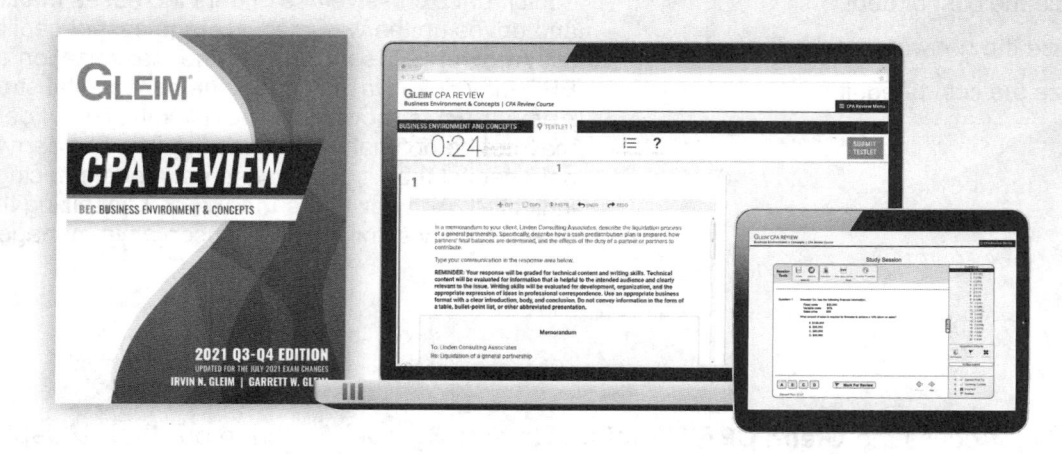

STUDY UNIT NINE
WORKING CAPITAL I: CASH AND RECEIVABLES

(11 pages of outline)

9.1	Working Capital Management	271
9.2	Liquidity Ratios -- Calculation	275
9.3	Liquidity Ratios -- Effects of Transactions	278
9.4	Receivables Management	279

All firms must hold a certain amount of current assets for daily operation. Manufacturers and distributors often hold as much as 50% of their total assets in the form of current assets. Thus, careful management of current assets is crucial to a firm's efficient operation.

Working capital management is the process of determining the optimal level and mix of current assets and the current liabilities that fund those assets. The focus of this study unit is on the most liquid current assets: cash and receivables.

9.1 WORKING CAPITAL MANAGEMENT

1. **Working capital**, as used by accountants, is calculated as follows:

    Working capital = Current assets − Current liabilities

    a. **Current assets** are the most liquid assets. They are expected to be converted to cash, sold, or consumed within 1 year or the operating cycle, whichever is longer. Accordingly, ratios involving current assets measure a firm's ability to continue operating in the short run.

        1) Current assets include, in descending order of liquidity,

            a) Cash and equivalents,
            b) Marketable securities,
            c) Receivables,
            d) Inventories, and
            e) Prepaid items.

    b. **Current liabilities** are the liabilities with the earliest due dates. They are expected to be settled or converted to other liabilities within 1 year or the operating cycle, whichever is longer.

        1) Current liabilities include

            a) Accounts payable,
            b) Notes payable,
            c) Current maturities of long-term debt,
            d) Unearned revenues,
            e) Taxes payable,
            f) Wages payable, and
            g) Other accruals.

2. **Permanent and Temporary Working Capital**

   a. In principle, current assets should be financed with current liabilities. However, this approach oversimplifies the requirements of working capital management for the following reasons:

      1) Some liquid current assets must be maintained to meet the firm's long-term minimum needs regardless of the firm's level of activity or profitability. This working capital is **permanent**.

      2) As the firm's needs for current assets change on a seasonal basis, **temporary** working capital is increased or decreased.

   b. Both elements tend to increase with the growth of the firm.

3. **Spontaneous Financing**

   a. Financing is spontaneous when current liabilities, such as trade payables and accruals, occur naturally in the ordinary course of business.

   b. Trade credit is created when a firm is offered credit terms by its suppliers.

EXAMPLE 9-1 Spontaneous Financing

A vendor has delivered goods and charged the firm $160,000 on terms of net 30. The firm effectively has received a 30-day interest-free $160,000 loan.

---

   c. Accrued expenses, such as (1) salaries, (2) wages, (3) interest, (4) dividends, and (5) taxes payable, are another source of (interest-free) spontaneous financing.

      1) For example, employees work 5, 6, or 7 days a week but are paid only every 2 weeks. Thus, employee salaries are paid periodically in lump sums, not on a perpetual basis with daily remittances, allowing the company to receive value that has not yet been paid for.

         a) Another periodic expense directly related to labor is the remittance of federal income taxes on a quarterly basis, even though the firm operates continuously.

      2) Accruals have the additional advantage of fluctuating directly with operating activity, satisfying the matching principle.

   d. The response to capital needs that cannot be satisfied spontaneously must be carefully planned.

4. **Short-Term vs. Long-Term Financing**

   a. The firm's temporary working capital usually cannot be financed by spontaneous financing alone. Thus, the firm must decide whether to use short-term or long-term financing.

      1) The interest rate on long-term debt is higher than the interest rate on short-term debt. Consequently, long-term financing is more expensive.

      2) However, the shorter the maturity schedule of a firm's debt obligations, the greater the risk that the firm will be unable to make principal and interest payments.

   b. In general, short-term financing is more risky and less expensive than long-term financing.

   c. The appropriate financing of the firm's working capital depends on management's attitude toward the tradeoff between profitability and risk.

5. Maturity Matching

a. A firm ideally should offset each element of its temporary working capital with a short-term liability with the same maturity. For example, a short-term loan could be obtained before the winter season and repaid with the collections from holiday sales. This ideal practice is maturity matching or hedging. It is rarely achievable because of uncertainty.

Maturity Matching

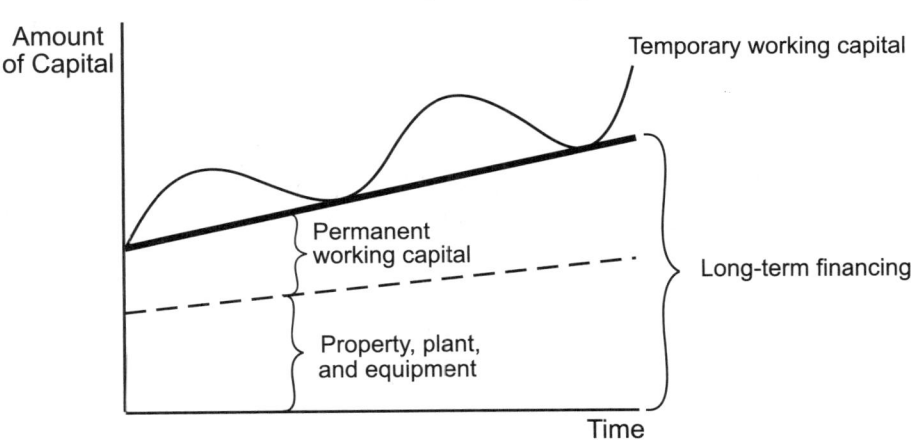

Figure 9-1

6. Conservative Policy

a. A firm that adopts a conservative financing policy seeks to minimize liquidity risk by financing its temporary working capital mostly with long-term debt.

Conservative Financing Policy

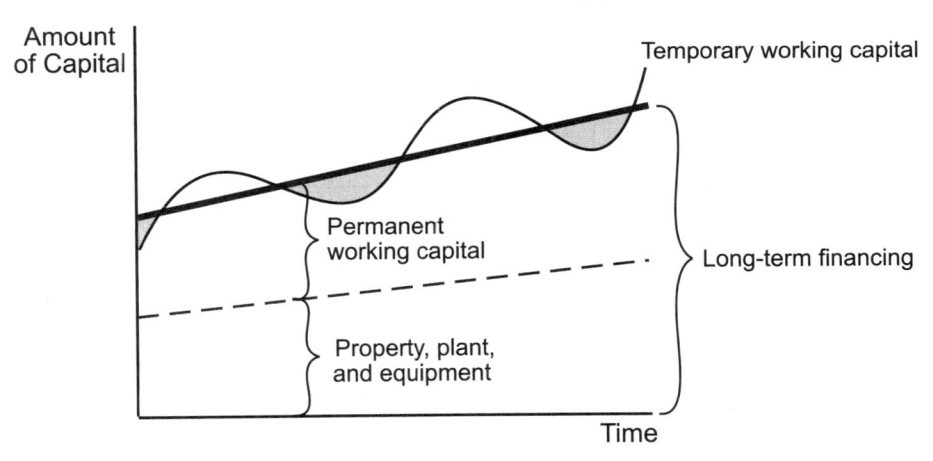

Figure 9-2

b. This approach takes advantage of the certainty inherent in long-term debt.

1) The locked-in interest rate mitigates interest rate risk (the risk that rates will rise in the short run). The long-term maturity date mitigates liquidity risk (the inability to repay a current obligation when due).

c. The disadvantages are that

1) Working capital is idle during periods when it is not needed, as represented by the shaded areas in Figure 9-2. This inefficiency is mitigated in part by investing in short-term securities.
2) Long-term debt is more expensive.

7. **Aggressive Policy**

    a. To increase profits, an aggressive financing policy reduces liquidity and accepts a higher risk of short-term cash flow shortages by financing part of its permanent working capital with short-term debt.

    Aggressive Financing Policy

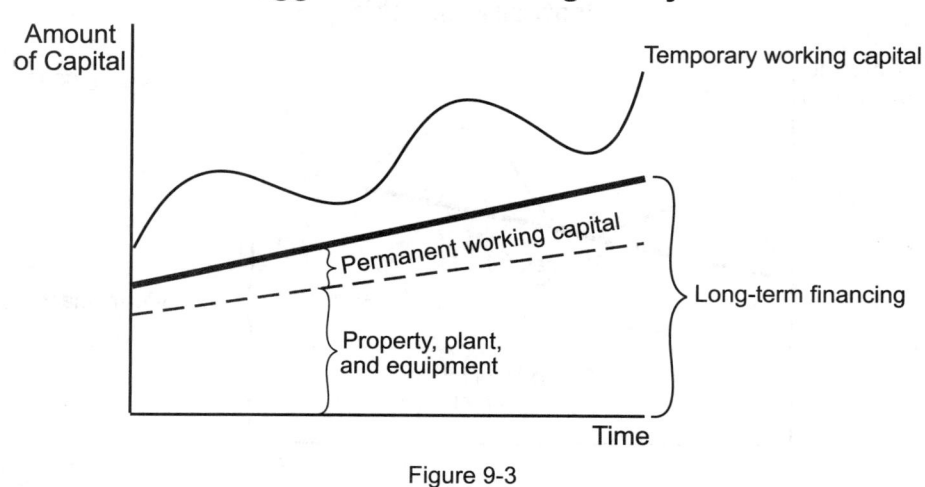

    Figure 9-3

    b. This approach avoids the opportunity cost of idle funds incurred under the conservative policy. But it risks either unexpectedly high interest rates or the total unavailability of financing in the short run.

8. **Summary**

    Risk in Relation to Financing

Working Capital Component	Financed with	
	Short-Term Debt	Long-Term Debt
Temporary	Medium risk	Low risk
Permanent	High risk	Medium risk

You have completed the outline for this subunit.
Study multiple-choice questions 1 through 5 beginning on page 282.

STOP & REVIEW

9.2 LIQUIDITY RATIOS -- CALCULATION

1. **Liquidity**

   a. Liquidity is a firm's ability to pay its current obligations as they come due and remain in business in the short run. Liquidity measures the ease with which assets can be converted to cash.

   b. Liquidity ratios measure this ability by relating a firm's liquid assets to its current liabilities.

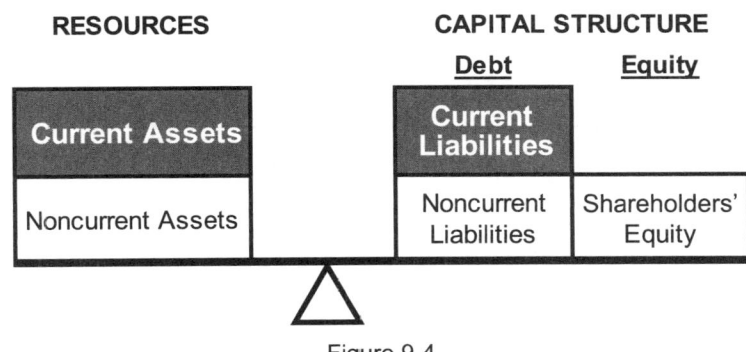

```
            RESOURCES                  CAPITAL STRUCTURE
                                       Debt          Equity

         ┌──────────────────┐       ┌──────────┐
         │ Current Assets   │       │ Current  │
         │                  │       │Liabilities│
         ├──────────────────┤       ├──────────┼──────────┐
         │                  │       │Noncurrent│Shareholders'│
         │ Noncurrent Assets│       │Liabilities│  Equity  │
         └──────────────────┘       └──────────┴──────────┘
                      △

                      Figure 9-4
```

EXAMPLE 9-2   Balance Sheet

The following balance sheet is used in this subunit:

RESOURCES			FINANCING		
CURRENT ASSETS:	Year 2	Year 3	**CURRENT LIABILITIES:**	Year 2	Year 3
Cash and equivalents	$ 275,000	$ 325,000	Accounts payable	$ 75,000	$ 150,000
Available-for-sale securities	145,000	165,000	Notes payable	50,000	50,000
Accounts receivable (net)	115,000	120,000	Accrued interest on note	5,000	5,000
Notes receivable	40,000	55,000	Current maturities of L.T. debt	100,000	100,000
Inventories	55,000	85,000	Accrued salaries and wages	10,000	15,000
Prepaid expenses	5,000	10,000	Income taxes payable	35,000	70,000
Total current assets	$ 635,000	$ 760,000	Total current liabilities	$ 275,000	$ 390,000
NONCURRENT ASSETS:			**NONCURRENT LIABILITIES:**		
Equity-method investments	$ 115,000	$ 120,000	Bonds payable	$ 600,000	$ 500,000
Property, plant, and equip.	900,000	1,000,000	Long-term notes payable	60,000	90,000
Minus: Accum. depreciation	(55,000)	(85,000)	Employee-related obligations	10,000	15,000
Goodwill	5,000	5,000	Deferred income taxes	5,000	5,000
Total noncurrent assets	$ 965,000	$1,040,000	Total noncurrent liabilities	$ 675,000	$ 610,000
			Total liabilities	$ 950,000	$1,000,000
			SHAREHOLDERS' EQUITY:		
			Preferred stock, $50 par	$ 0	$ 120,000
			Common stock, $1 par	500,000	500,000
			Additional paid-in capital	100,000	110,000
			Retained earnings	50,000	70,000
			Total shareholders' equity	$ 650,000	$ 800,000
Total assets	$1,600,000	$1,800,000	Total liabilities and shareholders' equity	$1,600,000	$1,800,000

SUCCESS TIP: Candidates should know the formulas used to calculate the various financial ratios and be able to analyze the results. Certain ratios that may have more than one commonly agreed upon definition will be provided or defined by the AICPA, but you are expected to know simple ratios, such as the current ratio. Similarly, the numbers necessary to calculate a ratio often are not given directly. As a CPA candidate, you will be expected to determine these numbers using information given in the question and then calculate the ratio.

2. **Liquidity Ratios**

   a. **Net working capital** equals the resources the firm must have to continue operating in the short run if it must liquidate all of its current liabilities.

   Current assets − Current liabilities = Net working capital

EXAMPLE 9-3	Net Working Capital

   Year 2: $635,000 − $275,000 = $360,000
   Year 3: $760,000 − $390,000 = $370,000

   Although the firm's current liabilities increased, its current assets increased by $10,000 more.

   b. The **current ratio** (working capital ratio) is the most common measure of liquidity.

   $$\frac{\text{Current assets}}{\text{Current liabilities}} = \text{Current ratio}$$

EXAMPLE 9-4	Current Ratio

   Year 2: $635,000 ÷ $275,000 = 2.31
   Year 3: $760,000 ÷ $390,000 = 1.95

   Although working capital increased in absolute terms ($10,000), current assets now provide less proportional coverage of current liabilities than in the prior year.

   1) A low current ratio indicates a possible lack of liquidity. An overly high ratio indicates that management may not be investing idle assets productively. This varies by industry, but often a 2:1 ratio is desirable.

   c. The **quick (acid-test) ratio** excludes inventories and prepaid items from the numerator. Such assets are difficult to liquidate at their carrying amounts. The quick ratio is therefore a more conservative measure than the current ratio.

   $$\frac{\text{Cash \& equivalents} + \text{Short-term marketable securities} + \text{Net receivables}}{\text{Current liabilities}} = \text{Quick ratio}$$

EXAMPLE 9-5	Quick Ratio

   Year 2: ($275,000 + $145,000 + $115,000 + $40,000) ÷ $275,000 = 2.09
   Year 3: ($325,000 + $165,000 + $120,000 + $55,000) ÷ $390,000 = 1.71

   Despite its increase in total working capital, the firm's position in its most liquid assets deteriorated significantly.

   1) This ratio measures the firm's ability to pay its short-term debts easily. It also avoids the problem of inventory valuation.
   2) The higher the quick ratio, the more favorable for the firm. Maintaining a quick ratio of at least 1:1 is desirable.
   3) If cash is classified as a compensating balance per a loan agreement, with no contractual agreement that restricts the use of the cash, the compensating balance can be reported as part of cash and cash equivalents.

Ratio Value	Current Ratio	Quick Ratio
1:2	Indicates the firm has less current assets than current liabilities. This typically means that a firm may be losing money, at least in the short run. The firm would have to sell long-term debt to satisfy its current liabilities, if possible.	Indicates the firm would not have adequate funds to pay current liabilities if the firm liquidated its current assets. In this situation, a firm would have to sell long-term liabilities to satisfy its current liabilities, if possible.
1:1	Indicates the firm would have adequate funds to pay current liabilities if the firm liquidated its current assets.	Indicates the firm would have adequate funds to pay current liabilities if the firm liquidated its current assets.
2:1	Indicates the firm has more current assets than current liabilities. It typically indicates the firm is profitable, at least in the short run. Moreover, the firm would have more funds than necessary to pay current liabilities if the firm liquidated its current assets.	Indicates the firm would have more funds than necessary to pay current liabilities if the firm liquidated its current assets. However, it may also indicate that management is not investing idle assets productively.

d. The **operating cash flow ratio** is a measure of a company's ability to settle its current liabilities with cash flows from operations.

$$\frac{\text{Cash flow from operations}}{\text{Current liabilities}} = \text{Operating cash flow ratio}$$

EXAMPLE 9-6 Operating Cash Flow Ratio

The company's cash flow from operations for Year 2 and Year 3 were $291,000 and $382,000, respectively.

Year 2: $291,000 ÷ $275,000 = 1.06
Year 3: $382,000 ÷ $390,000 = 0.98

Unlike in Year 2, the cash flows generated by the company in Year 3 were not sufficient to cover current liabilities.

You have completed the outline for this subunit.
Study multiple-choice questions 6 through 10 beginning on page 284.

STOP & REVIEW

9.3 LIQUIDITY RATIOS -- EFFECTS OF TRANSACTIONS

1. **Effects of Transactions**
   a. If a ratio is less than 1.0, the numerator is lower than the denominator.
      1) A transaction that causes equal changes in the numerator and denominator has a proportionally greater effect on the numerator, resulting in a change in the ratio in the same direction.
         a) If the current (or quick) ratio is less than 1.0, paying a current liability with current (or quick) assets decreases the numerator and the denominator by the same amount. The effect is a **decrease** in the ratio, which means less liquidity.

         EXAMPLE: $\dfrac{3-1}{4-1} = \dfrac{2}{3}$ and $\dfrac{3}{4} > \dfrac{2}{3}$

   b. If a ratio is equal to 1.0, the numerator and denominator are the same.
      1) A transaction that causes equal changes in the numerator and denominator does not affect the ratio, which does not affect liquidity.

      EXAMPLE: $\dfrac{4-1}{4-1} = \dfrac{3}{3}$ and $\dfrac{4}{4} = \dfrac{3}{3}$

   c. If a ratio is greater than 1.0, the numerator is higher than the denominator.
      1) A transaction that causes equal changes in the numerator and denominator has a proportionally greater effect on the denominator, resulting in a change in the ratio in the opposite direction.
         a) If the current (or quick) ratio is greater than 1.0, paying a current liability with current (or quick) assets decreases the numerator and denominator by the same amount. The effect is an **increase** in the ratio, which means the firm is more liquid.

         EXAMPLE: $\dfrac{4-1}{3-1} = \dfrac{3}{2}$ and $\dfrac{4}{3} < \dfrac{3}{2}$

Ratio range	Effect on ratio of equal increase of numerator and denominator	Effect on ratio of equal decrease of numerator and denominator
< 1.0	Increase – more liquid	Decrease – less liquid
= 1.0	No effect	No effect
> 1.0	Decrease – less liquid	Increase – more liquid

STOP & REVIEW

You have completed the outline for this subunit.
Study multiple-choice questions 11 through 15 beginning on page 286.

9.4 RECEIVABLES MANAGEMENT

> **BACKGROUND 9-1 Effect of Lowering Credit Standards**
>
> In 1969, in a desperate attempt to increase sales, the department store chain W.T. Grant drastically lowered its credit standards. As a result, sales boomed. However, during the economic downturn of 1970-71, cash inflows dried up as customer accounts began to turn delinquent. The firm finally went bankrupt in 1974. Grant's creditors were completely unaware because its accrual-basis income statement reported consistently positive results, and Grant never stopped paying a dividend. The inadequacy of the traditional income statement for assessing liquidity was made obvious by the Grant bankruptcy. This incident was one of the reasons for the FASB's requirement of a statement of cash flows.

1. **Overview**
   a. The goal of receivables management is to offer the **terms of credit** that maximize profits, not sales.
      1) Maximizing sales is easily done by raising discount percentages, offering longer payment periods, and accepting riskier customers. But this strategy could lead to cash flow shortages.
      2) Default risk can be minimized by raising credit standards, but the effect is loss of sales. Thus, the firm must achieve the proper balance.
   b. Credit terms are expressed in these terms: "Discount percentage"/"Pay by date to receive discount rate," net "Balance must be paid by date." The most common credit term is 2/10, net 30. This term means that the customer may either
      1) Subtract 2% of the invoice amount if it is paid within 10 days or
      2) Pay the entire balance by the 30th day.
   c. **Factoring** is an arrangement in which a firm sells its accounts receivable at a discount to a factor, an entity that specializes in collections.
      1) The seller receives cash and eliminates bad debts. Also, the seller need not maintain a credit department and an accounts receivable staff.
      2) Credit card companies are examples of factors. The credit card company remits the cash proceeds to the seller minus a typical fee in the range of 1.5%-4%. The credit card company assumes the risk that purchasers may not pay their credit card bills.

2. **Speeding Cash Collections of Receivables**
   a. The period of time from when a payor puts a check in the mail to the availability of the funds in the payee's bank is called float. Firms attempt to decrease float for receipts (collection float) and increase float for payments (disbursement float).
   b. A **lockbox** system expedites the receipt of funds from cashing checks.
      1) Customers submit their payments to a post office box. Bank personnel remove the envelopes from the mailbox and immediately deposit the checks in the firm's account. The remittance advices then must be transferred to the firm for entry into the accounts receivable system. The bank generally charges a flat monthly fee for this service.
      2) For firms doing business nationwide, a lockbox network is appropriate. The country is divided into regions according to customer population patterns. A lockbox arrangement then is established with a bank in each region.
   c. A firm using a lockbox network also participates in concentration banking. The regional banks that provide lockbox services automatically transfer their daily collections to the firm's principal bank, where they can be used for payments and short-term investment.

3. **Receivables Ratios**

EXAMPLE 9-7   **Balance Sheet and Selected Income Statement Data**

The following is from an income statement:

	Year 3	Year 2
Net sales	$1,800,000	$1,400,000
Cost of goods sold	(1,650,000)	(1,330,000)
Gross profit	$ 150,000	$ 70,000

The following balance sheet is used in this subunit:

RESOURCES

CURRENT ASSETS:	Year 3	Year 2
Cash and equivalents	$ 325,000	$ 275,000
Available-for-sale securities	165,000	145,000
Accounts receivable (net)	120,000	115,000
Notes receivable	55,000	40,000
Inventories	85,000	55,000
Prepaid expenses	10,000	5,000
Total current assets	$ 760,000	$ 635,000

NONCURRENT ASSETS:	Year 3	Year 2
Equity-method investments	$ 120,000	$ 115,000
Property, plant, and equip.	1,000,000	900,000
Minus: Accum. depreciation	(85,000)	(55,000)
Goodwill	5,000	5,000
Total noncurrent assets	$1,040,000	$ 965,000

Total assets	$1,800,000	$1,600,000

FINANCING

CURRENT LIABILITIES:	Year 3	Year 2
Accounts payable	$ 150,000	$ 75,000
Notes payable	50,000	50,000
Accrued interest on note	5,000	5,000
Current maturities of L.T. debt	100,000	100,000
Accrued salaries and wages	15,000	10,000
Income taxes payable	70,000	35,000
Total current liabilities	$ 390,000	$ 275,000

NONCURRENT LIABILITIES:	Year 3	Year 2
Bonds payable	$ 500,000	$ 600,000
Long-term notes payable	90,000	60,000
Employee-related obligations	15,000	10,000
Deferred income taxes	5,000	5,000
Total noncurrent liabilities	$ 610,000	$ 675,000
Total liabilities	$1,000,000	$ 950,000

SHAREHOLDERS' EQUITY:	Year 3	Year 2
Preferred stock, $50 par	$ 120,000	$ 0
Common stock, $1 par	500,000	500,000
Additional paid-in capital	110,000	100,000
Retained earnings	70,000	50,000
Total shareholders' equity	$ 800,000	$ 650,000

Total liabilities and shareholders' equity	$1,800,000	$1,600,000

---

a. The **accounts receivable turnover ratio** is the number of times in a year the total balance of receivables is converted to cash. In other words, the accounts receivable turnover ratio measures how often a business collects its average accounts receivable per year.

    1) Thus, if the accounts receivable turnover ratio equals 2.3, it means that the firm receives an amount of cash equal to 2.3 times its average accounts receivable.

    2) Alternatively, one can also view the accounts receivable turnover ratio as the number of times per year the accounts receivable account turns over. In this regard, the accounts receivable turnover ratio indicates how efficient the firm is at obtaining cash from credit sales.

    3) Therefore, the accounts receivable turnover ratio also provides insight into how liquid a firm is because the higher the ratio, the easier it is for the firm to generate cash flows, which indicates fewer credit sales are written off.

$$\text{Accounts receivable turnover} = \frac{\text{Net credit sales}}{\text{Average balance in accounts receivable (net)}}$$

SU 9: Working Capital I: Cash and Receivables

> **EXAMPLE 9-8**   **Accounts Receivable Turnover**
>
> In Example 9-7, all of the firm's sales are on credit. Net trade receivables at the balance sheet date for Year 1 were $105,000.
>
> Year 3: $1,800,000 ÷ [($120,000 + $115,000) ÷ 2] = 15.3 times
> Year 2: $1,400,000 ÷ [($115,000 + $105,000) ÷ 2] = 12.7 times
>
> The firm turned over its trade receivables balance 2.6 more times during Year 3, even as receivables increased. Thus, the firm's collection effectiveness improved.

    b.   The **average collection period (days' sales in receivables or days' sales in accounts receivable)** measures the average number of days between the time of sale and receipt of payment. This indicates how well and how quickly a firm converts a credit sale into cash.

        1)   The lower the ratio, the quicker the firm receives cash and is able to take advantage of the time value of money. On the other hand, the higher the ratio, the longer it takes a firm to receive the cash from a credit sale and, consequently, the firm is not able to take advantage of the time value of money (i.e., loses the ability to earn interest on cash on hand).

        2)   This ratio also provides insight into the amount of credit sales written off. The more credit sales written off, the higher this ratio will become.

$$\text{Days' sales in receivables} = \frac{\text{Ending accounts receivable (net)}}{\text{Net credit sales} \div \text{Days in year}}$$

NOTE: We anticipate, based on AICPA sample exams, that the days' sales in receivables formula given above is what you will see on the CPA Exam. This formula uses the ending balance. An alternative formula, shown below, uses the average balance.

$$\text{Days' sales in receivables} = \frac{\text{Days in year}}{\text{Accounts receivable turnover ratio}}$$

> **EXAMPLE 9-9**   **Days' Sales in Receivables**
>
> Year 3: $120,000 ÷ ($1,800,000 ÷ 365 days) = 24.3 days
> Year 2: $115,000 ÷ ($1,400,000 ÷ 365 days) = 30 days
>
> Days' sales in receivables decreased, which indicates that the company receives cash quicker. In addition to improving its collection practices, the firm may have better assessed the creditworthiness of potential customers. Some firms (and CPA questions) use a business year of 12 months at 30 days per month for a total of 360 days per year.

	Accounts Receivable Turnover Ratio	Average Collection Period
Higher	More Liquid	Less Liquid
Lower	Less Liquid	More Liquid

STOP & REVIEW

You have completed the outline for this subunit.
Study multiple-choice questions 16 through 20 beginning on page 288.

QUESTIONS

9.1 Working Capital Management

1. As a company becomes more conservative in its working capital policy, it tends to have a(n)

A. Decrease in its acid-test ratio.
B. Increase in the ratio of current liabilities to noncurrent liabilities.
C. Increase in the ratio of current assets to current liabilities.
D. Increase in funds invested in common stock and a decrease in funds invested in marketable securities.

Answer (C) is correct.
REQUIRED: The effect of a more conservative working capital policy.
DISCUSSION: A conservative working capital policy minimizes liquidity risk by increasing net working capital (Current assets − Current liabilities). The result is that the company forgoes the potentially higher returns available from using the additional working capital to acquire long-term assets. A conservative working capital policy is characterized by a higher current ratio (Current assets ÷ Current liabilities) and acid-test ratio (Quick assets ÷ Current liabilities). Thus, the firm will increase current assets or decrease current liabilities. A conservative policy finances assets using long-term or permanent funds rather than short-term sources.
Answer (A) is incorrect. A decrease in the acid-test ratio suggests an aggressive policy. A conservative firm wants a higher acid-test ratio, that is, more liquid assets relative to liabilities. **Answer (B) is incorrect.** A conservative firm wants working capital to be financed from long-term sources. **Answer (D) is incorrect.** A conservative firm seeks more liquid (marketable) investments.

2. Which one of the following provides a spontaneous source of financing for a firm?

A. Accounts payable.
B. Mortgage bonds.
C. Accounts receivable.
D. Debentures.

Answer (A) is correct.
REQUIRED: The spontaneous source of financing.
DISCUSSION: Trade credit is a spontaneous source of financing because it exists automatically as part of a purchase transaction. Because of its ease in use, trade credit is the largest source of short-term financing for many firms, both large and small.
Answer (B) is incorrect. Mortgage bonds and debentures do not arise automatically as a result of a purchase transaction. **Answer (C) is incorrect.** The use of receivables as a financing source requires an extensive factoring arrangement and often involves the creditor's evaluation of the credit ratings of the borrower's customers. **Answer (D) is incorrect.** Mortgage bonds and debentures do not arise automatically as a result of a purchase transaction.

3. Net working capital is the difference between

A. Current assets and current liabilities.
B. Fixed assets and fixed liabilities.
C. Total assets and total liabilities.
D. Shareholders' investment and cash.

Answer (A) is correct.
REQUIRED: The definition of net working capital.
DISCUSSION: Net working capital is defined by accountants as the difference between current assets and current liabilities. Working capital is a measure of liquidity.
Answer (B) is incorrect. Working capital refers to the difference between current assets and current liabilities; fixed assets are not a component. **Answer (C) is incorrect.** Total assets and total liabilities are not components of working capital; only current items are included. **Answer (D) is incorrect.** Shareholders' equity is not a component of working capital; only current items are included in the concept of working capital.

4. Determining the appropriate level of working capital for a firm requires

A. Changing the capital structure and dividend policy of the firm.

B. Maintaining short-term debt at the lowest possible level because it is generally more expensive than long-term debt.

C. Offsetting the benefit of current assets and current liabilities against the probability of technical insolvency.

D. Maintaining a high proportion of liquid assets to total assets in order to maximize the return on total investments.

Answer (C) is correct.
REQUIRED: The requirement for determining the appropriate level of working capital.
DISCUSSION: Working capital finance addresses the determination of the optimal level, mix, and use of current assets and current liabilities. The objective is to minimize the cost of maintaining liquidity while guarding against the possibility of technical insolvency. Technical insolvency is the inability to pay debts as they come due.
Answer (A) is incorrect. Capital structure and dividends relate to capital structure finance, not working capital finance. **Answer (B) is incorrect.** Short-term debt is usually less expensive than long-term debt. **Answer (D) is incorrect.** Liquid assets do not ordinarily earn high returns relative to long-term assets, so holding the former will not maximize the return on total assets.

5. Carter Co. had the following items on its balance sheet at the end of the current year:

Cash and cash equivalents	$ 200,000
Short-term investments	100,000
Accounts receivable	400,000
Inventories	600,000
Patent–10 years	300,000
Equipment	1,000,000
Accumulated depreciation	200,000

The amount of current liabilities at the end of the current year was $640,000. What is Carter's working capital at the end of the current year?

A. $60,000

B. $560,000

C. $660,000

D. $960,000

Answer (C) is correct.
REQUIRED: The working capital at the end of the year.
DISCUSSION: Working capital is calculated as current assets minus current liabilities. The current assets in this question total $1,300,000 ($200,000 + $100,000 + $400,000 + $600,000). The current liabilities are given as $640,000. Therefore, the working capital at the end of the current period is $660,000 ($1,300,000 – $640,000).
Answer (A) is incorrect. Inventories should also be considered in the calculation of current assets. **Answer (B) is incorrect.** Short-term investments should be included in the calculation of current assets. **Answer (D) is incorrect.** The patent is not included in current assets.

9.2 Liquidity Ratios -- Calculation

6. Given an acid-test ratio of 2.0, current assets of $5,000, and inventory of $2,000, the value of current liabilities is

A. $1,500
B. $2,500
C. $3,500
D. $6,000

Answer (A) is correct.
REQUIRED: The value of current liabilities given the acid-test ratio, current assets, and inventory.
DISCUSSION: The acid-test, or quick, ratio equals the ratio of the quick assets (cash, net accounts receivable, and marketable securities) divided by current liabilities. Current assets equal the quick assets plus inventory and prepaid expenses. This question assumes that the entity has no prepaid expenses. Given current assets of $5,000, inventory of $2,000, and no prepaid expenses, the quick assets must be $3,000. Because the acid-test ratio is 2.0, the quick assets are double the current liabilities. Current liabilities therefore are equal to $1,500 ($3,000 quick assets ÷ 2.0).
Answer (B) is incorrect. Dividing the current assets by 2.0 results in $2,500. Current assets includes inventory, which should not be included in the calculation of the acid-test ratio. Answer (C) is incorrect. Adding inventory to current assets rather than subtracting it results in $3,500. Answer (D) is incorrect. Multiplying the quick assets by 2 instead of dividing by 2 results in $6,000.

Questions 7 through 9 are based on the following information. Tosh Enterprises reported the following account information:

Accounts receivable	$400,000	Inventory	$800,000
Accounts payable	260,000	Land	500,000
Bonds payable, due in 10 years	600,000	Short-term prepaid expense	80,000
Cash	200,000		
Interest payable, due in 3 months	20,000		

---

7. The current ratio for Tosh Enterprises is

A. 1.68
B. 2.14
C. 5.00
D. 5.29

Answer (D) is correct.
REQUIRED: The current ratio.
DISCUSSION: The current ratio equals current assets divided by current liabilities. Current assets consist of accounts receivable, cash, inventory, and prepaid expenses, a total of $1,480,000 ($400,000 + $200,000 + $800,000 + $80,000). Current liabilities consist of accounts payable and interest payable, a total of $280,000 ($260,000 + $20,000). Hence, the current ratio is 5.29 ($1,480,000 ÷ $280,000).
Answer (A) is incorrect. The ratio of 1.68 includes long-term bonds payable among the current liabilities. Answer (B) is incorrect. The ratio of 2.14 is the quick ratio. Answer (C) is incorrect. The ratio of 5.00 excludes prepaid expenses from current assets.

8. What is Tosh Enterprises' quick (acid-test) ratio?

A. 0.68
B. 1.68
C. 2.14
D. 2.31

Answer (C) is correct.
REQUIRED: The quick ratio.
DISCUSSION: The quick ratio equals quick assets divided by current liabilities. For Tosh, quick assets consist of cash ($200,000) and accounts receivable ($400,000), a total of $600,000. Current liabilities consist of accounts payable ($260,000) and interest payable ($20,000), a total of $280,000. Thus, the quick ratio is 2.14 ($600,000 ÷ $280,000).
Answer (A) is incorrect. The ratio of 0.68 includes long-term bonds payable among the current liabilities. **Answer (B) is incorrect.** The ratio of 1.68 includes long-term bonds payable among the current liabilities and inventory and short-term prepaid expenses among the quick assets. **Answer (D) is incorrect.** The ratio of 2.31 excludes interest payable from the current liabilities.

9. Tosh Enterprises' amount of working capital is

A. $600,000
B. $1,120,000
C. $1,200,000
D. $1,220,000

Answer (C) is correct.
REQUIRED: The amount of working capital.
DISCUSSION: Working capital equals current assets minus current liabilities. For Tosh Enterprises, current assets consist of accounts receivable, cash, inventory, and prepaid expenses, a total of $1,480,000 ($400,000 + $200,000 + $800,000 + $80,000). Current liabilities consist of accounts payable and interest payable, a total of $280,000 ($260,000 + $20,000). Accordingly, working capital is $1,200,000 ($1,480,000 – $280,000).
Answer (A) is incorrect. The amount of $600,000 includes long-term bonds payable among the current liabilities. **Answer (B) is incorrect.** The amount of $1,120,000 excludes prepaid expenses from current assets. **Answer (D) is incorrect.** The amount of $1,220,000 excludes interest payable from current liabilities.

10. Blue Co. has current assets of $130 million, current liabilities of $50 million, and equity of $30 million. The current ratio for the company's peer group is 2.5. Which of the following statements is correct regarding Blue's current ratio?

A. Blue's current ratio is 2.6, which is more liquid than its peer group.
B. Blue's current ratio is 2.6, which is less liquid than average.
C. Blue's current ratio is 1.625, which is more liquid than its peer group.
D. Blue's current ratio is 1.625, which is less liquid than its peer group.

Answer (A) is correct.
REQUIRED: The correct statement regarding Blue's current ratio.
DISCUSSION: The current ratio is the most common measure of liquidity. It is calculated as a company's current assets divided by its current liabilities. Blue Co.'s current ratio is 2.6 ($130 million ÷ $50 million). Because this amount is larger than the peer group's ratio, Blue Co. is considered to be more liquid than its peers.
Answer (B) is incorrect. Blue Co. is more liquid than its peers because it has a higher current ratio. **Answer (C) is incorrect.** The current ratio is calculated as current assets divided by current liabilities. **Answer (D) is incorrect.** The current ratio is calculated as current assets divided by current liabilities.

9.3 Liquidity Ratios -- Effects of Transactions

11. Bond Corporation has a current ratio of 2 to 1 and a (acid test) quick ratio of 1 to 1. A transaction that would change Bond's quick ratio but **not** its current ratio is the

A. Sale of inventory on account at cost.
B. Collection of accounts receivable.
C. Payment of accounts payable.
D. Purchase of a patent for cash.

Answer (A) is correct.
REQUIRED: The transaction affecting the quick ratio but not the current ratio.
DISCUSSION: The quick ratio is determined by dividing the sum of cash, short-term marketable securities, and accounts receivable by current liabilities. The current ratio is equal to current assets divided by current liabilities. The sale of inventory (a nonquick current asset) on account increases accounts receivable (a quick asset), changing the quick ratio. The sale of inventory on account, however, replaces one current asset with another, and the current ratio is unaffected.
Answer (B) is incorrect. Neither ratio is changed.
Answer (C) is incorrect. The current, not the quick, ratio changes. Answer (D) is incorrect. Both ratios decrease.

12. Rice, Inc., uses the allowance method to account for uncollectible accounts. An account receivable that was previously determined uncollectible and written off was collected during May. The effect of the collection on Rice's current ratio and total working capital is

	Current Ratio	Working Capital
A.	None	None
B.	Increase	Increase
C.	Decrease	Decrease
D.	None	Increase

Answer (A) is correct.
REQUIRED: The effect on the current ratio and working capital of collecting an account previously written off.
DISCUSSION: The entry to record this transaction is to debit receivables, credit the allowance for credit losses, debit cash, and credit receivables. The result is to increase both an asset (cash) and a contra asset (allowance for credit losses, formerly bad debts). These appear in the current asset section of the balance sheet. Thus, the collection changes neither the current ratio nor working capital because the effects are offsetting. The credit for the journal entry is made to the allowance account on the assumption that another account will become uncollectible. The firm had previously estimated its bad debts and established an appropriate allowance for credit losses. It then (presumably) wrote off the wrong account. Accordingly, the journal entry reinstates a balance in the allowance account to absorb future uncollectibles.

13. Windham Company has current assets of $400,000 and current liabilities of $500,000. Windham Company's current ratio will be increased by

A. The purchase of $100,000 of inventory on account.
B. The payment of $100,000 of accounts payable.
C. The collection of $100,000 of accounts receivable.
D. Refinancing a $100,000 long-term loan with short-term debt.

Answer (A) is correct.
REQUIRED: The transaction increasing a current ratio less than 1.0.
DISCUSSION: The current ratio equals current assets divided by current liabilities. An equal increase in both the numerator and denominator of a current ratio less than 1.0 causes the ratio to increase. Windham Company's current ratio is .8 ($400,000 ÷ $500,000). The purchase of $100,000 of inventory on account would increase the current assets to $500,000 and the current liabilities to $600,000, resulting in a new current ratio of .83.
Answer (B) is incorrect. The payment of $100,000 of accounts payable decreases the current ratio.
Answer (C) is incorrect. The current ratio is unchanged.
Answer (D) is incorrect. Refinancing a $100,000 long-term loan with short-term debt decreases the current ratio.

SU 9: Working Capital I: Cash and Receivables

14. Peters Company has a 2-to-1 current ratio. This ratio would increase to more than 2 to 1 if

A. A previously declared stock dividend were distributed.
B. The company wrote off an uncollectible receivable.
C. The company sold merchandise on open account that earned a normal gross margin.
D. The company purchased inventory on open account.

Answer (C) is correct.
REQUIRED: The transaction increasing a current ratio greater than one.
DISCUSSION: The current ratio is current assets divided by current liabilities. Thus, an increase in current assets or a decrease in current liabilities, by itself, increases the current ratio. The sale of inventory at a profit increases current assets without changing liabilities. Inventory decreases, and receivables increase by a greater amount. Thus, total current assets and the current ratio increase.
Answer (A) is incorrect. The distribution of a stock dividend affects only shareholders' equity accounts (debit common stock dividend distributable and credit common stock). **Answer (B) is incorrect.** Writing off an uncollectible receivable does not affect total current assets. The allowance account absorbs the bad debt. Thus, the balance of net receivables is unchanged. **Answer (D) is incorrect.** The purchase of inventory increases current assets and current liabilities by the same amount. The transaction reduces a current ratio in excess of 1.0 because the numerator and denominator of the ratio increase by the same amount.

Question 15 is based on the following information. Depoole Company is a manufacturer of industrial products that uses a calendar year for financial reporting purposes. Assume that total quick assets exceeded total current liabilities both before and after the transaction described. Further assume that Depoole has positive profits during the year and a credit balance throughout the year in its retained earnings account.

15. Depoole's purchase of raw materials for $85,000 on open account will

A. Increase the current ratio.
B. Decrease the current ratio.
C. Increase net working capital.
D. Decrease net working capital.

Answer (B) is correct.
REQUIRED: The effect of a credit purchase of raw materials on the current ratio or working capital.
DISCUSSION: The purchase increases both the numerator and denominator of the current ratio by adding inventory to the numerator and payables to the denominator. Because the ratio before the purchase was greater than 1, the ratio is decreased.
Answer (A) is incorrect. The current ratio is decreased. **Answer (C) is incorrect.** The purchase of raw materials on account has no effect on working capital (current assets and current liabilities change by the same amount). **Answer (D) is incorrect.** The purchase of raw materials on account has no effect on working capital (current assets and current liabilities change by the same amount).

9.4 Receivables Management

16. Aaron Co.'s vendor will be offering a credit term of 5/15, net 30 next year. Which of the following descriptions is correct about the credit term?

A. Aaron Co. can take a discount of 5% if it pays within 20 days.
B. Aaron Co. will be required to pay the entire balance by the 15th day.
C. The vendor will offer a discount of 15% if Aaron Co. pays by the 30th day.
D. The vendor will not offer any discount if Aaron Co. pays on the 25th day.

Answer (D) is correct.
REQUIRED: The correct description of the credit term.
DISCUSSION: Credit terms are expressed in these terms: "Discount percentage"/"Pay by date to receive discount rate," net "Balance must be paid by date." The term 5/15, net 30 means that the customer may either (1) subtract 5% of the invoice amount if it is paid within 15 days or (2) pay the entire balance by the 30th day. Hence, if Aaron Co. pays on the 25th day, the vendor will not offer any discount.
Answer (A) is incorrect. Aaron Co. has to pay within 15 days, not 20 days, to take the 5% discount. **Answer (B) is incorrect.** Aaron Co. can pay within 15 days to take the discount and is required to pay the entire balance by the 30th day. **Answer (C) is incorrect.** The vendor will offer a 5% discount if Aaron Co. pays by the 15th day.

17. An organization would usually offer credit terms of 2/10, net 30 when

A. The organization can borrow funds at a rate exceeding the annual interest cost.
B. The organization can borrow funds at a rate less than the annual interest cost.
C. The cost of capital approaches the prime rate.
D. Most competitors are offering the same terms, and the organization has a shortage of cash.

Answer (D) is correct.
REQUIRED: The reason for offering credit terms of 2/10, net 30.
DISCUSSION: Because these terms involve an annual interest cost of over 36%, a company would not offer them unless it desperately needed cash. Also, credit terms are typically somewhat standardized within an industry. Thus, if most companies in the industry offer similar terms, a firm will likely be forced to match the competition or lose market share.
Answer (A) is incorrect. If the company does not need cash, it would not offer cash discounts, regardless of its cost of capital, unless required to match competition. **Answer (B) is incorrect.** The ability to borrow at a lower rate is a reason for not offering cash discounts. **Answer (C) is incorrect.** The relationship between the cost of capital and the prime rate may not be relevant if the firm cannot borrow at the prime rate.

SU 9: Working Capital I: Cash and Receivables

18. A company with $4.8 million in credit sales per year plans to relax its credit standards, projecting that this will increase credit sales by $720,000. The company's average collection period for new customers is expected to be 75 days, and the payment behavior of the existing customers is not expected to change. Variable costs are 80% of sales. The firm's opportunity cost is 20% before taxes. Assuming a 360-day year, what is the company's benefit (loss) on the planned change in credit terms?

A. $0
B. $28,800
C. $120,000
D. $144,000

Answer (C) is correct.
REQUIRED: The annual benefit or loss resulting from a change in credit terms.
DISCUSSION: The company can calculate the net benefit (loss) from the proposed change in credit policy as follows:

Increase in sales	$720,000
Times: variable cost ratio	× 80%
Increase in variable costs	$576,000

Increased investment in receivables
= $576,000 × (75 days ÷ 360 days)
= $120,000

Increased investment in receivables	$120,000
Times: opportunity cost of funds	× 20%
Cost of new credit plan	$ 24,000

Increase in sales	$720,000
Times: contribution margin ratio	× 20%
Increase in contribution margin	$144,000
Less: cost of new credit plan	(24,000)
Benefit of new credit plan	$120,000

Answer (A) is incorrect. The company benefits from the change in credit terms. Answer (B) is incorrect. The amount of $28,800 results from multiplying the contribution margin by the 20% interest rate. Answer (D) is incorrect. The amount of $144,000 results from ignoring the costs incurred by having funds invested in receivables for 75 days.

19. The main reason that a firm would strive to reduce the number of days sales outstanding is to increase

A. Accounts receivable.
B. Cash.
C. Cost of goods sold.
D. Contribution margin.

Answer (B) is correct.
REQUIRED: The effect the number of days sales outstanding (accounts receivable collection period) has on other accounts.
DISCUSSION: A low days sales outstanding value means that it takes a company fewer days to collect accounts receivables. A company that collects accounts receivables quickly will have an increase in cash.
Answer (A) is incorrect. A low days sales outstanding value means that it takes a company fewer days to collect accounts receivables. Thus, accounts receivables will decrease, not increase. Answer (C) is incorrect. Days sales outstanding is a measure of the average number of days that it takes for a company to collect revenue after a sale has been made. Cost of goods sold is not used in the calculation of days sales outstanding. Answer (D) is incorrect. Days sales outstanding is a measure of the average number of days that it takes for a company to collect revenue after a sale has been made. Contribution margin is not used in the calculation of days sales outstanding.

20. A company has credit sales of $20,000 in January, $30,000 in February, and $50,000 in March. The company collects 75% in the month of sale and 25% in the following month. The balance in accounts receivable on January 1 was $25,000. What amount is the balance in accounts receivable at closing on March 31?

A. $7,500

B. $12,500

C. $37,500

D. $45,000

Answer (B) is correct.
REQUIRED: The balance in accounts receivable at closing on March 31.
DISCUSSION: The company collects 75% of credit sales in the month of sale and 25% in the following month. Accordingly, the accounts receivable balance of $25,000 on January 1 (carried over from December) was collected in January; the credit sales of $20,000 in January were fully collected in February; the credit sales of $30,000 in February were fully collected in March; and $37,500 ($50,000 × 75%) of the $50,000 in credit sales in March were collected in March. Therefore, the balance in accounts receivable at closing on March 31 is $12,500 ($50,000 × 25%).
Answer (A) is incorrect. The amount of $7,500 ($30,000 × 25%) is the balance in accounts receivable as of March 1. **Answer (C) is incorrect.** The amount of $37,500 includes the balance in accounts receivable on January 1 of $25,000. The balance on January 1 represents the 25% of credit sales occurring in December collected in January. Therefore, these credit sales should not be included in the accounts receivable balance as of March 31. **Answer (D) is incorrect.** The amount of $45,000 includes the January 1 beginning accounts receivable of $25,000 and the March 1 beginning accounts receivable of $7,500. However, these balances were collected in January and March, respectively. Thus, neither balance should be included in the accounts receivable balance on March 31.

Access the **Gleim CPA Premium Review System** featuring our SmartAdapt technology from your Gleim Personal Classroom to continue your studies. You will experience a personalized study environment with exam-emulating multiple-choice questions.

STUDY UNIT TEN
WORKING CAPITAL II: INVENTORY AND SHORT-TERM FINANCING

(14 pages of outline)

10.1	Inventory Management -- Methods	292
10.2	Inventory Management -- Ratios	295
10.3	The Operating Cycle and Cash Conversion Cycle	298
10.4	Multiple Ratio Analysis	300
10.5	Short-Term Financing	301

In addition to managing cash and receivables in their daily operations, companies must consider the crucial role of inventory management in the operating cycle. More specifically, they must determine the optimal level and mix of inventories while balancing different inventory costs.

Generally, entities finance daily operations with capital from outside sources. These sources include (1) spontaneous financing in the form of trade credit offered by vendors and (2) bank loans. Successful working capital management, besides managing current assets, also aims at controlling the related financing costs.

10.1 INVENTORY MANAGEMENT -- METHODS

1. **Overview**

    a. Minimizing the total cost of inventory involves constant evaluation of the tradeoffs among the four components of total cost.

        Purchase costs + Carrying costs + Ordering costs + Stockout costs

        1) **Purchase costs** are the actual invoice amounts charged by suppliers. It is the investment in inventory.
        2) **Carrying costs** is a broad category. It consists of all costs associated with holding inventory: (a) storage, (b) insurance, (c) security, (d) depreciation or rent of facilities, (e) interest, (f) obsolescence, (g) spoilage, and (h) the opportunity cost of funds invested in inventory (percentage investment in inventory).
        3) **Ordering costs** are the fixed costs of placing an order with a vendor. They are not affected by the number of units ordered. If units are manufactured internally, **setup costs** for production lines are calculated instead.
        4) **Stockout costs** are the opportunity costs of not being able to fill customer orders. They also include the costs of expediting special shipments required because of insufficient inventory.

    b. Minimization of total inventory cost is difficult because of the following factors:

        1) Stockout costs can be minimized only by incurring higher carrying costs.
        2) Carrying costs can be minimized only by incurring the high fixed costs of placing many small orders.
        3) Ordering costs can be minimized only by incurring the higher carrying costs of larger inventories.

2. **Inventory Replenishment Factors**

    a. **Lead time** is the time between placing an order and receipt of goods from the supplier.

        1) When lead time is known and demand is uniform, the goods can be timed to arrive just as inventory is eliminated. This is the basis of the just-in-time model discussed later in this subunit.

    b. **Safety stock** is inventory held as a hedge against contingencies.

        1) Determining the appropriate safety stock requires a probabilistic calculation that balances the variability of demand with the risk of stockouts the firm is willing to accept.

    c. The **reorder point** is the inventory amount indicating that a new order should be placed. It is calculated using the following equation:

        (Average daily demand × Lead time in days) + Safety stock

3. **The Economic Order Quantity Model**

    a. The economic order quantity (EOQ) model determines the order quantity that minimizes the sum of ordering costs and carrying costs.

    $$EOQ = \sqrt{\frac{2OD}{c}}$$

    If: O = **o**rdering cost per purchase order
    D = periodic **d**emand in units/usage of units
    c = periodic **c**arrying costs per unit

Inventory Management

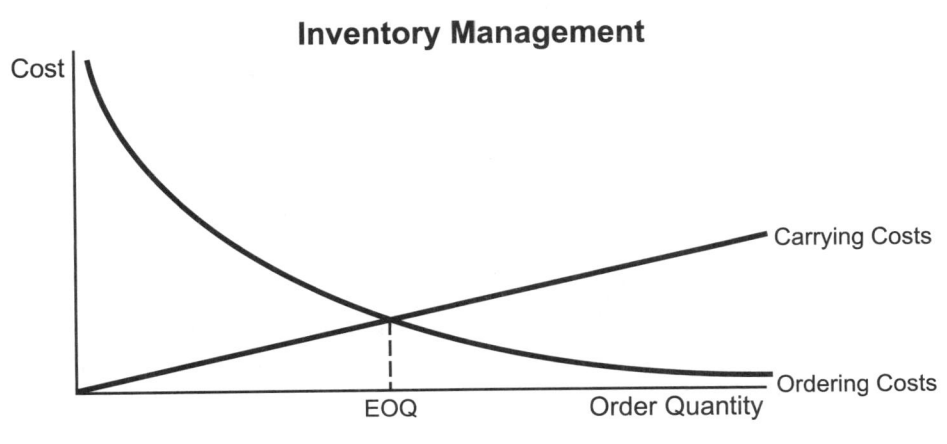

Figure 10-1

- b. The assumptions underlying the EOQ model are that
    1) Demand or production is uniform.
    2) Order (setup) costs and carrying costs are constant.
    3) No quantity discounts are allowed.
- c. A change in any variable changes the EOQ. If demand or ordering costs increase, each order must contain more units. If carrying costs increase, each order contains fewer units.

EXAMPLE 10-1   EOQ Calculation

A firm plans to use 40,000 inventory units (D) during the 180-day period. The ordering cost per order is $40 (O). The carrying costs per inventory unit are $20 (c). In order to minimize the total inventory cost for the 180-day period, the firm should order 400 inventory units (EOQ) in each order.

$$EOQ = \sqrt{\frac{2 \times \$40 \times 40,000}{\$20}} = 400$$

The firm should make 100 orders during that period (40,000 ÷ 400).

---

4. **Just-in-Time Inventory**

    a. In a just-in-time (JIT) inventory system, the moving, handling, and storage of inventory are treated as nonvalue-adding activities.

    1) Not just safety stock but all materials inventories (and their associated carrying costs) are reduced or eliminated entirely. Binding agreements with suppliers ensure that materials arrive exactly when they are needed and not before.

    2) JIT is a **pull** system that is demand-driven. In a manufacturing environment, production of goods does not begin until an order has been received. In this way, finished goods inventories also are eliminated.

    3) The purpose of the JIT inventory system is to minimize the cost associated with inventory control and maintenance by reducing the lag time between inventory's arrival and use.

    4) Conventional accounting systems track raw materials, work-in-process, and finished goods in sequence. The system provides comprehensive inventory control information and enables the calculation of manufacturing variances. However, a JIT system maintains minimal inventory and is demand-driven (sales volumes and productions are almost equal). Thus, there is no need to present a detailed view of inventory under a JIT system.

5. **MRP and MRP II**

   a. Materials requirements planning (MRP) is a computerized system for moving materials through a production process according to a predetermined schedule.

      1) MRP is a **push** system. The demand for materials is driven by the forecasted demand for the final product as programmed into the system.

         a) MRP, in effect, creates schedules of when items of inventory are needed in the production departments.

         b) If an outage of a given item is projected, the system automatically generates a purchase order on the proper date (considering lead times) so that deliveries arrive on time.

      2) MRP consists of three essential components:

         a) The master production schedule (MPS) is a table of the projected demand for end products along with the dates they are needed.

         b) The bill of materials (BOM) is a table of every component part required by every end product (and by every subassembly).

         c) Perpetual inventory records must be used to ensure that a true count of every component, subassembly, and finished good is available at all times.

      3) In essence, MRP embodies the principle of dependent (derived) demand.

         a) Demand-dependent goods are components of other goods. Their demand is driven by the demand for the final goods of which they are a part.

   b. MRP is a common function contained in enterprise resource planning (ERP) software systems.

      1) Although ERP and MRP are similar, they are not interchangeable. ERP includes many functions not included in MRP.

         a) For example, an ERP system allows a firm to determine what hiring decisions need to be made or whether it should invest in new capital assets.

            i) A firm that only needs to control materials should implement MRP.

      2) ERP is described in further detail in Study Unit 12, Subunit 6.

   c. Manufacturing resource planning (MRP II) does not replace, but extends the scope of, an MRP system.

      1) MRP is based on programmed demand, regardless of capacity considerations or changes in the market for the end product.

      2) MRP II is a closed-loop system that adds a feedback loop to allow analysis of capacity, market changes, and other variables.

STOP & REVIEW

You have completed the outline for this subunit.
Study multiple-choice questions 1 through 7 beginning on page 304.

10.2 INVENTORY MANAGEMENT -- RATIOS

SUCCESS TIP: Candidates should know the formulas used to calculate the various financial ratios and be able to analyze the results. Certain ratios that may have more than one commonly agreed upon definition will be provided or defined by the AICPA, but you are expected to know simple ratios, such as the current ratio. Similarly, the numbers necessary to calculate a ratio often are not given directly. As a future CPA, you will be expected to determine these numbers using information given in the question and then calculate the ratio.

1. **Inventory Ratios**

    a. Two ratios measure the efficiency of the management of inventory: inventory turnover and days' sales in inventory.

      1) **Inventory turnover** is the number of times in a year the total balance of inventory is converted to cash or receivables.

         a) Inventory turnover is affected by two departments: purchasing and sales.

            i) The purchasing department is responsible for ensuring that the firm either has product to sell or to use in manufacturing. Typically, a firm wants to minimize the amount of inventory without being detrimental to operations. Generally, the higher the inventory turnover rate, the more efficient the inventory management.

            ii) The sales department also needs to meet or exceed the sales budget so that the firm is not holding excess inventory longer than budgeted (or expected).

            iii) A high inventory turnover may imply that the firm is **not** carrying excess inventory or that the inventory is **not** obsolete. Thus, inventory turnover can be an indication of how well the firm's departments are interoperating.

$$\text{Inventory turnover} = \frac{\text{Cost of goods sold}}{\text{Average balance in inventory}}$$

         b) If business is seasonal, a simple average of beginning and ending balances is inadequate. The monthly balances should be averaged instead.

         c) Because cost of goods sold is in the numerator, higher sales (and a higher cost of goods sold) without an increase in inventory results in higher turnover.

            i) Because inventory is in the denominator, reducing inventory results in a higher turnover ratio.

         d) The ratio of a firm that uses LIFO may not be comparable with that of a firm with a higher inventory measurement, such as FIFO or Average Methods.

EXAMPLE 10-2   Inventory Turnover

The following is from an income statement:

	Year 3	Year 2
Net sales	$1,800,000	$1,400,000
Cost of goods sold	(1,650,000)	(1,330,000)
Gross profit	$ 150,000	$ 70,000

The following balance sheet is used in this subunit and in Subunit 10.3:

RESOURCES			FINANCING		
CURRENT ASSETS:	Year 3	Year 2	**CURRENT LIABILITIES:**	Year 3	Year 2
Cash and equivalents	$ 325,000	$ 275,000	Accounts payable	$ 150,000	$ 75,000
Available-for-sale securities	165,000	145,000	Notes payable	50,000	50,000
Accounts receivable (net)	120,000	115,000	Accrued interest on note	5,000	5,000
Notes receivable	55,000	40,000	Current maturities of L.T. debt	100,000	100,000
Inventories	85,000	55,000	Accrued salaries and wages	15,000	10,000
Prepaid expenses	10,000	5,000	Income taxes payable	70,000	35,000
Total current assets	$ 760,000	$ 635,000	Total current liabilities	$ 390,000	$ 275,000
NONCURRENT ASSETS:			**NONCURRENT LIABILITIES:**		
Equity-method investments	$ 120,000	$ 115,000	Bonds payable	$ 500,000	$ 600,000
Property, plant, and equip.	1,000,000	900,000	Long-term notes payable	90,000	60,000
Minus: Accum. depreciation	(85,000)	(55,000)	Employee-related obligations	15,000	10,000
Goodwill	5,000	5,000	Deferred income taxes	5,000	5,000
Total noncurrent assets	$1,040,000	$ 965,000	Total noncurrent liabilities	$ 610,000	$ 675,000
			Total liabilities	$1,000,000	$ 950,000
			SHAREHOLDERS' EQUITY:		
			Preferred stock, $50 par	$ 120,000	$ 0
			Common stock, $1 par	500,000	500,000
			Additional paid-in capital	110,000	100,000
			Retained earnings	70,000	50,000
			Total shareholders' equity	$ 800,000	$ 650,000
Total assets	$1,800,000	$1,600,000	Total liabilities and shareholders' equity	$1,800,000	$1,600,000

The balance in inventories at the balance sheet date of Year 1 was $45,000.

Year 3: $1,650,000 ÷ [($85,000 + $55,000) ÷ 2] = 23.6 times
Year 2: $1,330,000 ÷ [($55,000 + $45,000) ÷ 2] = 26.6 times

The firm did not turn over its inventories as many times during Year 3. This result is expected during a period of increasing sales (and increased inventory). Accordingly, lower turnover does not necessarily indicate poor inventory management.

SU 10: Working Capital II: Inventory and Short-Term Financing

2) **Days' sales in inventory (days in inventory)** measures the average number of days between the acquisition of inventory and its sale. It also indicates how many days the firm's current inventory level will last before stockout.

   a) Days' sales in inventory is important because it signifies the age of the firm's inventory. The older the inventory, the greater risk of it being obsolete (especially if the firm is in the consumer electronics industry).

      i) In addition, the lower the days' sales in inventory, the easier it is for the firm to generate sales and turn inventory into cash. This is beneficial to liquidity and working capital.

      ii) A lower days' sales in inventory also means the firm's inventory is liquid and, if necessary, creditors could liquidate it easily in a bankruptcy scenario.

$$\text{Days' sales in inventory} = \frac{\text{Ending inventory}}{\text{Cost of goods sold} \div \text{Days in year}}$$

NOTE: We anticipate, based on AICPA sample exams, that the days' sales in inventory formula given above is what you will see on the CPA Exam. This formula uses the ending balance. An alternative formula, shown below, uses the average balance.

$$\text{Days' sales in inventory} = \frac{\text{Days in year}}{\text{Inventory turnover ratio}}$$

EXAMPLE 10-3   Days' Sales in Inventory

Year 3: $85,000 ÷ ($1,650,000 ÷ 365 days) = 18.8 days
Year 2: $55,000 ÷ ($1,330,000 ÷ 365 days) = 15.1 days

Days' sales in inventory increased, which indicates that inventory is less liquid. This phenomenon is common during a period of increasing sales.

	Inventory Turnover	Days' Sales in Inventory
Higher	Good – More Liquid	Bad – Less Liquid
Lower	Bad – Less Liquid	Good – More Liquid

STOP & REVIEW

You have completed the outline for this subunit.
Study multiple-choice questions 8 and 9 on page 307.

10.3 THE OPERATING CYCLE AND CASH CONVERSION CYCLE

1. **Operating Cycle**

    a. A firm's **operating cycle** is the time between the acquisition of inventory and the collection of cash for its sale. The operating cycle dictates cash flow.

       1) The length of the operating cycle provides information on the company's need for liquidity. The longer the operating cycle, the greater the need for liquidity.

          a) A company with a short operating cycle is able to quickly recover its investments in inventory.

          b) A company with a long operating cycle will have less cash available to meet short-term needs, which can result in increased borrowing.

    Operating cycle = Days' sales in receivables + Days' sales in inventory

    ---

    EXAMPLE 10-4   Operating Cycle

    Year 3: 24.3 days + 18.8 days = 43.1 days
    Year 2: 30 days + 15.1 days = 45.1 days

    The firm has reduced its operating cycle while increasing sales and inventories.

    The days' sales in receivables for Year 3 (24.3 days) and Year 2 (30 days) are calculated in Example 9-9 in Study Unit 9, Subunit 4. The days' sales in inventory for Year 3 (18.8 days) and Year 2 (15.1 days) are calculated in Example 10-3 in Subunit 10.2.

    ---

    b. The diagram to the right depicts the phases of the operating cycle:

2. **Slowing Cash Payments**

    a. A **zero-balance account** has a balance of $0. At the end of each processing day, the bank transfers just enough from the firm's master account to cover all checks presented against the zero-balance account that day.

       1) This practice allows the firm to maintain higher balances in the master account from which short-term investments can be made. The bank generally charges a fee for this service.

**Operating Cycle
43.1 Days**

Acquire Inventory

Collect Receivables

Days' Sales in Inventory (18.8 days)

Days' Sales in Receivables (24.3 days)

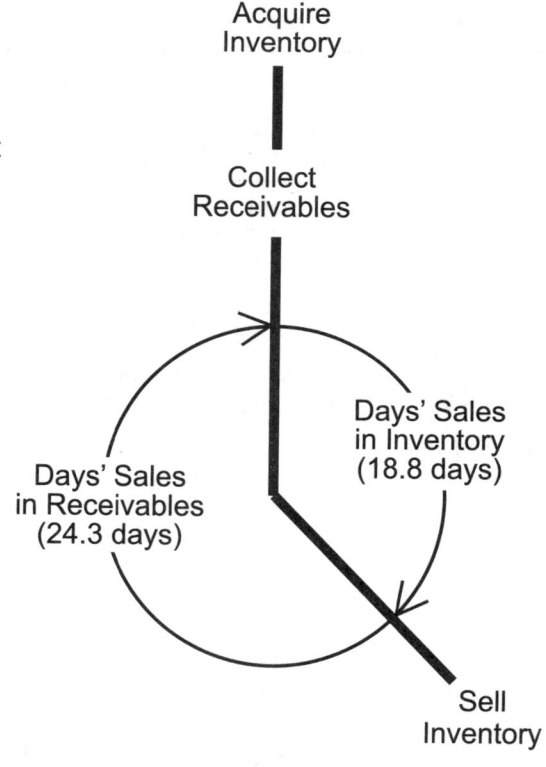

Sell Inventory

Figure 10-2

SU 10: Working Capital II: Inventory and Short-Term Financing

3. **Cash Conversion Cycle**

   a. A firm's cash conversion cycle is the time between the payment of cash for inventory and the collection of cash from its sale. This describes the efficacy of the firm's investment in operations. Firms with highly demanded products that are well run by management have lower cash conversion cycles than other firms.

   $$\text{Cash conversion cycle} = \frac{\text{Days' sales in receivables}}{\text{(average collection period)}} + \frac{\text{Days' sales}}{\text{in inventory}} - \frac{\text{Average}}{\text{payables period}}$$

   1) The **accounts payable turnover ratio** is the number of times during a period that the firm pays its accounts payable.

      a) The higher the accounts payable turnover, the more frequently a firm is able to pay all of its accounts payable.

      b) When a firm attempts to obtain credit from suppliers or banks, accounts payable turnover is used to determine whether credit should be extended.

   $$\text{Accounts payable turnover} = \frac{\text{Cost of goods sold}}{\text{Average balance in accounts payable}}$$

   2) The **average payables period** (payables turnover in days or days of payables outstanding) is the average time between the purchase of inventory and the payment of cash. This ratio provides insight on how often a firm can settle its average accounts payable per year.

   $$\text{Average payable period} = \frac{\text{Ending accounts payable}}{\text{Cost of goods sold} \div \text{Days in year}}$$

   NOTE: We anticipate, based on AICPA sample exams, that the average payable period formula given above is what you will see on the CPA Exam. This formula uses the ending balance. An alternative formula, shown below, uses the average balance.

   $$\text{Average payable period} = \frac{\text{Days in year}}{\text{Accounts payable turnover}}$$

      a) This ratio is used by creditors to determine a firm's liquidity, so a lower value is advantageous.

   b. The operating cycle and the cash conversion cycle differ because the firm's purchases of inventory are made on credit. Thus, the cash conversion cycle equals the operating cycle minus the average payables period.

	Accounts Payable Turnover	Average Payable Period
Higher	More Liquid	Less Liquid
Lower	Less Liquid	More Liquid

STOP & REVIEW

You have completed the outline for this subunit.
Study multiple-choice questions 10 through 12 on page 308.

10.4 MULTIPLE RATIO ANALYSIS

Some multiple-choice questions require candidates to combine their knowledge of the different categories of ratios. This subunit consists entirely of such questions. The ratios presented in Study Unit 9, Subunit 2, and Subunit 10.2 should be thoroughly reviewed before answering the questions. The following is a summary of ratio analysis:

1. **Liquidity Ratios**

$$\text{Net working capital} = \text{Current assets} - \text{Current liabilities}$$

$$\text{Current ratio} = \frac{\text{Current assets}}{\text{Current liabilities}}$$

$$\text{Quick (acid-test) ratio} = \frac{\text{Cash and equivalents} + \text{Marketable securities} + \text{Net receivables}}{\text{Current liabilities}}$$

$$\text{Cash flow ratio} = \frac{\text{Cash flow from operations}}{\text{Current liabilities}}$$

2. **Receivable Ratios**

$$\text{Accounts receivable turnover} = \frac{\text{Net credit sales}}{\text{Average balance in accounts receivable (net)}}$$

$$\text{Days' sales in receivables} = \frac{\text{Ending accounts receivable (net)}}{\text{Net credit sales} \div \text{Days in year}}$$

3. **Inventory Ratios**

$$\text{Inventory turnover} = \frac{\text{Cost of goods sold}}{\text{Average balance in inventory}}$$

$$\text{Days' sales in inventory} = \frac{\text{Ending inventory}}{\text{Cost of good sold} \div \text{Days in year}}$$

4. **Operating Performance Ratios**

$$\text{Operating cycle} = \text{Days' sales in receivables} + \text{Days' sales in inventory}$$

$$\text{Cash conversion cycle} = \begin{array}{c}\text{Days' sales in receivables}\\\text{(average collection period)}\end{array} + \begin{array}{c}\text{Days' sales}\\\text{in inventory}\end{array} - \begin{array}{c}\text{Average}\\\text{payables period}\end{array}$$

$$\text{Accounts payable turnover} = \frac{\text{Cost of goods sold}}{\text{Average balance in accounts payable}}$$

$$\text{Average payable period} = \frac{\text{Ending accounts payable}}{\text{Cost of goods sold} \div \text{Days in year}}$$

STOP & REVIEW

You have completed the outline for this subunit.
Study multiple-choice questions 13 through 16 beginning on page 309.

10.5 SHORT-TERM FINANCING

1. Firms often need short-term financing to meet their needs in cases where working capital management was not optimally mixed or during times of slow sales.

2. **Spontaneous Financing -- Trade Credit**

    a. A supplier may offer an early payment discount. For example, payment terms may be 2/10, n/30. These terms provide a 2% discount if payment is within 10 days. Otherwise, the entire balance is due in 30 days (an interest-free 30-day loan). Taking the discount ordinarily is advantageous. The annualized cost of **not** taking a discount can be calculated using the following formula:

    $$\frac{\text{Discount \%}}{100\% - \text{Discount \%}} \times \frac{\text{Days in year}}{\text{Total payment period} - \text{Discount period}}$$

    > **EXAMPLE 10-5**   Cost of Not Taking Discount -- Effective Rate
    >
    > A vendor has sold goods to a firm on terms of 2/10, net 30. The firm has chosen to pay on day 30. The effective annual rate paid by forgoing the discount is calculated as follows (using a 360-day year):
    >
    > Cost of not taking discount = [2% ÷ (100% − 2%)] × [360 days ÷ (30 days − 10 days)]
    >   = (2% ÷ 98%) × (360 days ÷ 20 days)
    >   = 2.0408% × 18
    >   = 36.73%
    >
    > Only firms with extreme cash-flow problems are willing to pay a 36.73% rate.

3. **Formal Financing Arrangements**

    a. Commercial banks offer short-term loans and lines of credit.

        1) A **term loan**, such as a note, must be repaid by a definite time.

        2) A **line of credit** allows the firm to reborrow amounts continuously up to a maximum amount if minimum payments are made each month. This arrangement is similar to a consumer's credit card.

4. Simple Interest Short-Term Loans

a. Interest on a simple interest loan is paid at the end of the loan term. The amount to be paid is based on the nominal (stated) rate and the principal of the loan (amount needed).

$$\text{Interest expense} = \text{Principal of loan} \times \text{Stated rate} \times \text{Time}$$

> **EXAMPLE 10-6 Simple Interest**
>
> A firm obtained a short-term bank loan of $15,000 at an annual interest rate of 8%. The interest expense on the loan is $1,200 ($15,000 × 8% × 1) per year.
>
> The stated rate of 8% also is the effective rate.

b. The **effective rate** of any financing arrangement is the ratio of the amount the firm must pay to the amount it can use. Often there are fees associated with loans, and the face value of the loan is not received.

$$\text{Effective interest rate} = \frac{\text{Interest expense (interest to be paid)}}{\text{Usable funds (net proceeds)}}$$

> **EXAMPLE 10-7 Effective Interest Rate**
>
> A firm obtained a short-term bank loan of $15,000 at an annual interest rate of 8%. The bank charges a loan origination fee of $500.
>
> Effective rate = Interest paid ÷ Net proceeds
> = ($15,000 × 8%) ÷ ($15,000 − $500)
> = $1,200 ÷ $14,500
> = 8.28%
>
> The effective interest rate (8.28%) is higher than the stated interest rate (8%) because the net proceeds are lower than the principal.

5. Discounted Loans

a. For a discounted loan, the interest and finance charges are paid at the beginning of the loan term.

$$\text{Total borrowings} = \frac{\text{Amount needed}}{(1.0 - \text{Stated rate})}$$

> **EXAMPLE 10-8 Discounted Loan -- Effective and Nominal Rates**
>
> A firm needs $90,000 of usable funds. Its bank has offered to make a loan at an 8% nominal rate on a discounted basis.
>
> Loan amount = Usable funds ÷ (1.0 − Stated rate)
> = $90,000 ÷ (100% − 8%)
> = $90,000 ÷ 92%
> = $97,826
>
> Because the borrower has the use of a smaller amount, the effective rate on a discounted loan is higher than its nominal rate.
>
> Effective rate = Net interest expense ÷ Usable funds
> = ($97,826 × 8%) ÷ $90,000
> = $7,826 ÷ $90,000
> = 8.696%

b. In all financing arrangements, the effective rate can be calculated without dollar amounts.

$$\text{Effective rate on discounted loan} = \frac{\text{Stated rate}}{(1.0 - \text{Stated rate})}$$

EXAMPLE 10-9   **Effective Interest Rate Discounted Loan**

The firm from Example 10-8 calculates the effective rate on this loan without dollar amounts.

Effective rate = Stated rate ÷ (1.0 − Stated rate)
= 8% ÷ (100% − 8%)
= 8% ÷ 92%
= 8.696%

---

6. **Loans with Compensating Balances**

    a. Banks may require a borrower to maintain a compensating balance during the term of a financing arrangement to reduce risk and increase their returns.

$$\text{Total borrowings} = \frac{\text{Amount needed}}{(1.0 - \text{Compensating balance \%})}$$

EXAMPLE 10-10   **Total Borrowing with Compensatory Balance**

A firm has received a loan of $120,000 with terms of 2/10, net 30. The firm's bank will lend the necessary amount for 20 days. Thus, the discount can be taken on the 10th day at a nominal annual rate of 6% and a compensating balance of 10%.

Total borrowings = Amount needed ÷ (1.0 − Compensated balance %)
= ($120,000 × 98%) ÷ (100% − 10%)
= $117,600 ÷ 90%
= $130,667

---

b. Because the bank requires a compensating balance, the borrower can use a smaller amount than the face amount of the loan and therefore pays an effective rate higher than the nominal rate.

EXAMPLE 10-11   **Effective Rate with Compensatory Balance**

A firm has an outstanding loan of $130,667 at a stated interest rate of 6%. The firm is required to maintain $13,067 as a minimum compensating balance.

Effective rate = Net interest expense (annualized) ÷ Usable funds
= (Principal × Interest rate) ÷ (Principal − Compensating balances)
= ($130,667 × 6%) ÷ ($130,667 − $13,067)
= $7,840 ÷ $117,600
= 6.667%

The effective interest rate (6.667%) is higher than the stated interest rate (6%) because the face amount is reduced by the compensating balance, resulting in smaller usable funds.

---

c. Again, the effective rate can be determined without dollar amounts.

$$\text{Effective rate with compensatory balance} = \frac{\text{Stated rate}}{(1.0 - \text{Compensating balance \%})}$$

EXAMPLE 10-12   **Effective Interest Rate with Compensatory Balance**

Effective rate = Stated rate ÷ (1.0 − Compensating balance %)
= 6% ÷ (100% − 10%)
= 6% ÷ 90%
= 6.667%

7. **Lines of Credit with Commitment Fees**

   a. A line of credit is the right to draw cash at any time up to a specified maximum. A line of credit may have a definite term, or it may be revolving; that is, the borrower can continuously pay off and reborrow from it.

   1) Sometimes a bank charges a borrower a commitment fee on the unused portion.

EXAMPLE 10-13   Line of Credit with Commitment Fees -- Annual Cost

A firm's bank extended a $1,000,00-250 line of credit at a nominal rate of 8% with a 0.5% commitment fee on the unused portion. The average loan balance during the year was $400,000.

Annual cost = Interest expense on average balance + Commitment fee on unused portion
= (Average balance × Stated rate) + [(Credit limit − Average balance) × Commitment fee %]
= ($400,000 × 8%) + [($1,000,000 − $400,000) × 0.5%]
= $32,000 + $3,000
= $35,000

STOP & REVIEW

You have completed the outline for this subunit.
Study multiple-choice questions 17 through 21 beginning on page 311.

QUESTIONS

10.1 Inventory Management -- Methods

1. Which of the following methods is a push system used to control inventory and minimize total inventory costs?

I.   Just-in-time (JIT) system
II. Kanban method
III. Materials requirements planning
IV. Manufacturing resource planning

   A. I and II only.
   B. I, III, and IV only.
   C. III and IV only.
   D. II and III only.

Answer (C) is correct.
   REQUIRED: The push inventory control system(s).
   DISCUSSION: A push inventory system is a system that controls inventory based on forecasted demand. Materials requirements planning (MRP) is a push system. The demand for materials is driven by the forecasted demand for the final product as programmed into the system. MRP, in effect, creates schedules of when items of inventory are needed in the production departments and thus reduces unnecessary inventory costs. Manufacturing resource planning (MRP II) is an advanced MRP system that extends the scope of an MRP system. Thus, both MRP and MRP II are push systems.
   JIT is a pull system that is demand-driven. In a manufacturing environment, production of goods does not begin until an order has been received. In this way, finished goods inventories also are eliminated. Kanban is also a pull system. It uses tickets to control the flow of production or parts so that they are produced or obtained in the needed amounts at the needed times.
   Answer (A) is incorrect. Both JIT and Kanban are pull systems, not push systems. **Answer (B) is incorrect.** A JIT system is a pull system, not a push system. **Answer (D) is incorrect.** A Kanban system is a pull system, not a push system. Both materials requirements planning and manufacturing resource planning are push systems.

2. Which changes in costs are most conducive to switching from a traditional inventory ordering system to a just-in-time ordering system?

	Cost per Purchase Order	Inventory Unit Carrying Costs
A.	Increasing	Increasing
B.	Decreasing	Increasing
C.	Decreasing	Decreasing
D.	Increasing	Decreasing

Answer (B) is correct.
REQUIRED: The changes in costs most conducive to switching to a JIT ordering system.
DISCUSSION: A JIT system is intended to minimize inventory. Thus, if inventory carrying costs are increasing, a JIT system becomes more cost-effective. Moreover, purchases are more frequent in a JIT system. Accordingly, a decreasing cost per purchase order is a reason to switch to a JIT system.

3. Stewart Co. uses the economic order quantity (EOQ) model for inventory management. A decrease in which one of the following variables would increase the EOQ?

A. Annual sales.
B. Cost per order.
C. Safety stock level.
D. Carrying costs.

Answer (D) is correct.
REQUIRED: The decrease in a variable that increases the EOQ.
DISCUSSION: The EOQ model minimizes the total of ordering and carrying costs. The EOQ is calculated as follows:

$$\sqrt{\frac{2 \times \text{Periodic demand} \times \text{Ordering costs per order}}{\text{Carrying costs per unit}}}$$

Increases in the numerator (demand or ordering costs) increase the EOQ, but decreases in the numerator decrease the EOQ. Also, a decrease in the denominator (carrying costs) increases the EOQ.
Answer (A) is incorrect. A decrease in demand (annual sales), which is in the numerator, decreases the EOQ. **Answer (B) is incorrect.** A decrease in ordering costs, which is in the numerator, encourages more orders, or a decrease in the EOQ. **Answer (C) is incorrect.** A decrease in safety stock does not affect the EOQ, although it might lead to a different ordering point.

4. Which of the following assumptions is associated with the economic order quantity formula?

A. The carrying cost per unit will vary with quantity ordered.
B. The cost of placing an order will vary with quantity ordered.
C. Periodic demand is known.
D. The purchase cost per unit will vary based on quantity discounts.

Answer (C) is correct.
REQUIRED: The assumption associated with the EOQ formula.
DISCUSSION: The economic order quantity (EOQ) model is a mathematical tool for determining the order quantity that minimizes the sum of ordering costs and carrying costs. The following assumptions underlie the EOQ model: (1) demand is uniform, (2) order (setup) costs and carrying costs are constant, and (3) no quantity discounts are allowed.
Answer (A) is incorrect. An assumption of the EOQ model is that the carrying cost per unit is constant. **Answer (B) is incorrect.** The cost of placing an order is constant when using the EOQ formula. **Answer (D) is incorrect.** An assumption of the EOQ model is that no quantity discounts are allowed.

5. In inventory management, the safety stock will tend to increase if the

A. Carrying cost increases.
B. Cost of running out of stock decreases.
C. Variability of the lead time increases.
D. Variability of the usage rate decreases.

Answer (C) is correct.
REQUIRED: The factor that increases safety stock.
DISCUSSION: A firm maintains safety stock to protect itself against the losses caused by stockouts. These can take the form of lost sales or lost production time. Safety stock is necessary because of the variability in lead time and usage rates. As the variability in lead time increases, a firm tends to carry larger safety stock.
Answer (A) is incorrect. An increase in inventory carrying costs makes carrying safety stock less efficient. **Answer (B) is incorrect.** If the cost of stockouts declines, the incentive to carry large safety stock is reduced. **Answer (D) is incorrect.** A decline in the variability of usage makes planning easier and safety stock less necessary.

6. The following information regarding inventory policy was assembled by the TKF Corporation. The company uses a 50-week year in all calculations.

Sales	12,000 units per year
Order quantity	4,000 units
Safety stock	1,500 units
Lead time	5 weeks

The reorder point is

A. 5,500 units.
B. 2,700 units.
C. 1,200 units.
D. 240 units.

Answer (B) is correct.
REQUIRED: The level of inventory at which an order should be placed.
DISCUSSION: The reorder point is the inventory level at which an order should be placed. It can be quantified using the following equation:

Reorder point = (Average weekly demand × Lead time) + Safety stock
= [(12,000 units ÷ 50 weeks) × 5 weeks] + 1,500 units
= 1,200 units + 1,500 units
= 2,700 units

Answer (A) is incorrect. The amount of 5,500 units equals the order size plus the safety stock. **Answer (C) is incorrect.** The amount of 1,200 units omits safety stock. **Answer (D) is incorrect.** The average weekly usage is 240 units.

7. A company serves as a distributor of products by ordering finished products once a quarter and using that inventory to accommodate the demand over the quarter. If it plans to ease its credit policy for customers, the amount of products ordered for its inventory every quarter will be

A. Increased to accommodate higher sales levels.
B. Reduced to offset the increased cost of carrying accounts receivable.
C. Unaffected if safety stock is part of the current quarterly order.
D. Unaffected if the JIT inventory control system is used.

Answer (A) is correct.
REQUIRED: The effect on the quantity of products ordered as a result of relaxing credit policy.
DISCUSSION: Relaxing the credit policy for customers leads to increased sales because more people are eligible for more credit. As sales increase, the amount ordered on each purchase order increases to accommodate the higher sales.
Answer (B) is incorrect. Inventory should be increased to accommodate higher sales levels. **Answer (C) is incorrect.** Safety stock is based on expected sales, which are expected to rise. **Answer (D) is incorrect.** A just-in-time system is not used when a company orders inventory once a quarter.

10.2 Inventory Management -- Ratios

8. The selected information below (in thousands) pertains to Devlin Company.

	December 31	
	Year 2	Year 1
Assets		
Current assets		
Cash	$ 45	$ 38
Trading securities	30	20
Accounts receivable (net)	68	48
Inventory	90	80
Prepaid expenses	22	30
Total current assets	$255	$216
Net sales	$480	$460
Costs and expenses		
Costs of goods sold	330	315
Selling, general, and administrative	52	51
Interest expense	8	9
Income before taxes	$ 90	$ 85
Income taxes	36	34
Net income	$ 54	$ 51

Devlin Company's inventory turnover for Year 2 was

A. 3.67 times.
B. 3.88 times.
C. 5.33 times.
D. 5.65 times.

Answer (B) is correct.
    REQUIRED: The inventory turnover.
    DISCUSSION: Inventory turnover equals cost of goods sold divided by the average balance in inventory. Thus, the inventory turnover is 3.88 times per year {$330 COGS ÷ [($90 + $80) ÷ 2]}.
    Answer (A) is incorrect. The ratio of 3.67 times is based on ending inventory. **Answer (C) is incorrect.** The ratio of 5.33 times equals sales divided by ending inventory. **Answer (D) is incorrect.** The ratio of 5.65 times is based on sales, not cost of goods sold.

9. Selected information (in thousands) from the statement of financial position for King Products Corporation for the fiscal years ended December 31, Year 2, and Year 1, is presented below. Net credit sales and cost of goods sold for Year 2 were $600,000 and $440,000, respectively.

	December 31	
	Year 2	Year 1
Cash	$ 60	$ 50
Marketable securities (at market)	40	30
Accounts receivable (net)	90	60
Inventories (at lower of cost or market)	120	100
Prepaid items	30	40
Total current assets	$340	$280

King Products Corporation's inventory turnover ratio for Year 2 was

A. 3.7
B. 4.0
C. 4.4
D. 6.0

Answer (B) is correct.
    REQUIRED: The inventory turnover ratio for Year 2.
    DISCUSSION: The inventory turnover ratio equals cost of goods sold divided by the average balance in inventory. Consequently, the inventory turnover is 4 times per year {$440,000 ÷ [($120,000 + $100,000) ÷ 2]}.
    Answer (A) is incorrect. The ratio of 3.7 is based on year-end inventory. **Answer (C) is incorrect.** The ratio of 4.4 is based on beginning inventory. **Answer (D) is incorrect.** The ratio of 6.0 is based on sales and beginning inventory.

10.3 The Operating Cycle and Cash Conversion Cycle

10. The following computations were made from Bruckner Co.'s current-year books:

Number of days' sales in inventory	55
Number of days' sales in trade accounts receivable	26

What was the number of days in Bruckner's current-year operating cycle?

A. 26
B. 40.5
C. 55
D. 81

Answer (D) is correct.
REQUIRED: The number of days in the operating cycle.
DISCUSSION: The operating cycle is the time needed to turn cash into inventory, inventory into receivables, and receivables back into cash. It is equal to the sum of the number of days' sales in inventory (average number of days to sell inventory) and the number of days' sales in receivables (the average collection period). The number of days' sales in inventory is given as 55 days. The number of days' sales in receivables is given as 26 days. Hence, the number of days in the operating cycle is 81 (55 + 26).
Answer (A) is incorrect. The number of days' sales in receivables is 26. **Answer (B) is incorrect.** The figure of 40.5 equals the sum of the number of days' sales in inventory and the number of days' sales in receivables, divided by 2. **Answer (C) is incorrect.** The number of days' sales in inventory is 55.

11. To determine the operating cycle for a retail department store, which one of the following pairs of items is needed?

A. Days' sales in accounts receivable and average merchandise inventory.
B. Cash turnover and net sales.
C. Days' sales in accounts receivable and days' sales in inventory.
D. Asset turnover and return on sales.

Answer (C) is correct.
REQUIRED: The pair of items needed to determine the operating cycle for a retailer.
DISCUSSION: The operating cycle is the time needed to turn cash into inventory, inventory into receivables, and receivables back into cash. For a retailer, it is the time from purchase of inventory to collection of cash. Thus, the operating cycle of a retailer is equal to the sum of the number of days' sales in inventory and the number of days' sales in receivables.

12. A company purchases inventory on terms of net 30 days and resells to its customers on terms of net 15 days. The inventory conversion period averages 60 days. What is the company's cash conversion cycle?

A. 15 days.
B. 45 days.
C. 75 days.
D. 105 days.

Answer (B) is correct.
REQUIRED: The length of the company's cash conversion cycle.
DISCUSSION: A firm's cash conversion cycle is the amount of time that passes between the actual outlay of cash for inventory purchases and the collection of cash from the sale of that inventory. Accordingly, the cash conversion cycle is equal to the average collection period plus days' sales in inventory minus the average payables period. Per the formula, the company's cash conversion cycle is 45 days (15 days average collection period + 60 days' sales in inventory – 30 days average payables period).
Answer (A) is incorrect. The period of 15 days is the average collection period, not the cash collection cycle. **Answer (C) is incorrect.** The period of 75 days is the company's operating cycle, not the cash conversion cycle. **Answer (D) is incorrect.** The period of 105 days results from adding the average payables period to the company's operating cycle instead of subtracting it.

10.4 Multiple Ratio Analysis

13. Which of the following ratios would most likely be used by management to evaluate short-term liquidity?

A. Return on total assets.
B. Sales to cash.
C. Accounts receivable turnover.
D. Acid-test ratio.

Answer (D) is correct.
REQUIRED: The ratio most likely used by management to evaluate short-term liquidity.
DISCUSSION: Liquidity is a firm's ability to pay its current obligations as they come due. Liquidity ratios relate a firm's liquid assets to its current liabilities. The current ratio is the most common measure of short-term liquidity. It is calculated by dividing current assets by current liabilities. The acid-test (quick) ratio equals the sum of (1) cash and cash equivalents, (2) marketable securities, and (3) net receivables, divided by current liabilities. It is a more conservative short-term liquidity ratio. It excludes inventories and prepayments (recognized as assets) from the numerator.
Answer (A) is incorrect. Return on total assets measures corporate performance. **Answer (B) is incorrect.** The sales to cash ratio measures the effectiveness of credit and collection policies. **Answer (C) is incorrect.** Accounts receivable turnover measures effectiveness in collecting accounts receivable.

14. Selected data from Sheridan Corporation's year-end financial statements are presented below. The difference between average and ending inventory is immaterial.

Current ratio	2.0
Quick ratio	1.5
Current liabilities	$120,000
Inventory turnover (based on cost of goods sold)	8 times
Gross profit margin	40%

Assuming no prepaid expenses are included in current assets, Sheridan's net sales for the year were

A. $800,000
B. $480,000
C. $1,200,000
D. $240,000

Answer (A) is correct.
REQUIRED: The net sales for the year.
DISCUSSION: Net sales can be calculated indirectly from the inventory turnover ratio and the other ratios given. If the current ratio is 2.0, and current liabilities are $120,000, current assets must be $240,000 (2.0 × $120,000). Similarly, if the quick ratio is 1.5, the total quick assets must be $180,000 (1.5 × $120,000). The difference between quick assets and current assets is that inventory is not included in the quick assets. Consequently, ending inventory must be $60,000 ($240,000 – $180,000). The inventory turnover ratio (COGS ÷ Average inventory) is 8. Thus, cost of goods sold must be 8 times average inventory, or $480,000, given no material difference between average and ending inventory. If the gross profit margin is 40%, the cost of goods sold percentage is 60%, cost of goods sold equals 60% of sales, and net sales must be $800,000 ($480,000 ÷ 60%).
Answer (B) is incorrect. Cost of goods sold is $480,000. **Answer (C) is incorrect.** The amount of $1,200,000 is based on a 60% gross profit margin. **Answer (D) is incorrect.** Current assets equal $240,000.

15. On July 14, Avila Co. collected a receivable due from a major customer. Which of the following ratios is increased by this transaction?

A. Inventory turnover ratio.
B. Receivable turnover ratio.
C. Current ratio.
D. Quick ratio.

Answer (B) is correct.
REQUIRED: The ratio increased by collection of a receivable.
DISCUSSION: The accounts receivable turnover is equal to net credit sales divided by the average accounts receivable. Collection of a receivable decreases the denominator and increases the ratio.
Answer (A) is incorrect. The inventory turnover ratio equals the cost of goods sold divided by the average inventory. Collection of a receivable does not affect it.
Answer (C) is incorrect. A decrease in a receivable and an equal increase in cash have no effect on the current ratio. **Answer (D) is incorrect.** A decrease in a receivable and an equal increase in cash have no effect on the quick ratio.

16. Which of the following ratios, if any, are useful in assessing a company's ability to meet currently maturing or short-term obligations?

	Acid-Test Ratio	Debt-to-Equity Ratio
A.	No	No
B.	No	Yes
C.	Yes	Yes
D.	Yes	No

Answer (D) is correct.
REQUIRED: The ratios, if any, useful in assessing a company's ability to meet currently maturing obligations.
DISCUSSION: Liquidity ratios measure the ability of a company to meet its short-term obligations. A commonly used liquidity ratio is the acid-test, or quick, ratio, which equals quick assets (net accounts receivable, current marketable securities, and cash) divided by current liabilities. The debt-to-equity ratio is a leverage ratio. Leverage ratios measure the impact of debt on profitability and risk.
Answer (A) is incorrect. The acid-test ratio is useful in assessing a company's ability to meet currently maturing or short-term obligations. **Answer (B) is incorrect.** The acid-test ratio is useful in assessing a company's ability to meet currently maturing or short-term obligations, but the debt-to-equity ratio does not exclude long-term obligations. **Answer (C) is incorrect.** The debt-to-equity ratio includes long-term obligations.

10.5 Short-Term Financing

> Questions 17 through 19 are based on the following information. Skilantic Company needs to pay a supplier's invoice of $60,000 and wants to take a cash discount of 2/10, net 40. The firm can borrow the money for 30 days at 11% per annum plus a 9% compensating balance.

17. The amount Skilantic Company must borrow to pay the supplier within the discount period and cover the compensating balance is

A. $60,000
B. $65,934
C. $64,615
D. $58,800

Answer (C) is correct.
REQUIRED: The amount to borrow to pay the supplier within the discount period and cover the compensating balance requirement.
DISCUSSION: Skilantic's total borrowings on this loan can be calculated as follows:

Total borrowings = Amount needed ÷
                   (1.0 − Compensating balance %)
  = ($60,000 × 98%) ÷ (100% − 9%)
  = $58,800 ÷ 91%
  = $64,615

Answer (A) is incorrect. The amount of $60,000 is the invoice amount. Answer (B) is incorrect. The amount of $65,934 assumes the amount paid to the supplier is $60,000. Answer (D) is incorrect. The amount of $58,800 is the amount to be paid to the supplier.

18. Assuming Skilantic Company borrows the money on the last day of the discount period and repays it 30 days later, the effective interest rate on the loan is

A. 11%
B. 10%
C. 12.09%
D. 9.90%

Answer (C) is correct.
REQUIRED: The effective interest rate when borrowing to take a discount.
DISCUSSION: Skilantic's effective rate on this loan can be calculated as follows:

Effective rate = Stated rate ÷
                 (1.0 − Compensating balance %)
  = 11% ÷ (100% − 9%)
  = 11% ÷ 91%
  = 12.09%

Answer (A) is incorrect. The contract rate is 11%. Answer (B) is incorrect. The effective rate is greater than the contract rate. The usable funds are less than the face amount of the note. Answer (D) is incorrect. The effective rate is greater than the contract rate. The usable funds are less than the face amount of the note.

19. Skilantic fails to take the discount and pays on the 40th day. Assuming a 360-day year, what effective rate of annual interest does it pay the vendor?

A. 2%
B. 24%
C. 24.49%
D. 36.73%

Answer (C) is correct.
REQUIRED: The effective interest rate paid when a discount is not taken.
DISCUSSION: By failing to take the discount, Skilantic is essentially borrowing $58,800 for 30 days. Thus, at a cost of $1,200, it acquires the use of $58,800, resulting in a rate of 2.0408% ($1,200 ÷ $58,800) for 30 days. Assuming a 360-day year, the effective annual rate is 24.49% [2.0408% × (360 days ÷ 30 days)].

Answer (A) is incorrect. The discount rate for a 30-day period is 2%. Answer (B) is incorrect. The percentage of 24% assumes that the available funds equal $60,000. Answer (D) is incorrect. The percentage of 36.73% assumes a 20-day discount period.

20. A company obtained a short-term bank loan of $250,000 at an annual interest rate of 6%. As a condition of the loan, the company is required to maintain a compensating balance of $50,000 in its checking account. The checking account earns interest at an annual rate of 2%. Ordinarily, the company maintains a balance of $25,000 in its account for transaction purposes. What is the effective interest rate of the loan?

A. 6.44%
B. 7.00%
C. 5.80%
D. 6.66%

Answer (A) is correct.
REQUIRED: The effective interest rate on a loan that requires a compensating balance above the normal working balance.
DISCUSSION: The $50,000 compensating balance requirement is partially satisfied by the practice of maintaining a $25,000 balance for transaction purposes. Thus, only $25,000 of the loan is not available for current use. At 6% interest, the $250,000 loan requires an interest payment of $15,000 per year. This amount is partially offset by the 2% interest earned on the $25,000 incremental balance, or $500. Subtracting the $500 interest earned from the $15,000 of expense results in net interest expense of $14,500 for the use of $225,000 ($250,000 − $25,000).ABy dividing $14,500 by $225,000 produces an effective interest rate of 6.44%.
Answer (B) is incorrect. The percentage of 7.00% fails to consider that the $25,000 currently being maintained counts toward the compensating balance requirement. Answer (C) is incorrect. The percentage of 5.80% fails to consider the compensating balance requirement. Answer (D) is incorrect. The percentage of 6.66% fails to consider the interest earned on the incremental balance being carried.

21. If a firm purchases raw materials from its supplier on a 3/10, net 30, cash discount basis, the equivalent annual interest rate (using a 360-day year) of forgoing the cash discount and making payment on the 30th day is

A. 3%
B. 37.11%
C. 55.67%
D. 31.81%

Answer (C) is correct.
REQUIRED: The equivalent annual interest charge for not taking the discount.
DISCUSSION: The buyer could satisfy the $100 obligation by paying $97 on the 10th day. By choosing to wait until the 30th day, the buyer is effectively paying a $3 interest charge for the use of $97 for 20 days (30-day credit period − 10-day discount period). The annualized cost of not taking this discount can be calculated as follows:

$$\frac{\text{Discount \%}}{100\% - \text{Discount \%}} \times \frac{\text{Days in year}}{\text{Total paymt. period} - \text{Discount period}}$$

Cost of not taking discount = [3% ÷ (100% − 3%)] × [360 days ÷ (30 days − 10 days)]
= (3% ÷ 97%) × (360 days ÷ 20 days)
= 3.0928% × 18
= 55.67%

Answer (A) is incorrect. The discount rate is 3%. Answer (B) is incorrect. The percentage of 37.11% is based on the 40-day credit period. Answer (D) is incorrect. The percentage of 31.81% is based on a 45-day credit period.

STUDY UNIT ELEVEN
CAPITAL BUDGETING

(24 pages of outline)

11.1	Capital Budgeting -- Basics	313
11.2	Capital Budgeting -- Net Present Value (NPV)	319
11.3	Capital Budgeting -- Internal Rate of Return (IRR)	327
11.4	Capital Budgeting -- Payback Methods	329
11.5	Ranking Capital Projects	331
11.6	Comparison of Capital Budgeting Methods	333

Firms retain some of their net income and use this plus other financing to expand production, develop new products, enter new business markets through acquisition or internal development, or make speculative investments. Firms must decide whether to invest in new product lines or means of production. This process, called capital budgeting, involves

1) Identifying investments,
2) Determining the resources required,
3) Projecting the expected amounts and timing of returns, and
4) Ranking the identified investments.

11.1 CAPITAL BUDGETING -- BASICS

1. **Capital Budgeting**

    a. Capital budgeting is the process of planning and controlling investments for long-term projects.

    1) Most financial and management accounting topics, such as calculating the allowance for credit losses (formerly bad debt) or accumulating product costs, require reporting activity for a single accounting or reporting cycle, such as 1 month or 1 year.

    2) Capital projects affect multiple accounting periods and limit the firm's future financial planning. Thus, capital budgeting decisions tend to be relatively permanent and inflexible.

    b. A capital project usually involves substantial expenditures and financing. Planning is important because of uncertainties about capital markets, inflation, interest rates, and the money supply.

    c. The following are capital budgeting applications:

    1) Buying equipment
    2) Building facilities
    3) Acquiring a business
    4) Developing a product or product line
    5) Expanding into new markets
    6) Replacing equipment

d. Capital budgeting involves screening decisions and preference decisions.
 1) The **screening decision** examines all potential projects and determines whether each of them meets a predefined criterion or hurdle.
    a) For example, a screening criterion for a business could be a required return on investment of at least 15% to accept a project.
 2) The **preference decision** ranks all the acceptable projects identified in the screening phase and selects from only the acceptable projects.
    a) The ranking or preference decision is sometimes referred to as **capital rationing**.
       i) For example, assume seven projects meet a firm's screening criteria during the screening decision. The total investment required for all seven projects is $5 million, but the firm only plans to invest $2 million. The preference decision determines how the firm ranks the potential projects to ration the use of the limited investment funds.
e. Capital projects can be independent or mutually exclusive.
 1) Projects that are **independent** do not affect each other. If the firm possesses enough available funds and both projects meet the screening criteria, the firm can proceed with both projects.
 2) If projects are **mutually exclusive**, proceeding with one project results in the other project not taking place. Only one project can be accepted for investment.

2. **Relevant Cash Flows**
   a. Many capital budgeting techniques used for screening and preference decisions require the identification of the relevant cash flows (future uncertain cash flows) for the project.
      1) Relevant cash flows do **not** include sunk costs, those already paid or irrevocably committed to be paid.
   b. The following are relevant cash flows for capital budgeting:
      1) Operating cash flow (the annual after-tax cash savings or inflows)
      2) Net capital expenditure, including
         a) Cost of new equipment
         b) Proceeds from disposal of old equipment (residual or salvage value)
         c) Proceeds from disposal of new equipment (residual or salvage value)
      3) Net change in working capital
         a) At project initiation, working capital is built up (increased) to serve the liquidity needs. This represents a cash outflow.
         b) At the end of the project, working capital is recovered. This represents a cash inflow.

3. **Depreciation Tax Shield**

   a. The amount by which depreciation shields or protects the taxpayer from income taxes is the applicable tax rate multiplied by the amount of depreciation (Depreciation expense × Tax rate). Tax shields are an important component of the decision-making process when making investment decisions.

EXAMPLE 11-1	Depreciation Tax Shield

   Debt Co. has depreciation on machinery of $10,000. The tax rate is 40%. The depreciation tax shield is $4,000 ($10,000 × 40%).

EXAMPLE 11-2	Relevant Cash Flows

   The following is a firm's relevant financial information based on the acquisition of a new machine:

Sales	$500,000
COGS	$340,000
SG&A expense	$40,000
Depreciation expense	$20,000
Tax rate	40%

   Required: To calculate the after-tax annual cash flows, the effect of annual depreciation expense on tax payments must be considered.

   After-tax cash flow formulas:

   Operating cash income net of taxes + Depreciation tax shield = After-tax cash flow

   [Operating income × (1 − Tax rate)] + Depreciation expense = After-tax cash flow

   NOTE: Depreciation expense affects cash flows only because it reduces tax payments.

   Approach 1:

Operating cash income	$120,000	($500,000 − $340,000 − $40,000)
Operating cash income after tax	$ 72,000	[$120,000 × (1 − 40%)]
Add: Depreciation tax shield	8,000	($20,000 × 40%)
After-tax cash flow	$ 80,000	

   Approach 2:

Operating income	$100,000	($500,000 − $340,000 − $40,000 − $20,000)
Operating income after tax	$ 60,000	[$100,000 × (1 − 40%)]
Add: Depreciation expense	20,000	
After-tax cash flow	$ 80,000	

   b. The free cash flow of a project can be calculated using the following equation:

Free cash flow = Operating cash flow − Net capital expenditure − Net change in working capital

EXAMPLE 11-3	Relevant Cash Flows

An investment project has the following information:

Operating income after tax	$ 60,000
Depreciation expense	20,000
Net capital expenditure	50,000
Net change in working capital	(10,000)

Free cash flow to the project = Operating cash flow − Net capital expenditure − Net change in working capital
 = $60,000 + $20,000 − $50,000 − $(10,000)
 = $40,000

4. **Time Value of Money**

    a. People prefer to hold money now rather than in the future. "A dollar today is worth more than a dollar tomorrow."

    b. This principle of desiring money sooner rather than later is the basis for the concept of interest.

    c. **Interest** is the cornerstone of investment because interest represents the price charged by investors (or creditors) to permit others to use their money. Investors are willing to forgo the use of money now in exchange for a return at a later moment in time.

    d. The relationship between a dollar today and its value in the future is depicted in the graph below.

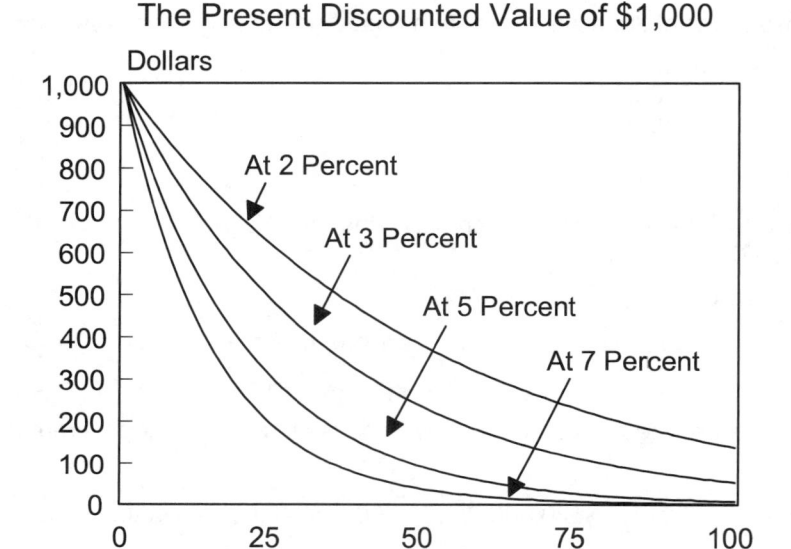

    The Present Discounted Value of $1,000

    Figure 11-1

e. The formula for compound interest and present value/future value computations is

$$FV = PV \times (1 + i)^n$$

FV = Future value
PV = Present value
i = Interest rate for the period
n = Number of periods

EXAMPLE 11-4   Future Value

Assume
  PV = $100
  i = 5% per year
  n = 2 years

The future value of the $100 held for 2 years earning 5% per year, compounded annually, is calculated as follows:

  FV = $100 × (1 + 0.05)²
     = $110.25

---

5. **Simple Interest vs. Compound Interest**

   a. The interest generated by an investment can either be paid periodically in cash or added to the investment principal in a process known as **compounding**.

EXAMPLE 11-5   Simple Interest and Compound Interest

A mutual fund offers its investors an annual 4% return. It can be received in cash or compounded. The following tables illustrate the difference in cash flows under the two methods:

	Using Simple Interest				Using Compound Interest			
	Beginning Balance	Annual Return		Cash Disbursed	Added to Balance	Beginning Balance	Annual Return	Added to Balance	Cash Disbursed
Year 1	$10,000.00 ×	4%	=	$400.00	--	$10,000.00 × 4% = $400.00	--
Year 2	10,000.00 ×	4%	=	400.00	--	10,400.00 × 4% = 416.00	--
Year 3	10,000.00 ×	4%	=	400.00	--	10,816.00 × 4% = 432.64	--
Year 4	10,000.00 ×	4%	=	400.00	--	11,248.64 × 4% = 449.95	--
Year 5	10,000.00 ×	4%	=	400.00	--	11,698.59 × 4% = 467.94	--

At the end of 5 years, the investor who received periodic payments had the use of $400 cash every year but has only the original $10,000 principal. An investor who chose compounding received no periodic cash flow but has a principal of $12,166.53 ($11,698.59 Year 5 beginning balance + $467.94 Year 5 return).

6. Accounting Rate of Return

a. The accounting rate of return is used to assess potential capital projects. It ignores the time value of money.

b. The accounting rate of return is based on readily available GAAP numbers. There are two methods to determine accounting rate of return.

$$\text{Accounting rate of return} = \frac{\text{Annual increase in GAAP net income}}{\text{Required investment}} = \frac{\text{Annual cash inflow} - \text{Depreciation}}{\text{Initial investment}}$$

EXAMPLE 11-6 Accounting Rate of Return

The following is a firm's relevant financial information for the acquisition of a new machine:

Initial cost: $250,000
Depreciation expense: $25,000 annually
Annual after-tax savings: $40,000

$$\frac{\text{Annual cash inflow} - \text{Depreciation}}{\text{Initial investment}} = \frac{\$40,000 - \$25,000}{\$250,000}$$
$$= 6\%$$

---

c. However, certain characteristics of the accounting rate of return limit its usefulness for selecting capital projects.

1) The accounting rate of return is affected by the accounting methods chosen.

   a) Accountants must choose which expenditures to capitalize and which to expense immediately. They also choose how quickly to depreciate capitalized assets.

   b) A project's true rate of return cannot be dependent on such decisions.

   c) The accounting rate of return does not take into account the time value of money.

   d) The accounting rate of return is not useful for projects in which the investments are made in multiple installments at different times.

   e) The accounting rate of return fails to consider increased risk of long-term projects. For example, a project with a 10% return earned in 10 years is preferred over a project with an 8% return earned in 3 years.

   f) Another distortion occurs when comparing a single project's accounting rate of return with the total return for all of the firm's capital projects.

   g) The decreasing book value of a depreciable investment implies the return on assets increases over the life of the investment.

SUCCESS TIP

The AICPA has tested the accounting rate of return by asking for its calculation. Questions also have asked for the components of the accounting rate of return.

STOP & REVIEW

You have completed the outline for this subunit.
Study multiple-choice questions 1 through 3 on page 337.

11.2 CAPITAL BUDGETING -- NET PRESENT VALUE (NPV)

1. **Discounted Cash Flow Analysis**

   a. A more sophisticated method for evaluating potential capital projects than the accounting rate of return is discounted cash flow analysis. It discounts the relevant cash flows to present value using the required rate of return as the discount rate. (This discount rate also is called the **hurdle rate** or **opportunity cost of capital**.)

      1) A hurdle rate is the minimum acceptable rate when choosing to invest in a project. There is a wide range of approaches to determine the hurdle rate. In practice, firms begin with their weighted-average cost of capital (WACC) and then adjust this interest rate in relation to other risks. **For the CPA Exam, the hurdle rate will be provided.**

2. **Considerations for the Required Rate of Return or the Hurdle Rate**

   a. Adjusting for Inflation

      1) In an inflationary environment, future cash inflows consist of inflated dollars. To compensate for this decline in purchasing power, hurdle rates must be adjusted upward.

   b. Adjusting for Risk

      1) Particularly risky projects may be assigned higher hurdle rates to ensure that only those whose potential returns are proportionate to their risks are accepted.

   c. Division-Specific Rates of Return

      1) When the divisions of a large, complex firm have specific risk attributes and capital costs, using a single firm-wide hurdle rate may result in bad decisions.

3. **Time Value of Money**

   a. A quantity of money to be received or paid in the future ordinarily is worth less than the same amount now. The difference is measured in terms of interest calculated using the appropriate discount rate.

      1) Interest is paid by a borrower or investee to a lender or investor for the use of money. It is a percentage of the amount (the principal) borrowed or invested.

   b. Time value of money concepts have many applications. For example, they need to be considered in calculating net present value, internal rate of return, and discounted payback.

4. **Present and Future Value**

    a. Standard tables have been developed to facilitate the calculation of present and future values. Each entry in one of these tables represents the factor by which any monetary amount can be modified to obtain its present or future value.

    b. The **present value (PV) of a single amount** is the value today of some future payment.

        1) It equals the future payment times the present value of 1 (a factor found in a standard table) for the given number of periods and interest rate.

EXAMPLE 11-7 PV -- Single Amount

	Present Value		
No. of Periods	6%	8%	10%
1	0.943	0.926	0.909
2	0.890	0.857	0.826
3	0.840	0.794	0.751
4	0.792	0.735	0.683
5	0.747	0.681	0.621

The present value of $1,000, to be received in 3 years and discounted at 8%, is $794 ($1,000 × 0.794).

---

    c. The **future value (FV) of a single amount** is the amount available at a specified time in the future based on a single investment (deposit) today. The FV is the amount to be computed if one knows the present value and the appropriate discount rate.

        1) It equals the current payment times the future value of 1 (a factor found in a standard table) for the given number of periods and interest rate.

EXAMPLE 11-8 FV -- Single Amount

	Future Value		
No. of Periods	6%	8%	10%
1	1.0600	1.0800	1.1000
2	1.1236	1.1664	1.2100
3	1.1910	1.2597	1.3310
4	1.2625	1.3605	1.4641
5	1.3382	1.4693	1.6105

The future value of $1,000 invested today for 4 years at 10% interest will be $1,464 ($1,000 × 1.464).

SUCCESS TIP

In questions, the CPA Exam will provide candidates with the present value or future value factor. Candidates need to know how to use the factor to calculate the answer.

SU 11: Capital Budgeting

d. **Annuities**
1) An annuity is usually a series of equal payments at equal intervals of time, e.g., $1,000 at the end of every year for 10 years.
    a) An **ordinary annuity (also called an annuity in arrears)** is a series of payments occurring at the end of each period.
        i) The first payment of an ordinary annuity is discounted.
        ii) Interest is not earned for the first period of an ordinary annuity.
    b) An **annuity due (also called an annuity in advance)** is a series of payments at the beginning of each period.
        i) The first payment of an annuity due is not discounted.
        ii) Interest is earned on the first payment of an annuity due.

EXAMPLE 11-9   **Present Value -- Annuities**

	Present Value		
No. of Periods	6%	8%	10%
1	0.943	0.926	0.909
2	1.833	1.783	1.736
3	2.673	2.577	2.487
4	3.465	3.312	3.170
5	4.212	3.993	3.791

Calculating the Present Value of an Ordinary Annuity

Terms of the annuity: 4 years with payments at the end of each year
Amount of each payment: $1,000
Rate: 10%

Step 1: Determine the present value factor using an annuity table.

In the chart above, the number corresponding to 4 periods at a 10% rate is 3.170.

Step 2: Calculate the present value using the present value factor.

$1,000 × 3.170 = $3,170

Calculating the Present Value of an Annuity Due

Terms of the annuity: 4 years with payments at the beginning of each year
Amount of each payment: $1,000
Rate: 10%

Step 1: The first payment occurs on day zero, so the present value of the first payment equals the first payment.

Step 2: Determine the number of annuity periods to discount, which is one less than the entire term of the annuity.

4 periods − 1 period = 3 periods

Step 3: Determine the present value factor using an annuity table.

In the chart above, the number corresponding to 3 periods at a 10% rate is 2.487.

Step 4: Calculate the present value using the present value factor.

$1,000 × 2.487 = $2,487

Step 5: Add the initial payment in Step 1 to the present value determined in Step 4.

$1,000 + $2,487 = $3,487

The present value of the annuity due ($3,487) is greater than the present value of the ordinary annuity ($3,170) because the payments occur 1 year sooner.

c) The FV of an annuity is the value that a series of equal payments will have at a certain moment in the future if interest is earned at a given rate.

EXAMPLE 11-10   **Future Value -- Annuities**

No. of Periods	Future Value 6%	8%	10%
1	1.0000	1.0000	1.0000
2	2.0600	2.0800	2.1000
3	3.1836	3.2464	3.3100
4	4.3746	4.5061	4.6410
5	5.6371	5.8667	6.1051

Calculating the Future Value of an Ordinary Annuity

Terms of the annuity: 3 years with payments at the end of each year
Amount of each payment: $1,000
Rate: 6%

Step 1: Determine the future value factor using an annuity table.

In the chart above, the number corresponding to 3 periods at a 6% rate is 3.1836.

Step 2: Calculate the future value using the future value factor.

$1,000 × 3.1836 = $3,183.60

Calculating the Future Value of an Annuity Due

Terms of the annuity: 3 years with payments at the beginning of each year
Amount of each payment: $1,000
Rate: 6%

Future value of an annuity due = Future value of ordinary annuity × (1 + Rate)

Step 1: Follow the same steps as for an ordinary annuity to determine the future value of the annuity as if it were an ordinary annuity.

Step 2: An annuity due earns 1 more year of interest than an ordinary annuity because payments are made on the first day of the period rather than the last day of the period. Consequently, the future value of an annuity due can be determined by multiplying the future value factor of an ordinary annuity calculated in Step 1 by (1 + .06).

Future value of an annuity due = $3,183.60 × 1.06 = $3,374.62

The future value of the annuity due ($3,375) is greater than the future value of an ordinary annuity ($3,184).

---

5. **NPV**

   a. A capital project's net present value (NPV) is the present value of all benefits minus the present value of all costs.

   b. The following is the equation:

        Net present value = PV of cash inflows − PV of cash outflows

   c. If NPV is

      1) **Positive**, the project should be **accepted**. The project is desirable because it has a higher rate of return than the company's desired rate.

      2) **Negative**, the project should be **rejected**. The project is not desirable because the project's rate of return is lower than the company's desired rate.

EXAMPLE 11-11   NPV with Salvage Value

The following information pertains to a capital project:

Item: A new machine with a useful life of 2 years
Initial investment: $100,000
Salvage value: $15,000
Depreciation method: Straight-line depreciation (required by the IRS)
Cash savings:

    Year 1 $80,000
    Year 2 $60,000

    Required rate of return = 12%
    PV of $1 for one period at 12% = 0.8929
    PV of $1 for two periods at 12% = 0.7972

Tax rate: 40%
IRS depreciation method: 50% Year 1 and 50% Year 2

Step 1: Determine the annual depreciation expense.

    Annual depreciation expense = (Cost − Salvage value) ÷ Years to depreciate
                                = ($100,000 − $15,000) ÷ 2
                                = $42,500

Step 2: Determine the annual depreciation tax shield (also called the tax benefit).

    Depreciation tax shield = Depreciation expense × Tax rate
                           = $42,500 × 40%
                           = $17,000

Step 3: Determine the after-tax inflow from the resale of the machine.

Resale of machine (salvage value)		
Expected proceeds	$15,000	
Tax basis of machine	--	(because fully depreciated)
Gain on expected disposal	$15,000	
Tax expense ($15,000 × 40%)	(6,000)	
Expected cash inflow after taxes	$ 9,000	

Step 4: Determine the after tax cash savings.

    Year 1: $80,000 × (1 − Tax rate) = $80,000 × .6 = $48,000
    Year 2: $60,000 × (1 − Tax rate) = $60,000 × .6 = $36,000

Step 5: Determine the cash flows for each year.

	Year 0	Year 1	Year 2
Initial investment in equipment	$(100,000)		
Net annual savings (cash inflow)		$48,000	$36,000
Depreciation tax shield		17,000	17,000
Inflow from resale (salvage value)			9,000
After-tax net expected cash flows	$(100,000)	$65,000	$62,000

Step 6: Determine the NPV of the cash flows.

	Year 0	Year 1	Year 2	
	$(100,000)	$65,000	$62,000	
Discount rate (rounded PV factor at 12%)	× 1	× 0.8929	× 0.7972	
NPV	$(100,000) +	$58,039 +	$49,426	= $7,465

The positive NPV indicates that the project should be accepted. The project's rate of return is higher than the company's 12% required rate of return.

NOTE: In accordance with the basic formula, cash inflows are positive amounts and the cash outflows are treated as positive amounts subtracted from the sum of the cash inflows.

NPV can easily be calculated without using present value tables. If you encounter an NPV problem in a simulation, you can use the spreadsheet function to calculate NPV. This is actually more accurate because the present value tables are rounded. Note that r represents the required rate of return.

$$NPV = \left[-1 \times \text{Amount of initial investment}\right] + \left[\frac{\text{Cash flow Year 1}}{(1+r)^1} + \frac{\text{Cash flow Year 2}}{(1+r)^2} + \frac{\text{Cash flow Year 3}}{(1+r)^3} + \ldots\right]$$

- Cash outflow (negative value)
- Cash inflow (positive value)

SUCCESS TIP

Using the information from Example 11-11, NPV is calculated as follows:

NPV = ($100,000 × –1) + [$65,000 ÷ (1 + .12)^1] + [$62,000 ÷ (1 + .12)^2]
NPV = –$100,000 + $58,036 + $49,426
NPV = $7,462*

Positive → Accept Investment

*The difference between $7,465 and $7,462 is the rounding difference associated with using PV factors. This second method is always exact.

EXAMPLE 11-12   NPV with No Salvage Value

Lumen Corporation is considering the purchase of a machine for $250,000 that has a useful life of 10 years and no residual (salvage) value. The machine is expected to generate an annual operating cash savings of $60,000 over its useful life. It will be depreciated on the straight-line basis, resulting in annual depreciation expense of $25,000 ($250,000 ÷ 10 years). Lumen's required rate of return is 12%, and its effective tax rate is 40%.

The present value of $1 for 10 periods at 12% is 0.322, and the present value of an ordinary annuity of $1 for 10 periods at 12% is 5.650. Lumen calculates the NPV of this investment as follows:

NOTE: Unlike the previous examples, the information above is presented in a format that a candidate may see on a simulation.

Step 1: Calculate the annual depreciation tax shield.

   Depreciation expense × Tax rate = $25,000 × 40% = $10,000

Step 2: Determine the annual after-tax cash savings.

   Cash savings × (1 – Tax rate) = $60,000 × (1 – 40%) = $60,000 × .6 = $36,000

Step 3: Determine the annual cash flows.

   Annual depreciation tax shield + Annual cash savings = $10,000 + $36,000 = $46,000

Step 4: Determine the present value of annual cash flows, which is a 10-year ordinary annuity.

After-tax net annual savings (cash inflow)	$ 46,000
Times: PV factor for an ordinary annuity	× 5.650
Present value of net savings (cash inflow)	$259,900

Step 5: Determine the PV of the required investment.

The investment occurs at Year 0. The present value of the investment is equal to the value of the investment $(250,000).

Step 6: Combine the PV of cash outflows and cash inflows.

$(250,000) + $259,900 = $9,900

The positive NPV indicates that the project should be accepted.

---

    d. Use of the NPV method implicitly assumes cash flows are reinvested at the firm's **required rate of return**.

6. **Lease vs. Buy Decision**

    a. A discounted cash flows analysis can be useful in making a decision whether to lease or purchase an asset.

    b. A lease is a contractual agreement in which the lessor (owner) conveys to the lessee (borrower) the right to control the use of specific property, plant, or equipment for a stated period in exchange for a stated payment.

    c. The lease is classified for **tax purposes** as either of the following:

        1) An operating lease is essentially a regular rental contract in which the ownership of the leased asset is not transferred to the lessee.

            a) The entire lease payment can be expensed (deducted) for tax purposes.

        2) A finance lease is treated as a purchase of the leased asset by borrowing to finance the transaction. The following can be expensed (deducted) for tax purposes:

            a) Depreciation of the leased asset
            b) Interest expense on finance lease payments

    d. The decision whether to purchase or lease the asset is based on the **discounted cash flows** of the two financing options.

    e. The financing option with the **lower present value of cash outflows** is the less expensive option for obtaining the asset.

    f. The key is to identify the following relevant net cash flows for each financing option:

        1) **Operating lease:**

            After-tax cash outflows = Lease payments × (1 – Tax rate)

        2) **Finance lease and purchase of the asset by borrowing:**

            Lease payments or loan payments
            – Depreciation tax shield (Depreciation expense × Tax rate)
            – Tax savings on interest expense (Interest expense × Tax rate)
            – After-tax cash flows from salvage (scrap) value received from sale of asset

        3) For buying the asset without borrowing, the cash flows include the purchase price of the asset, the depreciation tax shield, and the after-tax salvage value of the asset.

EXAMPLE 11-13 — Lease vs. Buy

An entity can borrow to buy a new machine for $350,000. The following information is relevant:

	Year 1	Year 2	Year 3	Year 4	Year 5
Annual cash revenue	$200,000.00	$180,000.00	$150,000.00	$100,000.00	$50,000.00

The most likely salvage value of the machine is $10,000, and the IRS requires the machine to be depreciated at 50% in Year 1, 20% in Year 2, and 10% in Years 3-5. Equal annual payments (consisting of both interest and principal payments) will be made at the end of each year to repay the loan.

Present value factor of an ordinary annuity for 5 years at 12% = 3.604776

Assuming the entity's tax rate is 25% and its cost to borrow is 12%, should the machine be leased or purchased based on a net present value (NPV) analysis?

Step 1: Determine the annual lease or loan payment.

Equal annual payment = $350,000 ÷ 3.604776 = $97,093.41

Step 2: Determine the depreciation tax shield for the buying/finance lease option.

	Year 1	Year 2	Year 3	Year 4	Year 5
Initial cost	$350,000.00	$350,000.00	$350,000.00	$350,000.00	$350,000.00
Depreciation rate	× 50%	× 20%	× 10%	× 10%	× 10%
Depreciation expense	$175,000.00	$70,000.00	$35,000.00	$35,000.00	$35,000.00
Tax rate	× 25%	× 25%	× 25%	× 25%	× 25%
Depreciation tax shield	$43,750.00	$17,500.00	$8,750.00	$8,750.00	$8,750.00

Step 3: Determine the interest tax savings for the buying/finance lease option.

	Year 1	Year 2	Year 3	Year 4	Year 5
Beginning balance	$350,000.00	$294,906.59	$233,201.97	$164,092.79	$86,690.51
Annual payment	97,093.41	97,093.41	97,093.41	97,093.41	97,093.41
Interest payment	42,000.00	35,388.79	27,984.23	19,691.13	10,402.90
Principal payment	55,093.41	61,704.62	69,109.18	77,402.28	86,690.51
Ending balance	294,906.59	233,201.97	164,092.79	86,690.51	0

	Year 1	Year 2	Year 3	Year 4	Year 5
Interest payment	$42,000.00	$35,388.79	$27,984.23	$19,691.13	$10,402.90
Tax rate	× 25%	× 25%	× 25%	× 25%	× 25%
Tax savings	$10,500.00	$8,847.20	$6,996.06	$4,922.79	$2,600.72

Step 4: Determine the present value of cash outflows for the buying/finance lease option.

	Year 1	Year 2	Year 3	Year 4	Year 5	Total
Annual lease payment	$97,093.41	$97,093.41	$97,093.41	$97,093.41	$97,093.41	
Depreciation tax shield	43,750.00	17,500.00	8,750.00	8,750.00	8,750.00	
Interest tax savings	10,500.00	8,847.20	6,996.06	4,922.79	2,600.72	
After-tax scrap value					7,500	
After-tax cash outflow	$42,843.41	$70,746.21	$81,347.35	$83,420.62	$85,742.69	
Discount factor	× 0.89286	× 0.79719	× 0.71178	× 0.63552	× 0.56743	
Present value	$38,253.17 +	$56,398.17 +	$57,901.42 +	$53,015.48 +	$48,652.97	= $254,221.21

Step 5: Determine the present value of cash outflows for the operating lease option.

	Year 1	Year 2	Year 3	Year 4	Year 5	Total
Lease payment	$97,093.41	$97,093.41	$97,093.41	$97,093.41	$97,093.41	
Tax rate	× (1-25%)	× (1-25%)	× (1-25%)	× (1-25%)	× (1-25%)	
After-tax cash outflow	$72,820.06	$72,820.06	$72,820.06	$72,820.06	$72,820.06	
Discount factor	× 0.89286	× 0.79719	× 0.71178	× 0.63552	× 0.56743	
Present value	$65,018.12 +	$58,051.42 +	$51,831.86 +	$46,278.60 +	$41,320.29	= $262,500.29

Step 6: Compare the PV of cash outflows of the buying/finance lease and the operating lease options. The PV of outflows of buying/a finance lease is $254,221.21. The PV of cash outflows of an operating lease is $262,500.29. Buying or having a finance lease is preferred as it has a lower PV of cash outflows.

STOP & REVIEW

You have completed the outline for this subunit.
Study multiple-choice questions 4 through 9 beginning on page 338.

11.3 CAPITAL BUDGETING -- INTERNAL RATE OF RETURN (IRR)

1. **IRR**

   a. The IRR of a project is the discount rate at which the investment's NPV equals zero. Thus, the IRR equates the present value of the expected cash inflows with the present value of the expected cash outflows.

EXAMPLE 11-14   **How IRR Is Calculated**

Project initial cost: $250,000
After-tax revenues:

Year 1	Year 2	Year 3
$100,000	$100,000	$100,000

NOTE: Candidates will not need to use algebra on the exam to calculate the IRR. The calculation below is simply an aid to understanding of the concept. However, Gleim suggests being familiar with the IRR spreadsheet function because it may calculate the IRR in a simulation.

How the IRR is calculated:

Step 1:

$$NPV = (\$250{,}000) + \frac{\$100{,}000}{(1+r)} + \frac{\$100{,}000}{(1+r)^2} + \frac{\$100{,}000}{(1+r)^3}$$

Step 2:

Let NPV equal $0 and solve for r.

$$\$0 = (\$250{,}000) + \frac{\$100{,}000}{(1+r)} + \frac{\$100{,}000}{(1+r)^2} + \frac{\$100{,}000}{(1+r)^3}$$

$$\$250{,}000 = \frac{\$100{,}000}{(1+r)} + \frac{\$100{,}000}{(1+r)^2} + \frac{\$100{,}000}{(1+r)^3}$$

r = 9.70%

---

   b. If the IRR is higher than the hurdle rate (required rate of return), the investment is accepted. If the IRR is lower, the project should be rejected.

   IRR > Hurdle rate → Accept project

   IRR < Hurdle rate → Reject project

EXAMPLE 11-15   IRR and the Hurdle Rate

NOTE: Candidates could calculate the IRR using a present value table. The payback period is the applicable present value factor.

Cork Company has a hurdle rate of 12% for all capital projects. Cork is considering a project with an initial cash outlay of $200,000 that will save $52,000 of after-tax cash costs in each of the next 5 years.

Step 1: Determine the payback period (applicable present value factor)

$$\text{Payback period} = \frac{\text{Initial investment}}{\text{After-tax annual revenues}} = \frac{\$200{,}000}{\$52{,}000 \text{ per year}} = 3.846 \text{ years}$$

Step 2: Determine the IRR

The time required to repay the initial $200,000 outlay is 3.846 years. The annual savings is for a 5-year annuity. Furthermore, the table for the present value of an ordinary annuity indicates that the present value factor (also the payback period) is less than 3.890 (9% interest rate) and more than 3.791 (10% interest rate). Because the lower the present value factor, the higher the interest rate, the IRR must be greater than 9% and less than 10%.

Step 3: Compare the IRR with the hurdle rate or required rate of return

Because a rate below 10% is less than the hurdle rate, the project should be rejected.

Present Value of Ordinary Annuity Table

	1%	2%	3%	4%	5%	6%	7%	8%	9%	10%	12%
1	0.990	0.980	0.971	0.962	0.952	0.943	0.935	0.926	0.917	0.909	0.893
2	1.970	1.942	1.913	1.886	1.859	1.833	1.808	1.783	1.759	1.736	1.690
3	2.941	2.884	2.829	2.775	2.723	2.673	2.624	2.577	2.531	2.487	2.402
4	3.902	3.808	3.717	3.630	3.546	3.465	3.387	3.312	3.240	3.170	3.037
5	4.853	4.713	4.580	4.452	4.329	4.212	4.100	3.993	**3.890**	**3.791**	3.605

STOP & REVIEW

You have completed the outline for this subunit.
Study multiple-choice questions 10 through 12 beginning on page 341.

SU 11: Capital Budgeting

11.4 CAPITAL BUDGETING -- PAYBACK METHODS

1. **Payback Period**

   a. The payback period is the number of years required for the net cash savings or inflows to equal the original investment, i.e., the time necessary for an investment to pay for itself. It is the breakeven point expressed as time.

      1) Firms using the payback method set a maximum length of time within which projects must pay for themselves to be acceptable.

   b. If the cash flows are constant, the formula is

   $$\text{Payback period} = \frac{\text{Initial investment}}{\text{Annual after-tax savings (cash inflow)}}$$

      1) This method ignores the time value of money.

EXAMPLE 11-16   Constant Cash Flows

The following information is pertinent to the determination of the payback period for Company's capital projects:

Company requirement: 4-year payback period test
Potential initial cash outlay: $200,000
Total after-tax costs saved: $260,000 over 5 years equally

Step 1: Determine the annual after-tax cash flow.

$260,000 ÷ 5 years = $52,000 annual after-tax cash flow

Step 2: Calculate the payback period using the formula.

Initial investment ÷ Annual after-tax savings = $200,000 ÷ $52,000 = 3.846 years

Step 3: Compare the calculated payback period with the requirement.

3.846 years is less than the 4-year requirement. The company therefore should invest in the project.

---

   c. If the cash flows are not constant, the calculation must be in cumulative form.

EXAMPLE 11-17   Variable Cash Flows

Use the information from Example 11-16, except Company's initial investment is $160,000 and the project's cash flows are expected to vary as shown below. The payback period is calculated as follows:

End of Year	Cash Savings	Initial Investment to Be Recovered
Initial investment	$ --	$160,000
Year 1	48,000	112,000
Year 2	54,000	58,000
Year 3	54,000	4,000
Year 4	60,000	--

The project is acceptable because its payback period is between 3 and 4 years and is less than Company's maximum.

d. The advantage of the payback method is its simplicity.

1) The payback period measures the risk and liquidity of an investment. The longer the period, the riskier and less liquid the investment.

e. The payback method has the following significant disadvantages:

1) Weighting all cash flows equally disregards the time value of money.
2) All cash inflows after the payback cutoff date are disregarded. Applying a single cutoff date to every project results in potentially accepting marginal projects and rejecting good ones.
3) Overall profitability is ignored.
4) It assumes cash flows occur evenly throughout the year.

2. **Discounted Payback**

a. The discounted payback method is sometimes used to overcome the major disadvantage of the basic payback method. The only difference between the two methods is that the discounted payback method considers the time value of money.

1) The net cash flows in the denominator are discounted to calculate the period required to recover the initial investment.

EXAMPLE 11-18   Discounted Payback

Company has a 12% cost of capital.

Period	Cash Savings		12% PV Factor		Discounted Cash Savings	Initial Investment to Be Recovered
Initial investment	$ --		--		$ --	$160,000
Year 1	48,000	×	0.89286	=	42,857	117,143
Year 2	54,000	×	0.79719	=	43,048	74,095
Year 3	54,000	×	0.71178	=	38,436	35,659
Year 4	60,000	×	0.63552	=	38,131	--

The project is acceptable because its discounted payback period is between 3 and 4 years and is less than Company's maximum.

The discounted payback period in years is calculated as follows:

1) Full payback occurs sometime in Year 4. The remaining investment at the beginning of Year 4 is $35,659.

2) The following is the percentage of Year 4 at which the amount of $35,659 is recovered:

$$\frac{\text{Amount of initial investment to be recovered in final year}}{\text{Discounted cash savings in final year}} = \frac{\$35,659}{\$38,131} = 0.935$$

3) The discounted payback period in years is **3.935 years** (3 + 0.935), or 3 years, 11 months, and 7 days.

SU 11: Capital Budgeting

b. The **breakeven time** is the time required for the discounted cash flows of an investment to equal its initial cost.
c. The discounted payback method's advantage is that it reflects the time value of money.
   1) Its disadvantages are
      a) Its greater complexity and
      b) Not considering cash flows after the arbitrary cutoff date.

> You have completed the outline for this subunit.
> Study multiple-choice questions 13 through 15 beginning on page 342.

11.5 RANKING CAPITAL PROJECTS

1. **Profitability Index**
   a. When sufficient resources are available, every project with a positive NPV should be accepted.
      1) However, few firms have the resources to accept every capital project with a return exceeding the hurdle rate.
      2) Under **capital rationing**, management determines which investments provide not necessarily the highest total return but the highest per dollar invested.
   b. The **profitability index** (or excess present value index) is a method for ranking projects to ensure that limited resources are allocated to the investments with the highest return per dollar invested.

$$\text{Profitability index} = \frac{\text{PV of future net cash flows or NPV of project}}{\text{Initial investment}}$$

EXAMPLE 11-19   Profitability Index

Dexter Company has $200,000 to invest and has a 6% hurdle rate. Dexter can invest either in (1) Project F or (2) Projects G and H:

	Project F	OR	Project G	AND	Project H
Initial investment	$(200,000)		$(150,000)		$(50,000)
Year 1	145,000		50,000		40,000
Year 2	145,000		50,000		30,000
Year 3			50,000		10,000
Year 4			77,452		

Step 1: Calculate each project's NPV

	Project F			OR	Project G			AND	Project H		
Initial Investment	Undiscounted Cash Flows	PV Factor	Discounted Cash Flows		Undiscounted Cash Flows	PV Factor	Discounted Cash Flows		Undiscounted Cash Flows	PV Factor	Discounted Cash Flows
(Year 0)	$(200,000)		$(200,000)		$(150,000)		$(150,000)		$(50,000)		$(50,000)
Year 1	145,000	0.9434	136,793		50,000	0.9434	47,170		40,000	0.9434	37,736
Year 2	145,000	0.8900	129,050		50,000	0.8900	44,500		30,000	0.8900	26,700
Year 3					50,000	0.8396	41,980		10,000	0.8396	8,396
Year 4					77,452	0.7921	61,350				
NPV			$ 65,843				$ 45,000				$ 22,832

Step 2: Calculate the profitability index for each project

Investing in Projects G and H is the alternative to investing in Project F. Thus, their NPVs and initial investments are combined in the Project G + H column below.

		Project F	Project G	Project H	Project G + H
Profitability index =	NPV	$65,843	$45,000	$22,832	$67,832
	Initial investment	$200,000	$150,000	$50,000	$200,000
	Profitability index =	0.3292	0.3000	0.4566	0.3392

Dexter should invest in Projects G and H. Their combined probability index of 0.3392 is higher than Project F's (0.3292).

NOTE: A profitability index calculation based on the present value of future cash inflows has the same outcomes as the NPV calculation.

	Project F	Project G	Project H	Project G + H
Year 1	$136,793	$ 47,170	$37,736	$ 84,906
Year 2	129,050	44,500	26,700	71,200
Year 3	-	41,980	8,396	50,376
Year 4	-	61,350	-	61,350
Total PV of future cash inflows	$265,843	$195,000	$72,832	$267,832

		Project F	Project G	Project H	Project G + H
Profitability index =	PV of future cash inflows	$265,843	$195,000	$72,832	$267,832
	Initial investment	$200,000	$150,000	$50,000	$200,000
	Profitability index =	1.3292	1.3000	1.4566	1.3392

SU 11: Capital Budgeting

    c.   When the initial investment is the same, one can simply choose the independent project with the higher NPV because it will always be the project with the higher profitability index.

STOP & REVIEW

You have completed the outline for this subunit.
Study multiple-choice questions 16 through 18 on page 344.

11.6 COMPARISON OF CAPITAL BUDGETING METHODS

1. Some CPA Exam questions involve selecting the best capital budgeting method for a given set of facts rather than the mechanics of the calculation.
2. NPV is the value today of all future cash flows.
3. IRR is the rate at which the NPV of all cash flows from an investment equals zero. It is the hurdle rate that equals the breakeven point.
4. **Comparing Cash Flow Patterns**

       a.   A decision maker may need to choose between two mutually exclusive projects, one with high initial cash flows and one with relatively constant cash flows.

             1)   The higher the hurdle rate, the more quickly a project must be profitable.
             2)   Firms with low hurdle rates prefer a steady payback.

EXAMPLE 11-20 — Two Project Comparisons

The following are the net cash flows of two projects with the same initial investment:

	Initial Investment	Year 1	Year 2	Year 3	Year 4
Project K	$(200,000)	$140,000	$100,000	–	–
Project L	(200,000)	65,000	65,000	$65,000	$65,000

A graph of the two projects at various discount rates illustrates the factors a decision maker must consider.

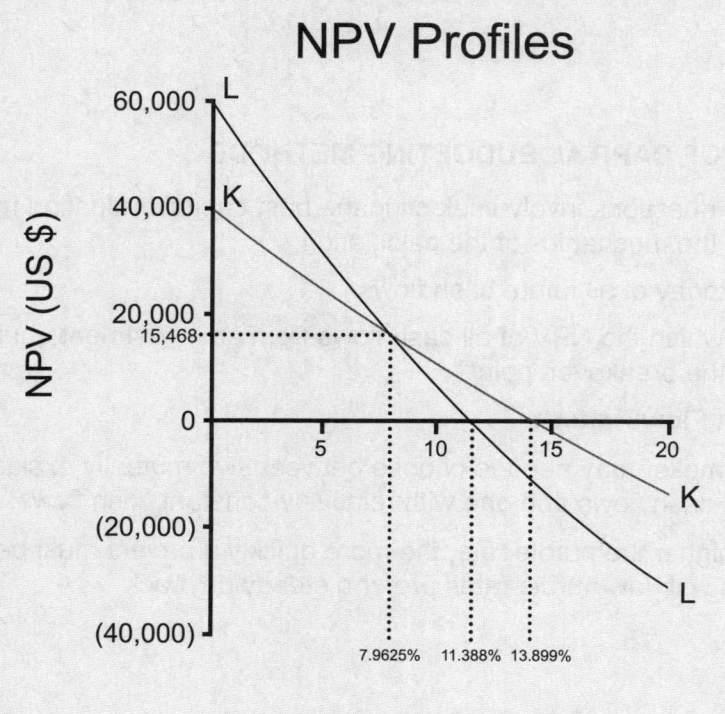

NPV Profiles

(Graph showing NPV profiles for Projects K and L. X-axis: Discount Rate (%), ranging from 0 to 20. Y-axis: NPV (US $), ranging from (40,000) to 60,000. The two lines cross at a discount rate of 7.9625% with NPV of $15,468. Project L's IRR is 11.388%. Project K's IRR is 13.899%.)

Figure 11-2

Project K's IRR is 13.899%. Project L's is 11.388%.

The NPV profile helps a manager determine how sensitive a project's profitability is to changes in the discount rate.

- At a hurdle rate of **exactly** 7.9625%, a decision maker is **indifferent** toward the two projects. The NPV of both K and L is $15,468 at that discount rate.
- At hurdle rates **below** 7.9625%, the project whose **inflows last longer** into the future is the better investment (L).
- At hurdle rates **above** 7.9625%, the project whose **inflows are received more quickly** is the better choice (K).

5. **Comparing NPV and IRR**

   a. The NPV and IRR methods will indicate the same capital budgeting decision (accept or reject) if projects have unrelated cash flows (are independent). Accordingly, all acceptable, independent projects can be chosen.

      1) However, if projects are **mutually exclusive** (i.e., only one project can be accepted for investment), the NPV and IRR methods may rank them differently if

         a) The cost of one project is greater than the cost of another.
         b) The timing, amounts, and directions of cash flows differ among projects.
         c) The projects have different useful lives.
         d) The cost of capital or desired rate of return varies over the life of a project. The NPV can be determined easily using different desired rates of return for different periods. The IRR determines one rate for the project.
         e) Multiple investments are involved in a project. NPV amounts are cumulative; IRR rates are not. The IRR for the whole is not the sum of the IRRs for the parts.

   b. The reinvestment rate is important in choosing between the NPV and IRR methods.

      1) NPV assumes the cash flows from the investment can be reinvested at the project's **required rate of return**.

         a) The NPV method provides a better understanding of the problem in many decision situations because reinvestment is assumed to be at the required rate of return.

      2) The IRR method assumes reinvestment is at the **IRR**. Consequently, the IRR is an accurate representation of a project's annual return only when (a) the reinvestment is at the actual IRR or (b) the project generates no interim cash flows.

         a) Interim cash flows are the cash flows of each year except the first and last years. Thus, if some years have no cash flows, the IRR is less accurate (dependable) than the NPV method.

      3) If the project's funds are not reinvested at the IRR, the ranking calculations obtained may be in error.

         a) When a project has an IRR that is close to the reinvestment rate (e.g., required rate of return), the annual return is less distorted by the IRR calculation. If the IRR is 10% or more above the reinvestment rate, annual return may be significantly distorted.

EXAMPLE 11-21   Comparing NPV and IRR

	Initial Investment	Year 1	NPV	IRR
Project A	$(10,000)	$25,000	$12,174.21	150%
Project B	$(25,000)	$50,000	$19,718.79	100%
Hurdle rate	8.00%			

- If the projects are independent, both projects could be good investments because both IRRs exceed the hurdle rate and the NPVs are positive.
- If the projects are mutually exclusive, the IRR method prefers Project A, but the NPV method prefers Project B.
- The question for the firm is whether to risk $10,000 to earn $15,000 or to risk $25,000 to earn $25,000.
  - No correct answer is possible. The decision depends on the entity's risk tolerance and therefore whether to use the NPV or IRR model.

Capital Budgeting Assessment Tools

	Accounting Rate of Return	Payback Method	Discounted Payback Method	NPV	IRR
Reflects time value of money?	No	No	Yes	Yes	Yes
Considers breakeven point?	No	Yes	Yes	No	Yes
Considers all cash flows (including beyond breakeven point)?	No	No	No	Yes	Yes

Quick Reference Guide
Advantages and Disadvantages of Capital Budgeting Assessment Tools

	Accounting Rate of Return	Payback Method	Discounted Payback Method	Net Present Value	Internal Rate of Return
ADVANTAGES	1. Based on GAAP 2. Easily understood 3. Simple to calculate	1. Simplicity 2. Measures more risk than accounting rate of return because the longer the period to achieve a payback, the riskier the investment 3. Focuses on assessing liquidity of a project	1. Considers the time value of money 2. Focuses on assessing risk and liquidity of a project	1. Considers the time value of money with all cash flows, including cash flows after the payback period 2. Indicates the quality of an investment by quantifying its risk in the form of a dollar value	1. Considers the time value of money with all cash flows, including cash flows after the payback period 2. Indicates the efficiency or quality of an investment by quantifying its risk in the form of an interest rate
DISADVANTAGES	1. Manipulated by accounting choices such as capitalization and depreciation 2. Does not consider the time value of money 3. Distorts investments made at multiple installments 4. Fails to consider increased risk of long-term projects	1. Weighting all cash flows equally disregards the time value of money 2. All cash flows after the payback date are disregarded 3. Ignores long-term profitability	1. Greater complexity than the payback method 2. All cash flows after the payback date are disregarded 3. Ignores overall profitability	1. Assumes the cash flows are reinvested at the firm's required rate of return, which is not always true 2. Creates difficulty when comparing two projects of different sizes because only dollar amounts are used	1. Assumes the cash flows are reinvested at the IRR, which is not necessarily true 2. Generates multiple IRRs when the cash flow changes between positive and negative more than once

SUCCESS TIP: For both the NPV and IRR, expect to see questions asking for calculations as well as an understanding of the underlying theories.

STOP & REVIEW: You have completed the outline for this subunit. Study multiple-choice questions 19 through 21 on page 345.

SU 11: Capital Budgeting

QUESTIONS

11.1 Capital Budgeting -- Basics

1. Of the following decisions, capital budgeting techniques would **least** likely be used in evaluating the

   A. Acquisition of new aircraft by a cargo company.
   B. Design and implementation of a major advertising program.
   C. Trade for a star quarterback by a football team.
   D. Adoption of a new method of allocating nontraceable costs to product lines.

Answer (D) is correct.
   REQUIRED: The decision least likely to be evaluated using capital budgeting.
   DISCUSSION: Capital budgeting is the process of planning expenditures for investments on which the returns are expected to occur over a period of more than 1 year. Thus, capital budgeting applies to the acquisition or disposal of long-term assets and the financing ramifications of such decisions. The adoption of a new method of allocating nontraceable costs to product lines has no effect on a firm's cash flows, the acquisition of long-term assets, and financing. Thus, capital budgeting is irrelevant to such a decision.
   Answer (A) is incorrect. A new aircraft is a long-term investment in a capital good. Answer (B) is incorrect. A major advertising program is a high cost investment with long-term effects. Answer (C) is incorrect. A star quarterback is a costly asset who is expected to have a substantial effect on the team's long-term profitability.

2. Which of the following is irrelevant in projecting the cash flows of the final year of a capital project?

   A. Cash devoted to use in project.
   B. Disposal value of equipment purchased specifically for project.
   C. Depreciation tax shield generated by equipment purchased specifically for project.
   D. Historical cost of equipment disposed of in the project's first year.

Answer (D) is correct.
   REQUIRED: The irrelevant information in projecting the cash flows for the final year of a capital project.
   DISCUSSION: After disposal of an old piece of equipment, its historical cost no longer affects a firm's cash flows.
   Answer (A) is incorrect. The recovery of working capital devoted to a capital project is a relevant cash flow in the final year. Answer (B) is incorrect. The disposal value of equipment acquired for the project is relevant in the final year. Answer (C) is incorrect. The depreciation tax shield generated by equipment acquired for the project is relevant to the final year.

3. Which one of the following items is **least** likely to directly impact an equipment replacement capital expenditure decision?

   A. The net present value of the equipment that is being replaced.
   B. The depreciation rate that will be used for tax purposes on the new asset.
   C. The amount of additional accounts receivable that will be generated from increased production and sales.
   D. The sales value of the asset that is being replaced.

Answer (A) is correct.
   REQUIRED: The item least likely to directly affect an equipment replacement capital expenditure decision.
   DISCUSSION: The only relevant valuation of existing equipment is its salvage value at the time of the decision.
   Answer (B) is incorrect. The depreciation rate for tax purposes on the new asset will determine the depreciation tax shield. Answer (C) is incorrect. The additional working capital associated with the new equipment is relevant to the decision. Answer (D) is incorrect. The salvage value of the existing equipment is relevant to the decision.

11.2 Capital Budgeting -- Net Present Value (NPV)

4. For capital budgeting purposes, management would select a high hurdle rate of return for certain projects because management

A. Wants to use equity funding exclusively.
B. Believes too many proposals are being rejected.
C. Believes bank loans are riskier than capital investments.
D. Wants to factor risk into its consideration of projects.

Answer (D) is correct.
REQUIRED: The reason for selecting a high hurdle rate for certain projects.
DISCUSSION: Risk analysis measures the likelihood of the variability of future returns from the proposed investment. Risk can be incorporated into capital budgeting decisions in various ways, one of which is to use a hurdle rate (desired rate of return) higher than the firm's cost of capital, that is, a risk-adjusted discount rate. This method adjusts the interest rate used for discounting upward as an investment becomes riskier. The expected flow from the investment must be relatively larger, or the increased discount rate will generate a negative NPV, and the proposed acquisition will be rejected.
Answer (A) is incorrect. The nature of the funding may not be a sufficient reason to use a risk-adjusted rate. The type of funding is just one factor affecting the risk of a project. Answer (B) is incorrect. A higher hurdle will result in rejection of more projects. Answer (C) is incorrect. A risk-adjusted high hurdle rate is used for capital investments with greater risk.

5. Assume that the interest rate is greater than zero. Which of the following cash-inflow streams should you prefer?

	Year 1	Year 2	Year 3	Year 4
A.	$400	$300	$200	$100
B.	$100	$200	$300	$400
C.	$250	$250	$250	$250

D. Any of these, since they each sum to $1,000.

Answer (A) is correct.
REQUIRED: The cash flows that are most advantageous.
DISCUSSION: The concept of present value gives greater value to inflows received earlier than later. Thus, the declining inflows are superior to increasing inflows or even inflows.
Answer (B) is incorrect. The cash flow shown does not produce the greatest present value. Answer (C) is incorrect. The cash flow shown does not produce the greatest present value. Answer (D) is incorrect. Present value of the cash flows must be considered.

6. Bell Co. is purchasing new equipment. The new equipment is expected to increase Bell's sales by $60,000 and costs by $10,000 annually. The expected depreciation expense of the new equipment is $10,000 annually. Bell's marginal tax rate is 40%. What is the annual depreciation tax shield for the purchase of equipment?

A. $6,000
B. $10,000
C. $3,000
D. $4,000

Answer (D) is correct.
REQUIRED: The annual depreciation tax shield.
DISCUSSION: The annual tax benefit (shield) equals depreciation expense times the applicable tax rate. The annual tax benefit therefore, is $4,000 ($10,000 depreciation expense × 40% marginal tax rate).
Answer (A) is incorrect. A $6,000 tax benefit results from multiplying depreciation expense by 1 minus the tax rate [($10,000 × (1 − .40)]. Answer (B) is incorrect. The amount of $10,000 does not consider the 40% marginal tax rate. Answer (C) is incorrect. The amount of $3,000 is based on a marginal tax rate of 30%.

SU 11: Capital Budgeting

Question 7 is based on the following information. Jorelle Company's financial staff has been requested to review a proposed investment in new capital equipment. Applicable financial data is presented below. There will be no salvage value at the end of the investment's life and, due to realistic depreciation practices, it is estimated that the salvage value and net book value are equal at the end of each year. All cash flows are assumed to take place at the end of each year. For investment proposals, Jorelle uses a 12% after-tax target rate of return.

Investment Proposal

Year	Purchase Cost and Book Value	Annual Net After-Tax Cash Flows	Annual Net Income
0	$250,000	$ 0	$ 0
1	168,000	120,000	35,000
2	100,000	108,000	39,000
3	50,000	96,000	43,000
4	18,000	84,000	47,000
5	0	72,000	51,000

Discounted Factors for a 12% Rate of Return

Year	Present Value of $1.00 Received at the End of Each Period	Present Value of an Annuity of $1.00 Received at the End of Each Period
1	.89	.89
2	.80	1.69
3	.71	2.40
4	.64	3.04
5	.57	3.61
6	.51	4.12

7. The net present value for the investment proposal is

A. $106,160
B. $(97,970)
C. $356,160
D. $96,560

Answer (A) is correct.
REQUIRED: The NPV.
DISCUSSION: The NPV is the sum of the present values of all cash inflows and outflows associated with the proposal. If the NPV is positive, the proposal should be accepted. The NPV is determined by discounting each expected cash flow using the appropriate 12% interest factor for the present value of $1. Thus, the NPV is $106,160 [(.89 × $120,000) + (.80 × $108,000) + (.71 × $96,000) + (.64 × $84,000) + (.57 × $72,000) − (1.00 × $250,000)].

Answer (B) is incorrect. The amount of $(97,970) is based on net income instead of cash flows. **Answer (C) is incorrect.** The amount of $356,160 excludes the purchase cost. **Answer (D) is incorrect.** The amount of $96,560 equals average after-tax cash inflow times the interest factor for the present value of a 5-year annuity, minus $250,000.

8. The Hopkins Company has estimated that a proposed project's 10-year annual net cash benefit, received each year end, will be $2,500 with an additional terminal benefit of $5,000 at the end of the 10th year.

Information on present value factors is as follows:

Present value of $1 at 8% at the end
of 10 periods .463
Present value of an ordinary annuity
of $1 at 8% for 10 periods 6.710

Assuming that these cash inflows satisfy exactly Hopkins' required rate of return of 8%, what is the initial cash outlay?

A. $16,775
B. $19,090
C. $25,000
D. $30,000

Answer (B) is correct.
REQUIRED: The initial cash outlay.
DISCUSSION: If the 8% return exactly equals the present value of the future flows (the NPV is zero), the present value of the future inflows equals the initial cash outlay. Thus, the initial cash outlay is $19,090 [($2,500)(present value of an ordinary annuity at 8% for 10 periods) + ($5,000)(present value of a single amount at 8% for 10 periods) = ($2,500)(6.710) + ($5,000)(.463)].
Answer (A) is incorrect. The amount of $16,775 failed to include the present value of the $5,000 terminal benefit. **Answer (C) is incorrect.** The amount of $25,000 is not a result of using present value analysis. **Answer (D) is incorrect.** The amount of $30,000 is not a result of using present value analysis.

9. Jackson Corporation uses net present value techniques in evaluating its capital investment projects. The company is considering a new equipment acquisition that will cost $100,000, fully installed, and have a zero salvage value at the end of its 5-year productive life. Jackson will depreciate the equipment on a straight-line basis for both financial and tax purposes. Jackson estimates $70,000 in annual recurring operating cash income and $20,000 in annual recurring operating cash expenses. Jackson's desired rate of return is 12% and its effective income tax rate is 40%.

The present value factors for 12% are as follows:

Present value of $1 at the end of
five periods .567
Present value of an ordinary annuity of
$1 for five periods 3.605

What is the net present value of this investment on an after-tax basis?

A. $28,840
B. $8,150
C. $36,990
D. $80,250

Answer (C) is correct.
REQUIRED: The NPV on an after-tax basis.
DISCUSSION: Annual cash outflow for taxes is $12,000 {[$70,000 inflows – $20,000 cash operating expenses – ($100,000 ÷ 5) depreciation] × 40%}. The annual net cash inflow is therefore $38,000 ($70,000 – $20,000 – $12,000). The present value of these net inflows for a 5-year period is $136,990 ($38,000 × 3.605 present value of an ordinary annuity for 5 years at 12%), and the NPV of the investment is $36,990 ($136,990 – $100,000 investment).
Answer (A) is incorrect. The amount of $28,840 is the present value of the depreciation tax savings. **Answer (B) is incorrect.** The amount of $8,150 ignores the depreciation tax savings. **Answer (D) is incorrect.** The amount of $80,250 ignores taxes.

11.3 Capital Budgeting -- Internal Rate of Return (IRR)

10. What is the approximate IRR for a project that costs $50,000 and provides cash inflows of $20,000 for 3 years?

Rate of Return	Present Value of an Annuity of $1 Received at the End of 3 Years
6%	2.673
8%	2.577
10%	2.487
12%	2.402

A. 10%
B. 12%
C. 22%
D. 27%

Answer (A) is correct.
REQUIRED: The approximate IRR.
DISCUSSION: To determine the IRR:

Step 1: Determine the payback period

$$\text{Payback period} = \frac{\text{Initial investment}}{\text{After-tax annual revenues}} = \frac{\$50,000}{\$20,000} = 2.5 \text{ years}$$

Step 2: Determine the IRR

Comparing the payback period with the PV factors given, a payback period of 2.5 years is closest to the PV factor of 2.487. The corresponding IRR is 10%.
Answer (B) is incorrect. Discounting the cash inflows at 12% would not produce a NPV of zero.
Answer (C) is incorrect. Discounting the cash inflows at 22% would not produce a NPV of zero. **Answer (D) is incorrect.** Discounting the cash inflows at 27% would not produce a NPV of zero.

11. Brown and Company uses the internal rate of return (IRR) method to evaluate capital projects. Brown is considering four independent projects with the following IRRs:

Project	IRR
I	10%
II	12%
III	14%
IV	15%

Brown's cost of capital is 13%. Which one of the following project options should Brown accept based on IRR?

A. Projects I and II only.
B. Projects III and IV only.
C. Project IV only.
D. Projects I, II, III and IV.

Answer (B) is correct.
REQUIRED: The acceptable projects given a certain cost of capital.
DISCUSSION: When sufficient funds are available, any capital project whose IRR exceeds the firm's cost of capital should be accepted.
Answer (A) is incorrect. Projects I and II have rates of return lower than the company's cost of capital. **Answer (C) is incorrect.** The rate of return for Project III also exceeds the company's cost of capital. **Answer (D) is incorrect.** Projects I and II should be rejected; their rates of return are lower than the company's cost of capital.

12. Pena Company is considering a project that calls for an initial cash outlay of $50,000. The expected net cash inflows from the project are $7,791 for each of 10 years.

Rate of Return	Present Value of an Annuity of $1 Received at the End of 10 Years
6%	7.360
8%	6.710
9%	6.418
10%	6.145
12%	5.650

What is the IRR of the project?

A. 6%

B. 7%

C. 8%

D. 9%

Answer (D) is correct.
REQUIRED: The IRR.
DISCUSSION: To determine the IRR:

Step 1: Determine the payback period

$$\text{Payback period} = \frac{\text{Initial investment}}{\text{After-tax annual revenues}} = \frac{\$50,000}{\$7,791} = 6.418 \text{ years}$$

Step 2: Determine the IRR

Comparing the payback period with the PV factors given, a payback period of 6.418 years corresponds with an IRR of 9%.
Answer (A) is incorrect. Discounting the cash inflows at 6% would not produce a NPV of zero.
Answer (B) is incorrect. Discounting the cash inflows at 7% would not produce a NPV of zero. **Answer (C) is incorrect.** Discounting the cash inflows at 8% would not produce a NPV of zero.

11.4 Capital Budgeting -- Payback Methods

13. A characteristic of the payback method (before taxes) is that it

A. Incorporates the time value of money.

B. Neglects total project profitability.

C. Uses accrual accounting inflows in the numerator of the calculation.

D. Uses the estimated expected life of the asset in the denominator of the calculation.

Answer (B) is correct.
REQUIRED: The characteristic of the payback method.
DISCUSSION: The payback method calculates the number of years required to complete the return of the original investment. This measure is determined by dividing the net investment required by the average expected cash flow to be generated, resulting in the number of years required to recover the original investment. Payback is easy to calculate but has two principal problems: (1) It ignores the time value of money, and (2) it does not consider returns after the payback period. Thus, it ignores total project profitability.
Answer (A) is incorrect. The payback method does not incorporate the time value of money. **Answer (C) is incorrect.** The payback method uses the net investment in the numerator of the calculation. **Answer (D) is incorrect.** Payback uses the net annual cash inflows in the denominator of the calculation.

14. Jasper Company has a payback goal of 3 years on new equipment acquisitions. A new sorter is being evaluated that costs $450,000 and has a 5-year life. Straight-line depreciation will be used; no salvage is anticipated. Jasper is subject to a 40% income tax rate. To meet the company's payback goal, the sorter must generate reductions in annual cash operating costs of

A. $60,000
B. $100,000
C. $150,000
D. $190,000

Answer (D) is correct.
REQUIRED: The cash savings that must be generated to achieve a targeted payback period.
DISCUSSION: Given a periodic constant cash flow, the payback period is calculated by dividing cost by the annual after-tax cash inflows, or cash savings. To achieve a payback period of 3 years, the annual increment in net cash inflow generated by the investment must be $150,000 ($450,000 ÷ 3-year targeted payback period). This amount equals the total reduction in cash operating costs minus related taxes. Depreciation is $90,000 ($450,000 ÷ 5 years). Because depreciation is a noncash deductible expense, it shields $90,000 of the cash savings from taxation. Accordingly, $60,000 ($150,000 – $90,000) of the additional net cash inflow must come from after-tax net income. At a 40% tax rate, $60,000 of after-tax income equals $100,000 ($60,000 ÷ 60%) of pre-tax income from cost savings, and the outflow for taxes is $40,000. Thus, the annual reduction in cash operating costs required is $190,000 ($150,000 additional net cash inflow required + $40,000 tax outflow).
Answer (A) is incorrect. The amount of $60,000 is after-tax net income from the cost savings. **Answer (B) is incorrect.** The amount of $100,000 is the pre-tax income from the cost savings. **Answer (C) is incorrect.** The amount of $150,000 ignores the impact of depreciation and income taxes.

15. Whatney Co. is considering the acquisition of a new, more efficient press. The cost of the press is $360,000, and the press has an estimated 6-year life with zero salvage value. Whatney uses straight-line depreciation for both financial reporting and income tax reporting purposes and has a 40% corporate income tax rate. In evaluating equipment acquisitions of this type, Whatney uses a goal of a 4-year payback period. To meet Whatney's desired payback period, the press must produce a minimum annual before-tax operating cash savings of

A. $90,000
B. $110,000
C. $114,000
D. $150,000

Answer (B) is correct.
REQUIRED: The minimum annual before-tax operating cash savings yielding a specified payback period.
DISCUSSION: Payback is the number of years required to complete the return of the original investment. Given a periodic constant cash flow, the payback period equals net investment divided by the constant expected periodic after-tax cash flow. The desired payback period is 4 years, so the constant after-tax annual cash flow must be $90,000 ($360,000 ÷ 4). Assuming that the company has sufficient other income to permit realization of the full tax savings, depreciation of the machine will shield $60,000 ($360,000 ÷ 6) of income from taxation each year, an after-tax cash savings of $24,000 ($60,000 × 40%). Thus, the machine must generate an additional $66,000 ($90,000 – $24,000) of after-tax cash savings from operations. This amount is equivalent to $110,000 [$66,000 ÷ (1.0 – .4)] of before-tax operating cash savings.
Answer (A) is incorrect. The amount of $90,000 is the total desired annual after-tax cash savings. **Answer (C) is incorrect.** The amount of $114,000 results from adding, not subtracting, the $24,000 of tax depreciation savings to determine the minimum annual after-tax operating savings. **Answer (D) is incorrect.** The amount of $150,000 assumes that depreciation is not tax deductible.

11.5 Ranking Capital Projects

16. Wood, Inc., is considering four independent investment proposals. Wood has $3 million available for investment during the present period. The investment outlay for each project and its projected net present value (NPV) is presented below.

Project	Investment Cost	NPV
I	$ 500,000	$ 40,000
II	900,000	120,000
III	1,200,000	180,000
IV	1,600,000	150,000

Which of the following project options should be recommended to Wood's management?

A. Projects I, II, and III only.

B. Projects I, II, and IV only.

C. Projects II, III, and IV only.

D. Projects III and IV only.

Answer (A) is correct.
REQUIRED: The acceptable capital projects given NPV.
DISCUSSION: When available funds are limited, potential projects should be ranked by profitability index. The indexes for the potential projects can be calculated as follows:

Project	NPV		Investment Cost		Profitability Index
I	$ 40,000	÷	$ 500,000	=	0.080
II	120,000	÷	900,000	=	0.133
III	180,000	÷	1,200,000	=	0.150
IV	150,000	÷	1,600,000	=	0.094

Ranked in order of desirability, they are III, II, IV, and I. Because only $3 million is available for funding, only III, II, and I will be selected.
Answer (B) is incorrect. Project III is more desirable than Project IV. Answer (C) is incorrect. Project IV is more desirable than Project I, but funding is not sufficient. Answer (D) is incorrect. Projects I and II also are desirable, and sufficient funding is available.

17. The profitability index approach to investment analysis

A. Fails to consider the timing of project cash flows.

B. Considers only the project's contribution to net income and does not consider cash flow effects.

C. Always yields the same accept/reject decisions for independent projects as the net present value method.

D. Always yields the same accept/reject decisions for mutually exclusive projects as the net present value method.

Answer (C) is correct.
REQUIRED: The true statement about the profitability index.
DISCUSSION: The profitability index is the ratio of a discounted cash flow amount to the initial investment. It is a variation of the net present value (NPV) method and facilitates the comparison of different-sized investments. Because it is based on the NPV method, the profitability index yields the same decision as the NPV for independent projects. However, decisions may differ for mutually exclusive projects of different sizes.
Answer (A) is incorrect. The profitability index, like the NPV method, discounts cash flows based on the cost of capital. Answer (B) is incorrect. The profitability index is cash-based. Answer (D) is incorrect. The NPV and the profitability index may yield different decisions if projects are mutually exclusive and of different sizes.

18. Mesa Company is considering an investment to open a new banana processing division. The project involves an initial investment of $45,000, and cash inflows of $20,000 can be expected in each of the next 3 years. The hurdle rate is 10%. The present value of an ordinary annuity of 1 discounted at 10% for 3 periods is 2.487. The present value of 1 due in 3 periods discounted at 10% is .751. What is the profitability index for the project?

A. 1.0784

B. 1.1053

C. 1.1379

D. 1.1771

Answer (B) is correct.
REQUIRED: The profitability index.
DISCUSSION: At a 10% hurdle rate, the present value of the future cash inflows is $49,740 (20,000 × 2.487). The NPV for the project is $4,740 ($49,740 – $45,000). The profitability index is therefore 1.1053 ($49,740 ÷ $45,000).

11.6 Comparison of Capital Budgeting Methods

19. Which limitation is common to the calculations of the payback period, discounted payback, internal rate of return (IRR), and net present value (NPV)?

A. They do not consider the time value of money.
B. They require multiple trial and error calculations.
C. They require knowledge of a firm's cost of capital.
D. They rely on forecasts of future data.

Answer (D) is correct.
REQUIRED: The limitation common to the calculations of the given capital budgeting evaluation methods.
DISCUSSION: The long-term aspect of capital budgeting presents the accountant with specific challenges. A firm must forecast accurately future changes in demand to have the necessary production capacity when demand increases. But it must avoid excess idle capacity when demand decreases. Because capital budgeting requires choosing among investment proposals, a ranking procedure is needed. The ranking procedure also requires reliable estimates of future cost savings or revenues to calculate the estimated cash flows.
Answer (A) is incorrect. Discounted cash flow, IRR, and NPV all consider the time value of money.
Answer (B) is incorrect. Multiple trial and error calculations only are required for determining the IRR.
Answer (C) is incorrect. The payback period calculation does not require knowledge of the cost of capital.

20. The method that divides a project's annual after-tax net income by the average investment cost to measure the estimated performance of a capital investment is the

A. Internal rate of return method.
B. Accounting rate of return method.
C. Payback method.
D. Net present value (NPV) method.

Answer (B) is correct.
REQUIRED: The capital budgeting method that divides annual after-tax net income by the average investment cost.
DISCUSSION: The accounting rate of return uses undiscounted net income (not cash flows) to determine a rate of profitability. Annual after-tax net income is divided by the average carrying amount (or the initial value) of the investment in assets.
Answer (A) is incorrect. The IRR is the rate at which the project's NPV is zero. **Answer (C) is incorrect.** The payback period is the time required to recover the original investment. This method does not consider the time value of money or returns after the payback period. **Answer (D) is incorrect.** The NPV method calculates the discounted present value of future cash inflows to determine whether it is greater than the initial cash outflow.

21. The technique that measures the number of years required for the after-tax cash flows to recover the initial investment in a project is called the

A. Net present value method.
B. Payback method.
C. Profitability index method.
D. Accounting rate of return method.

Answer (B) is correct.
REQUIRED: The capital budgeting method that measures the number of years required for the after-tax cash flows to recover the initial investment.
DISCUSSION: The usual payback formula divides the initial investment by the constant net annual cash inflow. The payback method is unsophisticated because it ignores the time value of money. But it is widely used because of its simplicity and emphasis on recovery of the initial investment.
Answer (A) is incorrect. The NPV method first discounts the future cash flows to their present value. **Answer (C) is incorrect.** The profitability index method divides the present value of the future net cash inflows by the initial investment. **Answer (D) is incorrect.** The accounting rate of return divides the annual net income by the average investment in the project.

STUDY UNIT TWELVE
IT ROLES, SYSTEMS, AND PROCESSING

(23 pages of outline)

12.1	Roles and Responsibilities within the IT Function	347
12.2	Role of Information Systems in the Modern Organization	350
12.3	IT Governance -- Vision and Strategy	353
12.4	Transaction Processing	356
12.5	Application Processing Phases	358
12.6	Systems that Support Routine Processes	362
12.7	Systems that Support Decision Making	366

While the use of information technology (IT) was once restricted to financial applications, it has permeated every area of the modern organization over the last 40 years. No entity, whether for-profit or not-for-profit, can fulfill its mission without the use of sophisticated electronic technologies and their accompanying procedures.

This study unit describes the various broad categories of information systems and the functions they perform, the standardized modes of processing transactions, and standardized phases of processing.

12.1 ROLES AND RESPONSIBILITIES WITHIN THE IT FUNCTION

SUCCESS TIP

In the early days of computing, maintaining a rigid segregation of duties was a simple matter because the roles surrounding a mainframe computer were so specialized. As IT became more and more decentralized over the years, clear lines that once separated jobs such as systems analyst and programmer became blurred and then disappeared.

Recent CPA Exams have contained questions regarding the duties and responsibilities of various IT personnel, as well as the segregation of duties within the IT function. Understand the responsibilities of IT personnel from the standpoint of duty segregation.

1. **Segregation of Duties -- IT Function**

   a. Organizational controls concern the proper segregation of duties and responsibilities within the information systems department.

   b. Controls should ensure the efficiency and effectiveness of IT operations. They include proper segregation of the duties within the IT environment. Thus, the responsibilities of systems analysts, programmers, operators, file librarians, the control group, and others should be assigned to different individuals, and proper supervision should be provided.

   c. Segregation of duties is vital because traditional segregation of responsibilities for authorization, recording, and custody of assets may not be feasible in an IT environment.

      1) For example, a computer may print checks, record disbursements, and generate information for reconciling the account balance, which are activities customarily segregated in a manual system.

         a) If the same person provides the input and receives the output for this process, a significant control weakness exists. Accordingly, certain tasks should not be combined.

         b) Thus, compensating controls may be necessary, such as library controls, effective supervision, and rotation of personnel. Segregating test programs makes concealment of unauthorized changes in production programs more difficult.

2. **Responsibilities of IT Personnel**

   a. **Database administrators (DBAs)** are responsible for developing and maintaining the organization's databases and for establishing controls to protect their integrity.

      1) Thus, only the DBA should be able to update data dictionaries.

      2) In small systems, the DBA may perform some functions of a database management system (DBMS). In larger applications, the DBA uses a DBMS as a primary tool.

   b. **Data administrators (DAs)** are responsible for maintaining the data within the databases.

   c. The **network administrator** manages data and network communication, which includes, but is not limited to, managing local area networks (LANs), metropolitan area networks (MANs), wide area networks (WANs), Internet systems or other forms of data, and network communication.

      1) Network administrator responsibilities include installing network systems (e.g., switched networks, routed networks, and wireless networks), maintaining and upgrading network systems, and resolving network problems.

   d. **Network technicians** maintain the bridges, hubs, routers, switches, cabling, and other devices that interconnect the organization's computers. They are also responsible for maintaining the organization's connection to other networks, such as the Internet.

SU 12: IT Roles, Systems, and Processing 349

- e. The **webmaster** is responsible for the content of the organization's website. (S)he works closely with programmers and network technicians to ensure that the appropriate content is displayed and that the site is reliably available to users.
- f. **Computer operators** are responsible for the day-to-day functioning of the data center, whether the organization runs a mainframe, servers, or anything in between.
    1) Operators load data, mount storage devices, and operate the equipment. Operators should not be assigned programming duties or responsibility for systems design. Accordingly, they also should have no opportunity to make changes in programs and systems as they operate the equipment.
        a) Ideally, computer operators should not have programming knowledge or access to documentation not strictly necessary for their work.
- g. **Librarians** maintain control over and accountability for documentation, programs, and data storage media.
- h. **Systems programmers** maintain and fine-tune the operating systems on the organization's medium- and large-scale computers. The operating system is the core software that performs three of a computer's four basic tasks, i.e., input, output, and storage.
    1) Programmers, as well as analysts, may be able to modify programs, data files, and controls. Thus, they should have no access to data center operations or to production programs or data.
- i. **Applications programmers** design, write, test, and document computer programs according to specifications provided by the end users. Like systems programmers, they should not have access to data center operations or data.
- j. A **systems analyst** uses his or her detailed knowledge of the organization's databases and applications programs to determine how an application system should be designed to best serve the users' needs. These duties are often combined with those of applications programmers.
    1) Systems analysts should not have access to data center operations, production programs, or data files.
- k. **Help desk personnel** log problems reported by users, resolve minor difficulties, and forward more difficult problems to the appropriate person, such as a database administrator or the webmaster. Help desk personnel are often called on to resolve such issues as desktop computers crashing or problems with email.
- l. **Information security officers** are typically in charge of developing information security policies, commenting on security controls in new applications, and monitoring and investigating unsuccessful login attempts.
- m. **End users** must be able to change production data but not programs. They include users who input data or access data from a system, as opposed to persons who install, develop, or program applications.

You have completed the outline for this subunit.
Study multiple-choice questions 1 though 4 beginning on page 370.

STOP & REVIEW

12.2 ROLE OF INFORMATION SYSTEMS IN THE MODERN ORGANIZATION

1. **Overview**

   a. Information technology (IT) is an all-encompassing term that refers to the electronic storage, retrieval, and manipulation of data; its conversion into human-usable form (i.e., information); and its transmission from one point to another.

      1) The Information Technology Association of America has defined IT as "the study, design, development, application, implementation, support or management of computer-based information systems."

   b. For the purposes of the CPA Exam, IT is a synonym for computers, computer networks, and the use of computer programs (i.e., software).

   Block Diagram of Information Technology

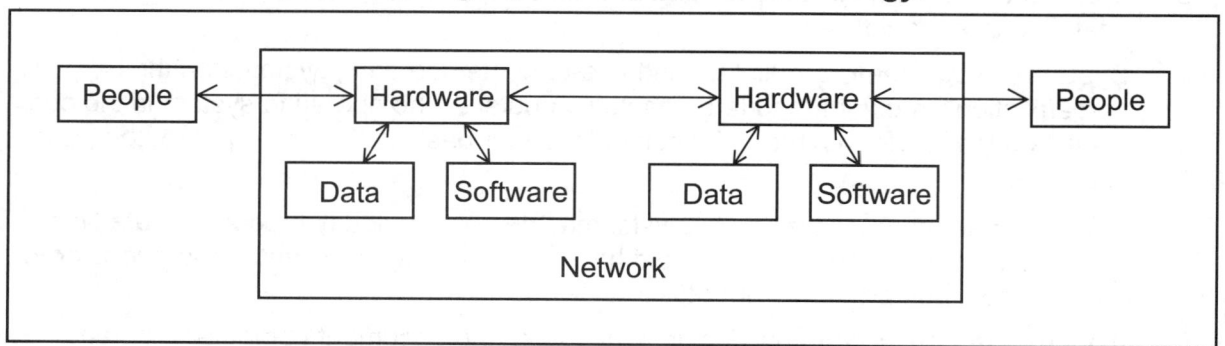

   ```
   ┌─────────────────────────────────────────────────────────────────────┐
   │  ┌────────┐    ┌──────────┐         ┌──────────┐     ┌────────┐    │
   │  │ People │<──>│ Hardware │<───────>│ Hardware │<───>│ People │    │
   │  └────────┘    └──────────┘         └──────────┘     └────────┘    │
   │                  ↕      ↕              ↕     ↕                      │
   │               ┌────┐ ┌────────┐    ┌────┐ ┌────────┐                │
   │               │Data│ │Software│    │Data│ │Software│                │
   │               └────┘ └────────┘    └────┘ └────────┘                │
   │                              Network                                │
   └─────────────────────────────────────────────────────────────────────┘
   ```

   Figure 12-1

2. **Definitions**

   a. **Hardware** is any physical item that comprises a computer system. This could refer to the monitor, keyboard, mouse, microchips, disk drives, etc. In other words, hardware is anything in information technology that can be touched.

   b. **Software** is a combination of computer programs that manipulate data and instruct the hardware on what to do. Software provides instructions to the computer hardware and may also serve as input to other pieces of software. Software is intangible and is anything in the computer system that is not hardware.

      1) Examples are Microsoft Word, CCH's TaxWise, or IDEA Data Analysis Software.

   c. A **network** is a collection of hardware devices that are interconnected so they can communicate among themselves. This allows different hardware to share software and communicate data. The Internet is an example of a network, but many offices have intranets where office computers can communicate with other office computers.

   d. **Data** are information, not instructions, that are stored in hardware. Data may be financial sales data or could be calculations provided by a software program.

   e. **People** refers to anyone who uses hardware (i.e., a computer). This could be an IT professional, an accountant, or a young adult who is surfing the Internet.

3. **Business Information Systems (BIS)**

   a. A business information system is any combination of hardware, software, data, people, and procedures employed to pursue an organizational objective.

      1) The first generation of business information systems served the finance and accounting functions, since computing lends itself so readily to quantitative tasks.
      2) Business information systems have evolved to serve the needs of users at all levels of the organizational hierarchy and, with the advent of fast telecommunications, even users outside the organization.

   b. Business information systems have three strategic roles:

      1) Support business processes and operations, such as creating purchase orders.
      2) Support decision making, such as creating an accounts receivable aging report so a manager can ascertain if a customer's credit is still acceptable.
      3) Support managers in planning for the future, such as the development of long-range planning and strategies.

   c. Any information system performs four major tasks:

      1) **Input.** The system must acquire (capture) data from within or outside of the entity.
      2) **Processing/transformation.** Raw materials (data) are converted into knowledge useful for decision making (information).
      3) **Output.** The ultimate purpose of the system is communication of results to internal or external users.
      4) **Storage.** Before, during, and after processing, data must be temporarily or permanently stored, for example, in files or databases.

EXAMPLE 12-1   Information System Tasks

All four tasks can be identified in the following description:

A firm collects sales and expense data in its automated accounting system. At year end, adjusting and closing entries are added to the system, and the data are processed into a special format from which the annual report is produced. The firm owns a database server on which all of its transactions and formatted financial statements are kept.

---

   d. Stakeholders in business information systems are those who affect, or are affected by, the output of the information system. They have an interest in the system's effective and efficient functioning.

      1) Hence, they include users such as managers, employees, suppliers, and customers.

4. **Electronic Communication (Networks)**
   a. Computer-based systems have been woven into almost every facet of the modern organization, from back-office functions, such as human resources and payroll, to instantaneous customer order placement over the Internet.
   b. The use of high-speed communication networks, such as the Internet, has enabled the growth of the truly global organization.
      1) Markets can be tapped in any part of the globe.
      2) Customer support and supply chain functions can be performed around the clock by personnel located on different continents.
   c. Organizations can make use of social networking sites, such as **Facebook** and **Twitter**, to disseminate information and gather customer feedback.
   d. **RSS**, which stands for rich site summary, allows the content of a website that changes often to be downloaded and stored automatically to a user's computer. This saves the user the need to constantly revisit the site to get the latest information.
   e. The newest stage of evolution is **cloud computing**, through which organizations are relieved of the need to manage the storage of both applications and data since all the software and data they need are maintained in the service providers' facilities (the Cloud).
      1) Cloud computing is defined as a standardized IT capability (services, software, infrastructure) delivered via the Internet in a pay-per-use, self-service way.
      2) Advantages of cloud computing include lower infrastructure investments and maintenance costs, increased mobility, and lower personnel and utility costs.
      3) Disadvantages of cloud computing include less control than there would be over an internal IT department, more difficulty ensuring data security and privacy, and less compatibility with existing tools and software.

STOP & REVIEW

You have completed the outline for this subunit.
Study multiple-choice question 5 on page 372.

12.3 IT GOVERNANCE -- VISION AND STRATEGY

1. **Overview**

    a. Information systems (IS) and information technology (IT) are vital to ensure the successful implementation of an organization's strategy. IT strategy should be driven by the business needs and not by the functions of available technology when formulating a plan to achieve goals.

    1) An IT strategic plan should be aligned with organizational goals and integrated with the overall business strategy.
    2) Individual departments may function well in terms of their own goals but still not serve the goals of the organization.
    3) IS infrastructure purchases need to be implemented in accordance with the IT strategic plan to ensure business needs are met.
    4) Business owners, employees, customers, and financiers such as banks have a vested interest in the strategy.

    b. Key people play a role in determining and supporting an entity's overall vision and strategy. Examples include but are not limited to the following:

    1) **Board of directors.** All major corporate decisions (including the establishment of IT governance and strategy) are made or approved by the board. The board has an oversight role.
    2) **Officers.** The corporation's officers (i.e., executive management) are responsible for carrying out the entity's day-to-day operations, such as implementing effective security governance. Officers include the Chief Executive Officer (CEO), Chief Information Officer (CIO), Chief Information Security Officer (CISO), etc.
    3) **IT Steering Committee.** The IT Steering Committee (or Information Systems Steering Committee) is responsible for overseeing the IT function of an organization. Responsibilities of the IT Steering Committee include, but are not limited to, deciding which information system to deploy, facilitating its implementation, and overseeing the controls over the system.

    NOTE: Information about the role IT personnel play in determining and supporting an entity's overall vision and strategy is presented in Subunit 12.1.

2. Organizations generally develop IT strategies at three different levels.

    a. **Corporate-level strategy** is concerned with market definition (i.e., business and markets to focus resources).
    b. **Business-level strategy** applies to organizations that have independent business units that each develop their own strategy.
    c. **Functional-level strategy** concentrates on a specific functional area of the organization such as treasury, information systems, human resources, and operations.

3. Strategic drivers are the critical elements that help determine the success or failure of an organization's strategy. IS has become a strategic driver in most, if not all, organizations.

   a. New technologies create opportunities for improvement and competitive advantage.

   b. **Customer relationship management (CRM)** is a term that refers to practices, strategies, and technologies that companies use to manage and analyze customer interactions and data throughout the customer lifecycle. CRM

      1) Has a goal of improving business relationships with customers, assisting in customer retention, and driving sales growth.
      2) Is designed to compile information on customers across different channels or points of contact between the customer and the company.
      3) Should manage customer relationships on a long-term basis in order to add value.

4. Samples of strategic analysis approaches include the following:

   a. **SWOT analysis** is a structured planning method that evaluates the **S**trengths, **W**eaknesses, **O**pportunities, and **T**hreats of a project or business venture. It

      1) Specifies the objective of the business venture or project and
      2) Identifies internal and external factors that are favorable and unfavorable to achieve that objective.

         a) Strengths and weaknesses (internal factors) usually are identified by considering the firm's capabilities and resources.
         b) Opportunities and threats (external factors) are identified by considering macroenvironmental factors (e.g., economic, political, social, technical factors) and microenvironmental factors (e.g., suppliers, customers, competitors, distributors).
         c) Strategic fit is the degree to which the internal environment of the firm matches the external environment.

   b. **Porter's five forces analysis** is a framework that analyzes the level of competition within an industry and business strategy development.

      1) According to this framework, the five forces determine the competitive intensity and attractiveness of an industry.

         a) Three forces are from "horizontal" competition:

            i) The threat of substitute products or services,
            ii) The threat of established rivals, and
            iii) The threat of new entrants.

         b) Two forces are from "vertical" competition:

            i) The bargaining power of suppliers and
            ii) The bargaining power of customers.

      2) Attractiveness, in this context, refers to the overall industry profitability. An unattractive industry is one in which the combination of these five forces drives down overall profitability. A very unattractive industry would be one approaching pure competition.

         a) The stronger the forces, the more intense the competition and thus the less attractive the industry is.

c. **Environmental scanning with the use of the Internet** is a process that systematically surveys and interprets relevant data to identify external opportunities and threats. An organization gathers information about the external world, its competitors, and itself. Examples of environmental scanning with the use of the Internet include

   1) Innovative blogs, which can be a good source for early discussion of emerging trends and cutting-edge ideas

   2) Web-crawlers or text mining software systems that scan the Internet automatically in search of emerging innovations and trends

d. **Big data** is an evolving term that describes a voluminous amount of structured, semi-structured, and unstructured data that can be mined to reveal relationships and dependencies or to predict outcomes and behaviors. (Analytics and big data are covered in greater detail in Study Unit 20.)

5. A control framework is a model for establishing a system of internal control. Although the framework does not prescribe the actual controls themselves, it does influence management to focus on risk areas and design controls accordingly.

   a. Generally, an IT control framework describes "families" of controls (i.e., groupings) that attempt to address a particular type of risk exposure. Examples of methodologies used to assess risk and design controls to mitigate those risks include

      1) **ISO 9000**, a group of standards and technical reports that provide guidance for establishing and maintaining a **quality management system (QMS)**. Quality management contributes to the effectiveness and efficiency of IT governance. This is discussed in more detail in Study Unit 16, Subunit 7.

      2) **Information Technology Infrastructure Library (ITIL)**, a product of AXELOS, which assists organizations by focusing on allocating IT efforts on the needs of the business and supporting core processes.

      3) **Control Objectives for Information and Related Technology (COBIT)**, the best-known control and governance framework that addresses information technology. This is discussed in more detail in Study Unit 15, Subunit 2.

STOP & REVIEW

You have completed the outline for this subunit.
Study multiple-choice questions 6 and 7 on page 372.

12.4 TRANSACTION PROCESSING

1. **Overview**

   a. The most common type of system used in the business information systems (BIS) environment is a **transaction processing system (TPS)**.

      1) A transaction is a single discrete event that can be stored in an information system.
      2) Examples include the movement of raw materials from storage to production, the issuance of a purchase order, the recording of a new employee's personal data, or the sale of merchandise.

   b. A TPS captures the fundamental data that reflect the economic life of an organization. An example of a TPS is an **accounting information system (AIS)**.

2. **Two Modes of Transaction Processing**

   a. The phrase "transaction processing modes" refers to the way in which a system is updated with new data. The methods in use can be classified into one of two categories: batch or online.

   b. **Batch Processing**

      1) In this mode, transactions are accumulated and submitted to the computer as a single "batch." In the early days of computers, this was the only way a set of transactions could be processed.
      2) Inherent in batch processing is a time delay between the batching of the transactions and the updating of the records. Sometimes this delay can be as long as overnight.

         a) Thus, errors in a batch processing system caused by incorrect programs or data may not be detected immediately.

   c. **Online Processing or Interactive Processing**

      1) In this mode, the computer processes each transaction individually as the user enters it. The user is in direct communication with the computer and gets **immediate processing/feedback** on whether the transaction was accepted.

         a) A common example is an accounts payable system in which a payables clerk can enter each individual invoice as (s)he verifies the paperwork.

      2) In online systems, having the latest information available at all times is crucial so that users can make immediate decisions. A common example is an airline reservation system, which is constantly updated from moment to moment and must be available all the time.

         a) These are called **real-time systems**. A thermostat is another example, constantly monitoring the temperature in the room and engaging the heating or cooling system accordingly.

   d. Many applications use combined batch and online modes.

      1) In such systems, users continuously enter transactions in online mode throughout the workday, collecting them in batches. The computer can then take advantage of the efficiencies of batch mode overnight when there are fewer users logged on to the system.

   e. The use of batch processing tends to be restricted to TPSs and systems that get their input from TPSs. Systems that support decision making are almost always of the online type.

3. **IT Infrastructure**
    a. Centralization. During the early days of computer processing, computers were very large and expensive, and only organizations such as large banks and governmental agencies could afford them.
        1) As a result, all processing and systems development were done at a single, central location. Users connected to the mainframe via "dumb terminals," i.e., simple monitor-and-keyboard combinations with no processing power of their own.
        2) Since hardware, information security, and data integrity functions were located in one office, economies of scale were achieved and controls were strong.
    b. Decentralization. As the data processing industry evolved, computers became smaller (so-called minicomputers), and branch offices of large organizations could have their own.
        1) **Distributed processing** involves the decentralization of processing tasks and data storage and the assignment of these functions to multiple computers, often in separate locations.
            a) **Cooperative processing** involves the splitting of an application into tasks performed on separate computers. Physical connectivity can occur via a direct channel connection, a local-area network (LAN), a peer-to-peer communication link, or a master/slave link. The application software can exist in a distributed processing environment, but this is not a requirement.
            b) Advantages of distributed processing:
                i) Data are dispersed to match business requirements.
                ii) Data access is much faster because users use only a subset of company data.
                iii) Data processing speed improves because processing occurs at multiple sites.
                iv) New sites can be added to the network without affecting operations at other sites.
                v) Communications become easier to manage because local sites are smaller and closer to customer operations.
                vi) It is easier and more cost-effective to add workstations to a network than to upgrade or add another mainframe to the network.
                vii) The chance of a single-point failure is minimized because processing and/or data storage is distributed. For example, if a workstation goes down, its processing and data storage can be picked up by other workstations with minimal disruption.
            c) Disadvantages of distributed processing:
                i) Database management activities become more complex to manage because data and processing are dispersed over different computers at different locations.
                ii) Control and data anomalies, as well as security, backup, and recovery procedures, must be coordinated and issues resolved with minimal disruption. For example, employees working remotely using their personal computers are subject to higher security risks.

Centralization Advantages	Decentralization Advantages
• Better and more efficient security • Consistent processing because it occurs at a set time in one location	• Remote locations have increased accountability over their data and processes • Remote locations can get data without concern of traffic bottlenecks over networks

STOP & REVIEW

You have completed the outline for this subunit. Study multiple-choice questions 8 through 10 on page 373.

12.5 APPLICATION PROCESSING PHASES

SUCCESS TIP

This subunit explains how data are entered into a transaction processing system (TPS), specifically the accounting information system (AIS). CPA candidates will need to understand how data are entered into a TPS (especially the AIS) and how the data in a TPS are processed.

1. **Data Capture**

    a. Data capture is the process of entering data into an information system. Two methods of capture are identical to their respective processing modes, discussed in item 2. in the previous subunit.

    1) **Batch entry** involves loading a group of records at one time.
    2) **Online entry** involves entering single records, usually in an interactive environment where the user gets immediate feedback.

    b. One type of online entry for capturing input is the optical scanner, such as that used in retail checkout lines (called **point-of-sale**, or POS, transactions). Besides instant updating of accounting and inventory records, POS transaction systems can help management

    1) Identify and respond to trends,
    2) Make sales forecasts,
    3) Determine which products are or are not in demand,
    4) Improve customer service,
    5) Target products and promotions to customers with different demographic traits, and
    6) Evaluate the effects of promotions, including coupons.

2. **Processing**

    a. Processing is the act of converting raw data into usable information. This is performed by the combination of hardware and software that makes up the organization's IT infrastructure.

3. Data Types

a. A data type stipulates the value of a variable and defines the relational or non-relational operations that can be incorporated into a program with the expectation of a valid outcome. Data types include but are not limited to the following:

1) A **string** is used to classify text (i.e., MEEN85).
2) A **float** is a number containing a decimal point (i.e., 10.98).
3) An **integer** classifies whole numbers (i.e., 10).
4) **Boolean** represents logical outcomes (i.e., Yes or No).
5) An **array** is a collection of objects of the same data type.

b. The data type defines the method of storage that can be used.

4. Types of Data Files

a. An understanding of the application processing phases requires an explanation of the two types of computer data files, **master files** and **transaction files**. These types are applicable whether the files are stored on tape, disk, flash drive, or other media and whether they are "flat" files or structured databases.

b. A master file may be fairly static or very volatile.

1) An example of a **fairly static master file** is an authorized vendor file containing each vendor's number, name, and address.

EXAMPLE 12-2   Fairly Static Master File

Authorized Vendor

vendor_num	vendor_name	address_1	city	state	zip	credit_limit	last_updated
0187634	Neyland's Nuts	101 Dandridge Av	Knoxville	TN	37915	$10,000	01/19/2020
1264428	Basic Barbecue	2224 Blossom St	Columbia	SC	29201	$50,000	06/25/2018
4552170	Bayou Bakery	10118 Florida St	Baton Rouge	LA	70801	$15,000	03/04/2018
5006321	Bulldog Barcoding	9085 Old West Point Rd	Starkville	MS	39759	$5,000	10/01/2017
8981463	Razorback Restaurant Supply	3510 West Maple St	Fayetteville	AR	72701	$20,000	07/01/2019

2) An example of a **volatile master file** is a general ledger file that, at any given moment, holds the balances of all accounts in the ledger.

EXAMPLE 12-3   Volatile Master File

General Ledger

account_num	account_name	balance	last_transaction_posted
A1209	Cash	$89,580.22	01/10/2020
G6573	Accounts Receivable	$72,024.57	01/10/2020
J0226	Accounts Payable	$(15,156.89)	01/10/2020
K4411	Sales	$(100,558.60)	01/10/2020
M2020	Cost of Goods Sold	$70,005.64	01/10/2020
Y3577	Administrative Expenses	$21,110.33	01/10/2020

3) **Volatility** is the relative frequency with which the records in a file are added, deleted, or changed during a period.

c. A transaction file contains the data that reflect ongoing business activity, such as individual purchases from vendors or general journal entries.

EXAMPLE 12-4 Transaction File

General Journal

transaction	transaction_date	debit_acct	debit_amt	credit_acct	credit_amt
GL5261904	01/10/2020	A1209	$1,001.56	G6573	$(1,001.56)
GL5261905	01/10/2020	G6573	$660.48	K4411	$(660.48)
GL5261906	01/10/2020	G6573	$898.15	K4411	$(898.15)
GL5261907	01/10/2020	Y3577	$150.75	J0226	$(150.75)

d. Transaction files and master files are constantly interacting.

1) Before an invoice can be paid, the payables transaction file must be matched against the vendor master file to see whether the vendor really exists.
2) The general ledger balance file must be updated every day by posting from the general journal transaction file.

5. **REA (Resources, Events, Agents) Processing**

   a. REA contrasts with the traditional TPS that uses double entry (debit and credit) by using single entry.
   b. It uses a relational database to store and process transactions.
   c. Each transaction (event) is stored in a table chronologically and linked to other tables with the details of the transaction (resources, agents, or other attributes).

   1) For example, a sales event would be recorded in the sales table and linked to a customer table, inventory table, salesperson table, etc.

   d. Processing is accomplished through queries to the tables. Examples include calculating

   1) The sales for a period by summing the amounts in the sales table from the beginning of the period to the end of the period and
   2) The accounts receivable balance for a period end by summing all sales from the sales table and subtracting the sum of all receipts from the accounts receivable cash collections table.

   e. Advantages include the following:

   1) Debits and credits are not considered.
   2) No general ledger is maintained since all balances are calculated through queries.
   3) Ad hoc reports are easily produced. For example, a report listing all customers who purchased a particular product between certain dates can be produced with a simple query.

   f. A major disadvantage is implementation cost because it is usually so high that it is prohibitive. Reasons for this include the following:

   1) Considerable computer storage and processing power are needed.
   2) Many accountants and auditors are not familiar with REA, so training costs are high and acceptance may be low.

6. **Reporting**
    a. **Reporting in General**
        1) The term "report" in this context does not necessarily refer to a printed hard copy. Advances in technology allow for report viewing on a computer screen or mobile device with the option of printing granted to the user.
    b. **Periodic Routine Reports**
        1) Certain reports are required at regular intervals. Examples are monthly trial balances and ledger summaries to assist in closing the books.
    c. **On-Demand and Ad Hoc Reports**
        1) Systems can be designed so that users can generate reports at times they specify. An on-demand report is one whose design is programmed into the system. The user specifies the date and time the report is run.
        2) Advances in processing power and software have given users the ability to design their own reports "on the fly."
            a) These ad hoc (sometimes called "quick-and-dirty") reports can be designed to the user's own specifications without the involvement of IT personnel. Database queries are a common example.
    d. **Exception Reports (also called error listing)**
        1) It is a common practice after daily processing to generate reports of transactions or activities that lie outside predefined boundaries. The appropriate personnel can then follow up and determine the reasons for these exceptions.
        2) Examples are batches whose debits and credits do not match and instances of multiple unsuccessful attempts to access the network (which may indicate hacking).
    e. **Electronic Distribution of Reports**
        1) The advent of email and other forms of digital communication has greatly enhanced the ability of organizations to distribute reports. Rather than wait for paper copies to be hand delivered, reports can be sent digitally to the appropriate personnel. This is sometimes referred to as **push reporting**.
    f. **Audit Trail**
        1) An audit trail of activities is a crucial part of monitoring security over a system. The audit trail includes not only the reports described above, but also such reports as logs of system sign-in and sign-out times to monitor who was doing what on the system.

STOP & REVIEW

You have completed the outline for this subunit.
Study multiple-choice questions 11 through 14 beginning on page 374.

12.6 SYSTEMS THAT SUPPORT ROUTINE PROCESSES

> **SUCCESS TIP**
>
> This subunit introduces other types of business information systems (BISs) used in the corporate environment to perform transaction type processes. The knowledge level of many CPA candidates is most likely highest with the accounting information systems (AIS). However, there are many other types of information systems that comprise the BIS and help corporations perform their day-to-day activities. CPA candidates will need to understand how each of these transaction information systems work and how they interrelate to each other and BISs.

1. **Management Information System (MIS)**

   a. An MIS typically receives input from a transaction processing system, aggregates it, then reports it in a format useful to middle management in running the business. For this reason, MISs are often classified by function or activity, such as the following:

      1) Accounting: general ledger, accounts receivable, accounts payable, payroll processing, fixed asset management, and tax accounting; other aspects of accounting information systems are described in item 2. below.
      2) Finance: capital budgeting, operational budgeting, and cash management
      3) Manufacturing: production planning, cost control, and quality control
      4) Logistics: inventory management and transportation planning
      5) Marketing: sales analysis and forecasting
      6) Human resources: projecting payroll, projecting benefits obligations, employment-level planning, and employee evaluation tracking

   b. These single-function systems, often called stovepipe systems because of their limited focus, are gradually being replaced by integrated systems that link multiple business activities across the enterprise.

      1) The most comprehensive integrated system is termed an enterprise resource planning (ERP) system (discussed in item 4. beginning on page 364).

2. **Accounting Information System (AIS)**

   a. An AIS is a subsystem of an MIS that processes routine, highly structured financial and transactional data relevant to financial as well as managerial accounting. An AIS is composed of the **general ledger/financial reporting system (GL/FRS), management reporting system (MRS)**, and TPS (discussed in Subunit 12.4).

      1) The **GL/FRS** is concerned with transactions with external parties (e.g., customers, suppliers, governments, owners, and creditors) reflected in financial statements prepared in conformity with GAAP.

         a) The GL/FRS typically produces the income statement, balance sheet, statement of cash flow, and other reports required by management.

      2) The **MRS** provides information useful to decision making and internal management, including the internal activities recorded in the cost accounting system and the preparation of related reports and analysis.

         a) The MRS typically produces production reports, pro forma financial statements, budgets, cost-volume-profit analysis, and other internal reports.

SU 12: IT Roles, Systems, and Processing

3. **Business Controls**

    a. Accounting and financial reporting systems encompass the methodology and related records to identify, assemble, analyze, classify, record, and report the company's transactions to make optimum economic decisions related to its assets and liabilities.

        1) Accounting and financial reporting systems create the ledger balances necessary to prepare financial statements.
        2) Accounting and financial reporting systems also help management control the company's assets and provide operational information to its decision makers as well as provide external decision makers the ability to make investment decisions.

Types of Accounting and Financial Reporting Systems	Examples
Material requirements planning (MRP)	Oracle, NetSuite, Sage 100cloud, Prodsmart, DELMIAworks, E2 Manufacturing System
Manufacturing resource planning (MRP II)	Fishbowl, FactoryEdge, Epicor
Computer-integrated manufacturing (CIM)	CNC Software Solutions, OpenCIM, CIMGLUE, ARMAGARD
Flexible manufacturing systems (FMSs)	Predator RCM, L2L, Intelitek OpenFMS
Enterprise resource planning (ERP)	Acumatica Cloud ERP, QT9 ERP, ALERE ERP Software, Brightpearl, Wrike
Financial reporting software	Quickbooks, Sage Intacct, FundCount, CCH Tagetik, Zoho Books

Author's Note: The examples of accounting and financial reporting systems above are included to help candidates relate these concepts to day-to-day accounting systems. They will not be tested on the Exam, and they should not be memorized.

    b. All accounting and financial reporting systems contain the following characteristics:

        1) Documentation of the accounting system, such as a chart of accounts
        2) An audit trail (or the ability to provide documentary evidence for each transaction)
        3) Communication or upstream flow of information from individual transactions to upper management
        4) Monitoring of communication (or the ongoing process of determining the quality of the information being synthesized/communicated to upper management)
        5) Synthesis of information into the double-entry system of accounting

    c. **The Control Process**

        1) Control requires feedback on the results of organizational activities for the purposes of measurement and correction.
        2) The control process includes
            a) Establishing standards for the operation to be controlled,
            b) Measuring performance against the standards,
            c) Examining and analyzing deviations,
            d) Taking corrective action, and
            e) Reappraising the standards based on experience.
        3) Internal control only provides reasonable assurance of achieving objectives. It cannot provide absolute assurance.

4. **Enterprise Resource Planning (ERP)**

   a. ERP is the latest phase in the development of computerized systems for managing organizational resources. ERP is intended to integrate enterprise-wide information systems by creating one database linked to all of an organization's applications.

   1) ERP subsumes traditional MISs.
   2) Figure 12-2 contrasts the less integrated MIS with the more integrated ERP system.

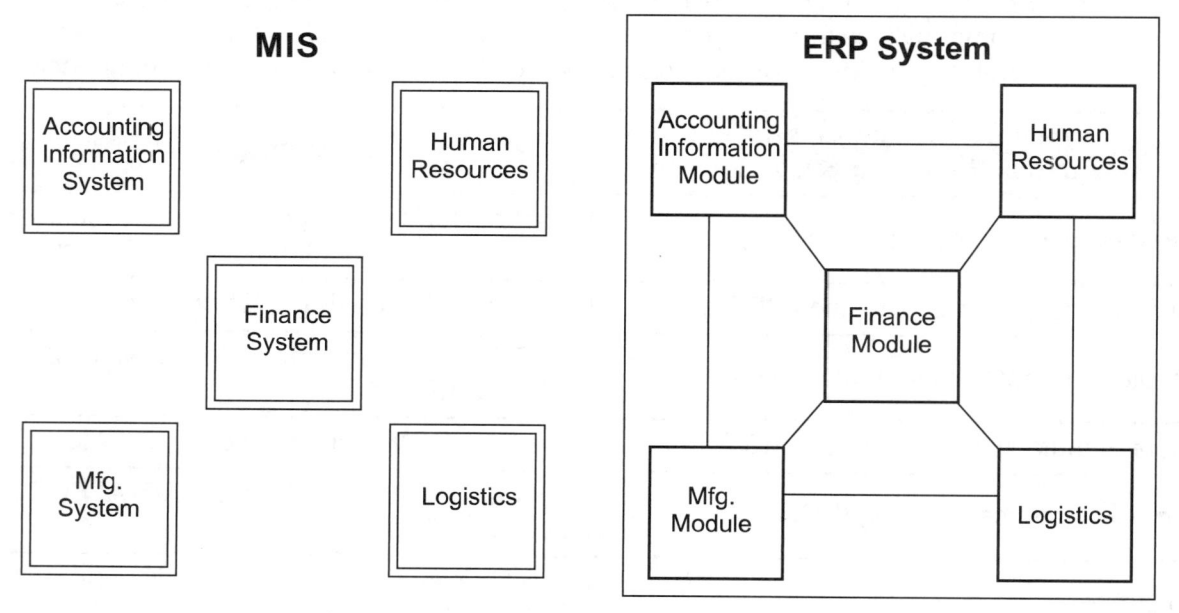

   Figure 12-2

   b. In the traditional ERP system, subsystems share data and coordinate their activities. Thus, if sales receives an order, it can quickly verify that inventory is sufficient to notify shipping to process the order.

   1) Otherwise, production is notified to manufacture more of the product, with a consequent automatic adjustment of output schedules.
   2) If materials are inadequate for this purpose, the system will issue a purchase order.
   3) If more labor is needed, human resources will be instructed to reassign or hire employees.
   4) The foregoing business processes (and others) should interact seamlessly in an ERP system.

   c. The subsystems in a traditional ERP system are internal to the organization. Hence, they are often called **back-office functions**. The information produced is principally (but not exclusively) intended for **internal** use by the organization's managers.

d. The current generation of ERP software has added **front-office functions**. These connect the organization with customers, suppliers, owners, creditors, and strategic allies (e.g., the members of a trading community or other business association).

   1) Moreover, the current generation of ERP software also provides the capability for smooth (and instant) interaction with the business processes of **external parties**.
   2) A newer ERP system's integration with the firm's back-office functions enables supply-chain management (SCM), customer relationship management (CRM), and partner relationship management (PRM).

e. The disadvantages of ERP are its extent and complexity, which make implementation difficult and costly.

f. Companies with legacy ERP systems are moving to cloud-based ERP systems. Advantages include

   1) Flexibility and agility of the cloud ERP's centralized data storage
   2) Sharing of data-processing tasks
   3) Internet-based access to services and resources
   4) Reduced development and implementation costs

BACKGROUND 12-1   ERP Packages

Because ERP software is costly and complex, it is usually installed only by the largest enterprises, although mid-size organizations are increasingly likely to buy ERP software. Major ERP packages include SAP ERP Central Component from SAP SE and Oracle e-Business Suite, PeopleSoft, and JD Edwards EnterpriseOne, all from Oracle Corp.

BACKGROUND 12-2   IRM

The tremendous variety of forms that information systems can take and the diverse needs of users have led to the concept of information resources management (IRM), which takes a global view of the information holdings and needs of an organization. This view is promoted by the Information Resources Management Association of Hershey, PA (www.irma-international.org).

STOP & REVIEW

You have completed the outline for this subunit.
Study multiple-choice questions 15 through 18 beginning on page 376.

12.7 SYSTEMS THAT SUPPORT DECISION MAKING

> **SUCCESS TIP**
>
> This subunit will acquaint you with information systems that support the decision-making process. In contrast to transaction-type processes, these types of programs assist humans with making decisions. CPA candidates will need to understand how these decision-making systems work.

1. **Data Warehouse**
   a. A data warehouse is a central database for transaction-level data from more than one of the organization's transaction processing systems (TPS).
      1) A data warehouse is strictly a query-and-reporting system. It is not used to carry on the enterprise's routine operations.
      2) Rather, a data warehouse gets its input from the various TPSs in the organization.
   b. Data warehouses store a large quantity of data and require that the transaction records be converted to a standard format.
      1) The ability of the data warehouse to relate data from multiple systems makes it a very powerful tool for ad hoc queries.
      2) The data warehouse can also be accessed using analytical and graphics tools, a technique called **online analytical processing (OLAP)**.
         a) An important component of OLAP is drill-down analysis, in which the user is first presented with the data at an aggregate level and then can display successive levels of detail for a given date, region, product, etc., until finally reaching the original transactions.
         b) OLAP is an example of a diagnostic analytics tool (discussed in more detail in Study Unit 20).
      3) The following technologies are replacing OLAP:
         a) **In-memory analytics** is an approach that queries data when it resides in a computer's random access memory (RAM), as opposed to querying data that is stored on physical disks. This results in shortened query response times and allows business intelligence and analytic applications to support faster business decisions.
         b) **Search engine technology** stores data at a document/transaction level, and data is not pre-aggregated like it would be when contained in an OLAP or in-memory technology application. Users are able to have full access to their raw data and create the aggregations themselves.

c. A data warehouse enables **data mining**, i.e., the search for unexpected relationships among data.

Data Warehouse and Data Mining

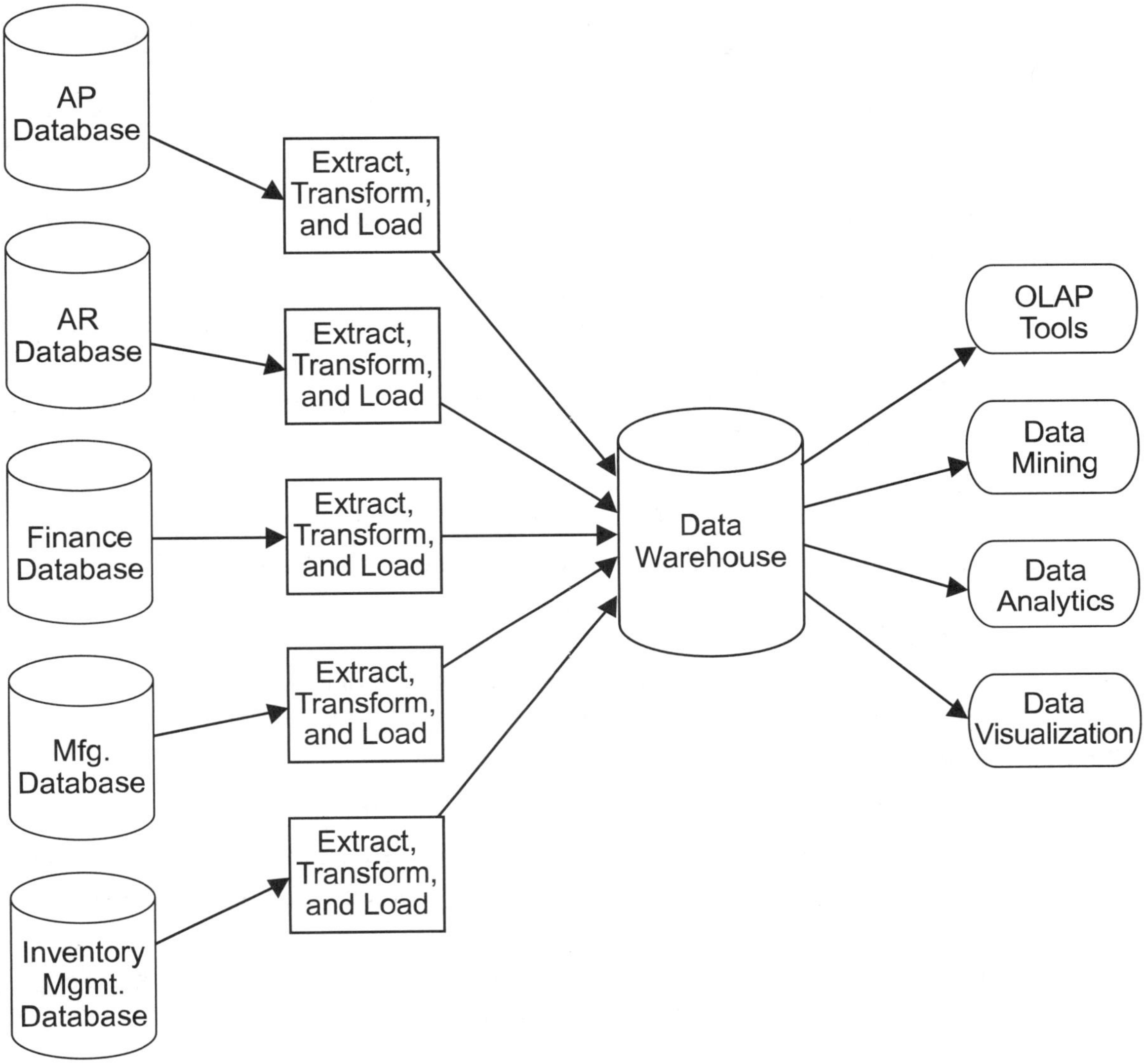

Figure 12-3

2. **Decision Support System (DSS)**

   a. A DSS is an interactive system that is useful in solving semistructured problems, that is, those with a structured portion (which the computer can solve) and an unstructured portion (which requires the manager's insight and judgment).

      1) This point requires emphasis: A DSS does not automate a decision. It examines the relevant data and presents a manager with choices between alternative courses of action.

      2) Similar to an AIS, a DSS is a subsystem of an MIS.

3. **Robotic Process Automation (RPA)**
   a. RPA is a form of machine learning technology that enables a computer, through software, to acquire knowledge and mimic the actions of the person(s) using it to perform a task.
      1) The software, referred to as a robot, can perform a set of instructions predefined by humans.
      2) RPA robots utilize the same user interface as humans to conduct a process. However, robots are faster, process more data, and eliminate the potential for human error.
      3) RPA systems capture data through a graphical interface and process the data used for repetitive tasks.
         a) For example, a company copies information such as a customer's name, items ordered, number of each item ordered, and address from the customer's order and pastes it into its system to create an invoice for the customer. Using RPA, the company can set instructions that direct a robot to perform this function. The robot can finish this repetitive task faster and more accurately than a human.
   b. Benefits of RPA include, but are not limited to, the following:
      1) Robots can perform continuously without needing to take time off.
      2) RPA eliminates the element of human error and improves efficiency (subsequent to successful programming and implementation).
      3) Although the initial implementation requires a capital investment, long-term costs associated with RPA are considerably lower than labor costs.

4. **Artificial Intelligence (AI)**
   a. AI is computer software designed to perceive, reason, and understand.
      1) Historically, computer software works through a series of if/then conditions in which every operation has exactly two possible outcomes (yes/no, on/off, true/false, one/zero).
         a) Human reasoning, on the other hand, is extremely complex, based on deduction, induction, intuition, emotion, and biochemistry, resulting in a range of possible outcomes.
      2) AI attempts to imitate human decision making, which hinges on this combination of knowledge and intuition (i.e., remembering relationships between variables based on experience).
      3) The advantage of AI in a business environment is that IT systems
         a) Can work 24 hours a day
         b) Will not become ill, die, or be hired away
         c) Are extremely fast processors of data, especially if numerous rules (procedures) must be evaluated
   b. There are several types of AI:
      1) **Neural networks** are a collection of processing elements working together to process information much like the human brain, including learning from previous situations and generalizing concepts.
      2) **Case-based reasoning systems** use a process similar to that used by humans to learn from previous, similar experiences.

SU 12: IT Roles, Systems, and Processing

      3) **Rule-based expert systems** function on the basis of set rules to arrive at an answer. These cannot be changed by the system itself. They must be changed by an outside source (i.e., the computer programmer).

      4) **Intelligent agents** are programs that apply a built-in or learned knowledge base to execute a specific, repetitive, and predictable task, for example, showing a computer user how to perform a task or searching websites for particular financial information.

      5) An **expert system** is an interactive system that attempts to imitate the reasoning of a human expert in a given field. It is useful for addressing unstructured problems when there is a local shortage of human experts.

5. **RPA vs. AI**

   a. The major difference between RPA and AI is that RPA cannot learn throughout a process because it can only replicate rules-based human actions. In item 3.a.3)a) on the previous page, the robot copies and pastes information from customer orders to invoices. If there are errors in the data, such as data in the wrong format, the robot will continue to process the data without adjusting for the errors because it can only do exactly what it was programmed to do.

   b. However, RPA and AI can work together. To continue the same example, when the format of the data is incorrect, AI can automatically execute necessary processes to correct the data's format, and the robot can continue to copy and paste.

6. **Executive Support System (ESS)**

   a. At the strategic level, high-level decision makers get the information they need to set, and monitor progress toward, the organization's long-term objectives from an ESS, also called an executive information system (EIS). An ESS assists senior management in making nonroutine decisions, such as identifying problems and opportunities. The information in an ESS comes from sources both within and outside the organization, including information from nontraditional computer sources.

7. **Business Intelligence (BI)**

   a. Business intelligence is what gives upper management the information it needs to know where the organization is and how to steer it in the intended direction. BI gives an executive immediate information about an organization's critical success factors.

      1) BI is replacing the older ESS model.

   b. BI tools display information about the organization as bar graphs, pie charts, columnar reports, or any other format considered appropriate to upper management's decision making. These displays are sometimes grouped by a particular executive's needs into what is termed a **digital dashboard**. (Data visualization is covered in Study Unit 20, Subunit 4.)

      1) Stock price trends, sales by region and date, on-time delivery performance, instantaneous cash balances, and profitability by customer are possible metrics to be included.

   c. BI tools use data both from within and outside the organization.

STOP & REVIEW

You have completed the outline for this subunit.
Study multiple-choice questions 19 through 22 beginning on page 378.

QUESTIONS

12.1 Roles and Responsibilities within the IT Function

1. The risks created by rapid changes in IT have **not** affected which concepts of internal control?

I. Cost-benefit analysis
II. Control environment
III. Reasonable assurance
IV. Management's responsibility

A. I and II only.
B. III and IV only.
C. II, III, and IV only.
D. I, II, III, and IV.

Answer (D) is correct.
REQUIRED: The concepts of control not affected by rapid IT change.
DISCUSSION: Internal control objectives remain essentially the same although technology, risks, and control methods change. Thus, many concepts of control (management's responsibility, the role of the control environment, reasonable assurance, monitoring, and cost-benefit analysis) are relevant regardless of IT changes.
Answer (A) is incorrect. IT control processes and procedures must provide reasonable assurance that objectives are achieved and risks are reduced. Moreover, management continues to be responsible for control and for coordinating activities to achieve objectives.
Answer (B) is incorrect. Cost-benefit analysis remains an essential tool for determining which controls mitigate identified risks at an acceptable cost. Furthermore, the control environment in an IT setting reflects the tone of the organization, influences control consciousness, and provides a foundation for the other components of control.
Answer (C) is incorrect. Cost-benefit analysis remains an essential tool for determining which controls mitigate identified risks at an acceptable cost.

2. In the organization of the information systems function, the most important segregation of duties is

A. Not allowing the data librarian to assist in data processing operations.
B. Assuring that those responsible for programming the system do not have access to data processing operations.
C. Having a separate information officer at the top level of the organization outside of the accounting function.
D. Using different programming personnel to maintain utility programs from those who maintain the application programs.

Answer (B) is correct.
REQUIRED: The most important segregation of duties.
DISCUSSION: Segregation of duties is a general control that is vital in a computerized environment. Some segregation of duties common in noncomputerized environments may not be feasible in an IT environment. However, certain tasks should not be combined. Systems analysts and programmers should be segregated from computer operators. Both programmers and analysts may be able to modify programs, files, and controls, and should therefore have no access to data center operations or to production programs or data. Operators should not be assigned programming duties or responsibility for systems design, and should have no opportunity to make changes in programs and systems.
Answer (A) is incorrect. Librarians maintain control over documentation, programs, and data files; they should have no access to equipment, but they can assist in data processing operations. **Answer (C) is incorrect.** A separate information officer outside of the accounting function would not be as critical a segregation of duties as that between programmers and processors. **Answer (D) is incorrect.** Programmers usually handle all types of programs.

3. Which of the following should **not** be the responsibility of a database administrator?

A. Design the content and organization of the database.

B. Develop applications to access the database.

C. Protect the database and its software.

D. Monitor and improve the efficiency of the database.

Answer (B) is correct.
REQUIRED: The choice not a responsibility of a database administrator.
DISCUSSION: The database administrator (DBA) is the person who has overall responsibility for developing and maintaining the database. One primary responsibility is to design the content of the database. Another responsibility of the DBA is to protect and control the database. A third responsibility is to monitor and improve the efficiency of the database. The responsibility of developing applications to access the database belongs to systems analysts and programmers.
Answer (A) is incorrect. Designing the content and organization of the database is a responsibility of the database administrator. **Answer (C) is incorrect.** Protecting the database and its software is a responsibility of the database administrator. **Answer (D) is incorrect.** Monitoring and improving the efficiency of the database is a responsibility of the database administrator.

4. If a payroll system continues to pay employees who have been terminated, control weaknesses most likely exist because

A. Procedures were not implemented to verify and control the receipt by the computer processing department of all transactions prior to processing.

B. There were inadequate manual controls maintained outside the computer system.

C. Programmed controls such as limit checks should have been built into the system.

D. Input file label checking routines built into the programs were ignored by the operator.

Answer (B) is correct.
REQUIRED: The reason control weaknesses most likely exist.
DISCUSSION: The authorization to pay employees comes from outside the computer department. Thus, inadequate controls external to the computer processing department are most likely the cause of allowing the payments to terminated employees to continue without detection.
Answer (A) is incorrect. Batch totals constitute adequate controls over properly authorized transactions but provide no control over unauthorized transactions. **Answer (C) is incorrect.** A limit check tests the reasonableness of a particular transaction but not whether it was authorized. **Answer (D) is incorrect.** Paying proper attention to input file labels (header labels) will not detect unauthorized transactions.

12.2 Role of Information Systems in the Modern Organization

5. The four major tasks that any system must perform are

A. Input, transformation, output, and storage.
B. Input, backup, output, and storage.
C. Input, transformation, output, and maintenance.
D. Input, transformation, storage, and feedback.

Answer (A) is correct.
REQUIRED: The four major tasks that any system must perform.
DISCUSSION: The four major tasks that any system must perform are input, transformation, output, and storage.

12.3 IT Governance -- Vision and Strategy

6. Information technology (IT) strategy is determined by

A. Business needs.
B. Individual department needs.
C. The technology available.
D. Competitors' strategies.

Answer (A) is correct.
REQUIRED: The item that determines information technology (IT) strategy formulation.
DISCUSSION: Information systems (IS) and IT are vital to the successful implementation of an organization's strategy. IT strategy should be driven by the business needs and not by the functions of available technology when formulating a plan to achieve goals.
Answer (B) is incorrect. Individual departments may function well in terms of their own goals but still not serve the goals of the organization. **Answer (C) is incorrect.** Technology is vital to the successful implementation of an organization's strategy. IS infrastructure purchases need to be implemented in accordance with the IT strategic plan to ensure business needs are met. **Answer (D) is incorrect.** Although being familiar with the strategies of competitors is useful, strategy should be driven by the business's needs. Competitors' strengths and weaknesses may differ from those of the business.

7. Which of the following is (are) a type(s) of business strategy(ies)?

A. Corporate-level strategy.
B. Business-level strategy.
C. Functional-level strategy.
D. All are types of strategies.

Answer (D) is correct.
REQUIRED: The item(s) that is (are) a type of business strategy.
DISCUSSION: Organizations generally develop strategies at three different levels. Corporate-level strategy is concerned with market definition (i.e., business and markets to focus resources). Business-level strategy applies to organizations that have independent business units that each develop their own strategy. Functional-level strategy concentrates on a specific functional area of the organization such as treasury, information systems, human resources, and operations.

12.4 Transaction Processing

8. An interactive system environment is best characterized by

A. Data files with records arranged sequentially.
B. The processing of groups of data at regular intervals.
C. Sorting the transaction file before processing.
D. The processing of data immediately on input.

Answer (D) is correct.
REQUIRED: The characteristic of an interactive system environment.
DISCUSSION: In an interactive (inquiry) system, users employ interactive devices to converse directly with the system. The system is characterized by online entry and processing, direct access, and time sharing.
Answer (A) is incorrect. An interactive system requires direct-access files. **Answer (B) is incorrect.** An interactive system permits immediate, online processing of single transactions. **Answer (C) is incorrect.** The transaction file need not be sorted before processing.

9. Information processing made possible by a network of computers dispersed throughout an organization is called

A. Online processing.
B. Interactive processing.
C. Time sharing.
D. Distributed data processing.

Answer (D) is correct.
REQUIRED: The method of information processing by dispersed computers.
DISCUSSION: Distributed processing is characterized by a merger of computer and telecommunications technology. Distributed systems permit not only remote access to a computer but also the performance of local processing at local sites. The result is greater flexibility in systems design and the possibility of an optimal distribution of processing tasks.
Answer (A) is incorrect. Online processing is a method of processing data that permits both immediate posting (updating) and inquiry of master files as transactions occur. **Answer (B) is incorrect.** Interactive processing is a method of processing data immediately upon input. **Answer (C) is incorrect.** Time sharing is the processing of a program by the CPU until an input or output operation is required. In time sharing, the CPU spends a fixed amount of time on each program.

10. An insurance company that has adopted cooperative processing is planning to implement new standard software in all its local offices. The new software has a fast response time, is very user friendly, and was developed with extensive user involvement. The new software captures, consolidates, edits, validates, and finally transfers standardized transaction data to the headquarters server. Local managers, who were satisfied with existing locally written personal computer applications, opposed the new approach because they anticipated

A. Increased workloads.
B. Centralization of all processing tasks.
C. More accountability.
D. Less computer equipment.

Answer (C) is correct.
REQUIRED: The reason for opposing introduction of new software.
DISCUSSION: Cooperative processing implies a tighter coupling than previously existed between the personal computers and the server. The result may threaten the managers' perceived autonomy by increasing the control exercised by headquarters and therefore the accountability of local managers.
Answer (A) is incorrect. Given that only existing systems would be converted, the transaction volume would likely remain relatively constant. **Answer (B) is incorrect.** In a cooperative processing environment, different computers execute different parts of an application. **Answer (D) is incorrect.** Compared with mainframe-only processing, cooperative processing typically requires more computer equipment at distributed locations.

12.5 Application Processing Phases

11. A company updates the payroll master file at the end of the week. The payroll time cards are transported to the computer center for processing. The sequence of events followed by the computer center in updating its master file should be

A. Converting to machine-readable form, batching records of transactions, validating input, updating the master.

B. Batching records of transactions, converting to machine-readable form, validating input, updating the master.

C. Validating input, batching records of transactions, converting to machine-readable form, updating the master.

D. Batching records of transactions, validating input, converting to machine-readable form, updating the master.

Answer (B) is correct.
REQUIRED: The sequence of events for updating a master file.
DISCUSSION: Batching is the collection and grouping of similar input records for processing. Information must be converted to machine language so the computer can read it. Validating input is checking the validity of account numbers, customer numbers, etc., included in the batched input records. The master file contains current or almost current records. The transaction (i.e., batch) file must be processed against the master file to bring the almost current records to a current state.
Answer (A) is incorrect. Data must be batched before it is converted. **Answer (C) is incorrect.** Data must be batched first. **Answer (D) is incorrect.** Data are validated by various computer checks after, not before, conversion to machine-readable form.

12. At a remote computer center, management installed an automated scheduling system to load data files and execute programs at specific times during the day. The best approach for verifying that the scheduling system performs as intended is to

A. Analyze job activity with a queuing model to determine workload characteristics.

B. Simulate the resource usage and compare the results with actual results of operations.

C. Use library management software to track changes to successive versions of applications programs.

D. Audit job accounting data for file accesses and job initiation/termination messages.

Answer (D) is correct.
REQUIRED: The best approach for verifying that the scheduling system performs as intended.
DISCUSSION: Job accounting data analysis permits programmatic examination of job initiation and termination, record counts, and processing times. Auditing job accounting data for file accesses and job initiation/termination messages will reveal whether the right data files were loaded/dismounted at the right times and the right programs were initiated/terminated at the right times.
Answer (A) is incorrect. Analyzing job activity with a queuing model to determine workload characteristics gives information about resource usage but does not verify that the system actually functioned as intended. **Answer (B) is incorrect.** A simulation helps management characterize the workload but does not verify that the system actually functioned as intended. **Answer (C) is incorrect.** Using library management software to track changes to successive versions of application programs permits control of production and test versions but does not verify that the system actually functioned as intended.

13. Mill Co. uses a batch processing method to process its sales transactions. Data on Mill's sales transaction file are electronically sorted by customer number and are subjected to programmed edit checks in preparing its invoices, sales journals, and updated customer account balances. One of the direct outputs of the creation of this file most likely would be a

A. Report showing exceptions and control totals.
B. Printout of the updated inventory records.
C. Report showing overdue accounts receivable.
D. Printout of the sales price master file.

Answer (A) is correct.
REQUIRED: The most likely direct output of the creation of a sales transaction file.
DISCUSSION: Batch processing is useful for processing large volumes of data, especially when sorted in sequential order, for example, by customer number. Editing (validation) of data should produce a cumulative automated error listing that includes not only errors found in the current processing run but also uncorrected errors from earlier runs. Each error should be identified and described, and the date and time of detection should be given. The creation of the file also generates various totals that serve as controls over the accuracy of the processing.
Answer (B) is incorrect. A batch system is less appropriate for printing records that require up-to-date information. **Answer (C) is incorrect.** Testing for overdue accounts receivable should be done prior to approving current sales orders. **Answer (D) is incorrect.** A complete listing of sales prices should not be in a sales transactions file.

14. A commonly used measure of the activity in a master file during a specified time period is

A. Volatility.
B. The index ratio.
C. The frequency ratio.
D. The volume ratio.

Answer (A) is correct.
REQUIRED: The commonly used measure of the activity in a master file.
DISCUSSION: File volatility is the relative frequency with which records are added, deleted, or changed during a specified period.

12.6 Systems that Support Routine Processes

15. An accounting information system (AIS) must include certain source documents in order to control purchasing and accounts payable. For a manufacturing organization, the best set of documents should include

A. Purchase requisitions, purchase orders, inventory reports of goods needed, and vendor invoices.

B. Purchase orders, receiving reports, and inventory reports of goods needed.

C. Purchase orders, receiving reports, and vendor invoices.

D. Purchase requisitions, purchase orders, receiving reports, and vendor invoices.

Answer (D) is correct.
REQUIRED: The best set of documents to be included in an AIS to control purchasing and accounts payable.
DISCUSSION: An AIS is a subsystem of a management information system that processes financial and transactional data relevant to managerial and financial accounting. The AIS supports operations by collecting and sorting data about an organization's transactions. An AIS is concerned not only with external parties but also with the internal activities needed for management decision making at all levels. An AIS is best suited to solve problems when reporting requirements are well defined. A manufacturer has well-defined reporting needs for routine information about purchasing and payables. Purchase requisitions document user department needs, and purchase orders provide evidence that purchase transactions were appropriately authorized. A formal receiving procedure segregates the purchasing and receiving functions and establishes the quantity, quality, and timeliness of goods received. Vendor invoices establish the liability for payment and should be compared with the foregoing documents.
Answer (A) is incorrect. Receiving reports should be included. **Answer (B) is incorrect.** Requisitions and vendor invoices should be included. **Answer (C) is incorrect.** Purchase requisitions should be included.

16. Which one of the following statements about an accounting information system (AIS) is **false**?

A. AIS supports day-to-day operations by collecting and sorting data about an organization's transactions.

B. The information produced by AIS is made available to all levels of management for use in planning and controlling an organization's activities.

C. AIS is best suited to solve problems where there is great uncertainty and ill-defined reporting requirements.

D. AIS is often referred to as a transaction processing system.

Answer (C) is correct.
REQUIRED: The false statement about an accounting information system (AIS).
DISCUSSION: An AIS is a subsystem of a management information system that processes financial and transactional data relevant to managerial and financial accounting. The AIS supports operations by collecting and sorting data about an organization's transactions. An AIS is concerned not only with external parties, but also with the internal activities needed for management decision making at all levels. An AIS is best suited to solve problems when reporting requirements are well-defined. A decision support system is a better choice for problems in which decision making is less structured.

17. A principal advantage of an ERP system is

A. Program-data dependence.
B. Data redundancy.
C. Separate data updating for different functions.
D. Centralization of data.

Answer (D) is correct.
REQUIRED: The principal advantage of an ERP system.
DISCUSSION: An advantage of an ERP system is the elimination of data redundancy through the use of a central database. In principle, information about an item of data is stored once, and all functions have access to it. Thus, when the item (such as a price) is updated, the change is effectively made for all functions. The result is reliability (data integrity).
Answer (A) is incorrect. An ERP system uses a central database and a database management system. A fundamental characteristic of a database is that applications are independent of the physical structure of the database. Writing programs or designing applications to use the database requires only the names of desired data items, not their locations. **Answer (B) is incorrect.** An ERP system eliminates data redundancy. **Answer (C) is incorrect.** An ERP system is characterized by one-time data updating for all organizational functions.

18. Enterprise resource planning (ERP) software packages, such as SAP ERP Central Component and Oracle e-Business Suite, are all-inclusive systems that attempt to provide entity-wide information. ERP systems provide advantages to an organization's auditors because they

A. Have proven difficult for some firms to install.
B. Typically require firms to reduce the division of duties and responsibilities found in traditional systems.
C. Typically have built-in transaction logs and ability to produce a variety of diagnostic reports.
D. Have been installed by smaller firms so, to date, few auditors have used them.

Answer (C) is correct.
REQUIRED: The advantage of an ERP for the auditor.
DISCUSSION: ERP systems have a variety of controls and report generation functions that allow auditors to abstract and monitor data collected and processed. Some ERP systems have built-in audit functions.
Answer (A) is incorrect. The difficulty of installing ERP systems is a disadvantage for the auditors.
Answer (B) is incorrect. ERP systems often require the client to depart from the traditional functional division of duties, such as accounting, finance, marketing, etc. The result is increased audit risk. **Answer (D) is incorrect.** ERP systems are very costly and therefore usually have been implemented by large organizations. However, the trend is for more and more organizations to install these systems.

12.7 Systems that Support Decision Making

19. Which of the following is the best example of the use of a decision support system (DSS)?

A. A manager uses a personal-computer-based simulation model to determine whether one of the company's ships would be able to satisfy a particular delivery schedule.

B. An auditor uses a generalized audit software package to retrieve several purchase orders for detailed vouching.

C. A manager uses the query language feature of a database management system (DBMS) to compile a report showing customers whose average purchase exceeds $2,500.

D. An auditor uses a personal-computer-based word processing software package to modify an internal control questionnaire for a specific audit engagement.

Answer (A) is correct.
REQUIRED: The best example of the use of a decision support system.
DISCUSSION: A decision support system (DSS) assists middle- and upper-level managers in long-term, nonroutine, and often unstructured decision making. The system contains at least one decision model, is usually interactive, dedicated, and time-shared, but need not be real-time. It is an aid to decision making, not the automation of a decision process. The personal-computer-based simulation model is used to provide interactive problem solving (i.e., scheduling) assistance, the distinguishing feature of a DSS.
Answer (B) is incorrect. The generalized audit software package does not provide interactive problem solving assistance in retrieving the purchase orders and thus is not a DSS. **Answer (C) is incorrect.** The query feature of a DBMS does not provide interactive problem solving assistance in compiling the report and thus is not a DSS. **Answer (D) is incorrect.** The word processing software package does not provide interactive problem solving assistance to the auditor and thus is not a DSS.

20. An expert system

A. Comprises a general ledger/financial reporting system and a management reporting system.

B. Is a central database for transaction-level data.

C. Solicits opinions from experts, summarizes the opinions, and feeds the summaries back to the experts.

D. Is useful in solving unstructured problems.

Answer (D) is correct.
REQUIRED: The characteristic of an expert system.
DISCUSSION: An expert system is an interactive system that attempts to imitate the reasoning of a human expert in a given field. It is useful for addressing unstructured problems when there is a local shortage of human experts.
Answer (A) is incorrect. An Accounting Information System (AIS), not an expert system, is composed of the general ledger/financial reporting system and a transaction processing system. **Answer (B) is incorrect.** A data warehouse, not an expert system, is a central database for transaction-level data from more than one of the organization's transaction processing systems. **Answer (C) is incorrect.** The Delphi approach, not an expert system, solicits opinions from experts, summarizes the opinions, and feeds the summaries back to the experts (without revealing participants to each other).

21. Business intelligence (BI) has all of the following characteristics **except**

A. Focusing on strategic objectives.
B. Giving immediate information about an organization's critical success factors.
C. Displaying information in graphical format.
D. Providing advice and answers to top management from a knowledge-based system.

Answer (D) is correct.
   REQUIRED: The item that is not a characteristic of business intelligence (BI).
   DISCUSSION: BI serves the needs of top management for managerial control and strategic planning. BI focuses on strategic (long-range) objectives and gives immediate information about a firm's critical success factors. BI is not a program for providing top management with advice and answers from a knowledge-based (expert) system.
   Answer (A) is incorrect. BI does focus on strategic objectives. **Answer (B) is incorrect.** BI gives immediate information about an organization's critical (strategic) success factors. **Answer (C) is incorrect.** BI often displays information in graphical format.

22. Which of the following can be discovered using a data-mining process?

A. Data structure.
B. Previously unknown information.
C. Artificial intelligence.
D. Standard query reporting.

Answer (B) is correct.
   REQUIRED: The item that can be discovered using a data-mining process.
   DISCUSSION: Data mining examines large amounts of data to discover patterns in the data (i.e., unexpected relationships among data). A classic example of the use of data mining is the discovery by convenience stores that diapers and beer often appear on the same sales transaction in the late evening. Thus, previously unknown information can be discovered using a data-mining process.
   Answer (A) is incorrect. Certain data structures, such as a relational data structure, can greatly facilitate the search for records. However, a data structure itself cannot be discovered using a data-mining process. **Answer (C) is incorrect.** Artificial intelligence (AI) is computer software designed to perceive, reason, and understand. AI attempts to imitate human decision making, which hinges on the combination of knowledge and intuition (i.e., remembering relationships between variables based on experience). AI cannot be discovered using a data-mining process. **Answer (D) is incorrect.** Similar to data mining, standard query reporting discovers queries within a database system. However, data mining will not discover standard query reporting itself.

Access the **Gleim CPA Premium Review System** featuring our SmartAdapt technology from your Gleim Personal Classroom to continue your studies. You will experience a personalized study environment with exam-emulating multiple-choice questions.

STUDY UNIT THIRTEEN
IT SOFTWARE, DATA, AND CONTINGENCY PLANNING

(26 pages of outline)

13.1	Software	381
13.2	Nature of Binary Data Storage	384
13.3	Data Management	386
13.4	Database Management Systems	391
13.5	Application Development and Maintenance	393
13.6	Business Resiliency	402

A computer's software consists of the sets of instructions, often called programs, that are executed by the hardware. Programs and data are stored in a computer in a series of ones and zeros, called binary code. The binary code is grouped into larger units of fields, records, and files. Files can be integrated into a database. When an organization acquires a new system, either by buying it or by creating it internally, a series of steps must be carefully followed to ensure that the system is stable and cost-effective. Business information systems are crucial to the continued existence of the modern organization; therefore, every entity must plan how it will continue processing in the case of an interruption to normal processing.

13.1 SOFTWARE

1. **Overview**

    a. Software refers to the programs (i.e., sets of computer instructions) that are executed by the hardware.

    b. Software can be described from two perspectives:

    1) Systems vs. application software and
    2) The programming language in which the software is written.

2. **Systems Software**

    a. Performs the fundamental tasks needed to manage computer resources. The three most common pieces of systems software are

    1) The **operating system**, which is the "traffic cop" of any computer system.

        a) The operating system negotiates the conversation between the computer's hardware, the application the user is running, and the data that the application is working with.
        b) Examples are Linux, Apple macOS, and Windows.

    2) **Utility programs**, which perform basic functions that are not particular to a certain application, such as anti-virus, file management, and network utilities.

    3) **Device driver programs**, which operate or control a particular type of device that is attached to the computer. For example, a printer requires a printer driver to function.

3. **Application Software**

    a. Programs designed to help people perform an activity that can manipulate text, numbers, graphics, or a combination of these elements.

        1) Examples of applications found on personal computers include word processors, spreadsheets, graphics, and databases.
        2) Applications found on dedicated servers are payroll, human resources, purchasing, accounts payable, general ledger, treasury, etc.

4. **Machine Learning**

    a. A form of artificial intelligence that enables computers, when exposed to new data, to learn, grow, change, and develop by themselves.

    b. The ability to adapt to new data by learning from previous computations and identifying trends in order to produce reliable results. Examples include

        1) Friend suggestions on Facebook based on connections with other friends
        2) Hulu listing movies and shows the user might like based on viewing patterns
        3) Amazon listing purchase suggestions based on previous purchase behavior

5. **Blockchain**

    a. In the late 15th century, the double-entry system and the general ledger were revolutionary concepts that changed commerce. The invention of the double-entry system allowed third parties to track the finances of a business. The firm maintains a private ledger of its transactions while a trusted independent party (i.e., the auditor) confirms the ledger's accuracy.

    b. A blockchain is an innovative technology that has the potential to revolutionize accounting.

        1) A **blockchain** is a type of digital database (or ledger) that provides proof of who owns what at any moment in time as each transaction has been added to the ledger.

            a) The **ledger** is encrypted, public, and distributed widely for anyone to view. Every transaction makes the ledger grow larger.

        2) The term "blockchain" derives from the nature of a ledger. It contains the history of every transaction and forms a **chain**. When a change of ownership occurs, a new "block" is linked to the original chain to extend the chain.

            a) A **block** is the current part of a blockchain. It records some or all of the recent transactions and becomes a permanent database in the blockchain.
            b) A blockchain is primarily used to verify financial transactions within digital currencies (i.e., cryptocurrency transactions), though it is possible to digitize, code, and insert practically any document into the blockchain.

                i) **Cryptocurrency** is a digital asset designed to be a medium of exchange using cryptography (encryption) to secure the transactions, control the creation of additional units of the currency, and verify the transfer of funds. Bitcoin is a type of cryptocurrency.

SU 13: IT Software, Data, and Contingency Planning

      c) Owning a **bitcoin**, which uses a blockchain, indicates that the owner has a piece of information (or a block) within the blockchain ledger.

      d) The blockchain enables each coin owner to transfer an amount of currency directly to any other party connected to the same network without the need for a financial institution to mediate the exchange.

3) The essence of a blockchain is that many third parties confirm that each new block is legitimate and part of the new complete chain. Each time a proposed transaction is entered in the form of a new block, **miners** authenticate the transaction by agreeing on what the current version of the blockchain should be.

      a) In the example of Bitcoin, the miners are paid with some new bitcoin for verifying the new chain.

4) A key element of a blockchain is a **consensus mechanism**. It is a cryptographic process that takes control of the ledger from one party (i.e., the firm) and allows it to be examined and maintained by multiple independent entities. No centralized organization controls the chain. The official chain is agreed upon by a majority of the participating miners.

      a) For example, blockchains and consensus mechanisms are similar to Google Docs. Users in a Google Doc can edit documents at the same time, and the most updated versions are always available. All users of the document must agree to any changes made.

5) In accounting, a company's ledger can be edited secretly, and the changes may not necessarily be obvious. But, using blockchain technology, edits to a chain are immediately obvious because the majority of third parties have a different chain. Thus, if anyone tries to alter a previous transaction, the public can see that the ledger has been tampered with and is presumably wrong. In the future, blockchain technology could potentially remove bookkeeping from private firms and turn it over to the public.

      a) Falsifying records using a blockchain requires changing over 50% of the peer chains in the ecosystem. In the case of Bitcoin, which has over 10,000 miners at any moment in time, a bad actor would have to control many computers to alter a chain.

STOP & REVIEW

You have completed the outline for this subunit.
Study multiple-choice questions 1 and 2 on page 407.

13.2 NATURE OF BINARY DATA STORAGE

1. **Binary Storage**

    a. Digital computers store all information in binary format, that is, as a pattern of ones and zeros. This makes arithmetic operations and true/false decisions at the lowest level extremely straightforward.

    b. A **bit** is either 0 or 1 (off or on) in binary code. Bits can be strung together to form a binary (i.e., base 2) number.

EXAMPLE 13-1	Bit
	0

    c. A **byte** is a group of bits, most commonly eight. A byte can be used to signify a character (a number, letter of the alphabet, or symbol, such as a question mark or asterisk).

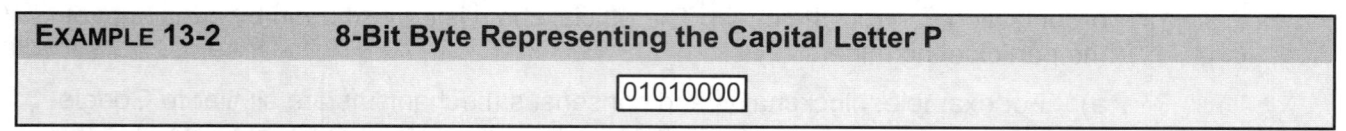

EXAMPLE 13-2	8-Bit Byte Representing the Capital Letter P
	01010000

    1) Quantities of bytes are measured with the following units:

    $$1,024\ (2^{10})\ bytes = \textbf{1 kilobyte} = 1\ KB$$
    $$1,048,576\ (2^{20})\ bytes = \textbf{1 megabyte} = 1\ MB$$
    $$1,073,741,824\ (2^{30})\ bytes = \textbf{1 gigabyte} = 1\ GB$$
    $$1,099,511,627,776\ (2^{40})\ bytes = \textbf{1 terabyte} = 1\ TB$$

    Authors' Note: Please do not memorize these numbers. The intent is to demonstrate the difference in size for each unit to help you better grasp these terms.

    d. A **field**, also called a data item, is a group of bytes. The field contains a unit of data about some entity, e.g., a composer's name.

EXAMPLE 13-3	Field
	Paul Hindemith

e. A **record** is a group of fields. All the fields contain information pertaining to an entity, e.g., a specific performance of an orchestral work.

EXAMPLE 13-4   Record

| Paul Hindemith | Violin Concerto | Chicago Symphony | Claudio Abbado | Josef Suk |

f. A **file** is a group of records. All the records in the file contain the same pieces of information about different occurrences, e.g., performances of several orchestral works.

EXAMPLE 13-5   File

Paul Hindemith	Violin Concerto	Chicago Symphony	Claudio Abbado	Josef Suk
Gustav Mahler	Das Lied von der Erde	New York Philharmonic	Leonard Bernstein	Dietrich Fischer-Dieskau
Bela Bartok	Piano Concerto No. 2	Chicago Symphony	Sir Georg Solti	Etsko Tazaki
Arnold Schoenberg	Gurrelieder	Boston Symphony	Seiji Ozawa	James McCracken
Leos Janacek	Sinfonietta	Los Angeles Philharmonic	Simon Rattle	None
Dmitri Shostakovich	Symphony No. 6	San Francisco Symphony	Kazuhiro Koizumi	None
Carl Orff	Carmina Burana	Berlin Radio Symphony	Eugen Jochum	Gundula Janowitz

STOP & REVIEW

You have completed the outline for this subunit.
Study multiple-choice questions 3 through 5 beginning on page 407.

13.3 DATA MANAGEMENT

1. **Flat Files**

    a. The oldest file structure is the flat file, in which all records are stored sequentially, one after the other, as on a reel of magnetic tape.

    　1) To find a certain record, every record on the tape has to be searched and bypassed until the desired one is found.

    　2) Also, the ways in which a user can perform a search on a flat file are extremely limited.

    b. As computers became more powerful, new ways of storing data became possible and permitted much more flexibility in searching and updating.

    　1) Databases allow companies to save information (data) in one place instead of having hundreds of specific files with similar information.

2. **Hierarchical Databases**

    a. The hierarchical, or tree, database model was a major development in file organization. Instead of the records being strung out one after the other, they form "branches" and "leaves" extending from a "root."

    　1) Note that the customer's address is stored only once in a hierarchical database; in a flat file, the address had to be stored every time the customer placed an order.

    　2) Another feature of the tree file structure is that every "parent" record can have multiple "child" records, but each child can have only one parent.

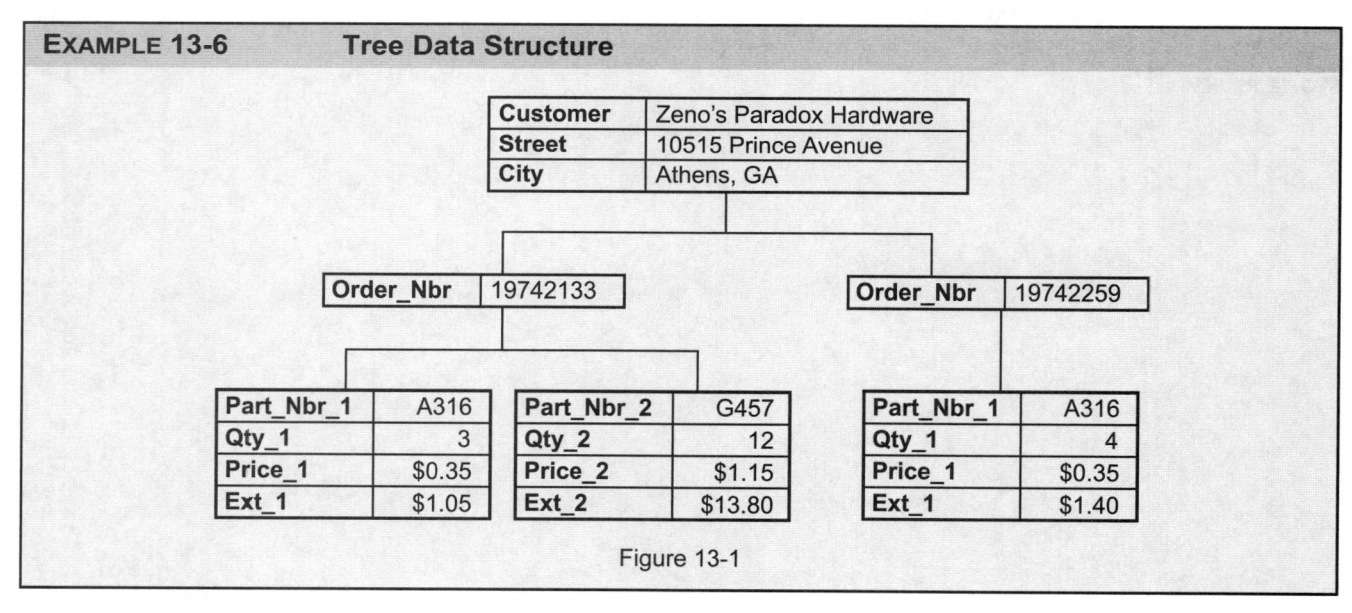

EXAMPLE 13-6　　　　**Tree Data Structure**

Customer	Zeno's Paradox Hardware
Street	10515 Prince Avenue
City	Athens, GA

Order_Nbr	19742133

Order_Nbr	19742259

Part_Nbr_1	A316
Qty_1	3
Price_1	$0.35
Ext_1	$1.05

Part_Nbr_2	G457
Qty_2	12
Price_2	$1.15
Ext_2	$13.80

Part_Nbr_1	A316
Qty_1	4
Price_1	$0.35
Ext_1	$1.40

Figure 13-1

---

    b. One customer has many orders, but each order can only be assigned to one customer.

    　1) The tree structure improves speed and storage efficiency for related data; for example, a parent record consisting of a customer may directly index the child records containing the customer's orders.

    　2) However, adding new records is much more difficult than with a flat file. In a flat file, a new record is simply inserted whole in the proper place. In a tree structure, the relationships between the parent and child records must be maintained.

3. **Relational Databases**
   a. Relational databases are the most commonly used databases today. They are used by companies such as Microsoft, Oracle, IBM, Amazon, and Google.
   b. When a relational database is used, a file like the one depicted in Example 13-7 on the next page is stored with every record in a single row and every column containing a value that pertains to that record.
      1) In database terminology, a file stored this way is called a table, and the columns are called attributes.
   c. Structured Query Language (SQL) is a database management language used to manage data in a relational database.
   d. Each data element is stored as few times as necessary. This reduction in data redundancy is accomplished through a process called **normalization**.
   e. Two features that make the relational data structure stand out are cardinality and referential integrity.
      1) **Cardinality** refers to how close a given data element is to being unique.
         a) A data element that can only exist once (a unique element) in a given table has high cardinality. In Example 13-7 on the next page, Customer_Nbr has high cardinality in the Customer Table.
         b) A data element that is not unique in a given table but that has a restricted range of possible values is said to have normal cardinality. Order_Nbr in the Order Table is an example.
         c) A data element that has a very small range of values is said to have low cardinality. A field that can contain only male/female or true/false is an example.
      2) **Referential integrity** means that for a record to be entered in a given table, there must already be a record in some other table(s).
         a) For example, the Order Table in Example 13-7 on the next page cannot contain a record where the part number is not already present in the Parts Table.
   f. Mandatory fields require an answer to be inputted in the field before updating the database can commence.
   g. The tremendous advantage of a relational data structure is that searching for records is greatly facilitated.
      1) For example, a user can specify a customer and see all the parts that customer has ordered, or the user can specify a part and see all the customers who have ordered it. Such queries were extremely resource-intensive, if not impossible, under older data structures.

h. A group of tables built following the principles of relational data structures is referred to as a **relational database**.

1) If the rules of cardinality, referential integrity, etc., are not enforced, a database will no longer be relational. To aid in the exceedingly challenging task of enforcing these rules, database management systems have been developed.

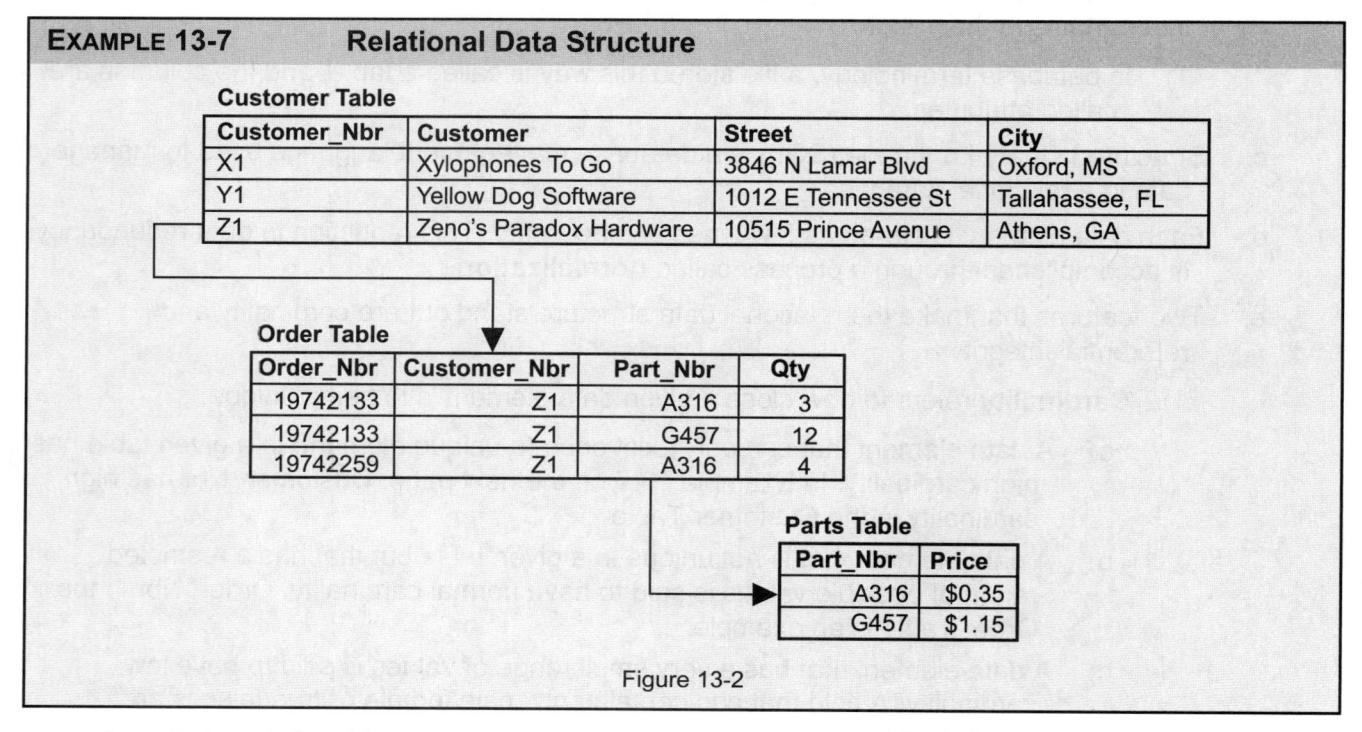

EXAMPLE 13-7   **Relational Data Structure**

Customer Table

Customer_Nbr	Customer	Street	City
X1	Xylophones To Go	3846 N Lamar Blvd	Oxford, MS
Y1	Yellow Dog Software	1012 E Tennessee St	Tallahassee, FL
Z1	Zeno's Paradox Hardware	10515 Prince Avenue	Athens, GA

Order Table

Order_Nbr	Customer_Nbr	Part_Nbr	Qty
19742133	Z1	A316	3
19742133	Z1	G457	12
19742259	Z1	A316	4

Parts Table

Part_Nbr	Price
A316	$0.35
G457	$1.15

Figure 13-2

---

i. Data relationships are situations in which records (rows) in relational database tables are referred to by records in different tables.

1) Records are referenced to each other by pairs of primary and foreign keys.

a) **Primary keys** are the data fields in a table that uniquely identify the records in the table.

b) **Foreign keys** are the data fields or groups of data fields that reference a primary key in another table.

c) Thus, the key in the referencing table is the foreign key, and that in the referenced table is the primary key.

2) In Example 13-7 above, the Part_Nbr attribute in the Parts Table uniquely identifies each part and is thus a primary key. The Part_Nbr attribute in the Order Table references the primary key in the Parts Table. Therefore, it is the foreign key in the Order-Parts relationship. Similarly, the Customer_Nbr attribute in the Customer Table is a primary key, and the Customer_Nbr attribute in the Order Table is the foreign key in the Customer-Order relationship.

3) If two tables use the same primary key, either primary key can be used as the foreign key to reference the other.

4) The primary key and the foreign key can be referenced using the following three relationships:

   a) **One-to-one.** A foreign key can only link to one primary key, and vice versa.
   b) **One-to-many.** A foreign key can link to many primary keys, but a primary key can only link to one foreign key.
   c) **Many-to-many.** A foreign key can link to many primary keys, and a primary key can also link to many foreign keys.

EXAMPLE 13-8   Data Relationships

Data relationships can be illustrated using a publisher-book-author-biography relationship.

1. Each book can have only one publisher, while one publisher may publish more than one book. Thus, the publisher-book relationship is a one-to-many relationship.
2. Each book can have more than one author, and each author can write more than one book. Thus, the book-author relationship is a many-to-many relationship.
3. Each author can have only one set of biographies written about them, and each set of biographies can only belong to one author. Thus, the author-biography relationship is a one-to-one relationship.

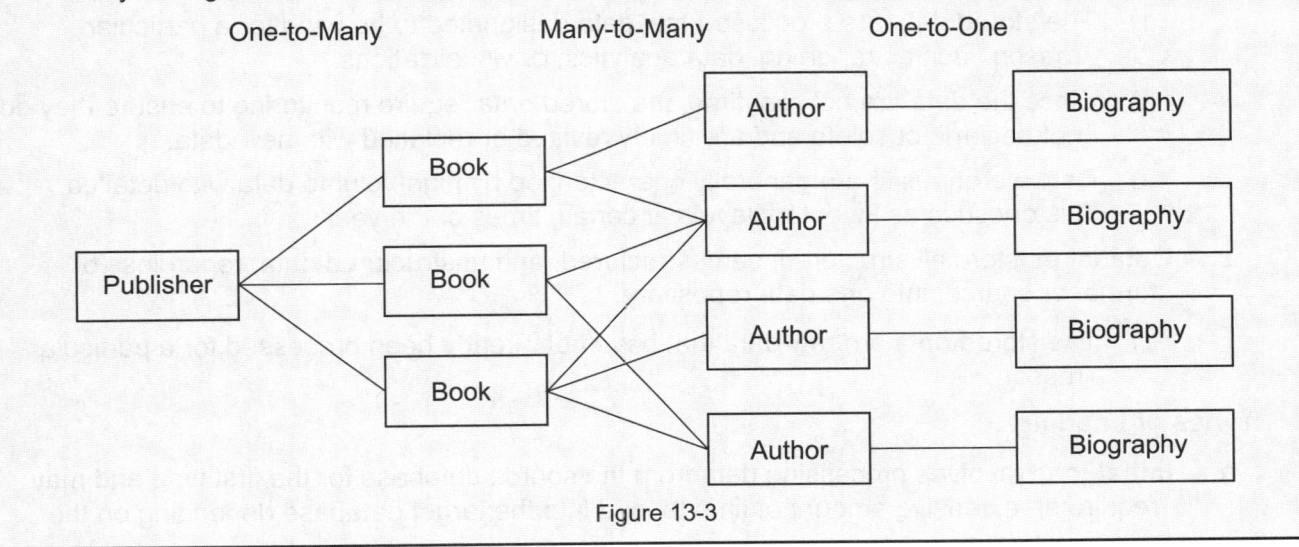

One-to-Many   Many-to-Many   One-to-One

Publisher — Book — Author — Biography (diagram)

Figure 13-3

---

4. **Non-Relational Databases**

   a. Provide a mechanism for storage and retrieval of data other than the tabular relations used in relational databases.

      1) The data structures used by NoSQL databases do not require joining tables, which allow operations to run faster.
      2) They capture all kinds of data (e.g., structured, semi-structured, and unstructured data), which allows for a flexible database that can easily and quickly accommodate any new type of data and is not disrupted by content structure changes.
      3) They provide better horizontal scaling (described in Subunit 13.5) to clusters of machines, which solves the problem when the number of concurrent users skyrockets for applications that are accessible via the Web and mobile devices.
      4) Storing all information in one document, in contrast to joining multiple tables together (relational), results in less code to write, debug, and maintain.

5. **Object-Oriented Databases**
    a. An object-oriented database is a response to the need to store graphics and multimedia applications used by object-oriented programming languages such as C++ and Java.
        1) Translating this type of data into tables and rows is difficult. However, in an object-oriented database, the objects can be stored along with the executable code that directs the behavior of the object.
6. **Loading Data into the Final Target Databases**
    a. **Operational data store repositories** store real-time (i.e., current) data to perform simple data analytics.
        1) The real-time data are constantly updated.
        2) The repositories are generally characterized by low-volume data with limited to no history, such as sales and the sales price right now.
    b. **Data warehouses** store structured, scrutinized data in one data repository for the purpose of performing complex data analytics.
        1) The stored data are processed raw data designated to be used for a particular reason such as reporting, data analytics, or visualizations.
        2) Since the data are not real-time, the stored data require monitoring to ensure they do not become obsolete and are timely revised or replaced with new data.
        3) Data warehouses are generally characterized by high-volume data with detailed history such as inventory levels at certain times of the year.
    c. **Data lakes** store all structured, semi-structured, and unstructured data, regardless of format or source, into one data repository.
        1) The stored data are raw data that have not already been processed for a particular reason.
7. **Types of Loading**
    a. **Initial load** involves processing data from the source database for the first time and may require an extensive amount of time to load into the target database depending on the volume of data.
    b. **Incremental load** is representative of the process of loading data from the source database to the target database subsequent to the initial load such as new or revised data.
        1) Maintenance of load dates is vital to ensure only new or revised data are loaded to the target database after the most recent data extraction from the source database.
    c. **Full refresh** completely wipes out data of one or multiple sections (i.e., tables, fields, etc.) of the database and loads new data into the database.
8. **Load verification** involves examining the data before and after loading to the target database to determine whether the data completely loaded and whether any discrepancies exist.

You have completed the outline for this subunit.
Study multiple-choice questions 6 through 8 beginning on page 408.

STOP & REVIEW

13.4 DATABASE MANAGEMENT SYSTEMS

1. **Overview**

    a. A **database management system (DBMS)** is an integrated set of software tools superimposed on the data files that helps maintain the integrity of the underlying database.

       1) Database management systems make the maintenance of vast relational databases practical. Without the sophisticated capabilities of database management systems, enforcing the rules that make the database relational would be overwhelmingly time-consuming.

    b. A DBMS allows programmers and designers to work independently of the physical and logical structure of the database.

       1) Before the development of DBMSs, programmers and systems designers needed to consider the logical and physical structure of the database with the creation of every new application. This was extremely time-consuming and therefore expensive.

       2) With a DBMS, the physical structure of the database can be completely altered without having to change any of the programs using the data items. Thus, different users may define their own views of the data (called subschemas).

          a) A **database view** is a virtual database table with which the user can query data. The view can be read-only or updatable.

             i) Insert, update, and delete commands can be executed on updatable views.

    c. Those in the IT function responsible for dealing with the DBMS are the database administrator (DBA) and the data administrator (DA).

       1) A DBA is responsible for supporting and maintaining the DBMS; a DA is responsible for maintaining the data within the database.

EXAMPLE 13-9   Available DBMSs

The three most prominent commercial relational database management systems are Oracle, IBM DB2, and Microsoft Access. A well-known open-source DBMS is MySQL.

2. **Aspects of a DBMS**
    a. A particular database's design, called its **schema**, consists of the layouts of the tables and the constraints on entering new records. To a great extent, a DBMS automates the process of enforcing the schema.
    b. Two vital parts of any DBMS are
        1) A **data definition language (DDL)**, which allows the user to specify how the tables will look and what kinds of data elements they will hold, and
        2) A **data manipulation language (DML)**, with which the DBMS retrieves, adds, deletes, or modifies records and data elements.
            a) Both of these roles are commonly fulfilled in the current generation of database management systems by SQL or one of its many variants.
    c. The **data dictionary** contains the physical and logical characteristics of every data element in a database. The data dictionary contains the size, format, usage, meaning, and ownership of every data element as well as what persons, programs, reports, and functions use the data element.
    d. A DBMS can maintain a **distributed database**, meaning one that is stored in two or more physical sites.
        1) In the **replication** (or **snapshot**) technique, the DBMS duplicates the entire database and sends it to multiple locations. Changes are periodically copied and similarly distributed.
        2) In the **fragmentation** (or **partitioning**) method, specific records are stored where they are most needed. For example, a financial institution may store a particular customer's data at the branch where (s)he usually transacts his or her business. If the customer executes a transaction at another branch, the pertinent data are retrieved via communications lines.
        3) **Concurrent update control (concurrency control)** is a database control that prevents simultaneous accessing or altering of data by multiple users. For example, two customers are booking train tickets for the last available seat. The first customer clicks "purchase" a few seconds before the second customer. The system will lock out the second customer so that only the first customer obtains the ticket.

STOP & REVIEW

You have completed the outline for this subunit.
Study multiple-choice questions 9 through 11 on page 410.

13.5 APPLICATION DEVELOPMENT AND MAINTENANCE

1. **Organizational Needs Assessment**
    a. The organizational needs assessment is a detailed process of study and evaluation of how information systems can be deployed to help an organization meet its goals. The steps in the assessment are as follows:
        1) Determine whether current systems support organizational goals
        2) Determine needs unmet by current systems
        3) Determine the capacity of current systems to accommodate projected growth
            a) Horizontal scalability increases computing capacity by adding to the number of computers in the system. For example, if the current system consists of five computers and five computers are added, the quantity of computers is doubled and computing capacity is increased.
            b) Vertical scalability increases computing capacity by adding more power (e.g., RAM or processors) to the existing computer(s) instead of adding to the number of computers.
        4) Propose a path for information systems deployment to achieve organizational goals within budgetary constraints

2. **Business Process Design**
    a. A business process is a flow of actions performed on goods and/or information to accomplish a discrete objective. Examples include hiring a new employee, recruiting a new customer, and filling a customer order.
    b. Some business processes are contained entirely within a single functional area; e.g., hiring a new employee is performed by the human resources function.
        1) Other processes cross functional boundaries. Filling a customer order requires the participation of the sales department, the warehouse, and accounts receivable.
    c. In the early days of automated system deployment, hardware and software were very expensive. Systems tended to be designed to serve a single process or even a single functional area. Tremendous gains in processing power and storage capacity have made integrated systems, i.e., those that combine multiple processes, the norm.
        1) The most advanced of these are enterprise resource planning (ERP) systems.
    d. The automation of a process, or the acquisition of an integrated system, presents the organization with an opportunity for business process reengineering.
        1) **Business process reengineering** involves a complete rethinking of and changes to how business functions are performed to provide value to customers, that is, **radical** innovation instead of mere improvement and a disregard for current jobs, hierarchies, and reporting relationships.
        2) **Process automation** refers to the automation of business processes and performance of routine tasks by mimicking the actions of humans. It involves **incremental** changes to how existing tasks are handled, as opposed to business process reengineering, which involves a complete and radical redesign of all tasks.
        3) A company may require its outsourced call center to automate the customer service with artificial intelligence. This is an example of process automation. The company may instead operate the call center itself and automate with artificial intelligence. This is an example of business process reengineering that involves both **disintermediation** and process automation. (If a new intermediary is added to the existing one, it is an example of **reintermediation**.)

3. **Participants in Business Process Design**
    a. The everyday functioning of a business process affects multiple stakeholder groups.
        1) Input from each group should be considered in the design of the process. However, some stakeholders will be more active participants.
    b. End-users are generally the drivers of a new or redesigned process.
        1) For example, the customers of a multi-division business may have open accounts with several of the divisions. Whenever a customer calls, the customer relations department would like the most up-to-date customer balance information for all divisions to be accessible at once.
        2) Although the motivation for the new process begins with the customer service department, personnel in various divisions, as well as the central IT function, will be affected.
    c. Because IT pervades every aspect of operations in a modern organization, the **IT steering committee** or information systems steering committee must study each request for a new process and either approve or deny it.
        1) Typical members of the steering committee include the chief information officer and the head of systems development from the IT function. Executive management from each division is also represented.
        2) The committee members have an understanding of the interactions of the organization's current systems and how they will affect and be affected by new or redesigned business processes.
        3) Roles and responsibilities of the IT steering committee include
            a) Engaging high-level management in planning information systems (e.g., build or buy) and setting IT policies
            b) Facilitating the implementation of information systems
            c) Overseeing the control over the information systems
    d. Once a new process or system has been approved, a project team is assembled, consisting of representatives of the end-users who requested it and the IT personnel who will design and build the software components that will support it.
    e. Upper management supports process design by making sufficient resources available to ensure successful implementation of the new process.
    f. If the new process or system crosses organizational boundaries, as is the case with electronic data interchange (EDI) systems, external parties, such as representatives of the vendor or customer businesses, are participants.

4. **Build or Buy**
    a. When an organization acquires a new system by purchasing from an outside vendor, contract management personnel oversee the process. The future end-users of the system, as well as IT personnel, are also involved, drawing up specifications and requirements.
        1) However, when a new system is to be created in-house, planning and managing the development process is one of the IT function's most important tasks.
        2) The needs of the end-users must be balanced with budget and time constraints; the decision to use existing hardware vs. the purchase of new platforms must be weighed.

SU 13: IT Software, Data, and Contingency Planning

    b. Extensive time and resources are devoted to the creation of a new application, and generally, the more important the business function being automated, the more complex the application is. Thus, having a well-governed methodology for overseeing the development process is vital.

        1) A **killer application** is one that is so useful that it may justify widespread adoption of a new technology.

    c. Both the end-users who specified the new system's functionality and IT management who are overseeing the development process must approve progress toward the completion of the system at the end of each of the stages described beginning below. This requirement for ongoing review and approval of the project is a type of implementation control.

5. **Systems Development Life Cycle (SDLC)**

> **SUCCESS TIP:** The AICPA has asked many questions concerning the systems development life cycle (SDLC). One of their favorite questions asks candidates to select the correct phase to which an activity belongs. Be sure you know each of the phases and the activities that occur in each.

    a. The SDLC approach is the traditional methodology applied to the development of large, highly structured application systems. A major advantage of the life-cycle approach is enhanced management and control of the development process. SDLC consists of the following five stages:

        1) **Systems strategy**, which requires understanding the organization's needs.

        2) **Project initiation** is the process by which systems proposals are assessed.

        3) **In-house development** is generally chosen for unique information needs.

        4) **Commercial packages** are generally chosen for common needs rather than developing a new system from scratch.

        5) **Maintenance and support** involves ensuring the system accommodates changing user needs.

    b. Once the need for a new system has been recognized, the seven steps of the SDLC proceed as depicted in the diagram below (portions of the phases can overlap).

Systems Development Life Cycle

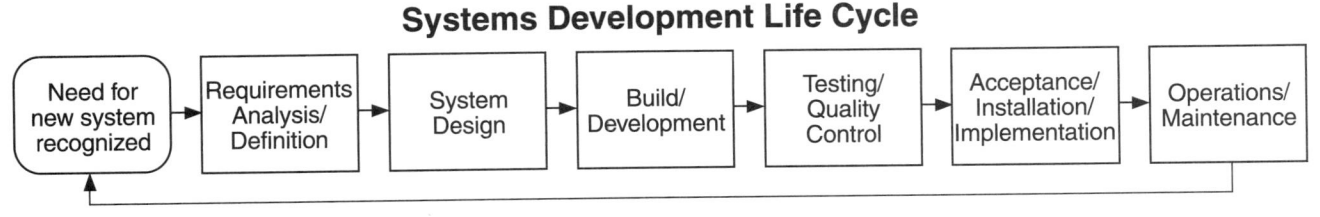

Need for new system recognized → Requirements Analysis/Definition → System Design → Build/Development → Testing/Quality Control → Acceptance/Installation/Implementation → Operations/Maintenance (with feedback loop back to "Need for new system recognized")

Figure 13-4

    c. Note that the feedback gathered during the maintenance of a system provides information for developing the next generation of systems, hence the name **life cycle**.

6. The **phases and component steps of the traditional SDLC** can be described as follows:
    a. **Initiation, Feasibility, and Planning**
        1) The SDLC begins with recognizing there is a need for a new system, gaining an understanding of the situation to determine whether it is feasible to create a solution, and formulating a plan.
    b. **Requirements Analysis and Definition**
        1) A formal proposal for a new system is submitted to the IT steering committee, describing the need for the application and the business function(s) that it will affect.
        2) Feasibility studies are conducted to determine
            a) What technology the new system will require
            b) What economic resources must be committed to the new system
            c) How the new system will affect current operations
        3) The steering committee gives its go-ahead for the project.
    c. **System Design**
        1) Logical design consists of mapping the flow and storage of the data elements that will be used by the new system and the new program modules that will constitute the new system.
            a) Data flow diagrams, system interface diagrams, and structured flowcharts are commonly used in this step.
            b) Some data elements may already be stored in existing databases. Good logical design ensures that they are not duplicated.
        2) Physical design involves planning the specific interactions of the new program code and data elements with the hardware platform (existing or planned for purchase) on which the new system will operate.
            a) Systems analysts are heavily involved in these two steps.
    d. **Build and Development**
        1) The actual program code and database structures that will be used in the new system are written.
        2) Hardware is acquired and physical infrastructure is assembled.
    e. **Testing and Quality Control**
        1) Testing is performed during system development with the intent of identifying errors or other defects. The job of testing is an iterative process because when one error is corrected, it can illuminate other errors or even create new ones. Testing determines whether the system
            a) Meets the requirements that guided its design and development.
            b) Responds correctly to all kinds of inputs.
            c) Performs its functions within an acceptable time.
            d) Achieves the general result its stakeholders desire.

SU 13: IT Software, Data, and Contingency Planning

2) Although the number of possible tests to apply is almost limitless, developers cannot test everything. All testing uses strategy to select tests that are feasible for the available time and resources.

   a) Combinatorial test design identifies the minimum number of tests needed to get the coverage developers desire.

3) The following are various methods available to test systems:

   a) **Static testing** examines the program's code and its associated documentation through reviews, walkthroughs, or inspections but does not require the program to be executed.

   b) **Dynamic testing** involves executing programmed code with a given set of test cases.

   c) **White-box testing** tests internal structures or workings of a program, as opposed to the functionality exposed to the end-user.

   d) **Black-box testing** treats the software as a "black box," examining functionality without any knowledge of the source code.

   e) **Gray-box testing** involves having knowledge of internal data structures and algorithms for purposes of designing tests, while executing those tests at the user, or black-box, level.

   f) **Sandbox testing** involves the use of a virtual testing environment that mimics the actual operating environment. Testing performed in the sandbox will not affect the live server.

4) There are four levels of tests:

   a) **Unit testing** refers to tests that verify

      i) The functionality of a specific section of code and

      ii) The handling of data passed between various units or subsystems components.

   b) **Integration testing** is any type of software testing that seeks to verify the interfaces between components against a software design. Integration testing works to expose defects in the interfaces and interaction between integrated components (modules).

   c) **System testing**, or end-to-end testing, tests a completely integrated system to verify that the system meets its requirements.

   d) **Acceptance testing** is conducted to determine whether the systems meets the organization's needs and is ready for release.

f. **Acceptance, Installation, and Implementation**
   1) User acceptance testing is the final step before placing the system in live operation.
      a) IT must demonstrate to the users that submitted the original request that the system performs the desired functionality.
      b) Once the users are satisfied with the new system, they acknowledge formal acceptance and implementation begins.
   2) Four strategies for converting to the new system can be used.
      a) With **parallel** conversion, the old and new systems both are run at full capacity for a given period.
         i) This strategy is the safest since the old system is still producing output (in case there are major problems with the new system), but it is also the most expensive and time-consuming.
      b) With **direct changeover** (direct cutover) conversion, the old system is shut down and the new one takes over processing at once.
         i) This is the least expensive and time-consuming strategy, but it is also the riskiest because the new system cannot be reverted to the original.
      c) Under **pilot** conversion, one branch, department, or division at a time is fully converted to the new system.
         i) Experience gained from each installation is used to benefit the next one. One disadvantage of this strategy is the extension of the conversion time.
      d) In some cases, **phased** conversion is possible. Under this strategy, one function of the new system at a time is placed in operation.
         i) For instance, if the new system is an integrated accounting application, accounts receivable could be installed, then accounts payable, cash management, materials handling, etc.
         ii) The advantage of this strategy is allowing the users to learn one part of the system at a time.
   3) Training and documentation are critical.
      a) The users must feel comfortable with the new system and have plenty of guidance available, either hard copy or online.
      b) Documentation consists of more than just operations manuals for the users. Layouts of the program code and database structures must also be available to the programmers for modifying and maintaining the system.

g. **Operations and Maintenance**

1) After a system becomes operational, the system should be monitored to ensure ongoing performance and continuous improvement.
2) Systems follow-up or post-audit evaluation is a subsequent review of the efficiency and effectiveness of the system after it has operated for a substantial time (e.g., 1 year).
    a) Post-audit evaluation can also help evaluate the decisions made by the steering committee by comparing the expectations with the actual results.

7. **Program Change Control**

    a. Over the life of an application, users are constantly asking for changes. The process of managing these changes is referred to as systems maintenance, and the relevant controls are called **program change controls**.
    b. Once a change to a system has been approved, the programmer should save a copy of the production program in a test area of the computer (a sandbox).
        1) Only in emergencies, and then only under close supervision, should a change be made directly to the production version of a computer program.
        2) The IT function must be able to revert to a prior version immediately if unexpected results are encountered during an emergency change.
    c. The programmer makes the necessary changes to this copy of the program's source code.
    d. The programmer transforms the changed program into a form that the computer can execute. The resulting machine-ready program is referred to as object code, or more precisely, executable code.
    e. Once the programmer has the executable version of the changed program, (s)he tests it to see if it performs the new task as expected.
        1) This testing process absolutely must not be run against production data. A special set of test data must be available for running test programs.
    f. The programmer demonstrates the new functionality for the user who made the request.
        1) Either the user accepts the new program or the programmer goes back and makes further changes.
    g. Once the program is in a form acceptable to the user, the programmer moves it to a holding area.
        1) Programmers (except in emergencies) should never be able to put programs directly into production.
    h. The programmer's supervisor reviews the new program, approves it, and authorizes its move into production, which is generally carried out by operations personnel.
        1) The compensating control is that operators generally lack the programming knowledge to put fraudulent code into production.

8. **Rapid Application Development**

    a. **Prototyping** is an alternative approach to application development. Prototyping involves creating a working model of the system requested, demonstrating it for the user, obtaining feedback, and making changes to the underlying code.

        1) This process repeats through several iterations until the user is satisfied with the system's functionality.

        2) Formerly, this approach was derided as being wasteful of resources and tending to produce unstable systems, but with vastly increased processing power and high-productivity development tools, prototyping can, in some cases, be an efficient means of systems development.

    b. **Computer-aided software engineering (CASE)** applies the computer to software design and development.

        1) It provides the capacity to

            a) Maintain on the computer all of the system documentation, e.g., data flow diagrams, data dictionaries, and pseudocode (structured English);

            b) Develop executable input and output screens; and

            c) Generate program code in at least skeletal form.

        2) Thus, CASE facilitates the creation, organization, and maintenance of documentation and permits some automation of the coding process.

9. **End-User vs. Centralized Computing**

    a. End-user computing (EUC) involves user-created or user-acquired systems that are maintained and operated outside of traditional information systems controls.

        1) Certain environmental control risks are more likely in EUC. They include copyright violations that occur when unauthorized copies of software are made or when the software is installed on multiple computers.

        2) Unauthorized access to application programs and related data is another concern. EUC lacks physical access controls, application-level controls, and other controls found in mainframe or networked environments.

        3) Moreover, EUC may not have adequate backup, recovery, and contingency planning. The result may be an inability to recreate the system or its data.

    b. Program development, documentation, and maintenance also may lack the centralized control found in larger systems.

        1) The risk of allowing end-users to develop their own applications is decentralization of control. These applications may not be reviewed by independent outside systems analysts and may not be created using a formal development methodology. They also may not be subject to appropriate standards, controls, and quality assurance procedures.

2) When end-users create their own applications and files, private information systems in which data are largely uncontrolled may proliferate. Systems may contain the same information, but EUC applications may update and define the data in different ways. Thus, determining the location of data and ensuring data consistency become more difficult.

3) The auditor should determine that EUC applications contain controls that allow users to rely on the information produced. Identification of applications is more difficult than in a traditional centralized computing environment because few people know about and use them. There are three steps that the auditor should take:

   a) The first step is to discover their existence and their intended functions. One approach is to take an organization-wide inventory of major EUC applications. An alternative is for the auditors and the primary user (a function or department) to review major EUC applications.

   b) The second step is risk assessment. EUC applications that represent high-risk exposures are chosen for audit, for example, because they support critical decisions or are used to control cash or physical assets.

   c) The third step is to review the controls included in the applications chosen in the risk assessment.

c. In a personal computer setting, the user is often the programmer and operator. Thus, the protections provided by the segregation of duties are eliminated.

d. The audit trail is diminished because of the lack of history files, incomplete printed output, etc.

e. In general, available security features for stand-alone machines are limited compared with those in a network.

f. Responsibility for the control of EUC exists at the organizational, departmental, and individual user levels. The end-user is directly responsible for the security of equipment. Acquisition of hardware and software, taking equipment inventories, and strategic planning of EUC are organizational- and departmental-level responsibilities.

STOP & REVIEW

You have completed the outline for this subunit.
Study multiple-choice questions 12 through 16 beginning on page 411.

13.6 BUSINESS RESILIENCY

1. **Overview**

    a. The information security goal of data availability is primarily the responsibility of the IT function.

    b. Business resiliency (also known as contingency planning) is the name commonly given to this activity.

    1) **Disaster recovery** is the process of resuming normal information processing operations after the occurrence of a major interruption.

    2) **Business continuity** is the continuation of business by other means during the period in which computer processing is unavailable or less than normal. **Business Continuity Management (BCM)** prepares the organization for IT failures through planning.

    c. Plans must be made for two major types of contingencies: those in which the data center is physically available and those in which it is not.

    1) Examples of the first type of contingency are (a) power failure; (b) random intrusions, such as viruses; and (c) deliberate intrusions, such as hacking incidents. The organization's physical facilities are sound, but immediate action is required to continue normal processing.

    2) The second type of contingency is much more serious. It is caused by disasters, such as floods, fires, hurricanes, or earthquakes. An occurrence of this type requires an alternate processing facility.

2. **Backup and Rotation**

    a. Periodic backup and offsite rotation of computer files is the most basic part of any disaster recovery or business continuity plan.

    b. An organization's data are more valuable than its hardware.

    1) Hardware can be replaced for a price, but each organization's data are unique and indispensable to operations. If they are destroyed, they cannot be replaced. For this reason, periodic backup and rotation are essential.

    c. A typical backup routine duplicates the data files and application programs. The frequency with which backups are created should depend on how often the data changes and the value of the data.

    1) A **mirror backup** is a full copy of the data and programs of the primary computer such that they can run on another system and immediately take up the place of the affected system. This is commonly used by organizations such as e-commerce companies and banks, whose downtime is costly.

    2) A **full backup** duplicates all data files and application programs. While this is the most effective and secure alternative, it is also the most costly and time-consuming.

    3) An **incremental backup** duplicates only the data that have changed since the previous backup. For example, if a full backup was performed on January 1, an incremental backup on January 2 would only contain the data that changed between January 1 and January 2. Similarly, an incremental backup on January 3 would only contain the data changed between January 2 and January 3.

4) A **differential backup** duplicates only the data that have changed since the previous full backup. For example, if a full backup was performed on January 1, a differential backup on January 2 would only contain the data that changed between January 1 and January 2. However, a differential backup on January 3 would contain the data that changed between January 1 and January 3.

5) Due to the larger sizes of backup files, a differential backup is generally slower than an incremental backup. However, due to its fragmented nature, an incremental backup takes longer than a differential backup to restore.

d. The offsite location must be temperature- and humidity-controlled and guarded against physical intrusion. Just as important, it must be far enough away from the site of main operations not to be affected by the same natural disaster. Adequate backup is useless if the files are not accessible or have been destroyed.

3. **Risk Assessment Steps**

   a. Identify and prioritize the organization's critical applications.

      1) Not all of an organization's systems are equally important. The firm must decide which vital applications it simply cannot do business without and in what order they should be brought back into operation.

   b. Determine the minimum recovery time frames and minimum hardware requirements.

      1) How long will it take to reinstall each critical application, and what platform is required? If the interruption has been caused by an attack, such as a virus or hacker, how long will it take to isolate the problem and eliminate it from the system?

   c. Develop a recovery plan.

4. **Disaster Recovery Plan (DRP)**

   a. Disaster recovery is the process of regaining access to data (e.g., hardware, software, and records), communications, work areas, and other business processes.

   b. Thus, a DRP that is established and tested must be developed in connection with the business continuity plan. It should describe IT recovery strategies, including details about procedures, vendors, and systems.

      1) Detailed procedures must be updated when systems and business processes change. The following are examples of items addressed by the DRP:

         a) Data center
         b) Applications and data needed
         c) Servers and other hardware
         d) Communications
         e) Network connections
         f) IT infrastructure (e.g., log-on services and software distribution)
         g) Remote access services
         h) Process control systems
         i) File rooms
         j) Document management systems

c. The following are considerations for choosing DRP strategies:
1) The DRP should be based on the business impact analysis.
2) The recovery abilities of critical service providers must be assessed.
3) The recovery of IT components often must be combined to recover a system.
4) Service providers (internal and external) must furnish recovery information, such as their
   a) Responsibilities,
   b) Limitations,
   c) Recovery activities,
   d) Recovery time and point objectives, and
   e) Costs.
5) Strategies for components may be developed independently. The objective is the best, most cost-effective solution that (a) allows user access and (b) permits components to work together, regardless of where systems are recovered.
6) Security and compliance standards must be considered.

5. **Contingencies with Data Center Available**

   a. The purchase of backup electrical generators protects against power failures. These can be programmed to begin running automatically as soon as a dip in electric current is detected. This practice is widespread in settings such as hospitals, where 24-hour availability is crucial.

   b. Attacks such as viruses and denial-of-service (DoS) require a completely different response. The system must be brought down "gracefully" to halt the spread of the infection. The IT staff must be well trained in the nature of the latest virus threats to know how to isolate the damage and bring the system back to full operation.

6. **Contingencies with Data Center Unavailable**

   a. The most extreme contingency is a disaster that makes the organization's main facility uninhabitable. To prepare for these cases, organizations seek alternate processing facilities.

   b. An **alternate processing facility** is a physical location maintained by the organization or an outside contractor for the purpose of providing processing facilities for customers in case of a disaster.
   1) The recovery center, like the off-site storage location for backup files, must be far enough away from the main facility that it is not affected by the same natural disaster. Usually, organizations contract for backup facilities in another city.
   2) Once processing is no longer possible at the principal site, the backup files are retrieved from the secure storage location and taken to the recovery center.

   c. Recovery centers include hot sites, warm sites, and cold sites. Organizations determine which facility is best by calculating the tradeoff between the cost of the contract and the cost of downtime.
   1) A **hot site** is a fully operational processing facility that is immediately available. It usually involves the use of a **mirror backup**. The organization generally contracts with a service provider.
      a) For a fee, the service provider agrees to have a hardware platform and communications lines substantially identical to the organization's ready for use 24 hours a day, 365 days a year.

- b) This solution is the least risky and most expensive.
- c) Any contract for a hot site must include a provision for periodic testing.
    - i) The service provider agrees to a window of time in which the organization can declare a fake disaster, load its backup files onto the equipment at the hot site, and determine how long it takes to resume normal processing.
- 2) A **cold site** is a shell facility with sufficient electrical power, environmental controls, and communications lines to permit the organization to install its own newly acquired equipment.
    - a) On an ongoing basis, this solution is much less expensive.
    - b) However, the time to procure replacement equipment can be weeks or months. Also, emergency procurement from equipment vendors can be very expensive.
- 3) A **warm site** is a compromise between a cold and hot site, combining features of both.
    - a) Resources are available at the site but may need to be configured to support the production system.
    - b) Some data may need to be restored.
    - c) Typical recovery time may range from several days to a week.

7. **Other Technologies for Restoration of Processing**
    a. Fault-tolerant computer systems (formerly called fail-soft systems) have additional hardware and software as well as a backup power supply. A fault-tolerant computer has additional processing capability and disk storage. This technology is used for mission-critical applications that cannot afford to suffer downtime.
        1) The technology that permits fault tolerance is the redundant array of inexpensive (or independent) disks, or RAID. It is a group of multiple hard drives with special software that allows for data delivery along multiple paths. If one drive fails, the other disks can compensate for the loss.
    b. High-availability computing is used for less critical applications because it provides for a short recovery time rather than the elimination of recovery time.

8. **Business Continuity Management (BCM) Overview**
    a. The objective of BCM is to restore critical processes and to minimize financial and other effects of a disaster or business disruption.
    b. BCM is the third component of an emergency management program. Its time frame is measured in hours and days if not weeks. The other components are
        1) Emergency response, the goal of which is lifesaving, safety, and initial efforts to limit the effects of a disaster to asset damage. Its time frame is measured in hours if not minutes.
        2) Crisis management, the focus of which is managing communications and senior management activities. Its time frame is measured in days if not hours.

9. **Elements of BCM**
    a. **Management Support**
        1) Management must assign adequate resources to prepare, maintain, and practice a business continuity plan.
    b. **Risk Assessment and Mitigation**
        1) The entity must (a) define credible risk events (threats), (b) assess their effects, and (c) develop risk mitigation strategies.
    c. **Business Impact Analysis**
        1) This analysis identifies business processes necessary to functioning in a disaster and determines how soon they should be recovered.
        2) The organization (a) identifies critical processes, (b) defines the recovery time objective and the recovery point objective for processes and resources, and (c) identifies the other parties (e.g., vendors and other divisions of the organization) and physical resources (e.g., critical equipment and records) needed for recovery.
            a) A recovery time objective is the duration of time and service level within which a process must be restored. A recovery point objective is the amount of data the organization can afford to lose.
            b) The cost of a recovery solution ordinarily increases as either objective decreases.
    d. **Business Recovery and Continuity Strategy**
        1) A crucial element of business recovery is the existence of a comprehensive and current disaster recovery plan, which addresses the actual steps, people, and resources required to recover a critical business process. (Disaster recovery plans were discussed in greater detail earlier.)
        2) The organization plans for
            a) **Alternative staffing** (e.g., staff remaining at the site, staff at another site, or staff of another organization),
            b) **Alternative sourcing** (e.g., use of nonstandard products and services, use of diverse suppliers, outsourcing to organizations that provide standard services, or reciprocal agreements with competitors),
            c) **Alternative work spaces** (e.g., another organization facility, remote access with proper security, or a commercial recovery site), and
            d) The **return to normal operations** (e.g., entry of manually processed data, resolution of regulatory and financial exceptions, return of borrowed equipment, and replenishment of products and supplies).
    e. **Awareness, Exercises, and Maintenance**
        1) Education and awareness (including training exercises) are vital to BCM and execution of the business continuity plan.
        2) The BCM capabilities and documentation must be maintained to ensure that they remain effective and aligned with business priorities.

You have completed the outline for this subunit.
Study multiple-choice questions 17 through 19 on page 413.

QUESTIONS

13.1 Software

1. A computer program processes payrolls. The program is a(n)

- A. Operating system.
- B. Application program.
- C. Report generator.
- D. Utility program.

Answer (B) is correct.
REQUIRED: The term associated with a computer program used to perform a business function.
DISCUSSION: Application programs are written to solve specific user problems; that is, they perform the ultimate computer functions required by system users. Thus, a program designed to process payroll is an application program.
Answer (A) is incorrect. An operating system is a set of programs used by the CPU to control operations.
Answer (C) is incorrect. A report generator is a component of a database management system that produces customized reports using data stored in the database. **Answer (D) is incorrect.** Utility programs are standardized subroutines that can be incorporated into other programs.

2. Cryptocurrency transactions are recorded on a(n)

- A. Private blockchain ledger.
- B. Distributed ledger.
- C. General ledger.
- D. Encryption ledger.

Answer (B) is correct.
REQUIRED: Where cryptocurrency transactions are recorded.
DISCUSSION: Cryptocurrency is a digital asset designed to be a medium of exchange using cryptography to secure the transactions, control the creation of additional units of the currency, and verify the transfer of funds. Cryptocurrency transactions are often recorded in a blockchain ledger. Owning a bitcoin (i.e., a type of cryptocurrency) indicates that the owner has a piece of information (or a block) within the blockchain ledger.
Answer (A) is incorrect. Blockchain ledgers are encrypted, public, and shared among participants.
Answer (C) is incorrect. A general ledger is a traditional accounting ledger. Cryptocurrency transactions are not recorded on general ledgers. **Answer (D) is incorrect.** Encryption ledger is a nonsense term.

13.2 Nature of Binary Data Storage

3. Computers understand codes that represent letters of the alphabet, numbers, or special characters. These codes require that data be converted into predefined groups of binary digits. Such chains of digits are referred to as

- A. Registers.
- B. ASCII code.
- C. Input.
- D. Bytes.

Answer (D) is correct.
REQUIRED: The term for the chains of digits that a computer is capable of understanding.
DISCUSSION: A byte is a grouping of bits that can define one unit of data, such as a letter or an integer.
Answer (A) is incorrect. A register is a location within the CPU where data and instructions are temporarily stored. **Answer (B) is incorrect.** ASCII (American Standard Code for Information Interchange) is the coding convention itself. **Answer (C) is incorrect.** Input is the data placed into processing (noun) or the act of placing the data into processing (verb).

4. Based only on the database file excerpt presented below, which one of the fields or combinations of fields is eligible for use as a key?

Column I	Column II	Column III	Column IV	Column V	Column VI
Florida	Sopchoppy	G9441	6	02/06/2017	$1823.65
Georgia	Hahira	H5277	2	02/06/2017	$412.01
Iowa	Clear Lake	B2021	1	02/06/2017	$6606.53
Iowa	Clear Lake	C2021	14	02/06/2017	$178.90
Kansas	Lawrence	A1714	2	02/06/2017	$444.28
Georgia	Milledgeville	A1713	1	02/06/2017	$195.60

A. Column I and Column II in combination.
B. Column I and Column V in combination.
C. Column III alone.
D. Column IV and Column V in combination.

Answer (C) is correct.
REQUIRED: The field or combination thereof that could be used as a key.
DISCUSSION: Some field or combination of fields on each record is designated as the key. The essence of a key is that it contains enough information to uniquely identify each record; i.e., there can be no two records with the same key. Of the choices presented, only Column III by itself uniquely identifies each record.
Answer (A) is incorrect. Column I and Column II in combination do not uniquely identify each record.
Answer (B) is incorrect. Column I and Column V in combination do not uniquely identify each record.
Answer (D) is incorrect. Column IV and Column V in combination do not uniquely identify each record.

5. Which one of the following correctly depicts the hierarchy of storage commonly found in computerized databases, from least complex to most complex?

A. Byte, field, file, record.
B. Byte, field, record, file.
C. Field, byte, record, file.
D. Field, byte, file, record.

Answer (B) is correct.
REQUIRED: The correct hierarchy in computerized databases.
DISCUSSION: A byte is a group of bits (binary 1s and 0s). A field is a group of bytes. A record is a group of fields. A file is a group of records.
Answer (A) is incorrect. A record is less complex than a file. **Answer (C) is incorrect.** A byte is less complex than a field. **Answer (D) is incorrect.** A byte is less complex than a field, and a record is less complex than a file.

13.3 Data Management

6. A database has three record types: (1) for suppliers, a type that contains a unique supplier number, a supplier name, and a supplier address; (2) for parts, a type that contains a unique part number, a part name, a description, and a location; and (3) for purchases, a type that contains a unique supplier number referencing the supplier number in the supplier record, a part number referencing the part number in the part record, and a quantity. This database has a

A. Single flat-file structure.
B. Hierarchical structure.
C. Relational structure.
D. Network structure.

Answer (C) is correct.
REQUIRED: The structure of the described database.
DISCUSSION: A relational structure organizes data in conceptual tables. One relation (a table or file) can be joined with (related to) another by the DBMS without pointers or linked lists if each contains one or more of the same fields (also known as columns or attributes). This database has a relational structure because it includes no links that are not contained in the data records themselves.
Answer (A) is incorrect. Each record type corresponds to a flat file, but there are multiple structures rather than a single flat-file structure. **Answer (B) is incorrect.** A hierarchical structure would have a tree structure with embedded links instead of explicit data values. **Answer (D) is incorrect.** A network structure would have bidirectional pointers instead of explicit data values.

7. Of the following, the greatest advantage of a database (server) architecture is that

A. Data redundancy can be reduced.
B. Conversion to a database system is inexpensive and can be accomplished quickly.
C. Multiple occurrences of data items are useful for consistency checking.
D. Backup and recovery procedures are minimized.

Answer (A) is correct.
REQUIRED: The greatest advantage of a database architecture.
DISCUSSION: Data organized in files and used by the organization's various application programs are collectively known as a database. In a database system, storage structures are created that render the applications programs independent of the physical or logical arrangement of the data. Each data item has a standard definition, name, and format, and related items are linked by a system of pointers. The programs therefore need only specify data items by name, not by location. A database management system handles retrieval and storage. Because separate files for different application programs are unnecessary, data redundancy can be substantially reduced.
Answer (B) is incorrect. Conversion to a database is often costly and time-consuming. **Answer (C) is incorrect.** A traditional flat-file system, not a database, has multiple occurrences of data items. **Answer (D) is incorrect.** Given the absence of data redundancy and the quick propagation of data errors throughout applications, backup and recovery procedures are just as critical in a database as in a flat-file system.

8. A database is

A. Essential for the storage of large data sets.
B. A collection of related files.
C. A real-time system.
D. A network of computer terminals.

Answer (B) is correct.
REQUIRED: The true statement about a database.
DISCUSSION: The use of a database system significantly reduces redundancy of stored data in a system. Data in a standardized form are ideally entered once into integrated files and then used for any and all related applications. The database is usually built to serve multiple applications. Consequently, the data are independent of particular applications and greater flexibility in meeting unanticipated demands is possible. The database approach also allows for better access by users and for more rapid updating of information.
Answer (A) is incorrect. The need for a database arises more from the multiplicity of applications than from the quantity of data stored. **Answer (C) is incorrect.** A database system need not provide immediate (real-time) responses. **Answer (D) is incorrect.** A database is an integrated, centralized group of files.

13.4 Database Management Systems

9. One advantage of a database management system (DBMS) is

A. Each organizational unit takes responsibility and control for its own data.
B. The cost of the data processing department decreases as users are now responsible for establishing their own data handling techniques.
C. A decreased vulnerability as the database management system has numerous security controls to prevent disasters.
D. The independence of the data from the application programs, which allows the programs to be developed for the user's specific needs without concern for data capture problems.

Answer (D) is correct.
REQUIRED: The advantage of a DBMS.
DISCUSSION: A fundamental characteristic of databases is that applications are independent of the database structure; when writing programs or designing applications to use the database, only the name of the desired item is necessary. Programs can be developed for the user's specific needs without concern for data capture problems. Reference can be made to the items using the data manipulation language, after which the DBMS takes care of locating and retrieving the desired items. The physical or logical structure of the database can be completely altered without having to change any of the programs using the data items. Only the schema requires alteration.
Answer (A) is incorrect. Each organizational unit develops programs to use the elements of a broad database. **Answer (B) is incorrect.** Data handling techniques are still the responsibility of the data processing department. It is the use of the data that is departmentalized. **Answer (C) is incorrect.** The DBMS is not necessarily safer than any other database system.

10. Which of the following is a **false** statement about a database management system application environment?

A. Data are used concurrently by multiple users.
B. Data are shared by passing files between programs or systems.
C. The physical structure of the data is independent of user needs.
D. Data definition is independent of any one program.

Answer (B) is correct.
REQUIRED: The false statement about data in a DBMS environment.
DISCUSSION: In this kind of system, applications use the same database. There is no need to pass files between applications.
Answer (A) is incorrect. The advantage of a DBMS is that data can be used concurrently by multiple users. **Answer (C) is incorrect.** When a DBMS is used, the physical structure of the data is independent of user needs. **Answer (D) is incorrect.** When a DBMS is used, the data are defined independently of the needs of any one program.

11. The function of a data dictionary is to

A. Mark the boundary between two consecutive transactions.
B. Describe and share information about objects and resources.
C. Specify systems users.
D. Specify privileges and security rules for objects and resources.

Answer (B) is correct.
REQUIRED: The function of a data dictionary.
DISCUSSION: A data dictionary is an organized and shared collection of information about the objects and resources used by the information system (IS) organization to deliver or exchange information internally and externally.
Answer (A) is incorrect. The database management system log contains checkpoint records that mark the boundary between two consecutive transactions. **Answer (C) is incorrect.** Specification of system users is a function of the security features of a DBMS. **Answer (D) is incorrect.** The data control language specifies privileges and security rules for objects and resources.

13.5 Application Development and Maintenance

12. An insurance firm that follows the systems development life cycle concept for all major information system projects is preparing to start a feasibility study for a proposed underwriting system. Some of the primary factors the feasibility study should include are

A. Possible vendors for the system and their reputation for quality.
B. Exposure to computer viruses and other intrusions.
C. Methods of implementation, such as parallel or cutover.
D. Technology and related costs.

Answer (D) is correct.
REQUIRED: The primary factors the feasibility study should include.
DISCUSSION: The feasibility study should consider the activity to be automated, the needs of the user, the type of equipment required, the cost, and the potential benefit to the specific area and the company in general. Thus, technical feasibility and cost are determined during this stage.
Answer (A) is incorrect. Possible vendors for the system and their reputation for quality would be determined after the feasibility study. **Answer (B) is incorrect.** Exposure to computer viruses and other intrusions is part of the information requirements phase. **Answer (C) is incorrect.** Methods of implementation, such as parallel or cutover, would be determined during the implementation and operations stage.

13. Which of the following is a component of the system design step in the traditional systems development life cycle?

A. Mapping the storage of the data elements.
B. Determining whether the system meets stakeholder expectations.
C. Assembling physical infrastructure.
D. Submitting a formal proposal to the IT steering committee.

Answer (A) is correct.
REQUIRED: The component of the system design step in the traditional systems development life cycle.
DISCUSSION: Logical design, a component phase of system design, consists of mapping the flow and storage of the data elements that will be used by the new system and the new program modules that will constitute the new system. System design also includes physical design.
Answer (B) is incorrect. During the testing and quality control phase, whether the system achieves the general results its stakeholder desire is determined. **Answer (C) is incorrect.** During the build and development phase, hardware is acquired and physical infrastructure is assembled. **Answer (D) is incorrect.** During the requirements analysis and definition phase, a formal proposal for a new system is submitted to the IT steering committee, describing the need for the application and the business function(s) that it will affect.

14. A benefit of using computer-aided software engineering (CASE) technology is that it can ensure that

A. No obsolete data fields occur in files.
B. Users become committed to new systems.
C. All programs are optimized for efficiency.
D. Data integrity rules are applied consistently.

Answer (D) is correct.
REQUIRED: The benefit of CASE.
DISCUSSION: CASE is an automated technology (at least in part) for developing and maintaining software and managing projects. A benefit of using CASE technology is that it can ensure that data integrity rules, including those for validation and access, are applied consistently across all files.
Answer (A) is incorrect. Obsolete data fields must be recognized by developers or users. Once recognized, obsolete data fields can be treated consistently in CASE procedures. **Answer (B) is incorrect.** Using CASE will not ensure user commitment to new systems if they are poorly designed or otherwise do not meet users' needs. **Answer (C) is incorrect.** Although it has the potential to accelerate system development, CASE cannot ensure that all programs are optimized for efficiency. In fact, some CASE-developed modules may need to be optimized by hand to achieve acceptable performance.

15. The process of learning how the current system functions, determining the needs of users, and developing the logical requirements of a proposed system is referred to as

A. Systems maintenance.
B. Systems analysis.
C. Systems feasibility study.
D. Systems design.

Answer (B) is correct.
REQUIRED: The term referring to the process of learning how a system functions, determining the needs of users, and developing the logical requirements of a proposed system.
DISCUSSION: A systems analysis requires a survey of the existing system, the organization itself, and the organization's environment to determine (among other things) whether a new system is needed. The survey results determine not only what, where, how, and by whom activities are performed but also why, how well, and whether they should be done at all. Ascertaining the problems and informational needs of decision makers is the next step. The systems analyst must consider the entity's key success variables (factors that determine its success or failure), the decisions currently being made and those that should be made, the factors important in decision making (timing, relation to other decisions, etc.), the information needed for decisions, and how well the current system makes those decisions. Finally, the systems analysis should establish the requirements of a system that will meet user needs.
Answer (A) is incorrect. Maintenance is the final stage of the life cycle in that it continues throughout the life of the system; maintenance includes the redesign of the system and programs to meet new needs or to correct design flaws. **Answer (C) is incorrect.** The systems feasibility study does not involve the process of learning how the current system works. **Answer (D) is incorrect.** Systems design is the process of developing a system to meet specified requirements.

16. The process of monitoring, evaluating, and modifying a system as needed is referred to as

A. Systems analysis.
B. Systems feasibility study.
C. Systems maintenance.
D. Systems implementation.

Answer (C) is correct.
REQUIRED: The term for the process of monitoring, evaluating, and modifying a system.
DISCUSSION: Systems maintenance must be undertaken by systems analysts and applications programmers continuously throughout the life of a system. Maintenance is the redesign of the system and programs to meet new needs or to correct design flaws. Ideally, these changes should be made as part of a regular program of preventive maintenance.
Answer (A) is incorrect. Systems analysis is the process of determining user problems and needs, surveying the organization's present system, and analyzing the facts. **Answer (B) is incorrect.** A feasibility study determines whether a proposed system is technically, operationally, and economically feasible. **Answer (D) is incorrect.** Systems implementation involves training and educating system users, testing, conversion, and follow-up.

13.6 Business Resiliency

17. Which of the following best describes the primary reason that organizations develop contingency plans for their computer-based information systems operations?

A. To ensure that they will be able to process vital transactions in the event of a disaster.
B. To ensure the safety of important records.
C. To help hold down the cost of insurance.
D. To plan for sources of capital for recovery from any type of disaster.

Answer (A) is correct.
REQUIRED: The primary reason that organizations develop contingency plans for their IS operations.
DISCUSSION: Contingency plans must be drafted so that the organization will be able to resume normal processing following a disaster.
Answer (B) is incorrect. The safety of records is a secondary reason. **Answer (C) is incorrect.** The reduction of insurance costs is a secondary reason. **Answer (D) is incorrect.** Planning for sources of capital is seldom included in disaster recovery planning.

18. Which of the following procedures would an entity most likely include in its computer disaster recovery plan?

A. Develop an auxiliary power supply to provide uninterrupted electricity.
B. Store duplicate copies of critical files in a location away from the processing facility.
C. Maintain a listing of all entity passwords with the network manager.
D. Translate data for storage purposes with a cryptographic secret code.

Answer (B) is correct.
REQUIRED: The most likely procedure to follow in a computer disaster recovery plan.
DISCUSSION: Off-site storage of duplicate copies of critical files protects them from a fire or other disaster at the computing facility. The procedure is part of an overall disaster recovery plan.
Answer (A) is incorrect. The use of an uninterruptible power supply ensures continued processing rather than recovery from a disaster. **Answer (C) is incorrect.** Maintaining a safeguarded copy of passwords protects against loss of passwords by personnel. **Answer (D) is incorrect.** Encrypting stored data files protects them from unauthorized use.

19. If High Tech Corporation's disaster recovery plan requires fast recovery with little or no downtime, which of the following backup sites should it choose?

A. Hot site.
B. Warm site.
C. Cold site.
D. Quick site.

Answer (A) is correct.
REQUIRED: The type of backup facility that has fast recovery and little or no downtime.
DISCUSSION: A company uses a hot site backup when fast recovery is critical. The hot site includes all software, hardware, and other equipment necessary for a company to carry out operations. Hot sites are expensive to maintain and may be shared with other organizations with similar needs.
Answer (B) is incorrect. A warm site provides an intermediate level of backup and causes more downtime than a hot site. **Answer (C) is incorrect.** A cold site is a shell facility suitable for quick installation of computer equipment. Disaster recovery would take more time in a cold site than a hot site. **Answer (D) is incorrect.** There is no backup site called a quick site.

Access the **Gleim CPA Premium Review System** featuring our SmartAdapt technology from your Gleim Personal Classroom to continue your studies. You will experience a personalized study environment with exam-emulating multiple-choice questions.

STUDY UNIT FOURTEEN
IT NETWORKS AND ELECTRONIC COMMERCE

(12 pages of outline)

14.1	Networks and the Internet	415
14.2	Electronic Commerce	420
14.3	Electronic Data Interchange (EDI)	424

Huge gains in productivity have resulted from the networking of computers. The traditional ways of carrying on business have found new channels through electronic networking. Now, the use of encryption is required to make electronic messages secure. As a licensed CPA, you will need to know how computers communicate over networks so you can ascertain their vulnerability. This study unit introduces you to the types of communications between computers. The next study unit focuses on how to assess and quantify information risks.

14.1 NETWORKS AND THE INTERNET

1. **Mainframe Communication**

   a. Large mainframe computers dominated the electronic data processing field in its first decades. Mainframes were arranged so that all processing and data storage were done in a single, centralized location.

   b. Communication with the mainframe was accomplished with the use of dumb terminals, simple keyboard-and-monitor combinations with no processing power (i.e., no CPU) of their own.

2. **Increasing Decentralization**

   a. Improvements in technology have led to the increasing decentralization of information processing.

      1) The mainframe-style computer was the only arrangement available in the early days of data processing. International Business Machines (IBM) dominated the marketplace.

      2) Mainframes are still in use at large institutions, such as governments, banks, insurance companies, and universities. However, remote connections to mainframes are usually through personal computers rather than through dumb terminals. This is known as terminal emulation.

      3) As minicomputers evolved, the concept of distributed processing arose.

         a) **Distributed processing** involves the decentralization of processing tasks and data storage and assigning these functions to multiple computers, often in separate locations.

         b) This allowed for a drastic reduction in the amount of communications traffic because data needed locally could reside locally.

SUCCESS TIP: Be sure you are able to describe distributed processing and the types of networks. Recent exams have included questions on this topic.

3. **Local Area Networks (LANs)**
    a. The need to increase productivity led to the development of the local area network (LAN). A LAN is any interconnection between devices in a single office or building.
        1) Very small networks with few devices can be connected using a peer-to-peer arrangement, where every device is connected directly to every other. Peer-to-peer networks become increasingly difficult to administer with each added device.
    b. The most cost-effective and easy-to-administer arrangement for LANs uses the client-server model.
        1) Client-server networks differ from peer-to-peer networks in that the devices play more specialized roles. Client processes (initiated by the individual user) request services from server processes (maintained centrally).
        2) In a client-server arrangement, servers are centrally located and devoted to the functions that are needed by all network users.
            a) Examples include
                i) Mail servers (to handle electronic mail),
                ii) Application servers (to run application programs),
                iii) File servers (to store databases and make user inquiries more efficient),
                iv) Internet servers (to manage access to the Internet), and
                v) Web servers (to host websites).
            b) Whether a device is classified as a server is not determined by its hardware configuration, but rather by the function it performs. A simple personal computer can be a server.
        3) Technically, a client is any object that uses the resources of another object. Thus, a client can be either a device or a software program.
            a) In common usage, however, "client" refers to a device that requests services from a server. This understanding of the term encompasses anything from a powerful graphics workstation to a personal mobile device.
            b) A client device normally displays the user interface and enables data entry, queries, and the receipt of reports. Moreover, many applications, e.g., word processing and spreadsheet software, run on the client computer.
        4) The key to the client-server model is that it runs processes on the platform most appropriate to that process while attempting to minimize traffic over the network.
            a) This is commonly referred to as the three-tiered architecture of **client**, **application**, and **database**.
            b) Because of the specialized roles, client-server systems are often assembled with equipment from multiple vendors.
        5) Security for client-server systems may be more difficult than in a highly centralized system because of the numerous access points.
    c. Along with the increased convenience and flexibility of decentralization came new security risks.
        1) Unauthorized software can be easily installed on the network from a desktop computer. This exposes the organization to both viruses and liability for copyright violation.
        2) Important files stored on a local computer may not be backed up properly by the user.
        3) Applications written by users of local computers may not adhere to the standards of the organization, making data sharing difficult.

4. Classifying Networks by Geographical Extent and Function

a. The range of networking has expanded from the earliest form (two computers in the same room) to the global reach of the Internet.

b. A **local area network (LAN)** connects devices within a single office or home or among buildings in an office park. The key aspect here is that a LAN is owned entirely by a single organization.

   1) The LAN is the network familiar to office workers all over the world. In its simplest conception, it can consist of a few personal computers and a printer.

c. A **wide area network (WAN)** consists of a conglomerate of LANs over widely separated locations. The key aspect here is that a WAN can be either publicly or privately owned.

   1) One advantage of a WAN is the possibility of spreading the cost of ownership among multiple organizations.

      a) WANs come in many configurations. In its simplest conception, it can consist of a lone personal computer using a slow dial-up line to connect to an Internet service provider.

   2) Publicly owned WANs, such as the public telephone system and the Internet, are available to any user with a compatible device. The assets of these networks are paid for by means other than individually imposed user fees.

      a) Public-switched networks use public telephone lines to carry data. This arrangement is economical, but the quality of data transmission cannot be guaranteed and security is highly questionable.

   3) Privately owned WANs are profit-making enterprises. They offer fast, secure data communication services to organizations that do not wish to make their own large investments in the necessary infrastructure.

      a) **Value-added networks (VANs)** are private networks that provide their customers with reliable, high-speed, secure transmission of data.

         i) To compete with the Internet, these third-party networks add value by providing their customers with error detection and correction services, electronic mailbox facilities for electronic data interchange (EDI) purposes, EDI translation, and security for email and data transmissions.

      b) **Virtual private networks (VPNs)** emerged as a relatively inexpensive way to solve the problem of the high cost of leased lines.

         i) A company connects each office or LAN to a local Internet service provider and routes data through the shared, low-cost public Internet.

         ii) The success of VPNs depends on the development of secure encryption products that protect data while in transit.

   4) Intranets and extranets are types of WANs.

      a) An **intranet** permits sharing of information throughout an organization by applying Internet connectivity standards and web software (e.g., browsers) to the organization's internal network.

         i) An intranet addresses the connectivity problems faced by organizations that have many types of computers. Its use is restricted to those within the organization.

      b) An **extranet** consists of the linked intranets of two or more organizations, for example, of a supplier and its customers. It typically uses the public Internet as its transmission medium but requires a password for access.

5. **Aspects and Terminology of the Internet**

    a. The Internet was initially restricted to email and text-only documents. **Hypertext markup language (HTML)** is the authoring software language commonly used to create and link websites. It allows users to click on a word or phrase (a hyperlink) on their screens and have another document automatically be displayed.

    b. **Hypertext transfer protocol (HTTP)** allows hyperlinking across the Internet rather than on just a single computer. A browser allows users to read HTML from any brand of computer. This system became known as the World Wide Web (often simply called "the Web").

        1) As the use of HTML and its successor languages spread, it became possible to display rich graphics and stream audio and video in addition to text.

        2) **Extensible markup language (XML)** was developed by an international consortium and released in 1998 as an open standard (e.g., not owned or controlled by any one entity) usable with many programs and platforms.

            a) XML is used to organize and define data online.

            b) It can be used to extract and tag structured data from a database for transmission and subsequent use in other applications.

    c. Extensible business reporting language (XBRL) is derived from XML. XBRL is the standard for transmitting business data by using a uniform format to tag each piece of business and financial information being transmitted to the published **taxonomy**. The tags allow computers to automatically search for and assemble data so the data can be readily accessed and analyzed by accountants, investors, analysts, etc.

        1) The SEC requires firms to provide their financial statements in XBRL format (e.g., Form 10-K) because XBRL allows the statements to be directly exported to spreadsheets for analyses.

    d. Every resource on the Web has a unique address, made up of alphanumeric characters, periods, and forward slashes, called a **uniform resource locator** (URL). A URL is recognizable by any web-enabled device. An example is https://www.gleim.com.

        1) However, just because the address is recognizable does not mean its content is accessible to every user. Security is a major feature of any organization's website.

6. **Outsourcing Arrangements**

    a. **Cloud computing ("the cloud")** is a popular term relating to on-demand access to resources that are accessed on the Internet and shared by others.

        1) Advantages of using cloud computing include fast access to software, a reduced need for investment in IT infrastructure, and the ability to use "pay as you go" services.

        2) IT security in the cloud is potentially more difficult due to the convenience and ease of access to sensitive data provided by cloud computing services.

3) There are three primary cloud services:

   a) **Infrastructure-as-a-Service (IaaS).** Under IaaS, an organization outsources hardware for information storage, security, and other networking components to service providers.

   b) **Platform-as-a-Service (PaaS).** Besides hardware, PaaS provides an organization with operating systems, servers, and software tools to develop applications. An example of PaaS is Amazon Web Services (AWS).

   c) **Software-as-a-Service (SaaS).** SaaS allows organizations to get immediate access to and use applications hosted by the service providers. Google Apps such as Google Docs are an example of SaaS.

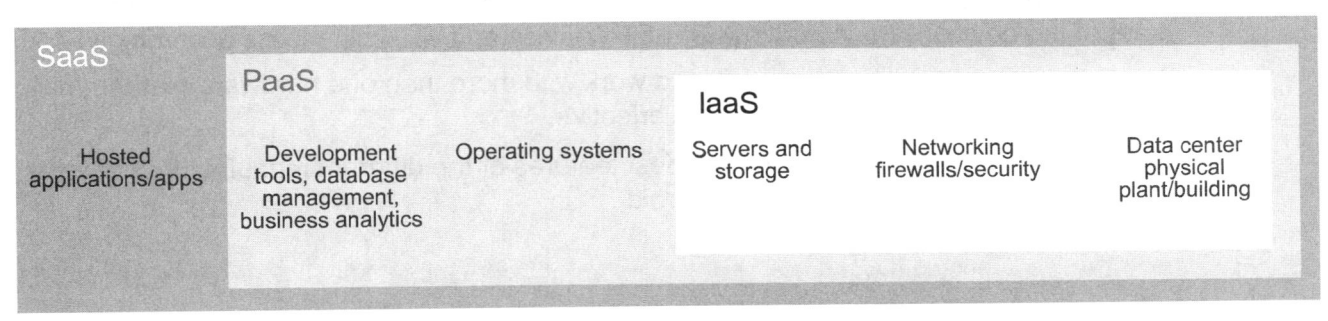

SaaS	PaaS		IaaS		
Hosted applications/apps	Development tools, database management, business analytics	Operating systems	Servers and storage	Networking firewalls/security	Data center physical plant/building

EXAMPLE 14-1   IaaS, PaaS, and SaaS

The differences between IaaS, PaaS, and SaaS can be visualized using a restaurant analogy. An entrepreneur is planning to open a restaurant. He has three options:

Option 1 (similar to IaaS): The entrepreneur leases a restaurant site equipped with dining tables, chairs, and cash registers. However, he needs to provide the ingredients, stove, oven, and other kitchen equipment and utensils to turn the ingredients into salable dishes.

Option 2 (similar to PaaS): The entrepreneur leases a restaurant site equipped with dining tables, chairs, and cash registers and is provided with a stove, oven, and other kitchen equipment and utensils. All he needs to provide are the ingredients and turn them into salable dishes.

Option 3 (similar to SaaS): The entrepreneur franchises a larger restaurant. The franchiser will provide all that the entrepreneur (franchisee) needs. The entrepreneur's only role will be to run the franchised restaurant.

4) Cloud computing has also benefited from the rise of smartphones and tablets.

   a) Because these devices have limited memory, personal data (e.g., pictures, contacts, etc.) may be stored on the cloud to be retrieved later so that available memory can be used for application software.

5) External service organizations providing cloud and other IT outsourcing services provide System and Organization Controls for Service Organization (SOC 2) reports to **user** organizations, which attest to whether controls address concerns associated with information security and privacy. SOC reports are discussed in Study Unit 2, Subunit 4.

b. An **application service provider (ASP)** is an entity that delivers computer software applications and other similar-type services to businesses and individuals over a network.

   1) Without using an ASP, similar applications and/or services would require installation on each computer.

   2) Examples of ASPs include Yahoo Mail, Gmail, Google Docs, and Microsoft Office 365.

7. **Mobile Technology**

   a. Mobile technology is essentially technology that is easily carried or moved. Examples of mobile devices include

      1) Smartphones
      2) Laptops
      3) Tablets
      4) Debit/credit card payment devices for smartphones

   b. Mobile devices generally are accessible via Wi-Fi, Bluetooth, data service providers (i.e., cellular phone providers), VANs, and VPNs.

   c. Security features for mobile devices have advanced to the point of detecting whether the user of the device is the actual owner of the device and will limit access accordingly.

   d. Cross-platform capabilities (i.e., ability to work with more than one hardware platform or operating system) are becoming more effective.

      1) Progressive web apps blend the best features of the different manufactured devices (i.e., Apple iOS and Google Android).

STOP & REVIEW

You have completed the outline for this subunit.
Study multiple-choice questions 1 through 9 beginning on page 427.

14.2 ELECTRONIC COMMERCE

SUCCESS TIP

Study Unit 2, Subunit 1, depicts the traditional flow of transactions in a business using flowcharts to display how documents are used to facilitate recording and integrate internal controls. In Study Units 14 and 15, that traditional flow is supplanted with electronic transmissions and related processing controls. You may find it helpful to review the traditional transaction flows presented in Study Unit 2, Subunit 1, as you consider this material.

1. **Overview**

   a. **E-business** is an umbrella term referring to all methods of conducting business electronically.

      1) This can include strictly internal communications as well as nonfinancial dealings with outside parties (e.g., contract negotiations).

   b. **E-commerce** is a narrower term referring to the conduct of financial transactions with outside parties electronically (e.g., the purchase and sale of goods and services).

      1) E-commerce introduces a new set of efficiencies into business relationships. Where orders previously were placed using a combination of phone calls and either mailed or faxed hard copy documents, e-commerce allows such transactions to take place entirely over the Internet.

2) There are six basic types of e-commerce:
   a) Business-to-Business (B2B) (e.g., IBM providing software and support to corporations)
   b) Business-to-Consumer (B2C) (e.g., corporations selling products to individual consumers)
   c) Consumer-to-Consumer (C2C) (e.g., transactions among consumers on Ebay)
   d) Consumer-to-Business (C2B) (e.g., individual consumers selling goods to corporations online)
   e) Business-to-Administration (B2A) (e.g., corporations hosting online marketing events for the government)
   f) Consumer-to-Administration (C2A) (e.g., consumers paying their taxes through a government website)
3) E-business and e-commerce are sometimes considered to be synonymous.

c. An extranet is one means of carrying on e-commerce.
   1) Extranets rely on the established communications protocols of the Internet. Thus, the expensive, specialized equipment needed for electronic data interchange (EDI) is unnecessary.
   2) Firewalls, which can be hardware- or software-based, provide security.
   3) The extranet approach is based on less formal agreements between the trading partners than in EDI and requires the sending firm to format the documents into the format of the receiving firm.

2. **Security and Reliability of E-Commerce**
   a. Because of the reduced level of human involvement in e-commerce, new security and reliability concerns arise.
   b. Specific concerns include the following:
      1) The transacting parties must be correctly identified, a process known as **authentication**. IDs and passwords are the most common tools for authentication.
      2) The circumstances in which a binding agreement can be made must be agreed to; in other words, who (or what system) is authorized to place (or promise to fill) an order? This is especially important in B2B applications, when entire production runs and large amounts of money are at stake.
      3) The confidentiality and integrity of information transmitted electronically must be maintained. Encryption is the most useful tool for this purpose.
      4) A reliable record of the transaction must be preserved such that disputes can be resolved and audits can be performed.
      5) Potential customers must be able to trust listed prices and discounts.
      6) Payment data must be verifiable.
      7) Both parties' systems must be robust; i.e., they are up and running at all times. This is usually aided by a mirror backup and hot sites in case of disaster.

3. **Business-to-Business (B2B) E-Commerce**
    a. B2B can be used to speed up the order and fulfillment process.
        1) A manufacturer in need of raw materials can initiate the transaction using the Internet or the vendor's extranet.
        2) The process can be further automated by establishing an EDI arrangement, in which the buyer's purchasing system automatically places an order with the vendor when inventories reach a predetermined level.
            a) The partners must have
                i) A common electronic document format and
                ii) A pre-existing agreement under which such orders will be accepted and filled without human intervention.
    b. **Benefits of B2B** include
        1) Reduced purchasing costs
            a) Purchasing products online saves time, and electronically processing an order simplifies the ordering process.
        2) Increased market efficiency
            a) By using the Internet, companies have easy access to price quotes from various suppliers. Buyers are more likely to get a better price, given the increased number of suppliers.
        3) Greater market intelligence
            a) B2B provides producers with better insights into the demand levels in any given market.
        4) Decreased inventory levels
            a) Companies can make better use of their inventory and raw materials. The Internet allows companies using just-in-time (JIT) manufacturing techniques to achieve better control of their operations, for example, by more precise coordination of delivery of raw materials. It also allows companies to use less working capital to do the same amount of work, which allows those funds to be invested elsewhere.
    c. The overriding principle of online B2B is that it can make companies more efficient.
        1) Increased efficiency means lower costs, which is a goal that interests every company. Thus, the potential of B2B online commerce is enormous.

4. **Business-to-Consumer (B2C) E-Commerce**
    a. B2C is one of the fastest growing segments of the economy. Consumers can order a vast array of merchandise from the comfort of their homes or mobile devices.
        1) B2C is almost exclusively conducted via the Internet.
        2) Traditional retailers have expanded their reach with B2C, and some firms use the Internet as their sole communication channel with customers.
    b. Many of the same benefits accrue to businesses as in the B2B model with reduced costs and increased efficiency.
        1) Many of the same security issues, such as authorization, also apply, but on a smaller scale. Also, the vendor need not concern itself with the IT infrastructure on the customer's end.

5. **Social Media**
    a. Social media is the interaction among people in virtual communities where they can share information and ideas.
        1) People access these virtual communities via platforms, apps, and websites that facilitate user interaction.
            a) Examples include Twitter, Facebook, LinkedIn, Instagram, and Snapchat.
        2) Sharing personal information over a virtual platform allows people to remain in contact, even if they are not physically close to each other.
    b. The spread and advancement of mobile technology has allowed people to stay regularly connected to their social networks.
        1) By embracing social media, many companies have been able to connect with their customers and the market on a more personal basis, increasing the rate of growth of B2C.
            a) This can be done in the form of special coupons, promotional videos, etc.
        2) Some companies may integrate social media and their customer relationship management (CRM) to provide better customer services or to tap potential customers. This is referred to as social CRM.
        3) Social media has also facilitated the growth of **consumer-to-consumer (C2C)** e-commerce.
    c. Laws and customs regarding privacy and ownership of material posted on social media websites are developing.

6. **Electronic Funds Transfer (EFT)**
    a. EFT is an e-commerce application provided by financial institutions worldwide that enables the transfer of funds via an access device, such as an ATM or POS terminal, telephone, computer, or chip (e.g., credit, debit, and check cards).
        1) A typical consumer application of EFT is the direct deposit of payroll checks in employees' accounts or the automatic withdrawal of payments for cable and telephone bills, mortgages, etc.
        2) EFT transaction costs are lower than for manual systems because documents and human intervention are eliminated from the transaction process. Moreover, transfer customarily requires less than a day.
        3) Another significant advantage is that the opportunities for clerical errors are greatly reduced.
        4) However, as EFT is usually conducted through third-party intermediaries, information security becomes a concern for both corporations and individuals.
    b. The most important application of EFT is check collection. To reduce the enormous volume of paper involved, the check-collection process has been computerized.
        1) The result has been to reduce the significance of paper checks because EFT provides means to make payments and deposit funds without physical transfer of negotiable instruments. Thus, wholesale EFTs among financial institutions and businesses (commercial transfers) are measured in the trillions of dollars.
        2) The two major systems for these "wire" or nonconsumer transfers are Fedwire (formerly known as the Federal Reserve Wire Network) and CHIPS (Clearing House Interbank Payment System). Private systems are also operated by large banks.

424   SU 14: IT Networks and Electronic Commerce

7. **EFT vs. Electronic Money**

   a. EFT differs from the use of electronic money, which may someday supplant traditional currency and coins.

   b. **Smart cards** contain computer chips rather than magnetized stripes. A smart card, therefore, can store data and security programs. It not only stores value but also authenticates transactions, such as by means of its digital signature.

   c. A disadvantage of electronic money is that most types are not covered by the insurance offered by the Federal Deposit Insurance Corporation (FDIC). Federal Reserve rules concerning EFT also do not extend to electronic money.

   d. Methods other than providing a credit card number or using electronic money may be used to make electronic payments.

      1) One such method is an online payment system, such as PayPal. A buyer makes a payment by a customary method to the online payment system, which then notifies the seller that payment has been made. The final step is to transfer the money to the seller's account.

STOP & REVIEW

You have completed the outline for this subunit.
Study multiple-choice questions 10 through 14 beginning on page 430.

14.3 ELECTRONIC DATA INTERCHANGE (EDI)

SUCCESS TIP

The AICPA has frequently tested the topic of EDI on recent exams. Questions have addressed such areas as the advantages of EDI and internal control and security for EDI transactions.

1. **Overview**

   a. Electronic data interchange (EDI) is the leading method of carrying on B2B e-commerce.

      1) EDI involves the communication of data in a format agreed to by the parties directly from a computer in one entity to a computer in another entity, for example, to order goods from a supplier or to transfer funds.

   b. EDI was the first step in the evolution of e-business.

      1) Successful EDI implementation begins with mapping the work processes and flows that support achievement of the organization's objectives.

      2) EDI was developed to enhance JIT inventory management.

   c. Advantages of EDI include the following:

      1) Reduction of clerical errors
      2) Increased speed of transactions
      3) Elimination of repetitive clerical tasks, such as document preparation, processing, and mailing
      4) Use of digital rather than physical record storage

SU 14: IT Networks and Electronic Commerce

 d. Disadvantages of EDI include the following:
 1) Information may be insecure.
 a) Thus, end-to-end data encryption should be used to protect data during EDI.
 2) Data may be lost.
 3) Transmissions to trading partners may fail.
 4) EDI is more complex and more costly than simpler B2B arrangements.
 a) In simpler B2B, each transaction is initiated over the Internet, with XML as the mediating language.
 b) EDI requires programming expertise and leased telephone lines or the use of a value-added or third-party network, whereas XML is simple and easy to understand.

2. **Costs of EDI**
 a. Specialized Software
 1) The software needed to convert data into the agreed-upon EDI format must be either purchased or developed in-house.
 b. Dedicated Hardware
 1) High-availability servers and high-speed communications devices must be available.
 c. Legal Costs
 1) Contracts with current trading partners must be negotiated when entering into an EDI arrangement.
 d. Process Reengineering
 1) Since existing procedures are being replaced, EDI arrangements may require significant changes to current internal processes. This also involves the cost of employee retraining.
 e. Enhanced Security and Monitoring
 1) EDI transactions are subject to the same risks as all electronic communications that cross organizational boundaries.

3. **Terms and Components of EDI**
 a. **Standards** concern procedures to convert written documents into a standard electronic document-messaging format to facilitate EDI.
 1) The current standards are ANSI X12 in the U.S. or UN/EDIFACT in Europe and most of the rest of the world.
 2) An alternative approach is XML language, which is not a standard at all. XML enables the creation of electronic business documents in a more flexible way, one that is not bound by the strict rules of data location.
 b. **Conventions** are the procedures for arranging data elements in specified formats for various accounting transactions, e.g., invoices, materials releases, and advance shipment notices.
 c. A **data dictionary** prescribes the meaning of data elements, including specification of each transaction structure.
 d. **Transmission protocols** are rules used to determine how each electronic envelope is structured and processed by the communications devices.
 1) Normally, a group of accounting transactions is combined in an electronic envelope and transmitted into a communications network.
 2) Rules are required for the separation and transmission of envelopes.

e. A crucial element of any EDI arrangement is the exchange of network and sender/recipient acknowledgment messages.

1) Acknowledgments serve as a nonrepudiation tool; i.e., one party cannot claim that a particular message was not received by a certain time or date.

f. Auditing an EDI application requires consideration of the **audit trail**. An essential element of an EDI audit trail is an **activity log**.

1) Because an audit trail allows for the **tracing** of a transaction from initiation to disposition, an activity log provides a key link in the process. Such a log provides information about the

   a) Users who have accessed the system,
   b) Files accessed,
   c) Processing accomplished,
   d) Time of access, and
   e) Amount of time the processing required.

4. **Methods of Communication between EDI Computers**

   a. A point-to-point system requires the use of dedicated computers by all parties.

   1) Each computer must be designed to be compatible with the other(s). This system is very similar to a network within one company. Dedicated lines or modems are used.

   b. Value-added networks (VANs) are private, third-party providers of common interfaces between organizations.

   1) Subscribing to a VAN eliminates the need for one organization to establish direct computer communication with a trading partner. VANs also eliminate the need for dedicated computers waiting for incoming messages.

5. **EDI Implications for Control**

   a. EDI eliminates the paper documents, both internal and external, that are the traditional basis for many controls, including internal and external auditing.

   b. Moreover, an organization that has reengineered its processes to take full advantage of EDI may have eliminated even the electronic equivalents of paper documents.

   1) For example, the buyer's point-of-sale (POS) system may directly transmit information to the seller, which delivers on a JIT basis. Purchase orders, invoices, and receiving reports are eliminated and replaced with

      a) A long-term contract establishing quantities, prices, and delivery schedules;
      b) Evaluated receipts settlements (authorizations for automatic periodic payment);
      c) Production schedules;
      d) Advance ship notices; and
      e) Payments by EFT.

STOP & REVIEW

You have completed the outline for this subunit. Study multiple-choice questions 15 through 20 beginning on page 432.

QUESTIONS

14.1 Networks and the Internet

1. Appropriate uses of an organization's internal communications network, or intranet, include all of the following **except**

A. Making the human resources policy manual available to employees.

B. Informing potential investors about company operations and financial results.

C. Providing senior management with access to the executive support system.

D. Enabling a project team that crosses departments to collaborate.

Answer (B) is correct.
REQUIRED: The item not one of the basic purposes of an organization's internal communications network.
DISCUSSION: An intranet permits sharing of information throughout an organization by applying Internet connectivity standards and web software (e.g., browsers) to the organization's internal network. An intranet addresses the connectivity problems faced by organizations that have many types of computers. Its use is restricted to those within the organization.
Answer (A) is incorrect. Making the human resources policy manual available to employees is an appropriate use of an organization's internal communications network. **Answer (C) is incorrect.** Providing senior management with access to the executive support system is an appropriate use of an organization's internal communications network. **Answer (D) is incorrect.** Enabling a project team that crosses departments to collaborate is an appropriate use of an organization's internal communications network.

2. Which one of the following network configurations is distinguished by the possibility of spreading the cost of ownership among multiple organizations?

A. Value-added network.

B. Baseband network.

C. Wide area network.

D. Local area network.

Answer (C) is correct.
REQUIRED: The network configuration that spreads its cost among multiple organizations.
DISCUSSION: Wide area networks consist of a conglomerate of local area networks (LANs) over widely separated locations. The key aspect here is that a WAN can be either publicly or privately owned.
Answer (A) is incorrect. A value-added network is a private network. **Answer (B) is incorrect.** Baseband refers to the signal-carrying capacity of a network, not the ownership of its hardware devices. **Answer (D) is incorrect.** All the equipment in a local area network (LAN) is owned by one organization.

3. A local area network (LAN) is best described as a(n)

A. Computer system that connects computers of all sizes, workstations, terminals, and other devices within a limited proximity.

B. System to allow computer users to meet and share ideas and information.

C. Electronic library containing millions of items of data that can be reviewed, retrieved, and analyzed.

D. Method to offer specialized software, hardware, and data-handling techniques that improve effectiveness and reduce costs.

Answer (A) is correct.
REQUIRED: The best description of a LAN.
DISCUSSION: A LAN is a local distributed computer system, often housed within a single building. Computers, communication devices, and other equipment are linked by cable. Special software facilitates efficient data communication among the hardware devices.

4. Which of the following control risks is more likely with personal computers than in a mainframe environment with dedicated terminals?

A. Copyright violations due to the use of unauthorized copies of purchased software.
B. Applications written by one department that cannot share data with existing organization-wide systems.
C. Lack of data availability due to inadequate data retention policies.
D. All of the answers are correct.

Answer (D) is correct.
REQUIRED: The control risk(s) likely in a personal computer environment.
DISCUSSION: When personal computers are used, likely control risks include copyright violations that occur when unauthorized copies of software are made or software is installed on multiple computers; locally written applications that do not adhere to the organization's standards; and inadequate backup, recovery, and contingency planning.
Answer (A) is incorrect. Copyright violations are a common risk with personal computers. **Answer (B) is incorrect.** Locally written applications that do not adhere to the organization's standards are a common risk with personal computers. **Answer (C) is incorrect.** Failure to follow proper backup procedures is a common risk with personal computers.

5. Which of the following networks provides the **least** secure means of data transmission?

A. Value-added.
B. Public-switched.
C. Local area.
D. Private.

Answer (B) is correct.
REQUIRED: The network that provides the least secure means of data transmission.
DISCUSSION: Public-switched networks are wide area networks that use public telephone lines. This arrangement may be the most economical, but data transmission may be of lower quality, no connection may be available, and security measures may be ineffective.
Answer (A) is incorrect. Value-added carriers provide data security and error detection and correction procedures. **Answer (C) is incorrect.** Local area networks inherently limit data transmission exposures. **Answer (D) is incorrect.** Private networks provide security through limited access and dedicated facilities.

6. Large organizations often have their own telecommunications networks for transmitting and receiving voice, data, and images. Small organizations, however, also can have remote locations that need to communicate. Such organizations are more likely to use

A. Public-switched lines.
B. Fast packet switches.
C. Internet.
D. A WAN.

Answer (C) is correct.
REQUIRED: The telecommunications networks likely to be used by small organizations.
DISCUSSION: Widespread use of the Internet has led to its becoming an efficient, low-cost transmission network.
Answer (A) is incorrect. Public-switched lines have been eclipsed in efficiency by the Internet. **Answer (B) is incorrect.** Fast packet switching networks are typically installed by telecommunication utility companies and other large companies that have their own networks. **Answer (D) is incorrect.** Small organizations lack the capital necessary for investment in a wide area network (WAN).

7. A company has abandoned the large array of dedicated servers it formerly used to store and provide access to its database. The company has entered into a contract with a provider who will guarantee storage of the database at its own location along with access over the Internet. This arrangement is an example of

A. Distributed computing.
B. Cloud computing.
C. Wide area network.
D. Ethernet.

Answer (B) is correct.
  REQUIRED: The type of arrangement described in the question.
  DISCUSSION: Cloud computing is a popular term relating to on-demand access to resources that are accessed on the Internet and shared by others. The entity has the ability to choose and pay for only the applications needed from the array (cloud) of resources, reducing the need for a large investment in IT infrastructure.
  Answer (A) is incorrect. Distributed processing involves the decentralization of processing tasks and data storage and assigning these functions to multiple computers, often in separate locations. **Answer (C) is incorrect.** A wide area network (WAN) consists of a conglomerate of local area networks over widely separated locations. **Answer (D) is incorrect.** Ethernet is a local area network transmission protocol.

8. Which of the following is **not** an advantage of using cloud computing?

A. Faster access to software.
B. Reduced IT costs.
C. Companies can choose to pay for services as needed.
D. Decreased risk of data exposure.

Answer (D) is correct.
  REQUIRED: The item that is not an advantage of using cloud computing.
  DISCUSSION: The risk of data exposure is increased by the convenience and ease of access to sensitive data provided by cloud computing services. This makes IT security in the cloud potentially more difficult.
  Answer (A) is incorrect. Fast access to software is an advantage of using cloud computing. **Answer (B) is incorrect.** A reduced need for investment in IT infrastructure is an advantage of using cloud computing. **Answer (C) is incorrect.** The ability to use "pay as you go" services is an advantage of using cloud computing.

9. A value-added network (VAN) adds value by

A. Reducing the cost of data transmission.
B. Providing the secure transmission of data over the Internet.
C. Routing data through a shared, low-cost Internet.
D. Providing error detection and correction services.

Answer (D) is correct.
  REQUIRED: The way value is added in a VAN.
  DISCUSSION: To compete with the Internet, VAN providers add value by providing their customers with error detection and correction and other services.
  Answer (A) is incorrect. A disadvantage of VANs is that they are more expensive than transmitting data over the Internet. **Answer (B) is incorrect.** VANs are private networks. Data are not transmitted through the Internet. **Answer (C) is incorrect.** VPNs route data through the shared, low-cost public Internet.

14.2 Electronic Commerce

10. An employee uses her company-issued ID and password to log into her employer's human resources system from home and change her choices of benefits. This is an example of

A. E-business.
B. Data warehouse.
C. Transmission protocol.
D. Extensible markup language.

Answer (A) is correct.
REQUIRED: The term for the transaction described.
DISCUSSION: E-business is an umbrella term referring to all methods of conducting business electronically. This can include strictly internal communications as well as nonfinancial dealings with outside parties (e.g., contract negotiations).
Answer (B) is incorrect. A data warehouse is a central database for transaction-level data from more than one of the organization's transaction processing systems. **Answer (C) is incorrect.** A transmission protocol is a necessary component of this transaction but does not describe the transaction itself. **Answer (D) is incorrect.** Extensible markup language (XML) is a way of coding information in such a way that a user can determine not only how it should be presented but also what it is; i.e., all computerized data may be tagged with identifiers.

11. Which of the following represents the greatest exposure to the integrity of electronic funds transfer data transmitted from a remote terminal?

A. Poor physical access controls over the data center.
B. Network viruses.
C. Poor system documentation.
D. Leased telephone circuits.

Answer (D) is correct.
REQUIRED: The greatest exposure to the integrity of EFT data transmitted from a remote terminal.
DISCUSSION: Leased telephone circuits represent a direct exposure to the risk of breached data integrity. They use public lines that can be easily identified and tapped.
Answer (A) is incorrect. Poor physical access controls represent a secondary exposure for compromise of remote data communications lines. **Answer (B) is incorrect.** Network viruses represent a secondary exposure for compromise of remote data communications lines. **Answer (C) is incorrect.** Poor system documentation represents a secondary exposure for compromise of remote data communications lines.

12. Which of the following risks is **not** greater in an electronic funds transfer (EFT) environment than in a manual system using paper transactions?

A. Unauthorized access and activity.
B. Duplicate transaction processing.
C. High cost per transaction.
D. Inadequate backup and recovery capabilities.

Answer (C) is correct.
REQUIRED: The risk not greater in an EFT environment than in a manual system using paper transactions.
DISCUSSION: EFT is a service provided by financial institutions worldwide that is based on EDI technology. EFT transaction costs are lower than for manual systems because documents and human intervention are eliminated from the transaction process.
Answer (A) is incorrect. Unauthorized access and activity is a risk specific to EFT. **Answer (B) is incorrect.** Inaccurate transaction processing (including duplication) is a risk specific to EFT. **Answer (D) is incorrect.** Inadequate backup and recovery capabilities is a risk specific to EFT.

13. Which one of the following is **not** a reason for a company to use EFT with an EDI system?

A. To take advantage of the time lag associated with negotiable instruments.
B. To allow the company to negotiate discounts with EDI vendors based upon prompt payment.
C. To improve its cash management program.
D. To reduce input time and input errors.

Answer (A) is correct.
REQUIRED: The item not a reason for using EFT.
DISCUSSION: The time lag between transmittal of a check (a negotiable instrument) and its clearance through regular banking channels is called float. Float is eliminated by EFT.
Answer (B) is incorrect. Payment schedules may be based on the time required to process invoices, prepare checks, and transmit checks. Using EFT, payment is instantaneous, and payment schedules can be based on other criteria, e.g., discounts for prompt payment.
Answer (C) is incorrect. EFT allows for more effective control of payments and transfers among accounts.
Answer (D) is incorrect. Integration of EDI and EFT eliminates manual input of transaction data, a process that introduces errors into the accounting system.

14. Which of the following significantly encouraged the development of electronic funds transfer (EFT) systems?

I. Response to competition
II. Cost containment
III. Advances in information technology

A. I and II.
B. I and III.
C. II only.
D. I, II, and III.

Answer (D) is correct.
REQUIRED: The items that most significantly encouraged the development of EFTs.
DISCUSSION: Competition has been a strong motivator in the financial services industry in the development of EFT systems, which are an application of EDI. Furthermore, containing costs in a highly competitive industry can be aided by leveraging information technology. Finally, advances in information technology, especially the wide acceptance of telecommunications standards and protocols, have made EFT systems possible.
Answer (A) is incorrect. Advances in information technology also significantly encouraged the development of EFT. **Answer (B) is incorrect.** Cost containment also significantly encouraged the development of EFT. **Answer (C) is incorrect.** Competitive forces and advances in information technology also significantly encouraged the development of EFT.

14.3 Electronic Data Interchange (EDI)

15. Which of the following is an accepted example of electronic data interchange (EDI)?

A. Request for an airline reservation by a travel agent.
B. Withdrawal of cash from an automated teller by a bank's customer.
C. Transfer of summary data from a local area network to a centralized mainframe.
D. Placement of order entry transactions from a customer to its supplier.

Answer (D) is correct.
REQUIRED: The accepted example of electronic data interchange.
DISCUSSION: EDI is the communication of electronic documents directly from a computer in one entity to a computer in another entity. Placement of order entry transactions from a customer to its supplier is an accepted use of EDI between trading partners.
Answer (A) is incorrect. A request for an airline reservation requires an online, real-time reservations system. Answer (B) is incorrect. Withdrawal of cash from an automated teller is accomplished via online transactions to copies of master files. Answer (C) is incorrect. The transfer of summary data to headquarters may be accomplished with point-to-point communications, known as distributed computing.

16. A system that permits suppliers and buyers to have direct access to portions of each others' databases, including inventory data, to enhance service and deliveries is

A. Electronic mail.
B. Interactive processing.
C. Electronic data interchange.
D. Distributed processing.

Answer (C) is correct.
REQUIRED: The system giving suppliers and buyers direct access to portions of each others' databases.
DISCUSSION: Electronic data interchange (EDI) is the communication of electronic documents directly from a computer in one entity to a computer in another entity. For example, a buyer's computer will issue a purchase order to a seller's computer. EDI was developed to enhance JIT inventory management. The advantages of EDI include reduction of clerical errors, increased speed of transactions, elimination of repetitive clerical tasks, and elimination of document preparing, processing, and mailing costs.
Answer (A) is incorrect. Electronic mail is the computer-to-computer exchange of messages. Answer (B) is incorrect. Interactive processing does not permit access to another company's database. Answer (D) is incorrect. Distributed processing distributes work among computers linked by a communications network.

17. Companies now can use electronic transfers to conduct regular business transactions. Which of the following terms best describes a system in which an agreement is made between two or more parties to electronically transfer purchase orders, sales orders, invoices, and/or other financial documents?

A. Electronic mail (email).
B. Electronic funds transfer (EFT).
C. Electronic data interchange (EDI).
D. Electronic data processing (EDP).

Answer (C) is correct.
REQUIRED: The term best describing electronic transfer of documents.
DISCUSSION: Electronic data interchange is the electronic transfer of documents between businesses. EDI was developed to enhance just-in-time (JIT) inventory management. Advantages include speed, reduction of clerical errors, and elimination of repetitive clerical tasks and their costs.
Answer (A) is incorrect. Email can send text or document files, but the term encompasses a wide range of transfers. EDI specifically applies to the system described in the question. Answer (B) is incorrect. EFT refers to the transfer of money. Answer (D) is incorrect. EDP is a generic term for computerized processing of transaction data within organizations.

18. Electronic data interchange (EDI) offers significant benefits to organizations, but it is not without certain major obstacles. Successful EDI implementation begins with which of the following?

A. Mapping the work processes and flows that support the organization's goals.
B. Purchasing new hardware for the EDI system.
C. Selecting reliable vendors for translation and communication software.
D. Standardizing transaction formats and data.

Answer (A) is correct.
  REQUIRED: The initial phase of EDI implementation.
  DISCUSSION: Marked benefits arise when EDI is tied to strategic efforts that alter, not mirror, previous practices. Applying EDI to an inefficient process results in continuing to do things the wrong way, only faster. Hence, the initial phase of EDI implementation includes understanding the organization's mission and an analysis of its activities as part of an integrated solution to the organization's needs.
  Answer (B) is incorrect. The prerequisite for EDI success is an understanding of the mission of the business and the processes and flows that support its goals, followed by cooperation with external partners. Purchasing new hardware is a subsequent step.
  Answer (C) is incorrect. Before applying EDI technology to the business, EDI must be viewed as part of an overall integrated solution to organizational requirements.
  Answer (D) is incorrect. EDI is not a solution by itself. Instead of considering how to transmit and receive transactions, a company must first analyze the entire process.

19. After a company implements electronic data interchange (EDI) to communicate with its customers, an appropriate control for ensuring authenticity of the electronic orders it receives is to

A. Encrypt sensitive messages such as electronic payments for raw materials received.
B. Perform reasonableness checks on quantities ordered before filling orders.
C. Verify the identity of senders and determine whether orders correspond to contract terms.
D. Acknowledge receipt of electronic payments with a confirming message.

Answer (C) is correct.
  REQUIRED: The control for ensuring the authenticity of the electronic orders the company receives.
  DISCUSSION: An EDI system is subject not only to the usual risk exposures for computer systems but also to those arising from the potential ineffectiveness of control on the part of the trading partner and the third-party service provider. Accordingly, authentication of users and messages received is a major security concern.
  Answer (A) is incorrect. Encrypting sensitive messages sent is an appropriate step but does not necessarily authenticate the transaction. **Answer (B) is incorrect.** Performing reasonableness checks on quantities ordered before placing orders is a control for ensuring the correctness of the company's own orders, not the authenticity of its customers' orders.
  Answer (D) is incorrect. Acknowledging receipt of electronic payments with a confirming message is good practice but will not authenticate orders from customers.

20. Before sending or receiving electronic data interchange (EDI) messages, a company should

- A. Execute a trading partner agreement with each of its customers and suppliers.
- B. Reduce inventory levels in anticipation of receiving shipments.
- C. Demand that all its suppliers implement EDI capabilities.
- D. Evaluate the effectiveness of its use of EDI transmissions.

Answer (A) is correct.
REQUIRED: The process to be performed before sending or receiving EDI messages.
DISCUSSION: Before sending or receiving EDI messages, a company should execute a trading partner agreement with its customers and suppliers. All parties should understand their responsibilities, the messages each will initiate, how they will interpret messages, the means of authenticating and verifying the completeness and accuracy of messages, the moment when the contract between the parties is effective, the required level of security, etc.
Answer (B) is incorrect. The company may intend to reduce inventory levels, but that intention is unrelated to the timing of its first EDI messages. **Answer (C) is incorrect.** The company may want to demand or encourage all its customers and suppliers to implement EDI capabilities, but that request is independent of sending and receiving messages. **Answer (D) is incorrect.** It is not possible to evaluate the effectiveness of EDI transmissions until after they occur.

Access the **Gleim CPA Premium Review System** featuring our SmartAdapt technology from your Gleim Personal Classroom to continue your studies. You will experience a personalized study environment with exam-emulating multiple-choice questions.

STUDY UNIT FIFTEEN
IT SECURITY AND CONTROLS

(27 pages of outline)

15.1	Risks Associated with Business Information Systems	435
15.2	COBIT -- A Framework for IT and Data Governance	438
15.3	Implementing the Cybersecurity Framework Using COBIT 2019	447
15.4	Electronic Transmission Security	450
15.5	Information Security	451
15.6	General Controls	455
15.7	Application Controls	459

The goals of a business information system are the same regardless of whether the system is manual or computerized; the risks of a computer-based system, however, are quite different.

SUCCESS TIP: The material included in this study unit overlaps with the enterprise risk management, internal control, and business processes topic on the AICPA Blueprint for the Business Environment and Concepts (BEC) section of the exam, covered in Study Units 2 and 3, as well as the internal control and information technology topic on the Blueprint for the Auditing and Attestation (AUD) section of the exam. We have attempted to include here those issues that are more likely to be tested on the BEC section of the exam. Many of these issues should be familiar for candidates who have already studied AUD.

15.1 RISKS ASSOCIATED WITH BUSINESS INFORMATION SYSTEMS

1. **Overview**
   a. Organizations need to be aware of the unique risks associated with a computer-based business information system.
   b. IT security (or **cybersecurity**) is information security applied to computer hardware, software, and computer networks.
   c. Safe computing can be achieved by using carefully crafted policies and procedures in conjunction with antivirus and access control software.
   d. The most comprehensive indicator of an information system's compliance with prescribed procedures is the control the system has over the data. This includes the capacity and complexity of the system, as well as the accessibility of the data to the end-user.

2. **System Availability**
   a. The ability to make use of any computer-based system is dependent on
      1) An uninterrupted flow of electricity
      2) Protection of computer hardware from environmental hazards (e.g., fire and water)
      3) Protection of software and data files from unauthorized access, alteration, and deletion
      4) Preservation of functioning communications channels among devices

3. **Volatile Transaction Trails**
   a. In any computer-based environment, a complete trail useful for audit purposes might exist for only a short time or in only computer-readable form. In online and real-time systems, data are entered directly into the computer, eliminating portions of the audit trail traditionally provided by source documents.

4. **Decreased Human Involvement**
    a. Because employees who enter transactions may never see the final results, the potential for detecting errors is reduced. Also, output from a computer system often carries a mystique of infallibility, reducing the incentive of system users to closely examine reports and transaction logs.
5. **Uniform Processing of Transactions**
    a. Computer processing uniformly subjects similar transactions to the same processing instructions, therefore virtually eliminating clerical error. Thus, it permits consistent application of predefined business rules and the performance of complex calculations in high volume.
    b. However, programming errors (or other similar systematic errors in either the hardware or software) will result in all like transactions being processed incorrectly.
6. **Unauthorized Access**
    a. When accounting records were kept in pen-and-ink format, physical access to them was the only way to carry out an alteration. Once they are computer-based, however, access may be gained by parties both internal and external to the organization.
    b. Security measures, such as firewalls and user ID-and-password combinations, are vital to maintaining security over data in an automated environment.
        1) A firewall limits access to a private network connected to the Internet rather than completely blocking information to and from the private network. Information with granted authorization (i.e., satisfying predefined security rules) is still accessible.
7. **Data Vulnerability**
    a. Destruction of hardware devices or units of storage media could have disastrous consequences if they contain the only copies of crucial data files or application programs.
    b. For this reason, an organization's computer files must be duplicated and stored offsite periodically.
8. **Reduced Segregation of Duties**
    a. Many functions once performed by separate individuals may be combined in an automated environment.

EXAMPLE 15-1   Reduced Segregation of Duties

Receiving cash, issuing a receipt to the payor, preparing the deposit slip, and preparing the journal entry may once have been performed by separate individuals. In a computer-based system, the receipt, deposit slip, and journal entry may be automatically generated by the computer. If the same employee who receives the cash is also responsible for entering the relevant data into the system, the potential for fraud or error is increased.

---

9. **Reduced Individual Authorization of Transactions**
    a. Certain transactions may be initiated automatically by a computer-based system. This is becoming even more widespread as an increasing number of business processes become automated.

EXAMPLE 15-2   Reduced Individual Authorizations

An enterprise resource planning system at a manufacturing concern may automatically generate a purchase order when raw materials inventory reaches a certain level. If the company shares an EDI system with the vendor, the purchase order may be sent to the vendor electronically without any human intervention.

b. This reduced level of oversight for individual transactions requires careful coding to ensure that computer programs accurately reflect management's goals for business processes.

   1) Independent verification of transactions is an important compensating control in the absence of segregation of duties and reduced individual authorization. A third party performs the verification to ensure that the transactions were appropriately processed.

10. **Malicious Software (Malware)**

   a. Malware is a term describing any program code that enters a computer system that has the potential to degrade that system. Common forms of malware include the following:

      1) A **Trojan horse** is an apparently innocent program (e.g., a spreadsheet) that includes a hidden function that may do damage when activated.

      2) A **virus** is a program that copies itself from file to file. The virus may destroy data or programs. A common way of spreading a virus is by email attachments and downloads.

         a) **Logic bombs** are a type of virus triggered by a predetermined event (such as Friday the 13th, April Fool's day, etc.).

      3) A **worm** copies itself not from file to file but from computer to computer, often very rapidly. Repeated replication overloads a system by depleting memory or overwhelming network traffic capacity.

      4) A **denial-of-service (DoS) attack** is an attempt to overload a system (e.g., a network or web server) with messages so that it cannot function (a system crash).

         a) A distributed denial-of-service (DDoS) attack comes from multiple sources, for example, the machines of innocent parties infected by Trojan horses. When activated, these programs send messages to the target and leave the connection open.

      5) **Phishing** is a method of electronically obtaining confidential information, such as a password or credit card number, through deceit. The perpetrator may set up a website that appears to be legitimate but actually serves no other purpose than to obtain the victim's information.

         a) Phishing scams are often initiated through email spoofing, in which the perpetrator sends out emails that appear to be from a real financial institution. When the victim clicks on the link to what (s)he thinks is the institution's website, the victim is unknowingly redirected to the perpetrator's website.

      6) A **back door** is a program that allows unauthorized access to a system and bypasses the normal login procedures (front door).

         a) Trojan horses and viruses can create a back door that allows unauthorized access to the system or data.

STOP & REVIEW

You have completed the outline for this subunit.
Study multiple-choice questions 1 through 3 beginning on page 462.

15.2 COBIT -- A FRAMEWORK FOR IT AND DATA GOVERNANCE

1. **Overview**

    a. COBIT is the best-known control and governance framework that addresses IT-related governance and management.

        1) In its original version, COBIT was focused on controls for specific IT processes.

        2) Over the years, information technology has gradually pervaded every facet of the organization's operations and functions. IT can no longer be viewed as a function distinct from other aspects of the organization.

            a) The evolution of COBIT has reflected this change in the nature of IT within the organization.

BACKGROUND 15-1   COBIT

When originally published in 1996, COBIT was an acronym for Control Objectives for Information and Related Technology. COBIT 2019, the most recent version, was published in 2018 by ISACA (formerly known as the Information Systems Audit and Control Association) and is available at www.isaca.org/resources/cobit.

---

2. **Information Criteria**

    a. **Effectiveness (doing right things)** deals with information's relevance to the business process and receipt in a timely, correct, consistent, and usable manner.

    b. **Efficiency (doing things right)** concerns the provision of information through the optimal (most productive and economical) use of resources.

    c. **Confidentiality** concerns the protection of sensitive information from unauthorized disclosure.

    d. **Integrity** relates to the accuracy and completeness of information, as well as to its validity in accordance with business values and expectations.

    e. **Availability** relates to information being available when required by the business process now and in the future. It also concerns the safeguarding of necessary resources and associated capabilities.

    f. **Compliance** deals with complying with the laws, regulations, and contractual arrangements to which the business process is subject, i.e., externally imposed business criteria as well as internal policies.

    g. **Reliability** relates to the provision of appropriate information for management to operate the entity and exercise its fiduciary and governance responsibilities.

SU 15: IT Security and Controls 439

3. **IT Governance Focus Areas**

   a. **Strategic alignment** focuses on ensuring the linkage of business and IT plans; defining, maintaining, and validating the IT value proposition; and aligning IT operations with enterprise operations.

   b. **Value delivery** is about executing the value proposition throughout the delivery cycle, ensuring that IT delivers the promised benefits against the strategy, concentrating on optimizing costs, and proving the intrinsic value of IT.

   c. **Resource management** is about the optimal investment in, and the proper management of, critical IT resources.

   d. **IT risk** is the business risk associated with the use, ownership, operation, involvement, influence, and adaption of IT within an enterprise or organization.

   e. **Risk management** involves risk awareness by senior corporate officers, understanding of compliance requirements, transparency about the significant risks to the enterprise, and embedding of risk management responsibilities into the organization.

   f. **Performance measurement** tracks and monitors strategy implementation, project completion, resource usage, process performance, and service delivery.

4. **COBIT 5 -- Five Key Principles**

   a. **Principle 1: Meeting Stakeholder Needs**

      1) COBIT 5 asserts that value creation is the most basic stakeholder need. Thus, the creation of stakeholder value is the fundamental goal of any enterprise, commercial or not.

         a) Value creation in this model is achieved by balancing three components:

            i) Realization of benefits
            ii) Optimization **(not minimization)** of risk
            iii) Optimal use of resources

      2) COBIT 5 also recognizes that stakeholder needs are not fixed. They evolve under the influence of both internal factors (e.g., changes in organizational culture) and external factors (e.g., disruptive technologies).

         a) These factors are collectively referred to as stakeholder drivers.

      3) In response to the identified stakeholder needs, enterprise goals are established.

         a) COBIT 5 supplies 17 generic enterprise goals that are tied directly to the balanced scorecard model.

         b) Next, IT-related goals (referred to as alignment goals) are drawn up to address the enterprise goals.

         c) Finally, enablers (referred to as components by COBIT 2019) that support the pursuit of the IT-related goals are identified. Categories of the enablers are identified in principle 4 on the next page.

         d) COBIT 5 refers to the process described above as the goals cascade.

b. **Principle 2: Covering the Enterprise End-to-End**
   1) COBIT 5 takes a comprehensive view of all of the enterprise's functions and processes. Information technology pervades them all; it cannot be viewed as a function distinct from other enterprise activities.
      a) Thus, IT governance must be integrated with enterprise governance.
   2) IT must be considered enterprise-wide and end-to-end, i.e., IT and non-IT functions and processes that govern and manage information "wherever that information may be processed" through the enablers.

c. **Principle 3: Applying a Single, Integrated Framework**
   1) In acknowledgment of the availability of multiple IT-related standards and best practices, COBIT 5 provides an overall framework for enterprise IT within which other standards can be consistently applied.
   2) COBIT 5 was developed to be an overarching framework that does not address specific technical issues; i.e., its principles can be applied regardless of the particular hardware and software in use.

d. **Principle 4: Enabling a Holistic Approach**
   1) COBIT 5 describes seven categories of enablers that support comprehensive IT governance and management:
      a) **Principles, policies, and frameworks** to translate desired behavior into guidance
      b) **Processes**, which are sets of practices to achieve the objectives
      c) **Organizational structures**, which are decision-making entities
      d) **Culture, ethics, and behavior** of individuals and the enterprise
      e) **Information** produced and used by the enterprise
      f) **Services, infrastructure, and applications** that provide the enterprise with IT processing and services
      g) **People, skills, and competencies** required for operations, error detections, and corrections
   2) Items e)-g) above are also classified as resources, the use of which must be optimized.
   3) Enablers are interconnected because they
      a) Need the input of other enablers to be fully effective and
      b) Deliver output for the benefit of other enablers.
   4) Enablers can be generic (usable in any given scenario) or variant (designed for a specific scenario).

e. **Principle 5: Separating Governance from Management**

1) The complexity of the modern enterprise requires governance and management to be treated as distinct activities.

   a) In general, governance is the setting of overall objectives and monitoring progress toward those objectives. COBIT 5 associates governance with the board of directors.

      i) Within any governance process, three practices must be addressed: evaluate, direct, and monitor.

   b) Management is the carrying out of activities in pursuit of enterprise goals. COBIT 5 associates these activities with executive management under the leadership of the CEO.

      i) Within any management process, four responsibility areas must be addressed: plan, build, run, and monitor.

2) COBIT 5 divides governance and management objectives into five domains (key areas):

   a) Governance

      i) **Evaluate, Direct, and Monitor (EDM)**

         - Evaluate. Evaluate stakeholder needs, conditions, and options.
         - Direct. Set direction through prioritization and decision making.
         - Monitor. Monitor performance and compliance.

   b) Management

      i) **Align, Plan, and Organize (APO).** Plan how IT can be used to achieve the company's goals and objectives.

      ii) **Build, Acquire, and Implement (BAI).** Identify IT requirements, build or acquire the technology, and incorporate into business processes.

      iii) **Deliver, Service, and Support (DSS).** Execute and support the application of the technology in business processes.

      iv) **Monitor, Evaluate, and Assess (MEA).** Monitor and evaluate whether the current IT system and internal control system meet the company's goals and objectives.

   c) Processes under each of the domains above are also defined.

5. **COBIT 5 Conversion to COBIT 2019**
    a. COBIT 2019 expands on COBIT 5's key principles for a governance system applicable to IT governance to include six **governance system** principles and three **governance framework** principles. A governance system is the rules, practices, and processes that direct and regulate an entity. A governance framework is the structure upon which the governance system is built.
        1) The six principles for a **governance system** are summarized as follows:
            a) Provide **stakeholder value**. Achieving value requires a strategy and governance system.
            b) **Holistic** approach. Create synergies among the components interconnected in the system.
                i) Governance system **components** were called "enablers" under COBIT 5. Components can be **generic** (components applied in principle to any circumstances) or **variant** (components designed for a given purpose or context in a focus area).
            c) **Dynamic** governance system. The governance system must be dynamic when dealing with a change in design factors (e.g., personnel, infrastructure, applications, etc.) and must be accompanied by consideration of its systemic effects.
            d) Governance **distinct** from management. Governance tasks should be differentiated from management tasks.
            e) Tailored to **enterprise needs**. The governance system must be designed to meet an organization's requirements.
                i) **Design factors** affect the blueprint of a governance system.
                ii) Design factors include, but are not limited to, threat landscape, technology adoption strategy, and enterprise strategy and goals.
            f) **End-to-end** governance system. The emphasis is not solely on the IT function but on all information, processes, and technology that contribute to organizational goal achievement.
        2) The following are three principles for a governance **framework**:
            a) It is **based on a conceptual model**. The governance framework achieves consistency and automation by identifying components and their relationships.
            b) It is **open and flexible**. The governance framework is flexible and permits inclusion of new content and issues without loss of consistency and integrity.
            c) It is **aligned with major standards**. The governance framework aligns with relevant regulations, standards, frameworks, and best practices (e.g., the latest IT standards and compliance regulations).

3) The COBIT implementation approach comprises seven phases, and each phase is represented by a question.

   a) Program initiation – **What are the drivers?**
      i) This phase involves recognizing change drivers and establishing management's desire to change.
   b) Problems and opportunities definition – **Where are we now?**
      i) This phase involves assessing the current state or capability and forming an implementation team.
   c) Road map definition – **Where do we want to be?**
      i) This phase involves defining the target state and identifying the gap as well as potential solutions.
   d) Program planning – **What needs to be done?**
      i) This phase involves planning implementation to close the gap.
   e) Plan execution – **How do we get there?**
      i) This phase involves implementing the plan and establishing monitoring systems.
   f) Benefits realization – **Did we get there?**
      i) This phase involves monitoring progress and achievement.
   g) Effectiveness review – **How do we keep the momentum going?**
      i) This phase involves reviewing the overall program and reinforcing improvements.

4) Generally, these phases can be matched with the principles of the governance system. However, note that Principle 6 and Phase 7 are not matched.

Governance System Principles	Implementation Phases
1. Provide stakeholder value	1. What are the drivers?
2. Holistic approach	2. Where are we now?
3. Dynamic governance system	3. Where do we want to be?
	4. What needs to be done?
4. Governance distinct from management	5. How do we get there?
5. Tailored to enterprise needs	6. Did we get there?
6. End-to-end governance system	
	7. How do we keep the momentum going?

b. COBIT 2019 includes 40 governance and management objectives organized into 5 domains, expanded from 37 processes organized into the same 5 domains under COBIT 5.

   1) Candidates need not memorize these objectives. They are included here because they represent one of the foundational shifts from COBIT 5 to COBIT 2019.

c. Performance management is a crucial element of a governance and management system. It directs all of the components at work towards accomplishing the goals of the organization by providing reliable and relevant outcomes.

1) The **COBIT Performance Management (CPM)** model measures performance using capability and maturity levels.

   a) **Capability levels.** The CPM measures performance by using the capability level to quantify how well a process is operating, ranging from 0 (no capability or not meeting the intent of any process practices) to 5 (well defined process or continuous improvement enabled).

   b) **Maturity levels.** The CPM measures performance by using focus area maturity levels. The six maturity levels, presented in order of maturity, are listed below.

      0 – Incomplete
      1 – Initial
      2 – Managed
      3 – Defined
      4 – Quantitative
      5 – Optimizing

      i) A **focus area** is a governance issue, domain, or topic that is associated with a group of objectives and their components. COBIT 2019 added new focus areas, including cloud computing, cybersecurity, privacy, and small and medium enterprises.

BACKGROUND 15-2   COBIT Product Family

The COBIT 2019 product family currently includes the following documents:
1. COBIT 2019 Framework: Introduction and Methodology
2. COBIT 2019 Framework: Governance and Management Objectives
3. COBIT 2019 Design Guide: Designing an Information and Technology Governance Solution
4. COBIT 2019 Implementation Guide: Implementing and Optimizing an Information and Technology Governance Solution

These documents can be obtained from www.isaca.org/resources/cobit.

---

6. **Starting a Data Management Program Using COBIT**

   a. Starting a data governance program or improving an existing program comes with the following challenges:

      1) Enterprises cannot easily quantify the benefits of data governance, which leads to a lack of management commitment
      2) Unclearly defined data ownership
      3) Disaggregated data sets from siloed departments

   b. In 2020, ISACA published *Rethinking Data Governance and Management: A Practical Approach for Data-Driven Enterprises*. The paper established a phased five-stage data management approach to overcome the challenges, which is discussed on the following pages.

c. Stage 1: Establish a Data Governance Foundation

1) A data governance foundation guides how to collect and use data by addressing legal, business intellectual property, and customer sensitivity considerations.

2) The data governance foundation should answer the following questions:

a) What data are owned, to be collected, and used?

i) **Data taxonomy**, the amount of data collected and the functional classification of the information (e.g., manufacturing data, product data, financial data, etc.), is defined.

ii) **Data classification** identifies data categories (e.g., public data, internal data, confidential data, or sensitive data) for data protection purposes.

b) When do data governance practices take place?

i) Data governance practices can be mapped to the data life cycle. An example is depicted in the following diagram.

Data Life Cycle Phases	Plan/Design	Build/Acquire	Store	Use	Share	Archive/Destroy
Security Management Activities	Identify security/privacy requirements Identify data classification Design security/privacy framework	Validate data	Implement data protection Implement data-retention rules	Monitor and control data access	Ensure compliance with laws/regulations	Data wiping

c) Who is responsible for data governance?

i) **Data governance structure** should first be created to **strategically** evaluate, direct, and monitor (EDM) data governance activities.

ii) After the data governance structure is set, a **data stewardship structure** is set to **operationally** define roles and responsibilities for data management activities.

- **Data owners** make decisions about data as well as their business definitions, e.g., forecasting sales using current sales data.

- **Data stewards** ensure that data assets are used and adopted properly, e.g., ensuring that the sales data used for forecasting are accurate and authorizing who can access the sales data.

- **Data custodians** ensure the IT controls and safeguards for the data, e.g., controlling the storage of the sales data and ensuring that only authorized personnel can access the data.

d) How are data managed?

i) Risk assessment is conducted to identify the gap between regulation requirements and current practices.

ii) Data governance policies and standards to close the gap are then established.

d. Stage 2: Establish and Evolve the Data Architecture

1) Data architecture is a description of the structure and interaction of the major types and sources of data, data assets, and data management resources.

2) To establish the data structure, **standardization** is required for
   a) Data rules (what data can be stored)
   b) Data models (how data are stored, grouped, and structured)
   c) Metadata (how data are described to improve usability)
   d) Master data (how data are uniquely identified)

e. Stage 3: Define, Execute, Assure Data Quality, and Clean Polluted Data

1) **Data quality criteria** are defined (these criteria are similar to the information criteria covered in item 2. on page 438).

2) Data quality programs are executed and assessed regularly (e.g., review data quality, identify exceptions, and take corrective measures).

3) Corrective measures primarily include cleansing the data against the standards.

f. Stage 4: Realize Data Democratization

1) **Data democratization** is the creation of a self-serviced enterprise-wide platform, which allows permitted users to access the data, facilitates the sharing of data and insights, and provides a single source of reference for searching data.

2) Data democratization is not the delegation of data control. It only changes the way data are accessed, shared, searched, and used.

3) Data security and privacy are fundamental to data democratization. Thus, while access to and sharing of data are enhanced, data security and privacy are not compromised.

g. Stage 5: Focus on Data Analytics

1) Data analytics adds value to the business by helping identify patterns, draw conclusions, and predict future events. (Data analytics is covered in detail in Study Unit 20.)

2) Data visualization represents the data using graphical elements to enhance understandability and presentational persuasiveness.

STOP & REVIEW

You have completed the outline for this subunit.
Study multiple-choice question 4 on page 463.

15.3 IMPLEMENTING THE CYBERSECURITY FRAMEWORK USING COBIT 2019

1. **Overview**

    a. The U.S. National Institute of Standards and Technology (NIST) created the Framework for Improving Critical Infrastructure Cybersecurity (commonly known as the Cybersecurity Framework, or CSF) to guide the controls over cybersecurity risks.

    b. The CSF defines the following five functions to control cyber risk activities and outcomes:

    1) **Identify** – Understanding of cybersecurity risk management
    2) **Protect** – Protection of critical services
    3) **Detect** – Detective measures to identify occurrence of cybersecurity breaches
    4) **Respond** – Corrective measures to tackle identified breaches
    5) **Recover** – Plans to restore services impacted by the breaches

    c. Management processes can be organized into the following four tiers:

    1) Tier 1: Partial

        a) Cybersecurity management practices are informal and not based on risks.
        b) Awareness of cyber risk is limited.
        c) Processes to enable internal sharing of cybersecurity information may not exist.
        d) The organization does not collaborate (receive and share) cybersecurity risk-related information with other entities.

    2) Tier 2: Risk-informed

        a) Cybersecurity management practices exist but are not included as formal policies.
        b) Awareness of cyber risk exists, but the consideration of risk is not at all levels.
        c) Processes to enable internal information sharing are informal.
        d) The organization receives cybersecurity risk-related information from other entities but may not share such information.

    3) Tier 3: Repeatable

        a) Cybersecurity management practices are established as formal policies.
        b) Awareness of cyber risks exists at all levels of the organization.
        c) Processes to enable internal information sharing are formal.
        d) The organization receives and shares cybersecurity risk-related information, but not proactively.

    4) Tier 4: Adaptive

        a) Cybersecurity management policies are constantly improving to respond to risks promptly.
        b) Awareness of current and evolving cyber risks is incorporated in the organization's culture.
        c) Information is continuously shared internally.
        d) The organization collaborates with other entities proactively in real time.

d. A summary of the four management processes is depicted in the following table:

	Cybersecurity Management Practices	Awareness of Cyber Risks	Processes to Internally Share Cybersecurity Information	Collaboration with Outside Parties
Tier 1: Partial	None/Informal	None/Limited	None	None
Tier 2: Risk-Informed	Exist but not as formal policies	Exists but not at all levels	Informal	Information received but not shared
Tier 3: Repeatable	Formal policies	Exists at all levels	Formal	Information received and shared but not proactively
Tier 4: Adaptive	Constantly improving	Incorporated in company culture	Continuous	Proactive, real-time collaboration

2. **Using COBIT 2019 to Implement the CSF**

    a. The CSF can be implemented in phases or across the entire organization simultaneously. According to ISACA's *Governance Playbook: Integrating Frameworks to Tackle Cybersecurity*, the CSF, in the context of COBIT 2019, is implemented **incrementally** in seven steps as depicted in the following diagram:

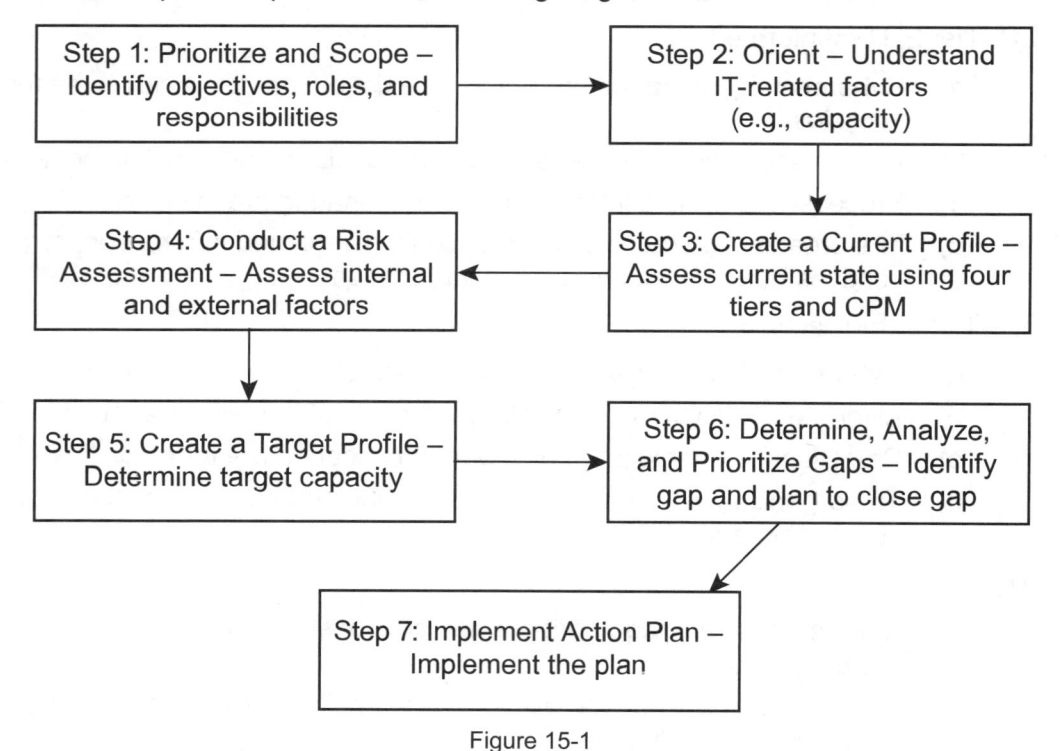

    Step 1: Prioritize and Scope – Identify objectives, roles, and responsibilities

    Step 2: Orient – Understand IT-related factors (e.g., capacity)

    Step 3: Create a Current Profile – Assess current state using four tiers and CPM

    Step 4: Conduct a Risk Assessment – Assess internal and external factors

    Step 5: Create a Target Profile – Determine target capacity

    Step 6: Determine, Analyze, and Prioritize Gaps – Identify gap and plan to close gap

    Step 7: Implement Action Plan – Implement the plan

    Figure 15-1

    NOTE: For Step 1, the goals cascade of COBIT 2019 is generally conducted.

    b. Upon conclusion of the seven steps for CSF implementation, organizations should proceed with the following:

       1) CSF Action Plan Review. Determine whether the action plan is appropriate and delivers the values desired.
       2) CSF Life Cycle Management. Continually review and improve the action plan.

c. The following table shows the alignment between the COBIT 2019 implementation phases and the CSF implementation steps. The last two items in the CSF column are not included in the seven-step model, but they are included in the playbook to align with the final two phases in COBIT 2019.

CSF Implementation Steps	COBIT 2019 Implementation Phases
1. Prioritize and Scope	1. What are the drivers?
2. Orient	2. Where are we now?
3. Create a Current Profile	
4. Conduct a Risk Assessment	3. Where do we want to be?
5. Create a Target Profile	
6. Determine, Analyze, and Prioritize Gaps	4. What needs to be done?
7. Implement Action Plan	5. How do we get there?
CSF Action Plan Review	6. Did we get there?
CSF Life Cycle Management	7. How do we keep the momentum going?

STOP & REVIEW

You have completed the outline for this subunit.
Study multiple-choice questions 5 and 6 on page 464.

15.4 ELECTRONIC TRANSMISSION SECURITY

1. **Encryption Technology**
   a. Encryption technology is vital for the security and therefore the success of electronic commerce, especially with regard to transactions carried out over public networks.
      1) The sender's encryption program encodes the data prior to transmission. The recipient's program decodes it at the other end. Unauthorized users may be able to intercept the data by eavesdropping on information (called a **sniffing** or a **sniffer attack**), but without the decryption key, they will be unable to decode it.
   b. Encryption performed by physically secure hardware is inherently more secure than encryption performed by software.
   c. The use of encryption increases system overhead. A certain amount of system resources must be used to execute the machine instructions necessary to encrypt and decrypt data.

2. **Public-Key vs. Symmetric Encryption**
   a. With public-key (asymmetric) encryption, the communicating parties create mathematically related pairs of keys. One of the keys in the pair is made public, and the other is kept secret.
      1) The sending party uses the public key to encrypt the message. Since only the intended recipient has access to the private key that relates to that public key, only that party will be able to decrypt the message.
   b. With symmetric encryption, the communicating parties agree on a single (private) key for use in that session.
      1) Symmetric encryption's strength is its length. The longer the key (measured in bits), the more resistant it is to decryption by unauthorized parties.
      2) However, the parties must have a secure way of sharing the key.

3. **Digital Certificates**
   a. Digital certificates are data files created by trusted third parties called certificate authorities (e.g., VeriSign, Thawte, GoDaddy).
      1) An entity who wishes to engage in e-commerce first establishes a relationship with a certificate authority, who verifies that party's identity.
      2) The certificate authority then creates a coded electronic certificate that contains (a) the holder's name, (b) its public key, (c) a serial number, and (d) an expiration date. The certificate authority makes its own public key widely available.
      3) A party wishing to do business over the Internet with the certificate holder seeks the holder's certificate on the authority's server and uses the authority's public key to decrypt it.
      4) The sender obtains the recipient's public key from the certificate, encodes the message, and sends it. The recipient uses its private key to decrypt the message.
   b. This system, called the public-key infrastructure, relieves the parties from the need to establish their own pairs of keys when they want to communicate securely.
      1) The public-key infrastructure allows buyers to securely exchange credit card numbers with Internet vendors.

4. **Digital Signatures**

    a. A digital signature is a means of authenticating an electronic document such as a purchase order, acceptance of a contract, or financial information.

        1) The sender uses its private key to encode all or part of the message, and the recipient uses the sender's public key to decode it. Hence, if that key decodes the message, the sender must have written it.

> **STOP & REVIEW**
> You have completed the outline for this subunit.
> Study multiple-choice questions 7 through 10 beginning on page 464.

15.5 INFORMATION SECURITY

1. **Overview**

    a. Information (proprietary and personal) security encompasses not only computer hardware and software but all of an organization's information, no matter what medium it resides on. It involves far more than just user IDs and passwords.

        1) The importance of a broad definition of information security becomes clear in light of recent incidents of firms accidentally disposing of documents containing confidential customer information with their regular trash.

    b. Organizations have three principal goals for their information security programs: data confidentiality, data availability, and data integrity.

        1) **Confidentiality** is protecting data from disclosure to unauthorized persons.

        2) **Availability** is ensuring that the organization's information systems are up and running so that employees and customers are able to access the data they need.

        3) **Integrity** is ensuring that data accurately reflect the business events underlying them and are not subject to tampering or destruction.

c. A set of data has integrity when it is consistent with the data definition, which should be clearly described to reduce the risk of data misuse or misinterpretation. In *Criteria for Describing a Set of Data and Evaluating Its Integrity*, the Assurance Services Executive Committee (ASEC) of the AICPA provides three criteria for documenting the description of the definition and evaluation of a set of data:

   1) The description of the set of data includes the **purpose** of the data.

      a) This includes identification of the intended users, how they are intended to use the data, and whether the planned use of the data aligns with its purpose.

   2) The description of the set of data is **complete and accurate** and includes the following:

      a) **Data population:** What specific information is to be included or excluded, and why the information is included or excluded (e.g., transactional data for a fiscal year include only data for transactions occurring during the year)

      b) **Nature of each data element (attribute):** How the data attribute relates to the event or instance (e.g., the "cost" attribute of a transaction record measures the cost of the product sold) and what each attribute means (e.g., the "cost" field presents unit cost)

      c) **Source of data:** Where and how the data are collected and how they are transformed (e.g., transactional data are collected from a company's POS system and automatically transformed by its accounting system)

      d) **Units of measurement:** The unit in which a data attribute is measured (e.g., costs are measured in U.S. dollars)

      e) **Accuracy, correctness, or precision:** The level of precision of the data (e.g., costs are measured at a precision of the nearest U.S. cent)

      f) **Uncertainty or confidence interval:** Potential deviation of an estimate and the person determining the estimate (e.g., historical variations or margin of error of a financial estimate prepared by the actuarial department)

      g) **Time period of measurement:** The measurement date or the period over which the events occurred (e.g., transactional data for a fiscal year include data for transactions occurring between April 1 of the prior year and March 31 of the current year)

      h) **Other factors:** Additional factors that determine the inclusion or exclusion of an item in the data elements and population (e.g., the version of the system from which the transactional data are retrieved or deviation from industry-wide practices in measuring sales)

   3) The description of the set of data identifies any information that **has not been included** within the set of data or the description but is **necessary for understanding** each data element and the population.

      a) For example, the description of the inventory of a diamond company needs to include the GIA color-grading scale.

d. **Cost-Benefit Analysis**

1) In deciding among information security risk responses, management must consider the costs and benefits of each risk response. A risk response should be ignored if its costs exceed its benefits.

2) The costs associated with a risk response include both direct and indirect costs. Such costs include the costs incurred to design, implement, and maintain the risk response. Management should also consider the opportunity costs associated with each risk response.

3) The costs and related benefits of each risk response can be measured quantitatively or qualitatively.

4) The Application Techniques portion of the COSO Framework provides the following guidance on preparing a cost-benefit analysis:

Virtually every risk response will incur some direct or indirect cost that is weighed against the benefits it creates. The initial cost to design and implement a response (processes, people, and technology) is considered, as is the cost to maintain the response on an ongoing basis. The costs, and associated benefits, can be measured quantitatively or qualitatively, with the unit of measure typically consistent with that used in establishing the related objective and risk tolerance.

2. **Steps in Creating an Information Security (or Response) Plan**

    a. Perform threat identification to identify risks related to information confidentiality, i.e., events that can potentially compromise an organization's information infrastructure.

    1) Threats to confidentiality include the improper disposal of customer records, threats to availability include viruses and denial-of-service attacks, and threats to integrity include employee errors and sabotage.

    b. Identify the risks that these threats entail.

    1) Risk analysis encompasses determining the likelihood of the identified threats and the level of damage that could potentially be done should the threats materialize.

        a) **Evaluate the significance of a threat.** In evaluating the significance of an identified threat, determine whether a threat is at an acceptable level. A threat is at an acceptable level when a reasonable and informed third party who is aware of the relevant information would be expected to conclude that the threat would not compromise the organization's ability to recover and continue business as usual.

    2) For example, an organization may conclude that, while the potential damage from sabotage is very high, its likelihood may be quite low.

    c. Design the controls that will compensate for the risks.

    1) Controls are designed based on the combination of likelihood and potential damage determined in the risk analysis.

    d. Incorporate the controls into a coherent, enterprise-wide information security plan.

    1) The plan lists the controls that will be put in place and how they will be enforced.

e. Set forth policies with expectations of all persons, both employees and external users, with access to the organization's systems.

1) The single most important policy is that which governs the information resources to which individuals have access and how the level of access will be tied to their job duties.

a) Carrying out such a policy requires the organization's systems to be able to tie data and program access to individual system IDs.

b) One provision of the policy must be for the immediate removal of access to the system by terminated employees.

3. **Preventive-Detective-Corrective Control Model**

a. IT controls can also be classified according to the traditional three-way division of internal controls.

b. **Preventive controls** prevent errors from entering the system. Preventive controls are often highly visible and are considered better than other forms of control because they stop problems before they occur.

1) Examples of physical preventive controls include fences, locked doors, security guards, and a segregation of duties policy.

2) Examples of logical preventive controls are the input controls described on page 459.

c. **Detective controls** call attention to errors that have already entered the system before an error causes a negative outcome.

1) Examples of detective accounting controls are petty cash counts and physical inventory counts.

a) An important detective control in IT is examination of system logs. These logs are reports automatically generated by the system of actions that require scrutiny, such as repeated failed login attempts and the use of powerful utility programs.

2) Examples in an automated systems context are the output controls described on page 461.

d. **Corrective controls** correct errors after they have been detected.

1) Examples include correcting errors reported on error listings, isolating and removing viruses, and restarting from system crashes.

4. **Broad Controls**

a. The two broad groupings of information systems control activities are **general controls** and **application controls** discussed in the next two subunits.

You have completed the outline for this subunit.
Study multiple-choice question 11 on page 466.

STOP & REVIEW

15.6 GENERAL CONTROLS

1. **General controls** are the umbrella under which the IT function operates. They affect the organization's entire processing environment and commonly include controls over

    a. Data center and network operations;
    b. Systems software acquisition, change, and maintenance;
    c. Access security; and
    d. Application system acquisition, development, and maintenance.

2. IT Administration Controls over Operations

    a. A modern organization should recognize information technology as a separate function with its own set of management and technical skills. An organization that allows every functional area to acquire and administer its own systems in isolation is not serious about proper control.

    b. Treating IT as a separate functional area of the organization involves the designation of a chief information officer (CIO) or chief technology officer (CTO) and the establishment of an information systems steering committee (or IT steering committee) to set a coherent direction for the organization's systems and prioritize information technology projects.

3. **Segregation of duties** is vital because a separation of functions (authorization, recording, and custody of assets) may not be feasible in an IT environment. For example, a computer may print checks, record disbursements, and generate information for reconciling the account balance. These activities customarily are segregated in a manual system. Segregation of duties within the IT function is discussed in Study Unit 12, Subunit 1.

4. Controls over software acquisition, change, and maintenance include

    a. **Controls over systems software**, which ensure that operating systems, utilities, and database management systems are acquired and changed only under close supervision and that vendor updates are routinely installed.

    b. **Controls over application software**, which ensure that programs used for transaction processing (e.g., payroll and accounts receivable) are cost-effective and stable.

5. **Hardware controls** are built into the equipment by the manufacturer. They ensure the proper internal handling of data as they are moved and stored.

    a. They include parity checks, echo checks, read-after-write checks, and any other procedure built into the equipment to ensure data integrity.

6. **Physical controls** limit physical access and environmental damage to computer equipment, data, and important documents.

   a. **Access Controls**

      1) Access controls prevent improper use or manipulation of data files and programs. They ensure that only those persons with a bona fide purpose and authorization have access. An example of such persons would be employees working remotely using their personal computers (an unsecured environment), who are more frequently subject to higher information security risks.

      2) No persons except operators should be allowed unmonitored access to the processing facility. This can be accomplished through the use of a security guard, a guard desk, a keypad, or a magnetic card reader.

      3) **Passwords and ID numbers.** The use of passwords and identification numbers (for example, a PIN used for an ATM) is an effective control in an online system to prevent unauthorized access to files. Lists of authorized persons are maintained online and should constantly be updated when there are personnel changes (e.g., promotion or resignation). To avoid unauthorized access, the entity may combine

         a) The entry of passwords or identification numbers;
         b) A prearranged set of personal questions; and
         c) The use of badges, magnetic cards, optically scanned cards, or biometric attributes.

      4) **Device authorization table.** This control grants access only to those physical devices that should logically need access. For example, because it is illogical for anyone to access the accounts receivable file from a manufacturing terminal, the device authorization table will deny access even when a valid password is used.

      5) **System access log.** This log records all uses and attempted uses of the system. The date and time, codes used, mode of access, data involved, and interventions by operators are recorded.

      6) **Encryption.** Encoding data before transmission over communication lines makes it more difficult for someone with access to the transmission to understand or modify its contents. Encryption technology converts data into unreadable code. Unauthorized users may still be able to access the data but, without the decryption key, will be unable to decode (decipher) the information.

      7) **Callback.** This feature requires the remote user to call, give identification, hang up, and wait for a call to an authorized number. This control ensures acceptance of data only from authorized modems. However, a call-forwarding device may thwart this control by transferring access from an authorized to an unauthorized number.

      8) **Controlled disposal of documents.** One method of enforcing access restrictions is to destroy data when they are no longer in use. Thus, paper documents may be shredded, and magnetic media may be erased. Company policies should be established regarding the disposal and destruction of records, as regulatory bodies may impose record retention requirements.

9) **Biometric technologies.** These are automated methods of establishing an individual's identity using physiological or behavioral traits. These characteristics include fingerprints, retina patterns, hand geometry, signature dynamics, speech, and keystroke dynamics. Biometric access controls can better verify the identity of an individual than passwords. Passwords may be leaked or stolen, while biometric attributes are less subject to these risks.

10) **Automatic log-off.** The disconnection of inactive data terminals may prevent the viewing of sensitive data on an unattended work station.

11) **Security personnel.** An entity may hire security specialists. For example, (a) developing an information security policy for the entity, (b) commenting on security controls in new applications, and (c) monitoring and investigating unsuccessful access attempts are appropriate duties of the information security officer.

b. **Environmental Controls**

1) The processing facility should be equipped with both a cooling and heating system (to maintain a year-round constant level of temperature and humidity) and a fire-suppression system.

7. **Logical controls** are established to limit access in accordance with the principle that all persons should have access only to those elements of the organization's information systems that are necessary to perform their job duties. Logical controls have a double focus: authentication and authorization.

a. **Authentication** is the act of ensuring that the person attempting to access the system is in fact who (s)he says (s)he is. The most widespread means of achieving this is through the use of IDs and passwords.

1) Authentication methods to identify the user include information known to the user (e.g., passwords), information owned by the user (e.g., a smartcard), and biometric attributes of the user (e.g., fingerprints).

2) A **single-factor authentication** requires the use of only one authentication method (e.g., the use of a password) to verify the user's identity.

3) A **multi-factor authentication** requires the use of more than one authentication method (e.g., a combination of a password, a token card, and facial recognition) to verify the user's identity.

b. The elements of user account management are as follows:

1) Anyone attempting access to one of the organization's systems must supply a unique identifier (e.g., the person's name or other series of characters) and a password that is known only to that person and is not stored anywhere in the system in unencrypted format.

a) Not even information security personnel should be able to view unencrypted passwords. Security personnel can change passwords, but the policy should require that the user immediately change it to something secret.

2) The organization's systems should force users to change their passwords periodically, e.g., every 90 days.

3) The policy should prohibit employees from leaving their IDs and passwords written down in plain view.

c. **Authorization** is the practice of ensuring that, once in the system, the user can only access those programs and data elements necessary for his or her job duties.

   1) In many cases, users should be able to view the contents of some data fields but not be able to change them (read-only).
   2) An example is an accounts receivable clerk who can view customers' credit limits but cannot change them. This same clerk can, however, change a customer's outstanding balance by entering or adjusting an invoice.
   3) To extend the example, only the head of the accounts receivable department should be able to execute the program that updates the accounts receivable master balance file. An individual clerk should have no such power.

8. A **firewall** is a combination of hardware and software that separates an internal network (e.g., an intranet) from an external network (e.g., the Internet) and prevents passage of traffic deemed suspicious. Two principal types of firewalls are network firewalls and application firewalls.

   a. **Network firewalls** regulate traffic to an entire network, such as an organization's LAN.

      1) The firewall examines each query and, depending on the rules set up by the network security administrator, denies entry to the network based on the source, destination, or other data in the header.
      2) Queries from a particular source address that repeatedly fail to gain access to the network might indicate a penetration attempt or DDoS attack. The firewall can notify network security personnel who can then investigate.

   b. **Application firewalls** regulate traffic to a specified application, such as email or file transfer.

      1) An application firewall is based on proxy server technology. The firewall becomes a proxy, or intermediary, between the computer actually sending the packet and the application in question. This arrangement allows for a high level of security over the application but at the cost of slowing down communications.
      2) Since an application firewall only provides security for a single application, it is not a substitute for a network firewall.

   c. A firewall alone is not an adequate defense against computer viruses. Specialized antivirus software is a must.

STOP & REVIEW

You have completed the outline for this subunit.
Study multiple-choice questions 12 though 16 beginning on page 466.

15.7 APPLICATION CONTROLS

> **SUCCESS TIP**: CPA Exam questions concerning application controls often give a description of a control, then ask for the name of it.

1. **Application Controls**
   a. Are built into each application (payroll, accounts payable, inventory management, etc.).
   b. Are designed to ensure that only correct, authorized data enter the system and that the data are processed and reported properly.
   c. Include input, processing, and output controls.

2. **Input Controls**
   a. Input controls provide reasonable assurance that data submitted for processing are (1) authorized, (2) complete, and (3) accurate. These controls vary depending on whether input is entered in online or batch mode.
   b. The most basic input control is thus authorization; e.g., a batch of accounts payable transactions must be authorized by the AP supervisor before being submitted for recording.
   c. Many input controls take the form of **edit routines**, i.e., controls programmed into the software that prevent certain types of errors from entering into the system.
      1) **Preformatting.** To avoid data entry errors in online systems, a preformatted screen may be designed to look exactly like the corresponding paper document.
      2) **Edit (field) checks.** Some data elements can only contain certain characters, and any transaction that attempts to use an invalid character is halted.
         a) Typical examples are Social Security numbers, which cannot contain letters, and drop-down menus, which restrict users' choices to only valid selections.
      3) **Limit (reasonableness)** and **range checks**. Based on known limits for given information, certain entries can be rejected by the system.
         a) For example, hours worked per week cannot exceed 80 without a special override by management, date of birth of an employee cannot be any date within the last 15 years, etc.
      4) **Validity checks.** In order for a transaction to be processed, some other record must already exist in another file.
         a) For example, for the system to accept a transaction requesting payment of a vendor invoice, the vendor must already have a record on the vendor master file.
      5) **Sequence checks.** Processing efficiency is greatly increased when files are sorted on some designated field(s), called the "key," before operations such as matching.
         a) For instance, the accounts payable transaction file and master file should both be sorted according to vendor number before the matching operation is attempted. If the system discovers a record out of order, it may indicate that the files were not properly prepared for processing.

6) **Prompting.** The system requests the input of each data item and waits for a response before requesting the next input. This ensures the completeness of the input data.

7) **Closed-loop verification.** Inputs by a user are transmitted to the computer and processed. Related records are displayed back to the user to verify the accuracy of the data.

   a) For example, an employee in the purchasing department enters a vendor number to place a purchase order. Related records, such as the vendor's name and address, are displayed for the employee to verify before placing the order.

   b) A closed-loop control system involves automatic feeding of data back to the user and validation of data accuracy without human intervention. It differs from an open loop control system, which requires manual input. For example, when the amount of money to be transferred is entered, ATMs automatically process the input and display the amount to the user for verification without the need of manual input by bank staff.

8) **Check-digit verification** (self-checking digits). An algorithm is applied to, for instance, a product number and incorporated into the number. This reduces keying errors, such as dropped and transposed digits.

EXAMPLE 15-3   **Check-Digit Verification**

A box of detergent has the product number 4187604. The last digit is actually a derived number, arrived at by applying the check-digit algorithm to the other digits.

In this example, the check digit is calculated by starting with the last position of the base product number (418760) and multiplying each successive digit to the left by 2, then by 1, then by 2, etc., and adding the results: $(0 \times 2) + (6 \times 1) + (7 \times 2) + (8 \times 1) + (1 \times 2) + (4 \times 1) = 0 + 6 + 14 + 8 + 2 + 4 = 34$. The last digit of this result becomes the check digit.

When the clerk enters 4187604 into the terminal, the system performs an immediate calculation and determines that this is a valid product number.

---

9) **Zero-balance checks.** The system will reject any transaction or batch thereof in which the sum of all debits and credits does not equal zero.

d. **Batch input controls** can be used when data are grouped for processing.

   1) **Management release.** A batch is not released for processing until a manager reviews and approves it.

   2) **Record count.** A batch is not released for processing unless the number of records in the batch, as reported by the system, matches the number calculated by the user.

   3) **Financial total.** A batch is not released for processing unless the sum of the dollar amounts of the individual items as reported by the system matches the amount calculated by the user.

   4) **Hash total.** The arithmetic sum of a numeric field, which has no meaning by itself, can serve as a check that the same records that should have been processed were processed. An example is the sum of all employee identification numbers. The hash total for the employee listing by the personnel department could be compared with the hash total generated during the payroll run to ensure the completeness and accuracy of input transaction data.

3. Processing Controls

a. Processing controls provide reasonable assurance that (1) all data submitted for processing are processed and (2) only approved data are processed. These controls are built into the application code by programmers during the systems development process.

b. Some processing controls repeat the steps performed by the **input controls**, such as limit checks and batch controls.

c. **Validation.** Identifiers are matched against master files to determine existence. For example, any accounts payable transaction in which the vendor number does not match a number on the vendor master file is rejected.

d. **Completeness.** Any record with missing data is rejected.

e. **Arithmetic controls.** Cross-footing compares an amount with the sum of its components. Zero-balance checking adds the debits and credits in a transaction or batch to ensure that their sum is zero.

f. **Sequence check.** Computer effort is expended most efficiently when data are processed in a logical order, such as by customer number. This check ensures the batch is sorted in the proper order before processing begins. Any out-of-sequence, duplicated, or missing records in a sequential file should be rejected for follow-up.

g. **Run-to-run control totals.** The controls associated with a given batch are checked after each stage of processing to ensure all transactions have been processed.

h. **Key integrity.** A record's key is the group of values in designated fields that uniquely identify the record. No application process should be able to alter the data in these key fields.

4. Output Controls

a. Output controls provide assurance that the processing result (such as account listings or displays, reports, files, invoices, or disbursement checks) is accurate and that only authorized personnel receive the output.

b. These procedures are performed at the end of processing to ensure that all transactions the user expected to be processed were actually processed.

   1) **Transaction logs.** Every action performed in the application is logged along with the date, time, and ID in use when the action was taken.

   2) **Error listings.** All transactions rejected by the system are recorded and distributed to the appropriate user department for resolution.

   3) **Record counts.** The total number of records processed by the system is compared to the number the user expected to be processed.

   4) **Record reconciliation.** Data processing results and control totals are reconciled.

   5) **Run-to-run control totals.** The new financial balance should be the sum of the old balance plus the activity that was just processed.

STOP & REVIEW

You have completed the outline for this subunit.
Study multiple-choice questions 17 though 20 beginning on page 468.

QUESTIONS

15.1 Risks Associated with Business Information Systems

1. Which of the following statements most accurately describes the impact that automation has on the controls normally present in a manual system?

A. Transaction trails are more extensive in a computer-based system than in a manual system because a one-for-one correspondence always exists between data entry and output.

B. Responsibility for custody of information assets is more concentrated in user departments in a computer-based system than it is in a manual system.

C. Controls must be more explicit in a computer-based system because many processing points that present opportunities for human judgment in a manual system are eliminated.

D. The quality of documentation becomes less critical in a computer-based system than it is in a manual system because data records are stored in machine-readable files.

Answer (C) is correct.
REQUIRED: The impact that automation has on the controls normally present in a manual system.
DISCUSSION: Using a computer does not change the basic concepts and objectives of control. However, the use of computers may modify the control techniques used. The processing of transactions may be combined with control activities previously performed separately, or control functions may be combined within the information system activity.
Answer (A) is incorrect. The audit trail is less extensive in an information system. Combining processing and controls within the system reduces documentary evidence. **Answer (B) is incorrect.** Information assets are more likely to be under the control of the information system function. **Answer (D) is incorrect.** Documentation is more important in an information system. Information is more likely to be stored in machine-readable form than in hard copy.

2. Attacks on computer networks may take many forms. Which of the following uses the computers of innocent parties infected with Trojan horse programs?

A. A distributed denial-of-service attack.
B. A man-in-the-middle attack.
C. A brute-force attack.
D. A password-cracking attack.

Answer (A) is correct.
REQUIRED: The attack on a network that uses the computers of innocent parties infected with Trojan horse programs.
DISCUSSION: A denial-of-service (DoS) attack is an attempt to overload a system (e.g., a network or web server) with false messages so that it cannot function (a system crash). A distributed DoS attack comes from multiple sources, for example, the machines of innocent parties infected by Trojan horses.
Answer (B) is incorrect. A man-in-the-middle attack takes advantage of network packet sniffing and routing and transport protocols to access packets flowing through a network. **Answer (C) is incorrect.** A brute-force attack uses password cracking software to try large numbers of letter and number combinations to access a network. **Answer (D) is incorrect.** Password-cracking software accesses a network by trying many letter and number combinations.

3. Spoofing is one type of malicious online activity. Spoofing is

A. Trying large numbers of letter and number combinations to access a network.
B. Eavesdropping on information sent by a user to the host computer of a website.
C. Accessing packets flowing through a network.
D. Identity misrepresentation in cyberspace.

Answer (D) is correct.
REQUIRED: The nature of spoofing.
DISCUSSION: Passwords, user account numbers, and other information may be stolen through spoofing. Spoofing is identity misrepresentation in cyberspace, for example, by using a false website to obtain information about visitors.
Answer (A) is incorrect. A brute-force attack uses password cracking software to try large numbers of letter and number combinations to access a network.
Answer (B) is incorrect. Sniffing is the use of software to eavesdrop on information sent by a user to the host computer of a website. **Answer (C) is incorrect.** A man-in-the-middle attack takes advantage of network packet sniffing and routing and transport protocols to access packets flowing through a network.

15.2 COBIT -- A Framework for IT and Data Governance

4. Which of the following statements is inconsistent with the key principles of the COBIT 5 framework?

A. Enterprise governance and management are treated as the same activity.
B. The needs of stakeholders are the focus of all organizational activities.
C. Information technology controls are considered to be intertwined with those of the organization's everyday operations.
D. COBIT 5 can be applied even when other IT-related standards have been adopted.

Answer (A) is correct.
REQUIRED: The statement inconsistent with the key principles of the COBIT 5 framework.
DISCUSSION: Under the COBIT 5 framework, the complexity of the modern enterprise requires governance and management to be treated as distinct activities.
Answer (B) is incorrect. COBIT 5 asserts that the creation of stakeholder value is the fundamental goal of any enterprise. **Answer (C) is incorrect.** COBIT 5 takes a comprehensive view of all of the enterprise's functions and processes. Information technology pervades them all; it cannot be viewed as a function distinct from other enterprise activities. **Answer (D) is incorrect.** In acknowledgment of the availability of multiple IT-related standards and best practices, COBIT 5 provides an overall framework for enterprise IT within which other standards can be applied.

15.3 Implementing the Cybersecurity Framework Using COBIT 2019

5. What approach is used to implement the CSF in the context of COBIT 2019?

A. Rapid approach.
B. Inclusive approach.
C. Radical approach.
D. Incremental approach.

Answer (D) is correct.
REQUIRED: The approach used to implement the NIST CSF in the context of COBIT 2019.
DISCUSSION: The CSF can be implemented in phases or across the entire organization simultaneously. In the context of COBIT 2019, the CSF is implemented incrementally in seven steps.
Answer (A) is incorrect. The rapid approach, which involves adopting the CSF across the entire organization simultaneously, is not consistent with the context of COBIT 2019. **Answer (B) is incorrect.** In the context of COBIT 2019, the CSF should not be implemented across the whole organization at once. **Answer (C) is incorrect.** In the context of COBIT 2019, adoption of the CSF is not characterized by radical changes.

6. Which of the following CSF implementation steps and COBIT 2019 implementation phases are paired correctly?

	CSF steps	COBIT 2019 phases
A.	Prioritize and Scope; Orient	Where are we now?
B.	Conduct a Risk Assessment; Create a Target Profile	Where do we want to be?
C.	Determine, Analyze, and Prioritize Gaps	How do we get there?
D.	Implement Action Plan	Did we get there?

Answer (B) is correct.
REQUIRED: The alignment of CSF implementation steps with COBIT 2019 implementation phases.
DISCUSSION: Step 4: Conduct a Risk Assessment and Step 5: Create a Target Profile of the CSF implementation approach align with COBIT 2019 phase 3 (Where do we want to be?) and involve assessing internal and external cybersecurity factors and determining the target capacity level for each process (e.g., based on best practices).
Answer (A) is incorrect. The CSF implementation step of prioritize and scope aligns with COBIT 2019 implementation phase 1 (What are the drivers?). **Answer (C) is incorrect.** The COBIT 2019 implementation phase 5 (How do we get there?) involves implementing the plan and establishing monitoring systems. It aligns with the CSF implementation step of implement action plan. **Answer (D) is incorrect.** The implement action plan step aligns with COBIT 2019 implementation phase 5 (How do we get there?).

15.4 Electronic Transmission Security

7. A client communicates sensitive data across the Internet. Which of the following controls will be most effective to prevent the use of the information if it were intercepted by an unauthorized party?

A. A firewall.
B. An access log.
C. Passwords.
D. Encryption.

Answer (D) is correct.
REQUIRED: The most effective control for preventing the use of intercepted information.
DISCUSSION: Encryption technology converts data into a code. Encoding data before transmission over communications lines makes it more difficult for someone with access to the transmission to understand or modify its contents.
Answer (A) is incorrect. A firewall prevents access from specific types of traffic to an internal network. After an unauthorized user has obtained information from the site, a firewall cannot prevent its use. **Answer (B) is incorrect.** An access log only records attempted usage of a system. **Answer (C) is incorrect.** Passwords prevent unauthorized users from accessing the system. If information has already been obtained, a password cannot prevent its use.

8. To ensure privacy in a public-key encryption system, knowledge of which of the following keys is required to decode the received message?

I. Private
II. Public

A. I only.
B. II only.
C. Both I and II.
D. Neither I nor II.

Answer (A) is correct.
REQUIRED: The key(s) required to decode messages in a public-key system to ensure privacy.
DISCUSSION: In a public-key system, the public key is used to encrypt the message prior to transmission. The private key is needed to decrypt (decode) the message.
Answer (B) is incorrect. The private key, not the public key, is needed to decrypt (decode) the message.
Answer (C) is incorrect. The public key is needed to encode, not decode, the message. **Answer (D) is incorrect.** The private key is needed to decrypt (decode) the message.

9. Which of the following IT developments poses the **least** risk to organizational security?

A. Adoption of wireless technology.
B. Use of public-key encryption.
C. Outsourcing of the IT infrastructure.
D. Enterprise-wide integration of functions.

Answer (B) is correct.
REQUIRED: The least risky IT developments.
DISCUSSION: Encryption is essential when electronic commerce is conducted over public networks, such as the Internet. Thus, the use of public-key encryption is a response to risk, not a source of risk.
Answer (A) is incorrect. Adoption of wireless technology increases the risk that communications will be intercepted. **Answer (C) is incorrect.** Outsourcing of the IT infrastructure means that ineffective controls over the outside service provider's operations could compromise the security of the organization's information. **Answer (D) is incorrect.** Enterprise-wide integration of functions, for example, in an ERP system with an organization-wide database, increases the difficulty of assuring the integrity of information. In an organization with discrete, closed functional subsystems, compromising one subsystem does not affect the others. In an ERP system, however, a breach of security may affect the entire organization.

10. Which of the following is an encryption feature that can be used to authenticate the originator of a document and ensure that the message is intact and has not been tampered with?

A. Heuristic terminal.
B. Perimeter switch.
C. Default settings.
D. Digital signatures.

Answer (D) is correct.
REQUIRED: The encryption feature used to authenticate the originator of a document and ensure that the original message is intact.
DISCUSSION: A digital signature is a means of authenticating an electronic document, such as a purchase order, acceptance of a contract, or financial information. Because digital signatures use public-key encryption, they are a highly secure means of ensuring security over the Internet.
Answer (A) is incorrect. The term "heuristic terminal" is not meaningful in this context. **Answer (B) is incorrect.** The term "perimeter switch" is not meaningful in this context. **Answer (C) is incorrect.** In a computer program, a default setting is a value that a parameter will automatically assume unless specifically overridden.

15.5 Information Security

11. Which of the following is a true statement regarding security over an entity's IT?

A. Controls should exist to ensure that users have access to and can update only the data elements that they have been authorized to access.
B. Controls over data sharing by diverse users within an entity should be the same for every user.
C. The employee who manages the computer hardware should also develop and debug the computer programs.
D. Controls can provide assurance that all processed transactions are authorized but cannot verify that all authorized transactions are processed.

Answer (A) is correct.
REQUIRED: The true statement regarding security over an entity's IT.
DISCUSSION: Authorization is the practice of ensuring that, once in a particular system, a user can only access those programs and data elements necessary for his or her job duties.
Answer (B) is incorrect. Certain data should not be accessed by all individuals, and those who do have access may have different levels of authority. Thus, the controls should vary among users regardless of whether the environment includes a database. **Answer (C) is incorrect.** These duties should be segregated. **Answer (D) is incorrect.** Controls can play multiple roles in a database or nondatabase environment by comparing authorized transactions with processed transactions and reporting anomalies.

15.6 General Controls

12. A client installed the sophisticated controls using the biometric attributes of employees to authenticate user access to the computer system. This technology most likely replaced which of the following controls?

A. Use of security specialists.
B. Reasonableness tests.
C. Passwords.
D. Virus protection software.

Answer (C) is correct.
REQUIRED: The control most likely replaced by biometric technologies.
DISCUSSION: The use of passwords is an effective control in an online system to prevent unauthorized access to computer systems. However, biometric technologies are more sophisticated and difficult to compromise.
Answer (A) is incorrect. Biometric technologies do not eliminate the need for specialists who evaluate and monitor security needs. **Answer (B) is incorrect.** Reasonableness tests are related to input controls, not access controls. **Answer (D) is incorrect.** Virus protection software prevents damage to data in a system, not access to a system.

13. The two broad groupings of information systems control activities are general controls and application controls. General controls include controls

A. Relating to the correction and resubmission of faulty data.
B. For developing, modifying, and maintaining computer programs.
C. Designed to assure that only authorized users receive output from processing.
D. Designed to ensure that all data submitted for processing have been properly authorized.

Answer (B) is correct.
REQUIRED: The general controls.
DISCUSSION: General controls are policies and procedures that relate to the entity's overall IT environment. They support the effective functioning of application controls by helping to ensure the continued proper operation of information systems. General controls include controls over (1) data center and network operations; (2) systems software acquisition and maintenance; (3) access security; and (4) application systems acquisition, development, and maintenance.
Answer (A) is incorrect. Control over correction of input errors is an application control. **Answer (C) is incorrect.** Control over report distribution (output) is an application control. **Answer (D) is incorrect.** Control over authorization of input is an application control.

14. The significance of hardware controls is that they

A. Ensure the proper execution of machine instructions.
B. Reduce the incidence of user input errors in online systems.
C. Ensure accurate programming of operating system functions.
D. Ensure that run-to-run totals in application systems are consistent.

Answer (A) is correct.
REQUIRED: The significance of hardware controls.
DISCUSSION: Hardware controls are built into the equipment by the manufacturer to detect and control errors arising from the use of the equipment. Examples include parity checks, read-after-write checks, and echo checks.
Answer (B) is incorrect. Use of input screens, limit tests, self-checking digits, and other input controls can reduce the incidence of input errors in online systems. Answer (C) is incorrect. Programmers and/or analysts must correct errors in computer programs. Answer (D) is incorrect. Run-to-run totals ensure the completeness of update in an online system by accumulating separate totals for all transactions processed throughout a period. This total is compared with the total of items accepted for processing.

15. One of the major problems in a computer system is that incompatible functions may be performed by the same individual. One compensating control is the use of

A. Echo checks.
B. A check digit system.
C. Computer-generated hash totals.
D. A computer log.

Answer (D) is correct.
REQUIRED: The control compensating for inadequate segregation of duties in a computer system.
DISCUSSION: A computer (console) log is a record of computer and software usage usually produced by the operating system. Proper monitoring of the log is a compensating control for the lack of segregation of duties. For instance, the log should list operator interventions.
Answer (A) is incorrect. Echo checks are hardware controls used to determine if the correct message was received by an output device. Answer (B) is incorrect. A check digit system is an input control that tests identification numbers. Answer (C) is incorrect. Hash totals are control totals used to check for losses or inaccuracies arising during data movement.

16. Authentication is the process by which the

A. System verifies that the user is entitled to enter the transaction requested.
B. System verifies the identity of the user.
C. User identifies himself or herself to the system.
D. User indicates to the system that the transaction was processed correctly.

Answer (B) is correct.
REQUIRED: The definition of authentication.
DISCUSSION: Identification is the process of uniquely distinguishing one user from all others. Authentication is the process of determining that individuals are who they say they are. For example, a password may identify but not authenticate its user if it is known by more than one individual.
Answer (A) is incorrect. Authentication involves verifying the identity of the user. This process does not necessarily confirm the functions the user is authorized to perform. Answer (C) is incorrect. User identification to the system does not imply that the system has verified the identity of the user. Answer (D) is incorrect. This procedure is an application control for accuracy of the transaction.

15.7 Application Controls

17. Which of the following computerized control procedures is most effective in ensuring that files of data uploaded from personal computers to a server are complete and that **no** additional data are added?

A. Self-checking digits to ensure that only authorized part numbers are added to the database.
B. Batch control totals, including control totals and hash totals.
C. Passwords that effectively limit access to only those authorized to upload the data to the server.
D. Field-level edit controls that test each field for alphanumerical integrity.

Answer (B) is correct.
REQUIRED: The most effective computerized control procedure.
DISCUSSION: Batch control totals for the data transferred can be reconciled with the batch control totals in the existing file. This comparison provides information on the completion of the data transfer. Batch totals may include record counts, totals of certain critical amounts, or hash totals. A hash total is a control total without a defined meaning, such as the total of employee numbers or invoice numbers, that is used to verify the completeness of data. Thus, the hash total for the employee listing by the personnel department could be compared with the total generated during the payroll run.
Answer (A) is incorrect. Self-checking digits detect inaccurate identification numbers. They are an effective control to ensure that the appropriate part has been identified but not that data transfer is complete. **Answer (C) is incorrect.** Passwords help ensure that only authorized personnel make the transfer, not that data transfer is complete. **Answer (D) is incorrect.** Field checks are effective input controls, but they do not ensure completeness of data transfer.

18. In an automated payroll processing environment, a department manager substituted the time card for a terminated employee with a time card for a fictitious employee. The fictitious employee had the same pay rate and hours worked as the terminated employee. The best control to detect this action using employee identification numbers is a

A. Reasonableness test.
B. Record count.
C. Hash total.
D. Financial total.

Answer (C) is correct.
REQUIRED: The best control technique to detect the action.
DISCUSSION: A hash total is a control total without a defined meaning, such as the total of employee numbers or invoice numbers, that is used to verify the completeness of data. Thus, the hash total for the employee listing by the personnel department could be compared with the total generated during the payroll run.
Answer (A) is incorrect. A reasonableness test is based on known limits for given information. **Answer (B) is incorrect.** A record count is a control total of the number of records processed during the operation of a program. **Answer (D) is incorrect.** Financial totals summarize dollar amounts in an information field in a group of records.

19. Certain payroll transactions were posted to the payroll file but were not uploaded correctly to the general ledger file on the main server. The best control to detect this type of error would be

A. A standard method for uploading mainframe data files.
B. An appropriate edit and validation of data.
C. A record or log of items rejected during processing.
D. Balancing totals of critical fields.

Answer (D) is correct.
REQUIRED: The best control to detect failure to upload correctly to the general ledger certain payroll transactions.
DISCUSSION: Balancing totals should be used to ensure completeness and accuracy of processing. For example, comparing totals of critical fields generated before processing with output totals for those fields tests for missing or improper transactions.
Answer (A) is incorrect. A standard method for uploading data may not include the controls necessary to detect errors in the uploading process. **Answer (B) is incorrect.** Edit and validation checks are typically designed to identify errors in data entry rather than in processing. **Answer (C) is incorrect.** A record or log of rejected items is a control for monitoring the subsequent correction and processing of the items.

20. Which of the following errors most likely would be detected by batch financial totals?

A. A transposition error on one employee's paycheck on a weekly payroll run.
B. A missing digit in an invoice number in a batch of daily sales.
C. A purchase order mistakenly entered into two different batches.
D. Malfeasance resulting from a receivable clerk's pocketing of a customer's payment and altering of the related records.

Answer (A) is correct.
REQUIRED: The error that will likely be detected by batch financial totals.
DISCUSSION: Batch financial totals compare the sum of the dollar amounts of the individual items as reported by the system, with the amount calculated by the user. Thus, batch financial totals would most likely detect a transposition error on an employee's paycheck.
Answer (B) is incorrect. Batch financial totals give information about the total dollar amounts of the invoices within the batch but do not detect errors in the digits of the invoice numbers themselves. **Answer (C) is incorrect.** Batch financial totals are not capable of detecting errors that are made in two separate batches. **Answer (D) is incorrect.** Batch financial totals alone are not capable of detecting the alteration of records or the theft of payment.

Access the **Gleim CPA Premium Review System** featuring our SmartAdapt technology from your Gleim Personal Classroom to continue your studies. You will experience a personalized study environment with exam-emulating multiple-choice questions.

STUDY UNIT SIXTEEN
PERFORMANCE MEASUREMENT AND PROCESS MANAGEMENT

(24 pages of outline)

16.1	Responsibility Centers	471
16.2	Performance Measurement -- Financial and Nonfinancial Measures	475
16.3	Performance Measurement -- Balanced Scorecard	481
16.4	Process Management	484
16.5	Tools for Process Management	488
16.6	Costs of Quality	492
16.7	TQM and the ISO Framework	493

Responsibility accounting allows each component of the organization to be judged based on the achievement of its own objectives. The performance of a responsibility center must be evaluated using appropriate criteria. Such criteria includes financial and nonfinancial performance measures. The balanced scorecard is a tool used for implementing the organization's strategies towards achieving its objectives.

Much practical and theoretical innovation has occurred in business processes and the ways of monitoring their efficiency. Quality is a special area of management scrutiny. Its costs can be quantified, and frameworks have been developed for systematizing the pursuit of quality.

16.1 RESPONSIBILITY CENTERS

1. **Decision Making and Decentralization**

    a. The primary distinction between centralized and decentralized organizations is in the degree of freedom of decision making by managers.

       1) In a centralized organization, decision making is consolidated so that activities may be more effectively coordinated from the top.

       2) In a decentralized organization, decision making is at the lowest level possible. The premise is that the local manager can make more informed decisions than a manager farther from the decision.

2. **Responsibility Centers**

    a. A decentralized organization is divided into **responsibility centers** (also called **strategic business units**, or SBUs) to facilitate local decision making. Four types of responsibility centers are generally recognized.

        1) A **cost center**, e.g., a maintenance department, is responsible for costs only.

            a) Cost drivers are the relevant performance measures. Variance analysis is used to measure performance.

            b) A disadvantage of a cost center is the potential for cost shifting, for example, replacement of variable costs for which a manager is responsible with fixed costs for which (s)he is not.

                i) Another disadvantage is that long-term issues may be disregarded when the emphasis is on, for example, annual costs.

            c) Allocation of service department costs to cost centers is another issue. Service centers provide specialized support to other organizational subunits. They are usually operated as cost centers.

        2) A **revenue center**, e.g., a sales department, is responsible for revenues only.

            a) Revenue drivers are the relevant performance measures. They are factors that influence unit sales, such as

                i) Changes in prices and products,
                ii) Customer service,
                iii) Marketing efforts, and
                iv) Delivery terms.

        3) A **profit center**, e.g., an appliance department in a retail store, is responsible for revenues and expenses. The contribution margin formatted income statement (covered in detail in Study Unit 18, Subunit 4) or segment income statement is used to evaluate the performance of a profit center.

        4) An **investment center**, e.g., a branch office, is responsible for revenues, expenses, and invested capital.

            a) The performance of an investment center can be compared with that of other responsibility centers or other potential investments on a return on investment (ROI) basis. ROI measures the effectiveness of asset usage.

3. **Performance Measures and Manager Motivation**
    a. In a responsibility center, a logical group of operations is directed by one manager.
        1) Measures are designed for every responsibility center to monitor performance.
    b. **Controllability.** The performance measures on which the manager's compensation is based should be, to the extent practicable, under the manager's influence.
        1) Controllable factors are those a manager can influence in a given period.
            a) But some costs, for example, the costs of central administration, cannot be traced to particular activities or responsibility centers.
            b) Most costs, revenues, etc., are not wholly controlled by one manager. They may be influenced by
                i) Factors external to the organization (e.g., prices of materials),
                ii) A team of managers, or
                iii) A person with no authority over incurrence of the cost (e.g., a purchasing manager with expert knowledge of price changes).
        2) Controllable cost is not synonymous with variable cost. Often, this classification depends on the level of the organization.
            a) For example, senior management may be responsible for selecting the carrier that will be used to ship inventory to all customers. The number of units sold will directly affect the cost incurred by the seller. Thus, the associated variable selling costs (e.g., freight costs) are directly selected by senior management. However, despite being variable in nature, a branch sales manager is unable to control the shipping costs incurred.
    c. **Goal congruence.** Performance measures must be designed so that they relate directly to accomplishment of the organization's goals.
        1) Suboptimization results when the goals of segments of the organization differ from the organization's goals.

4. **Transfer Pricing**
    a. Transfer prices are charged by one segment of an organization for goods and services it provides to another segment of the same organization.
        1) The principal challenge is determining a price that motivates both the selling and the buying manager.
    b. In a decentralized system, each responsibility center theoretically may be completely separate.
        1) Thus, the transferor (seller) should charge the same price to the transferee (buyer) as to an outsider buyer.
        2) Decentralization is intended in part to motivate managers. But the transferor's best interests may not be served by giving a discount to the transferee if the goods or services can be sold at the regular price to outside buyers. Nevertheless, the discount may be to the entity's advantage.

c. Three methods of transfer pricing are common.

1) **Market-based transfer prices**

   a) A market price often is the best transfer price. For example, a transferor may be operating at full capacity and can sell all of its output at the market price. Charging a lower price as the transfer price for intraentity transfers is therefore unjustified.

   b) However, if the transferor is not producing at full capacity, the use of market prices for internal transfers is not justified. A lower price might motivate either the buyer or the seller.

2) **Cost-based transfer prices**

   a) Transfer prices may be based on the transferor's variable cost or full cost.

3) **Negotiated transfer prices**

   a) A negotiated price gives the segments the freedom to agree on a price.

5. **Common Costs**

   a. Common costs are the costs of products, activities, facilities, services, or operations shared by two or more cost objects. Joint costs are the common costs of a single process that yields two or more joint products.

      1) The costs of service centers and central administration are examples.

   b. Because common costs are indirect, identification of a direct cause-and-effect relationship with the actions of the cost object to which it is allocated can be difficult.

6. **Management Reporting**

   a. Relevance is the most important attribute of management reporting. Relevance is determined by whether a revenue or cost element depends on a manager's decision.

You have completed the outline for this subunit.
Study multiple-choice questions 1 and 2 on page 495.

STOP & REVIEW

16.2 PERFORMANCE MEASUREMENT -- FINANCIAL AND NONFINANCIAL MEASURES

1. **Financial vs. Nonfinancial Measures**
   a. The appropriate financial performance measures vary with the type of responsibility center.
      1) Cost centers -- Variable costs, total costs
      2) Revenue centers -- Gross sales, net sales
      3) Profit centers -- Sales, gross margin, operating income, contribution margin, segment margin
      4) Investment centers
         a) Return on investment, residual income
         b) Return on assets, return on equity, return on common equity, economic rate of return on common stock, economic value added
   b. Nonfinancial performance measures are not standardized and thus can take any appropriate form.
      1) Product quality -- measures include returns and allowances and the number and types of customer complaints.
      2) Manufacturing systems -- measures include throughput time (i.e., the time required to convert raw materials into finished goods), the ratio of equipment setup time to total production time, and the ratio of reworked units to completed units.

2. **Profit Margin**
   a. **Gross profit margin** is the percentage of gross revenues retained by the firm after paying for merchandise. The key analysis with respect to the gross profit margin is whether it is stable despite an increase or decrease in sales.

   $$\text{Gross profit margin} = \frac{\text{Net sales} - \text{Cost of goods sold}}{\text{Net sales}}$$

   b. **Operating profit margin** is the percentage retained after selling and general administrative expenses have been paid.

   $$\text{Operating profit margin} = \frac{\text{Operating income}}{\text{Net sales}}$$

   1) The ratio of net operating income to sales also may be defined as earnings before interest and taxes (EBIT) divided by net sales.
   2) Operating profit margin also is known as return on sales (ROS).

   c. **Net profit margin** (profit margin) is the percentage retained after other gains, losses (including interest expense), and income taxes have been recognized.

   $$\text{Net profit margin} = \frac{\text{Net income}}{\text{Net sales}}$$

476   SU 16: Performance Measurement and Process Management

3. **Return on Investment (ROI) and Residual Income**
   a. The return provided to a corporation's owners most often is assessed using one of two measures to evaluate investment centers:
      1) Return on investment, stated in percentage terms
      2) Residual income, stated in dollar terms
   b. These measures allow an investor to assess how effectively and efficiently the firm is using assets to obtain a return.
   c. Operating income equals earnings before interest and tax.

4. **Return on Investment -- Basic Version**
   a. ROI is calculated as follows if the investment is defined as assets:

   $$\text{Return on investment (ROI)} = \frac{\text{Operating income}}{\text{Average invested capital}} = \frac{\text{Operating income}}{\text{Total assets}}$$

   1) If the firm's ROI is higher than its cost of capital, its activities are adding to shareholder value.

EXAMPLE 16-1   Basic ROI

A firm had the following information for the year just ended:

Sales	$100,000
Operating expenses	58,000
Invested capital (total assets)	800,000

Invested capital at the previous year end was $600,000. ROI for the year can be calculated as follows:

Return on investment (ROI) = Operating income ÷ Average invested capital
= ($100,000 − $58,000) ÷ [($800,000 + $600,000) ÷ 2]
= $42,000 ÷ $700,000
= 6%

---

5. **Return on Investment -- Component Version**
   a. ROI can be calculated as the product of two component ratios.

Return on Investment	Operating Profit Margin	Capital (Asset) Turnover
$\dfrac{\text{Operating income}}{\text{Average invested capital}}$ =	$\dfrac{\text{Operating income}}{\text{Sales}}$ ×	$\dfrac{\text{Sales}}{\text{Average invested capital}}$

EXAMPLE 16-2   Components of ROI

Invested capital at the previous year end was $600,000. ROI for the year can be calculated as follows:

Operating profit margin: Operating income ÷ Sales = $42,000 ÷ $100,000 = 42%
Capital turnover: Sales ÷ Average invested capital = $100,000 ÷ $700,000 = .143 times

The calculation can be checked by recombining the two ratios to generate ROI.

Return on investment: Operating profit margin × Capital turnover = 42% × .143 = 6%

SU 16: Performance Measurement and Process Management

6. **Residual Income**

    a. Residual income is calculated as follows:

       Residual income = Operating income − Target return on invested capital

       1) The target return amount equals average invested capital times an imputed interest rate. This imputed interest rate is the entity's required rate of return on investments.

    EXAMPLE 16-3   Residual Income

    The firm's capital has an imputed interest rate of 5.5%.

    Residual income = Operating income − Target return on invested capital
    = $42,000 − ($700,000 × 5.5%)
    = $42,000 − $38,500
    = $3,500
    ---

7. **Comparison of ROI and Residual Income**

    a. ROI is a percentage, and residual income is a monetary amount.

    b. ROI is widely used because it facilitates comparison with other percentage-based measures, such as the firm's cost of capital and the ROIs of competitors.

       1) But a disadvantage of ROI is the potential rejection of projects that decrease the ROI despite increasing shareholder value.

    EXAMPLE 16-4   ROI vs. Residual Income

    A firm assesses divisional performance based solely on ROI. If a division with a current ROI of 12% is considering a project that is estimated to return only 10%, management might reject it because divisional ROI would decrease.

    Nevertheless, if the project has a positive residual income, it should be accepted because it increases shareholder value.
    ---

    c. Example 16-4 indicates the reason residual income often is preferable.

       1) The distinction between ROI and residual income is similar to that between internal rate of return (IRR), a percentage, and net present value (NPV), a monetary amount.

          a) A percentage identifies the highest return per dollar invested. But the firm ultimately is most interested in the total monetary amount of the return.

    SUCCESS TIP: The AICPA has frequently asked questions about the determination of ROI and residual income as well as questions requiring their comparison.

8. Return on Assets

a. Return on assets (ROA) is an alternative to return on investment.

$$\text{Return on assets (ROA)} = \frac{\text{Net income}}{\text{Average total assets}}$$

EXAMPLE 16-5 ROA

A firm reports the following information for the year just ended:

Operating income	$ 90,000
Income taxes	27,000
Total assets	400,000

Total assets at the previous year end were $500,000. ROA for the year is calculated as follows:

Return on assets (ROA) = Net income ÷ Average total assets
= ($90,000 − $27,000) ÷ [($400,000 + $500,000) ÷ 2]
= $63,000 ÷ $450,000
= 14%
---

9. Internal Growth Rate

a. The internal growth rate measures the potential growth of a firm without external financing.

$$\text{Internal growth rate} = \frac{\text{Return on assets} \times \text{Retention}}{1 - (\text{Return on assets} \times \text{Retention})}$$

1) **Retention** (a rate) equals the addition to retained earnings divided by net income.

EXAMPLE 16-6 Internal Growth Rate

A firm has net income of $100,000 and average total assets of $500,000. The amount of net income retained was $80,000.

Return on assets: Net income ÷ Average total assets = $100,000 ÷ $500,000 = 0.2
Retention: Addition to retained earnings ÷ Net income = $80,000 ÷ $100,000 = 0.8

Thus,

Internal growth rate = (Return on assets × Retention) ÷ [1 − (Return on assets × Retention)]
= (0.2 × 0.8) ÷ [1 − (0.2 × 0.8)]
= 19%
---

10. Earnings per Share (EPS)

a. EPS is a ratio of interest to common shareholders. It is a profitability ratio that measures the amount of current-period earnings that can be associated with a single share of common stock.

$$\text{EPS} = \frac{\text{Net income} - \text{Preferred dividends}}{\text{Common shares outstanding}}$$

1) The numerator also is known as income available to common shareholders.

11. Return on Equity (ROE) -- Basic Version

a. ROE measures the amount of net income returned in relation to shareholder equity.

$$\text{ROE} = \frac{\text{Net income}}{\text{Average shareholder's equity}}$$

SU 16: Performance Measurement and Process Management

12. **Return on Equity -- Component Version**

    a. Using DuPont ROE equation, ROE can be calculated as the product of three component ratios.

Return on Equity		**Net Profit Margin**		**Assets Turnover**		**Equity Multiplier**
$\dfrac{\text{Net income}}{\text{Average total equity}}$	=	$\dfrac{\text{Net income}}{\text{Net sales}}$	×	$\dfrac{\text{Net sales}}{\text{Average total assets}}$	×	$\dfrac{\text{Average total assets}}{\text{Average total equity}}$

    1) The net profit margin component examines efficiency in generating earnings from sales.

    2) The assets turnover component examines how efficiently all resources are used to generate revenues.

    3) The equity multiplier measures financial leverage. Issuing debt to raise capital increases the equity multiplier and the return on equity.

        a) The equity multiplier also equals total assets divided by total equity.

13. **Return on Common Equity (ROCE)**

    a. ROCE measures the amount of income earned per dollar invested by the common shareholders.

    $$\text{ROCE} = \frac{\text{Net income} - \text{Preferred dividends}}{\text{Average common equity}}$$

14. **The Price-Earnings (P-E) Ratio**

    a. The P-E ratio measures the amount that investors are willing to pay for $1 of earnings.

    $$\text{P-E} = \frac{P}{E} = \frac{\text{Market price of share}}{\text{EPS}}$$

    1) Generally, the higher the ratio, the more confidence the market has in the firm's ability to provide higher returns to investors.

15. **Economic Rate of Return on Common Stock**

    a. The economic rate of return on common stock measures the amount of shareholder value generated during a period in relation to the investment.

    $$\text{Economic rate of return on common stock} = \frac{\text{Dividends paid} + \text{Change in share price}}{\text{Beginning share price}}$$

16. **Economic Value Added**

   a. Economic value added (EVA) is a performance measure to approximate economic profit. While the formula is similar to the formula for residual income, there are two differences:

      1) EVA uses after-tax operating income and adjusts for the opportunity cost of capital.
      2) EVA attempts to measure the "value added" by each segment or division.

   b. The following is the basic formula:

   EVA = After-tax operating income − (Invested capital × Weighted-average cost of capital[1])

   [1]The weighted-average cost of capital (WACC) is defined in Study Unit 8, Subunit 6.

      1) Invested capital equals total assets minus current liabilities.

EXAMPLE 16-7   EVA

A firm invested $200,000 in a new operating segment. Its current-year after-tax operating income was $21,000. The WACC is 9%.

After-tax operating income	$21,000
Investment × Cost of capital ($200,000 × 9%)	(18,000)
EVA	$ 3,000

The EVA is positive. Thus, the investment increased shareholder value.

---

   c. EVA represents a business unit's true economic profit primarily because it is determined by subtracting the cost of equity capital.

      1) The cost of equity is an opportunity cost, i.e., the return on the best alternative investment of similar risk.
      2) Accordingly, EVA measures the marginal benefit obtained by using resources in a specific way.

   d. EVA also differs from measures based on accounting income because it results from certain other adjustments.

      1) For example, R&D costs may be capitalized and amortized over 5 years for EVA purposes, and true economic depreciation rather than the amount used for accounting or tax purposes may be recognized. Adjustments vary from firm to firm.

SUCCESS TIP

Candidates should know the formulas used to calculate the various financial ratios and also should be able to analyze the results. Numerous CPA Exams have included questions on both the calculation and analysis of financial ratios. However, the numbers necessary to calculate a ratio often are not given directly.

NOTE: This tip also applies to Study Unit 9, Subunits 2 and 3, and Study Unit 10, Subunit 2.

STOP & REVIEW

You have completed the outline for this subunit.
Study multiple-choice questions 3 through 5 beginning on page 496.

16.3 PERFORMANCE MEASUREMENT -- BALANCED SCORECARD

1. **Critical Success Factors (CSFs)**

    a. The trend in performance evaluation is the balanced scorecard approach to managing the implementation of the firm's strategy. This includes multiple performance measures.

    1) The balanced scorecard is an accounting report that connects the firm's CSFs with measurements of its performance.

    b. The balanced scorecard is a goal congruence tool that informs managers about the nonfinancial factors that upper management believes to be important.

    1) Measures on the balanced scorecard may be financial or nonfinancial, internal or external, and short-term or long-term.

    2) The balanced scorecard facilitates best practice analysis. Best practices are methods of performing a business function that are superior to all other known methods.

    c. CSFs are specific, measurable financial and nonfinancial, internal and external, short-term and long-term elements of performance that are vital to competitive advantage.

    1) Multiple measures of performance determine whether a manager is achieving certain objectives but not others that may be more important. For example, an improvement in operating results at the expense of new product development is apparent using a balanced scorecard.

2. **SWOT Analysis**

    a. A firm identifies its CSFs by means of a SWOT analysis that addresses internal factors (its **S**trengths and **W**eaknesses) and external factors (its **O**pportunities and **T**hreats).

3. **Measures**

    a. Specific measures for each CSF should be relevant to the success of the firm and reliably stated.

    1) Thus, the balanced scorecard varies with the strategy adopted by the firm.

    b. The scorecard should include **lagging** indicators (such as output and financial measures) and **leading** indicators (such as many types of nonfinancial measures, e.g., customer satisfaction, sales returns, and repeat customers).

    1) The latter should be used only if they are predictors of ultimate financial performance.

    c. The scorecard should permit a determination of whether certain objectives are being achieved at the expense of others.

    1) For example, reduced spending on customer service may improve short-term financial results at a significant cost that is revealed by a long-term decline in customer satisfaction measures.

SUCCESS TIP: The AICPA has tested the balanced scorecard approach by asking for the perspective related to either measures or CSFs.

4. **Possible CSFs and Measures**

    a. A typical balanced scorecard classifies objectives into one of four perspectives:

    1) **Financial**

Possible CSF	Possible Measure
Sales	New product sales
Fair value of firm's stock	Price-earnings ratio
Profitability	Return on investment
Liquidity	Quick ratio, current ratio, days payables or receivables

    2) **Customer Satisfaction**

CSF	Financial Measure	Nonfinancial Measure
Customer satisfaction	Trends in dollar amounts of returns	Market share
Dealer and distributor relationships	Trends in dollar amounts of discounts taken	Lead time
Marketing and selling performance	Trends in dollar amounts of sales	Market research results
Prompt delivery	Trends in delivery expenses	On-time delivery rate
Quality	Dollar amounts of defects	Rate of defects

    3) **Internal Business Processes**

CSF	Financial Measure	Nonfinancial Measure
Quality	Scrap costs	Rate of scrap and rework
Productivity	Change in company revenue/change in company costs	Units produced per machine hour
Flexibility of response to changing conditions	Cost to repurpose machine for new use	Time to repurpose machine for new use
Operating readiness	Set-up costs	Downtime
Safety	Dollar amount of injury claims	Number and type of injury claims

    4) **Learning and Growth**

CSF	Financial Measure	Nonfinancial Measure
Development of new products	R&D costs	Number of new patents applied for
Promptness of their introduction	Lost revenue (from slow introduction of new product to market)	Length of time to bring a product to market
Human resource development	Recruiting costs	Personnel turnover
Morale	Orientation/team-building costs	Personnel complaints
Competence of workforce	Training/retraining costs	Hours of training

5. **Development**
   a. The active participation of senior management is essential.
      1) This involvement ensures the cooperation of lower-level managers in the identification of objectives, appropriate measures, targeted results, and methods of achieving the results.
   b. The scorecard should contain measures at the detail level that permit everyone to understand how his or her efforts affect the firm's results.
      1) The scorecard and the strategy it represents must be communicated to all managers and used as a basis for compensation decisions.
6. **Functionality**
   a. Each objective is associated with one or more measures that permit the organization to measure progress toward the objective.
      1) The organization should identify a cause-and-effect relationship between an action taken (or avoided) that affects a CSF. For example, if the R&D budget increases, the number of new patents applied for increases.
      2) Achievement of the objectives in one perspective makes it possible to achieve the objectives in other perspectives.
      3) A **strategy map** relates objectives and perspectives.
   b. To achieve its objectives, the organization must establish relevant
      1) Criteria to measure outcomes
      2) Performance drivers

EXAMPLE 16-8	Balanced Scorecard		
OBJECTIVES	PERFORMANCE MEASURES	TARGETS	INITIATIVES
PERSPECTIVE: Financial			
Increase sales	Gross revenues	Increase 15%	• Expand into new markets • Improve same-store sales
PERSPECTIVE: Customer Satisfaction			
Reduce returns	Number of returns	Decrease 10%	• Reduce number of defects • Determine customer needs prior to sale
PERSPECTIVE: Internal Business Processes			
Reduce scrap	Costs of scrap	Decrease 5%	• Employee training • Seek higher quality materials
PERSPECTIVE: Learning and Growth			
Reduce personnel turnover	Length of time employed	Increase 50%	• Improve hiring practices • Reevaluate compensation plan

You have completed the outline for this subunit. Study multiple-choice questions 6 and 7 on page 497.

STOP & REVIEW

16.4 PROCESS MANAGEMENT

1. **Learning Curve Analysis**

    a. Learning curve analysis reflects the increased rate at which people perform tasks as they gain experience.

    1) The time required to perform a given task decreases most rapidly during the early stages of production.

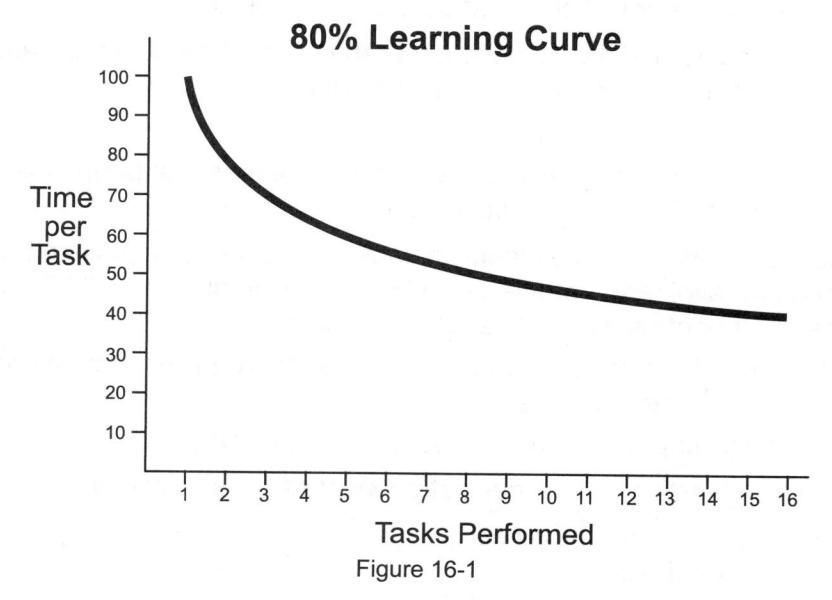

    80% Learning Curve

    Figure 16-1

    b. The curve is usually expressed as a percentage of reduced time to complete a task for each doubling of cumulative production. The most common percentage used in practice is 80%. The most common assumption is that the learning rate applies to the **cumulative average completion time per unit**.

    c. The limitation of the learning curve in practice is the difficulty in knowing the shape of the learning curve.

    1) The existence of the learning curve effect is widely accepted, but the percentage to be used may not be known while the information is still useful. As a result, many simply assume an 80% learning curve and make decisions based on those results.

2. **Performance-Improving Processes**

    a. The Process-Management-Driven Business

        1) Management emphasizes the effective and efficient performance of predefined business processes.

        2) Well-designed processes lead to the accomplishment of the organization's goals.

    b. Shared Services

        1) Shared services are centralized but with a nontraditional focus.

        2) The shared services model involves combining redundant services (e.g., combining separate human resources departments for each division into one single human resources department and sharing its services among divisions) so that its employees are motivated to be flexible and responsive to customer needs.

        3) Centralizing a firm's internal services at a single location can reduce costs but may delay services.

    c. Outsourcing

        1) Processes such as human resources, payroll, and information services may not be core competencies of an organization.

            a) Contracting with outside service providers who specialize in these functions may result in cost savings. The organization also is not affected by knowledge loss when key employees leave.

        2) Potential disadvantages include

            a) Loss of core knowledge,
            b) Loss of control over the outsourced function,
            c) Unexpected costs, and
            d) The challenges of contract management.

    d. Off-Shore Operations

        1) Cost advantages (lower taxes, lower wages, and less strict environmental and occupational safety regulations) can be gained by moving operations to foreign countries.

        2) The effects of currency exchange rate fluctuations and the possibility of political instability must be considered.

3. **Business Process Reengineering (BPR)**

    a. BPR is the complete, bottom-up revision of the way an organization performs a business process.

    b. Organizations undertaking BPR ignore how the process currently is performed.

    c. BPR is **not**

        1) A gradual, incremental streamlining of existing procedures (kaizen);
        2) Computerization of manual processes (automation); or
        3) A change in the nature of the business itself (paradigm shift).

d. The goals of BPR are usually stated in terms of increased efficiency or elimination of redundant jobs. These goals eventually can be stated in terms of cost savings.

e. But BPR often does not provide the promised benefits.

1) Business processes routinely cross organizational boundaries.

a) Redesigning the process of one department often requires the cooperation of other departments that may be reluctant to reduce their autonomy.

2) Upper management may have begun other strategic initiatives, such as total quality management or Six Sigma, that conflict with either the goals of, or the resources necessary for, BPR.

a) Any BPR program must be closely aligned with the overall organizational strategy.

4. **Lean Operation**

a. The ultimate goal of lean operation is a smooth, rapid flow of work through the system. To achieve this ultimate goal, three supporting goals are constantly pursued.

1) Elimination of Disruptions

a) A disruption is anything that interrupts the smooth flow of work, e.g., line stoppages, materials shortages, and excessive defects.

2) System Flexibility

a) A flexible system can be adapted to changes in product mix or quantities without creating a disruption.

3) Elimination of Waste

a) Waste is any unproductive use of resources. In accordance with a just-in-time philosophy, inventory is considered waste.

5. **Theory of Constraints (TOC)**

a. The theory of constraints is a system to improve human thinking about problems. It has been greatly extended to include manufacturing operations.

1) The basic premise of TOC as applied to business is that improving any process is best done not by trying to maximize efficiency in every part of the process but by focusing on a limiting factor, called the constraint (or bottleneck operation).

EXAMPLE 16-9   TOC

During the early days of the American Civil War, several units calling themselves legions were formed, consisting of combined infantry, artillery, and cavalry. This arrangement did not last because the entire unit could only maneuver as fast as the slowest part. The artillery was the constraint. The solution was to study the Barnum & Bailey Circus's use of trains to move and set up wagons.

---

2) Increasing the efficiency of processes that are not constraints merely creates backup in the system.

b. The following are the steps in a TOC analysis:
   1) Identify the constraint.
   2) Determine the most profitable product mix given the constraint.
   3) Maximize the flow through the constraint.
   4) Increase capacity at the constraint.
   5) Redesign the manufacturing process for greater flexibility and speed.

c. A basic principle of TOC analysis is that short-term profit maximization requires maximizing the contribution margin through the constraint (throughput contribution).
   1) Thus, the product with the highest output should be the one with the highest throughput contribution per unit, not necessarily the highest contribution margin per unit.
   2) Throughput margin is sales less direct materials and is also referred to as throughput contribution.

d. To determine the most profitable use of the bottleneck operation, a manager calculates the throughput contribution per unit of time spent in the constraint.
   1) Profits are maximized by maximizing the flow through the bottleneck operation of the product with the highest throughput contribution per unit of time.

6. **Six Sigma**

   a. Six Sigma is a quality improvement approach. The goal is to reduce the number of defects in a mass-production process.
      1) The name Six Sigma (sometimes written 6σ) is derived from statistics and probability theory. In a normal distribution (i.e., a bell curve), six standard deviations encompass 99.99966% of the items in the distribution.
      2) Because of the importance of statistical analysis in any Six Sigma program, accurate and verifiable data are a necessity.

   b. A Six Sigma program also involves role-filling by specific individuals in the organization. (The color coding system is based on martial arts belt rankings.)
      1) The executive level must demonstrate its commitment to the Six Sigma program and must empower those in the other roles with enough authority and resources to implement the program successfully.
      2) Champions have responsibility for oversight of the implementation of the Six Sigma program across the organization.
      3) Master black belts assist the champions in implementing the program.
      4) Black belts, like champions and master black belts, devote all of their time to the Six Sigma program. They oversee specific projects.
      5) Green belts and yellow belts do Six Sigma work in addition to their regular duties. They are closest to the production processes to be improved.

STOP & REVIEW

You have completed the outline for this subunit.
Study multiple-choice questions 8 through 11 beginning on page 498.

16.5 TOOLS FOR PROCESS MANAGEMENT

SUCCESS TIP: Past exam questions have asked for identification of the methods used to measure process performance.

1. **Statistical Process Control (SPC)**
    a. SPC is a method of quality control that uses statistical methods.
    b. Results of an operation are monitored to determine whether it is within certain limits or at certain capacities.
    c. SPC can be applied to any process in which a conforming product can be measured.
    d. The information learned from SPC should be used in planning and budgeting.

SUCCESS TIP: The AICPA has begun to test candidates' knowledge of data visualization, which is the placement of data in a visual context to help users understand their significance. Statistical control charts, Pareto diagrams, histograms, and fishbone diagrams are all types of visualizations. Other types of visualizations can be found in Study Unit 20, Subunit 4.

2. **Statistical Control Charts**
    a. Statistical control charts are graphic aids for monitoring the status of any process subject to acceptable or unacceptable variations during repeated operations.
        1) They also have applications of direct interest to auditors and accountants, for example, (a) unit cost of production, (b) direct labor hours used, (c) ratio of actual expenses to budgeted expenses, (d) number of calls by sales personnel, or (e) total accounts receivable.
    b. A control chart consists of three lines plotted on a horizontal time scale.
        1) The center line represents the overall mean or average range for the process being controlled. The other two lines are the upper control limit (UCL) and the lower control limit (LCL).
        2) The processes are measured periodically, and the values (X) are plotted on the chart.
            a) If the value falls within the control limits, no action is taken.
            b) If the value falls outside the limits, the result is abnormal, the process is considered out of control, and an investigation is made for possible corrective action.

c. Another advantage of the chart is that it makes trends and cycles visible.

1) A disadvantage of the chart is that it does not indicate the cause of the variation.

EXAMPLE 16-10   **Statistical Control Chart**

The chart below depicts 2 weeks of production by a manufacturer who produces a single precision part each day. To be usable, the part can vary from the standard by no more than +/− 0.1 millimeter.

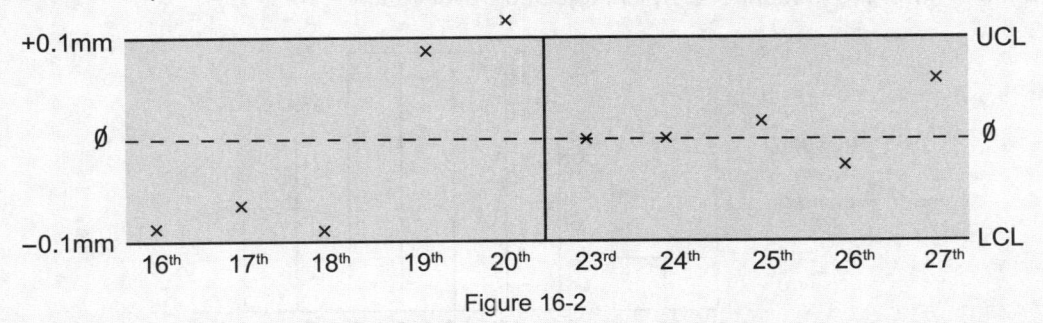

Figure 16-2

The part produced on the 20th had to be scrapped, and changes were made to the equipment to return the process to the controlled state for the following week's production.

---

3. **Pareto Diagrams**

   a. A Pareto diagram is a bar chart that assists managers in quality control analysis.

      1) In the context of quality control, managers optimize their time by focusing their effort on the relatively few sources of the most defects.

         a) The independent variable, plotted on the x axis, is the factor selected by the manager as the subject of interest, e.g., a department, time period, or geographical location. The frequency of occurrence of the defect (dependent variable) is plotted on the y axis.

         b) The occurrences of the independent variable are ranked from highest to lowest, allowing the manager to observe the sources of the most defects.

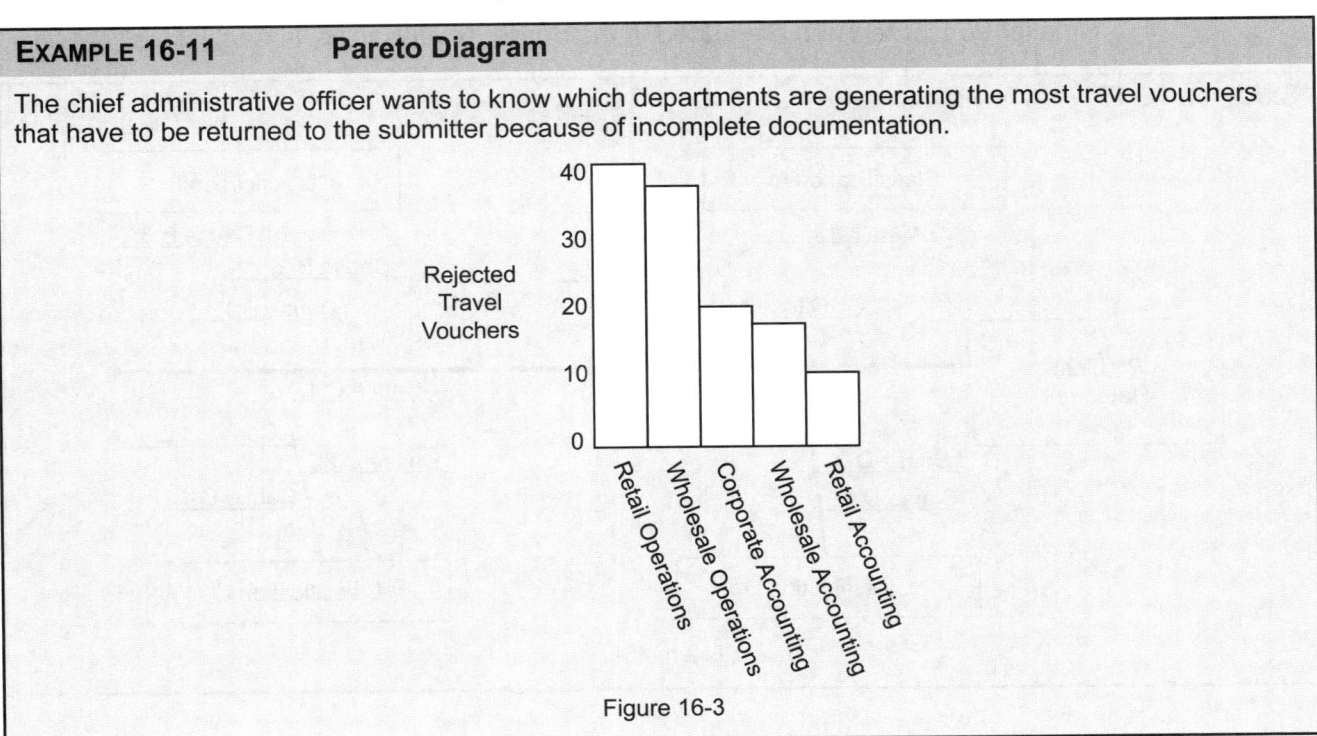

EXAMPLE 16-11   **Pareto Diagram**

The chief administrative officer wants to know which departments are generating the most travel vouchers that have to be returned to the submitter because of incomplete documentation.

Figure 16-3

4. **Histograms**

   a. A histogram is similar to a Pareto diagram. The major distinction is that histograms display a continuum for the independent variable.

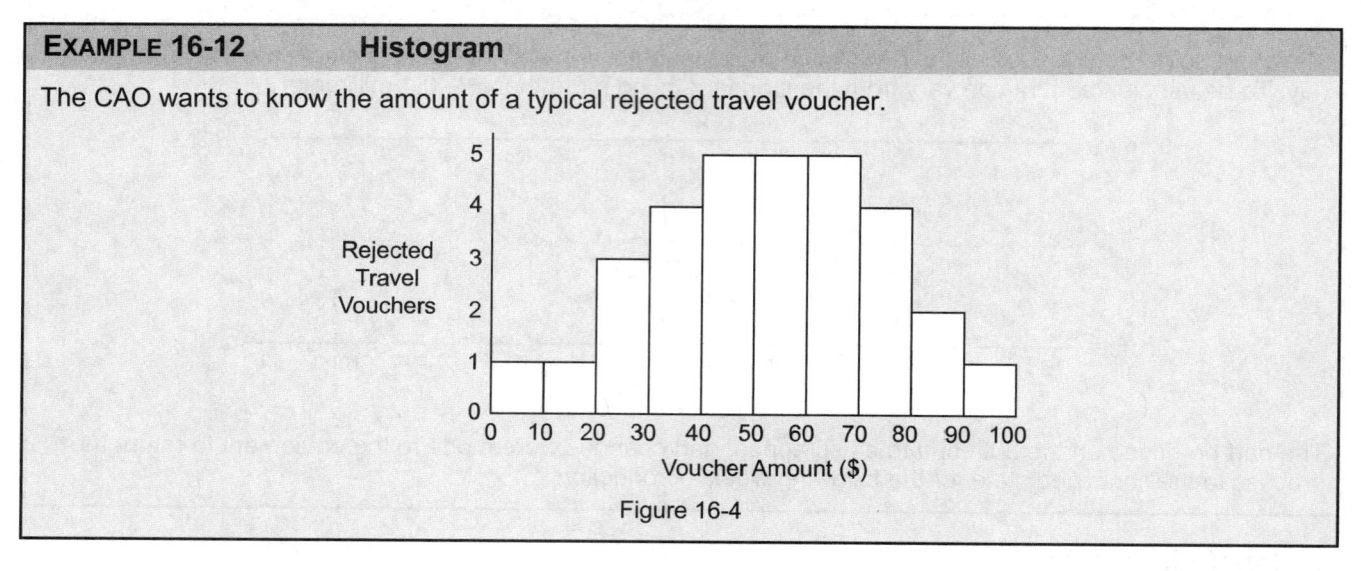

   EXAMPLE 16-12   Histogram

   The CAO wants to know the amount of a typical rejected travel voucher.

   [Histogram: Rejected Travel Vouchers (y-axis, 0–5) vs. Voucher Amount ($) (x-axis, 0–100). Bar heights at 10, 20, 30, 40, 50, 60, 70, 80, 90, 100 are approximately 1, 1, 3, 4, 5, 5, 5, 4, 2, 1.]

   Figure 16-4
   ---

5. **Fishbone Diagrams**

   a. A fishbone diagram (also called a cause-and-effect diagram) is a total quality management process improvement method that is useful in studying causation (why the actual and desired situations differ).

   1) The diagram organizes the analysis of causation and helps to identify possible interactions among causes.
   2) The head of the skeleton represents the statement of the problem.
   3) The principal classifications of causes are represented by lines (bones) drawn diagonally from the heavy horizontal line (the spine).
   4) Smaller horizontal lines are added in their order of probability in each classification.

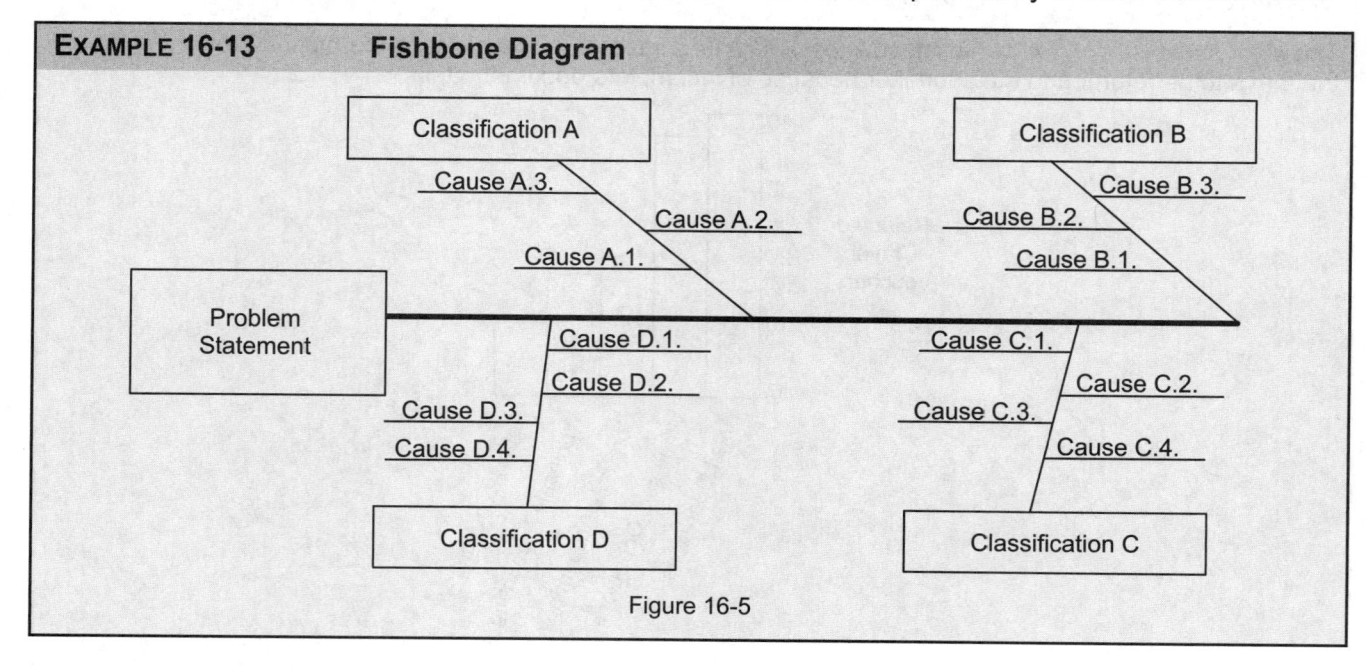

   EXAMPLE 16-13   Fishbone Diagram

   [Fishbone diagram with Problem Statement at left connected to spine. Classification A (upper left) with Cause A.1, A.2, A.3. Classification B (upper right) with Cause B.1, B.2, B.3. Classification D (lower left) with Cause D.1, D.2, D.3, D.4. Classification C (lower right) with Cause C.1, C.2, C.3, C.4.]

   Figure 16-5
   ---

6. Benchmarking

a. Benchmarking is a primary tool used in quality management. It applies to productivity management and business process analysis.

   1) Benchmarking involves analysis and measurement of key outputs against those of the best organizations. This procedure also identifies the underlying key actions and causes that contribute to the performance difference.

   2) Best practices are recognized by authorities in the field and by customers for their outstanding results. They generally are innovative technically or in the management of human resources.

   3) Benchmarking is an ongoing process that requires quantitative and qualitative measurement of the difference between the performance of an activity and the performance by the benchmark.

b. The following are kinds of benchmarking:

   1) Competitive benchmarking studies an organization in the same industry.

   2) Process (function) benchmarking studies operations of organizations with similar processes regardless of industry. Thus, the benchmark need not be a competitor or even a similar entity.

      a) This method may introduce new ideas that provide a significant competitive advantage.

   3) Strategic benchmarking is a search for successful competitive strategies.

   4) Internal benchmarking is the application of best practices in one part of the organization to its other parts.

> **EXAMPLE 16-14   Benchmarking**
>
> A team from an airline company charged with improving its aircraft ground turnaround time (refueling, maintenance, and service) might consider the benchmark of auto racing's pit stops and determine the applicability of their best practices.

7. Gamification

a. This method of problem solving involves thinking of business goals as if they were goals in a game, such as achieving a higher return on investment.

   1) Rewards are given to players who achieve certain goals.

      a) **Scores** can be published so that players are encouraged to compete.

      b) Due to the possibility that increased competition could lead to unethical behavior, the game should be monitored.

STOP & REVIEW

You have completed the outline for this subunit.
Study multiple-choice questions 12 through 15 beginning on page 499.

16.6 COSTS OF QUALITY

1. **Costs of Quality**

    a. The costs of quality must be assessed in terms of relative costs and benefits. Thus, an organization should attempt to optimize its total cost of quality.

        1) Moreover, nonquantitative factors also must be considered. For example, an emphasis on quality improves competitiveness, enhances employee expertise, and generates goodwill.

2. **Categories**

    a. **Conformance costs** include costs of prevention and costs of appraisal, which are financial measures of internal performance.

        1) **Prevention** attempts to avoid defective output. These costs include

            a) Preventive maintenance,
            b) Employee training,
            c) Review of equipment design, and
            d) Evaluation of suppliers.

        2) **Appraisal** includes such activities as statistical quality control programs, inspection, and testing.

    b. **Nonconformance costs** include internal failure costs (a financial measure of internal performance) and external failure costs (a financial measure of customer satisfaction).

        1) **Internal failure costs** occur when defective products are detected before additional costs are incurred on defective products. Examples are scrap, rework, tooling changes, and downtime.

        2) **External failure costs**, e.g., warranty costs, product liability costs, and loss of customer goodwill, result when problems occur after shipment.

            a) Environmental costs also are external failure costs, e.g., fines for nonadherence to environmental law and loss of customer goodwill.

STOP & REVIEW

You have completed the outline for this subunit.
Study multiple-choice questions 16 through 18 beginning on page 501.

16.7 TQM AND THE ISO FRAMEWORK

1. **Total Quality Management (TQM) Defined**

    a. TQM is the continuous pursuit of quality in every aspect of organizational activities through (1) a philosophy of doing it right the first time, (2) employee training and empowerment, (3) promotion of teamwork, (4) improvement of processes, and (5) attention to satisfaction of internal and external customers.

    1) TQM emphasizes the supplier's relationship with the customer and identifies customer needs. It also recognizes that everyone in a process is at some time a customer or supplier of someone else, either within or outside the organization.

    2) Thus, TQM (a) begins with external customer requirements, (b) identifies internal customer-supplier relationships and requirements, and (c) establishes requirements for external suppliers.

    3) Organizations tend to be vertically organized, but TQM requires strong horizontal linkages.

    > **BACKGROUND 16-1 Development of TQM**
    >
    > TQM was developed in the mid-1940s by statistician W. Edwards Deming, who aided Japanese industry in its recovery from World War II. The Deming Prize is awarded by the Union of Japanese Scientists and Engineers for outstanding contributions to the study or application of TQM (www.juse.or.jp/deming_en). While Deming was praised and deeply respected in Japan, it took 30 years for his principles to be applied in the U.S.

    b. TQM treats the pursuit of quality as a basic organizational function that is as important as production or marketing.

    c. TQM recognizes that quality improvement can increase revenues and decrease costs significantly. The following are TQM's core principles or critical factors:

    1) Emphasis on the customer

        a) Satisfaction of external customers
        b) Satisfaction of internal customers
        c) Requirements for external suppliers
        d) Requirements for internal suppliers

    2) Continuous improvement as a never-ending process, not a destination

    3) Engaging every employee in the pursuit of total quality

        a) Avoidance of defects in products or services and satisfaction of external customers requires that all internal customers be satisfied.

    d. The management of quality is not limited to quality management staff, engineers, and production personnel. It extends to everyone in the organization.

2. **Implementation**
    a. Implementation of TQM cannot be accomplished by application of a formula, and the process is lengthy and difficult. The following phases are typical:
        1) Establishing an executive-level quality council of senior managers with strong involvement by the CEO.
        2) Providing quality training programs for senior managers.
        3) Conducting a quality audit to evaluate the success of the process for gathering background information to develop the strategic quality improvement plan.
            a) The quality audit also may identify the best improvement opportunities and the organization's strengths and weaknesses compared with its benchmarked competitors.
        4) Preparing a gap analysis to determine what is necessary to close the gap between the organization and the quality leaders in its industry and to establish a database for the development of the strategic quality improvement plan.
        5) Developing strategic quality improvement plans for the short and long term.
        6) Conducting employee communication and training programs.
        7) Establishing quality teams, which ensure that goods and services conform to specifications.
        8) Creating a measurement system and setting goals.
        9) Revising compensation, appraisal, and recognition systems.
        10) Reviewing and revising the entire effort periodically.

3. **The ISO Standards**
    a. In 1987, the International Organization for Standardization (ISO) introduced ISO 9000, a group of 11 standards and technical reports that provide guidance for establishing and maintaining a **quality management system** (QMS). The ISO's rules specify that its standards be revised every 5 years to reflect technological and market developments.

> **BACKGROUND 16-2   Meaning of ISO**
>
> ISO is not an acronym. It means equal, suggesting that entities certified under ISO standards have equal quality. For specific and up-to-date information, see the ISO's website (www.iso.org).

    b. The intent of the standards is to ensure the quality of the process, not the product. The marketplace determines whether a product is good or bad.
        1) For this reason, the ISO deems it unacceptable for phrases referring to ISO certification to appear on individual products or packaging.

STOP & REVIEW

You have completed the outline for this subunit.
Study multiple-choice questions 19 through 21 on page 503.

QUESTIONS

16.1 Responsibility Centers

1. A segment of an organization is referred to as a profit center if it has

A. Authority to make decisions affecting the major determinants of profit including the power to choose its markets and sources of supply.

B. Authority to make decisions affecting the major determinants of profit including the power to choose its markets and sources of supply and significant control over the amount of invested capital.

C. Authority to make decisions over the most significant costs of operations including the power to choose the sources of supply.

D. Authority to provide specialized support to other units within the organization.

Answer (A) is correct.
REQUIRED: The definition of a profit center.
DISCUSSION: A profit center is responsible for both revenues and expenses. For example, the perfume department in a department store is a profit center. The manager of a profit center usually has the authority to make decisions affecting the major determinants of profit, including the power to choose markets (revenue sources) and suppliers (costs).
Answer (B) is incorrect. An investment center, not a profit center, has control over invested capital.
Answer (C) is incorrect. A cost center manager has authority over all significant costs but not of revenues or investments. **Answer (D) is incorrect.** A service center supports other organizational units.

2. Managers are most likely to accept allocations of common costs based on

A. Cause and effect.
B. Ability to bear.
C. Percent of revenues earned.
D. Top management decisions.

Answer (A) is correct.
REQUIRED: The criterion most likely to result in acceptable allocations of common costs.
DISCUSSION: The difficulty with common costs is that they are indirect costs whose allocation may be arbitrary. A direct cause-and-effect relationship between a common cost and the actions of the cost object to which it is allocated is desirable. Such a relationship promotes acceptance of the allocation by managers who perceive the fairness of the procedure, but identification of cause and effect may not be feasible.
Answer (B) is incorrect. Allocation using an ability-to-bear criterion punishes successful managers and rewards underachievers. **Answer (C) is incorrect.** Allocations based on the percentage of revenues earned use an ability-to-bear approach. **Answer (D) is incorrect.** Top management decisions on cost allocation tend to be arbitrary.

16.2 Performance Measurement -- Financial and Nonfinancial Measures

3. Which one of the following statements pertaining to the return on investment (ROI) as a performance measurement is **false**?

A. When the average age of assets differs substantially across segments of a business, the use of ROI may not be appropriate.

B. ROI relies on financial measures that are capable of being independently verified, while other forms of performance measures are subject to manipulation.

C. The use of ROI may lead managers to reject capital investment projects that can be justified by using discounted cash flow models.

D. The use of ROI can make it undesirable for a skillful manager to take on troubleshooting assignments such as those involving turning around unprofitable divisions.

Answer (B) is correct.
REQUIRED: The false statement about ROI as a performance measure.
DISCUSSION: ROI is calculated by dividing a segment's income by the invested capital. Thus, ROI can be manipulated by falsifying income or invested capital.
Answer (A) is incorrect. ROI can be misleading when the quality of the investment base differs among segments. Answer (C) is incorrect. Managers may reject projects that are profitable (a return greater than the cost of capital) but decrease ROI. For example, the manager of a segment with a 15% ROI may not want to invest in a new project with a 10% ROI, even though the cost of capital might be only 8%. **Answer (D) is incorrect.** The use of ROI does not reflect the relative difficulty of tasks undertaken by managers.

4. Charlie's Service Co. is an automobile service center. Charlie's had the following operating statistics for Year 6:

Sales	$750,000
Operating income	50,000
Net profit after taxes	6,000
Total assets available	700,000
Shareholders' equity	300,000
Cost of capital	8%

Charlie's has a

A. Return on investment of 6.67%.
B. Residual income of $(6,000).
C. Return on investment of 8%.
D. Residual income of $(10,000).

Answer (B) is correct.
REQUIRED: The true statement about operating performance.
DISCUSSION: Residual income is the excess of operating income (a pretax amount) over a targeted amount equal to an imputed interest charge on invested capital. Using total assets available as the investment base, Charlie's targeted amount is $56,000 ($700,000 total assets × 8% cost of capital). Subtracting this amount from operating income results in residual income of $(6,000).
Answer (A) is incorrect. The return on sales is 6.67% ($50,000 ÷ $750,000). **Answer (C) is incorrect.** The cost of capital is 8%. **Answer (D) is incorrect.** Residual income of $(10,000) results from improperly subtracting weighted sales rather than weighted assets.

5. Avionics Industrials reported at year end that operating income before taxes for the year equaled $2,400,000. The firm's weighted-average cost of capital (WACC) is 7.24%. The carrying amount of debt is $1,300,000, and the carrying amount of equity capital is $8,800,000. The income tax rate for Avionics is 30%. What is the economic value added (EVA)?

A. $731,240
B. $948,760
C. $1,668,760
D. $1,680,000

Answer (B) is correct.
REQUIRED: The EVA.
DISCUSSION: EVA equals after-tax operating income minus the product of the weighted-average cost of capital (WACC) and the investment base. After-tax operating income equals operating income multiplied by 1 minus the tax rate, or $1,680,000 [$2,400,000 × (1 − .3)]. The investment base is $10,100,000, consisting of $1,300,000 of debt and $8,800,000 of equity. Thus, EVA equals $948,760 [$1,680,000 − ($10,100,000 × 0.0724)].
Answer (A) is incorrect. The cost of capital is $731,240. **Answer (C) is incorrect.** Income taxes must be subtracted from operating income to compute EVA. **Answer (D) is incorrect.** The after-tax operating income is $1,680,000.

16.3 Performance Measurement -- Balanced Scorecard

6. Using the balanced scorecard approach, an organization evaluates managerial performance based on

A. A single ultimate measure of operating results, such as residual income.
B. Multiple financial and nonfinancial measures.
C. Multiple nonfinancial measures only.
D. Multiple financial measures only.

Answer (B) is correct.
REQUIRED: The nature of the balanced scorecard approach.
DISCUSSION: The trend in managerial performance evaluation is the balanced scorecard approach. Multiple measures of performance permit a determination as to whether a manager is achieving certain objectives at the expense of others that may be equally or more important. These measures may be financial or nonfinancial and usually include items with four perspectives: (1) financial; (2) customer satisfaction; (3) internal business processes; and (4) learning and growth.

7. On a balanced scorecard, which is more of an internal process measure than an external-based measure?

A. Cycle time.
B. Profitability.
C. Customer satisfaction.
D. Market share.

Answer (A) is correct.
REQUIRED: The measure more internal-process related on a balanced scorecard.
DISCUSSION: Cycle time is the manufacturing time to complete an order. Thus, cycle time is strictly related to internal processes. Profitability is a combination of internal and external considerations. Customer satisfaction and market share are related to how customers perceive a product and how competitors react.
Answer (B) is incorrect. Profitability is a measure that includes external considerations. **Answer (C) is incorrect.** Customer satisfaction is a measure that includes external considerations. **Answer (D) is incorrect.** Market share is a measure that includes external considerations.

16.4 Process Management

8. System flexibility, elimination of waste, and elimination of disruptions are characteristic goals of which business process?

A. Lean operation.
B. Six Sigma.
C. Delphi technique.
D. Monte Carlo technique.

Answer (A) is correct.
REQUIRED: The business process with the characteristic goals of system flexibility, elimination of waste, and elimination of disruptions.
DISCUSSION: The three supporting goals of lean operation are (1) elimination of disruptions, (2) system flexibility, and (3) elimination of waste. Inventory is considered a waste.
Answer (B) is incorrect. The goal of Six Sigma is to reduce the number of defects per million opportunities in a mass-production process to 3.4. Answer (C) is incorrect. The Delphi technique is a system for forecasting based on identifying a consensus among experts. Answer (D) is incorrect. Monte Carlo is a system for using random variables for forecasting in an environment of uncertainty.

9. Increasing the efficiency of all phases of a given process is specifically discouraged by which of the following models?

A. Lean operation.
B. Theory of constraints.
C. Six Sigma.
D. Demand flow technology.

Answer (B) is correct.
REQUIRED: The business process model that specifically discourages increasing the efficiency of all phases.
DISCUSSION: Under the theory of constraints, increasing the efficiency of processes that are not constraints (bottlenecks) merely creates backup in the system.
Answer (A) is incorrect. Lean operation does not specifically discourage increasing the efficiency of all phases. Answer (C) is incorrect. Six Sigma does not specifically discourage increasing the efficiency of all phases. Answer (D) is incorrect. Demand flow technology does not specifically discourage increasing the efficiency of all phases. It is based on a set of applied mathematical tools that help connect processes in a flow to daily changes in demand.

10. Which of the following is a characteristic of business process reengineering?

A. Gradual, incremental streamlining of existing procedures.
B. The movement of manual processes to computers.
C. A change in the nature of the business itself.
D. The bottom-up revision of the way the organization carries out a particular business process.

Answer (D) is correct.
REQUIRED: The characteristic of business process reengineering.
DISCUSSION: Business process reengineering (BPR) is the complete, bottom-up revision of the way an organization carries out a particular business process. Organizations undertaking BPR totally rethink how a particular business function should be carried out, without regard to how it is currently performed.
Answer (A) is incorrect. Gradual, incremental streamlining of existing procedures (kaizen) is specifically rejected by business process reengineering. Answer (B) is incorrect. Simply moving manual processes to computers (automation) is not a characteristic of business process engineering. Answer (C) is incorrect. A change in the nature of the business itself (paradigm shift) is not a characteristic of business process reengineering.

11. Given demand in excess of capacity, no spoilage or waste, and full use of a constant number of assembly hours, the number of components needed for an assembly operation with an 80% learning curve should

I. Increase for successive periods.
II. Decrease per unit of output.

A. I only.
B. II only.
C. Both I and II.
D. Neither I nor II.

Answer (A) is correct.
REQUIRED: The movement(s) of the number of components needed.
DISCUSSION: Learning curves reflect the increased rate at which people perform tasks as they gain experience. An 80% learning curve means that the cumulative average time required to complete a unit (or the time required to produce the last unit) declines by 20% when unit output doubles in the early stages of production. Thus, as the cumulative average time per unit (or the time to complete the last unit) declines, the number of units produced per period of time increases. As more units are produced, more components are needed for the production. The number of components per unit of output is not affected by an increase in output.
Answer (B) is incorrect. The number of components needed per unit of output produced should remain constant, assuming no spoilage or waste. Answer (C) is incorrect. The number of components needed per unit of output produced should remain constant, assuming no spoilage or waste. Answer (D) is incorrect. The number of components needed will increase for successive periods for an assembly operation with an 80% learning curve.

16.5 Tools for Process Management

12. The director of sales asks for a count of customers grouped in descending numerical rank by (1) the number of orders they place during a single year and (2) the dollar amounts of the average order. The visual format of these two pieces of information is most likely to be a

A. Fishbone diagram.
B. Cost of quality report.
C. Kaizen diagram.
D. Pareto diagram.

Answer (D) is correct.
REQUIRED: The appropriate process measurement tool.
DISCUSSION: A Pareto diagram displays the values of an independent variable such that managers can quickly identify the areas most in need of attention.
Answer (A) is incorrect. A fishbone diagram is useful for determining the unknown causes of problems, not for stratifying quantifiable variables. Answer (B) is incorrect. The contents of a cost of quality report are stated in monetary terms. This report is not helpful for determining when to adjust machinery. Answer (C) is incorrect. Kaizen diagram is not a meaningful term in this context.

13. Which of the following statements regarding benchmarking is **false**?

A. Benchmarking involves continuously evaluating the practices of best-in-class organization and adapting processes to incorporate the best of these practices.

B. Benchmarking, in practice, usually involves formation of benchmarking teams.

C. Benchmarking is an ongoing process that involves quantitative and qualitative measurement of the difference between the organization's performance of an activity and the performance by the best in the world or the best in the industry.

D. The benchmarked organization against which a firm is comparing itself must be a direct competitor.

14. A company, which has many branch stores, has decided to benchmark one of its stores for the purpose of analyzing the accuracy and reliability of branch store financial reporting. Which one of the following is the most likely measure to be included in a financial benchmark?

A. High turnover of employees.

B. High level of employee participation in setting budgets.

C. High amount of credit loss write-offs.

D. High number of suppliers.

Answer (D) is correct.
REQUIRED: The false statement about benchmarking.
DISCUSSION: Benchmarking is an ongoing process that involves quantitative and qualitative measurement of the difference between the organization's performance of an activity and the performance by a best-in-class organization. The benchmarked organization need not be a direct competitor. The important consideration is that it be an outstanding performer in its industry.
Answer (A) is incorrect. Benchmarking involves continuously evaluating the practices of best-in-class organization and adapting company processes to incorporate the best of these practices. **Answer (B) is incorrect.** Benchmarking, in practice, usually involves a formation of benchmarking teams. **Answer (C) is incorrect.** Benchmarking is an ongoing process that involves quantitative and qualitative measurement of the difference between the organization's performance of an activity and the performance by the best in the world or the best in the industry.

Answer (C) is correct.
REQUIRED: The most likely measure to be included in a financial benchmark.
DISCUSSION: High credit loss (bad debt) write-offs could indicate fraud, which compromises the accuracy and reliability of financial reports. Credit loss (bad debt) write-offs may result from recording fictitious sales.
Answer (A) is incorrect. Turnover of employees is not a financial benchmark. **Answer (B) is incorrect.** Employee participation in setting budgets is not a financial benchmark. **Answer (D) is incorrect.** The number of suppliers is not a financial benchmark.

15. A manufacturer that wants to improve its staging process compares its procedures against the check-in process for a major airline. Which of the following tools is the manufacturer using?

A. Total quality management.
B. Statistical process control.
C. Economic value added.
D. Benchmarking.

Answer (D) is correct.
REQUIRED: The tool that the manufacturer is using in comparing its procedures to the check-in process of a major airline.
DISCUSSION: Benchmarking is a primary tool used in quality management. It is a means of helping organizations with productivity management and business process analysis. Benchmarking involves analysis and measurement of key outputs against those of the best organizations. This procedure also involves identifying the underlying key actions and causes that contribute to the performance difference. The benchmark need not be a competitor or even a similar entity. Process (function) benchmarking studies operations of organizations with similar processes regardless of industry. Thus, a comparison to procedures against the check-in process for a major airline is an example of benchmarking.
Answer (A) is incorrect. Total quality management is the continuous pursuit of quality in every aspect of organizational activities through a philosophy of doing it right the first time, employee training and empowerment, promotion of teamwork, improvement of processes, and attention to satisfaction of both internal and external customers. This tool is not helpful in comparing the processes of two companies in different industries.
Answer (B) is incorrect. Statistical process control is used to monitor and measure the manufacturing process in real time. This tool is not helpful in comparing the processes of two companies in different industries.
Answer (C) is incorrect. Economic value added is calculated using monetary amounts and is thus a financial performance measure. It is not a helpful tool in improving the staging process of a company.

16.6 Costs of Quality

16. An example of an internal failure cost is

A. Maintenance.
B. Inspection.
C. Rework.
D. Product recalls.

Answer (C) is correct.
REQUIRED: The example of an internal failure cost.
DISCUSSION: In a quality management system, one of the costs of product nonconformance is internal failure cost, the cost of discovering, after appraisal but before shipment, that a completed product does not meet quality standards. An example is the cost of reworking the product.
Answer (A) is incorrect. A maintenance cost is a prevention cost. **Answer (B) is incorrect.** Inspection is an appraisal cost. **Answer (D) is incorrect.** Product recalls are external failure costs.

17. The cost of statistical quality control in a product quality cost system is categorized as a(n)

A. Internal failure cost.
B. Training cost.
C. External failure cost.
D. Appraisal cost.

Answer (D) is correct.
REQUIRED: The cost category that includes statistical quality control.
DISCUSSION: The four categories of quality costs are (1) prevention, (2) appraisal, (3) internal failure, and (4) external failure (lost opportunity). Appraisal costs include quality control programs, inspection, and testing. However, some authorities regard statistical quality and process control as preventive activities. They not only detect faulty work but also allow for adjustment of processes to avoid future defects.
Answer (A) is incorrect. Internal failure costs are incurred after poor quality has been found before shipment. Statistical quality control is designed to detect quality problems. **Answer (B) is incorrect.** Statistical quality control is not a training cost. **Answer (C) is incorrect.** External failure costs are incurred after the product has been shipped, including the costs associated with (1) warranties, (2) product liability, and (3) loss of customer goodwill.

18. The four categories of costs associated with product quality costs are

A. External failure, internal failure, prevention, and carrying.
B. External failure, internal failure, prevention, and appraisal.
C. Warranty, product liability, training, and appraisal.
D. Warranty, product liability, prevention, and appraisal.

Answer (B) is correct.
REQUIRED: The categories of product quality costs.
DISCUSSION: The four categories of quality costs are (1) prevention, (2) appraisal, (3) internal failure, and (4) external failure. Costs of prevention include attempts to avoid defective output, such as (1) employee training, (2) review of equipment design, (3) preventive maintenance, and (4) evaluation of suppliers. Appraisal includes quality control programs, inspection, and testing. Internal failure costs are incurred when detection of defective products occurs before shipment. They include costs of (1) scrap, (2) rework, (3) tooling changes, and (4) downtime. External failure costs are incurred after the product has been shipped. They include the costs associated with warranties, product liability, and loss of customer goodwill.
Answer (A) is incorrect. Carrying cost is an inventory cost. **Answer (C) is incorrect.** All training costs are not quality control related. Also, internal failure costs should be included. **Answer (D) is incorrect.** Internal failure costs should be included.

16.7 TQM and the ISO Framework

19. Which statement best describes total quality management (TQM)?

A. TQM emphasizes reducing the cost of inspection.
B. TQM emphasizes participation by all employees in the decision-making process.
C. TQM implementation is quick and easy.
D. TQM is the continuous pursuit of quality.

Answer (D) is correct.
REQUIRED: The best description of TQM.
DISCUSSION: TQM is the continuous pursuit of quality in every aspect of organizational activities through (1) a philosophy of doing it right the first time, (2) employee training and empowerment, (3) promotion of teamwork, (4) improvement of processes, and (5) attention to satisfaction of customers, both internal and external.
Answer (A) is incorrect. Reducing the cost of inspection helps achieve the lowest overall business cost. **Answer (B) is incorrect.** Participative management emphasizes participation by all employees in the decision-making process. **Answer (C) is incorrect.** TQM implementation is often lengthy and difficult.

20. If a company is customer-centered, its customers are defined as

A. Only people external to the company who have purchased something from the company.
B. Only people internal to the company who directly use its product.
C. Anyone external to the company and those internal who rely on its product to get their job done.
D. Everybody external to the company who is currently doing, or may in the future do, business with the company.

Answer (C) is correct.
REQUIRED: The definition of customers if a firm is customer-centered.
DISCUSSION: One of the principles of TQM is customer orientation, whether the customer is internal or external. An internal customer is a member of the organization who relies on another member's work to accomplish his or her task.

21. Which statement best describes the emphasis of total quality management (TQM)?

A. Reducing the cost of inspection.
B. Implementing better statistical quality control techniques.
C. Doing each job right the first time.
D. Encouraging cross-functional teamwork.

Answer (C) is correct.
REQUIRED: The emphasis of TQM.
DISCUSSION: The basic principles of TQM include (1) doing each job right the first time, (2) being customer-oriented, (3) committing the organizational culture to continuous improvement, and (4) promoting teamwork and employee empowerment.
Answer (A) is incorrect. Reducing the cost of inspection is a detail of the TQM emphasis. **Answer (B) is incorrect.** Implementing better statistical quality control is a detail of the TQM emphasis. **Answer (D) is incorrect.** Encouraging cross-functional teamwork is a detail of the TQM emphasis.

Access the **Gleim CPA Premium Review System** featuring our SmartAdapt technology from your Gleim Personal Classroom to continue your studies. You will experience a personalized study environment with exam-emulating multiple-choice questions.

STUDY UNIT SEVENTEEN
COSTING FUNDAMENTALS

(19 pages of outline)

17.1	Cost Measurement Terminology	505
17.2	Basic Cost Calculations	507
17.3	Other Cost Measurement Concepts	508
17.4	Absorption Costing and Variable Costing	511
17.5	Joint Product and By-Product Costing	520
17.6	Joint Cost Allocation Methods	522

Management accounting has specialized terminology. After reviewing this terminology, this study unit covers the most fundamental cost calculations and measurements.

17.1 COST MEASUREMENT TERMINOLOGY

1. **Manufacturing vs. Nonmanufacturing**

    a. The costs of manufacturing a product can be classified as one of two types: direct and indirect.

    1) Direct costs would be eliminated if the product was eliminated.

        a) **Direct materials** are tangible inputs to the manufacturing process that can feasibly be traced to the product, e.g., sheet metal welded together for a piece of heavy equipment.

            i) All costs of bringing materials to the production line, e.g., transportation-in, are included in the cost of direct materials.

        b) **Direct labor** is the cost of human labor that can feasibly be traced to the product, e.g., the wages of the welder.

    2) Indirect costs would not be eliminated if the product was eliminated.

        a) **Manufacturing overhead** consists of all costs of manufacturing that **are not direct** materials or direct labor.

            i) **Indirect materials** are tangible inputs to the manufacturing process that cannot feasibly be traced to the product, e.g., the welding compound used to put together a piece of heavy equipment.

            ii) **Indirect labor** is the cost of human labor connected with the manufacturing process that cannot feasibly be traced to the product, e.g., the wages of assembly line supervisors and janitorial staff.

            iii) Other manufacturing costs include utilities expense, real estate taxes, insurance, and depreciation on factory equipment. These costs are also known as factory overhead costs.

b. Manufacturing costs also may be classified as follows:
1) **Prime cost** – costs directly attributable to a product (equals direct materials plus direct labor).
2) **Conversion cost** – costs of converting materials into the finished product (equals direct labor plus manufacturing overhead).

c. A manufacturer incurs **nonmanufacturing costs (operating costs)**.
1) Selling (marketing) costs are incurred while getting the product to the consumer, e.g., sales personnel salaries and product transportation.
2) Administrative expenses are not directly related to producing or marketing the product, e.g., executive salaries and depreciation on the administration building.

2. **Direct vs. Indirect**
a. Costs can be classified by how they are assigned to cost objects.
1) **Direct costs** can be traced to a cost object in an economically feasible way.
a) Examples are direct materials and direct labor inputs.
2) **Indirect costs**, such as indirect materials and indirect labor, cannot be traced to a cost object in an economically feasible way. Thus, they must be allocated.
a) To simplify allocation, indirect costs often are collected in cost pools.
i) A cost pool is an account in which similar cost elements with a common cause (cost driver) are accumulated.
ii) Manufacturing overhead is a commonly used cost pool in which various indirect costs of manufacturing are accumulated prior to allocation.

3. **Product vs. Period**
a. An important issue in management accounting is whether to **capitalize** costs in inventory or to **expense** them in the period incurred.
1) Product costs (inventoriable costs) are capitalized as part of inventory. They eventually become components of cost of goods sold.
2) Period costs are expensed as incurred and are therefore excluded from cost of goods sold and inventory.

You have completed the outline for this subunit.
Study multiple-choice questions 1 through 3 on page 524.

STOP & REVIEW

17.2 BASIC COST CALCULATIONS

1. **Cost of Goods Sold and Cost of Goods Manufactured**

   a. Cost of goods sold is a straightforward computation for **retailers** because they have only one class of inventory.

   > Beginning inventory
   > \+ Purchases
   > − Ending inventory
   > = **Cost of goods sold**

   b. The calculation is more complex for **manufacturers** because they have three classes of inventory: raw (direct) material inventory, work-in-process inventory, and finished goods inventory.

   1) Cost of goods manufactured is an intermediate component of cost of goods sold. It is similar to a retailer's purchases account.

      > Beginning work-in-process inventory
      > \+ Total manufacturing costs
      > − Ending work-in-process inventory
      > = **Cost of goods manufactured**

   c. A comparison of these computations in full is as follows:

Cost of goods sold for a retailer:

Beginning inventory		$10,000
Plus: Purchases	$15,000	
Minus: Returns and discounts	(1,000)	
Net purchases	$14,000	
Plus: Freight-in	1,000	15,000
Goods available for sale		$25,000
Minus: Ending inventory		(5,000)
Cost of goods sold		$20,000

Cost of goods sold for a manufacturer:

Beginning direct materials inventory		$ 2,000	
Plus: Purchases	$ 4,000		
Minus: Returns and discounts	(1,000)		
Net purchases	$ 3,000		
Plus: Freight-in	1,000	4,000	
Direct materials available for use		$ 6,000	
Minus: Ending direct materials inventory		(1,000)	
Direct materials used in production			$ 5,000
Direct labor costs			5,000
Manufacturing overhead costs			4,000
Total manufacturing costs for the period			$14,000
Plus: Beginning work-in-process inventory			5,000
Minus: Ending work-in-process inventory			(4,000)
Cost of goods manufactured			$15,000
Plus: Beginning finished goods inventory			6,000
Goods available for sale			$21,000
Minus: Ending finished goods inventory			(11,000)
Cost of goods sold			$10,000

2. **Relevant vs. Sunk**

   a. Relevant costs are future costs that change depending on the action taken. All other costs are assumed to be constant and are irrelevant to the decision.

      1) An example is tuition that must be spent to attend a fourth year of college.

   b. Sunk costs already have been incurred or irrevocably committed to be incurred. Because they are unavoidable and do not vary with the option chosen, they are not relevant to future decisions.

      1) An example is 3 years of tuition already paid. The previous 3 years of tuition do not affect the decision to attend a fourth year.

3. **Additional Cost Concepts**

   a. **Value-adding costs** cannot be eliminated without reducing the quality, responsiveness, or quantity of the output required.

   b. **Incremental (differential or marginal) cost** is the difference in total cost between two decisions. Incremental cost never includes fixed costs or sunk costs.

   c. **Opportunity cost** is the maximum benefit forgone by using a scarce resource for a given purpose. This is usually the value of the second best option.

You have completed the outline for this subunit.
Study multiple-choice questions 4 through 6 on page 525.

STOP & REVIEW

17.3 OTHER COST MEASUREMENT CONCEPTS

1. **Variable vs. Fixed**

   a. Variable cost **per unit** is constant in the short run regardless of the level of production. But variable costs **in total** vary directly and proportionally with changes in volume. Typical variable costs are direct materials, direct labor, and manufacturing supplies.

   Variable Cost per Unit

   Figure 17-1

   Variable Cost in Total

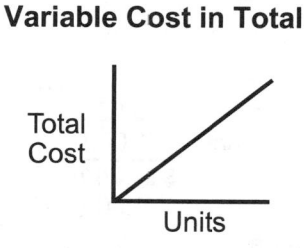

   Figure 17-2

SU 17: Costing Fundamentals

EXAMPLE 17-1 — Total Cost of Units

One unit of direct materials is to be used in each unit of a finished good.

Number of Units Produced		Cost per Unit		Total Cost of Units
0	×	$10	=	$ 0
100	×	$10	=	$ 1,000
1,000	×	$10	=	$ 10,000
5,000	×	$10	=	$ 50,000
10,000	×	$10	=	$100,000

b. **Fixed costs in total** are unchanged in the short run regardless of production level. Accordingly, the amount paid for an assembly line is the same even if nothing is produced. But fixed cost **per unit** varies indirectly with the activity level. Typical fixed costs are rent, depreciation, and insurance.

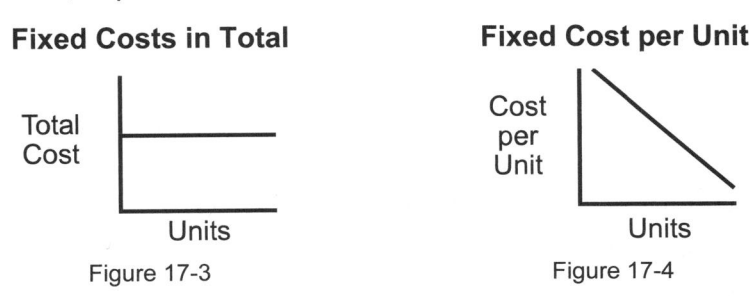

Fixed Costs in Total

Figure 17-3

Fixed Cost per Unit

Figure 17-4

EXAMPLE 17-2 — Unit Cost as Production Increases

The historical cost of an assembly line is fixed, but its cost per unit decreases as production increases.

Cost of Assembly Line		Number of Units Produced		Per-Unit Cost of Assembly Line
$1,000,000	÷	1	=	$1,000,000
$1,000,000	÷	100	=	$ 10,000
$1,000,000	÷	1,000	=	$ 1,000
$1,000,000	÷	5,000	=	$ 200
$1,000,000	÷	10,000	=	$ 100

c. **Mixed (semivariable) costs** combine fixed and variable elements, e.g., rental of a car for a flat fee per month plus an additional fee for each mile driven.

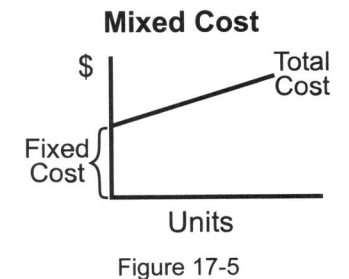

Mixed Cost

Figure 17-5

> **EXAMPLE 17-3**   **Mixed Costs**
>
> A piece of machinery is rented to improve the efficiency of a production line. The rent is $150,000 per year plus $1 for every unit produced.
>
> | Number of Units Produced | Fixed Cost of Extra Machine | | Variable Cost of Extra Machine | | Total Cost of Extra Machine |
> |---|---|---|---|---|---|
> | 0 | $150,000 | + | $ 0 | = | $150,000 |
> | 100 | $150,000 | + | $ 100 | = | $150,100 |
> | 1,000 | $150,000 | + | $ 1,000 | = | $151,000 |
> | 5,000 | $150,000 | + | $ 5,000 | = | $155,000 |
> | 10,000 | $150,000 | + | $10,000 | = | $160,000 |

        1) The fixed and variable portions of a mixed cost can be estimated using the high-low method (this method is covered in Study Unit 7, Subunit 2).

2. **Relevant Range**

   a. Relevant range is the **expected** range of activity.

   b. Within the relevant range, per-unit variable costs and total fixed costs do not change. It is synonymous with the **short run** because all costs are variable in the long run.

       1) The relevant range is established by the efficiency of current manufacturing operations, agreements with labor unions and suppliers, etc.

           a) Investment in more efficient equipment may result in higher total fixed costs and lower total and per-unit variable costs.

3. **Spoilage and Scrap**

   a. **Normal spoilage** occurs under normal, efficient operating conditions. It is essentially uncontrollable in the short run. Thus, it is accounted for as a product cost and included in the cost of the good output (predicted and unavoidable).

   b. **Abnormal spoilage** is **not** expected to occur under normal, efficient operating conditions. It is accounted for as a period cost (a loss).

   c. **Scrap** consists of materials left over from making a product. No cost is recognized for scrap, and it is not classified as normal or abnormal. Scrap also may be reused or discarded.

       1) If scrap is **common** to all jobs or **process costing** is used, the proceeds of its sale **reduce manufacturing overhead**. (Process costing is covered in Study Unit 18, Subunit 2.)

       2) If **job costing** is used, the proceeds **reduce work-in-process**. (Job-order costing is covered in Study Unit 18, Subunit 1.)

STOP & REVIEW

You have completed the outline for this subunit.
Study multiple-choice questions 7 through 9 on page 526.

17.4 ABSORPTION COSTING AND VARIABLE COSTING

1. **Two Ways of Treating Fixed Production Costs: Period vs. Product Costs**

    a. Recall that product costs are capitalized costs because they become a component of cost of goods sold.

    b. **Period costs** are expensed as incurred, i.e., they are not capitalized in finished goods inventory and are thus excluded from cost of goods sold.

    c. For **internal purposes**, decision making is improved by treating fixed overhead as a period cost so that only costs that are variable in the short run are included in the cost of the product.

       1) Fixed overhead costs are considered period costs and deducted in the period in which they are incurred.

       2) This practice is termed **variable**, or **direct**, **costing**. Variable costing is the preferred term because it concisely describes what is happening–namely that product costs are based only on variable costs.

    d. For **external reporting purposes (GAAP)**, the cost of a product must include **all** the costs of manufacturing it: direct labor, direct materials, and all factory overhead (both fixed and variable).

       1) This method is commonly known as **absorption, full costing,** or **full absorption costing**.

2. **Absorption Costing**

    a. Under absorption costing, the fixed portion of manufacturing overhead is "absorbed" into the cost of each unit of product.

       1) Product cost thus includes **all manufacturing costs**, both fixed and variable.

       2) Absorption-basis cost of goods sold is subtracted from sales to arrive at **gross margin** (also called gross profit).

       3) Gross margin is the net difference between sales revenue and absorption cost of goods sold. It represents the amount available to cover selling and administrative (S&A) expenses.

       4) Total S&A expenses (i.e., both fixed and variable) are then subtracted from gross margin to arrive at **operating income**.

       5) The inventoried cost of the product thus includes all production costs, whether variable or fixed.

    b. This method is required for external financial reporting purposes (GAAP) and for income tax purposes.

3. **Variable Costing**

   a. **Variable costs** are a direct function of production volume. They increase when production grows and decrease when production shrinks. Raw materials and labor directly involved with production are common variable costs.

   b. This method is more appropriate for internal reporting. It is sometimes called **direct costing**, although variable costing is the more accurate term (the phrase "direct costing" is considered misleading because it implies traceability).

      1) Product cost includes only the variable portion of manufacturing costs.

      2) Fixed manufacturing costs are considered period costs and are thus expensed as incurred. This technique is not allowed for external financial reporting but is very useful for internal decision making. It also stops management from manipulating income by overproducing during the period.

      3) Variable-basis cost of goods sold and the variable portion of S&A expenses are subtracted from sales to arrive at **contribution margin**.

         a) This amount (Sales – Total variable costs) is an important element of the variable costing income statement because it is the amount available for covering fixed costs (both manufacturing and S&A).

         b) Contribution margin is an important metric internally but is generally considered irrelevant to external financial statement users.

         c) Manufacturing contribution margin considers only the actual costs of manufacturing (i.e., direct materials, direct labor, and variable manufacturing overhead) to be product costs, i.e., inventoriable.

EXAMPLE 17-4   **Contribution Margin Income Statement**

Company X sells 20,000 units in the current year at a sales price of $60 per unit. X has the following costs:

Variable costs per unit		Total fixed costs	
Direct materials	$8	Overhead	$200,000
Direct labor	5	Selling and administrative	150,000
Overhead	2		
Selling	1		

Company X's contribution margin formatted income statement is prepared as follows:

Sales ($60 × 20,000)			$1,200,000
Less: Variable costs			
Direct materials ($8 × 20,000)		$160,000	
Direct labor ($5 × 20,000)		100,000	
Overhead ($2 × 20,000)		40,000	
Selling ($1 × 20,000)		20,000	(320,000)
Contribution margin			$ 880,000
Less: Fixed costs			
Overhead		$200,000	
Selling and administrative		150,000	(350,000)
Operating income			$ 530,000

SU 17: Costing Fundamentals

4. **Variable vs. Absorption Costing**

   a. The accounting for variable production costs and fixed S&A expenses is identical under the two methods.

   b. The difference lies in the varying treatment of fixed production costs and presentation of variable S&A expenses.

   c. Absorption and variable costing income statements can be illustrated as follows:

Absorption Costing	Variable Costing
Sales	Sales
− Cost of goods sold:	− Variable expenses:
Direct materials	Direct materials
Direct labor	Direct labor
Variable overhead	Variable overhead
Fixed overhead	Variable S&A expenses
= Gross margin	= Contribution margin
− Total S&A expenses	− Fixed expenses:
= Operating income	Fixed overhead
	Fixed S&A expenses
	= Operating income

   d. Note that ending finished goods inventory will differ between the two methods due to the different treatment of fixed production costs.

   1) This leads to a difference in cost of goods sold and operating income.

EXAMPLE 17-5   Absorption vs. Variable Costing

		Absorption Costing (Required for ext. rptg.)	Variable Costing (For internal reporting only)
	Sales	$100,000	$100,000
	Beg. finished goods inventory	$10,000	$10,000
Product Costs	Add: Variable production costs	20,000 (a)	20,000 (a)
	Add: Fixed production costs	30,000 (b)	−
	Goods available for sale	$60,000	$30,000
	Minus: End. finished goods inventory	(35,000)	(25,000)
	Cost of goods sold	$(25,000)	$(5,000)
Period Costs	Minus: Variable S&A expenses	−	(10,000) (c)
	Gross margin (abs.) / Contribution margin (var.)	$75,000	$85,000
	Minus: Fixed production costs	−	(30,000) (b)
	Minus: Variable S&A expenses	(10,000) (c)	−
	Minus: Fixed S&A expenses	(20,000) (d)	(20,000) (d)
	Operating income	$45,000	$35,000

Legend   Cost Component
- (a) Variable production costs
- (b) Fixed production costs
- (c) Variable selling and administrative expenses
- (d) Fixed selling and administrative expenses

The $10,000 difference in operating income ($45,000 − $35,000) is the difference between the ending inventory values ($35,000 − $25,000). In essence, the absorption method carries 33.33% of the fixed overhead costs ($30,000 × 33.33% = $10,000) on the balance sheet as an asset because 33.33% of the month's production is still in inventory.

> **SUCCESS TIP**
>
> CPA candidates must know how to calculate the various income statement components under the absorption and variable costing methods. The AICPA has frequently tested this topic, focusing especially on the differences between the amounts, such as operating income, determined by each method.

e. The following table summarizes product and period costs under both methods:

	Absorption Costing (Required under GAAP)	Variable Costing (For Internal Reporting Only)
Product Costs (Included in Cost of Goods Sold)	Variable production costs	
	Fixed production costs	
Period Costs (Excluded from Cost of Goods Sold)		Fixed production costs
	Variable S&A expenses	
	Fixed S&A expenses	

5. **Justification for Variable Costing**

   a. Under variable costing, fixed manufacturing overhead cost is considered a cost of maintaining capacity, not a cost of production.

      1) To illustrate, a company has a fixed rental expense of $10,000 per month on its factory building. That cost will be $10,000 regardless of whether there is any production.

         a) If the company produces zero units, the cost will be $10,000; if the company produces 10,000 units, the cost will be $10,000.

      2) Therefore, the $10,000 is not viewed as a cost of production and is not added to the cost of the inventories produced. The $10,000 is a cost of maintaining a certain level of production capacity.

   b. To emphasize, variable costing is used only for internal decision-making purposes; it is not permitted for external financial reporting or for tax calculation.

      1) The main advantage of the variable costing method is that income cannot be manipulated by management action, but management can manipulate income when using the absorption method. Additional advantages of variable costing are discussed in item 8. on page 517.

EXAMPLE 17-6 Absorption Basis vs. Variable Basis

During its first month in business, a firm produced 100 units and sold 80 while incurring the following costs:

Direct materials	$1,000
Direct labor	2,000
Variable overhead	1,500
Manufacturing costs used in variable costing	**$4,500**
Fixed overhead	3,000
Manufacturing costs used in absorption costing	**$7,500**

The effects on the financial statements of using one method rather than the other can be seen in these calculations:

	Absorption Basis	Variable Basis
Manufacturing costs	$7,500	$4,500
Divided by: Units produced	÷ 100	÷ 100
Per-unit cost	$ 75	$ 45
Times: Ending inventory	× 20	× 20
Value of ending inventory	**$1,500**	**$ 900**

The $600 difference ($1,500 − $900) in inventory value represents the fixed overhead that is charged to the absorption basis inventory. Because 20% of the units produced are still in inventory, 20% of the $3,000 of fixed costs, or $600, is still in inventory. Under the variable basis, all fixed costs are expended.

The per-unit selling price of the finished goods was $100, and the company incurred $200 of variable selling and administrative expenses and $600 of fixed selling and administrative expenses.

The following are partial income statements prepared using the two methods:

		Absorption Costing (Required under GAAP)	Variable Costing (For Internal Reporting Only)
	Sales	$ 8,000	$ 8,000
	Beginning finished goods inventory	$ 0	$ 0
Product Costs	Plus: Variable production costs	4,500 (a)	4,500 (a)
	Plus: Fixed production costs	3,000 (b)	
	Goods available for sale	$7,500	$4,500
	Less: Ending finished goods inventory	(1,500)	(900)
	Cost of goods sold	$(6,000)	$(3,600)
	Less: Variable S&A expenses		(200) (c)
	Gross margin (abs.) / Contribution margin (var.)	$ 2,000	$ 4,200
Period Costs	Less: Fixed production costs		(3,000) (b)
	Less: Variable S&A expenses	(200) (c)	
	Less: Fixed S&A expenses	(600) (d)	(600) (d)
	Operating income	**$ 1,200**	**$ 600**

The $600 difference in operating income ($1,200 − $600) is the difference between the two ending inventory values ($1,500 − $900). In essence, the absorption method carries 20% of the fixed overhead costs ($3,000 × 20% = $600) on the balance sheet as an asset because 20% of the month's production (100 available − 80 sold = 20 on hand) is still in inventory.

This calculation is for illustrative purposes only. The difference in operating income is exactly the difference in ending inventory only when beginning inventory is $0.

6. **Effects on Operating Income**
    a. As production and sales levels change, the two methods have varying effects on operating income.
        1) When everything produced during a period is sold that period, the two methods report the same operating income.
            a) Total fixed costs budgeted for the period are charged to sales revenue in the period under both methods.
        2) When production and sales are not equal for a period, the two methods report different operating income.
    b. When production exceeds sales, ending inventory expands.
        1) Under absorption costing, some fixed costs are embedded in ending inventory whereas, under variable costing, all costs have been expensed.
        2) **Therefore, when production exceeds sales, operating income is higher under absorption costing than it would be under variable costing.**
    c. When production is less than sales, ending inventory contracts.
        1) Under absorption costing, fixed costs embedded in beginning inventory get expensed whereas, under variable costing, only the current period's fixed costs are expenses.
        2) **Therefore, when production is less than sales, operating income is higher under variable costing than it would be under absorption costing.**
    d. Many companies prefer variable costing for internal reporting because of the perverse incentive inherent in absorption costing.
        1) Whenever production exceeds sales, fewer fixed costs are expensed under the absorption basis, and operating income always increases.
        2) A production manager can thus **increase absorption-basis operating income merely by increasing production**, whether there is any customer demand for the additional product or not.
            a) The company must also deal with the increased carrying costs resulting from swelling inventory levels.
        3) This practice, called producing for inventory, can be effectively discouraged by using variable costing for performance reporting and consequent bonus calculation.

7. **Summary of Effects on Income and Ending Inventory**
    a. The value of ending inventory is **never** higher under variable costing than it is under absorption costing because fixed manufacturing costs are not included in inventory under variable costing.
    b. Income and inventory levels will differ whenever sales and production differ.
        1) Income will be higher or lower under variable costing depending upon whether inventories are increased during the period or liquidated.
        2) If inventories increase during a period, the variable costing method will show a lower income because all fixed costs are being subtracted on the income statement, while under the absorption method, some fixed costs are being capitalized as inventories.
        3) Variable costing will show a higher income in periods when inventories decline because the absorption method forces the subtraction of current period fixed costs included in inventory sold, plus some fixed costs incurred (and capitalized) in prior periods.
    c. Under variable costing, profits always move in the same direction as sales volume. Profits reported under absorption costing behave erratically and sometimes move in the opposite direction from sales trends.
    d. In the long run, the two methods will report the same total profits if sales equal production. The inequalities between production and sales are usually minor over an extended period.

8. **Benefits of Variable Costing**
    a. Although the use of variable costing for financial statements is prohibited, most agree about its superiority for internal reporting. It is far better suited than absorption costing to the needs of management.
        1) Management requires a knowledge of cost behavior under various operating conditions. For planning and control, management is more concerned with treating fixed and variable costs separately than with calculating full costs.
        2) Full costs are usually of dubious value because they contain arbitrary allocations of fixed cost.

- b. Under the variable costing method, a production manager can manipulate income levels by deferring costs but not by overproducing. Given the same cost structure every year, the income levels will be based on sales, not the level of production.
- c. Under variable costing, the cost data for profit planning and decision making are readily available from accounting records and statements. Reference to auxiliary records and supplementary analyses is not necessary.
    1) For example, cost-volume-profit relationships and the effects of changes in sales volume on net income can easily be computed from the income statement prepared under the variable costing concept, but not from the conventional absorption cost income statement based on the same data.
- d. Profits and losses reported under variable costing have a relationship to sales revenue and are not affected by inventory or production variations.
- e. Absorption cost income statements may show decreases in profits when sales are rising and increases in profits when sales are decreasing, which may be confusing to management. Attempts at explanation by means of volume variances often compound rather than clarify the confusion.
- f. When variable costing is used, the favorable margin between selling prices and variable cost should provide a constant reminder of profits forgone because of lack of sales volume. A favorable margin justifies a higher production level.
- g. The full impact of fixed costs on net income, partially hidden in inventory values under absorption costing, is emphasized by the presentation of costs on an income statement prepared under variable costing.
- h. Proponents of variable costing maintain that fixed factory overhead is more closely correlated to capacity to produce than to the production of individual units.

9. **Further Aspects of Variable Costing**
   - a. Variable costing is also preferred over absorption costing for studies of relative profitability of products, territories, and other segments of a business. It concentrates on the contribution that each segment makes to the recovery of fixed costs that will not be altered by decisions to make and sell. Under variable costing procedures,
       1) The marginal income concept leads to better pricing decisions, which are a principal advantage of variable costing.
       2) The impact of fixed costs on net income is emphasized by showing the total amount of such costs separately in financial reports.
       3) Out-of-pocket expenditures required to manufacture products conform closely with the valuation of inventory.

4) The relationship between profit and the major factors of selling price, sales mix, sales volume, and variable manufacturing and nonmanufacturing costs is measured in terms of a single index of profitability.

   a) This profitability index, expressed as a positive amount or as a ratio, facilitates the analysis of cost-volume-profit relationships, compares the effects of two or more contemplated courses of action, and aids in answering many questions that arise in profit planning.

5) Inventory changes have no effect on the breakeven computations.

6) Marginal income amounts facilitate appraisal of products, territories, and other business segments without having the results hidden or obscured by allocated joint fixed costs.

7) Questions regarding whether a particular part should be made or bought can be more effectively answered if only variable costs are used.

   a) Management must consider whether to charge the product being made with variable costs only or to charge a percentage of fixed costs as well.

   b) Management must also consider whether the making of the part will require additional fixed costs and a decrease in normal production.

8) Disinvestment decisions are facilitated because whether a product or department is recouping its variable costs can be determined.

   a) If the variable costs are being covered, operating a department at an apparent loss may be profitable.

9) Management is better able to judge the differences between departments if certain fixed costs are omitted from the statements instead of being allocated arbitrarily.

10) Costs are guided by sales.

    a) Under variable costing, cost of goods sold will vary directly with sales volume, and the influence of production on gross profit is avoided.

    b) Variable costing also eliminates the possible difficulties of having to explain over- or underapplied factory overhead to higher management.

STOP & REVIEW

You have completed the outline for this subunit.
Study multiple-choice questions 10 through 13 beginning on page 527.

17.5 JOINT PRODUCT AND BY-PRODUCT COSTING

1. **Joint Product Costing**

    a. Joint products are separate products resulting from a common manufacturing process. They have high sales values compared with the sales values of other outputs (by-products).

        1) **Joint costs** are incurred up to the split-off point where the products become separately identifiable. They include direct materials, direct labor, and manufacturing overhead.

            a) Because joint costs are incurred before products can be identified separately, they must be allocated.

    b. Costs incurred after split-off are separable costs.

        1) Separable costs can be identified with a specific joint product.

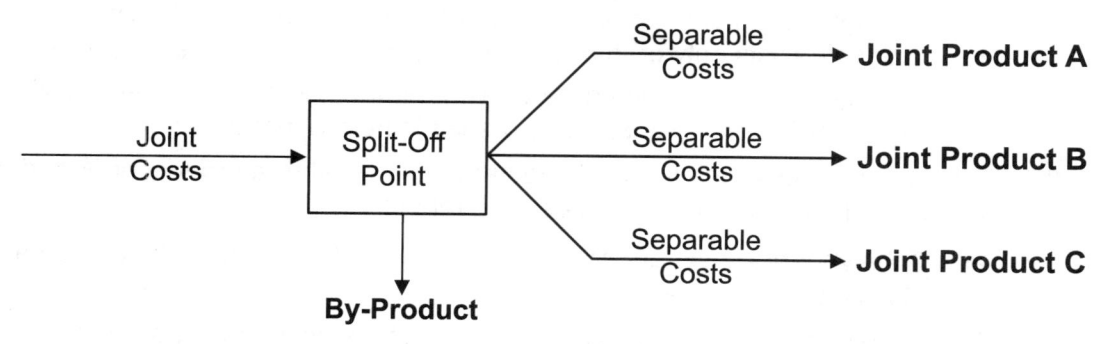

Figure 17-6

   c. The decision to **sell or process further** is made based on whether the incremental revenue from further processing exceeds the incremental cost. The joint cost of the product is irrelevant because it is a sunk cost.

EXAMPLE 17-7   **Sell As Is or Process Further**

Golden Company produces products A, B, and C. All three products are processed jointly in Department 1 for a total cost $100,000. After Department 1 processing, each product is identifiable and could be sold, or each product could be processed further in Department 2.

After Department 1 processing:

Product	Units Available	Sales Price per Unit
A	40,000	$24
B	20,000	30
C	15,000	32

Department 2 processing:

Product	Processing Cost	Sales Price per Unit after Further Processing
A	$160,000	$29
B	100,000	33
C	30,000	36

-- Continued on next page --

> **EXAMPLE 17-7 -- Continued**
>
> The Department 1 processing cost of $100,000 is an example of a joint cost and is therefore irrelevant to the decision.
>
> Compare the incremental revenue to incremental cost to determine if each product should be processed further.
>
> | Product | Incremental Revenue | Incremental Cost | Decision |
> |---------|---------------------|------------------|----------|
> | A | $29 − $24 = $5 | $160,000 ÷ 40,000 units = $4 | Process further |
> | B | $33 − $30 = $3 | $100,000 ÷ 20,000 units = $5 | Sell as is |
> | C | $36 − $32 = $4 | $30,000 ÷ 15,000 units = $2 | Process further |

2. **By-Product Costing**

    a. By-products are one or more products of relatively small total value that are produced simultaneously from a common manufacturing process with products of greater value (joint-products).

       1) Whether the benefits of further processing and sale exceed the costs must be determined.

          ```
          Selling price
          − Additional processing costs
          − Selling costs
          = Net realizable value
          ```

       2) If the net realizable value (NRV) is zero or negative, the by-products should be sold at the split-off point or discarded as scrap if they cannot be sold.

    b. The value of a by-product may be recognized when (1) production is complete or (2) the by-product is sold.

       1) If recognized when production is completed, the amount equals the expected net proceeds from its sale (or its expected NRV if the by-product is subject to further processing to be salable). Thus, by-product inventory is recognized.

    c. Any proceeds (revenue) from the sale of a by-product are recognized either as (1) a reduction of the cost of goods sold of the joint products or (2) a revenue.

       1) Cost of goods sold is not recognized for by-products.

    d. Regardless of the timing of their recognition in the accounts, by-products usually do not receive an allocation of joint costs. The cost of this accounting treatment ordinarily exceeds the benefit.

STOP & REVIEW

You have completed the outline for this subunit.
Study multiple-choice questions 14 through 17 beginning on page 528.

17.6 JOINT COST ALLOCATION METHODS

1. **Physical-Quantity Method**

    a. The physical-quantity method uses a physical measure, such as volume or weight.

        1) Joint production costs are allocated to each product based on its relative proportion of the measure selected.

EXAMPLE 17-8   **Physical-Quantity Method**

Processing 1,000 barrels of crude oil costs $100,000. The process results in the following outputs:

	Barrels	Selling price per barrel at a split-off point	Separable costs	Selling price per barrel after additional process
Asphalt	300	$ 60	$1,000	$ 70
Fuel oil	300	180	1,000	200
Diesel fuel	200	160	1,000	180
Kerosene	100	80	2,000	90
Gasoline	100	180	2,000	190

Under the physical-quantity method, the joint costs up to split-off are allocated as follows:

Asphalt	$100,000 × (300 barrels ÷ 1,000 barrels) =	$ 30,000
Fuel oil	$100,000 × (300 barrels ÷ 1,000 barrels) =	30,000
Diesel fuel	$100,000 × (200 barrels ÷ 1,000 barrels) =	20,000
Kerosene	$100,000 × (100 barrels ÷ 1,000 barrels) =	10,000
Gasoline	$100,000 × (100 barrels ÷ 1,000 barrels) =	10,000
Joint costs allocated		$100,000

---

   b. The physical-quantity method's simplicity is an advantage, but it does not match costs with the individual products' revenues.

2. **Market-Based Method**

    a. A market-based method assigns a proportionate amount of the total cost to each product on a quantitative basis. These allocations are **not** based on units sold because the joint costs were incurred for all units produced, not just those sold. The following are common methods of allocation:

        1) The **sales-value at split-off method** is based on the relative sales values of the separate products at split-off.

EXAMPLE 17-9 — Sales-Value at Split-Off Method

The five outputs can be sold for the following prices at split-off:

Asphalt	300 barrels × $ 60 per barrel =	$ 18,000
Fuel oil	300 barrels × $180 per barrel =	54,000
Diesel fuel	200 barrels × $160 per barrel =	32,000
Kerosene	100 barrels × $ 80 per barrel =	8,000
Gasoline	100 barrels × $180 per barrel =	18,000
	Total sales value at split-off	$130,000

The total sales value for the production run at split-off is $130,000. For each product, total joint cost to be allocated is multiplied by the proportion of the sales of each product:

Asphalt	$100,000 × ($18,000 ÷ $130,000) =	$ 13,846
Fuel oil	$100,000 × ($54,000 ÷ $130,000) =	41,538
Diesel fuel	$100,000 × ($32,000 ÷ $130,000) =	24,616
Kerosene	$100,000 × ($ 8,000 ÷ $130,000) =	6,154
Gasoline	$100,000 × ($18,000 ÷ $130,000) =	13,846
	Joint costs allocated	$100,000

2) The estimated **net realizable value (NRV) method** allocates joint costs based on the relative market values of the products after additional processing.

   a) NRV at split-off equals the sale price at the point of sale minus the cost to complete after split-off (separable costs).

   b) Under the estimated NRV method, all separable costs necessary to make the product salable are subtracted before the allocation.

EXAMPLE 17-10 — Net Realizable Value (NRV) Method

The following are the final estimated sales prices:

Asphalt	300 barrels × $ 70 per barrel =	$21,000
Fuel oil	300 barrels × $200 per barrel =	60,000
Diesel fuel	200 barrels × $180 per barrel =	36,000
Kerosene	100 barrels × $ 90 per barrel =	9,000
Gasoline	100 barrels × $190 per barrel =	19,000

From these amounts, separable costs are subtracted (these costs are given):

Asphalt	$21,000 − $1,000 =	$ 20,000
Fuel oil	$60,000 − $1,000 =	59,000
Diesel fuel	$36,000 − $1,000 =	35,000
Kerosene	$ 9,000 − $2,000 =	7,000
Gasoline	$19,000 − $2,000 =	17,000
	Total net realizable value	$138,000

The total NRV for the production run is $138,000. For each product, total joint cost to be allocated is multiplied by the proportion of the NRV of each product:

Asphalt	$100,000 × ($20,000 ÷ $138,000) =	$ 14,493
Fuel oil	$100,000 × ($59,000 ÷ $138,000) =	42,754
Diesel fuel	$100,000 × ($35,000 ÷ $138,000) =	25,362
Kerosene	$100,000 × ($ 7,000 ÷ $138,000) =	5,072
Gasoline	$100,000 × ($17,000 ÷ $138,000) =	12,319
	Joint costs allocated	$100,000

You have completed the outline for this subunit.
Study multiple-choice questions 18 and 19 on page 530.

STOP & REVIEW

QUESTIONS

17.1 Cost Measurement Terminology

1. If a product required a great deal of electricity to produce, and crude oil prices increased, which of the following costs most likely increased?

A. Direct materials.
B. Direct labor.
C. Prime costs.
D. Conversion costs.

Answer (D) is correct.
REQUIRED: The costs that most likely increase if overhead increases.
DISCUSSION: Conversion costs consist of direct labor and manufacturing overhead. Overhead includes the costs of utilities, such as electricity. An increase in the price of crude oil, which is used to generate electricity, is therefore likely to increase conversion costs.
Answer (A) is incorrect. Direct materials are tangible inputs to the manufacturing process that can practicably be traced to the product. Electricity is not a direct material. **Answer (B) is incorrect.** Direct labor is the cost of labor that can practicably be traced to the product. Electricity is not direct labor. **Answer (C) is incorrect.** Prime costs equal direct materials plus direct labor. Because electricity is neither a direct material nor direct labor, electricity is not a prime cost.

2. Inventoriable costs

A. Include only the prime costs of manufacturing a product.
B. Include only the conversion costs of manufacturing a product.
C. Are expensed when products become part of finished goods inventory.
D. Are regarded as assets before the products are sold.

Answer (D) is correct.
REQUIRED: The true statement about inventoriable costs.
DISCUSSION: Product (inventoriable) costs are capitalized as part of inventory. But period costs are expensed as they are incurred and are not capitalized as assets. Under an absorption costing system, inventoriable costs include variable and fixed costs of production. Under variable costing, inventoriable costs include only variable production costs.
Answer (A) is incorrect. Overhead costs and prime costs (direct materials and labor) are included in inventory. **Answer (B) is incorrect.** Materials costs also are included. **Answer (C) is incorrect.** Inventory costs are expensed when the goods are sold, not when they are transferred to finished goods.

3. The unit costs for direct materials, machining, and assembly of a manufactured product represent

A. Conversion costs.
B. Separable costs.
C. Committed costs.
D. Prime costs.

Answer (D) is correct.
REQUIRED: The type of cost represented by direct materials, machining, and assembly.
DISCUSSION: Prime costs are a manufacturer's direct cost. Direct materials and direct labor (such as machining and assembly) are examples.
Answer (A) is incorrect. Conversion costs consist of direct labor and overhead. **Answer (B) is incorrect.** Separable costs are incurred beyond the point at which jointly produced items become separately identifiable. **Answer (C) is incorrect.** Committed costs result when an entity holds fixed assets. Examples of committed costs include long-term lease payments and depreciation.

17.2 Basic Cost Calculations

4. Fab Co. manufactures textiles. Among Fab's manufacturing costs for the month just ended were the following salaries and wages:

Loom operators	$120,000
Factory foremen	45,000
Machine mechanics	30,000

What was the amount of Fab's direct labor for the month just ended?

A. $195,000
B. $165,000
C. $150,000
D. $120,000

Answer (D) is correct.
   REQUIRED: The amount of direct labor.
   DISCUSSION: Direct labor costs are wages paid to labor that can feasibly be specifically identified with the production of finished goods. Because the wages of loom operators are identifiable with the production of finished goods, the $120,000 wages are a direct labor cost. However, the salaries and wages of the factory foremen and machine mechanics are overhead. The $45,000 and $30,000 are indirect costs. Thus, $120,000 is the amount of direct labor.
   Answer (A) is incorrect. This amount includes the wages and salaries of machine mechanics and factory foremen. Answer (B) is incorrect. This amount includes the salary of factory foremen. Answer (C) is incorrect. This amount includes the wages of machine mechanics.

5. Following are Mill Co.'s production costs for the month just ended:

Direct materials	$100,000
Direct labor	90,000
Factory overhead	4,000

What amount of costs should be traced to specific products in the production process?

A. $194,000
B. $190,000
C. $100,000
D. $90,000

Answer (B) is correct.
   REQUIRED: The amount of direct costs.
   DISCUSSION: Direct materials and direct labor can feasibly be identified with the production of specific goods. Factory overhead cannot be traced to a specific product but is allocated to all products produced. Thus, the amount of costs traceable to specific products in the production process equals $190,000 ($100,000 + $90,000).
   Answer (A) is incorrect. This amount includes factory overhead. Answer (C) is incorrect. This amount excludes direct labor. Answer (D) is incorrect. This amount excludes direct materials.

6. For the year just ended, Abel Co. incurred direct costs of $500,000 based on a particular course of action during the year. If a different course of action had been taken, direct costs would have been $400,000. In addition, Abel's fixed costs were $90,000. The incremental cost was

A. $10,000
B. $90,000
C. $100,000
D. $190,000

Answer (C) is correct.
   REQUIRED: The incremental cost.
   DISCUSSION: Incremental cost is the difference in total cost between two decisions. Only the costs that will differ under the alternatives are relevant. Thus, Abel's incremental cost is $100,000 ($500,000 – $400,000). The fixed costs of $90,000 are not relevant.
   Answer (A) is incorrect. This amount results from subtracting the fixed costs. Answer (B) is incorrect. This amount equals the fixed costs. Answer (D) is incorrect. This amount results from including the fixed costs.

17.3 Other Cost Measurement Concepts

7. A decrease in production levels within a relevant range

A. Decreases variable cost per unit.
B. Decreases total costs.
C. Increases total fixed costs.
D. Increases variable cost per unit.

Answer (B) is correct.
REQUIRED: The effect on unit and total costs when production declines.
DISCUSSION: When production levels decrease within a relevant range, the total costs will decrease. Although the total fixed costs will remain constant, fixed costs per unit will increase because fewer units are available to absorb the constant amount of total fixed costs. Furthermore, total variable costs decrease assuming the unit variable costs remain constant.
Answer (A) is incorrect. Variable costs per unit are assumed to remain constant across the relevant range. Answer (C) is incorrect. Total fixed costs are assumed to remain constant across the relevant range. Answer (D) is incorrect. The relevant range is the decision-making time period in which variable costs per unit are assumed to remain constant.

8. In manufacturing its products for the month just ended, Elk Co. incurred normal spoilage of $10,000 and abnormal spoilage of $12,000. How much spoilage cost should Elk charge as a period cost for the month?

A. $22,000
B. $12,000
C. $10,000
D. $0

Answer (B) is correct.
REQUIRED: The spoilage charged as a period cost.
DISCUSSION: Normal spoilage occurs under efficient operating conditions and is therefore a product cost. Abnormal spoilage is not expected to occur under efficient operating conditions. It is accounted for as a period cost. Thus, the amount of spoilage charged as a period cost is the $12,000 related to abnormal spoilage.
Answer (A) is incorrect. The amount of $22,000 includes the normal spoilage ($10,000), which is a product cost. Answer (C) is incorrect. The $10,000 normal spoilage is a product cost. Answer (D) is incorrect. The abnormal spoilage ($12,000) is a period cost.

9. Dahl Co. uses a standard costing system in connection with the manufacture of a "one size fits all" article of clothing. Each unit of finished product contains 2 yards of direct materials. However, a 20% direct materials spoilage calculated on input quantities occurs during the manufacturing process. The cost of the direct materials is $3 per yard. The standard direct materials cost per unit of finished product is

A. $4.80
B. $6.00
C. $7.20
D. $7.50

Answer (D) is correct.
REQUIRED: The standard direct materials cost per unit of finished product.
DISCUSSION: If 2 yards remain in each unit after spoilage of 20% of the direct materials input, the total per unit input must have been 2.5 yards (2.0 ÷ 80%). The standard unit direct materials cost is therefore $7.50 (2.5 yards × $3).
Answer (A) is incorrect. The 2 yards of good output should be divided (not multiplied) by 80% to determine the standard yards of material per unit. Answer (B) is incorrect. The cost per unit before spoilage is added is $6.00. Answer (C) is incorrect. Adding 20% of the materials of the finished product as spoilage and then multiplying by the $3.00 cost per yard results in $7.20 [(2.00 × 1.20) × $3.00].

17.4 Absorption Costing and Variable Costing

10. The change in period-to-period operating income when using variable costing can be explained by the change in the

   A. Unit sales level multiplied by the unit sales price.
   B. Finished goods inventory level multiplied by the unit sales price.
   C. Unit sales level multiplied by a constant unit contribution margin.
   D. Finished goods inventory level multiplied by a constant unit contribution margin.

Answer (C) is correct.
   REQUIRED: The factor explaining the change in period-to-period operating income when using variable costing.
   DISCUSSION: In a variable costing system, only the variable costs are recorded as product costs. All fixed costs are expensed in the period incurred. Because changes in the relationship between production levels and sales levels do not cause changes in the amount of fixed manufacturing cost expensed, profits more directly follow the trends in sales, especially when the UCM (Selling price per unit − Variable costs per unit) is constant. Unit sales times the UCM equals the total CM, and operating income (a pretax amount) equals the CM minus fixed costs of operations. If the UCM is constant and fixed costs are stable, the change in operating income will approximate the change in the CM (Unit sales × UCM).

11. When a firm prepares financial reports by using absorption costing,

   A. Profits will always increase with increases in sales.
   B. Profits will always decrease with decreases in sales.
   C. Profits may decrease with increased sales even if there is no change in selling prices and costs.
   D. Decreased output and constant sales result in increased profits.

Answer (C) is correct.
   REQUIRED: The profit relationship between output and sales under absorption costing.
   DISCUSSION: In an absorption costing system, fixed overhead costs are included in inventory. When sales exceed production, more overhead is expensed under absorption costing because fixed overhead is carried over from the prior inventory. If sales exceed production, more than one period's fixed overhead is recognized as expense. Accordingly, if the increase in fixed overhead expensed is greater than the contribution margin of the increased units sold, less profit may result from an increased level of sales.
   Answer (A) is incorrect. Profit is a function of both sales and production, so profit may not increase with increases in sales. **Answer (B) is incorrect.** Profit is a function of both sales and production, so profit may not decrease with decreases in sales. **Answer (D) is incorrect.** Decreased output will increase the unit cost of items sold. Fixed overhead per unit will increase.

12. In an income statement prepared using the variable-costing method, fixed factory overhead would

   A. Not be used.
   B. Be used in the computation of operating income but not in the computation of the contribution margin.
   C. Be used in the computation of the contribution margin.
   D. Be treated the same as variable factory overhead.

Answer (B) is correct.
   REQUIRED: The treatment of fixed factory overhead in an income statement based on variable costing.
   DISCUSSION: Under the variable-costing method, the contribution margin equals sales minus variable expenses. Fixed selling and administrative costs and fixed factory overhead are deducted from the contribution margin to arrive at operating income. Thus, fixed costs are included only in the computation of operating income.
   Answer (A) is incorrect. Fixed factory overhead is deducted from the contribution margin to determine operating income. **Answer (C) is incorrect.** Only variable expenses are used in the computation of the contribution margin. **Answer (D) is incorrect.** Variable factory overhead is included in the computation of contribution margin and fixed factory overhead is not.

13. Which of the following statements is correct regarding the difference between the absorption costing and variable costing methods?

A. When production equals sales, absorption costing income is greater than variable costing income.
B. When production equals sales, absorption costing income is **less** than variable costing income.
C. When production is greater than sales, absorption costing income is greater than variable costing income.
D. When production is **less** than sales, absorption costing income is greater than variable costing income.

Answer (C) is correct.
REQUIRED: The true statement about the difference between absorption costing and variable costing.
DISCUSSION: When production exceeds sales, ending inventory increases. Under absorption costing, some fixed costs are included in ending inventory. Under variable costing, all fixed costs are expensed. Accordingly, income is higher under absorption costing.
Answer (A) is incorrect. When production and sales are equal, the two methods report the same income.
Answer (B) is incorrect. When production and sales are equal, the two methods report the same income.
Answer (D) is incorrect. When production is less than sales, ending inventory decreases. Under absorption costing, prior-period fixed costs included in beginning inventory are expensed. Under variable costing, only the current period's fixed costs are expensed. Thus, income is higher under variable costing.

17.5 Joint Product and By-Product Costing

14. For the purposes of cost accumulation, which of the following are identifiable as different individual products before the split-off point?

	By-Products	Joint Products
A.	Yes	Yes
B.	Yes	No
C.	No	No
D.	No	Yes

Answer (C) is correct.
REQUIRED: The products identifiable before the split-off point.
DISCUSSION: In a joint production process, at the split-off point, neither by-products nor joint products are separately identifiable as individual products. Joint costs up to the split-off point are usually related to both joint products and by-products. After split-off, additional (separable) costs can be traced and charged to the individual products. By-products usually do not receive an allocation of joint costs.
Answer (A) is incorrect. Neither by-products nor joint products are separately identifiable until split-off. Answer (B) is incorrect. By-products are also not separately identifiable until split-off. Answer (D) is incorrect. Joint products are also not separately identifiable until split-off.

15. In accounting for by-products, the value of the by-product may be recognized at the time of

	Production	Sale
A.	Yes	Yes
B.	Yes	No
C.	No	No
D.	No	Yes

Answer (A) is correct.
REQUIRED: The timing of recognition of by-products.
DISCUSSION: Practice with regard to recognizing by-products in the accounts is not uniform. The most cost-effective method for the initial recognition of by-products is to account for their value at the time of sale as a reduction in the joint cost or as a revenue. The alternative is to recognize the net realizable value at the time of production, a method that results in the recording of by-product inventory.
Answer (B) is incorrect. By-products also may be recognized initially at the time of sale. Answer (C) is incorrect. By-products may be initially recognized at the time of sale or at the time of production. Answer (D) is incorrect. By-products may also be recorded in the accounts when produced.

16. Kode Co. manufactures a major product that gives rise to a by-product called May. May's only separable cost is a $1 selling cost when a unit is sold for $4. Kode accounts for May's sales by deducting the $3 net amount from the cost of goods sold of the major product. There are no inventories. If Kode were to change its method of accounting for May from a by-product to a joint product, what would be the effect on Kode's overall gross margin?

A. No effect.
B. Gross margin increases by $1 for each unit of May sold.
C. Gross margin increases by $3 for each unit of May sold.
D. Gross margin increases by $4 for each unit of May sold.

Answer (B) is correct.
REQUIRED: The effect on gross margin (gross profit) of treating a product as a joint product rather than a by-product.
DISCUSSION: Gross margin is the difference between sales and the cost of goods sold. Subtracting the $3 net amount from cost of goods sold does not have the same effect on overall gross margin as recording the $4 sales revenue and subtracting the $1 cost. In the latter case, the $1 unit selling cost is not subtracted in arriving at the gross margin. Thus, gross margin increases by $1 for each unit of May sold.
Answer (A) is incorrect. Net income, not gross margin, is unaffected. Answer (C) is incorrect. The amount of $3 is the per-unit increase in net income using either by-product or joint-product costing. Answer (D) is incorrect. The amount of $4 is the per-unit increase in sales when switching to joint-product from by-product costing.

17. A lumber company produces two-by-fours and four-by-eights as joint products and sawdust as a by-product. The packaged sawdust can be sold for $2 per pound. Packaging costs for the sawdust are $.10 per pound and sales commissions are 10% of sales price. The by-product net revenue serves to reduce joint processing costs for joint products. Joint products are assigned joint costs based on board feet. Cost and production data are:

Joint processing costs	$50,000
Two-by-fours produced (board feet)	200,000
Four-by-eights produced (board feet)	100,000
Sawdust produced (pounds)	1,000

What is the cost assigned to two-by-fours?

A. $32,000
B. $32,133
C. $32,200
D. $33,333

Answer (C) is correct.
REQUIRED: The cost assigned to a joint product when joint products and a by-product are produced.
DISCUSSION: The net revenue from sale of the by-product is $1,700 [(1,000 lb. × $2 price) – (1,000 lb. × $.10) – (1,000 lb. × $2 × .1)]. Joint processing costs to be allocated to joint products are therefore $48,300 ($50,000 – $1,700 net by-product revenue). Of this amount, $32,200 should be assigned to the two-by-fours [$48,300 × (200,000 board feet of two-by-fours ÷ 300,000 total board feet)].
Answer (A) is incorrect. The net revenue from the sale of the by-product is $1,700, not $2,000. The costs related to the packaging and selling of the by-product must be deducted. Answer (B) is incorrect. The $.10-per-pound packaging cost for the sawdust must be subtracted from the by-product revenue. Answer (D) is incorrect. The net revenue of $1,700 [1,000 lb. × ($2 sale price – $.10 packaging – $.20 sales cost)] from the by-product should be subtracted from the joint processing costs before the joint processing costs are allocated.

17.6 Joint Cost Allocation Methods

18. A company manufactures two products, X and Y, through a joint process. The joint (common) costs incurred are $500,000 for a standard production run that generates 240,000 gallons of X and 160,000 gallons of Y. X sells for $4.00 per gallon, while Y sells for $6.50 per gallon. If there are no additional processing costs incurred after the split-off point, what is the amount of joint cost for each production run allocated to X on a physical-quantity basis?

A. $200,000
B. $240,000
C. $260,000
D. $300,000

Answer (D) is correct.
REQUIRED: The joint cost for each production run allocated to X on a physical-quantity basis.
DISCUSSION: The company produces products X and Y in each production run at a joint cost of $500,000. No additional processing costs are incurred. To allocate the common cost on a physical-quantity basis means to distribute the costs based on each product's pro-rata share of the total units produced. A production run produces 240,000 gallons of product X and 160,000 gallons of product Y, resulting in 400,000 total units. Thus, product X is allocated $300,000 of the cost [$500,000 × (240,000 ÷ 400,000)]. Product Y is allocated $200,000 [$500,000 × (160,000 ÷ 400,000)].
Answer (A) is incorrect. This amount is the joint cost allocated to Y. Answer (B) is incorrect. This amount is the joint cost allocated to X on a relative sales value basis. Answer (C) is incorrect. This amount is the joint cost allocated to Y on a relative sales value basis.

19. For purposes of allocating joint costs to joint products, the sales price at point of sale, reduced by cost to complete after split-off, is assumed to be equal to the

A. Joint costs.
B. Total costs.
C. Net sales value at split-off.
D. Sales price less a normal profit margin at point of sale.

Answer (C) is correct.
REQUIRED: The assumption about the sales price at point of sale, reduced by cost to complete after split-off.
DISCUSSION: The relative sales value method is the most frequently used method to allocate joint costs to joint products. It allocates joint costs based upon the products' proportion of total sales revenue. For joint products salable at the split-off point, the relative sales value is the selling price at split-off. However, if further processing is needed, the relative sales value is approximated by subtracting the additional anticipated processing costs from the final sales value to arrive at the estimated net sales value at split-off.
Answer (A) is incorrect. Joint costs are computed up to the split-off point. Answer (B) is incorrect. Total costs include the cost to complete after split-off. Answer (D) is incorrect. The normal profit margin does not necessarily equal the cost to complete after split-off.

STUDY UNIT EIGHTEEN
COSTING SYSTEMS AND DECISION MAKING

(27 pages of outline)

18.1	Job-Order Costing and Overhead Application	532
18.2	Process Costing	537
18.3	Activity-Based Costing (ABC)	543
18.4	Cost-Volume-Profit Analysis	548
18.5	Management Decision Making	553

Job-order costing and process costing are the fundamental methods for assigning costs to products. **Job-order costing** assigns costs to specific units, lots, or batches. It is appropriate when products have unique characteristics, such as custom-made furniture. **Process costing** assigns costs to large numbers of homogeneous products with costs accumulated by processes, departments, or cost centers. **Activity-based costing** is an alternative costing approach with advantages over traditional volume-based costing systems.

Overhead consists of indirect costs that cannot be traced feasibly to final products. They consist primarily of indirect materials, indirect labor, and indirect operating costs, such as utilities and depreciation. Overhead is accumulated in one or more cost pools and applied using a standard rate.

Cost-volume-profit analysis is one of the key areas where accountants use cost data to make decisions. Other decisions covered in this study unit include make or buy, special orders, and eliminating a segment.

18.1 JOB-ORDER COSTING AND OVERHEAD APPLICATION

1. **Uses of Job-Order Costing**

    a. Job-order costing is used when each end product is unique. Because the end products are few, tracking their costs is relatively simple.

    b. Manufacturers that use job-order costing include construction and shipbuilding. Service industries include software design and plumbing.

2. **Accumulation of Direct Costs**

    a. The accumulation of costs in a job-order system can best be described in terms of the flow of manual documents in the process. (These functions currently are performed most often with computers rather than physical documents.)

    b. The accounting process begins when a sales order is received from a customer. Because products are custom made, no finished goods inventory is held, but production cannot begin until an order is placed. After the sales order is approved, a production order is issued.

    c. The physical inputs required for production are obtained from suppliers.

    1) For example, $100,000 of direct materials are purchased on account. The journal entry is

Materials inventory	$100,000	
Accounts payable		$100,000

    d. A subsidiary account is created within the work-in-process ledger to track the costs for each job. The accumulation of direct costs (direct materials and direct labor) is simple.

    e. Materials requisition forms request direct materials to be sent from the warehouse to the production line.

    1) For example, the production line submits a materials requisition to the warehouse for $60,000 of direct materials for Job 1015. The journal entry is

Work-in-process -- Job 1015	$60,000	
Materials inventory		$60,000

    f. Time tickets track the direct labor by workers on various jobs.

    1) For example, workers accrue $45,000 in salaries on Job 1015. The journal entry is

Work-in-process -- Job 1015	$45,000	
Wages payable		$45,000

    g. Direct costs are recorded in the general ledger at their actual amounts. Job-order costing facilitates tracing the direct costs incurred for a given job.

3. **Accumulation of Indirect Costs**

   a. Accounting for overhead costs is more difficult because they are indirect costs. It is not feasible to trace them to final products. Thus, they must be accumulated in one or more indirect cost pools and allocated based on an appropriate cost driver.

      1) When one indirect cost pool is used, it is commonly called manufacturing overhead control. (Some manufacturers require a higher degree of accuracy in indirect cost assignment and use two overhead control accounts, one for variable overhead and one for fixed. For simplicity, the following examples use one pool.)

   b. Manufacturing overhead consists of three main categories of costs:

      1) Indirect materials are tangible inputs to the manufacturing process that cannot feasibly be traced to the product, e.g., lubricating oil for machines.

         a) For example, the production department requisitions $4,500 of lubricating oil for a machine that was due maintenance. The journal entry is

Manufacturing overhead control	$4,500	
Materials inventory		$4,500

      2) Indirect labor is the labor used in the manufacturing process that cannot feasibly be traced to the product, e.g., the wages of assembly line supervisors and janitorial staff.

         a) For example, $2,000 in wages are accrued for the janitorial staff. The journal entry is

Manufacturing overhead control	$2,000	
Wages payable		$2,000

      3) Other overhead operating costs include such items as utility expense, real estate taxes, insurance, and depreciation of equipment. The actual total of these costs is not known until the end of the period.

         a) For example, $8,500 of property taxes are accrued, $1,600 of insurance costs are prepaid, and $12,000 of depreciation expense is recognized. The journal entries are

Manufacturing overhead control	$8,500	
Property taxes payable		$8,500
Manufacturing overhead control	$1,600	
Prepaid insurance		$1,600
Manufacturing overhead control	$12,000	
Accumulated depreciation -- equipment		$12,000

   c. When an overhead control account is used, actual overhead costs do not affect work-in-process when they are incurred. The total actual overhead incurred is the debit balance in the control account.

4. **Allocation of Indirect Costs**
   a. Indirect costs are allocated to production using an overhead allocation rate. The first step is to estimate the total indirect costs for the next period.
      1) The overhead application rate is best derived using estimated annual totals rather than on a monthly basis. Many overhead costs are fixed and must be incurred every month regardless of the level of production. Calculating a new rate every month may cause large variations in product costs even though the underlying cost structure does not change.
   b. The following is the equation for the rate:

   $$\text{Overhead application rate} = \frac{\text{Estimated annual total overhead costs}}{\text{Estimated total units of allocation base}}$$

   (If more than one indirect cost pool is used, a different rate is used for each pool.)
      1) The numerator is estimated from annual budget data.
      2) The denominator (the allocation base) must be a cost driver that has a **direct cause-and-effect relationship** with the incurrence of overhead costs. When overhead costs change, the units of the allocation base also should change. Common allocation bases for one indirect cost pool are direct labor hours and machine hours.
         a) For example, an estimated $350,000 in overhead costs will be incurred during the year. The best way to allocate these costs is by machine hours (budgeted at 10,000 hours). The allocation rate is determined as follows:

   Overhead application rate ($350,000 ÷ 10,000) = $35 per machine hour

   c. At the end of each month, the number of units of the allocation base expended is multiplied by the application rate to determine the amount of overhead to be applied to that month's production.
      1) For example, Job 1015 has used 900 machine hours this month. The calculation is

   Overhead applied = Units of overhead driver × Application rate
   = 900 machine hours for Job 1015 × $35 per hour
   = $31,500

      2) This amount ordinarily is not credited to the control account. Instead, it is credited to manufacturing overhead applied (a contra account). The two accounts track actual and applied costs separately.
         a) For example, overhead is applied to Job 1015. The journal entry is

Work-in-process -- Job 1015	$31,500	
Manufacturing overhead applied		$31,500

      3) Separate tracking retains actual overhead amounts in the debit balance of the control account. It also permits comparison of actual and applied costs. The closer they are, the better the estimate.

5. Completion of Job

a. When a job order is completed, all costs are transferred to finished goods.

1) For example, when work on Job 1015 is completed, the product is prepared for sale. Total costs incurred for Job 1015 are $136,500. The journal entry is

   Finished goods $136,500
       Work-in-process -- Job 1015 $136,500

b. When the output is sold, the sale is recorded and the appropriate portion of the cost is transferred to cost of goods sold.

1) For example, the product created in Job 1015 is sold for $200,000 on account. The journal entry is

   Accounts receivable $200,000
       Sales $200,000
   Cost of goods sold $136,500
       Finished goods $136,500

6. Cost Flows

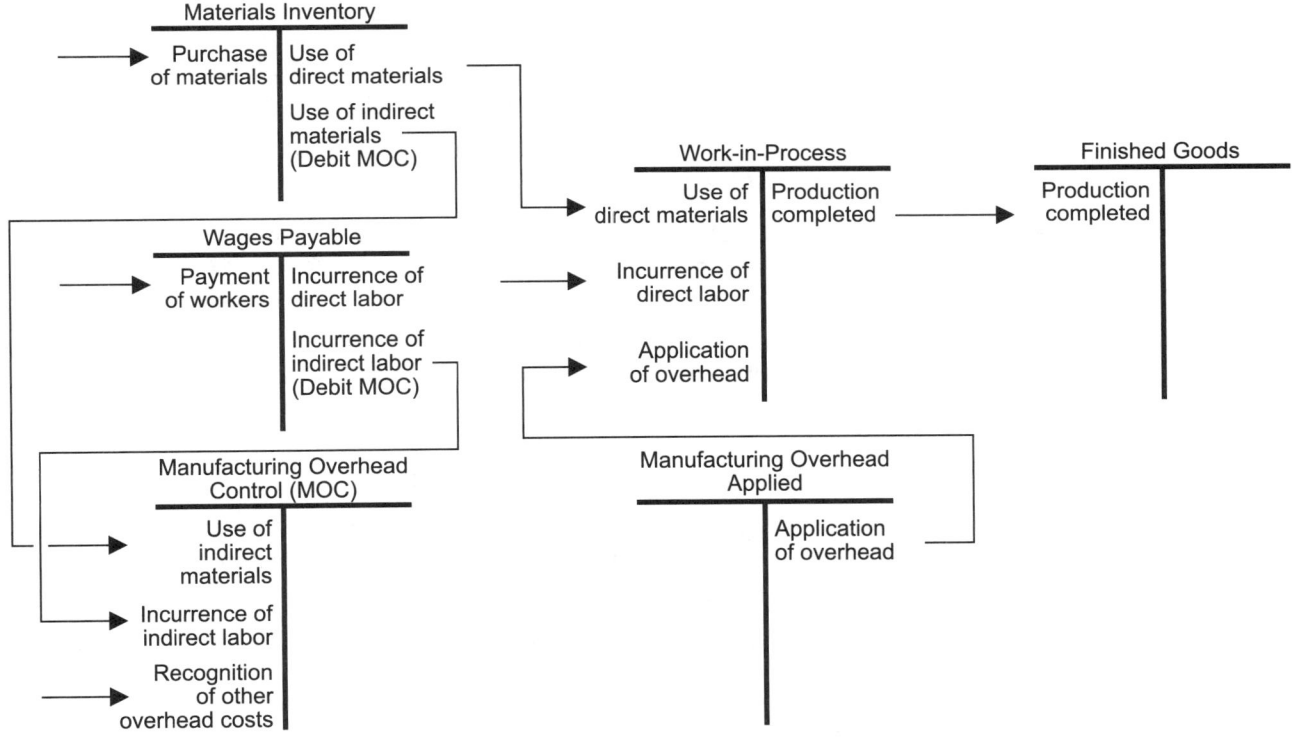

Figure 18-1

7. **Over- and Underapplied Overhead**
   a. At the end of the period, if the balance in the overhead control account (records actual amount incurred) is less than that in the overhead applied account (i.e., actual < applied), **overhead was overapplied**. If the balance in the overhead applied account is lower (i.e., actual > applied), **overhead was underapplied**.
      1) For example, overhead applied was $331,500 during the period, but the amount accrued was only $328,600.
      2) Given that more overhead was applied than was actually incurred, overhead was overapplied by $2,900.
         a) If the **variance is immaterial**, it may be closed directly to cost of goods sold.
            i) Overhead applied is debited and manufacturing overhead control is credited. The balancing credit is to cost of goods sold. The journal entry is

            Manufacturing overhead applied (balance) $331,500
                Cost of goods sold (difference) $ 2,900
                Manufacturing overhead control (balance)   328,600

            (If overhead is underapplied, cost of goods sold is debited.)
         b) If the **variance is material**, it should be allocated based on the relative values of work-in-process, finished goods, and cost of goods sold.
            i) For example, the amount overapplied has a 20:20:60 cost relationship. The journal entry is

            Manufacturing overhead applied (balance) $331,500
                Work-in-process (difference × 20%) $ 580
                Finished goods (difference × 20%)   580
                Cost of goods sold (difference × 60%)   1,740
                Manufacturing overhead control (balance)   328,600

      3) Actual overhead costs for the period eventually become product costs.
   b. The reason for the foregoing procedure is to identify **variance**.
      1) The variance between the control and applied amounts indicates whether production for the period sufficed to spread overhead costs among as many units as were expected when the annual budget was completed.
   c. A variance results from factors that affect the numerator or the denominator of the application rate.
      1) Factors affecting the numerator cause higher or lower costs than estimated.
      2) Factors affecting the denominator cause the activity level to vary from the estimate.

STOP & REVIEW

You have completed the outline for this subunit.
Study multiple-choice questions 1 through 3 beginning on page 557.

18.2 PROCESS COSTING

1. **Uses of Process Costing**

   a. Process cost accounting assigns costs to inventoriable goods or services. It applies to relatively homogeneous products that are mass produced on a continuous basis (e.g., petroleum products, thread, and computer monitors).

   b. Instead of using subsidiary ledgers to track specific jobs, process costing typically uses a **work-in-process** account for each department through which the production of output passes.

   c. Process costing calculates the average cost of all units as follows:

      1) Costs are accumulated for a **cost object** that consists of a large number of similar units of goods or services,
      2) Work-in-process is stated in terms of **equivalent units produced (EUP)**, and
      3) Cost per EUP is established.

2. **Accumulation of Costs**

   a. The accumulation of costs under a process costing system is by department to reflect the continuous, homogeneous nature of the process.

   b. The physical inputs required for production are obtained from suppliers.

Materials	$XXX	
Accounts payable		$XXX

   c. Direct materials are added by the first department in the process.

Work-in-process -- Department A	$XXX	
Materials		$XXX

   d. **Conversion costs** are the sum of direct labor and manufacturing overhead. The nature of process costing makes this accounting treatment more efficient. (Item 4., beginning on page 539, contains an outline of equivalent units.)

Work-in-process -- Department A	$XXX	
Wages payable (direct labor)		$XXX
Manufacturing overhead		XXX

   e. Products move from one department to the next.

Work-in-process -- Department B	$XXX	
Work-in-process -- Department A		$XXX

   f. The second department adds more direct materials and more conversion costs.

Work-in-process -- Department B	$XXX	
Materials		$XXX
Work-in-process -- Department B	$XXX	
Wages payable (direct labor)		$XXX
Manufacturing overhead		XXX

   g. When processing is finished in the last department, all costs are transferred to finished goods.

Finished goods	$XXX	
Work-in-process -- Department B		$XXX

h. As products are sold, sales are recorded and the costs are transferred to cost of goods sold.

Accounts receivable	$XXX	
Sales		$XXX
Cost of goods sold	$XXX	
Finished goods		$XXX

i. The changes in these accounts during the period can be summarized as follows:

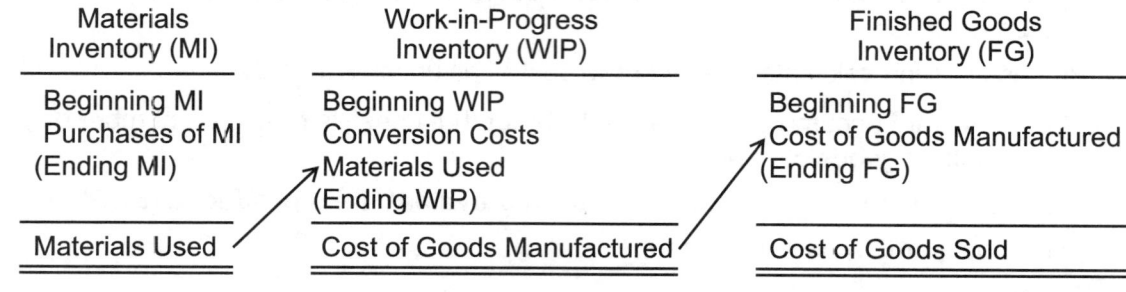

Materials Inventory (MI)	Work-in-Progress Inventory (WIP)	Finished Goods Inventory (FG)
Beginning MI Purchases of MI (Ending MI)	Beginning WIP Conversion Costs Materials Used (Ending WIP)	Beginning FG Cost of Goods Manufactured (Ending FG)
Materials Used	Cost of Goods Manufactured	Cost of Goods Sold

Figure 18-2

3. **Process Cost Flows**

Materials Inventory: Beginning MI, Purchase of materials | Use of direct materials; Ending MI

Wages Payable: | Use of direct and indirect labor

Manufacturing Overhead: | Manufacturing overhead applied

Work-in-Process Department A: Beginning WIP, Use of direct materials, Incurrence of conversion costs | Costs transferred out; Ending WIP

Work-in-Process Department B: Beginning WIP, Costs transferred in, Addition of direct materials, Addition of conversion costs | Costs of goods manufactured; Ending WIP

Finished Goods: Beginning FG, Cost of goods manufactured, Goods available for sale | To cost of goods sold; Ending FG

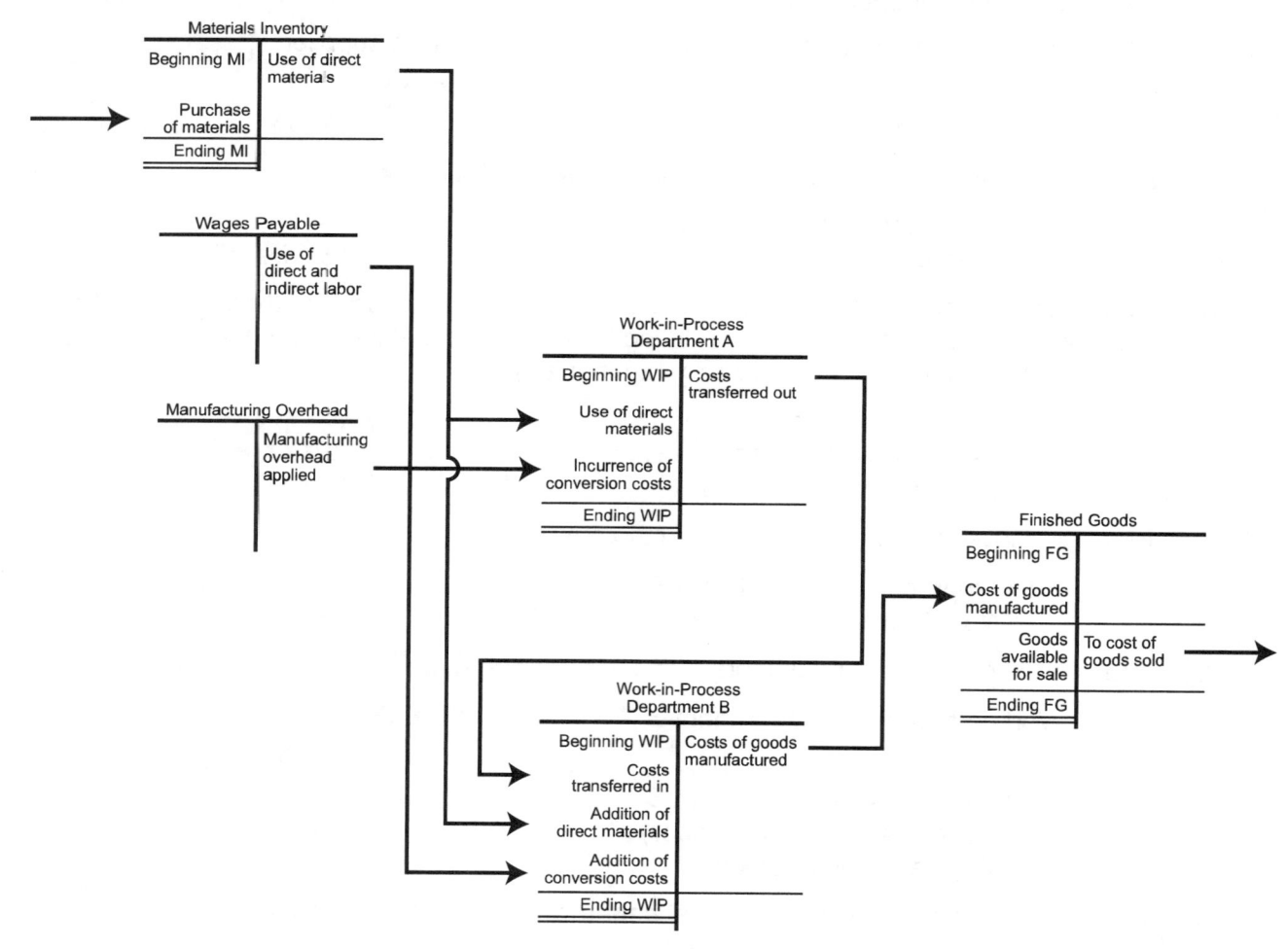

Figure 18-3

4. Equivalent Units of Production (EUP)

> **SUCCESS TIP**
>
> The AICPA frequently tests the calculation of equivalent units of production (EUP). This topic may be confusing to CPA candidates. To understand fully the calculation and use of EUP, work through the questions in the Gleim materials. Examples of how to calculate EUP are below and on the next page.

a. Some units are unfinished at the end of the period. To account for their costs, the units are restated in terms of EUP. EUP equal the number of finished goods that could have been produced using the inputs consumed during the period. EUP for direct materials or conversion costs is the amount required to complete one physical unit of production.

EXAMPLE 18-1   EUP

1,000 work-in-process units, 80% complete for direct materials and 60% for conversion costs, equal 800 EUP of direct materials (1,000 × 80%) and 600 EUP of conversion costs (1,000 × 60%).

1) Determining the costs of unfinished units requires two calculations (commonly performed by weighted-average method or FIFO method):

   a) Calculating the EUP and
   b) Calculating the cost per EUP.

2) The two calculations are made separately for direct materials and conversion costs. Conversion costs are assumed to be uniformly incurred.

   a) **Transferred-in** costs are by definition 100% complete. The units (costs) transferred in from the previous department should be included in the computation of the EUP of the second department.

      i) These costs are treated the same as direct materials added at the beginning of the period.

3) The actual production quantity flow is based on the following relationship:

   Beginning work-in-process + Units started this period = Units transferred out (completed) + Ending work-in-process

b. In all EUP calculations, three populations of units must be accounted for:

1) Units in beginning work-in-process (beginning WIP)

   a) Units in beginning WIP can be calculated as follows:

   $$\begin{array}{r}\text{Units transferred out}\\ +\ \text{Ending WIP}\\ -\ \text{Units started}\\ \hline \text{Beginning WIP}\end{array}$$

2) Units started and completed during the current period

   a) Units started and completed can be calculated as follows:

   $$\begin{array}{r}\text{Units transferred out}\\ -\ \text{Beginning WIP}\\ \hline \text{Units started and completed}\end{array} \quad \text{OR} \quad \begin{array}{r}\text{Units started}\\ -\ \text{Ending WIP}\\ \hline \text{Units started and completed}\end{array}$$

3) Units in ending work-in-process (ending WIP)

   a) Units in ending WIP can be calculated as follows:

   $$\begin{array}{r}\text{Beginning WIP}\\ +\ \text{Units started}\\ -\ \text{Units transferred out}\\ \hline \text{Ending WIP}\end{array}$$

   b) These units have not been completed during the period.

EXAMPLE 18-2   Beginning WIP, Units Started and Completed, and Ending WIP

A company's beginning inventory consists of 20,000 units that were 40% complete. At the end of the month, work-in-process inventory consisted of 15,000 units that were 30% complete. During the period, the company transferred 150,000 units to finished goods.

Three EUP populations to account for:
Beginning WIP   20,000 units
Units started and completed   130,000 units (150,000 transferred out – 20,000 beginning WIP)
Ending WIP   15,000 units

EXAMPLE 18-3   Beginning WIP, Units Started and Completed, and Ending WIP

A company's beginning work-in-process inventory included 7,000 units that were 60% complete. During the period, 100,000 units started production. By the end of the period, work-in-process inventory totaled 18,000 units that were 70% complete.

Three EUP populations to account for:
Beginning WIP   7,000 units
Units started and completed   82,000 units (100,000 started – 18,000 ending WIP)
Ending WIP   18,000 units

c. Under the **weighted-average** method, units in beginning work-in-process (WIP) are treated as if they had been started and completed during the current period. This method averages the costs of beginning WIP with the costs of current-period production.

   1) The calculation of EUP under the weighted-average method is as follows:

   $$\begin{array}{l} \text{Total units \textbf{completed} (transferred out) during the current period} \\ +\ \text{Ending work-in-process (WIP)} \times \text{Percent completed} \\ \hline =\ \text{EUP under weighted-average} \end{array}$$

   2) The cost per EUP under the weighted-average method is calculated as follows:

   $$\text{Weighted-average cost per EUP} = \frac{\text{Beginning WIP costs + Current-period costs}}{\text{Weighted-average EUP}}$$

d. Under the **first-in, first-out (FIFO)** method, the EUP in beginning work-in-process (work done in the prior period) must be excluded from the calculation. Only the costs incurred in the current period are considered. The EUP produced during the current period are based only on the work done during the current period.

   1) The calculation of EUP under the FIFO method is as follows:

   $$\begin{array}{l} \text{Beginning work-in-process (WIP)} \times \text{Percent left to complete} \\ +\ \text{Units \textbf{started and completed} during the current period} \\ +\ \text{Ending work-in-process (WIP)} \times \text{Percent completed} \\ \hline =\ \text{EUP under FIFO} \end{array}$$

   NOTE: Units **started and completed** during the current period are equal to units started minus ending WIP (or equal to units completed minus beginning WIP).

   2) Another version of this equation is below:

   $$\begin{array}{l} \text{Total units completed (transferred out) this period} \\ +\ \text{Ending work-in-process (WIP)} \times \text{Percent completed} \\ -\ \text{Beginning work-in-process (WIP)} \times \text{Percent completed in the prior period} \\ \hline =\ \text{EUP under FIFO} \end{array}$$

   3) The cost per EUP under FIFO is calculated as follows:

   $$\text{FIFO cost per EUP} = \frac{\text{Current-period costs}}{\text{FIFO EUP}}$$

EXAMPLE 18-4   Weighted-Average vs. FIFO

	Units	Completed for Direct Materials (DM)	Completed for Conversion Costs (CC)
Beginning work-in-process (BWIP)	100	30%	40%
Units started during period	3,000		
Units completed (transferred out)	2,600		
Ending work-in-process (EWIP)	500	15%	20%

	DM	CC
Costs to account for:		
BWIP costs	$ 1,200	$ 2,200
Costs incurred during the period	30,000	33,000
	$31,200	$35,200

Step 1: Determine the equivalent units produced (EUP).

	Weighted-Average		FIFO	
	DM	CC	DM	CC
BWIP				
100 units × (1 – 30%)			70	
100 units × (1 – 40%)				60
Units completed	2,600	2,600		
Units started and completed				
2,600 units completed – 100 units BWIP			2,500	2,500
EWIP				
500 units × 15%	75		75	
500 units × 20%		100		100
EUP	2,675	2,700	2,645	2,660

Step 2: Determine the cost per EUP.

	Weighted-Average		FIFO	
	DM	CC	DM	CC
(BWIP costs + current-period costs) ÷ EUP				
($1,200 + $30,000) ÷ 2,675 units	$11.66			
($2,200 + $33,000) ÷ 2,700 units		$13.04		
Current-period costs ÷ EUP				
$30,000 ÷ 2,645 units			$11.34	
$33,000 ÷ 2,660 units				$12.41

   e.   After the EUP have been calculated, the cost per EUP under each method can be determined.

        1)   Under the **weighted-average method**, all direct materials and conversion costs incurred in the current period and in beginning work-in-process are averaged.

        2)   Under the **FIFO method**, only the costs incurred in the current period are included in the calculation.

f. When beginning work-in-process is zero, the two methods have the same results.

> **SUCCESS TIP:** Beginning inventory is subtracted in the EUP calculation only when applying FIFO. The weighted-average method treats units in beginning inventory as if they had been started and completed during the current period.

> **STOP & REVIEW:** You have completed the outline for this subunit. Study multiple-choice questions 4 through 8 beginning on page 559.

18.3 ACTIVITY-BASED COSTING (ABC)

1. **Disadvantages of Volume-Based Systems**

    a. ABC is a response to the significant increase in the incurrence of **indirect costs** resulting from the rapid advance of technology. ABC is a refinement of an existing costing system (job-order or process).

       1) Under a **traditional (volume-based)** system, overhead is accumulated in **one cost pool** and allocated to all end products using one allocation base, such as direct labor hours or direct machine hours used.

       2) Under **ABC**, indirect costs are assigned to **activities** and then rationally allocated to end products.

          a) ABC may be used by manufacturing, service, or retailing firms.
          b) ABC may be used in a job-order system or a process cost system.

    b. The inaccurate averaging or spreading of indirect costs over products or service units that use different amounts of resources is called **peanut-butter costing**. Peanut-butter costing results in product-cost cross-subsidization. It miscosts one product and, as a result, miscosts other products.

    c. The peanut-butter effect of using a volume-based system can be summarized as follows:

       1) Direct labor and direct materials are traced to products or service units.
       2) One pool of indirect costs (overhead) is accumulated for a given organizational unit.
       3) Indirect costs from the pool are assigned using an allocative (rather than a tracing) procedure, such as using a single overhead rate for an entire department, e.g., $3 of overhead for every direct labor hour.

          a) The effect is an averaging of costs that may result in significant inaccuracy when products or service units do not use similar amounts of resources (i.e., cost shifting).

> **EXAMPLE 18-5   ABC vs. Volume-Based**
>
> The effect of product-cost cross-subsidization can be illustrated as follows:
>
> - Two products are produced. Both require 1 unit of direct materials and 1 hour of direct labor. Materials costs are $14 per unit, and direct labor is $70 per hour. Also, the manufacturer has no beginning or ending inventories.
> - During the month just ended, production equaled 1,000 units of Product A and 100 units of Product B. Manufacturing overhead for the month was $20,000.
>
> **Volume-Based**
>
> Using direct labor hours as the overhead allocation base, per-unit costs and profits are calculated as follows:
>
> | | Product A | Product B | Total |
> |---|---|---|---|
> | Direct materials | $ 14,000 | $ 1,400 | |
> | Direct labor | 70,000 | 7,000 | |
> | Overhead {$20,000 × [1,000 ÷ (1,000 + 100)]} | 18,182 | | |
> | Overhead {$20,000 × [100 ÷ (1,000 + 100)]} | | 1,818 | |
> | Total costs | $102,182 | $ 10,218 | $112,400 |
> | | | | |
> | Selling price | $ 119.99 | $ 139.99 | |
> | Cost per unit ($102,182 ÷ 1,000) | (102.18) | | |
> | Cost per unit ($10,218 ÷ 100) | | (102.18) | |
> | Profit per unit | $ 17.81 | $ 37.81 | |
>
> **ABC**
>
> Overhead consists almost entirely of production line setup costs, and the two products require equal setup times. Allocating overhead on this basis has different results.
>
> | | Product A | Product B | Total |
> |---|---|---|---|
> | Direct materials | $14,000 | $ 1,400 | |
> | Direct labor | 70,000 | 7,000 | |
> | Overhead ($20,000 × 50%) | 10,000 | | |
> | Overhead ($20,000 × 50%) | | 10,000 | |
> | Total costs | $94,000 | $18,400 | $112,400 |
> | | | | |
> | Selling price | $119.99 | $139.99 | |
> | Cost per unit ($94,000 ÷ 1,000) | (94.00) | | |
> | Cost per unit ($18,400 ÷ 100) | | (184.00) | |
> | Profit (loss) per unit | $ 25.99 | $ (44.01) | |
>
> Under volume-based costing, Product B appeared to be profitable. But ABC revealed that high-volume Product A has been subsidizing the setup costs for the low-volume Product B.

  d. Example 18-5 above assumed a single component of overhead for clarity. In reality, overhead consists of many components.

e. The peanut-butter effect of volume-based overhead allocation is illustrated in the following diagram:

Overhead Allocation in Volume-Based Costing

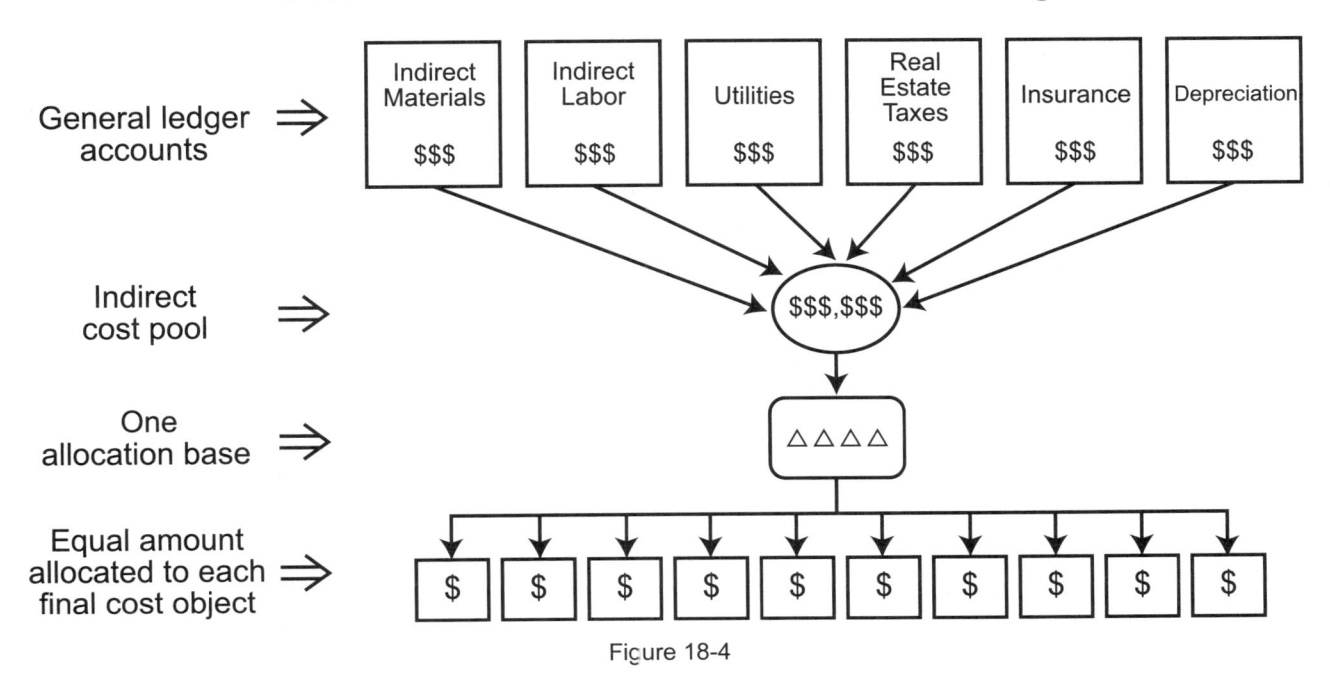

General ledger accounts ⇒ Indirect Materials $$$ | Indirect Labor $$$ | Utilities $$$ | Real Estate Taxes $$$ | Insurance $$$ | Depreciation $$$

Indirect cost pool ⇒ $$$,$$$

One allocation base ⇒ △△△△

Equal amount allocated to each final cost object ⇒ $ $ $ $ $ $ $ $ $ $

Figure 18-4

2. **Volume-Based vs. Activity-Based**

   a. Volume-based systems are appropriate when most manufacturing costs are homogeneously consumed. In these cases, one volume-based cost driver can be used to allocate the overhead costs. However, overhead costs do not always fluctuate with volume. ABC addresses the increasing complexity and variety of overhead costs.

   b. Activity-based systems involve

      1) Identifying organizational activities that incur overhead
      2) Assigning the costs of resources consumed by the activities
      3) Assigning the costs of the activities by appropriate cost drivers to final cost objects

3. **Step 1: Activity Analysis**

   a. An activity is a set of work actions undertaken, and a cost pool is established for each activity.

   b. Analysis identifies **value-adding** activities, which contribute to customer satisfaction. **Nonvalue-adding** activities should be reduced or eliminated.

   c. Activities are classified in a hierarchy according to the level of the production process where they occur.

4. **Step 2: Assign Resource Costs to Activities**
    a. After activities are identified, the next step is to assign the costs of resources to the activities, a **first-stage allocation**.
    b. Identifying resource costs is not as simple as in volume-based overhead allocation, which designates general ledger accounts to be combined in one general ledger cost pool.
        1) A separate accounting system may be necessary to track resource costs separately from the general ledger.
    c. After resource costs have been identified, resource drivers are designated to allocate resource costs to **activity cost pools**.
        1) **Resource drivers** are measures of the causes of resources consumed by an activity.

EXAMPLE 18-6   Resource Drivers

A job-order system accumulates costs for a product made in various models. But given increasing reliance on robots in the production process and computers for monitoring and control, overhead is now a greater percentage of total costs, and direct labor costs have decreased. Thus, implementation of an activity-based costing system has begun.

The following resources are used by the indirect cost processes:

Resource	Driver
Computer processing	CPU cycles
Production line	Machine hours
Materials management	Hours worked
Utilities	Square footage

---

5. **Step 3: Allocate Costs in Activity Cost Pools to Final Cost Objects**
    a. This final step is a **second-stage allocation**.
    b. Costs are reassigned to final-stage cost objects on the basis of activity cost drivers.
        1) **Activity cost drivers** are measures of the demands on an activity by next-stage cost objects (e.g., the number of parts in a product used to measure an assembly activity).
        2) A driver is a factor that causes a change in a cost. **Cost drivers** are cost assignment bases that are used in the allocation of manufacturing overhead costs to cost objects.

SU 18: Costing Systems and Decision Making

c. Drivers (both resource and activity) must be chosen on the basis of a **cause-and-effect** relationship with the resource or activity cost allocated.

EXAMPLE 18-7   Activity Cost Drivers

The following cost drivers have a cause-and-effect relationship with their corresponding activities:

Activity	Cost driver
Product design	Number of products
Production setup	Number of setups
Machining	Number of units produced
Inspection and testing	Number of units produced
Production orders	Number of orders

EXAMPLE 18-8   Volume-Based vs. ABC Systems

The following information pertains to current-month activities regarding the manufacture of X and Z:

Manufacturing overhead costs		Cost driver
Plant utilities and real estate taxes	$150,000	Square footage
Materials handling	40,000	Pounds of direct materials used
Inspection and testing	10,000	Number of units produced
	$200,000	

Current month activity level

	X	Z	Total
Direct labor hours	20,000	5,000	25,000
Plant square footage	400	600	1,000
Pounds of direct materials used	10,000	6,000	16,000
Number of units produced	15,000	3,000	18,000

Under a **volume-based system**, using direct labor hours as the overhead allocation base, the manufacturing overhead costs are allocated as follows:

X: $200,000 × (20,000 ÷ 25,000) = $160,000
Z: $200,000 × (5,000 ÷ 25,000) = $40,000

Manufacturing overhead costs per unit of X: $160,000 ÷ 15,000 = $10.67
Manufacturing overhead costs per unit of Z: $40,000 ÷ 3,000 = $13.33

Under an **ABC system**, the manufacturing overhead costs are allocated as follows:

	X	Z
Plant utilities and real estate taxes	$150,000 × (400 ÷ 1,000) = $60,000	$150,000 × (600 ÷ 1,000) = $ 90,000
Materials handling	$40,000 × (10,000 ÷ 16,000) = 25,000	$40,000 × (6,000 ÷ 16,000) = 15,000
Inspection and testing	$10,000 × (15,000 ÷ 18,000) = 8,333	$10,000 × (3,000 ÷ 18,000) = 1,667
	$93,333	$106,667

Manufacturing overhead costs per unit of X = $93,333 ÷ 15,000 = $6.22
Manufacturing overhead costs per unit of Z = $106,667 ÷ 3,000 = $35.56

STOP & REVIEW

You have completed the outline for this subunit. Study multiple-choice questions 9 through 13 beginning on page 561.

18.4 COST-VOLUME-PROFIT ANALYSIS

1. Cost-volume-profit (CVP) analysis (also called **breakeven analysis**) explains the effects of changes in assumptions about cost behavior and the relevant ranges in which those assumptions are valid. These changes may affect the relationships among revenues, variable costs, and fixed costs at different output levels.

    a. Thus, CVP analysis determines the probable effects of changes in unit sales, sales price, unit variable cost, fixed cost, and product mix.

2. **Simplifying Assumptions**

    a. Cost and revenue relationships are predictable and linear. They are true over the relevant range of activity and specified time span.
    b. Unit selling prices and market conditions are constant.
    c. Changes in inventory are insignificant in amount. Thus, production equals sales.
    d. Total variable costs change proportionally with volume, but unit variable costs are constant over the relevant range.
        1) Direct materials and direct labor are variable costs.
    e. Fixed costs are constant over the relevant range, but unit fixed costs vary indirectly with activity.

3. **Contribution Margin (CM)**

    a. The contribution margin formatted income statement is utilized in managerial accounting as it facilitates making decisions, such as those found in CVP analysis.
    b. Variable and fixed cost behaviors are highlighted in the preparation of the contribution margin formatted income statement.
    c. Contribution margin, in total and per unit, is key to calculating various items in CVP analysis.
        1) Contribution margin per unit can also be referred to as unit contribution margin (UCM).
    d. Contribution margin ratio (CMR) is the contribution margin as a percentage of sales. This ratio can be calculated using totals or per-unit data and is also key to calculating various items in CVP analysis.

4. **Breakeven Point in Units**

    a. The **breakeven point** is the output at which all fixed costs and cumulative variable costs have been covered. It is the output at which operating income is zero.
        1) Each additional unit produced above the breakeven point generates operating profit equal to the unit contribution margin (UCM). UCM equals unit selling price minus unit variable cost.

SU 18: Costing Systems and Decision Making

b. The simplest calculation for breakeven in units is to divide fixed costs by the UCM.

$$\text{Breakeven point in units} = \frac{\text{Fixed costs}}{\text{UCM}}$$

1) Breakeven point in units should always be rounded up to the next unit. For example, 3333.34 units should be rounded up to 3334 units.

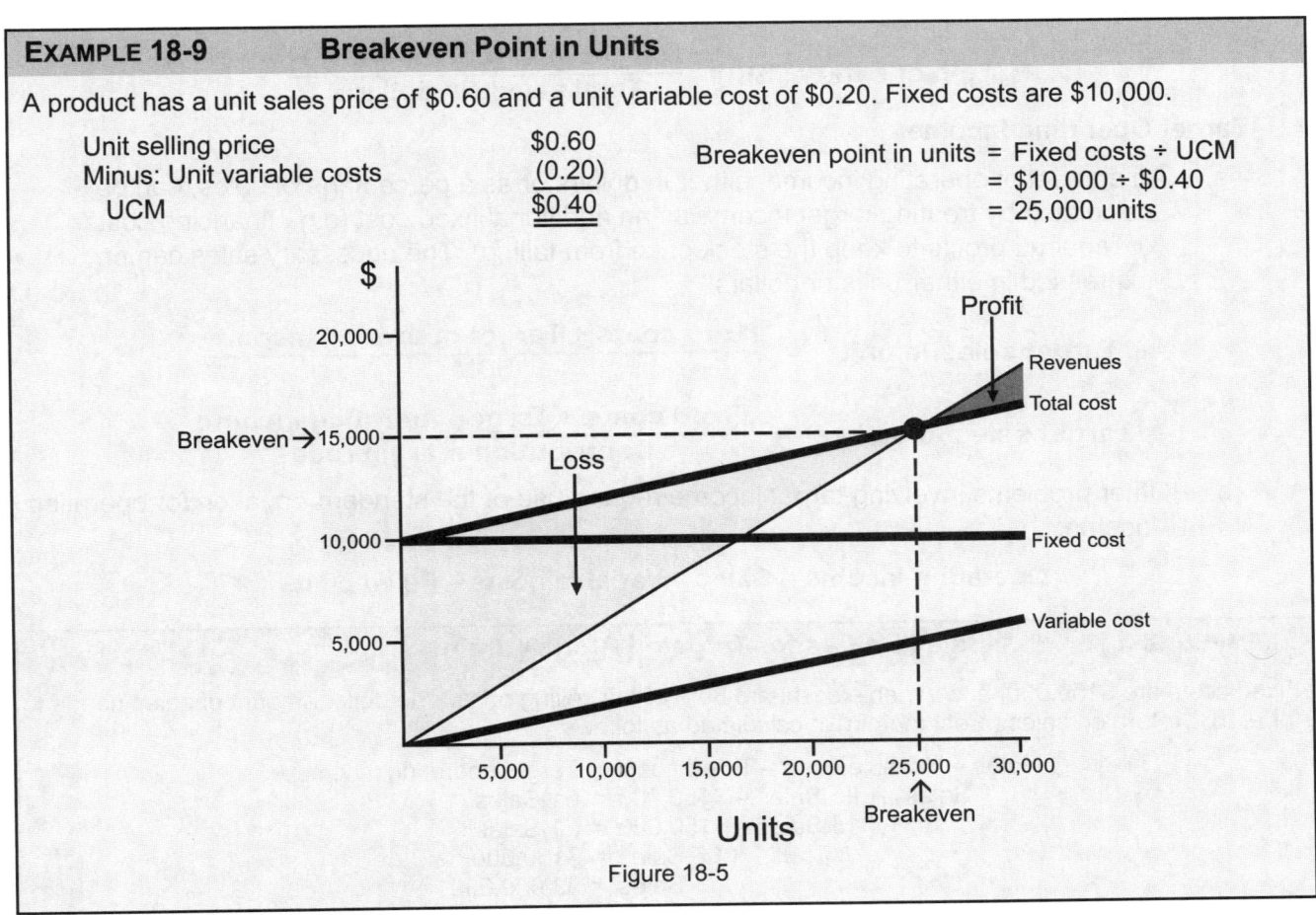

EXAMPLE 18-9   Breakeven Point in Units

A product has a unit sales price of $0.60 and a unit variable cost of $0.20. Fixed costs are $10,000.

Unit selling price	$0.60
Minus: Unit variable costs	(0.20)
UCM	$0.40

Breakeven point in units = Fixed costs ÷ UCM
= $10,000 ÷ $0.40
= 25,000 units

Figure 18-5

---

5. **Breakeven Point in Dollars**

   a. The breakeven point in sales dollars equals fixed costs divided by the contribution margin ratio (CMR). CMR is the ratio of contribution margin to sales price on either a total or per-unit basis.

   $$\text{Breakeven point in dollars} = \frac{\text{Fixed costs}}{\text{CMR}}$$

   b. The breakeven point in sales dollars also equals the breakeven point in units multiplied by the selling price.

EXAMPLE 18-10   Breakeven Point in Dollars

The contribution margin ratio is 66.667% ($0.40 ÷ $0.60).

Breakeven point in dollars = Fixed costs ÷ CMR
= $10,000 ÷ .66667
= $15,000

6. **Margin of Safety**

    a. The margin of safety is the excess of sales over breakeven sales. It is the amount by which sales can decline before losses occur.

    b. The margin of safety can be expressed as either a dollar amount or a percentage of sales.

    Margin of safety in dollars = Total sales in dollars − Breakeven point in dollars

    $$\text{Margin of safety (\%)} = \frac{\text{Margin of safety (in dollars)}}{\text{Total sales (in dollars)}}$$

7. **Target Operating Income**

    a. An amount of operating income, either in dollars or as a percentage of sales, can be calculated by treating target income as an additional fixed cost (e.g., financing costs or required profits to keep the stock price from falling). The necessary sales can be expressed in either units or dollars.

    $$\text{Target sales in units} = \frac{\text{Fixed costs} + \text{Target operating income}}{\text{UCM}}$$

    $$\text{Target sales in dollars} = \frac{\text{Fixed costs} + \text{Target operating income}}{\text{Contribution margin ratio}}$$

    b. Other problems involving target income require use of the standard equation for operating income.

    Operating income = Sales − Variable costs − Fixed costs

EXAMPLE 18-11   Sales Dollars for Targeted Profit Margin

Fixed costs are $150,000, and variable costs are 85% of the selling price. The dollar amount of sales needed for a 10% return on sales (profit margin) is calculated as follows:

$$\begin{aligned}
\text{Sales} - \text{Variable costs} - \text{Fixed costs} &= \text{Target operating income} \\
\text{Sales} - (.85)\text{Sales} - \$150,000 &= (.1)\text{Sales} \\
(.15)\text{Sales} - \$150,000 &= (.1)\text{Sales} \\
(.05)\text{Sales} &= \$150,000 \\
\text{Sales} &= \$3,000,000
\end{aligned}$$

Alternatively, it can be calculated as follows:

$$\begin{aligned}
\text{Sales} - \text{Variable costs} - \text{Fixed costs} - \text{Target operating income} &= 0 \\
\text{Sales} - (.85)\text{Sales} - \$150,000 - (.10)\text{Sales} &= 0 \\
\text{Sales}(1.00 - .85 - .10) - \$150,000 &= 0 \\
\text{Sales}(.05) &= \$150,000 \\
\text{Sales} &= \$3,000,000
\end{aligned}$$

EXAMPLE 18-12   Unit Sales for Targeted Operating Income

Assuming that target operating income is $25,000, unit sales are calculated as follows:

$$\begin{aligned}
\text{Target units} &= (\text{Fixed costs} + \text{Target operating income}) \div \text{UCM} \\
&= (\$10,000 + \$25,000) \div \$0.40 \\
&= \$35,000 \div \$.40 \\
&= 87,500 \text{ units}
\end{aligned}$$

8. Target Net Income

a. A problem may ask for net income (an after-tax amount) instead of operating income (a pretax amount).

$$\text{Net income} = \text{Operating income} - (\text{Operating income} \times \text{Tax rate})$$
$$= \text{Operating income} \times (1 - \text{Tax rate})$$
$$\text{Operating income} = \text{Net income} \div (1 - \text{Tax rate})$$

1) The calculation of unit sales or sales dollars for a given target net income is based on the same equations used for target operating income. The difference is that net income is substituted for target operating income.

$$\text{Target sales in units} = \frac{\text{Fixed costs} + [\text{Target net income} \div (1.0 - \text{Tax rate})]}{\text{UCM}}$$

EXAMPLE 18-13 — **Unit Sales for Target Net Income**

Assuming that target net income is $30,000 and the effective tax rate is 20%, unit sales are calculated as follows:

$$\text{Target units} = \{\text{Fixed costs} + [\text{Target net income} \div (1.0 - .20)]\} \div \text{UCM}$$
$$= [\$10,000 + (\$30,000 \div .80)] \div \$.40$$
$$= 118{,}750 \text{ units}$$

---

9. Multiple Products (or Services)

a. A multi-product breakeven point in units can be calculated as follows:

$$\text{Multi-product breakeven point} = \frac{\text{Total fixed costs}}{\text{Weighted-average selling price} - \text{Weighted-average variable cost}}$$

$$\text{Multi-product breakeven point} = \frac{\text{Total fixed expenses}}{\text{Weighted-average unit contribution margin (UCM)}}$$

1) The weighted-average selling price and weighted-average variable costs are calculated using the individual product sales percentages in the total sales mix.

2) The multi-product breakeven point provides the breakeven point of composite units, which is a mixture of all the different products. From this, individual breakeven points can be calculated.

3) No unique breakeven point exists in a multi-product problem. The breakeven point varies with the sales mix. It is lower if a greater quantity of high-contribution-margin product is sold and vice versa.

b. A multi-product breakeven point in sales dollars can be calculated as follows:

$$\text{Weighted-average contribution margin ratio (CMR)} = \frac{\text{Weighted-average UCM}}{\text{Weighted-average unit selling price}}$$

$$\text{Multi-product breakeven point} = \frac{\text{Total fixed costs}}{\text{Weighted-average CMR}}$$

EXAMPLE 18-14 — Multi-Product BEP

A manufacturer produces two products, Product V and Product W. Total fixed costs are $75,000. Variable cost and sales data for these products are as follows:

	Product V	Product W
Selling price per unit	$10	$18
Variable cost per unit	$7	$14
Budget sales (units)	6,000	18,000

The multi-product breakeven point in units can be calculated as follows:

Product V: UCM = $10 − $7 = $3
Product W: UCM = $18 − $14 = $4

Sales mix:

Product V: 6,000 ÷ (6,000 + 18,000) = 25%
Product W: 18,000 ÷ (6,000 + 18,000) = 75%

Weighted-average UCM = ($3 × 25%) + ($4 × 75%) = $3.75

Multi-product breakeven point = Total fixed costs ÷ Weighted-average UCM
= $75,000 ÷ $3.75
= 20,000 total units

Breakeven point in units:

Product V: 20,000 total units × 25% = 5,000 units
Product W: 20,000 total units × 75% = 15,000 units

The multi-product breakeven point in sales dollars can be calculated as follows:

Weighted-average CMR = Weighted-average UCM ÷ Weighted-average unit selling price
= $3.75 ÷ [($10 × 25%) + ($18 × 75%)]
= 0.234375

Multi-product breakeven point = Total fixed costs ÷ Weighted-average CMR
= $75,000 ÷ 0.234375
= $320,000

Breakeven sales:

Product V: 5,000 units × $10 selling price = $50,000
Product W: 15,000 units × $18 selling price = $270,000

SUCCESS TIP

Proficiency in using the CVP equations is needed to determine the information required by questions. The multiple-choice questions in the Gleim materials provide an opportunity to practice and improve proficiency in working with these equations.

STOP & REVIEW

You have completed the outline for this subunit.
Study multiple-choice questions 14 through 18 beginning on page 563.

18.5 MANAGEMENT DECISION MAKING

1. **Relevant vs. Irrelevant Factors**

   a. Decision making should focus only on relevant revenues and costs. To be relevant, they must

      1) Be **expected** to be earned or incurred, respectively, in the **future**.

         a) Costs already incurred or to which the organization is committed (sunk costs) do not affect current decisions.

         b) EXAMPLE: A manufacturer is considering the purchase of new equipment. The amounts paid for the existing equipment are sunk costs. They are irrelevant to the purchase decision.

         c) EXAMPLE: A union contract may require 6 months of wage continuance after a plant shutdown. Because the occurrence of a plant shutdown is a future event, the 6 months of wages represent relevant costs.

      2) Differ among the possible decisions.

      3) Be avoidable.

         a) A cost is avoidable if it can be eliminated by choosing a specific option. Avoidable costs may include variable materials costs or direct labor costs.

         b) An unavoidable cost must be incurred regardless of whether a specific option is chosen.

            i) For example, rent under a long-term lease on a building is not eliminated by closing the business in that building. Thus, the rent is an unavoidable cost.

   b. Marginal (incremental or differential) analysis relates to relevance.

      1) For example, throughout the relevant range, the marginal cost of an additional unit of output is usually the same. However, beyond a certain output, current production capacity is insufficient and additional fixed costs must be incurred.

      2) The basic decision model is, if marginal revenue exceeds marginal costs (i.e., the contribution margin is positive), accept the project.

EXAMPLE 18-15   Marginal Analysis

The following unit costs of a product are incurred:

Direct materials	$2.00
Direct labor	3.00
Variable overhead	.50
Fixed overhead	.50
Total cost	$6.00

The product normally sells for $10 per unit. Marginal analysis is necessary if a buyer, who has never before been a customer, offers to pay $5.60 per unit for a special order of the product. One possibility is to reject the offer because the selling price is less than the average cost of production.

However, marginal analysis results in a different decision. Assuming idle capacity is available, the only marginal costs are for direct materials, direct labor, and variable overhead. No additional fixed overhead costs are incurred. Because marginal revenue (the $5.60 selling price) exceeds marginal costs ($2 materials + $3 labor + $.50 variable OH = $5.50 per unit), accepting the special order is profitable (i.e., the contribution margin is positive: $5.60 − $5.50 = $0.10 per unit).

2. Add-or-Drop-a-Segment Decisions

a. Disinvestment decisions involve discontinuing an operation, product or product line, business segment, branch, or major customer. These decisions are also referred to as keep or drop decisions.

   1) In general, if the marginal cost of a project exceeds the marginal revenue, the firm should disinvest.

b. A firm making a disinvestment decision should

   1) Identify fixed costs that will be eliminated, e.g., insurance on equipment used.
   2) Determine the revenue that justifies continuing operations. In the short run, this amount should at least equal the variable cost of production or continued service.
   3) Establish the opportunity cost of alternatives.
   4) Determine whether the carrying amount of the assets equals their economic value. If not, the decision should be evaluated using current fair value.

c. When a firm disinvests, excess capacity may exist unless it is used immediately by another project. The cost of idle capacity is a relevant cost.

EXAMPLE 18-16   Keep-or-Drop Incremental Approach

JF Company is considering eliminating Product X. If Product X is eliminated, the sales of Product Y will decrease by 10%.

	Product X	Product Y	Product Z
Sales	$500,000	$800,000	$1,000,000
Variable costs	280,000	350,000	460,000
Fixed costs	300,000	320,000	450,000
Operating income	$(80,000)	$130,000	$ 90,000

Fixed costs include $100,000 of allocated corporate costs assigned to each product.

Using the incremental approach, the impact to the company's operating income if Product X were eliminated would be as follows:

Lost contribution margin from Product X ($500,000 – $280,000)	$(220,000)
Lost contribution margin from Product Y [($800,000 – $350,000) × 10%]	(45,000)
Fixed cost savings ($300,000 – $100,000 allocated corporate costs)	200,000
Increase (decrease) in operating income if Product X were eliminated	$ (65,000)

If Product X were eliminated, the company's operating income would decrease by $65,000. JF Company should keep Product X.

EXAMPLE 18-17   Keep-or-Drop Incremental Approach

Using the information from Example 18-16, assume the only change to the situation is that eliminating Product X would cause a 25% increase in the sales of Product Z.

Lost contribution margin from Product X ($500,000 – $280,000)	$(220,000)
Lost contribution margin from Product Y [($800,000 – $350,000) × 10%]	(45,000)
Gained contribution margin from Product Z [($1,000,000 – $460,000) × 25%]	135,000
Fixed cost savings ($300,000 – $100,000 allocated corporate costs)	200,000
Increase (decrease) in operating income if Product X were eliminated	$ 70,000

If Product X were eliminated, the company's operating income would increase by $70,000. JF Company should eliminate Product X.

3. **Special Orders When Excess Capacity Exists**

   a. When a manufacturer has excess production capacity, accepting a special order has no opportunity cost.

      1) The order should be accepted if the minimum price for the product is equal to or greater than the variable costs. When capacity is available, fixed costs are irrelevant.

      2) A special order might be rejected if acceptance affects the price of regular sales.

EXAMPLE 18-18   Special Orders -- Available Capacity

Normal unit pricing for a manufacture's product is as follows:

Direct materials and labor	$15.00
Variable overhead	3.00
Fixed overhead	5.00
Variable selling	1.50
Fixed selling and administrative	12.00
Total cost	$36.50

If the manufacturer receives a special order for which capacity exists, the lowest bid the company could offer is $19.50 ($15.00 + $3.00 + $1.50).

---

4. **Special Orders in the Absence of Excess Capacity**

   a. When a manufacturer lacks excess production capacity, the marginal costs of accepting the order must be considered.

      1) Besides the variable costs of the production run, the firm must consider the opportunity cost of redirecting productive capacity away from (possibly more profitable) products.

EXAMPLE 18-19   Special Orders -- No Available Capacity

Using the information from Example 18-18, if the manufacturer receives a special order for which capacity does not exist, the lowest bid the company could offer is $36.50.

In addition to fixed costs, any revenue lost from reducing or stopping production on other product lines would be relevant when determining the lowest acceptable bid price.

---

5. **Make-or-Buy Decisions (Insourcing vs. Outsourcing)**

   a. The firm should use available resources as efficiently as possible before outsourcing.

      1) If the total relevant costs of production are **less** than the costs to buy the item, it should be made in-house.

      2) If the total relevant costs of production are **more** than the costs to buy the item, it should be bought (outsourced).

b. As with a special order, the manager considers only the costs relevant to the investment decision. The key variable is total relevant costs, not total costs.

1) Sunk costs are irrelevant.
2) Costs that do not differ between two alternatives should be ignored because they are not relevant to the decision being made.
3) Opportunity costs must be considered when idle capacity (additional capacity) is not available. Opportunity cost is important because it represents the forgone opportunities of the firm.

    a) In some situations, a firm may decide to stop processing one product in order to free up capacity for another product, reducing relevant costs, and affecting the decision to make or buy.

c. The firm also should consider the qualitative aspects of the decision.

1) Will the product quality be as high if a component is outsourced rather than produced internally?
2) How reliable are the suppliers?
3) Will workers acquire new skills or efficiencies?

6. **Make-or-Buy Decisions**

   a. The relevant cost of making a component is the total of all avoidable costs.
   b. Avoidable costs include the variable manufacturing costs and relevant fixed costs that would be eliminated if the component were purchased from an outside supplier.

EXAMPLE 18-20   Make-or-Buy Decision

Hines Company currently produces all of the component parts of its top selling widget. Hines can purchase component J from an outside supplier for $8. Hines currently produces 35,000 units of component J each year.

Cost information for component J is as follows:

Direct materials	$4.00
Direct labor	2.50
Variable overhead	1.00
Fixed overhead	2.00*
Total unit cost	$9.50

*Fixed overhead includes $1.20 that would not be eliminated if component J were purchased from an outside supplier.

The relevant cost to produce component J is $8.30 ($4 + $2.50 + $1.00 + $0.80). The relevant cost to buy component J is $8.

If Hines buys component J from the outside supplier, operating income would increase by $10,500 ($0.30 × 35,000 units).

SU 18: Costing Systems and Decision Making

7. Opportunity costs must be considered when idle capacity is not available. They are of primary importance because they represent the forgone opportunities of the firm.

   a. In some situations, a firm may decide to stop processing one product in order to free up capacity for another product, reducing relevant costs and affecting the decision to make or buy.

EXAMPLE 18-21   Make-or-Buy Decision -- Opportunity Cost

MG Company currently produces toy tractors. An important part of the toy tractor is the wheels. MG produces 40,000 wheels each year. MG can purchase the wheels from an outside supplier for $3 per wheel. MG is operating at full capacity and would eliminate all fixed overhead costs related to wheel production if it purchased the wheels from the outside supplier. MG's cost data for each wheel follows:

Direct materials	$0.80
Direct labor	1.00
Variable overhead	0.20
Fixed overhead	0.75
Total unit cost	$2.75

With no other information, MG should make the wheels in-house. If MG bought from the outside supplier, operating income would decrease by $10,000 [($3 − $2.75) × 40,000 wheels]. Now assume the following:

If MG bought the wheels from the outside supplier, MG could begin producing toy trucks in the space currently occupied by the wheel production line. Annual operating income for the toy truck line would be $24,000.

The operating income for the toy truck line represents an opportunity cost that will change MG's decision. MG's decision would now be to purchase the wheels from the outside supplier. If MG bought from the outside supplier, operating income would increase by $14,000 ($24,000 opportunity cost − $10,000 additional cost to buy).

STOP & REVIEW

You have completed the outline for this subunit.
Study multiple-choice questions 19 through 22 beginning on page 565.

QUESTIONS

18.1 Job-Order Costing and Overhead Application

1. Lucy Sportswear manufactures a specialty line of T-shirts using a job-order cost system. During March, the following costs were incurred in completing Job ICU2: direct materials, $13,700; direct labor, $4,800; administrative, $1,400; and selling, $5,600. Overhead was applied at the rate of $25 per machine hour, and Job ICU2 required 800 machine hours. If Job ICU2 resulted in 7,000 good shirts, the cost of goods sold per unit would be

A. $6.50
B. $6.30
C. $5.70
D. $5.50

Answer (D) is correct.
  REQUIRED: The cost of goods sold per unit.
  DISCUSSION: Cost of goods sold is based on the manufacturing costs incurred in production but does not include selling or general and administrative expenses. Manufacturing costs equal $38,500 [$13,700 DM + $4,800 DL + (800 hours × $25) OH]. Thus, per-unit cost is $5.50 ($38,500 ÷ 7,000 units).
  Answer (A) is incorrect. The amount of $6.50 includes selling and administrative expenses. **Answer (B) is incorrect.** Including selling costs results in cost of goods sold per unit of $6.30. **Answer (C) is incorrect.** Including administrative expenses results in cost of goods sold per unit of $5.70.

2. Worley Company has underapplied overhead of $45,000 for the year. Before disposition of the underapplied overhead, selected year-end balances from Worley's accounting records were

Sales	$1,200,000
Cost of goods sold	720,000
Direct materials inventory	36,000
Work-in-process inventory	54,000
Finished goods inventory	90,000

Under Worley's cost accounting system, over- or underapplied overhead is assigned to appropriate inventories and COGS based on year-end balances. In its year-end income statement, Worley should report COGS of

A. $682,500
B. $684,000
C. $757,500
D. $765,000

Answer (C) is correct.
    REQUIRED: The amount of cost of goods sold after allocation of underapplied overhead.
    DISCUSSION: The assignment of underapplied overhead increases COGS. The underapplied overhead of $45,000 for the year should be assigned on a pro rata basis to work-in-process ($54,000), finished goods ($90,000), and COGS ($720,000). The sum of these three items is $864,000. Thus, $37,500 should be assigned to COGS [($720,000 ÷ $864,000) × $45,000]. COGS after assignment is $757,500 ($37,500 + $720,000). The remaining $7,500 should be assigned proportionately to work-in-process and finished goods.
    Answer (A) is incorrect. The appropriate COGS balance if overhead was overapplied by $45,000 and $37,500 was assigned to COGS is $682,500. **Answer (B) is incorrect.** The COGS balance if overhead was overapplied by $45,000 and direct materials inventory was incorrectly included in the denominator of the ratio used to assign overhead is $684,000. **Answer (D) is incorrect.** Debiting the full amount of underapplied overhead ($45,000) to COGS results in $765,000.

3. Felicity Corporation manufactures a specialty line of dresses using a job-order cost system. During January, the following costs were incurred in completing job J-1:

Direct materials	$27,400
Direct labor	9,600
Administrative costs	2,800
Selling costs	11,200

Overhead was applied at the rate of $50 per direct labor hour, and job J-1 required 400 direct labor hours. If job J-1 resulted in 4,000 good dresses, the cost of goods sold per unit is

A. $9.25
B. $14.25
C. $14.95
D. $17.75

Answer (B) is correct.
    REQUIRED: The cost of goods sold per unit.
    DISCUSSION: Cost of goods sold is based on the manufacturing costs incurred in production. It does not include selling or general and administrative expenses. Manufacturing costs consist of direct materials ($27,400), direct labor ($9,600), and overhead (400 direct labor hours × $50 per hour = $20,000). The total of these cost elements is $57,000. Dividing the $57,000 of total manufacturing costs by the 4,000 units produced results in a per-unit cost of $14.25.
    Answer (A) is incorrect. Failing to include overhead results in $9.25. **Answer (C) is incorrect.** Including administrative costs results in $14.95. **Answer (D) is incorrect.** The amount of $17.75 includes selling and administrative costs.

18.2 Process Costing

4. The units transferred in from the first department to the second department should be included in the computation of the equivalent units for the second department under which of the following methods of process costing?

	FIFO	Weighted-Average
A.	Yes	Yes
B.	Yes	No
C.	No	Yes
D.	No	No

Answer (A) is correct.
REQUIRED: The cost flow method(s) that include(s) transferred-in costs in EUP calculations.
DISCUSSION: The units transferred from the first to the second department should be included in the computation of EUP for the second department regardless of the cost flow assumption used. The transferred-in units are considered materials added at the beginning of the period.
Answer (B) is incorrect. Units transferred in also should be included in the EUP computation under the weighted-average method. Answer (C) is incorrect. Units transferred in also should be included in the EUP computation under the FIFO method. Answer (D) is incorrect. Units transferred in should be included in the EUP computation under both methods.

5. Purchased direct materials are added in the second department of a three-department process. This addition does **not** increase the number of units produced in the second department and will

A. Not change the dollar amount transferred to the next department.
B. Decrease total ending work-in-process inventory.
C. Increase the factory overhead portion of the ending work-in-process inventory.
D. Increase total unit cost.

Answer (D) is correct.
REQUIRED: The effect of adding direct materials in a subsequent department given constant production.
DISCUSSION: Adding materials to a production process without changing the number of units produced increases the unit cost. The numerator (total cost) increases while the denominator (total units) remains the same.
Answer (A) is incorrect. If purchased materials are added to the process, the cost will be added to the total cost transferred to the next department. Answer (B) is incorrect. The unit cost, and therefore the cost of EWIP, increases when materials are added. Answer (C) is incorrect. Materials cost is separate from overhead.

6. Assuming no beginning work-in-process inventory, and that the ending work-in-process inventory is 100% complete as to materials costs, the number of equivalent units as to materials costs is

A. The same as the units placed in process.
B. The same as the units completed.
C. Less than the units placed in process.
D. Less than the units completed.

Answer (A) is correct.
REQUIRED: The number of EUP as to materials costs.
DISCUSSION: Given no BWIP, whether the FIFO or weighted-average method is used is immaterial. Because EWIP is 100% complete as to materials costs, the EUP for materials costs are equal to the number of units placed in process (units in EWIP + units transferred to finished goods).
Answer (B) is incorrect. The number of EUP is equal to the units completed only if there is no EWIP. Answer (C) is incorrect. The number of EUP is less than the units placed in process when EWIP is less than 100% complete as to materials costs. Answer (D) is incorrect. The EUP must at least equal the number of units completed.

7. A company employs a process cost system using the first-in, first-out (FIFO) method. The product passes through both Department 1 and Department 2 in order to be completed. Units enter Department 2 upon completion in Department 1. Additional direct materials are added in Department 2 when the units have reached the 25% stage of completion with respect to conversion costs. Conversion costs are added proportionally in Department 2. The production activity in Department 2 for the current month was as follows:

Beginning work-in-process inventory (40% complete with respect to conversion costs)	15,000
Units transferred in from Department 1	80,000
Units completed and transferred to finished goods	85,000
Ending work-in-process inventory (20% complete with respect to conversion costs)	10,000

How many equivalent units for direct materials were added in Department 2 for the current month?

A. 70,000 units.
B. 80,000 units.
C. 85,000 units.
D. 90,000 units.

Answer (A) is correct.
REQUIRED: The EUP for direct materials added in Department 2 for the current month.
DISCUSSION: Beginning inventory is 40% complete. Thus, direct materials have already been added. Ending inventory has not reached the 25% stage of completion, so direct materials have not yet been added to these units. Thus, the EUP for direct materials calculated on a FIFO basis are equal to the units started and completed in the current period (85,000 units completed – 15,000 units in BWIP = 70,000 units started and completed).
Answer (B) is incorrect. The amount transferred in from Department 1 was 80,000 total units. Answer (C) is incorrect. The EUP for direct materials calculated on a weighted-average basis equals 85,000. Answer (D) is incorrect. The sum of units transferred in from Department 1 and ending work-in-process inventory equals 90,000 units.

8. The following data pertain to a company's cracking-department operations in December:

	Units	Completion
Work-in-process, Dec. 1	20,000	50%
Units started	170,000	
Units completed and transferred to the distilling department	180,000	
Work-in-process, Dec. 31	10,000	50%

Materials are added at the beginning of the process, and conversion costs are incurred uniformly throughout the process. Assuming use of the FIFO method of process costing, the equivalent units of production (EUP) with respect to conversion performed during December were

A. 170,000
B. 175,000
C. 180,000
D. 185,000

Answer (B) is correct.
REQUIRED: The EUP for conversion.
DISCUSSION: Under the FIFO method, EUP are determined based only on work performed during the current period. Thus, units in beginning work-in-process must be excluded.

	Conversion
Units transferred out	180,000
Add: EWIP (10,000 × 50%)	5,000
Total completed units	185,000
Less: BWIP (20,000 × 50%)	(10,000)
Equivalent units of production	175,000

Answer (A) is incorrect. The number of EUP of materials for the period is 170,000. Answer (C) is incorrect. The total amount of work done on the completed units is 180,000. Answer (D) is incorrect. The amount determined using the weighted-average method is 185,000.

18.3 Activity-Based Costing (ABC)

Question 9 is based on the following information.

Zeta Company is preparing its annual profit plan. As part of its analysis of the profitability of individual products, the controller estimates the amount of overhead that should be allocated to the individual product lines from the information given in the next column:

	Wall Mirrors	Specialty Windows
Units produced	25	25
Material moves per product line	5	15
Direct labor hours per unit	200	200
Budgeted materials handling costs		$50,000

9. Under a costing system that allocates overhead on the basis of direct labor hours, Zeta Company's materials handling costs allocated to one unit of wall mirrors would be

A. $1,000
B. $500
C. $2,000
D. $5,000

Answer (A) is correct.
REQUIRED: The amount of materials handling costs allocated to one unit of wall mirrors when direct labor hours is the activity base.
DISCUSSION: If direct labor hours are used as the allocation base, the $50,000 of costs is allocated over 400 hours of direct labor. Multiplying the 25 units of each product times 200 hours results in 5,000 labor hours for each product, or a total of 10,000 hours. Dividing $50,000 by 10,000 hours results in a cost of $5 per direct labor hour. Multiplying 200 hours times $5 results in an allocation of $1,000 of overhead per unit of product.
Answer (B) is incorrect. The amount of $500 is the allocation based on number of material moves.
Answer (C) is incorrect. The amount of $2,000 assumes that all the overhead is allocated to the wall mirrors.
Answer (D) is incorrect. The amount of $5,000 assumes overhead of $250,000.

10. A company with three products classifies its costs as belonging to five functions: design, production, marketing, distribution, and customer services. For pricing purposes, all company costs are assigned to the three products. The direct costs of each of the five functions are traced directly to the three products. The indirect costs of each of the five business functions are collected into five separate cost pools and then assigned to the three products using appropriate allocation bases. The allocation base that will most likely be the best for allocating the indirect costs of the distribution function is

A. Number of customer phone calls.
B. Number of shipments.
C. Number of sales persons.
D. Dollar sales volume.

Answer (B) is correct.
REQUIRED: The allocation base that will most likely be the best for allocating the indirect costs of the distribution function.
DISCUSSION: The number of shipments is an appropriate cost driver. A cause-and-effect relationship may exist between the number of shipments and distribution costs.
Answer (A) is incorrect. The number of customer phone calls has little relation to distribution. It is probably more closely related to customer service. Answer (C) is incorrect. The number of sales persons is not related to distribution. It is more closely related to marketing.
Answer (D) is incorrect. The dollar sales volume is not necessarily related to distribution. It is more likely related to marketing.

11. Pelder Products Company manufactures two types of engineering diagnostic equipment used in construction. The two products are based on different technologies, X-ray and ultrasound, but are manufactured in the same factory. Pelder has computed the manufacturing cost of the X-ray and ultrasound products by adding together direct materials, direct labor, and overhead cost applied based on the number of direct labor hours. The factory has three overhead departments that support the single production line that makes both products. Budgeted overhead spending for the departments is as follows:

Department			
Engineering design	Material handling	Setup	Total
$6,000	$5,000	$3,000	$14,000

Pelder's budgeted manufacturing activities and costs for the period are as follows:

Activity	Product	
	X-Ray	Ultrasound
Units produced and sold	50	100
Direct materials used	$5,000	$8,000
Direct labor hours used	100	300
Direct labor cost	$4,000	$12,000
Number of parts used	400	600
Number of engineering changes	2	1
Number of product setups	8	7

The budgeted cost to manufacture one ultrasound machine using the activity-based costing method is

A. $225
B. $264
C. $293
D. $305

Answer (B) is correct.
REQUIRED: The ABC cost of a single ultrasound machine.
DISCUSSION: Charges for direct materials and direct labor are traceable to each type of machine ($8,000 and $12,000 respectively for the ultrasound). The departmental costs must be allocated based on each machine's proportional driver level. Engineering design costs can be allocated to the ultrasound machine at a rate of 33.3% [1 ÷ (1 + 2)], material handling at a rate of 60% [600 ÷ (600 + 400)], and setup at a rate of 46.7% [7 ÷ (7 + 8)]. Pelder's cost for a single ultrasound machine can thus be calculated as follows:

	For 100 Units
Direct materials ($8,000)	$ 80
Direct labor ($12,000)	120
Engineering changes ($6,000 × 33.3%)	20
Materials handling ($5,000 × 60%)	30
Setup ($3,000 × 46.7%)	14
Total	$264

Answer (A) is incorrect. The amount of $225 results from using X-ray direct labor rather than ultrasound direct labor. Answer (C) is incorrect. The amount of $293 results from improperly using the units of production to allocate the engineering, handling, and setup costs. Answer (D) is incorrect. The amount of $305 results from improperly using direct labor hours to allocate the engineering, handling, and setup costs.

12. A company is considering the implementation of an activity-based costing and management program. The company

A. Should focus on manufacturing activities and avoid implementation with service-type functions.
B. Would probably find a lack of software in the marketplace to assist with the related recordkeeping.
C. Would normally gain added insights into causes of cost.
D. Would likely use fewer cost pools than it did under more traditional accounting methods.

Answer (C) is correct.
REQUIRED: The most likely result of an ABC and ABM program.
DISCUSSION: One of the benefits of activity-based costing is the discovery of cost relationships that are unnoticed using traditional accounting methods.
Answer (A) is incorrect. Activity-based costing is suitable for service-type functions. Answer (B) is incorrect. Software exists to help firms implement activity-based management. Answer (D) is incorrect. Activity-based costing generally results in many more cost pools than under traditional accounting methods.

SU 18: Costing Systems and Decision Making

13. The Chocolate Baker specializes in chocolate baked goods. The firm has long assessed the profitability of a product line by comparing revenues to the cost of goods sold. However, Barry Love, the firm's new accountant, wants to use an activity-based costing system that takes into consideration the cost of the delivery person. Listed below are activity and cost information relating to two of Chocolate Baker's major products.

	Muffins	Cheesecake
Revenue	$53,000	$46,000
Cost of goods sold	26,000	21,000
Delivery activity:		
Number of deliveries	150	85
Average length of delivery	10 min.	15 min.
Cost per hour for delivery	$20.00	$20.00

Using activity-based costing, which one of the following statements is correct?

A. The muffins are $2,000 more profitable.
B. The cheesecakes are $75 more profitable.
C. The muffins are $1,925 more profitable.
D. The muffins have a higher profitability as a percentage of sales and therefore are more advantageous.

Answer (C) is correct.
REQUIRED: The true statement given activity-based costing.
DISCUSSION: The first step is to calculate the gross margin on the two products:

	Muffins	Cheesecake
Revenues	$53,000	$46,000
Cost of goods sold	(26,000)	(21,000)
Gross margin	$27,000	$25,000

The next step is to calculate total delivery cost for each product:

	Muffins	Cheesecake
Number of deliveries	150	85
Times: Minutes per delivery	× 10	× 15
Total delivery minutes	1,500	1,275
Divided by: Minutes per hour	÷ 60	÷ 60
Total delivery hours	25.00	21.25
Times: Delivery cost per hour	× $20	× $20
Total delivery cost	$500	$425

The operating profits on these two products, and the difference between them, can now be determined:

Muffins	($27,000 – $500)	$26,500
Cheesecake	($25,000 – $425)	(24,575)
Excess		$ 1,925

Answer (A) is incorrect. Muffins exceed cheesecake by $2,000 only at the gross margin, not the total profitability level. Answer (B) is incorrect. The total delivery cost for muffins exceeds that of cheesecake by $75. Answer (D) is incorrect. Muffins ($26,500 ÷ $53,000 = 50.0%) have a lower profitability percentage than cheesecake ($24,575 ÷ $46,000 = 53.4%).

18.4 Cost-Volume-Profit Analysis

14. The breakeven point in units increases when unit costs

A. Increase and sales price remains unchanged.
B. Decrease and sales price remains unchanged.
C. Remain unchanged and sales price increases.
D. Decrease and sales price increases.

Answer (A) is correct.
REQUIRED: The event that causes the breakeven point in units to increase.
DISCUSSION: A BEP ratio can be increased either by raising the numerator or lowering the denominator. The breakeven point in units is calculated by dividing fixed costs by the unit contribution margin. If selling price is constant and costs increase, the unit contribution margin decreases. The effect is to decrease the denominator and increase the ratio.
Answer (B) is incorrect. A decrease in costs decreases the breakeven point. The unit contribution margin increases. Answer (C) is incorrect. An increase in the selling price also increases the unit contribution margin, resulting in a lower breakeven point. Answer (D) is incorrect. The unit contribution margin is increased by a cost decrease and a sales price increase, resulting in a lower breakeven point.

15. The following information pertains to Sisk Co.:

Sales (25,000 units)	$500,000
Direct materials and direct labor	150,000
Factory overhead:	
Variable	20,000
Fixed	35,000
Selling and general expenses:	
Variable	5,000
Fixed	30,000

Sisk's breakeven point in number of units is

A. 4,924
B. 5,000
C. 6,250
D. 9,286

Answer (B) is correct.
    REQUIRED: The breakeven point in units.
    DISCUSSION: The breakeven point in units equals the fixed costs divided by the unit contribution margin (UCM). The fixed costs are $65,000 ($35,000 manufacturing overhead + $30,000 SG&A). The UCM is calculated as follows:

	Dollars	Units	Per Unit
Sales	$500,000 ÷	25,000 =	$20.00
Variable costs:			
Prime costs	$150,000		
Variable overhead	20,000		
Variable SG&A	5,000		
Total var. costs	$175,000 ÷	25,000 =	(7.00)
Contribution margin			$13.00

    Thus, the breakeven point in units is 5,000 ($65,000 fixed costs ÷ $13 UCM).
    Answer (A) is incorrect. The amount of 4,924 does not include the variable selling and general expenses in the unit contribution margin calculation. **Answer (C) is incorrect.** The amount of 6,250 includes the unit fixed manufacturing overhead and unit fixed selling and general expenses in the unit contribution margin. **Answer (D) is incorrect.** The amount of 9,286 results from using the total variable costs of $7 rather than the contribution margin of $13.

16. Wren Co. manufactures and sells two products with selling prices and variable costs as follows:

	A	B
Selling price	$18.00	$22.00
Variable costs	12.00	14.00

Wren's total annual fixed costs are $38,400. Wren sells four units of A for every unit of B. If operating income last year was $28,800, what was the number of units Wren sold?

A. 5,486
B. 6,000
C. 9,600
D. 10,500

Answer (D) is correct.
    REQUIRED: The number of units sold.
    DISCUSSION: The contribution margins of the two products are $6 and $8, respectively ($18 – $12 and $22 – $14). The units sold can be calculated as follows:

$$\text{Target unit volume} = \frac{\text{Fixed costs} + \text{Target operating income}}{\text{Weighted UCM}}$$

$$= (\$38{,}400 + \$28{,}800) \div (\$6A + \$8B)$$
$$\$6A + \$8B = \$67{,}200$$
$$\$6(4B) + \$8B = \$67{,}200$$
$$\$32B = \$67{,}200$$
$$B = 2{,}100 \text{ units}$$

    Because 4 units of A are sold for every unit of B, the volume of A was 8,400 units (2,100 × 4). Thus, the total number of units sold was 10,500 (8,400A + 2,100B).
    Answer (A) is incorrect. The amount of 5,486 units equals the fixed costs divided by the contribution margin from product B. **Answer (B) is incorrect.** The amount of 6,000 units does not include the operating income of $28,800 in the calculation. **Answer (C) is incorrect.** The operating income plus the fixed costs are divided by the contribution margin for product B, giving the number of units sold of 9,600.

SU 18: Costing Systems and Decision Making

17. The following information pertains to Clove Co. for the month just ended:

Budgeted sales	$1,000,000
Breakeven sales	700,000
Budgeted contribution margin	600,000
Cash flow breakeven	200,000

Clove's margin of safety is

A. $300,000
B. $400,000
C. $500,000
D. $800,000

Answer (A) is correct.
REQUIRED: The margin of safety.
DISCUSSION: The margin of safety measures the amount by which sales may decline before losses occur. It is the excess of budgeted or actual sales over the breakeven sales. Given that the budgeted sales are $1,000,000 and the breakeven sales are $700,000, the margin of safety is $300,000 ($1,000,000 − $700,000).
Answer (B) is incorrect. The budgeted sales minus the budgeted contribution margin is $400,000. Answer (C) is incorrect. The breakeven sales minus the cash flow breakeven is $500,000. **Answer (D) is incorrect.** The budgeted sales minus the cash flow breakeven is $800,000.

18. In using cost-volume-profit analysis to calculate expected unit sales, which of the following should be added to fixed costs in the numerator?

A. Predicted operating loss.
B. Predicted operating income.
C. Unit contribution margin.
D. Variable costs.

Answer (B) is correct.
REQUIRED: The addition to fixed costs when calculating expected unit sales.
DISCUSSION: CVP analysis can be used to restate the equation for target net income to determine the required level of unit sales.

$$\text{Target unit volume} = \frac{\text{Fixed costs} + \text{Target operating income}}{\text{UCM}}$$

Answer (A) is incorrect. Predicted operating loss is subtracted from fixed costs, not added. Answer (C) is incorrect. Unit contribution margin is the denominator. Answer (D) is incorrect. Variable costs are a component of unit contribution margin.

18.5 Management Decision Making

19. Clay Co. has considerable excess manufacturing capacity. A special job order's cost sheet includes the following applied manufacturing overhead costs:

Fixed costs	$21,000
Variable costs	33,000

The fixed costs include a normal $3,700 allocation for in-house design costs, although no in-house design will be done. Instead, the job will require the use of external designers costing $7,750. What is the total amount to be included in the calculation to determine the minimum acceptable price for the job?

A. $36,700
B. $40,750
C. $54,000
D. $58,050

Answer (B) is correct.
REQUIRED: The total amount to be included in the calculation to determine the minimum acceptable price.
DISCUSSION: Given excess capacity, neither increased fixed costs nor opportunity costs are incurred by accepting the special order. Thus, the marginal cost of the order (the minimum acceptable price) is $40,750 ($33,000 variable costs + $7,750 cost of external design).
Answer (A) is incorrect. The amount of $36,700 equals variable costs plus the in-house design costs. Answer (C) is incorrect. The amount of $54,000 equals the fixed costs plus the variable costs. **Answer (D) is incorrect.** The amount of $58,050 equals the fixed costs, plus the variable costs, minus the in-house design costs, plus the external design costs.

SU 18: Costing Systems and Decision Making

20. Mili Co. plans to discontinue a division with a $20,000 contribution to overhead. Overhead allocated to the division is $50,000, of which $5,000 cannot be eliminated. The effect of this discontinuance on Mili's pretax income would be an increase of

- A. $5,000
- B. $20,000
- C. $25,000
- D. $30,000

Answer (C) is correct.
REQUIRED: The effect of discontinuing a division.
DISCUSSION: This disinvestment decision eliminates $45,000 of overhead ($50,000 – $5,000) and the $20,000 contribution to overhead. The net effect on pretax income is therefore a $25,000 increase ($45,000 – $20,000).
Answer (A) is incorrect. The overhead allocated to the division, which cannot be eliminated, is $5,000. The net effect is a $25,000 increase in pretax income ($45,000 overhead that can be eliminated – $20,000 contribution to overhead). **Answer (B) is incorrect.** The contribution to overhead is $20,000. **Answer (D) is incorrect.** The $5,000 of overhead that cannot be eliminated from the $50,000 overhead allocated should be subtracted.

21. In a make-versus-buy decision, the relevant costs include variable manufacturing costs as well as

- A. Factory management costs.
- B. General office costs.
- C. Avoidable fixed costs.
- D. Depreciation costs.

Answer (C) is correct.
REQUIRED: The relevant costs in a make-versus-buy decision.
DISCUSSION: The relevant costs in a make-versus-buy decision are those that differ between the two decision choices. These costs include any variable costs plus any avoidable fixed costs. Avoidable fixed costs will not be incurred if the "buy" decision is selected.
Answer (A) is incorrect. Factory management costs are unlikely to differ regardless of which decision is selected. **Answer (B) is incorrect.** General office costs are unlikely to differ regardless of which decision is selected. **Answer (D) is incorrect.** Depreciation costs are unlikely to differ regardless of which decision is selected.

22. A company's approach to an insourcing vs. outsourcing decision

- A. Depends on whether the company is operating at or below normal volume.
- B. Involves an analysis of avoidable costs.
- C. Should use absorption (full) costing.
- D. Should use activity-based costing.

Answer (B) is correct.
REQUIRED: The true statement about a company's approach to a make-or-buy decision.
DISCUSSION: Available resources should be used as efficiently as possible before outsourcing. If the total relevant costs of production are less than the cost to buy the item, it should be produced in-house. The relevant costs are those that can be avoided.
Answer (A) is incorrect. Whether operations are at normal volume is less important than the amount of idle capacity. The company is less likely to buy if it has sufficient unused capacity. **Answer (C) is incorrect.** Total costs (absorption costing) are not as important as relevant costs. **Answer (D) is incorrect.** Activity-based costing is used to allocate fixed overhead. Fixed overhead is not relevant in an insourcing vs. outsourcing decision unless it is avoidable.

STUDY UNIT NINETEEN
BUDGETING AND VARIANCE ANALYSIS

(24 pages of outline)

19.1	Standard Costs	567
19.2	The Master Budget and Its Components	569
19.3	The Operating Budget	571
19.4	The Financial Budget	575
19.5	Flexible Budgeting and Variance Analysis	578
19.6	Variance Analysis -- Materials and Labor	581
19.7	Variance Analysis -- Overhead	584
19.8	Sales Variances	590

A standard cost is an estimate of what a cost should be under normal operating conditions based on accounting and engineering studies. Standard costs are used to assign costs to products and control actual costs. To be effective, a budget must be based on reasonably determined standard costs. The preparation of a comprehensive budget has two stages: the operating budget and the financial budget. A flexible budget is prepared for better analysis of budget variances. Comparing actual and standard costs permits evaluation of managerial performance using variance analysis. This analysis also can be applied to revenue amounts.

19.1 STANDARD COSTS

1. **Standard Costs**

    a. Standard costs are **predetermined expectations** about how much a unit of input, a unit of output, or a given activity should cost.

    1) The use of standard costs in budgeting allows the standard cost system to alert management when the actual costs of production differ significantly from the standard.

    $$\text{Standard cost of input per unit of output} = \text{Units of input per single unit of output} \times \text{Price per unit of input}$$

    b. A standard cost is not just an average of past costs but is an **objectively determined estimate** of what a cost should be. Standards may be based on accounting, engineering, or statistical quality control studies.

SUCCESS TIP

Standard costs have been tested by asking for the calculation of a cost for a standard unit of input. Candidates may be asked to explain the use of standard costs.

2. **Ideal vs. Attainable Standards**
   a. **Ideal (theoretical) standards** are standard costs that are set for production under optimal conditions. For this reason, they also are called perfection or maximum efficiency standards.
      1) They are based on the work of the most skilled workers **with no allowance** for spoilage, waste, machine breakdowns, or other downtime.
      2) Often called tight standards, they can have positive behavioral effects if workers are motivated to strive for excellence. However, they are not in wide use because they can have negative effects if the standards are impossible to attain.
      3) Ideal standards ordinarily are replaced by **currently attainable** standards for cash budgeting, product costing, and budgeting departmental performance. Otherwise, accurate financial planning is impossible.
   b. **Practical (currently attainable)** standards are the results expected to be achieved by reasonably well-trained workers **with an allowance** for normal spoilage, waste, and downtime.
      1) Compared to ideal standards, attainable practical standards serve as a better motivating target for manufacturing personnel.
3. A company's standard cost card identifies the standard quantity of each input and the standard price for each input. The total standard cost per unit is found on the standard cost card.

EXAMPLE 19-1   **Standard Cost Card**

	Standard Quantity	Standard Price	Standard Cost
Direct materials	4 pounds per unit	$28.00 per pound	$112.00
Direct labor	5.6 hours per unit	$22.00 per hour	123.20
Variable overhead	2 machine hours per unit	$12.50 per machine hour	25.00
			$260.20

The standard cost per unit for this product is $260.20.

The predetermined variable overhead rate, also referred to as the budgeted application rate, is $12.50.

---

4. **Activity Analysis**
   a. Activity analysis identifies, describes, and evaluates the activities and resources needed to produce a particular output. This process aids in the development of standard costs.
   b. Each operation requires a unique set of inputs and preparations. Activity analysis describes what these inputs are and who performs these preparations.
      1) Inputs include the amounts and kinds of equipment, facilities, materials, and labor. Engineering analysis, cost accounting, time-and-motion study, and other approaches may be useful.
   c. Historical data, adjusted for current conditions, may be used to set standards if an entity lacks the resources to engage in the complex task of activity analysis.

STOP & REVIEW

You have completed the outline for this subunit.
Study multiple-choice questions 1 through 3 on page 591.

19.2 THE MASTER BUDGET AND ITS COMPONENTS

1. **The Master Budget Process -- Sequence**

   a. The **master budget** (also called the comprehensive budget, static budget, or annual profit plan) encompasses the organization's operating and financial plans for a specified period (ordinarily a year or single operating cycle).

   b. The master budget consists of the **operating budget** and the **financial budget**. Both consist of inputs from interrelated sub-budgets.

      1) For example, the production budget cannot be prepared until after completion of the sales budget. The direct materials budget and the direct labor budget cannot be prepared until after completion of the production budget.

2. **The Operating Budget**

   a. In the operating budget, the emphasis is on obtaining and using current resources. It contains the following components:

      1) Sales budget
      2) Production budget
      3) Direct materials budget
      4) Direct labor budget
      5) Manufacturing overhead budget
      6) Cost of goods sold budget
      7) Nonmanufacturing budget

         a) Research and development budget
         b) Selling and administrative budget

            i) Design budget
            ii) Marketing budget
            iii) Distribution budget
            iv) Customer service budget
            v) Administrative budget

      8) Pro forma income statement

3. **The Financial Budget**

   a. In the financial budget, the emphasis is on obtaining the funds needed to purchase operating assets. It contains the following components:

      1) Capital budget
      2) Cash budget

         a) Projected cash collection schedule
         b) Projected cash disbursement schedule

      3) Pro forma balance sheet
      4) Pro forma statement of cash flows

4. Master Budget Process -- Graphical Depiction

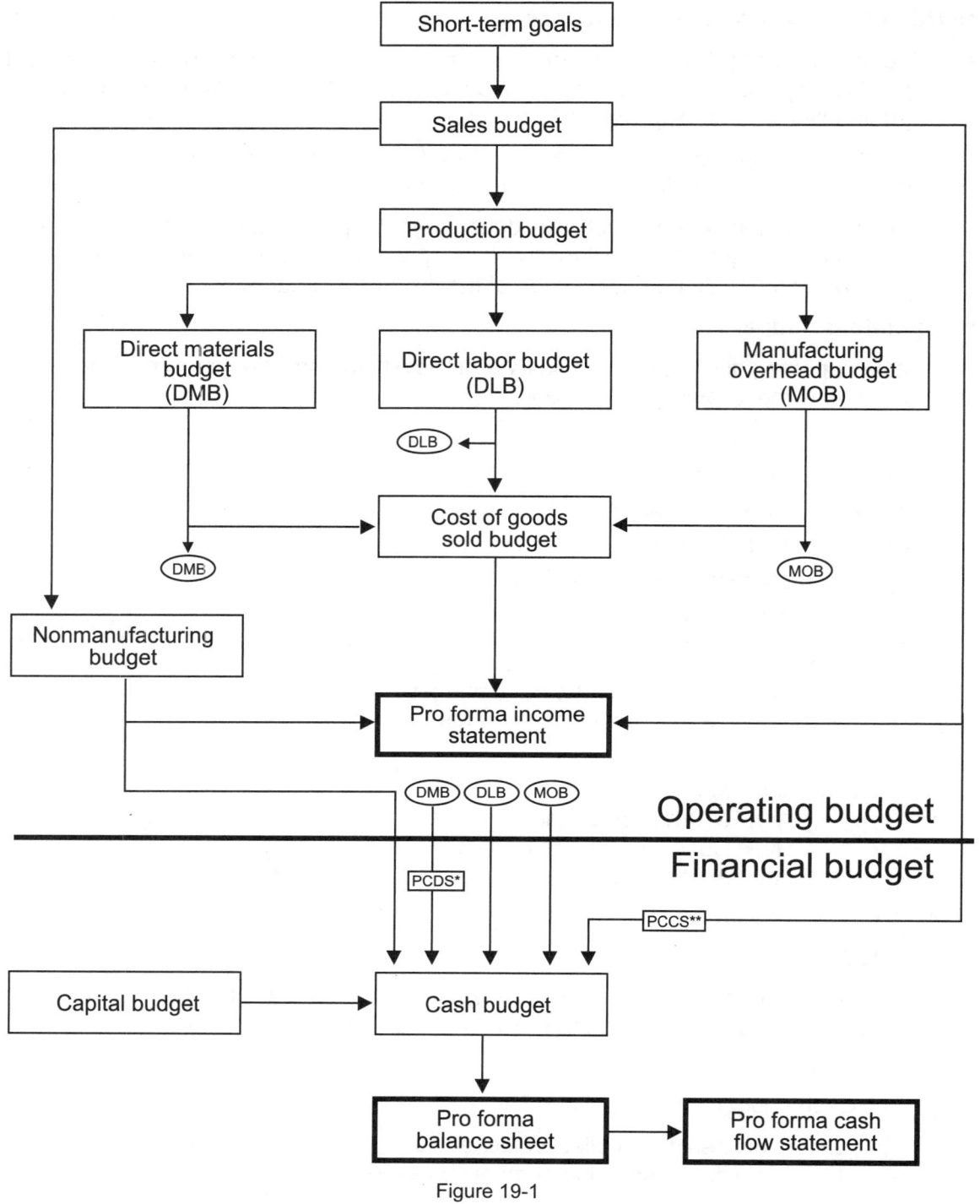

```
                    Short-term goals
                           │
                           ▼
        ┌──────────── Sales budget ────────────┐
        │                  │                    │
        │                  ▼                    │
        │           Production budget           │
        │       ┌──────────┼──────────┐         │
        │       ▼          ▼          ▼         │
        │  Direct      Direct     Manufacturing │
        │  materials   labor      overhead      │
        │  budget      budget     budget        │
        │  (DMB)       (DLB)      (MOB)         │
        │    │          │ (DLB)←    │           │
        │    │          ▼           │           │
        │    └──→ Cost of goods ←───┘           │
        │         sold budget                   │
        │   (DMB)     │        (MOB)            │
        ▼             ▼                         │
   Nonmanufacturing                             │
   budget       →  Pro forma income  ←──────────┘
                   statement
                  (DMB)(DLB)(MOB)      Operating budget
   ─────────────────────────────────────────────────────
                    (PCDS*)             Financial budget
                                  (PCCS**)
                      │ │ │ │ │      │
                      ▼ ▼ ▼ ▼ ▼      ▼
   Capital budget → Cash budget
                      │
                      ▼
                  Pro forma    →   Pro forma cash
                  balance sheet    flow statement
```

Figure 19-1

* PCDS = projected cash disbursements schedule
** PCCS = projected cash collection schedule

STOP & REVIEW

You have completed the outline for this subunit.
Study multiple-choice questions 4 through 6 on page 592.

19.3 THE OPERATING BUDGET

1. **Sales Budget**

    a. The sales budget (also called the revenue budget) is the starting point for the cycle that produces the annual profit plan (the master budget).

    b. The sales budget is based on the sales forecast. The forecast reflects (1) recent sales trends, (2) overall conditions in the economy and industry, (3) market research, (4) activities of competitors, and (5) credit and pricing policies.

    c. The sales budget must specify both projected unit sales and dollar revenues.

EXAMPLE 19-2   **Sales Budget**

	April	Ref.
Projected sales in units	1,000	SB1
Selling price	× $400	
Projected total sales	$400,000	SB2

---

2. **Production Budget**

    a. The production budget follows directly from the sales budget. The production budget is stated in units only. Product pricing is ignored because the purpose is only to plan output and inventory levels and the necessary manufacturing activity.

    b. To minimize finished goods carrying costs and obsolescence, the levels of production are dependent upon the projections in the sales budget.

    c. The desired ending inventory level is often expressed as a percentage of the next month's sales.

EXAMPLE 19-3   **Production Budget**

Finished goods beginning inventory consists of 100 units at $125 cost per unit (a total of $12,500), and the desired finished goods ending inventory is 120 units.

	Source	April	Ref.
Projected sales in units	SB1	1,000	
Plus: Desired ending inventory		120	
Minus: Beginning inventory		(100)	
Units to be produced		1,020	PB

---

d. The **purchases budget** for a retailer is prepared after projected sales are estimated.

   1) It is prepared on a monthly or even a weekly basis.
   2) Purchases can be planned so that stockouts are avoided.
   3) Inventory should be at an appropriate level to avoid unnecessary carrying costs while acting as a "shock absorber."
   4) It is similar to Example 19-3 above. However, the units are purchased rather than produced.

SUCCESS TIP: Questions asked by the AICPA about budgeting often require calculations. Always read and think through the scenario very carefully. For example, you may encounter a question regarding budgeted materials required for a time period. If it asks for the budgeted number of legs necessary for tables produced, be sure to calculate the amount using the appropriate number of legs per table.

3. **Direct Materials Budget**

    a. The direct materials budget reflects both units and input prices. (Direct materials is defined in Study Unit 17.)

        1) Two dollar amounts are calculated in the direct materials budget:

            a) The cost of materials actually **used** in production and
            b) The total cost of materials **purchased**.

    b. The direct materials budget begins with the results from the production budget. Plans for materials are based on the number of units being produced during the period (not the sales for the period).

EXAMPLE 19-4   Direct Materials Budget

The materials beginning inventory is 1,000 units at $18 cost per unit, and the desired materials ending inventory is 980 units.

Materials Used (Quantity)	Source	April	Ref.
Finished units to be produced	PB	1,020	
Times: Materials per finished product		× 4	
Total units needed for production		4,080	DMB1

Materials Purchased	Source	April	Ref.
Units needed for production	DMB1	4,080	
Plus: Desired units in ending inventory		980	
Minus: Beginning inventory		(1,000)	
Materials to be purchased		4,060	
Times: Materials cost per unit*		× $20	
Cost of materials to be purchased		$81,200	DMB2

Materials Used ($)	Source	April	Ref.
Beginning inventory (1,000 × $18)		$18,000	
Plus: Purchases of material	DMB2	81,200	
Minus: Desired ending inventory (980 × $20)		(19,600)	
Cost of materials used in production		$79,600	DMB3

*For the month of April.

---

4. **Direct Labor Budget**

    a. The direct labor budget depends on wage rates, amounts and types of production, numbers and skill levels of employees to be hired, etc.

    b. In addition to the regular wage rate, the total direct labor cost per hour also may include employer FICA taxes, health insurance, life insurance, and pension contributions. (Direct labor is explained in detail in Study Unit 17.)

    c. The direct labor budget begins with the results from the production budget. Plans for direct labor are based on the number of units being produced during the period (not the sales for the period).

> **EXAMPLE 19-5**   **Direct Labor Budget**
>
> The Human Resources department has determined that the total cost per labor hour is $18.
>
> | | Source | April | Ref. |
> |---|---|---|---|
> | Units to be produced | PB | 1,020 | |
> | Times: Direct labor hours per unit | | × 2 | |
> | Projected total direct labor hours | | 2,040 | DLB1 |
> | Times: Direct labor cost per hour | | × $18 | |
> | Total projected direct labor cost | | $36,720 | DLB2 |

5. **Manufacturing Overhead Budget**

   a. The manufacturing overhead budget has variable and fixed components because overhead is a mixed cost. (Mixed costs are defined in Study Unit 17.)

   $$\text{Total costs} = \text{Fixed costs} + (\text{Variable cost each item} \times \text{Quantity used})$$

   $$TC = FC + (VC_{EA} \times Q)$$

   b. Variable overhead contains elements that vary with the level of production.

      1) Indirect materials
      2) Some indirect labor
      3) Variable factory operating costs (e.g., electricity)
      4) Depreciation using the units-of-production method

         a) An example is miles on a motor vehicle.

> **EXAMPLE 19-6**   **Variable Overhead Budget**
>
> Variable overhead is applied to production on the basis of direct labor hours.
>
> | | Source | April | Ref. |
> |---|---|---|---|
> | Projected total direct labor hours | DLB1 | 2,040 | |
> | Variable OH rate per direct labor hour | | × $3 | |
> | Projected variable overhead | | $6,120 | MOB1 |

   c. Fixed overhead contains elements that do **not** change regardless of the level of production.

      1) Real estate taxes
      2) Insurance
      3) Depreciation using the straight line method

> **EXAMPLE 19-7**   **Fixed Overhead Budget**
>
> | | April | Ref. |
> |---|---|---|
> | Projected fixed overhead | $9,000 | MOB2 |

6. **Cost of Goods Sold Budget**

    a. The cost of goods sold budget combines the projections for the three major inputs (materials, labor, and overhead). The result directly affects the pro forma income statement. Cost of goods sold is the largest cost for a manufacturer.

EXAMPLE 19-8   Cost of Goods Sold Budget

	Source	April	Ref.
Beginning finished goods inventory		$ 12,500	
Manufacturing costs:			
Direct materials used	DMB3	$79,600	
Direct labor used	DLB2	36,720	
Variable overhead	MOB1	6,120	
Fixed overhead	MOB2	9,000	
Cost of goods manufactured		131,440	
Cost of goods available for sale		$143,940	
Ending finished goods inventory			
(120 units × $129*)		(15,480)	
Cost of goods sold		$128,460	CGSB

*Rounded to the nearest whole number (131,440 COGM ÷ 1,020 units to be produced)

---

7. **Nonmanufacturing Budget**

    a. The nonmanufacturing budget consists of the individual budgets for (1) R&D, (2) design, (3) marketing, (4) distribution, (5) customer service, and (6) administrative costs. The development of separate budgets for these functions is based on a value chain approach.

        1) An alternative is to prepare a single budget for selling and administrative (S&A) costs of nonproduction functions.

    b. The variable and fixed portions of selling and administrative costs must be treated separately.

        1) Some S&A costs vary directly and proportionately with the level of sales. As more products are sold, sales representatives must travel more miles and serve more customers.

        2) Other S&A expenses, such as sales support staff, are fixed. They must be paid at any level of sales.

8. **Pro Forma Income Statement**

    a. The pro forma income statement is prepared after the operating budget process.

        1) Financial statements are pro forma when they report projected, not actual, results.

    b. The pro forma income statement is used to decide whether the budgeted activities will result in an acceptable level of income. If the initial projection is a loss or otherwise unacceptable, adjustments can be made to the components of the master budget.

> **EXAMPLE 19-9**   **Pro Forma Income Statement**
>
> **Manufacturing Company**
> **Pro Forma Statement of Income**
> **Month of April**
>
> | | |
> |---|---:|
> | Sales | $400,000 |
> | Cost of goods sold | (128,460) |
> | Gross margin | $271,540 |
> | Minus: Selling and administrative expenses | (82,000) |
> | Operating income | $189,540 |
> | Minus: Other revenues, expenses, gains, and losses | (15,000) |
> | Earnings before interest and taxes | $174,540 |
> | Minus: Interest expense | (45,000) |
> | Earnings before income taxes | $129,540 |
> | Minus: Income taxes (40%) | (51,816) |
> | Net income | $ 77,724 |

STOP & REVIEW

You have completed the outline for this subunit.
Study multiple-choice questions 7 and 8 on page 593.

19.4 THE FINANCIAL BUDGET

1. **Capital Budget**

   a. The preparation of the capital budget is separate from the operating budget cycle.

   b. The capital budget, which often must be approved by the board of directors, addresses financing of major expenditures for long-term assets. It therefore must have a multi-year perspective. Productive assets must be acquired to enable the entity to achieve its projected levels of output.

   c. A procedure for ranking projects according to their risk and return characteristics is necessary because every organization has finite resources. [These procedures (net present value, internal rate of return, etc.) are covered in Study Unit 11.]

   d. The capital budget is a direct input to the cash budget and the pro forma balance sheet and statement of cash flows.

      1) Principal and interest on debt acquired to finance capital purchases require regular **cash outflows**. The acquired debt also appears in the liabilities section of the pro forma balance sheet.

      2) The output produced by new productive assets generates regular **cash inflows**. The new assets also appear in the assets section of the pro forma balance sheet.

2. **Cash Budget**
   a. The cash budget is the part of the financial budget cycle that connects all the schedules from the operating budget. A cash budget projects cash flows for planning and control purposes. Thus, it helps prevent not only cash emergencies but also excessive idle cash.
      1) A cash budget is vital because an organization must have adequate cash at all times. Almost all organizations, regardless of size, prepare a cash budget.
         a) Even with plenty of other assets, an organization with a temporary shortage of cash can become bankrupt.
      2) Proper planning can help prevent financial difficulty. Thus, cash budgets are prepared not only for annual and quarterly periods but also for monthly and weekly periods.
         a) They are particularly important for organizations operating in seasonal industries.
         b) The factors needed to prepare a cash forecast include all other elements of the budget preparation process plus consideration of
            i) Collection policies,
            ii) Credit loss (bad debt) estimates, and
            iii) Changes in the economy.
      3) Credit and purchasing policies directly affect the cash budget.
         a) Loose customer credit policies delay cash receipts.
         b) Use of purchase discounts accelerates cash payments.
   b. The cash budget process begins with preparation of a **projected cash collection schedule**. It forecasts the inflows of cash from customer payments.

EXAMPLE 19-10   **Cash Collection Schedule for April**

Sales are made on credit. Note the assumption that 5% of sales will be uncollectible.

	February Sales (Actual)	March Sales (Actual)	Source	April Sales (Projected)	Totals	Ref.
Sales	$180,000	$220,000	SB2	$400,000		
Projection of collection in April	× 30%	× 50%		× 15%		
From 2nd prior-month sales	$ 54,000				$ 54,000	
From prior-month sales		$110,000			110,000	
From current-month sales				$ 60,000	60,000	
Total cash collections from sales					$224,000	PCCS

c. The next step is preparation of a **projected cash disbursements schedule**.

EXAMPLE 19-11   Cash Disbursements Schedule for April

Materials purchases are the only purchases made on credit.

	March Purchases (Actual)	Source	April Purchases (Projected)	Totals	Ref.
Cost of materials purchased	$72,000	DMB2	$81,200		
Projection of payments in April	× 40%		× 60%		
For prior-month purchases	$28,800			$28,800	
For current-month purchases			$48,720	48,720	
Total cash disbursements for materials				$77,520	PCDS

---

d. The **cash budget** is the key element of the financial budget.

1) A comprehensive statement of the sources and uses of the entity's cash flows combines the operating budget and the cash flow schedules.

2) The cash budget can be used to plan financing activities. E.g., if the budget projects a cash deficit, the entity can plan to borrow the necessary funds or sell stock.

3) Dividend policy can also be planned using the cash budget. For example, dividend payment dates should correspond to a time when the entity has excess cash. For publicly held companies, dividends are usually paid quarterly.

EXAMPLE 19-12   Cash Budget

The bottom line is the expected cash surplus or the financing required.

	Source	April
Beginning cash balance		$100,000
Cash collections from sales	PCCS	224,000
Cash available for disbursement		$324,000
Cash disbursements:		
For materials	PCDS	$ 77,520
For direct labor	DLB2	36,720
For variable overhead	MOB1	6,120
For fixed overhead	MOB2	9,000
For nonmanufacturing costs*		26,000
For equipment purchases		110,000
Total disbursements		(265,360)
Excess of cash available over disbursements		$ 58,640
Desired ending cash balance		100,000
Short-term financing required		$ 41,360

*Note that any noncash expenses (such as depreciation) from the operating budget for nonmanufacturing costs would be deducted to arrive at the planned cash disbursements.

3. **Pro Forma Balance Sheet and Cash Flow Statement**

    a. The **pro forma balance sheet** is prepared using the cash and capital budgets and the pro forma income statement.

        1) The pro forma balance sheet is the beginning-of-the-period balance sheet updated for projected changes in cash, receivables, payables, inventory, etc.
        2) If the balance sheet indicates that a contract may be breached, the budgeting process must be repeated.

            a) For example, some loan agreements require that

                i) Owners' equity be maintained at some percentage of total debt or
                ii) Current assets be maintained at a given multiple of current liabilities.

    b. The **pro forma statement of cash flows** classifies cash flows depending on whether they are from operating, investing, or financing activities.

    c. The pro forma statements are interrelated. For example, the pro forma cash flow statement includes anticipated borrowing. The interest on this borrowing appears in the pro forma income statement.

STOP & REVIEW

You have completed the outline for this subunit.
Study multiple-choice questions 9 through 11 on page 594.

19.5 FLEXIBLE BUDGETING AND VARIANCE ANALYSIS

1. **Flexible Budget**

    a. A flexible budget is an annual profit plan prepared for various levels of production or sales. It reports the operating income for each level.

        1) A flexible budget can be used for any component of the budget process that varies with the level of activity. Examples are

            a) Sales revenue,
            b) Direct labor and materials,
            c) Marketing expenses, and
            d) Sales and administrative expenses.

2. **Static vs. Flexible Budgeting**

    a. The **static (master) budget** is prepared before the period begins and is not changed. The static budget is based on only one level of **expected activity** (output planned at the beginning of the period).

EXAMPLE 19-13 Static Budget

The following static (master) budget for the upcoming month is based on production and sales of 1,000 units:

Sales revenue ($400 per unit)	$400,000
Minus: Variable costs ($160 per unit)	(160,000)
Contribution margin	$240,000
Minus: Fixed costs	(200,000)
Operating income	$ 40,000

    b.   The **flexible budget** is prepared

        1) Based on the **actual output** sold (produced) during the period.
        2) Using the same drivers as those used to prepare the master budget.
        3) After the end of the period when all actual results are known.

EXAMPLE 19-14 Flexible Budget

	Flexible Budget Based on 800 Units	Static Budget Based on 1,000 Units
Sales revenue ($400 per unit)	$320,000	$400,000
Minus: Variable costs ($160 per unit)	(128,000)	(160,000)
Contribution margin	$192,000	$240,000
Minus: Fixed costs	(200,000)	(200,000)
Operating income	$ (8,000)	$ 40,000

3. **Variance Analysis Using Flexible Budgeting**

    a.   The most common use of the flexible budget is for analysis of budget variances.

        1) Variance analysis helps management in monitoring and measuring performance.

    b.   A variance is the difference between the actual results for the period and a budgeted amount for the period.

        1) A **favorable** variance (F) occurs when actual revenues are greater than standard (budgeted) or actual costs are less than standard (budgeted), i.e., income increases.

        2) An **unfavorable** variance (U) occurs when actual revenues are less than standard (budgeted) or actual costs are greater than standard (budgeted), i.e., income decreases.

EXAMPLE 19-15 Budget Variances

Actual results for the month were as follows:

Sales revenue	$342,000 (800 units × $427.50 price per unit)
Variable costs	$153,000
Fixed costs	$220,000

	Actual Results	Budget Variances	Master Budget
Sales revenue	$342,000	$(58,000) U	$400,000
Minus: Variable costs	(153,000)	7,000 F	(160,000)
Contribution margin	$189,000	$(51,000) U	$240,000
Minus: Fixed costs	(220,000)	(20,000) U	(200,000)
Operating income (loss)	$ (31,000)	$(71,000) U	$ 40,000

c. To analyze performance for the period, the budget variances should be subdivided into sales volume variances and flexible budget variances.

1) **Sales volume** variances result from inaccurate forecasting of the output sold for the period. They are measured as the difference between the flexible budget and the static (master) budget amounts.

2) **Flexible budget** variances report the differences between (a) the actual revenues and costs for the period and (b) the amounts that should have been earned and expended given the achieved level of production.

EXAMPLE 19-16 — Flexible Budget and Sales Volume Variances

	Actual Results 800 Units	Flexible Budget Variances	Flexible Budget Based on Actual Sales of 800 Units	Sales Volume Variances	Master (Static) Budget Based on 1,000 Units
Sales revenue	$342,000	$ 22,000 F	$320,000	$(80,000) U	$400,000
Minus: Variable costs	(153,000)	(25,000) U	(128,000)	32,000 F	(160,000)
Contribution margin	$189,000	$ (3,000) U	$192,000	$(48,000) U	$240,000
Minus: Fixed costs	(220,000)	(20,000) U	(200,000)	– –	(200,000)
Operating income (loss)	$ (31,000)	$(23,000) U	$ (8,000)	$(48,000) U	$ 40,000

The net of the two variances equals the difference between the master budget and the actual results, the **static budget variance**.

Flexible budget variance	$(23,000) U	Actual results	$(31,000)
Sales volume variance	(48,000) U	Master (static) budget	40,000
Static budget variance	$(71,000) U	Static budget variance	$(71,000) U

---

a) Flexible budget variances are measured as the difference between the actual results and the flexible budget. More extensive analysis of flexible budget variances can be made by using standard costing.

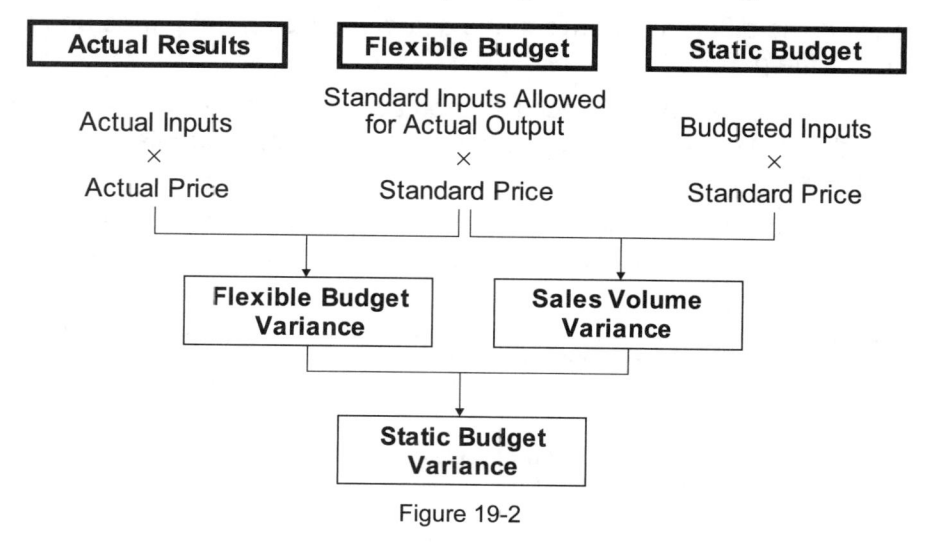

```
    Actual Results              Flexible Budget             Static Budget
                           Standard Inputs Allowed
    Actual Inputs             for Actual Output           Budgeted Inputs
         ×                            ×                          ×
    Actual Price                Standard Price             Standard Price
         └──────────┬───────────────┘  └─────────────┬────────────┘
              Flexible Budget                   Sales Volume
                 Variance                         Variance
                        └──────────────┬──────────────┘
                                 Static Budget
                                    Variance
```

Figure 19-2

You have completed the outline for this subunit.
Study multiple-choice questions 12 through 14 on page 595.

STOP & REVIEW

19.6 VARIANCE ANALYSIS -- MATERIALS AND LABOR

> **SUCCESS TIP**: The AICPA frequently tests variance analysis. Be certain to learn how to calculate the different variances. However, variance analysis is complex, and the terminology is not standardized.

1. **Use of Variance Analysis**

    a. Variance analysis is the basis of performance evaluation using standard costs (i.e., budgeted costs).

    1) A **favorable** variance **(F)** increases net income and occurs when actual costs are **less** than standard.

    2) An **unfavorable** variance **(U)** decreases net income and occurs when actual costs are **greater** than standard.

    b. Variance analysis enables management by exception, the practice of emphasizing significant deviations from expectations (whether favorable or unfavorable). A variance alerts management that corrective action may be needed.

2. **Framework for Variance Calculation**

    a. Variable inputs (direct materials and direct labor) can be analyzed in terms of a price (rate) variance and a quantity (efficiency) variance.

    1) **Price (rate) variances** result from a difference between (a) the actual price of resources used in production and (b) the standard price if **quantity** is constant.

    2) **Quantity (efficiency) variances** result from differences between (a) the actual resources used in production and (b) the standard amount if **price** is constant.

    b. The following abbreviations are used in the calculation of variances:

    AQP = Actual quantity of materials purchased
    AQ = Actual quantity of materials or hours
    AP = Actual price (rate) of materials or hours consumed
    SQ = Standard quantity of materials or hours for the actual production
    SP = Standard price (rate) of materials or hours

3. **Direct Materials**

   a. The **total direct materials variance** is the difference between (1) the actual materials cost of the actual units of output and (2) the standard materials cost of that output. Direct materials variances have price and quantity components.

   1) The **materials price variance** equals the actual quantity of input purchased during the period times the difference between (a) the standard price of materials and (b) the actual price.

   $$\text{Direct materials price variance} = \text{Actual quantity purchased (AQP)} \times \left(\text{Standard materials price (SP)} - \text{Actual materials price (AP)} \right)$$

   2) The **materials quantity variance** (also called usage or efficiency variance) equals the standard price times the difference between (a) the standard quantity of materials and (b) the actual quantity used in production.

   $$\text{Direct materials quantity variance} = \left(\text{Standard quantity of input allowed (SQ)} - \text{Actual quantity consumed (AQ)} \right) \times \text{Standard materials price (SP)}$$

EXAMPLE 19-17   **Direct Materials Variances**

Budgeted use is 980 tons of materials at a cost of $54 per ton. The actual amounts purchased and used during the month were 1,150 tons and 1,078 tons, respectively. The actual cost for the period was $50 per ton. If the materials price variance is recognized at purchase, variances for direct materials are calculated as follows:

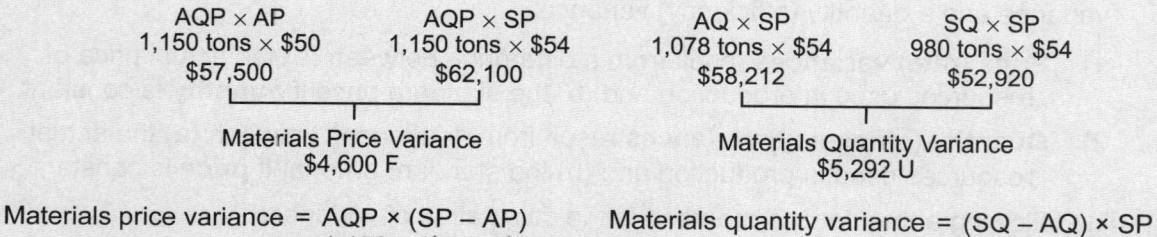

AQP × AP	AQP × SP	AQ × SP	SQ × SP
1,150 tons × $50	1,150 tons × $54	1,078 tons × $54	980 tons × $54
$57,500	$62,100	$58,212	$52,920

Materials Price Variance: $4,600 F (between AQP × AP and AQP × SP)

Materials Quantity Variance: $5,292 U (between AQ × SP and SQ × SP)

Materials price variance = AQP × (SP − AP)
= 1,150 × ($54 − $50)
= 1,150 × $4
= $4,600 favorable

Materials quantity variance = (SQ − AQ) × SP
= (980 − 1,078) × $54
= −98 × $54
= $5,292 unfavorable

SU 19: Budgeting and Variance Analysis

4. **Direct Labor**

   a. The **total variance for direct labor** is the sum of the two components below:

      1) The **labor rate variance** equals the actual number of hours worked times the difference between (a) the standard hourly wage rate and (b) the actual hourly rate.

      $$\text{Direct labor rate variance} = \text{Actual hours worked (AQ)} \times (\text{Standard hourly rate (SP)} - \text{Actual hourly rate (AP)})$$

      2) The **labor efficiency variance** equals the difference between (a) the standard number of hours allowed and (b) the actual number of hours worked, times the standard hourly wage rate.

      $$\text{Direct labor efficiency variance} = (\text{Standard number of hours allowed (SQ)} - \text{Actual number of hours worked (AQ)}) \times \text{Standard hourly rate (SP)}$$

      ```
      AQ × AP              AQ × SP              SQ × SP
         └──────────┬──────────┘└──────────┬──────────┘
            Labor Rate Variance     Labor Efficiency Variance
      ```

      Figure 19-3

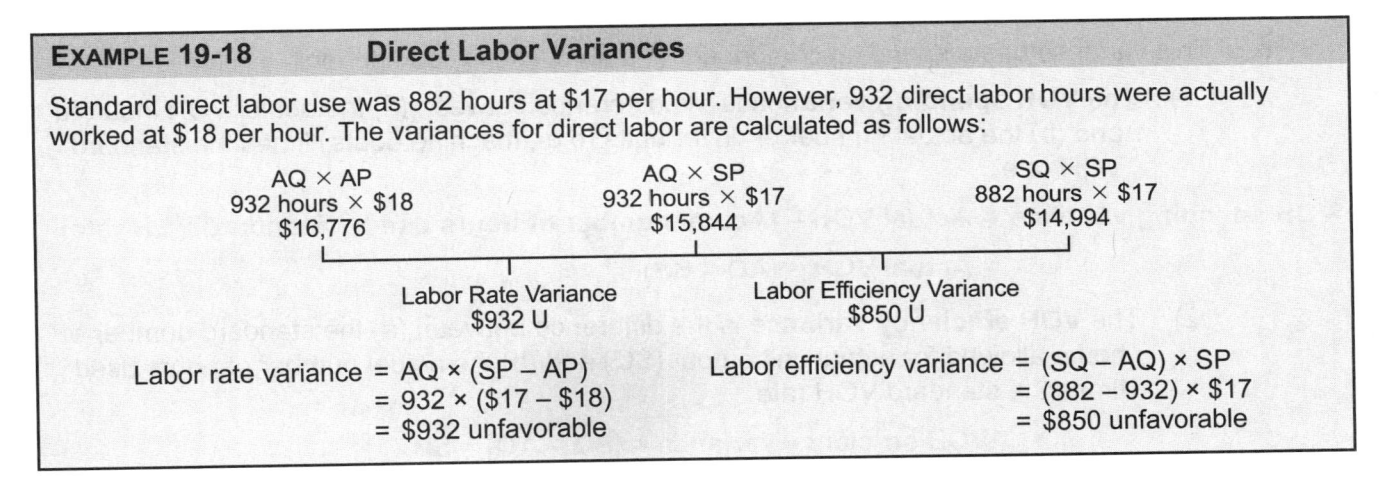

EXAMPLE 19-18   Direct Labor Variances

Standard direct labor use was 882 hours at $17 per hour. However, 932 direct labor hours were actually worked at $18 per hour. The variances for direct labor are calculated as follows:

AQ × AP	AQ × SP	SQ × SP
932 hours × $18	932 hours × $17	882 hours × $17
$16,776	$15,844	$14,994

Labor Rate Variance
$932 U

Labor Efficiency Variance
$850 U

Labor rate variance = AQ × (SP − AP)
= 932 × ($17 − $18)
= $932 unfavorable

Labor efficiency variance = (SQ − AQ) × SP
= (882 − 932) × $17
= $850 unfavorable

STOP & REVIEW

You have completed the outline for this subunit.
Study multiple-choice questions 15 and 16 on page 596.

19.7 VARIANCE ANALYSIS -- OVERHEAD

1. **Variable Overhead**

   a. The amount of variable overhead (VOH) **under- or overapplied** for the period is the **variable overhead flexible budget variance**.

      1) Overhead is **underapplied (U)** when actual overhead costs exceed applied overhead costs. Conversely, overhead is **overapplied (F)** when applied overhead costs exceed actual overhead costs.
      2) Overhead is applied based on the standard quantity (SQ) allowed given the actual output.
      3) For simplicity, assume that the variable overhead is applied based on **direct machine hours used**.

   $$\text{VOH flexible budget variance} = \text{Actual VOH costs incurred} - (SQ \times SP)$$

   $$\text{VOH over- or underapplied} = \text{Actual VOH costs incurred} - \text{VOH applied}$$

   $$= \text{Actual VOH incurred} - \left(\text{Actual unit output} \times \text{Standard hours allowed per unit of output} \times \text{Standard VOH rate} \right)$$

   b. This variance has a spending component and an efficiency component.

      1) The **VOH spending variance** is the difference between (a) the actual VOH incurred and (b) the actual number of driver units (e.g., machine hours) times the standard VOH rate.

   $$\text{VOH spending variance} = \text{Actual VOH} - (\text{Actual number of hours used} \times \text{Standard VOH rate})$$
   $$= \text{Actual VOH} - (AQ \times SP)$$

      2) The **VOH efficiency variance** is the difference between (a) the standard number of hours allowed for actual unit output (SQ) and (b) the actual number of hours used, times the standard VOH rate.

   $$\text{VOH efficiency variance} = (SQ - AQ) \times SP$$

   Variable Overhead Variances

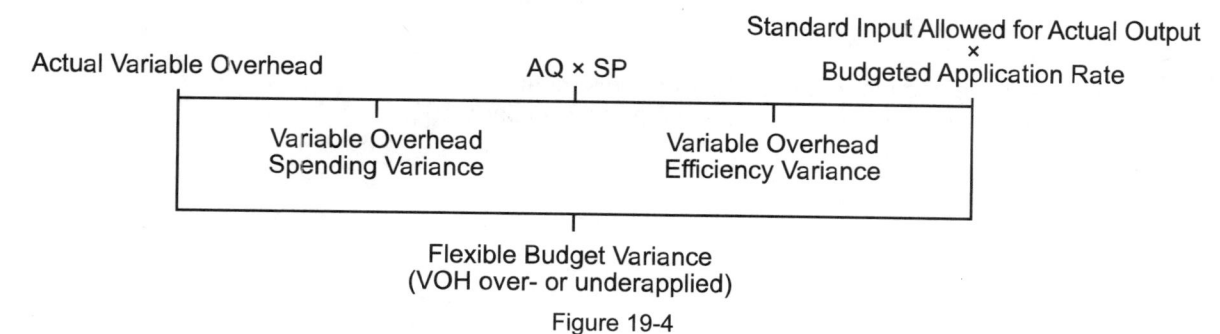

   ```
   Actual Variable Overhead        AQ × SP        Standard Input Allowed for Actual Output
                                                   ×
                                                   Budgeted Application Rate
   |_____|_____|
   |    Variable Overhead          |    Variable Overhead          |
   |    Spending Variance          |    Efficiency Variance        |
   |_____|
                   Flexible Budget Variance
                   (VOH over- or underapplied)
   ```

   Figure 19-4

SU 19: Budgeting and Variance Analysis

> **EXAMPLE 19-19   Variable Overhead Variances**
>
> Variable overhead is applied at the rate of $4 per machine hour. The use of 10 machine hours is budgeted for each unit produced. The planned output was 90 units. Actual output is 98 units. The number of machine hours used was 900, and actual variable overhead was $4,000. The variances for variable overhead are calculated as follows:
>
> | Actual Variable Overhead | AQ × SP | Standard Input Allowed for Actual Output × SP |
> |---|---|---|
> | $4,000 | 900 hours × $4 = $3,600 | (98 output units × 10 hours) × $4 = $3,920 |
>
> Variable Overhead Spending Variance = $400 U
>
> Variable Overhead Efficiency Variance = $320 F
>
> These calculations can be reconciled with the following equation:
>
> Amount applied − Actual costs incurred = VOH flexible budget variance
> = VOH spending variance + VOH efficiency variance
> $3,920 − $4,000 = $400 U + $320 F
> $80 underapplied = $80 U

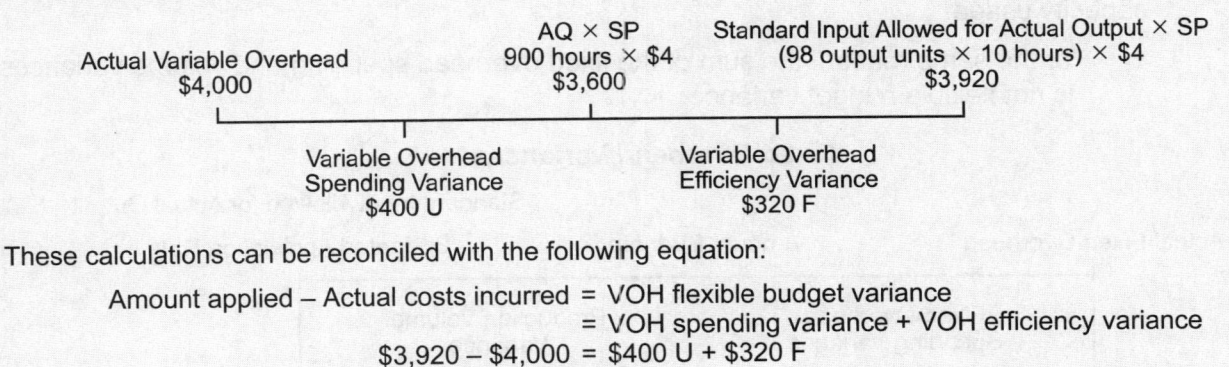

2. **Fixed Overhead**

   a. The amount of fixed overhead (FOH) that was under- or overapplied for the period consists of a spending component and a volume component.

   FOH over- or underapplied = Actual FOH incurred − FOH applied

   = Actual FOH incurred − (Actual unit output × Standard hours allowed per unit of output × Standard FOH rate)

   1) The **FOH spending variance** is the difference between (a) the actual costs incurred and (b) the amount budgeted. This variance is also referred to as the budget variance.

   FOH spending variance = Actual FOH incurred − Amount budgeted

   = Actual FOH incurred − (Budgeted unit output × Standard hours allowed per unit of output × Standard FOH rate)

   2) The **FOH volume variance** is the difference between (a) the amount of fixed overhead budgeted and (b) the amount applied.

   FOH volume variance = Amount budgeted − FOH applied

   a) This variance results when production capacity differs from capacity usage. A favorable (unfavorable) variance occurs when overhead applied is more (less) than budgeted fixed costs. For example, the variance is favorable when actual production exceeds planned production.

b. Fixed overhead has a volume variance instead of an efficiency variance. The fixed overhead volume variance is referred to as the production volume variance. Fixed costs by definition do not change within the relevant range of the budgeting cycle. The same amount of fixed cost is budgeted regardless of the number of driver units actually used or the actual unit output. This variance results when production capacity differs from capacity usage.

   1) For the same reason, the sum of the fixed overhead spending and volume variances is not flexible budget variance.

Fixed Overhead Variances

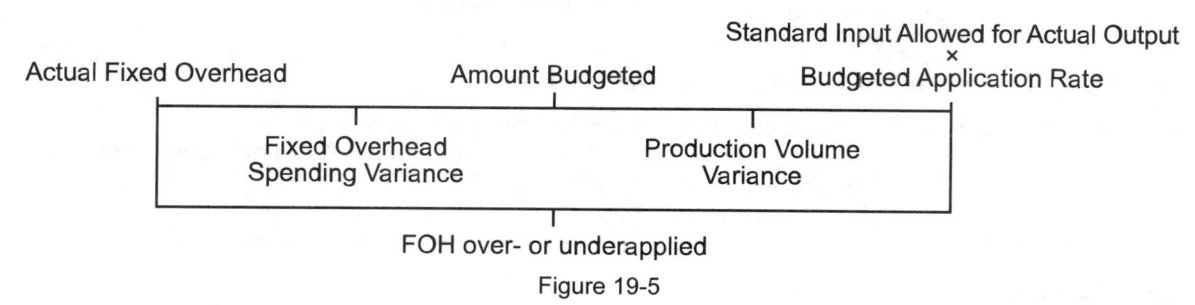

```
                                           Standard Input Allowed for Actual Output
                                                            ×
Actual Fixed Overhead      Amount Budgeted         Budgeted Application Rate
       |_____|_____|
                    |                           |
             Fixed Overhead              Production Volume
           Spending Variance                  Variance
       |_____|
                              |
                  FOH over- or underapplied
```
Figure 19-5

EXAMPLE 19-20   Fixed Overhead Variances

The budget for fixed overhead during the period is $1,440 based on budgeted output of 90 units. Actual output is 98 units. The fixed overhead allocation rate is $1.60 per machine hour, and 10 hours are required per output unit. Actual fixed overhead for the period is $1,600.

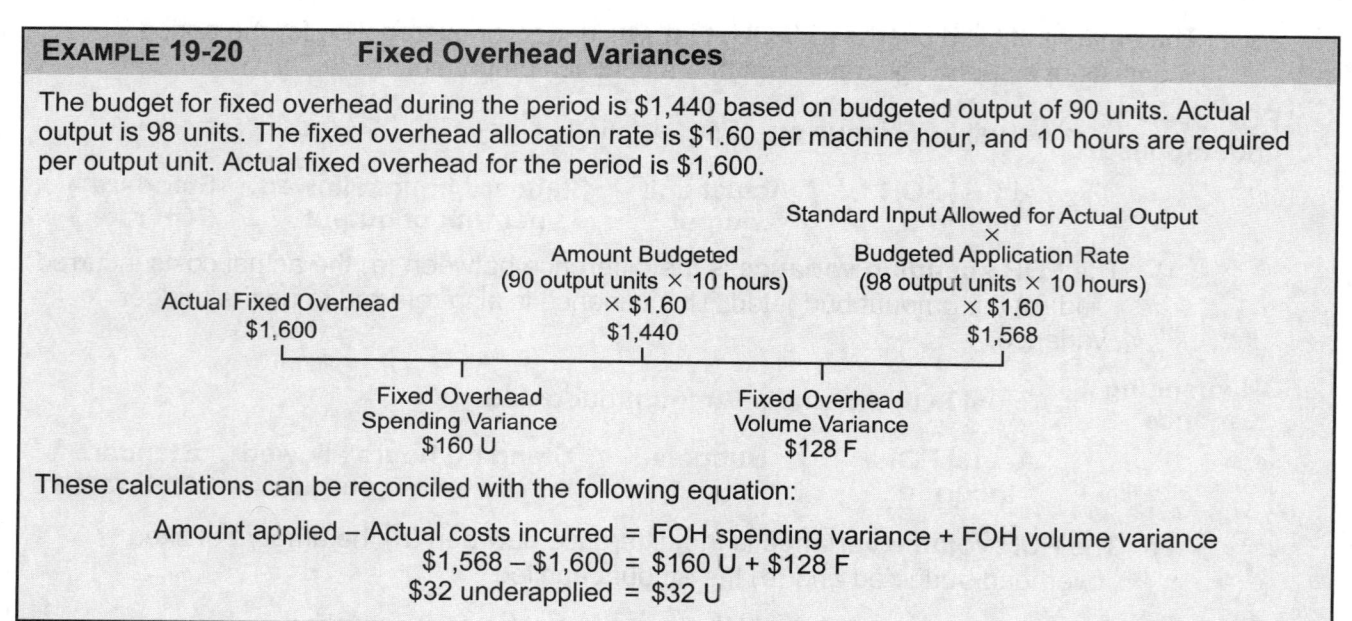

```
                                                    Standard Input Allowed for Actual Output
                                                                     ×
                              Amount Budgeted              Budgeted Application Rate
                         (90 output units × 10 hours)     (98 output units × 10 hours)
   Actual Fixed Overhead          × $1.60                          × $1.60
         $1,600                   $1,440                           $1,568
       |_____|_____|
                    |                                  |
             Fixed Overhead                     Fixed Overhead
           Spending Variance                    Volume Variance
                $160 U                              $128 F
```

These calculations can be reconciled with the following equation:

Amount applied − Actual costs incurred = FOH spending variance + FOH volume variance
$1,568 − $1,600 = $160 U + $128 F
$32 underapplied = $32 U

SU 19: Budgeting and Variance Analysis

3. **Integrated Overhead Variance Analysis**

   a. **Three-way overhead variance analysis** combines the variable and fixed spending variances ($400 U + $160 U = $560 U) and reports the other two variances separately.

EXAMPLE 19-21	Three-Way Analysis of Overhead			
		Spending Variance	Efficiency Variance	Volume Variance
	Total overhead	$560 U	$320 F	$128 F

   b. **Two-way overhead variance analysis** combines the spending and efficiency variances into one budget variance ($400 U + $160 U + $320 F = $240 U) and reports the volume variance separately.

EXAMPLE 19-22	Two-Way Analysis of Overhead		
		Budget Variance	Volume Variance
	Total overhead	$240 U	$128 F

   1) The budget variance in two-way analysis is also called the **controllable variance**. It is the portion of the total not attributable to the volume variance.

   c. The **net overhead variance** (one-way overhead variance analysis) combines all the components into one amount ($240 U + $128 F = **$112 U**).

   1) The net overhead variance equals the difference between (a) the total actual overhead incurred of $5,600 ($4,000 actual VOH + $1,600 actual FOH) and (b) the total overhead applied of $5,488 [(98 × 10) standard hours applied to actual output produced × ($4 + $1.6) standard total overhead rate].

   $$\$5,600 - \$5,488 = \$112 \text{ U}$$

4. Comprehensive Example

	STANDARD COSTS	ACTUAL COSTS (AC)
DIRECT MATERIALS	600,000 units of materials at $2.00 each	700,000 units purchased and used at $1.90
DIRECT LABOR	60,000 hours allowed for actual output at $7 per hour	65,000 hours at $7.20
OVERHEAD	$8.00 per direct labor hour on normal capacity of 50,000 direct labor hours:	
	$6.00 for variable overhead	$396,000 variable
	$2.00 for fixed overhead	$130,000 fixed

MATERIALS VARIANCES

Price

$$\begin{aligned}
AQP \times (SP - AP) &= \text{Actual quantity purchased} \times (\text{Standard price} - \text{Actual price}) \\
&= 700{,}000 \text{ units} \times (\$2.00 - \$1.90) \\
&= 700{,}000 \times \$0.10 \\
&= \$70{,}000 \text{ F}
\end{aligned}$$

Quantity

$$\begin{aligned}
(SQ - AQ) \times SP &= (\text{Standard quantity} - \text{Actual quantity used}) \times \text{Standard price} \\
&= (600{,}000 \text{ units} - 700{,}000 \text{ units}) \times \$2.00 \\
&= -100{,}000 \times \$2.00 \\
&= \$200{,}000 \text{ U}
\end{aligned}$$

LABOR VARIANCES

Rate

$$\begin{aligned}
AQ \times (SP - AP) &= \text{Actual hours} \times (\text{Standard rate} - \text{Actual rate}) \\
&= 65{,}000 \text{ hours} \times (\$7.00 - \$7.20) \\
&= 65{,}000 \times -\$0.20 \\
&= \$13{,}000 \text{ U}
\end{aligned}$$

Efficiency

$$\begin{aligned}
(SQ - AQ) \times SP &= (\text{Standard hours} - \text{Actual hours}) \times \text{Standard rate} \\
&= (60{,}000 \text{ hours} - 65{,}000 \text{ hours}) \times \$7.00 \\
&= -5{,}000 \times \$7.00 \\
&= \$35{,}000 \text{ U}
\end{aligned}$$

SU 19: Budgeting and Variance Analysis

VARIABLE OVERHEAD VARIANCES

Spending

(AQ × SP) − AC = (Actual hours × Standard rate) − Actual costs incurred
            = (65,000 × $6.00) − $396,000
            = $390,000 − $396,000
            = $6,000 U

Efficiency

(SQ − AQ) × SP = (Standard hours allowed for actual production − Actual hours) × Standard rate
            = (60,000 − 65,000) × $6.00
            = −5,000 × $6.00
            = $30,000 U

Total VOH Variance

            = Actual VOH incurred − VOH applied
            = $396,000 − (60,000 × $6.00)
            = $36,000 U

FIXED OVERHEAD VARIANCES

Spending

            = Flexible/Static budget − Actual costs incurred
            = (50,000 hours × $2.00) − $130,000
            = $30,000 U

Volume

            = (Standard hours allowed for actual output × Standard rate) − Flexible/Static budget
            = (60,000 hours × $2.00) − (50,000 hours × $2.00)
            = $120,000 − $100,000
            = $20,000 F

Total FOH Variance

            = FOH incurred − FOH applied
            = $130,000 − (60,000 hours × $2.00)
            = $10,000 U

STOP & REVIEW

You have completed the outline for this subunit.
Study multiple-choice questions 17 and 18 on page 597.

19.8 SALES VARIANCES

1. **Sales, Contribution Margin, and Operating Income**

    a. Variance analysis is useful for evaluating not only the production function but also the selling function.

      1) If sales differ from the amount budgeted, the difference could consist of a **sales price variance**, a **sales volume variance**, or both.
      2) The analysis of these variances concentrates on **contribution margins** because fixed costs are assumed to be constant.

EXAMPLE 19-23   Budgeted vs. Actual Results

Budgeted sales of a product are 10,000 units at $17 per unit. Variable costs are expected to be $10 per unit, and fixed costs are budgeted at $50,000. The following compares budgeted and actual results:

	Budget Computation	Budget Amount	Actual Computation	Actual Amount
Sales	10,000 units × $17 per unit	$170,000	11,000 units × $16 per unit	$176,000
Variable costs	10,000 units × $10 per unit	(100,000)	11,000 units × $10 per unit	(110,000)
Contribution margin		$ 70,000		$ 66,000
Fixed costs		(50,000)		(50,000)
Operating income		$ 20,000		$ 16,000
Unit contribution margins	$70,000 ÷ 10,000 units	$ 7	$66,000 ÷ 11,000 units	$ 6

---

2. **Sales Variances**

    a. In Example 19-23 above, sales were greater than budgeted, but the contribution margin is lower. The difference can be analyzed in terms of the sales price variance and the sales volume variance. If net income increases (decreases) the variance is favorable (unfavorable).

      1) The **sales price variance** is the change in the contribution margin attributable solely to the change in selling price (if quantity is constant).

    $$\text{Sales price variance} = \text{Actual units sold} \times \left(\text{Actual selling price per unit} - \text{Budgeted selling price per unit} \right)$$

      2) In Example 19-23, the actual selling price of $16 per unit is $1 less than expected. Thus, the sales price variance is $11,000 U (11,000 actual units sold × $1).

    b. The **sales volume variance** is the change in the contribution margin attributable solely to the difference between the actual and budgeted unit sales (if price is constant).

    $$\text{Sales volume variance} = \text{Budgeted contribution margin per unit} \times \left(\text{Actual units sold} - \text{Budgeted units sold} \right)$$

      1) In Example 19-23, it equals $7,000 F (1,000 unit increase in sales × $7).

    c. The sales price variance ($11,000 U) plus the sales volume variance ($7,000 F) equals the total change in the contribution margin ($4,000 U).

You have completed the outline for this subunit.
Study multiple-choice questions 19 and 20 on page 598.

STOP & REVIEW

QUESTIONS

19.1 Standard Costs

1. The best basis upon which cost standards should be set to measure controllable production inefficiencies is

- A. Engineering standards based on ideal performance.
- B. Normal capacity.
- C. Recent average historical performance.
- D. Engineering standards based on attainable performance.

Answer (D) is correct.
REQUIRED: The best basis upon which cost standards should be set.
DISCUSSION: Standards must be accepted by those who will carry them out if they are to have maximum effectiveness. Subordinates should believe that standards are both fair and achievable. Otherwise, they may tend to sabotage, ignore, or circumvent them.
Answer (A) is incorrect. Employees may not cooperate with standards based on ideal performance. Attainable standards are usually better for motivational purposes. **Answer (B) is incorrect.** Normal capacity may not suffice to control production inefficiencies. **Answer (C) is incorrect.** Historical performance may not always be a guide to future performance, and standards should be based on anticipated future conditions.

2. When compared with ideal standards, practical standards

- A. Produce lower per-unit product costs.
- B. Result in a less desirable basis for the development of budgets.
- C. Incorporate very generous allowance for spoilage and worker inefficiencies.
- D. Serve as a better motivating target for manufacturing personnel.

Answer (D) is correct.
REQUIRED: The correct statement regarding practical standards when compared to ideal standards.
DISCUSSION: Practical standards, also called attainable standards, are more likely to be accepted by workers than standards based on an unachievable ideal.
Answer (A) is incorrect. The effect of one type of standard over another cannot guarantee lower costs. **Answer (B) is incorrect.** Practical standards are more appropriate in most cases than ideal standards in the development of budgets. **Answer (C) is incorrect.** An acceptance of high levels of spoilage and worker inefficiencies cannot be overcome through the use of standards.

3. After performing a thorough study of Michigan Company's operations, an independent consultant determined that the firm's labor standards were too tight. Which of the following is **inconsistent** with the consultant's conclusion?

- A. A review of performance reports revealed the presence of many unfavorable efficiency variances.
- B. Michigan's budgeting process was based on a top-down (authoritative) philosophy.
- C. Management noted that minimal incentive bonuses have been paid in recent periods.
- D. Production supervisors found several significant fluctuations in manufacturing volume, with short-term increases in output being followed by rapid, sustained declines.

Answer (D) is correct.
REQUIRED: The statement inconsistent with the consultant's conclusion.
DISCUSSION: The situation described is indicative of rush jobs being too common, which is a result of poor production planning, not tight labor standards.
Answer (A) is incorrect. Many unfavorable efficiency variances indicate standards are too tight. **Answer (B) is incorrect.** A budgeting process based on a top-down (authoritative) philosophy is more likely than a bottom-up approach to set standards that are too tight. **Answer (C) is incorrect.** The widespread failure to earn expected bonuses indicates standards are too tight.

19.2 The Master Budget and Its Components

4. In an organization that plans by using comprehensive budgeting, the master budget is

A. A compilation of all the separate operational and financial budget schedules of the organization.
B. The booklet containing budget guidelines, policies, and forms to use in the budgeting process.
C. The current budget updated for operations for part of the current year.
D. A budget of a not-for-profit organization after it is approved by the appropriate authoritative body.

Answer (A) is correct.
REQUIRED: The nature of the master budget.
DISCUSSION: The overall budget, often called the master or comprehensive budget, encompasses the organization's operating and financial plans for a specified period (ordinarily a year). Thus, all other budgets are subsets of the master budget.
Answer (B) is incorrect. The booklet containing budget guidelines, policies, and forms to use in the budgeting process is the budget manual. **Answer (C) is incorrect.** The current budget updated for operations for part of the current year is a continuous budget. **Answer (D) is incorrect.** A master budget may be prepared by a for-profit entity.

5. Pro forma financial statements are part of the budgeting process. Normally, the **last** pro forma statement prepared is the

A. Capital expenditure plan.
B. Income statement.
C. Statement of cost of goods sold.
D. Statement of cash flows.

Answer (D) is correct.
REQUIRED: The last pro forma financial statement prepared.
DISCUSSION: The statement of cash flows is usually the last of the listed items prepared. All other elements of the budget process must be completed before it can be developed.
Answer (A) is incorrect. The capital expenditure plan must be prepared before the cash budget. Cash may be needed to pay for capital purchases. **Answer (B) is incorrect.** The income statement must be prepared before the statement of cash flows, which reconciles net income and net operating cash flows. **Answer (C) is incorrect.** Cost of goods sold is included in the income statement, which is an input to the statement of cash flows.

6. Wilson Company uses a comprehensive planning and budgeting system. The proper order for Wilson to prepare certain budget schedules would be

A. Cost of goods sold, balance sheet, income statement, and statement of cash flows.
B. Income statement, balance sheet, statement of cash flows, and cost of goods sold.
C. Statement of cash flows, cost of goods sold, income statement, and balance sheet.
D. Cost of goods sold, income statement, balance sheet, and statement of cash flows.

Answer (D) is correct.
REQUIRED: The order in which budget schedules should be prepared.
DISCUSSION: The cost of goods sold budget is an input for the pro forma income statement. The entire operating budget process must be completed before the pro forma balance sheet and statement of cash flows can be prepared.
Answer (A) is incorrect. The balance sheet should not precede the income statement. **Answer (B) is incorrect.** The income statement cannot precede cost of goods sold. **Answer (C) is incorrect.** The statement of cash flows cannot precede the cost of goods sold. The latter is an input of the former.

19.3 The Operating Budget

7. When budgeting, the items to be considered by a manufacturing firm in going from a sales quantity budget to a production budget would be the

A. Expected change in the quantity of work-in-process inventories.
B. Expected change in the quantity of finished goods and work-in-process inventories.
C. Expected change in the quantity of finished goods and raw material inventories.
D. Expected change in the availability of raw material without regard to inventory levels.

Answer (B) is correct.
REQUIRED: The items to be considered in developing a production budget from a sales quantity budget.
DISCUSSION: Production quantities are not identical to sales because of changes in inventory levels. Both finished goods and work-in-process inventories may change during a period, necessitating an analysis of both inventory levels before the production budget can be set.
Answer (A) is incorrect. Finished goods inventories cannot be ignored. Answer (C) is incorrect. Work-in-process inventory should be considered. Answer (D) is incorrect. Existing inventories determine production levels.

8. Superior Industry's sales budget shows quarterly sales for the next year as follows:

Quarter	Units
1	10,000
2	8,000
3	12,000
4	14,000

Company policy is to have a finished goods inventory at the end of each quarter equal to 20% of the next quarter's sales. Budgeted production for the second quarter of the next year would be

A. 7,200 units.
B. 8,000 units.
C. 8,800 units.
D. 8,400 units.

Answer (C) is correct.
REQUIRED: The budgeted production for the second quarter given ending inventory for each quarter.
DISCUSSION: The finished units needed for sales (8,000), plus the units desired for ending inventory (12,000 units to be sold in the third quarter × 20% = 2,400), minus the units in beginning inventory (8,000 units to be sold in the second quarter × 20% = 1,600) equals budgeted production for the second quarter of 8,800 units.
Answer (A) is incorrect. Subtracting the beginning inventory twice results in 7,200 units. Answer (B) is incorrect. Assuming no change in inventory results in 8,000 units. Answer (D) is incorrect. Including the beginning inventory for the first quarter, not the second quarter, in the calculation results in 8,400 units.

19.4 The Financial Budget

9. Which one of the following is the best characteristic concerning the capital budget? The capital budget is a(n)

A. Plan to ensure that there are sufficient funds available for the operating needs of the company.
B. Exercise that sets the long-range goals of the company including the consideration of external influences caused by others in the market.
C. Plan that results in the cash requirements during the operating cycle.
D. Plan that assesses the long-term needs of the company for plant and equipment purchases.

Answer (D) is correct.
REQUIRED: The true statement about the capital budget.
DISCUSSION: Capital budgeting is the process of planning expenditures for long-lived assets. It involves choosing among investment proposals using a ranking procedure. Evaluations are based on various measures involving the IRR.
Answer (A) is incorrect. Capital budgeting involves long-term investment needs, not immediate operating needs. **Answer (B) is incorrect.** Establishing long-term goals in the context of relevant factors in the environment is strategic planning. **Answer (C) is incorrect.** Cash budgeting determines operating cash flows. Capital budgeting evaluates the rate of return on specific investment alternatives.

10. Which one of the following items would have to be included for a company preparing a schedule of cash receipts and disbursements for Calendar Year 1?

A. A purchase order issued in December Year 1 for items to be delivered in February Year 2.
B. Dividends declared in November Year 1 to be paid in January Year 2 to shareholders of record as of December Year 1.
C. The amount of uncollectible customer accounts for Year 1.
D. The borrowing of funds from a bank on a note payable taken out in June Year 1 with an agreement to pay the principal and interest in June Year 2.

Answer (D) is correct.
REQUIRED: The item included in a cash budget for Year 1.
DISCUSSION: A schedule of cash receipts and disbursements (cash budget) should include all cash inflows and outflows during the period without regard to the accrual accounting treatment of the transactions. Thus, it should include all checks written and all sources of cash, including borrowings. A borrowing from a bank in June Year 1 should appear as a cash receipt for Year 1.
Answer (A) is incorrect. The cash disbursement presumably will not occur until Year 2. **Answer (B) is incorrect.** The cash flow will not occur until dividends are paid in Year 2. **Answer (C) is incorrect.** Credit loss (formerly bad debt) expense is a noncash item.

11. Which one of the following may be considered an independent item in the preparation of the annual master budget?

A. Ending inventory budget.
B. Capital investment budget.
C. Pro forma income statement.
D. Pro forma statement of financial position.

Answer (B) is correct.
REQUIRED: The independent item in the preparation of the annual master budget.
DISCUSSION: The capital investment budget may be prepared more than a year in advance, unlike the other elements of the master budget. Because of the long-term commitments that must be made for some types of capital investments, planning must be done far in advance and is based on needs in future years as opposed to the current year's needs.
Answer (A) is incorrect. The ending inventory budget is based on the current production budget. **Answer (C) is incorrect.** The pro forma income statement is based on the sales budget, expense budgets, and all other elements of the current master budget. **Answer (D) is incorrect.** The pro forma balance sheet is based on the other elements of the current master budget.

19.5 Flexible Budgeting and Variance Analysis

12. The use of the master budget throughout the year as a constant comparison with actual results signifies that the master budget is also a

A. Flexible budget.
B. Capital budget.
C. Zero-based budget.
D. Static budget.

Answer (D) is correct.
REQUIRED: The type of budget that is used throughout the year for comparison with actual results.
DISCUSSION: If an unchanged master budget is used continuously throughout the year for comparison with actual results, it must be a static budget, that is, one prepared for just one level of activity.
Answer (A) is incorrect. A flexible budget can be used in conjunction with standard costs to provide budgets for different activity levels. **Answer (B) is incorrect.** A capital budget addresses only long-term investments. **Answer (C) is incorrect.** A zero-based budget is one that requires its preparer to fully justify every item in the budget for each period.

13. Which one of the following statements regarding the difference between a flexible budget and a static budget is true?

A. A flexible budget primarily is prepared for planning purposes, while a static budget is prepared for performance evaluation.
B. A flexible budget provides cost allowances for different levels of activity, whereas a static budget provides costs for one level of activity.
C. A flexible budget includes only variable costs, whereas a static budget includes only fixed costs.
D. A flexible budget is established by operating management, while a static budget is determined by top management.

Answer (B) is correct.
REQUIRED: The difference between a flexible and a static budget.
DISCUSSION: A flexible budget provides cost allowances for different levels of activity, but a static budget provides costs for only one level of activity. Thus, a flexible budget conceptually is a series of budgets prepared for many different levels of activity.
Answer (A) is incorrect. Both budgets are prepared for both planning and performance evaluation purposes. **Answer (C) is incorrect.** Both budgets include both fixed and variable costs. **Answer (D) is incorrect.** Either budget can be established by any level of management.

14. Flexible budgets

A. Provide for external factors affecting company profitability.
B. Are used to evaluate capacity use.
C. Are budgets that project costs based on anticipated future improvements.
D. Accommodate changes in activity levels.

Answer (D) is correct.
REQUIRED: The true statement about flexible budgets.
DISCUSSION: A flexible budget conceptually is a series of budgets prepared for various levels of activity. A flexible budget adjusts the master budget for changes in activity so that actual results can be compared with meaningful budget amounts.
Answer (A) is incorrect. Flexible budgets address external factors only to the extent that activity is affected. **Answer (B) is incorrect.** A flexible budget essentially restates variable costs for different activity levels within the relevant range. Thus, a flexible budget variance does not address capacity use. An output level (production volume) variance is a fixed cost variance. **Answer (C) is incorrect.** By definition, flexible budgets address differences in activity levels only within the relevant range.

19.6 Variance Analysis -- Materials and Labor

15. The difference between the actual labor rate multiplied by the actual hours worked and the standard labor rate multiplied by the standard labor hours is the

A. Total labor variance.
B. Labor rate variance.
C. Labor usage variance.
D. Labor efficiency variance.

Answer (A) is correct.
REQUIRED: The variance defined by the difference between total actual labor costs and total standard costs allowed.
DISCUSSION: The total actual labor cost equals the actual labor rate times the actual labor hours. The total standard cost for good output equals the standard rate times the standard hours allowed. The total labor rate variance is the difference between the total actual labor costs and the total standard labor costs.
Answer (B) is incorrect. The labor rate variance is AQ × (SP – AP). **Answer (C) is incorrect.** The labor usage variance is (SQ – AQ) × SP. **Answer (D) is incorrect.** The labor efficiency variance is the same as the labor usage variance: (SQ – AQ) × SP.

16. The standard unit cost is used in the calculation of which of the following variances?

	Materials Price Variance	Materials Usage Variance
A.	No	No
B.	No	Yes
C.	Yes	No
D.	Yes	Yes

Answer (D) is correct.
REQUIRED: The variance(s) using standard unit costs.
DISCUSSION: The materials price variance is isolated at either the time of purchase or use in production. It is calculated by multiplying the actual quantity of units purchased (or used) by the difference between actual price and standard price. The materials quantity (usage) variance is calculated by multiplying the difference between (1) the standard quantity of units (the actual output times the standard number of inputs per unit of output) and (2) the actual quantity of units consumed, times standard price. Thus, the standard unit cost is used to compute both the materials price variance and the materials quantity variance.
Answer (A) is incorrect. Standard unit cost is used in the calculation of materials price variance and materials quantity variance. **Answer (B) is incorrect.** Standard unit cost also is used in the calculation of the materials price variance. **Answer (C) is incorrect.** Standard unit cost also is used in the calculation of the materials quantity variance.

19.7 Variance Analysis -- Overhead

17. Which of the following variances would be useful in calling attention to a possible short-term problem in the control of overhead costs?

	Spending Variance	Volume Variance
A.	No	No
B.	No	Yes
C.	Yes	No
D.	Yes	Yes

Answer (C) is correct.
REQUIRED: The variance(s) useful for controlling overhead costs.
DISCUSSION: The volume variance is the difference between fixed overhead applied and fixed overhead budgeted. Thus, the volume variance has no relation to cost control because the amount of fixed costs is constant. The variance results only from a change in the level of the application base. However, the spending variance is simply a price variance for manufacturing overhead. Consequently, it is the spending variance, not the volume variance, that is useful in detecting problems in the control of overhead costs.
Answer (A) is incorrect. The spending variance is a price variance. **Answer (B) is incorrect.** The spending variance, not the volume variance, is useful for calling attention to a possible short-term problem in the control of overhead costs. **Answer (D) is incorrect.** The volume variance does not indicate whether problems exist in the control of costs.

18. During the month just ended, a department's fixed overhead standard costing system reported unfavorable spending and volume variances. The activity level selected for allocating overhead to the product was based on 80% of practical capacity. If 100% of practical capacity had been selected instead, how would the reported unfavorable spending and volume variances be affected?

	Spending Variance	Volume Variance
A.	Increased	Unchanged
B.	Increased	Increased
C.	Unchanged	Increased
D.	Unchanged	Unchanged

Answer (C) is correct.
REQUIRED: The effects on unfavorable spending and volume variances of increasing the budgeted activity level.
DISCUSSION: The fixed overhead spending variance equals the actual costs incurred minus the budgeted amount. Thus, the spending variance is not affected by the denominator level of the overhead application driver. However, the volume variance equals the budgeted amount minus the amount applied. Because the fixed overhead applied depends on the activity level of the driver used for application, a change in the denominator affects the volume variance. If the denominator increases, the application rate and the amount applied decrease, causing the variance to increase.

19.8 Sales Variances

19. The following data are available for July:

	Budget	Actual
Sales	40,000 units	42,000 units
Selling price	$6 per unit	$5.70 per unit
Variable cost	$3.50 per unit	$3.40 per unit

What is the sales volume variance for July?

A. $5,000 favorable.
B. $4,600 favorable.
C. $12,000 unfavorable.
D. $12,600 unfavorable.

Answer (A) is correct.
REQUIRED: The sales volume variance for a particular month.
DISCUSSION: The sales volume variance is the difference between the actual volume and the budgeted volume in units, times the budgeted contribution margin per unit.

= (Actual volume − Budgeted volume) ×
  (Selling price − Unit variable cost)
= (42,000 − 40,000) × ($6 − $3.50)
= $5,000 F

Answer (B) is incorrect. The budgeted selling price and budgeted variable cost must be used to determine the sales volume variance, not the actual selling price and actual variable cost. Answer (C) is incorrect. The budgeted variable cost must be subtracted from the selling price before multiplying by the 2,000 unit difference actually sold from budgeted sales. Answer (D) is incorrect. The sales volume variance is found by multiplying the 2,000 unit difference between actual and budgeted sales by the $2.50 budgeted contribution margin.

20. A decrease in direct materials costs often results in a(n)

A. Unfavorable sales volume variance.
B. Favorable sales volume variance.
C. Unfavorable sales price variance.
D. None of the answers are correct.

Answer (D) is correct.
REQUIRED: The effect of a decrease in direct materials costs on sales variances.
DISCUSSION: The sales volume variance is the change in contribution margin attributable solely to the difference between the actual and budgeted unit sales (if contribution margin is constant). A decrease in direct materials costs will not change standard price, actual unit sales, or budgeted unit sales unless the materials are defective, unsuitable, or otherwise of poor quality. Thus, a decrease in direct materials costs will not result in a sales volume variance. The sales price variance is the change in contribution margin attributable solely to the change in selling price (if quantity is constant). A simple decrease in direct materials costs will not change actual unit sales, actual price, or standard price. Thus, a decrease in direct materials costs usually will not result in a sales price variance. However, a favorable materials cost decrease due to poor quality materials may affect sales.

STUDY UNIT TWENTY
DATA ANALYTICS

(28 pages of outline)

20.1	Definitions: Data Analytics	599
20.2	Big Data and Data Analytics	600
20.3	Implementing Data Analytics	605
20.4	Data Visualization	608

CPAs have always utilized data to help their clients create value. Traditionally, data were mostly financial. In the 21st century, CPAs are expected to help clients analyze nonfinancial and external data to derive business data insights. Data analytics is now as important to a CPA's knowledge as understanding debits and credits.

This study unit covers Area I of the Blueprint for BEC but is presented last so the data analysis can cover all aspects of the blueprint. Therefore, the practice questions will test candidates on data analytics and other topics, such as finance or cost accounting, jointly. This is how the AICPA will test candidates' knowledge on the CPA Exam.

20.1 DEFINITIONS: DATA ANALYTICS

1. **Data Analytics (DA)**

    a. Data analytics involves qualitative and quantitative methodologies and procedures to retrieve data out of data sources and then inspect the data (in accordance with predetermined requirements) based on data type to facilitate the decision-making process.

    1) A **data type** specifies the type of value and the applicable mathematical or logical operation methodologies that can be applied without resulting in an error. For example, an error will occur if mathematical computations are performed on text data.

    b. For-profit entities, not-for-profit entities, and government agencies (federal, state, and local) utilize DA to reach conclusions based on evidence and reasoning to make well-supported decisions and formulate strong business models.

    1) Organizations can also use business analytics to rule out proposed strategic plans and models that would not be beneficial or work for the organization.

    c. Management utilizes DA to evaluate operational, financial, and other data to identify any deviations from the norm (e.g., anomaly detection, potential risks) and opportunities for enhancement or advancement.

2. **Data management.** Data need to be high quality and well-governed before they can be reliably analyzed. Thus, businesses need to establish

    a. Repeatable processes to build and maintain standards for data quality and
    b. A master data management program.

3. **Data mining** examines large amounts of data to discover patterns, usually unexpected, in the data.

    a. Data mining sifts through all the chaotic and repetitive noise in data, pinpoints what is relevant, uses that information to assess likely outcomes, and then accelerates the pace of making informed decisions.

4. Apache **Hadoop** is an open source software for distributed clusters of computers to store and analyze data sets. The software is scalable and reliable, so much so that Microsoft, Cloudera, Oracle, HP, SAP, and other large technology firms use Hadoop as a base platform for their proprietary systems.

   a. As a distributed software system, Hadoop leverages the bandwidth, memory, and processing power of clusters of commodity hardware (computers) rather than using a mainframe computer.

      1) It also allows massive storage by utilizing multiple machines.

5. **In-memory analytics** analyzes data from system memory instead of secondary storage. This approach

   a. Derives immediate results by removing data preparation and analytical processing delays and

   b. More efficiently enables iterative and interactive analytic scenarios.

6. **Text mining** analyzes text data from the Web, comment fields, books, and other text-based sources through the use of machine learning or natural language processing technology.

   a. It can be used to identify new topics and term relationships.

STOP & REVIEW

You have completed the outline for this subunit.
Study multiple-choice questions 1 and 2 on page 627.

20.2 BIG DATA AND DATA ANALYTICS

1. The accountant's role has become one of a data scientist and storyteller because the manipulation of data reveals trends that can be used to make business decisions.

2. Gradually, since the prevalence of the Internet, accountants have been able to easily analyze external data in addition to internal data.

   a. The Internet of Things (IoT), which is the widespread use of sensors within products, has generated massive amounts of data to the point where batch processing is no longer viable and continuous processing is necessary.

      1) The resulting flood of data, and the availability of such large amounts of information, leads to the term "big data."

      2) For example, big data includes information collected from social media, data from Internet-enabled devices, machine data, videos, and voice recordings. Each type of data is not valuable on its own, but collectively it becomes data that has value.

   b. Examples of big data sets (as of January 2021):

Tweets	6,000 tweets per second, or 200 billion per year
Facebook Photos	4,000 photos uploaded per second, or over 127 billion per year
Amazon Sales	$4,722 in sales per second, or over $17 million per hour

3. Big data is an evolving term that describes any voluminous amount of structured, semi-structured, or unstructured data that has the potential to be mined for information.
   a. **Structured data** refers to data that are highly organized into predefined groupings and are typically maintained in relational databases. The data are predefined such that each item falls into a specific anticipated data type (e.g., string, float, integer, date, Boolean) that can easily be sorted and searched by computer programs. For example, sales data are mostly structured.
   b. **Semi-structured data** refers to data that are not as highly organized as structured data but still have some identifying information that can be used for organization by computer programs. With certain processes, semi-structured data can be stored in relational databases, which can be handled in the same way as structured data. For example, XML and XBRL data can be converted and stored in relational databases for analysis.
   c. **Unstructured data** refers to information that has little or no predefined organizational structure. This lack of organization makes such data much more difficult for computer programs to search, sort, and analyze. For example, tweets, audios, videos, and images are data types that are difficult for computer programs to analyze.
4. The sheer volume of structured data, unstructured data, and streaming data makes collecting, archiving, accessing, and interpreting the information to make optimal business decisions a daunting task. However, big data processed with analytic and algorithmic tools can reveal meaningful information.
5. Big data uses inductive statistics and concepts from nonlinear system identification (i.e., the output is not directly proportional to the input) to infer laws from large sets of data to reveal relationships and dependencies or to predict outcomes and behaviors.
   a. The goal is to have large data sets that are detailed, relational, and flexible.
      1) Firms monetize data by interpreting it to gain a competitive advantage.
   b. Data analytics of big data enables accountants to help their clients or firms by analyzing data to identify opportunities. Examples include, but are not limited to,
      1) Enhanced strategic decisions
      2) Insights for improved productivity, such as minimizing expenses (e.g., inefficiencies, waste, or errors)
      3) Maximizing revenues (e.g., improving customer satisfaction, retention, or attraction of new customers)
      4) Faster and proactive decision making
      5) New product development and optimized offerings
   c. Big data provides statistics. However, statistics are not facts. Data can be biased, and statistical bias can lead accountants to infer the wrong facts.
      1) Volume does not imply facts.
      2) Volume can make facts difficult to uncover.
   d. Big data analytics tools complete missing pieces through **data fusion**, the process of integrating data and knowledge representing the same real-world object into a more consistent, accurate, and useful representation than the individual sources.

6. **Big Data Sources**
    a. Internal structured data
    b. Internal unstructured data
    c. External structured data accessible to the company
        1) Examples include government data, almanacs, etc.
    d. External unstructured data accessible to the company
        1) Examples include tweets, blog posts, etc.
    e. Data the company cannot readily obtain
        1) Sometimes data can be bought. The company often does not know the value of a data set until after buying it.
        2) Data from Google, Facebook, Twitter, Amazon, and any entity possessing personally identifiable information are valuable.
        3) Transactions contribute to the largest data sets.

7. **Big Data**
    a. Big data has four dimensions and is often characterized by the "4 Vs."
        1) **Volume**
            a) Volume is used to describe the extreme amount of data captured over time.
                i) Depending on the amount of data required to be captured, the number of servers required could range from a single server to thousands of servers.
            b) Real-time sensors used in the IoT have become one of the top sources of data.
                i) IoT is a system of interrelated computing devices, mechanical and digital machines, objects, animals, or people that are provided with real-time sensors and with the ability to transfer data over a network without requiring human-to-human or human-to-computer interaction. For example, a smart home device that is connected to a thermostat and temperature sensor such that room temperature is automatically adjusted based on the sensor data.
        2) **Variety**
            a) Data exist in a wide variety of file types.
                i) Structured data file types are generally maintained by Structured Query Language (SQL), which is used for managing relational databases and performing various operations on the data in them. They include numbers, addresses, dates, etc.
                ii) Unstructured data file types (e.g., streaming data from sensors, text, audios, images, and videos) are maintained by non-relational databases (i.e., NoSQL).

3) **Velocity**

   a) Velocity refers to the speed at which big data are generated and must be analyzed.

      i) Analysts must have a detailed understanding of the available data and possess some sense of what answer(s) they are looking for.

      ii) The computing power required to quickly process huge volumes and varieties of data can overwhelm a single server or multiple servers. Organizations must apply adequate computing power to big data tasks to achieve the desired velocity.

      iii) Businesses are hesitant to invest in an extensive server and storage infrastructure that might only be used occasionally to complete big data tasks. As a result, cloud computing has emerged as a primary source for hosting big data projects.

4) **Veracity**

   a) Veracity refers to the trustworthiness of the data (relevance and reliability).

      i) Can the user rely on the fact the data are representative?

b. The "5th V"

   1) More and more businesses are using big data because of the **value** of the information resulting from the culmination of analyzing large information flows and identifying opportunities for improvement.

      a) Use of big data is only as valuable as the business outcomes it makes possible. It is how businesses make use of data that allows full recognition of its true value and potential to improve decision-making capabilities and enhance positive business outcomes.

         i) **Volume-based value.** The more data businesses have on customers, both recent and historical, the greater the insights. This leads to generating better decisions around acquiring, retaining, increasing, and managing those customer relationships.

         ii) **Variety-based value.** In the digital era, the capability to acquire and analyze varied data is extremely valuable. This in turn provides deep insights into successfully developing and personalizing customer platforms for businesses to be more engaged and aware of customer needs and expectations.

         iii) **Velocity-based value.** The faster businesses process data, the more time they will have to ask the right questions and seek answers. Rapid analysis capabilities provide businesses with the right data in time to achieve their customer relationship management goals.

         iv) **Veracity-based value.** Once data is validated, the data transforms into "smart data." Collecting large amounts of statistics and numbers is of little value if they cannot be relied upon and used.

8. Limitations of Big Data

    a. Big data is not suitable for all applications and analyses. Situations in which big data may be unsuitable include but are not limited to those in which

        1) **User-level data results are incomplete.** Generally, the data available to an organization are restricted to data obtained from individuals who visited the organization's Internet resources (i.e., website) or viewed the organization's advertisements on the Internet.

            a) The data are only representative of the target market; thus, untapped markets could potentially exist, the data of which are not being captured.

        2) **Providing the answer to why the analysis results are what they are is difficult.** Data are processed by (a) separating data into groups and applying analytic methods or (b) analyzing data directly using algorithmic methods. Both processes can result in forecasting outcomes and providing guidance, but algorithmic analytic methods tend to make it more difficult for non-technical people to justify choosing a certain course of action over another course of action (e.g., spending more capital expenditures on product Z over product P).

        3) **Data are subject to useless information (commonly known as noise).** A single incorrect or useless variable can corrupt the results and require additional labor hours to work with the data in order to attain meaningful results.

        4) **User-level data results require interpretation prior to use.** Generally, collected data are converted from text format to data visualizations. Data visualizations assist with identifying trends and correlations that run the risk of going undetected in text-based data.

STOP & REVIEW

You have completed the outline for this subunit.
Study multiple-choice questions 3 through 8 beginning on page 628.

20.3 IMPLEMENTING DATA ANALYTICS

1. Data analytics contains five stages as follows:

   a. **Define questions**

      1) Goals and objectives that the organization is trying to achieve should be identified. Key performance indicators (KPIs) must be identified to assist with measuring whether an organization is progressing toward its goals and objectives. Examples of KPIs include

         a) Current ratio
         b) Net profit margin
         c) Budget variance
         d) Debt to equity ratio
         e) Payment error rate

      2) Clearly defined goals and objectives assist the IT team with selecting the most appropriate technology source to use for the analysis.

      3) Early adoption of goals and KPIs helps keep the analysis on course and avoid worthless analysis.

   b. **Obtain relevant data** (commonly referred to as **information discovery**)

      1) Access to every piece of data available allows for

         a) Valuable analysis,
         b) More precise correlations,
         c) Construction of meaningful analysis models and forecasts, and
         d) Identification of actionable insights.

   c. **Clean/scrub/normalize data**

      1) Data cleaning consists of, but is not limited to, flushing out useless information (e.g., duplicated data) and identifying missing data.

      2) Data governance assists with ensuring data are accurate and usable.

      3) Data normalization involves storing each data element as few times as necessary. It results in a reduction in data and strengthened data integrity for use of a specific purpose.

         a) **Integrity** is ensuring that data accurately reflect the business events underlying them and that any anomalies are rectified.

d. **Analyze data**

1) As a collection of data is analyzed, a determination can be made as to whether it is comprised of the exact data needed. This process involves

    a) Assessing whether additional data are needed,
    b) Collecting new and/or different data,
    c) Revising the original question, and
    d) Formulating additional questions.

2) Data analytics methods include the following application types:

    a) **Descriptive analysis** is the most basic and most used method. It concentrates on reporting historical information, such as financial results (e.g., the change in profit margin from the previous month).
    b) **Diagnostic analysis** is an additional step after descriptive analysis. It provides insight into the reason certain results occur (e.g., what caused the change in profit margin).
    c) **Predictive analysis** examines historical information to determine what will happen in the future. It involves applying assumptions to data and predicting future results (e.g., if a measure is taken, what will be the profit margin for the current month).
    d) **Prescriptive analysis** uses descriptive, diagnostic, and prediction analytics to improve business strategy. Specifically, it concentrates on what an organization needs to do for the predicted future results to actually occur [e.g., what needs to be done (such as cutting costs) to increase the profit margin to a certain level].
    e) **Anomaly detection** is used to identify unusual patterns or deviations from the norm or expected results (e.g., any deviation in change in profit margin not attributable to seasonal effects).
    f) **Network analysis** consists of analyzing network data and statistics to find patterns.
    g) **Text analysis** involves the utilization of text mining and natural language algorithms to find patterns in unstructured text.

3) Personnel generally will select data to trace to supporting source documentation, such as invoices, contracts, and payments, and perform the following additional procedures:

    a) Review and confirm the details of the data selected.
    b) Analyze the findings and determine compliance or noncompliance with policy.
    c) Analyze the findings for accuracy.
    d) Identify internal controls requiring enhancement or, if no controls exist, assist with the creation of a control.

Type of Data Analytics	Types of Questions to Ask	How
Descriptive	Report: What happened?	Query, reporting, and search functions
Diagnostic	Analysis: Why did it happen?	Online analytical processing (OLAP) and visualization tools
Diagnostic	Monitoring: What is happening now?	Dashboards and score cards
Predictive	What might happen?	Regression, experience, and judgment
Prescriptive	What needs to be done?	Experience and judgment

- e. **Communicate results**
    1) The primary purpose of communicating results with appropriate management is to ensure the accuracy of the information used, conclusions, and recommendations.
    2) Data visualization or graphic illustrations (e.g., charts, graphs, network analysis), written repetition (e.g., summaries), and itemized lists (bulleted or numbered) are good ways of emphasizing information. Detailed examples of graphic illustrations are found in Subunit 20.4.
        a) Using visual aids to support a discussion of major points results in the greatest retention of information.
    3) Generally, language should be fact-based and neutral.
        a) Using too strong a word or a word inappropriate for the particular recipient may induce an unwanted response. Thus, high-connotation language should be chosen carefully to appeal to the specific recipient.

2. **Examples of Data Analytics Application**
    a. **Accounts receivable.** Payment patterns can alert the accountant to whether a client will be able to pay.
        1) If a client typically pays between the 14th and 16th of every month, and customer payment has not been received by the 20th, a phone call may be necessary to identify whether the client intends to or can pay.
        2) Those clients who are always late may need credit restriction or other approaches to improve payment timeliness.
    b. **Accounts payable.** Errors or duplicate payments have historically required time-intensive research. Through data analytics, the time spent can be shortened by downloading annual disbursement data.
        1) By sorting payments by invoice number, dates, and amounts, duplicates or similarities can be identified quickly.
            a) Many times, duplicates are added by having a sample " - ," "space," or "A" to fool the software's internal control.

c. **Inventory.** Slow-moving inventory may indicate inventory obsolescence and valuation issues.

   1) Inventories unsold or unmoved for a long period of time or with fair values lower than their costs should be written down.

d. **Procurement cards.** Excessive purchases without a respective increase in demand may indicate abuse and waste.

   1) Comparing price lists of purchases with other suppliers may reveal abuse.
   2) Purchases from related parties should also be investigated.

e. **Payroll and time sheets.**

   1) Analyze time reported to identify previously unidentified patterns that may indicate errors or fraud.

   2) Analyze time for operating hours, weekends, closures, or holidays to identify possible mistakes or fraud in time reporting.

   3) Compare time sheets (hours worked) and the payroll register (hours paid).

STOP & REVIEW

You have completed the outline for this subunit. Study multiple-choice questions 9 through 12 beginning on page 630.

20.4 DATA VISUALIZATION

1. Elements of Visualization

   a. Title

      1) A title helps establish an expectation of the information. For example, the title "GDP of United States, 1970-2020" gives three pieces of information about the data being presented: (a) GDP but not other measures, (b) United States but not other countries, and (c) the period between 1970 and 2020 but not others.

      2) An expectation and an understanding of what is being conveyed help determine what to look for or whether the data supports or contradicts what to look for. For instance, in the above example, it is immediately clear that the GDP of Mexico will not be available. If data for 1920 are shown, the visualization is problematic.

b. Axes

1) Axes convey how the data are measured and presented. They deliver the following pieces of information:

   a) The label is what the axis measures and presents. For example, in a 2-dimensional graph, the y-axis can be used to depict revenue growth rate and the x-axis can be used to depict the market share, and vice versa. Knowing what the axis measures is critical for data interpretation.

   b) The range shows whether the axis captures all the data. For example, if a data set contains sales between $1,000 and $10,000,000, a range between $0 and $5,000,000 is insufficient to capture and present all the data.

   c) The scale is also important to consider. A bad-axis scale has been among one of the most common examples of bad visualization. For example, consider the following two graphs that present the same set of data. Using a different scale may lead to deceptive conclusions.

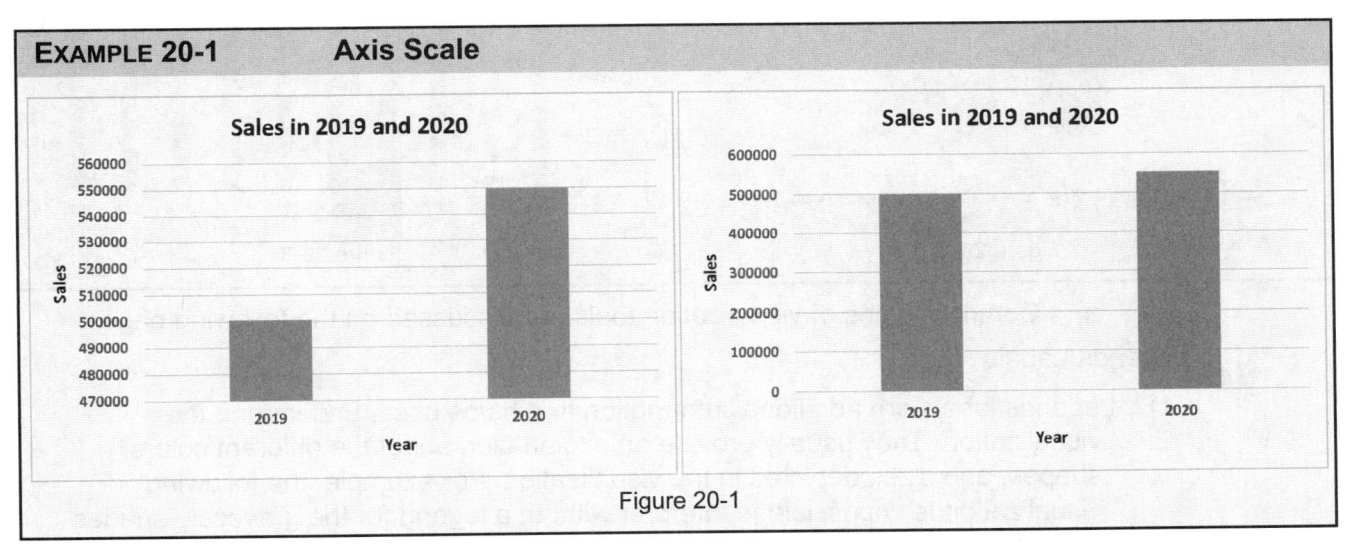

EXAMPLE 20-1   Axis Scale

Figure 20-1

c. Presentation

1) Presentation determines what and how to look for the information. After establishing an expectation and understanding of the visualization from the title, the way in which the data are presented determines whether the visualization can be utilized to achieve the objectives. The objectives determine the type of visualization used. For example, consider the following two graphs that present the same set of data. A pie chart cannot intuitively convey information about the changes in sales over time, but this is feasible if a bar chart is used.

EXAMPLE 20-2   Presentation -- Type of Visualization Used

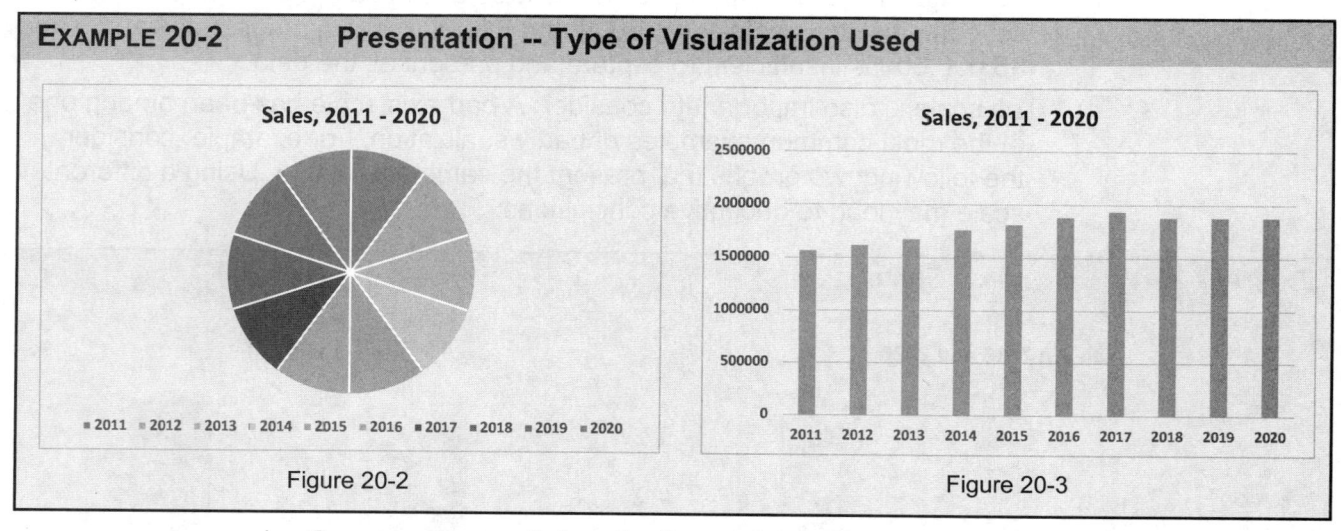

Figure 20-2

Figure 20-3

a) Common types of visualization tools are discussed on the following pages.

d. Legends/Labels

1) Legends/labels are additional information that helps users understand the visualization. They usually provide an explanation about the different colors, shapes, and sizes depicted in the visualization. For example, the following visualization is impossible to interpret without a legend for the grayscale shades presented.

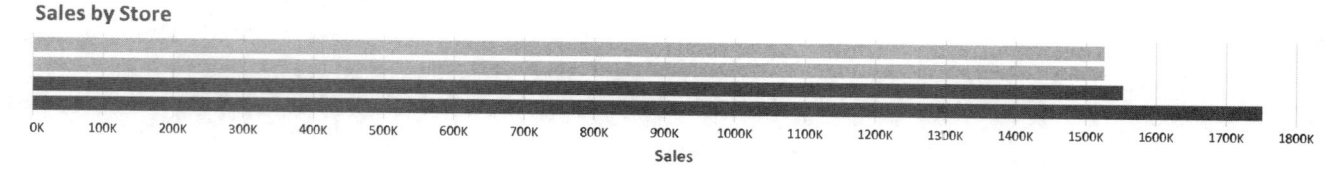

Figure 20-4

2. Interpreting Types of Visualization

a. Tables

1) Tables present data as close to their raw form as possible. Although a tabular presentation is able to retain the details of the data, it is less intuitive for understanding. Also, as the size of the data set increases, the difficulty of interpreting the tabular data also increases.

a) Tables present data in columns, which are called attributes or dimensions.

EXAMPLE 20-3 — Tabular Visualization

The following table lists a sample of 20 vouchers of a grocery store, each with 8 attributes (dimensions).

Voucher ID	Store	Customer Type	Product Line	Total Revenue	Total Cost	Profit Margin	Voucher Date
V0000001	Alachua	Member	Health and beauty	510	275	46.08%	2018-04-03
V0000002	Alachua	NonMember	Food and beverages	450	243	46.00%	2018-05-06
V0000003	Duval	NonMember	Electronic accessories	630	372	40.95%	2018-06-25
V0000004	Duval	NonMember	Home and lifestyle	770	385	50.00%	2018-07-14
V0000005	Alachua	Member	Health and beauty	490	372	24.08%	2019-01-28
V0000006	Alachua	NonMember	Health and beauty	750	533	28.93%	2019-04-23
V0000007	Clay	Member	Sports and travel	590	425	27.97%	2019-05-29
V0000008	Alachua	Member	Health and beauty	550	402	26.91%	2019-06-21
V0000009	Clay	Member	Food and beverages	170	134	21.18%	2019-07-29
V0000010	Clay	Member	Electronic accessories	110	80	27.27%	2019-08-01
V0000011	Alachua	Member	Health and beauty	80	61	23.75%	2019-09-09
V0000012	Duval	NonMember	Electronic accessories	80	60	25.00%	2019-09-30
V0000013	Alachua	Member	Electronic accessories	430	340	20.93%	2019-11-13
V0000014	Alachua	NonMember	Home and lifestyle	340	289	15.00%	2020-04-29
V0000015	Clay	Member	Fashion accessories	60	53	11.67%	2020-05-10
V0000016	Alachua	NonMember	Sports and travel	630	554	12.06%	2020-06-05
V0000017	Alachua	NonMember	Food and beverages	170	145	14.71%	2020-06-26
V0000018	Alachua	NonMember	Sports and travel	460	396	13.91%	2020-07-06
V0000019	Alachua	NonMember	Electronic accessories	250	218	12.80%	2020-09-30
V0000020	Clay	Member	Health and beauty	200	172	14.00%	2020-11-25

A table retains the different categories and details of the data without using complex visualization. However, as the number of vouchers or attributes (dimensions) increases, data interpretation becomes increasingly difficult.

b. Bar Graphs
1) Bar graphs use the heights of vertical bars (or lengths of horizontal bars) to show the quantitative comparison among qualitative (categorical) items, such as the sales revenues of different stores. When combined with time-series data, the relative heights (or lengths) can also be used to show trends, cyclicality, or variability over time.

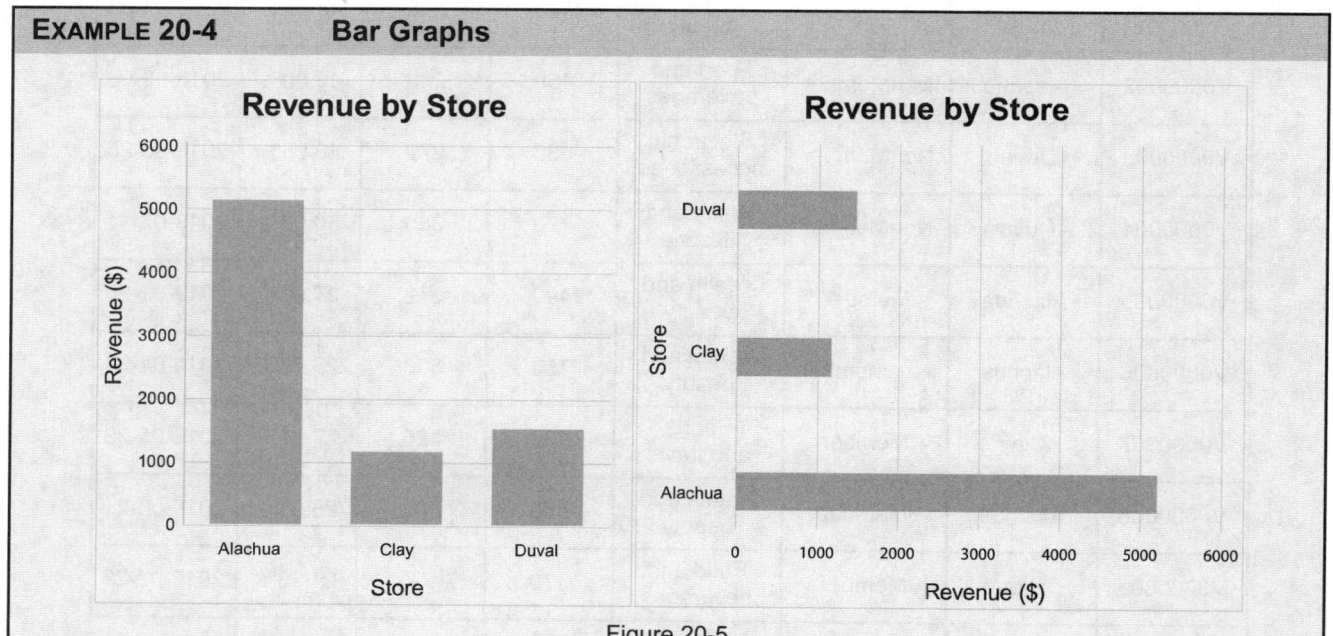

EXAMPLE 20-4   Bar Graphs

Figure 20-5

The two bar graphs above present the same set of data using vertical bars and horizontal bars. Based on the relative heights (or lengths) of the bars, it can be observed that the revenue for the store in Alachua is the highest among the three stores, followed by the store in Duval.

EXAMPLE 20-5   Bar Graph with Time-Series Data

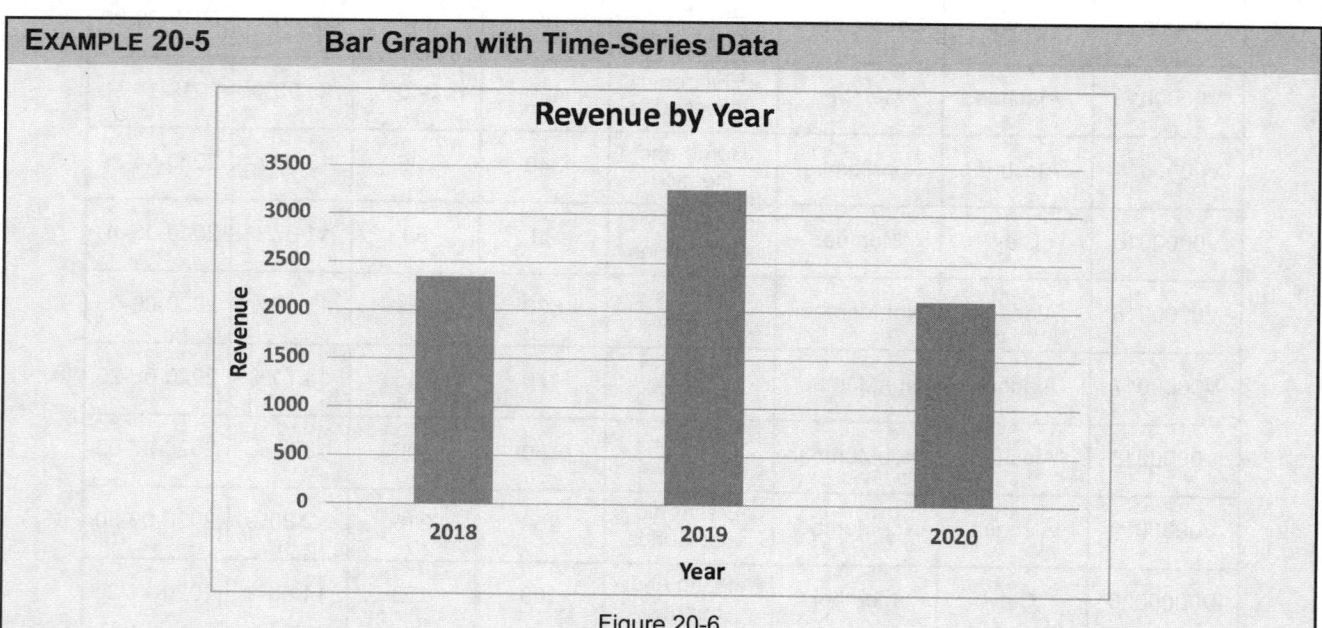

Figure 20-6

The bar graph above depicts the revenue (quantitative data) by year (time-series data). Thus, by observing the relative heights of the bars, it can be concluded that the revenue increased between 2018 and 2019 but decreased between 2019 and 2020.

EXAMPLE 20-6   Bar Graph with Colors or Patterns

Revenue by Store and by Customer Type

Store	Cust. Type
Alachua	Member
	Nonmember
Clay	Member
Duval	Nonmember

Total Revenue (0 – 3200)

Customer Type: Member, Nonmember

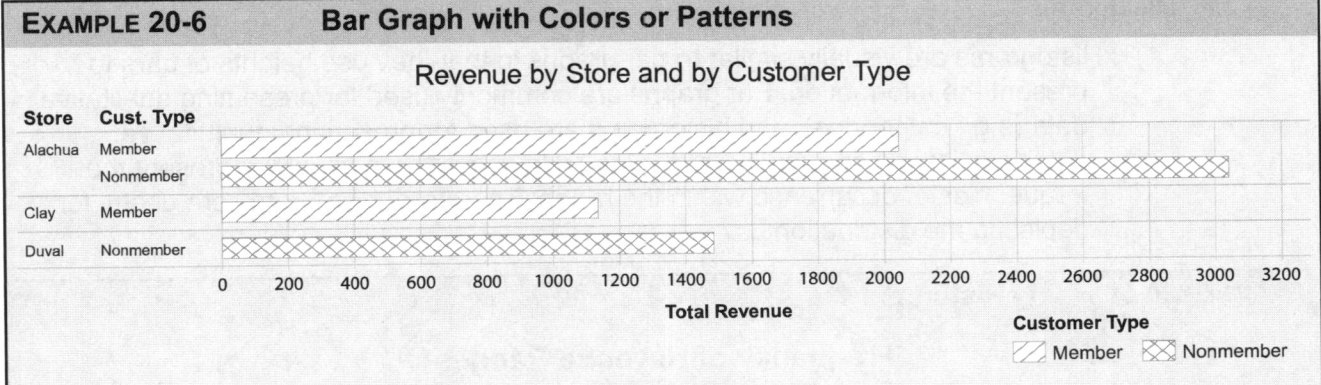

Figure 20-7

Sometimes, bars with different colors or patterns are used to add dimensions to bar graphs. The bar graph above displays the revenue by store. To add the dimension of customer type, two different patterns are used to denote whether the customer is a member or nonmember. The graph above denotes the following pieces of information:

1. All revenue in the Duval store was contributed by nonmembers.
2. All revenue in the Clay store was contributed by members.
3. Revenue in the Alachua store was contributed by both customer types.

EXAMPLE 20-7   Bar Graph with Varying Bar Widths

Revenue by Store and by Customer Type

Store	Cust. Type
Alachua	Member
	Nonmember
Clay	Member
Duval	Nonmember

Total Revenue (0 – 3200)

Customer Type: Member, Nonmember

Count of Customer Type: 3, 4, 5, 6, 7

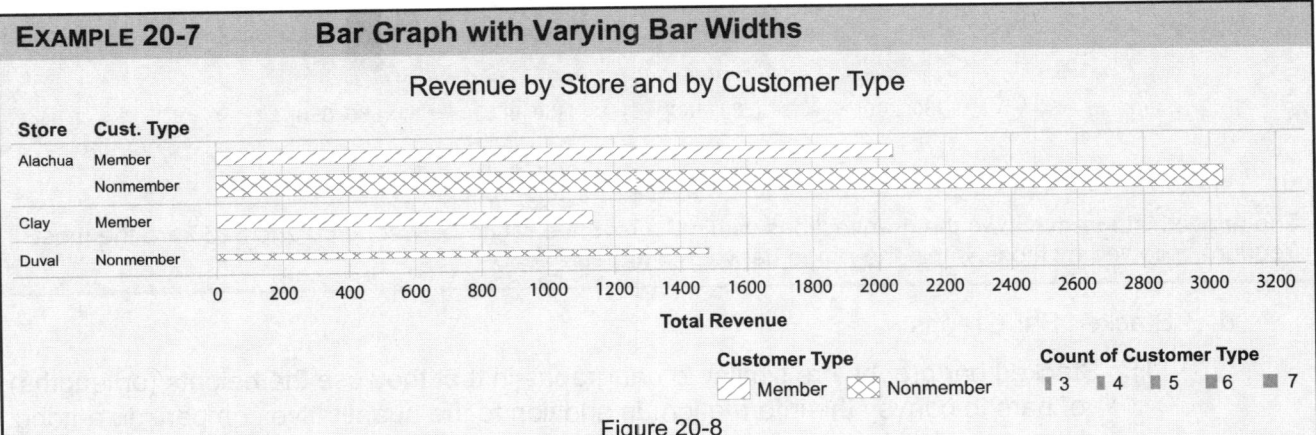

Figure 20-8

Besides color/pattern, sizes (widths) of the bars can be used to provide additional data. The bar widths in the bar graph above depict the number of customers of each customer type.

From the widths of the bars, the following observations can be made:

1. The number of customers of both types in the Alachua store were relatively high (indicated by their widths). The higher number of customers may explain the higher revenue.
2. Despite a lower number of customers than the Clay store, the Duval store has higher revenue. This may indicate that the average revenue is higher in the Duval store than the Clay store.

c. Histograms

1) Histograms are visually similar to bar graphs in that they use heights of bars to present the information. Bar graphs are commonly used for presenting qualitative data (e.g., categories), and histograms are used for presenting quantitative data (e.g., range of quantity, price, etc.). Heights of bars usually represent the frequencies of occurrence within the range. Therefore, histograms are useful for depicting the distribution.

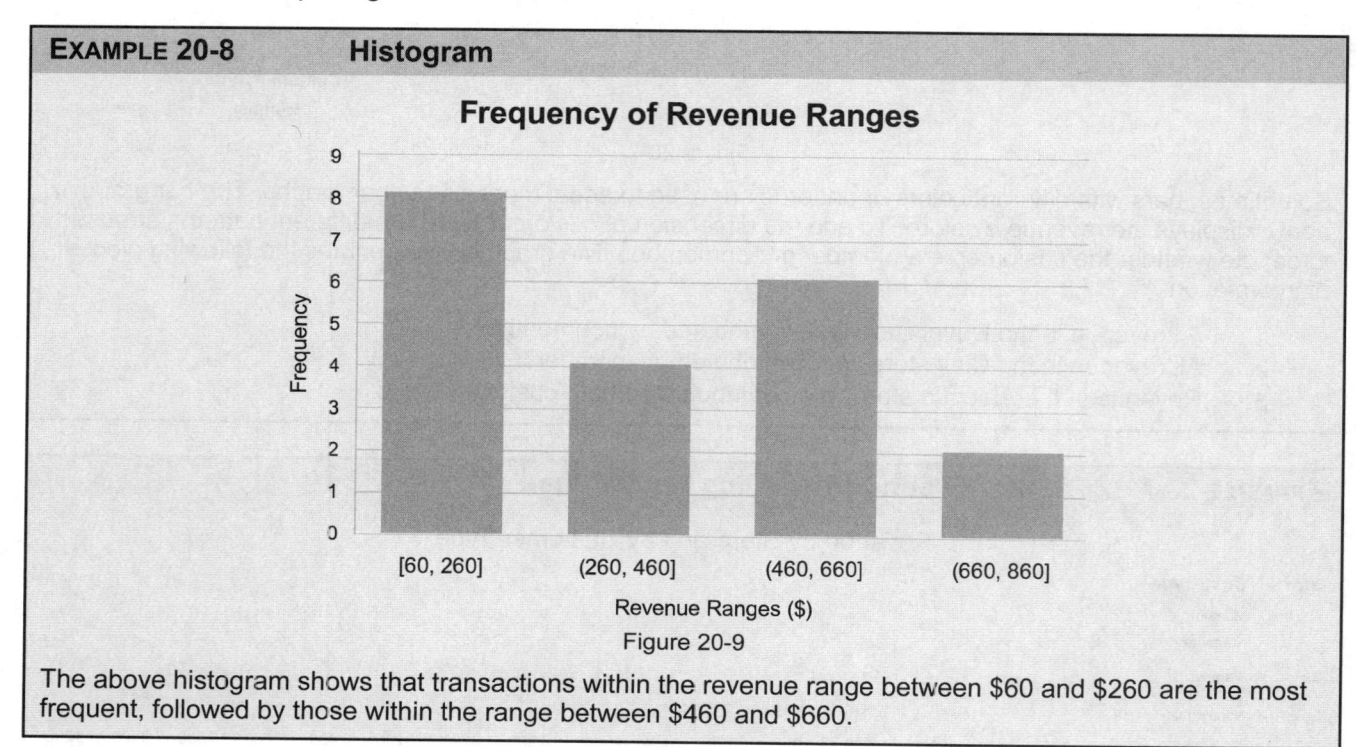

EXAMPLE 20-8   **Histogram**

Frequency of Revenue Ranges

Revenue Range ($)	Frequency
[60, 260]	8
(260, 460]	4
(460, 660]	6
(660, 860]	2

Figure 20-9

The above histogram shows that transactions within the revenue range between $60 and $260 are the most frequent, followed by those within the range between $460 and $660.

---

d. Stacked Bar Graphs

1) Stacked bar graphs are similar to bar graphs in that they use the heights (or lengths) of bars to convey the information. In addition to the quantitative comparison among items, stacked bar graphs are also used to represent the components of the items, such as the proportion of sales from different types of customers. By combining a stacked bar graph with time-series data and cross-referencing the relative heights (lengths) of the stacked bars over time, changes in the components can also be visualized.

   a) Sometimes bar graphs are stacked in terms of percentages of the total using 100% stacked bar graphs. By presenting the components as percentages of the totals, 100% stacked bar graphs eliminate the biases caused by the different magnitudes of the items. Similar to stacked bar graphs, 100% stacked bar graphs can be used to show the comparison among items and changes in the components over time.

EXAMPLE 20-9 — Stacked Bar Graph

Revenue by Year and by Customer Type

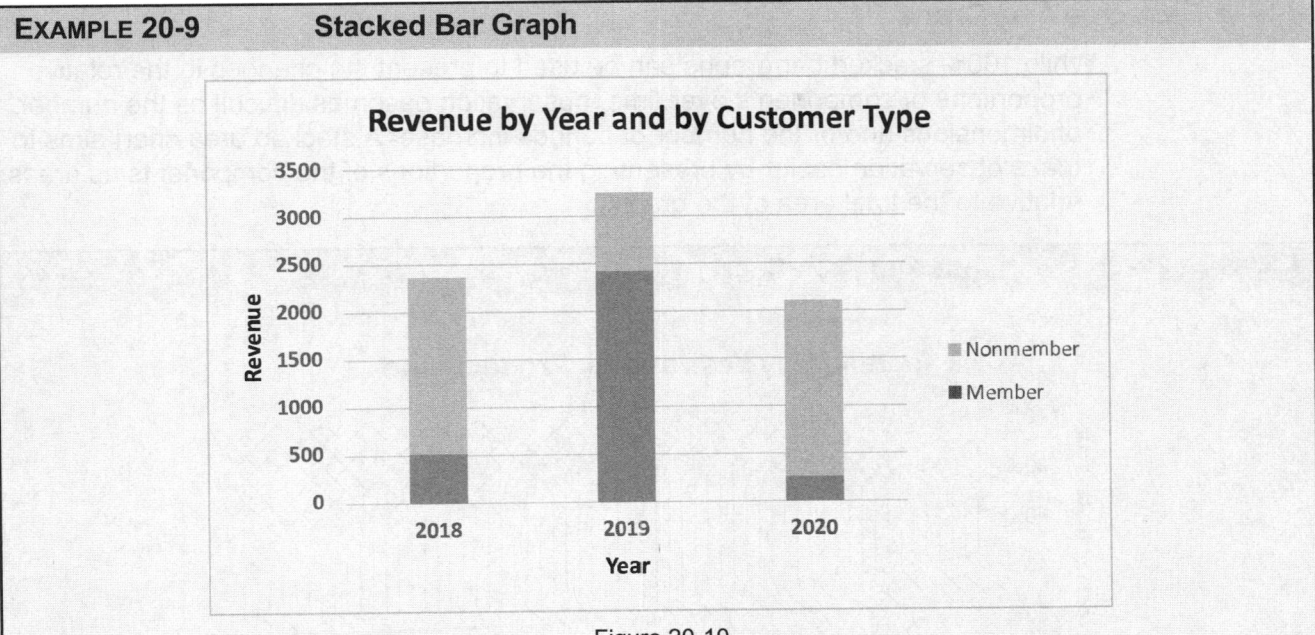

[Stacked bar graph showing Revenue (0–3500) by Year (2018, 2019, 2020), with Member and Nonmember segments]

Figure 20-10

The stacked graph above conveys the following pieces of information:

1. In 2018 and 2020, revenues contributed by nonmembers are higher than those by members. In 2019, members contributed more revenue than nonmembers.
2. Revenue contributed by members increased from 2018 to 2019 and decreased from 2019 to 2020.
3. Revenue contributed by nonmembers decreased from 2018 to 2019 and increased from 2019 to 2020.

EXAMPLE 20-10 — 100% Stacked Bar Graph

Revenue by Year and by Customer Type

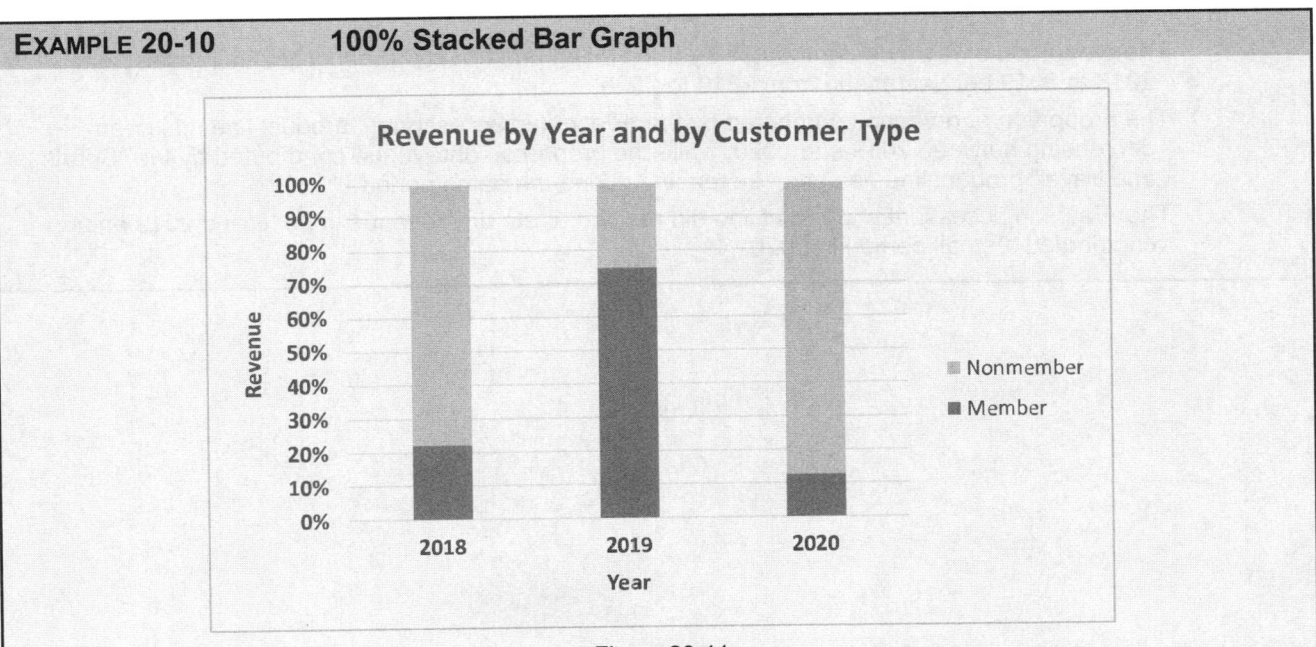

[100% stacked bar graph showing Revenue proportions (0%–100%) by Year (2018, 2019, 2020), with Member and Nonmember segments]

Figure 20-11

The 100% stacked bar graph above visualizes the relative proportions of the revenues contributed by the two customer types. This allows for more accurate comparison if the proportion of the component and its change are more relevant than the absolute magnitude of the component and its change.

e. Stacked Area Charts

1) While 100% stacked bar graphs can be used to present the changes in the relative proportions of components over time, observation becomes difficult as the number of dimensions and/or the number of periods increase. A stacked area chart aims to make observation easier by presenting the proportions of the components as areas relative to the total area of the graph.

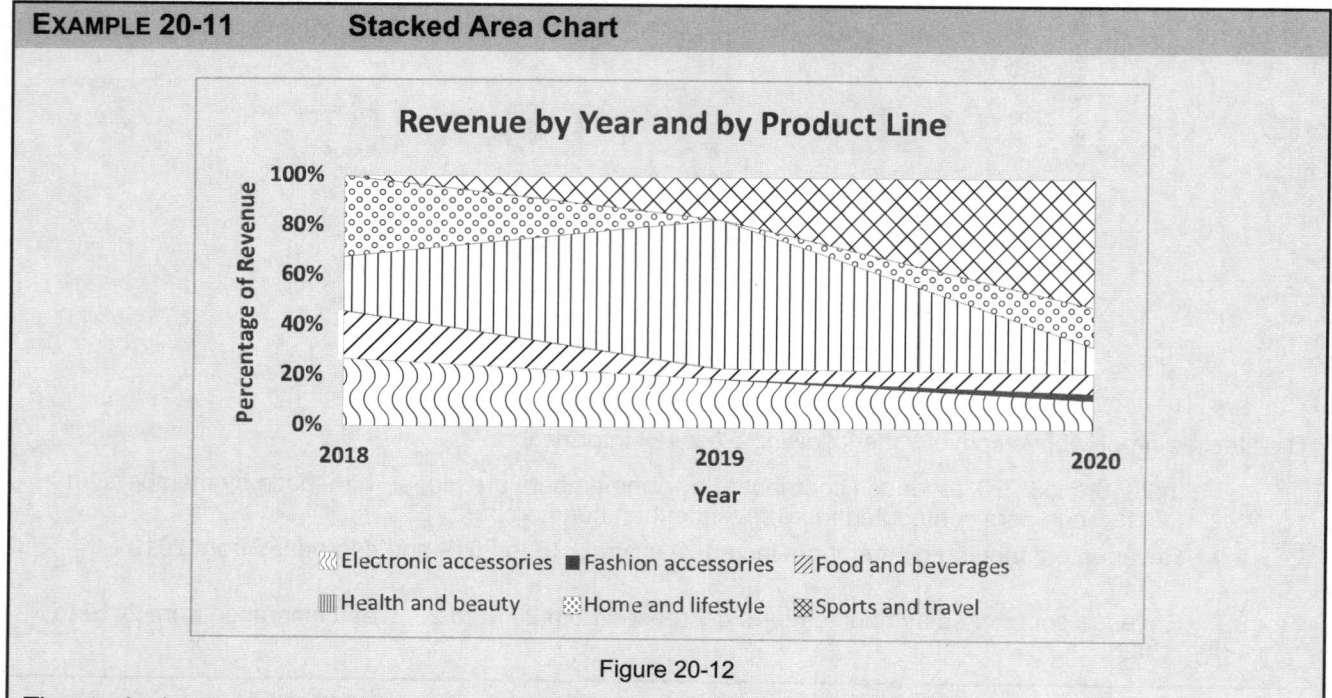

EXAMPLE 20-11 **Stacked Area Chart**

Revenue by Year and by Product Line

(Chart showing Percentage of Revenue from 0% to 100% across years 2018, 2019, 2020)

Legend: Electronic accessories, Fashion accessories, Food and beverages, Health and beauty, Home and lifestyle, Sports and travel

Figure 20-12

The stacked area chart above presents the following pieces of information:

1. The proportion of revenue contributed by the "Health and beauty" product line increased from 2018 to 2019 but decreased from 2019 to 2020.
2. The proportion of revenue contributed by the "Electronic accessories" product line has been decreasing between 2018 and 2020, while the proportion of revenue contributed by the "Sports and travel" product line has been increasing during the same period.
3. The "Fashion accessories" product line did not contribute any revenue in 2018 and 2019 and contributed a small portion in 2020.

f. Line Charts
   1) Line charts are similar to bar graphs combined with time-series data in that they are often used to show trends, cyclicality, or variability over time. Instead of heights of bars, line charts use dots and connect the dots with lines, such that changes over time are more observable.
      a) Line charts also can be used to present changes over time for several different categories (e.g., revenues and costs) by utilizing different lines to represent the different categories.

EXAMPLE 20-12   **Line Chart**

Revenue and Cost By Year

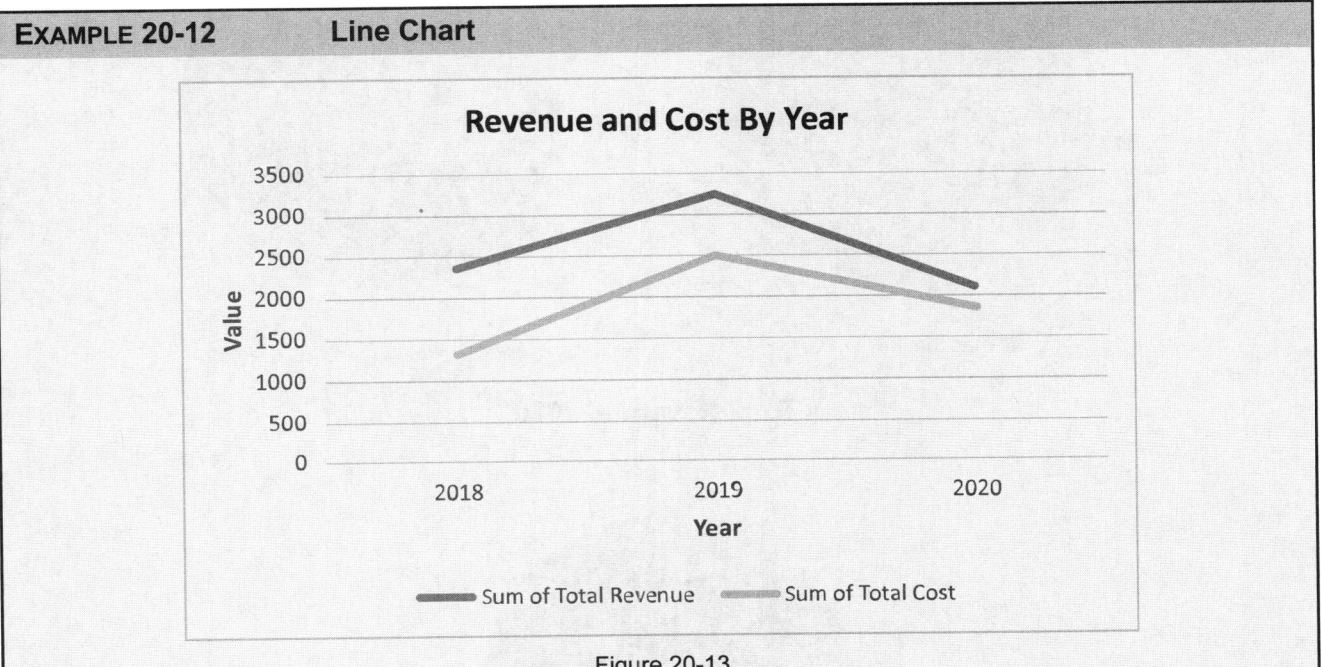

(Line chart showing Sum of Total Revenue and Sum of Total Cost for years 2018, 2019, and 2020, with values ranging from 0 to 3500.)

Figure 20-13

From the line chart above, it can be observed that both revenue and cost increased between 2018 and 2019 and decreased between 2019 and 2020. Also, it can be observed that the differences between total cost and total revenue decreased between 2018 and 2020, indicating a decline in profit margin throughout the 3 years.

---

g. Pie Charts
   1) Pie charts use circles (pies) to display the whole set of data, with each category displayed as a segment of the circle (percentage of the total). The area of the segment represents the proportion of the category to the total.
      a) This is similar to a 100% stacked bar graph, which also presents the relative proportions of different categories. However, 100% stacked bar graphs can be used to depict the change in the relative proportions over time, while pie charts generally can only depict the relative proportions at a specific period. Changes in the relative proportions have to be observed by cross-referencing pie charts for different periods.

EXAMPLE 20-13   Pie Chart

Total Revenue, 2018
- Alachua 41%
- Duval 59%

Total Revenue, 2019
- Alachua 71%
- Clay 27%
- Duval 2%

Total Revenue, 2020
- Alachua 88%
- Clay 12%

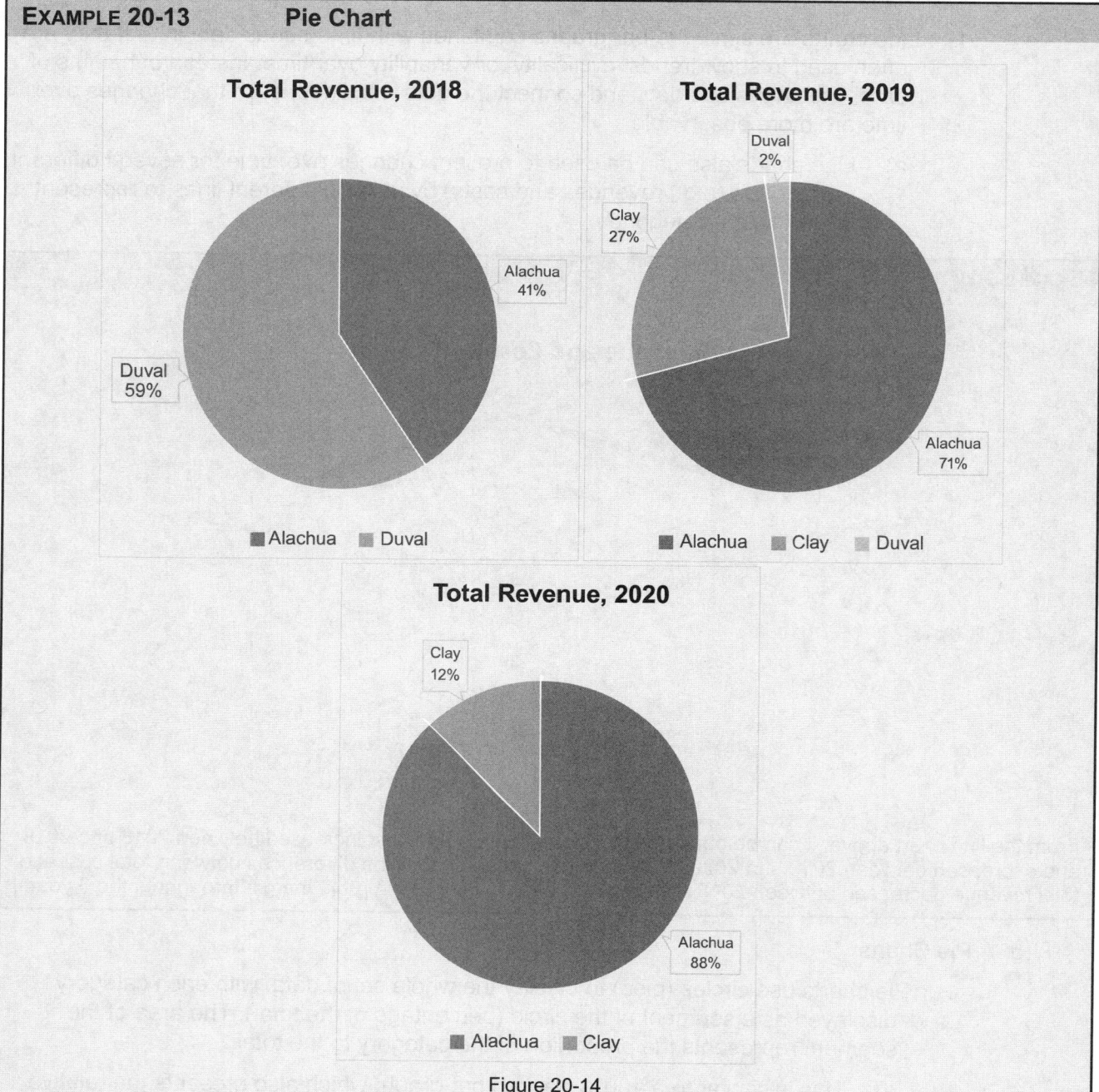

Figure 20-14

The charts above convey the following pieces of information:

1. In 2018, over half of the revenue was contributed by the Duval store. The rest was contributed by the Alachua store.
2. In 2019, the Alachua store contributed the majority of the revenue, the Clay store contributed approximately 1/4 of the revenue, and the Duval store contributed only 2% of the revenue.
3. By cross-referencing the 2018 and 2019 pie charts, it can be observed that the proportion of revenue contributed by the Alachua store increased, while the proportion of revenue contributed by the Duval store decreased dramatically. Also, the revenue in 2019 was contributed by 3 stores, compared to 2 stores in 2018.
4. In 2020, the revenue was contributed by the Clay and Alachua stores. The Duval store did not contribute any revenue. An implication may be that the Duval store was relocated to Alachua during 2019.

SU 20: Data Analytics

h. **Scatter Plots**

1) Scatter plots show the relationship between two quantitative variables. For data with multiple dimensions (e.g., revenue and cost), one dimension is plotted on the x-axis and the other is plotted on the y-axis, creating points on a graph. The overall pattern of the points depicts the relationships between the two variables.

   a) The most common relationship between two variables is the linear relationship, meaning that if one variable changes in one direction (increases or decreases), the other variable changes in the same or the opposite direction, or does not change at all. The strength of the linear relationship is depicted by how closely the pattern of charted points resembles a straight line. The direction of the relationship is indicated by the slope of the line; a positive slope represents a positive relationship (as one variable increases, the other variable also increases), while a negative slope represents a negative relationship (as one variable increases, the other variable decreases).

EXAMPLE 20-14   Scatter Plot

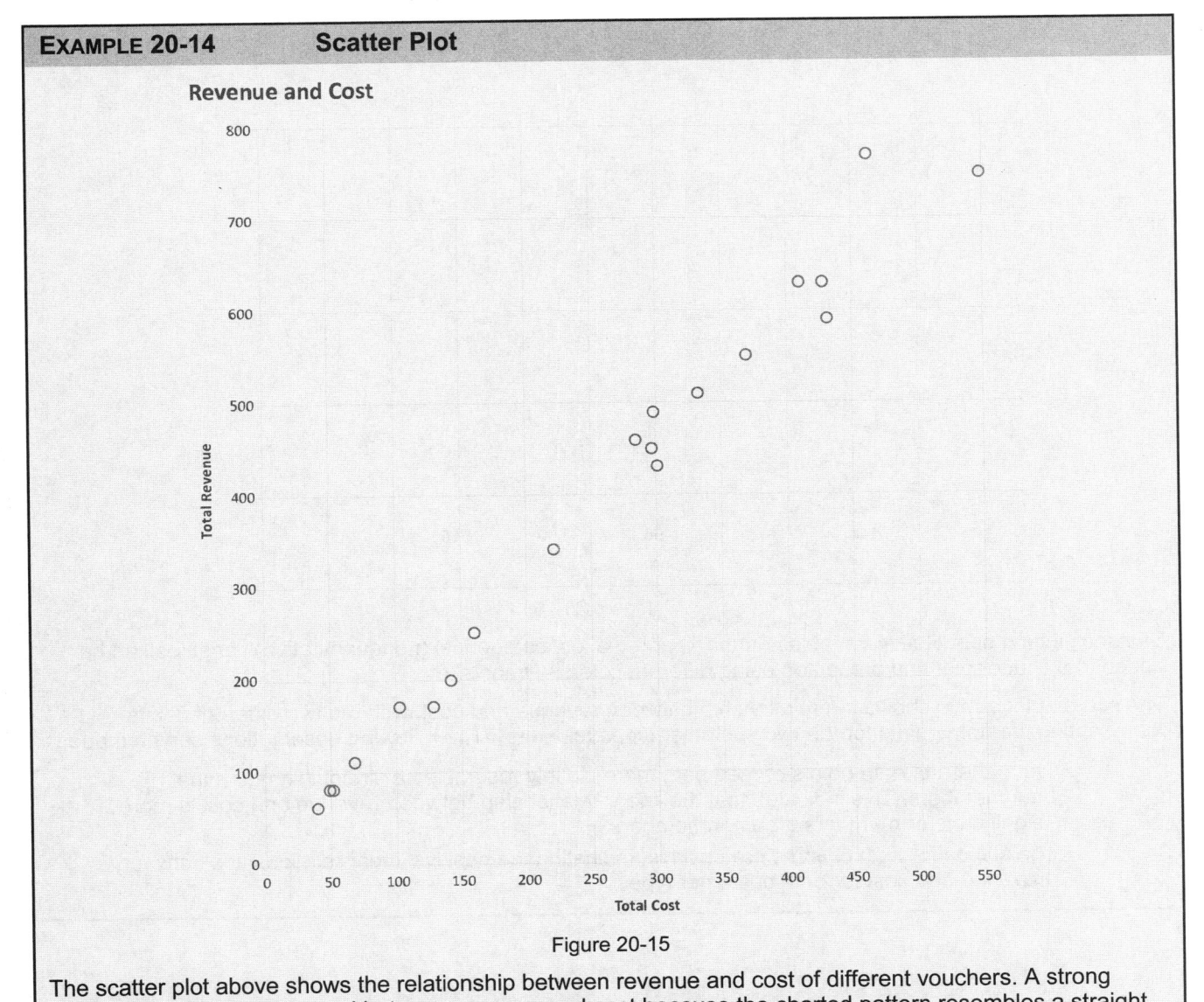

Revenue and Cost

[Scatter plot with Total Cost on x-axis (0 to 550) and Total Revenue on y-axis (0 to 800), showing points forming a positive linear pattern]

Figure 20-15

The scatter plot above shows the relationship between revenue and cost of different vouchers. A strong linear relationship is observed between revenue and cost because the charted pattern resembles a straight line. The slope of the line is positive, indicating a positive linear relationship between revenue and cost–as cost increases, revenue increases. However, note that a linear relationship does not imply causation. That is, an increase in revenue may not be caused by an increase in cost, and vice versa.

EXAMPLE 20-15   Clustered Scatter Plot

Revenue and Cost

Customer Type
- Member
- NonMember

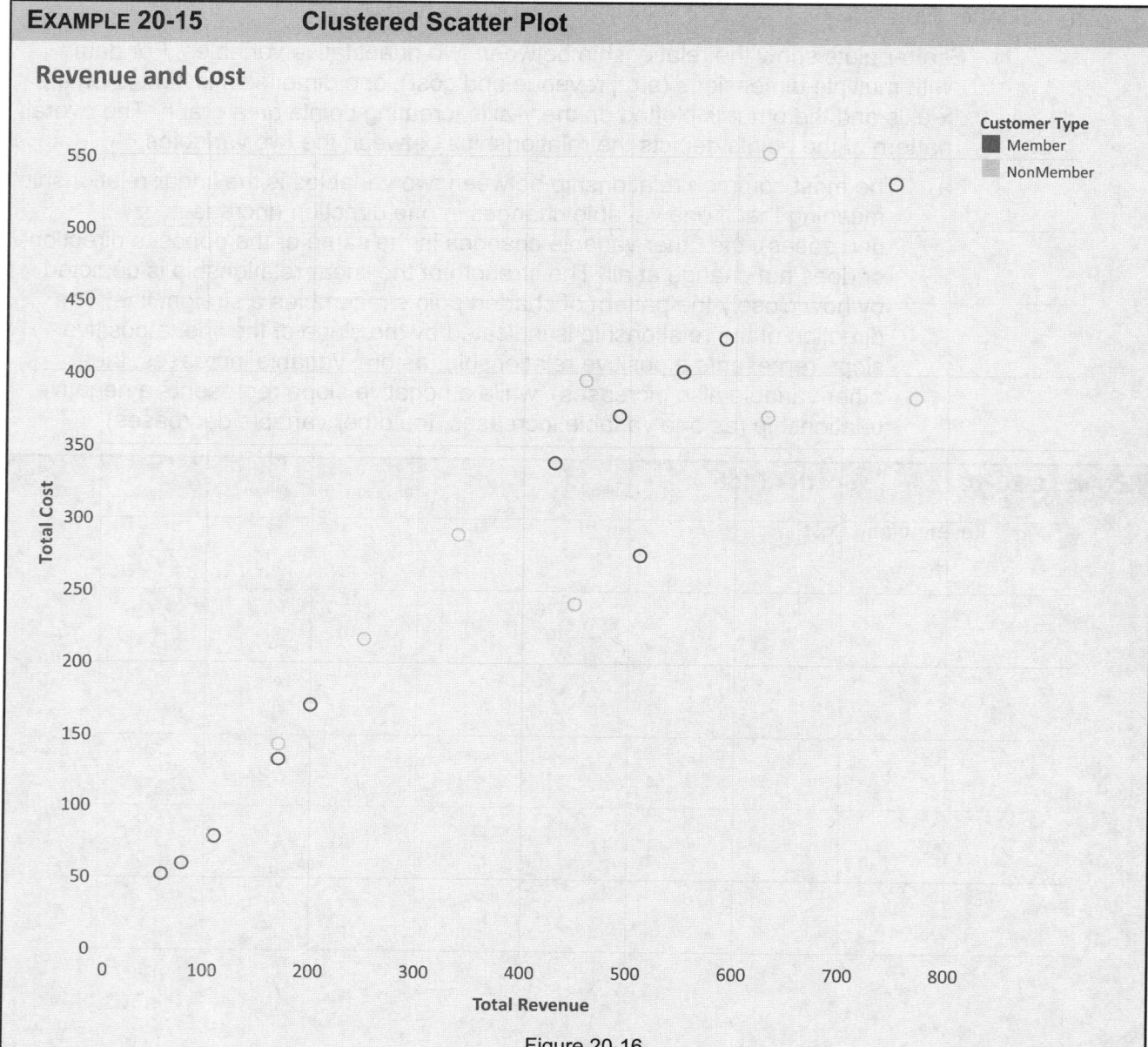

Figure 20-16

Besides plotting quantitative variables on the x- and y-axes, categorical (nonquantitative) variables can be added to a scatter plot and presented using different colors, symbols, etc.

The scatter plot above shows the relationship between revenue and cost, with the two different colors representing the data points for the two customer types (clusters). The following observations can be made:

1. The pattern of data points of members more closely resembles a straight line than that of nonmembers. This indicates that the linear relationship between revenue and cost is more significant for members than nonmembers.
2. The slopes for both clusters are positive, indicating the positive linear relationships between revenue and cost for both customer types.

i. Bubble Charts
   1) Bubble charts are similar to scatter plots, with two quantitative variables plotted on the x- and y-axes to depict the relationship between the variables. Bubble charts add a third variable to scatter plots by utilizing the sizes of the data points. That is, the relative sizes of the data points convey information about the third variable.

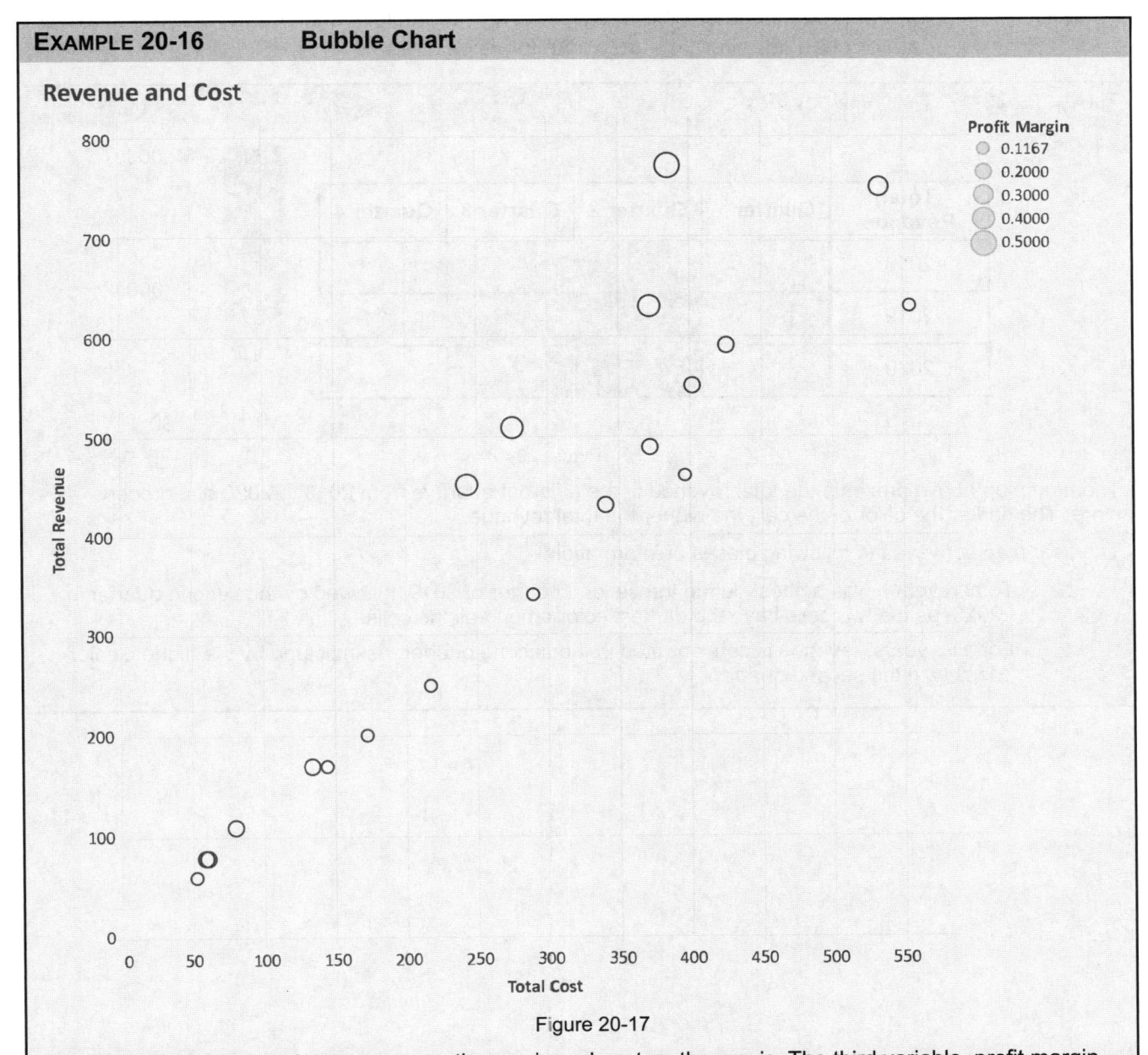

EXAMPLE 20-16   Bubble Chart

Revenue and Cost

[Bubble chart plotting Total Revenue (y-axis, 0 to 800) against Total Cost (x-axis, 0 to 550). Profit Margin legend: 0.1167, 0.2000, 0.3000, 0.4000, 0.5000.]

Figure 20-17

The bubble chart above plots revenue on the y-axis and cost on the x-axis. The third variable, profit margin, is depicted by the sizes of the data points. Besides the significance and direction of the linear relationship between revenue and cost, the sizes of the data points show that vouchers with higher revenues and/or higher costs tend to have higher profit margins.

j. Heat Maps

1) Heat maps present data using colors and shadings. Compared to tables, which present data in as close to their raw forms as possible, heat maps provide graphical presentations of data such that they are more understandable at a glance. Generally, greater values are represented by darker colors and lower values are represented by lighter colors. By observing the color density, the relative values of data or changes over time are more intuitive.

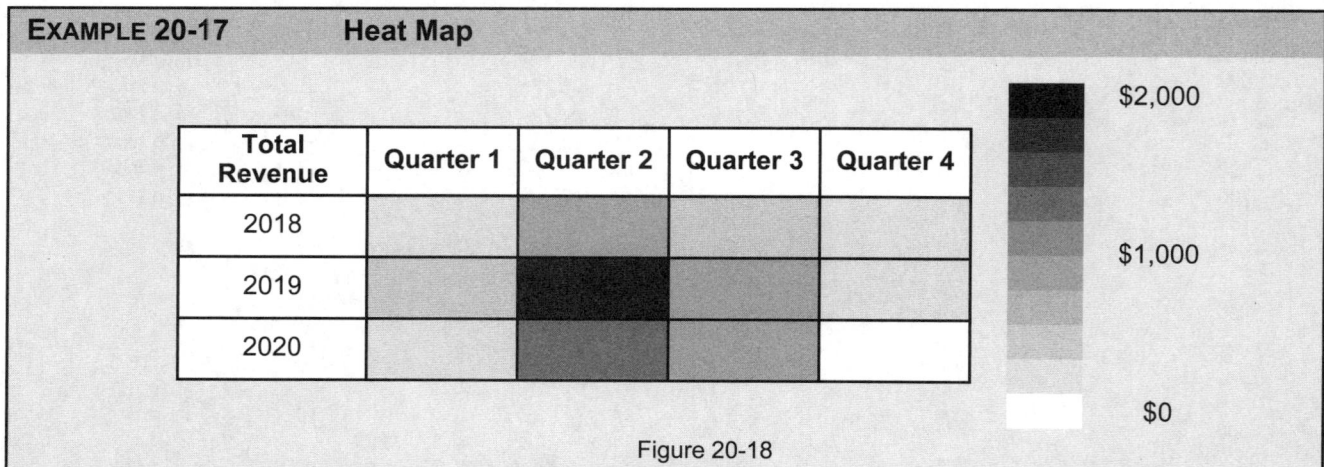

EXAMPLE 20-17   **Heat Map**

Total Revenue	Quarter 1	Quarter 2	Quarter 3	Quarter 4
2018				
2019				
2020				

Figure 20-18

The heat map above presents the total revenue in the different quarters from 2018 to 2020 of a grocery store. The darker the color of the cell, the higher the total revenue.

The heat map conveys the following pieces of information:

1. Total revenue was highest during the second quarter of 2019, followed by the second quarter in 2020, as the two cells have the darkest color among all the cells.
2. For all 3 years, revenue is concentrated in the second quarter, as indicated by the highest color density in the second quarter.

SU 20: Data Analytics

k. Choropleth (Filled Map)

1) A choropleth is a combination of a map and a heat map. It uses a color scale to visualize quantitative values across geographical areas. Generally, the darker the color for a geographical area on the choropleth, the greater the value, and vice versa. A choropleth is commonly used for data sets with greater amounts of geographical data (e.g., counties).

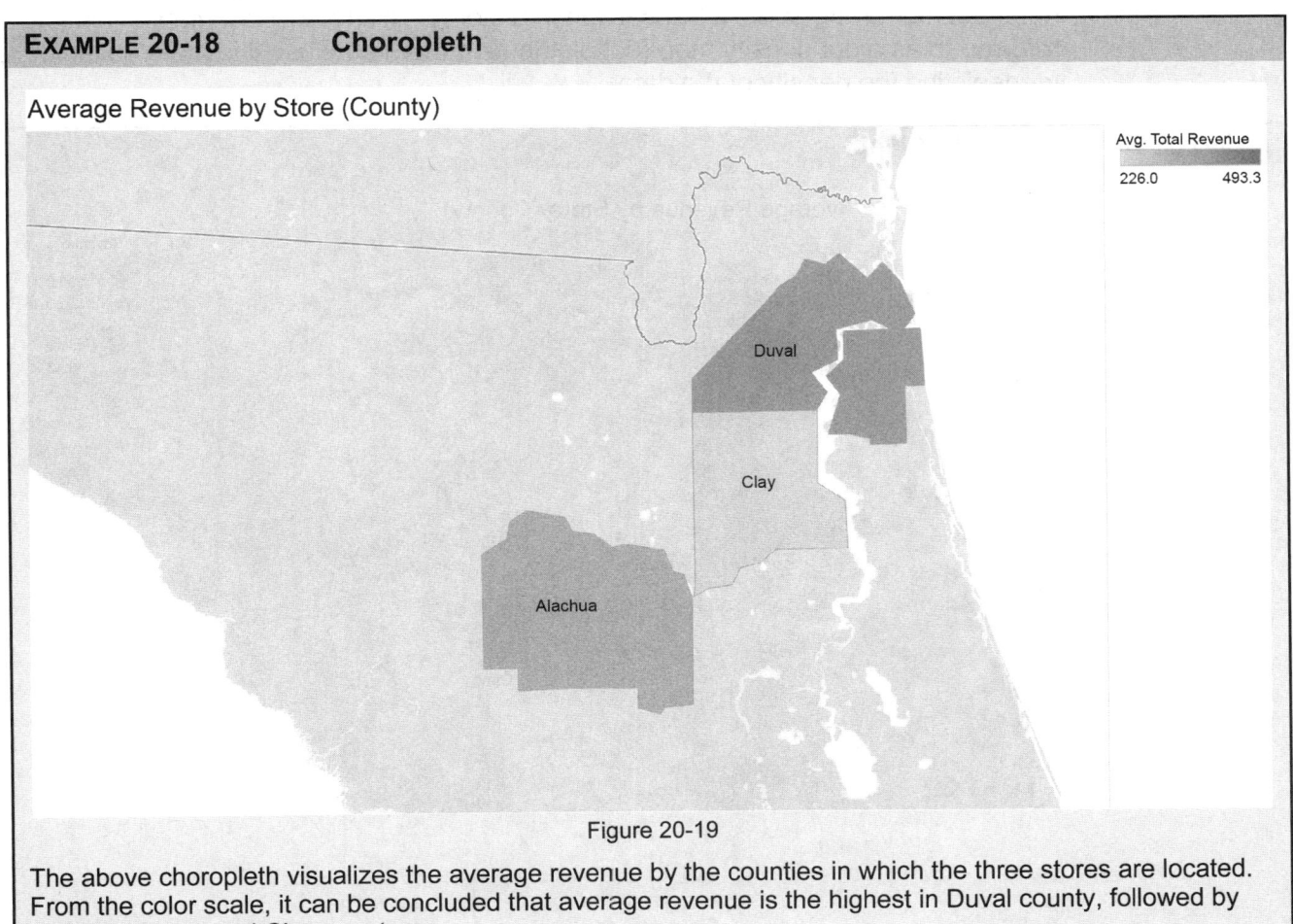

EXAMPLE 20-18   Choropleth

Average Revenue by Store (County)

Avg. Total Revenue
226.0   493.3

Figure 20-19

The above choropleth visualizes the average revenue by the counties in which the three stores are located. From the color scale, it can be concluded that average revenue is the highest in Duval county, followed by Alachua county and Clay county.

l. Dot maps

1) Dot maps are similar to choropleths except that quantitative values across geographical areas are visualized using dots with different sizes. Compared to choropleths, dot maps are commonly used for smaller data sets. Comparing quantitative data by color scale may be more intuitive than comparing it by size. Sometimes, dots with the same size are used to give equal weighting to the data (e.g., each dot represents a transaction in a store). This type of dot map is usually referred to as a dot density map (dot distribution map) because it is more suitable for depicting the density of the data.

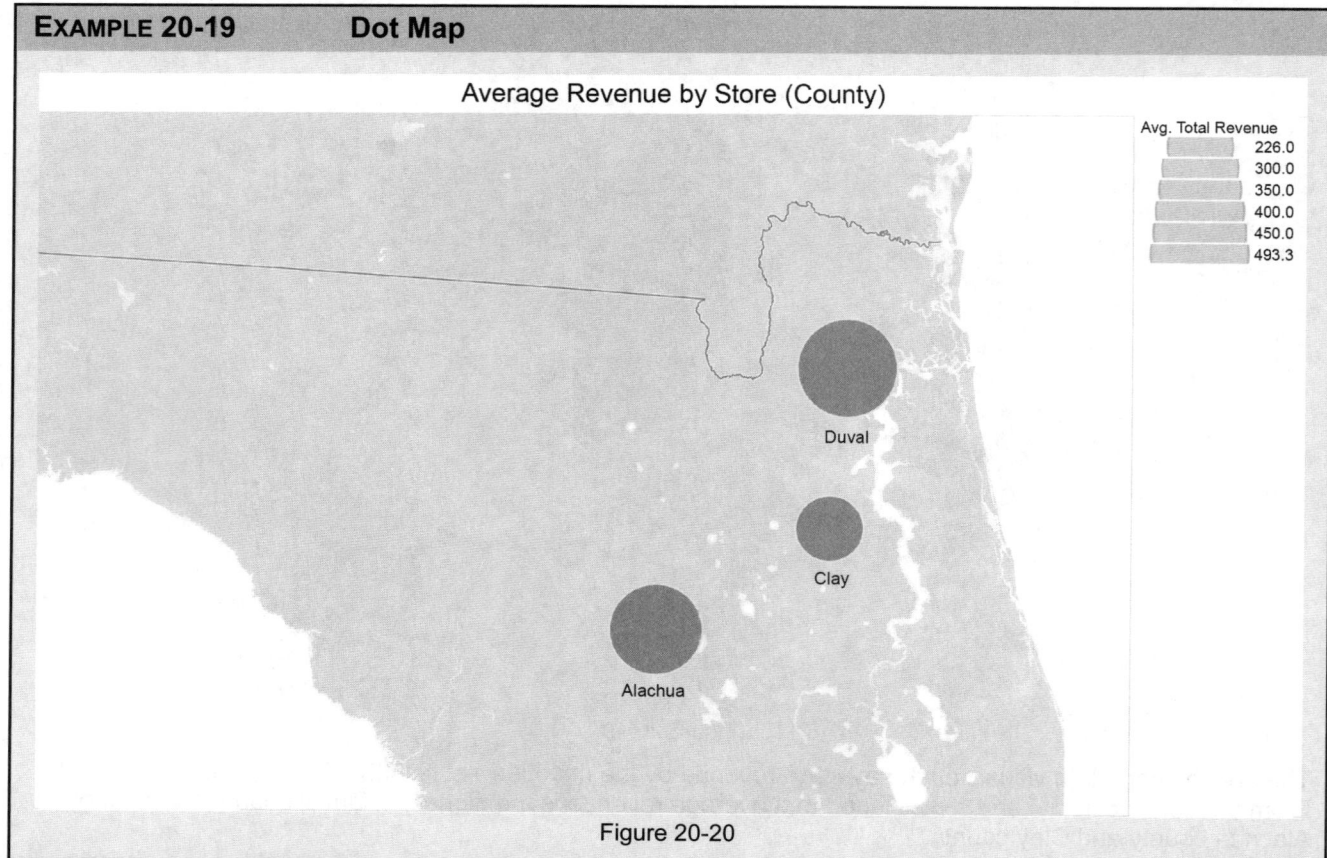

EXAMPLE 20-19 Dot Map

Average Revenue by Store (County)

Avg. Total Revenue
226.0
300.0
350.0
400.0
450.0
493.3

Figure 20-20

The above dot map presents the same information as the choropleth in Example 20-18. For smaller data sets (i.e., data sets with smaller geographical areas), comparison of dot sizes may be more intuitive than comparison of color scales.

m. Treemap

1) Treemaps provide an alternative way to present the composition of data besides pie charts and stacked bar graphs. Typically, treemaps are composed of rectangles of different colors and sizes. Colors are used for presenting categories of the data and sizes are used for presenting the quantitative values. One common application of treemaps is to show the composition of the stocks in a market index (e.g., S&P 500). The colors of the rectangles represent the industry to which the stock belongs, and the sizes of the rectangles represent the market values of the stock.

EXAMPLE 20-20   Treemap

Revenue by Store and by Product Line

Figure 20-21

The above treemap shows the total revenue by store and by product line. The three colors depict the stores, and the rectangles within each color depict the product lines. It conveys the following pieces of information:

1. The Alachua store accounted for the majority of total revenue.
2. The most profitable product line (in terms of revenue) for the Alachua store was health and beauty. Those for the Clay and Duval stores were home and lifestyle and sports and travel, respectively.
3. Revenue from the health and beauty product line from the Alachua store was greater than the total revenue of the Clay store or the Duval store (depicted by the sizes of the rectangles).

n. Combined Visualization

1) Combined visualization refers to the combination of types of visualization. It is often used to present two or more dimensions of a data set when the scales of the dimensions differ.

a) A common example is a dual-axis graph, which utilizes two y-axes (a primary y-axis and a secondary y-axis) to present two dimensions of a data set with different scales. For example, one may want to plot the revenue (in millions of dollars) and the revenue growth rate (in percentages) on the same graph. Due to the different scales of revenues and revenue growth rates, two y-axes can be used.

EXAMPLE 20-21   Dual-Axis Graph

Revenue and Growth By Quarter, 2019

Figure 20-22

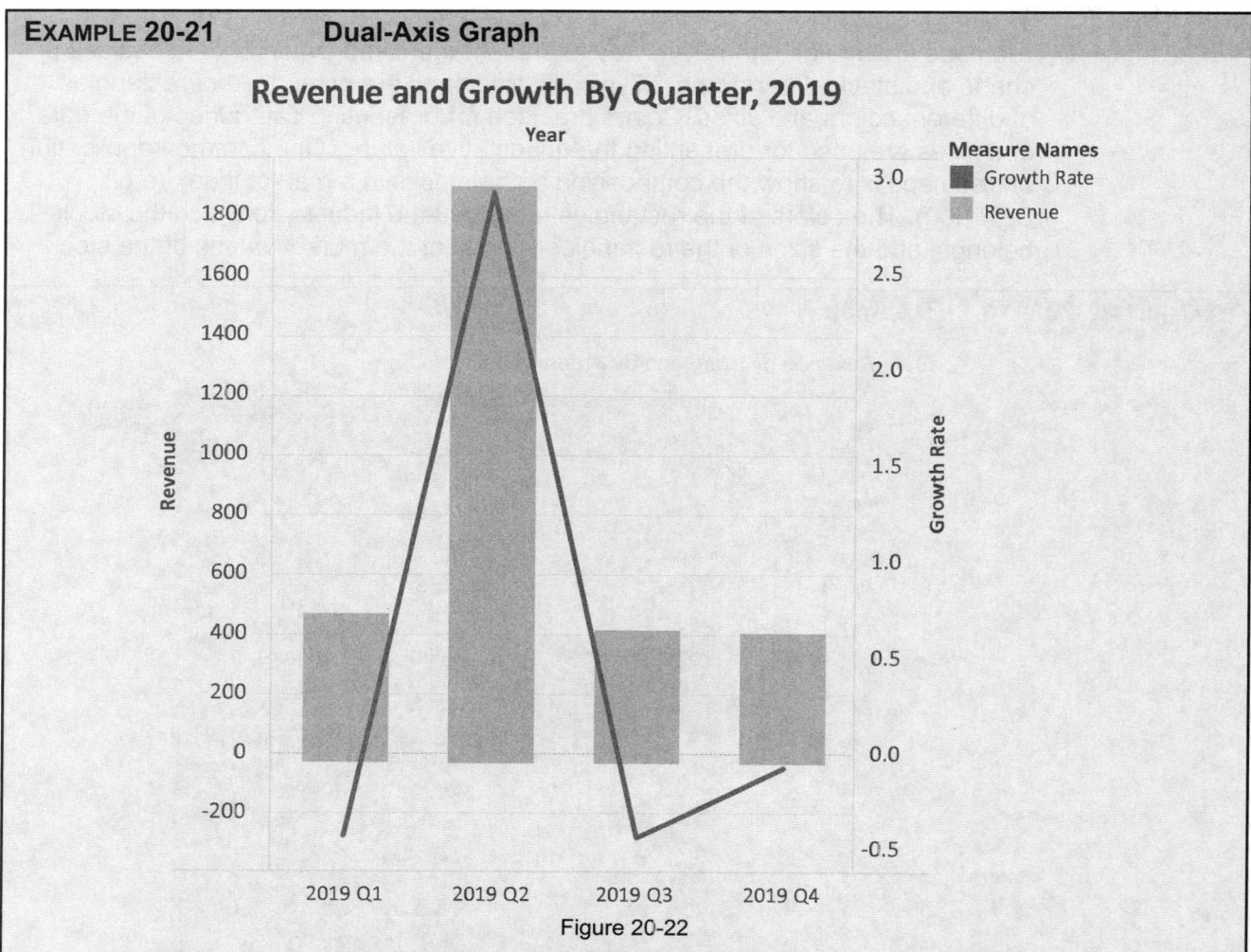

The dual-axis graph above shows the revenues and revenue growth rates by quarter in the year of 2019. The primary y-axis on the left plots the revenues and uses a bar graph to show the absolute magnitudes of the revenues. The secondary y-axis on the right plots the revenue growth rates and uses a line chart to present the changes in the growth rates.

From the line graph, it can be observed that the revenue growth rate changed from negative to positive (from a decline to growth) between the first and second quarter. The growth turned into a decline in the third quarter. In the fourth quarter, the rate of decline (indicated by a negative number) was much lower than that in the third quarter.

STOP & REVIEW

You have completed the outline for this subunit.
Study multiple-choice questions 13 through 20 beginning on page 632.

SU 20: Data Analytics

QUESTIONS

20.1 Definitions: Data Analytics

1. Which of the following is a correct statement regarding in-memory analytics?

A. It is an open source software framework that stores large amounts of data and runs applications on clusters of commodity hardware.

B. It analyzes data from system memory instead of hard drives.

C. It is a technology that uses data, statistical algorithms, and machine-learning techniques to identify the likelihood of future outcomes based on historical data.

D. It examines large amounts of data to discover patterns in the data.

Answer (B) is correct.
REQUIRED: The correct statement regarding in-memory analytics.
DISCUSSION: In-memory analytics analyzes data from system memory instead of hard drives.
Answer (A) is incorrect. Hadoop is an open source software framework that stores large amounts of data and runs applications on clusters of commodity hardware. **Answer (C) is incorrect.** Predictive analytics is technology that uses data, statistical algorithms, and machine-learning techniques to identify the likelihood of future outcomes based on historical data. **Answer (D) is incorrect.** Data mining examines large amounts of data to discover patterns in the data.

2. To ensure data quality, the IT department of a company establishes a master program to build standards for data quality. These standards are maintained and improved iteratively with inputs from personnel from different levels within the company. This process is an example of

A. Data management.
B. Data mining.
C. Data scrubbing.
D. Data normalization.

Answer (A) is correct.
REQUIRED: The term describing the tasks performed.
DISCUSSION: Data need to be high-quality and well-governed in order to be reliably analyzed. Data management consists of repeatable processes to ensure data quality and governance by establishing a master data management program and to build and maintain standards for data quality.
Answer (B) is incorrect. Data mining examines large amounts of data to discover patterns, usually unexpected, in the data. The examination of data is performed after data quality is ensured. **Answer (C) is incorrect.** Data scrubbing (cleaning) consists of, but is not limited to, flushing out useless information and identifying missing data. Although data scrubbing increases data quality, it does not encompass building and maintaining standards for data quality. Data quality standards are set before data scrubbing is performed. **Answer (D) is incorrect.** Data normalization involves storing each data element as few times as necessary. Although data normalization increases data quality, it does not encompass building and maintaining data quality standards.

20.2 Big Data and Data Analytics

3. Financial statements and their notes are examples of

	Financial Statements	Notes to Financial Statements
A.	Structured data	Structured data
B.	Structured data	Unstructured data
C.	Unstructured data	Unstructured data
D.	Unstructured data	Structured data

Answer (B) is correct.
REQUIRED: The classification of data.
DISCUSSION: Structured data refers to data that are highly organized into predefined groupings and typically maintained in relational databases. The data are predefined such that each item falls into a specific anticipated data type. Unstructured data refers to information that has little or no predefined organizational structure, which makes it more difficult for computer programs to search, sort, and analyze. Financial statement amounts are reported in XBRL and stored as floats that can easily be sorted and searched by computer programs. Notes to financial statements usually have little predefined organizational structure and are difficult to sort and analyze using computer programs.
Answer (A) is incorrect. Notes to financial statements are usually not organized into predefined groupings and are difficult to sort and analyze using computer programs. **Answer (C) is incorrect.** Financial statements can be organized into predefined groupings and can be easily searched, sorted, and analyzed by computer programs. **Answer (D) is incorrect.** Financial statement amounts can be organized into predefined groupings and can be easily searched, sorted, and analyzed by computer programs. Notes to financial statements are usually not organized into predefined groupings and are difficult to sort and analyze using computer programs.

4. All of the following are correct statements regarding big data **except**

A. Big data is an evolving term that describes any voluminous amount of structured, semi-structured, and unstructured data that has the potential to be mined for information.

B. Big data includes information collected from social media, data from Internet-enabled devices, machine data, video, and voice recordings. The information collected is converted from high-density data into low-density data.

C. Big data is often characterized by the "4 Vs" - volume, variety, velocity, and veracity.

D. Big data processes data with analytic and algorithmic tools to reveal meaningful information.

Answer (B) is correct.
REQUIRED: The false statement about big data.
DISCUSSION: Big data includes information collected from social media, data from Internet-enabled devices, machine data, video, and voice recordings. The information collected is converted from low-density data into high-density data, not from high-density data to low-density data.

5. Which of the following best describes unstructured data?

A. Data with a high level of organization.
B. Data systematically stored with markers to enforce hierarchies of records and fields within the data.
C. Information that is not organized in a pre-defined manner (e.g., text-heavy facts, dates, numbers, and images).
D. Conforms with the organization of data models associated with relational databases.

Answer (C) is correct.
   REQUIRED: The description of unstructured data.
   DISCUSSION: Unstructured data refers to information that is not organized in a pre-defined manner (e.g., text-heavy facts, dates, numbers, and images).
   Answer (A) is incorrect. Structured data refers to data with a high level of organization. **Answer (B) is incorrect.** Semi-structured data does not conform with the formal structure of data models associated with relational databases or other forms of data tables; however, markers exist to enforce hierarchies of records and fields within the data. **Answer (D) is incorrect.** Structured data conforms with the organization of data models associated with relational databases.

6. Each of the following represents a characteristic of big data **except**

A. Size.
B. Mixture.
C. Speed.
D. Uniformity.

Answer (D) is correct.
   REQUIRED: The item not a characteristic of big data.
   DISCUSSION: Big data is often characterized by the "4 Vs" - volume, variety, velocity, and veracity. Thus, uniformity is not a characteristic of big data.

7. A company uses big data analytics in marketing. Which of the following is a limitation of using big data?

A. The company can use big data to predict customer behaviors.
B. Data results cannot be visualized to identify and forecast customer trends.
C. Big data often cannot explain why customers behave in certain ways.
D. Data collected only represent untapped customers but not tapped customers.

Answer (C) is correct.
   REQUIRED: The limitation of using big data.
   DISCUSSION: One limitation of big data is that determining why the analysis results are what they are is difficult. While big data analysis can show that there is a certain pattern in monthly sales, it fails to show what causes the pattern. Further and more complicated analyses are needed, the results of which tend to be more difficult for non-technical people to understand.
   Answer (A) is incorrect. Predicting customer behaviors is an advantage of big data. **Answer (B) is incorrect.** Data results can usually be visualized using data visualization tools to enhance understanding. **Answer (D) is incorrect.** Generally, the data available to an organization are restricted to data obtained from individuals who visited the organization's Internet resources (i.e., website) or viewed the organization's advertisement on the Internet. Thus, collected data is more likely to be from tapped customers than untapped customers.

8. The Department of Transportation collects and combines acoustic, image, and other sensor data to better monitor the real-time traffic of a city. This is an example of

A. Data scrubbing.
B. Data normalization.
C. Data fusion.
D. Data mining.

Answer (C) is correct.
REQUIRED: The term describing the tasks performed.
DISCUSSION: Acoustic, image, and other sensor data are individual sources of data. The combination of the individual sources of data to better monitor real-time traffic is an example of data fusion, the process of integrating data and knowledge representing the same real-world object into a more consistent, accurate, and useful representation than their individual sources.
Answer (A) is incorrect. Data scrubbing (cleaning) consists of, but is not limited to, flushing out useless information and identifying missing data. Integrating data from different sensors does not involve data cleaning. **Answer (B) is incorrect.** Data normalization involves storing each data element as few times as necessary. Data normalization does not involve the integration of different sources of data to derive more insights than the individual sources. **Answer (D) is incorrect.** Data mining examines large amounts of data to discover patterns, usually unexpected, in the data. The purpose of integrating data from different sources to monitor the real-time traffic is not to discover unexpected patterns.

20.3 Implementing Data Analytics

9. Which of the following best represents the application of predictive analytics?

A. The human resource manager prepares an analysis to show which departments have the highest employee turnover.
B. The website recommends pet toys and bedding after the customer purchases pet food.
C. A consultant organizes an analysis of causation for dissatisfied workers and possible interactions among causes.
D. A cost accountant monitors whether direct materials used are within the acceptable variations for the last 6 months.

Answer (B) is correct.
REQUIRED: The example of predictive analysis.
DISCUSSION: A common use of predictive analytics in the retail sector occurs when a customer selects an item to purchase online and prepares to finalize the transaction; the web page then displays additional products other customers purchased in conjunction with the initial item.
Answer (A) is incorrect. This example represents the application of pareto diagrams. A pareto diagram can be used to rank the departments based on the employee turnover and assist the manager to identify the departments having the greatest employee turnover. **Answer (C) is incorrect.** This example represents the application of fishbone diagrams. A fishbone diagram is a total quality management process improvement method that is useful in studying causation (why the actual and desired situations differ). **Answer (D) is incorrect.** This example represents the application of statistical control charts. Statistical control charts are graphic aids for monitoring the status of any process subject to acceptable or unacceptable variations during repeated operations.

10. Under which category of data analysis should "anomaly detection" be classified?

A. Descriptive analysis.
B. Diagnostic analysis.
C. Predictive analysis.
D. Prescriptive analysis.

Answer (A) is correct.
REQUIRED: The category of data analysis under which anomaly detection is classified.
DISCUSSION: The purpose of anomaly detection is to identify unusual patterns or deviations from the norm or expected results. The focus of anomaly detection is on the reporting of historical information (i.e., descriptive analysis).
Answer (B) is incorrect. The focus of anomaly detection is on the reporting of an anomaly; it does not identify the root cause of the anomaly. **Answer (C) is incorrect.** The focus of anomaly detection is on the reporting of an anomaly; it does not forecast future results. **Answer (D) is incorrect.** The focus of anomaly detection is on the reporting of an anomaly; it does not identify the actions that should be taken to realize a predicted future result.

11. The type of data analytics that is most likely to yield the most impact for an organization but is also the most complex is called

A. Diagnostic analysis.
B. Predictive analysis.
C. Descriptive analysis.
D. Prescriptive analysis.

Answer (D) is correct.
REQUIRED: The type of data analytics that is the most complex but is likely to yield the most impact.
DISCUSSION: Prescriptive analysis uses descriptive, diagnostic, and predictive analytics to improve business strategy. It concentrates on what an organization needs to do in order for the predicted future results to actually occur. This type of analytics provides the most benefit but requires the most inputs.
Answer (A) is incorrect. Diagnostic analysis provides insight into the reason certain results occur. It is not the most complex type of data analytics. **Answer (B) is incorrect.** Predictive analysis examines historical information to determine what will happen in the future. It involves applying assumptions to data and predicting future results. It is less complex than prescriptive analysis. **Answer (C) is incorrect.** Descriptive analysis concentrates on reporting historical information, such as financial results. It is the most basic and most used method.

12. Fishbone diagrams are most often used in

A. Descriptive analysis.
B. Diagnostic analysis.
C. Predictive analysis.
D. Prescriptive analysis.

Answer (B) is correct.
REQUIRED: The type of analytics in which fishbone diagrams are most often used.
DISCUSSION: A fishbone diagram is a total quality management process improvement method that is useful in studying causation (why the actual and desired situations differ). It is often used in diagnostic analysis, which provides insights into the reason certain results occur.
Answer (A) is incorrect. A fishbone diagram is often used to study causation but not to report historical information. **Answer (C) is incorrect.** A fishbone diagram is not used to predict future results. **Answer (D) is incorrect.** A fishbone diagram shows only the possible causes of an event and does not provide insights into what needs to be done.

20.4 Data Visualization

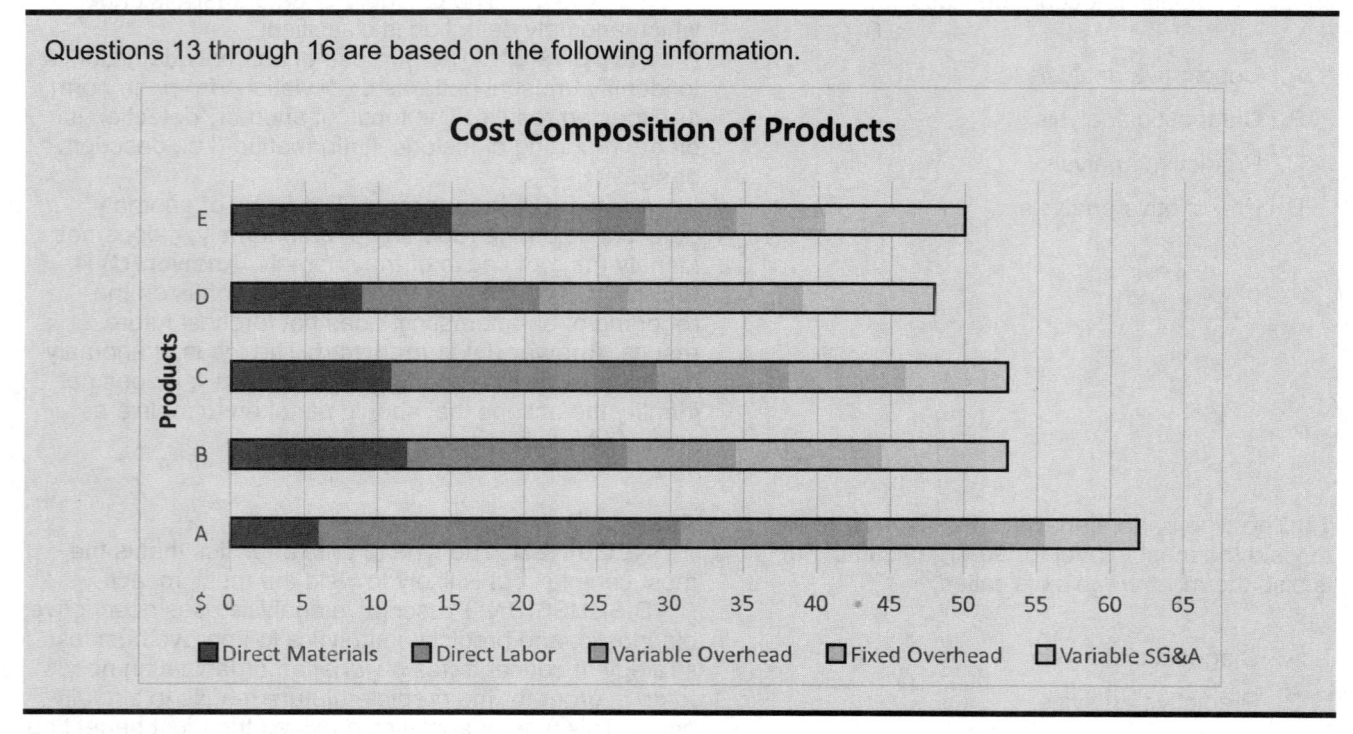

Questions 13 through 16 are based on the following information.

Cost Composition of Products

(Horizontal stacked bar chart showing Products A–E with cost categories: Direct Materials, Direct Labor, Variable Overhead, Fixed Overhead, Variable SG&A, on a $ scale from 0 to 65.)

13. Which of the following is a **false** conclusion regarding Product A?

A. Product costs for Product A are the highest among the products.
B. Period costs for Product A are the highest among the products.
C. Direct costs for Product A are the highest among the products.
D. Indirect costs for Product A are the highest among the products.

Answer (B) is correct.
REQUIRED: The false conclusion drawn from a visualization.
DISCUSSION: Period costs are costs that are expensed as incurred but not capitalized as part of inventory. In the cost categories listed in the visualization, the selling, general, and administrative (SG&A) costs are the period costs. Among the five products, Product A does not have the highest period costs (i.e., the bar for SG&A costs is not the longest).
Answer (A) is incorrect. Product costs are costs that are capitalized as part of inventory. In the cost categories listed in the visualization, all costs are product costs except for selling, general, and administrative (SG&A) costs. Among the five products, Product A has the highest product costs (i.e., the total length of the bars representing the product costs is the highest). **Answer (C) is incorrect.** Direct costs are costs that can be directly traced to a cost object in an economically feasible way. In the cost categories listed in the visualization, direct materials and direct labor costs are direct costs. Among the five products, direct costs for Product A are the highest (i.e., the total length of the bars representing direct materials and direct labor costs is the highest). **Answer (D) is incorrect.** Indirect costs are costs that cannot be directly traced to a cost object in an economically feasible way. In the cost categories listed in the visualization, variable and fixed overhead costs are indirect costs. Among the five products, indirect costs for Product A are the highest (i.e., the total length of the bars representing variable and fixed overhead costs is the highest).

14. Which of the following conclusions can be drawn from the visualization?

A. The range for product costs of the five products is between $48 and $62.

B. Variable costs of Product B are higher than those of Product C.

C. The ratio of direct labor cost to total cost for Product C is higher than that for Product B.

D. The price of Product A is the highest among the products.

Answer (C) is correct.
REQUIRED: The true conclusion drawn from the visualization.
DISCUSSION: Product B has the same total costs as Product C but lower direct labor costs than Product C. Thus, the ratio of direct labor cost to total cost for Product C is higher than that for Product B.
Answer (A) is incorrect. The range for total costs, not product costs, of the five products is between $48 and $62. **Answer (B) is incorrect.** Variable costs in the cost categories presented in the visualization are all costs except fixed overhead costs. Product B has the same total costs as Product C but higher fixed overhead costs than Product C. Therefore, variable costs of Product B are lower than those of Product C. **Answer (D) is incorrect.** The visualization presents only information about costs. Without additional information about prices (e.g., pricing method and profit margins), conclusions about prices cannot be made.

15. What is the approximate ratio between direct materials costs and product costs for Product E?

A. 30%
B. 37%
C. 43%
D. 54%

Answer (B) is correct.
REQUIRED: The ratio between two cost categories in a visualization.
DISCUSSION: Direct materials costs for Product E are $15 per unit. Product costs of Product E are the sum of direct materials costs, direct labor costs, and variable and fixed overhead costs, which are approximately $40. Thus, the ratio between direct materials costs and product costs for Product E is about 37% ($15 ÷ $40).
Answer (A) is incorrect. The ratio between direct materials costs and total costs of Product E is 30%. **Answer (C) is incorrect.** The ratio between direct materials costs and total variable product costs of Product E is 43%. **Answer (D) is incorrect.** The ratio between direct materials costs and direct costs of Product E is 54%.

16. Rank the products in ascending order of direct labor costs.

A. E, B, C, D, A.
B. A, C, B, E, D.
C. A, D, C, B, E.
D. D, E, B, C, A.

Answer (D) is correct.
REQUIRED: The ranking of products in terms of direct labor costs.
DISCUSSION: The direct labor costs of the five products can be compared by the relative lengths of the bars. Among the five products, Product D has the shortest bar for direct labor costs, followed by Products E, B, C, and A, indicating that the ranking in ascending order of direct labor costs is D, E, B, C, A.
Answer (A) is incorrect. This order is the ranking in descending order of direct materials costs. **Answer (B) is incorrect.** This order is the ranking in descending order of direct labor costs. **Answer (C) is incorrect.** This order is the ranking in ascending order of direct materials costs.

17. Which of the following is a true statement regarding data visualization?

A. Data visualization is the use of computers to convey information.
B. Data visualization is always the most appropriate way for presenting data.
C. Data visualization can take various forms.
D. Data visualization tends to convey more complete information than raw data.

Answer (C) is correct.
REQUIRED: The true statement about data visualization.
DISCUSSION: Data visualization may take various forms depending on the purposes and needs of a given situation. Examples of data visualization includes tables, graphs, charts, maps, and images.
Answer (A) is incorrect. Data visualization is not limited to the use of computers to convey information. It has been available since before computers were invented. **Answer (B) is incorrect.** Data can be presented in various ways and through various media, including data visualization. Depending on the purposes and needs in certain circumstances, data visualization may not be the most appropriate way to present data. **Answer (D) is incorrect.** Data visualization conveys information in a more visually appealing way. However, compared to raw data, completeness of information may be sacrificed in data visualization.

18. Match the following purposes with the elements of data visualization.

	Help convey how data are measured and presented	Provide additional information for understanding the visualization
A.	Title	Legend(s)
B.	Presentation	Legend(s)
C.	Presentation	Axes
D.	Axes	Legend(s)

Answer (D) is correct.
REQUIRED: The purposes of data visualization elements.
DISCUSSION: Axes convey how the data are measured and presented through the use of (1) labels (i.e., what the axis measures and presents), (2) range (i.e., whether the axis captures all the data), and (3) scale (i.e., the intervals or scaling used to present data). Legends provide additional information that helps users understand the visualization. They usually provide an explanation about the different colors, shapes, and sizes depicted in the visualization.
Answer (A) is incorrect. A title helps establish an expectation of the information presented (i.e., what information is presented) but not how data are measured and presented. **Answer (B) is incorrect.** Presentation determines whether the way in which the data are presented can be utilized to achieve the objectives. Presentation focuses on objective achievement but not how data are measured and presented. An accurately measured and presented visualization may not achieve the desired objectives. **Answer (C) is incorrect.** Presentation determines whether the way in which the data are presented can be utilized to achieve the objectives. Presentation focuses on objective achievement but not how data are measured and presented. Also, axes do not provide additional information for understanding the visualization.

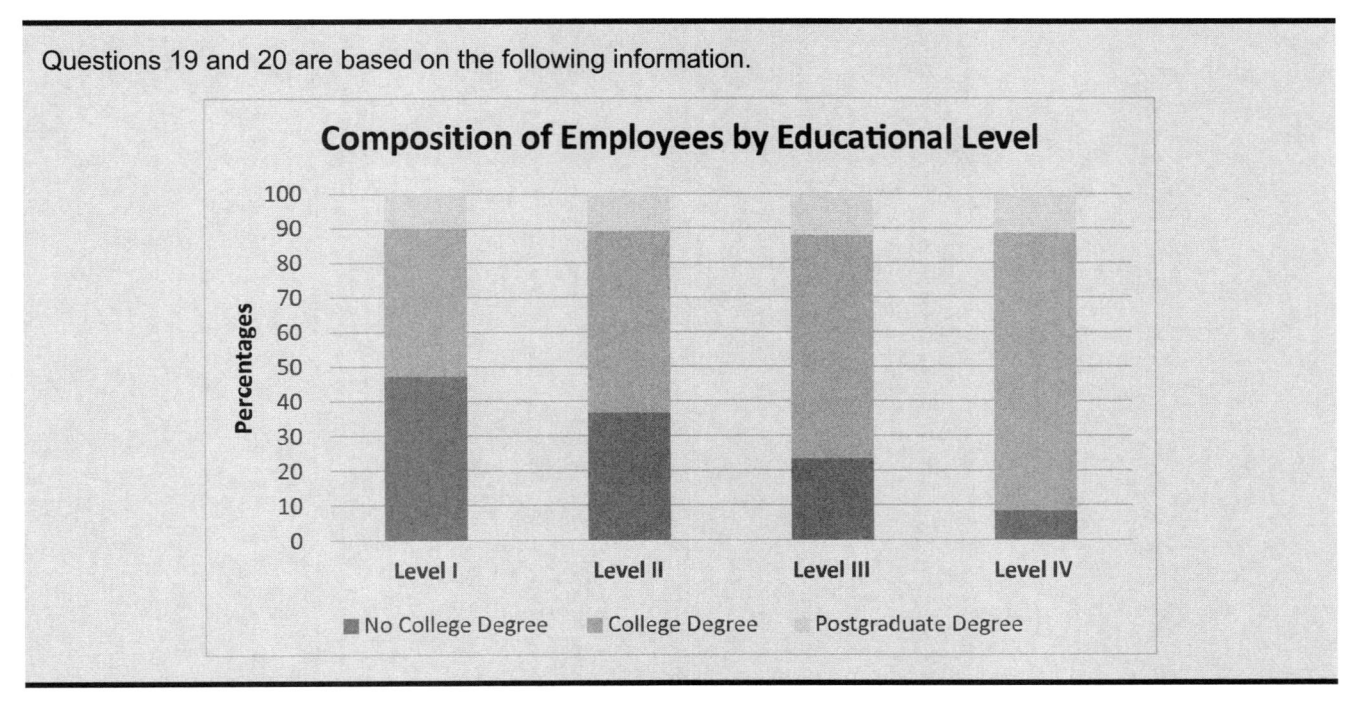

Questions 19 and 20 are based on the following information.

Composition of Employees by Educational Level

[Bar chart showing percentages across Level I, Level II, Level III, and Level IV, with categories: No College Degree, College Degree, Postgraduate Degree]

19. What is the approximate percentage of Level III employees with a college degree or above?

A. 52%
B. 65%
C. 77%
D. 92%

Answer (C) is correct.
REQUIRED: The percentage of Level III employees with a college degree or above.
DISCUSSION: Employees with a college degree or above include those with a college degree and those with a postgraduate degree. The percentage of Level III employees without a college degree is about 23%. Thus, the percentage of Level III employees with a college degree or above is about 77% (100% − 23%).
Answer (A) is incorrect. The percentage of Level II employees with a college degree is 52%. **Answer (B) is incorrect.** The amount of 65% excludes the percentage of Level III employees with a postgraduate degree. **Answer (D) is incorrect.** The percentage of Level IV employees with a college degree or above is 92%.

20. Which of the following is a true conclusion based on the visualization?

A. Level IV contains the largest number of employees with a college degree.
B. Employees with a college degree account for the majority of employees among the four levels.
C. Employees with a college degree account for the majority of Level II employees.
D. The higher the level of employment, the higher the proportion of employees with a postgraduate degree.

Answer (C) is correct.
REQUIRED: The true conclusion based on the visualization.
DISCUSSION: Among the three categories of Level II employees, employees with a college degree account for about 52% (90% − 38%).
Answer (A) is incorrect. A 100% stacked bar graph shows only the relative percentages, not the absolute number of employees. **Answer (B) is incorrect.** Among Level I employees, employees without a college degree are a larger proportion than those with a college degree. **Answer (D) is incorrect.** The proportion of Level IV employees with a postgraduate degree is lower than that of Level III employees.

APPENDIX A
ACRONYMS

ABC	Activity-based costing	DTL	Degree of total (combined) leverage
ACL	Audit command language	EAR	Earnings at risk
AD	Aggregate demand	EBIT	Earnings before interest and taxes
AFC	Average fixed costs	EDI	Electronic data interchange
AI	Artificial intelligence	EFT	Electronic funds transfer
AIS	Accounting information system	EIS	Executive information system
AS	Aggregate supply	EMH	Efficient market hypothesis
ATC	Average total costs	EOQ	Economic order quantity
AVC	Average variable costs	EPS	Earnings per share
B2A	Business-to-Administration e-commerce	ERM	Enterprise risk management
B2B	Business-to-Business e-commerce	ERP	Enterprise resource planning
B2C	Business-to-Consumer e-commerce	ESS	Executive support system
BASIC	Beginner's All-purpose Symbolic Instruction Code	EUC	End-user computing
		EUP	Equivalent units of production
BCM	Business continuity management	EVA	Economic value added
BI	Business intelligence	FC	Total fixed costs
BIS	Business information system	FDIC	Federal deposit insurance corporation
BPR	Business process reengineering	FIFO	First-in, first-out
C2A	Consumer-to-Administration e-commerce	FOH	Fixed overhead
C2B	Consumer-to-Business e-commerce	FOMC	Federal Open Market Committee
C2C	Consumer-to-Consumer e-commerce	FV	Future value
CAAT	Computer-assisted audit techniques	GAS	Generalized audit software
CAPM	Capital asset pricing model	GDSS	Group decision support system
CASE	Computer-aided software engineering	GDP	Gross domestic product
CD	Certificates of deposit	GL/FRS	General ledger/financial reporting system
CEO	Chief executive officer	HTML	Hypertext markup language
CFAR	Cash flow at risk	HTTP	Hypertext transfer protocol
CIO	Chief information officer	IaaS	Infrastructure-as-a-Service
CMR	Contribution margin ratio	IDEA	Interactive data extraction and analysis
COBIT	Control objectives for information and related technology	IPO	Initial public offering
		IRM	Information resources management
COBOL	COmmon Business-Oriented Language	IS	Information systems
COGS	Cost of goods sold	ISO	International Organization for Standardization
CPI	Consumer price index		
CPM	COBIT performance management	ISP	Internet service provider
CRM	Customer relationship management	IT	Information technology
CSF	Critical success factor	ITIL	Information Technology Infrastructure Library
CTO	Chief technology officer		
CV	Coefficient of variation	IRR	Internal rate of return
CVP	Cost-volume-profit	JIT	Just-in-time
DBA	Database administrator	LAN	Local-area network
DBMS	Database management system	LCL	Lower control limit
DDoS	Distributed denial-of-service attack	LIFO	Last-in, first out
DFL	Degree of financial leverage	LRATC	Long-run average total cost
DFT	Demand flow technology	MC	Marginal cost
DI	Disposable income	MIS	Management information system
DOL	Degree of operating leverage	MPC	Marginal propensity to consume
DoS	Denial-of-service attack	MR	Marginal revenue
DRP	Disaster recovery plan	MRP	Marginal revenue product
DSS	Decision support system	MRP	Materials requirements planning

MRP II	Manufacturing resource planning
MRS	Management reporting system
NDP	Net domestic product
NI	National income
NPV	Net present value
NRV	Net realizable value
OLAP	Online analytical processing
PaaS	Platform-as-a-Service
PCAOB	Public Company Accounting Oversight Board
PI	Personal income
POS	Point-of-sale
PV	Present value
QMS	Quality management system
RAID	Redundant array of inexpensive disks
RAM	Random access memory
REA	Resources, events, agents
ROA	Return on assets
ROCE	Return on common equity
ROE	Return on equity
ROI	Return on investment
ROS	Return on sales
RPA	Robotic process automation
RSS	Rich site summary
SaaS	Software-as-a-Service
SBU	Strategic business unit
SDLC	Systems development life cycle
SEC	Securities and Exchange Commission
SML	Security market line
SOX	Sarbanes-Oxley Act of 2002
SPC	Statistical process control
SQL	Structured query language
SRAS	Short-run aggregate supply
SRATC	Short-run average total cost
TCP/IP	Transmission Control Protocol/Internet Protocol
TOC	Theory of constraints
TPS	Transaction processing system
TQM	Total quality management
UCL	Upper control limit
UCM	Unit contribution margin
URL	Uniform resource locator
VAN	Value-added network
VAR	Market value at risk
VPN	Virtual private network
VC	Total variable costs
VOH	Variable overhead
WACC	Weighted-average cost of capital
WAN	Wide area network
XBRL	eXtensible business reporting language
XML	eXtensible markup language

APPENDIX B
OPTIMIZING YOUR SCORE ON THE TASK-BASED SIMULATIONS (TBSs) AND WRITTEN COMMUNICATIONS (WCs)

Each section of the CPA Exam contains multiple testlets of Task-Based Simulations. The number of TBS testlets and the number of TBSs in each testlet are the same for each exam section except BEC.

TBSs per Exam Section

	Testlet 3	Testlet 4	Testlet 5	Total
AUD	2	3	3	8
BEC	2	2	N/A*	4
FAR	2	3	3	8
REG	2	3	3	8

*Testlet 5 of BEC is Written Communications.

Task-Based Simulations are constructive response questions with information presented either with the question or in separate exhibits. Question responses may be in the form of entering amounts into a spreadsheet, choosing the correct answer from a list in a pop-up box, or reviewing and completing or correcting a draft of a document. In the AUD, FAR, and REG exam sections, you will also have to complete a Research task, which requires you to research the relevant authoritative literature and cite the appropriate guidance as indicated. You will not have to complete a Research task in BEC.

In the BEC section of the exam, your last testlet will be the written communication tasks, which test your ability to logically organize and communicate information. This testlet will contain three written communication scenarios (two graded, one pretest) that you must respond to in the form of a memo by typing with a word processor.

It is not productive to practice TBSs or WCs on paper. Instead, you should use your online Gleim CPA Review Course to complete truly interactive TBSs and WCs that emulate exactly how they are tested on the CPA Exam. As a CPA candidate, you must become an expert on how to approach TBSs and WCs, how to budget your time in the last three testlets, and the different types of TBSs. This appendix covers all of these topics for you and includes examples of typical TBSs and WCs. Use this appendix only as an introduction to TBSs and WCs, and then practice hundreds of exam-emulating TBSs and WCs in your Gleim CPA Review Course.

TASK-BASED SIMULATIONS

Toolbar Icons and Operations

The following information and toolbar icons are located at the top of the testlet screen of each TBS. All screenshots are taken from the AICPA Sample Test (www.aicpa.org). The examples that follow are taken from our online course. The CPA Exam, the Sample Test, and all screenshots are Copyright 2021 by the AICPA with All Rights Reserved. The AICPA requires all candidates to review the Sample Tests and Tutorials before sitting for the CPA Exam.

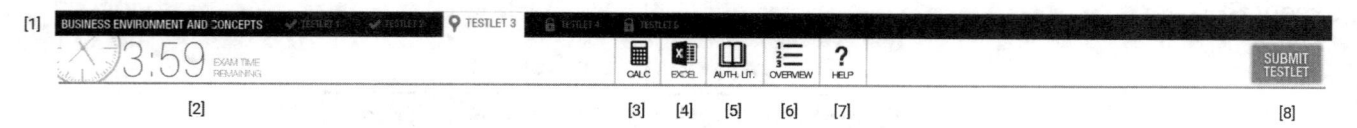

1. **Exam Section and Testlet Number:** The testlet number will always be 3 or 4 of 5 for the simulations in BEC.
2. **Time Remaining:** This information box displays how much time you have remaining in the entire exam. Consistently check the amount of time remaining to stay on schedule.
3. **Calculator:** The calculator icon launches a basic tool for simple computations. It is similar to calculators used in common software programs. The calculator tape is saved and accessible throughout the entire testlet; it does not clear until a new testlet is entered or the "Clear Tape" function is employed. Numbers (but not text) can be copied and pasted between the calculator, any exhibits, the question content and answer fields, and Excel.

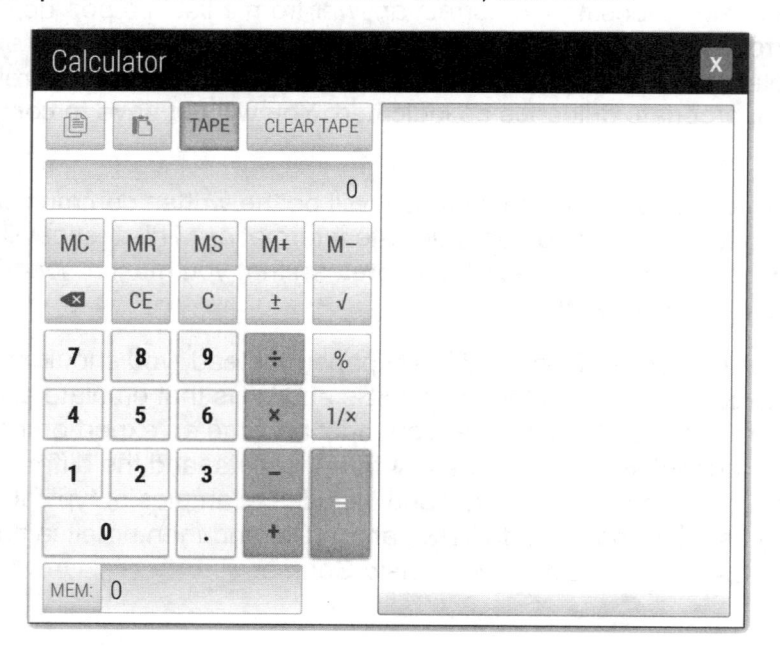

4. **Excel:** Instead of the proprietary spreadsheet used previously, candidates have access to the desktop version of Excel, which launches by clicking the spreadsheet icon found in the top toolbar.
    - The exam spreadsheet will perform the same essential functions as a regular desktop Excel spreadsheet.
    - Candidates can easily transfer data out of and into Excel, for example, by copying from Excel and pasting to the answer fields of a simulation or into the calculator, and vice versa. Excel will retain all of the information entered while in a testlet, even if Excel is closed and/or when navigating between simulations. Excel will only clear when beginning a new testlet. There is also an option to manually save any work.
    - Work done and calculations performed within Excel will not be graded. Many of Excel's less relevant features and some functions of Excel that may threaten user security will not work.
5. **Authoritative Literature:** The Authoritative Literature for AUD, FAR, and REG is available in every TBS testlet. You can use either the table of contents or the search function to locate the correct guidance. Note that although the AUD, FAR, and REG Authoritative Literature will be available for BEC TBSs, you do not need it. Practically speaking, it is just a distraction on the BEC section, and you should not spend any of your valuable time looking at it.
6. **Overview:** The overview lets you review and navigate the questions within a testlet. You can also use it to view, add, and remove bookmarks.
7. **Help:** The help icon provides important information about certain functions and tool buttons specific to the type of task you are working in. It also provides directions and general information but does not include information related specifically to the test content. It can be navigated via either the table of contents or the search bar.
8. **Submit Testlet:** There are two options when you choose this icon from the toolbar.
    - In any of the first four testlets, you will be asked to select either Return to Testlet or Submit Testlet. Return to Testlet allows you to review and change your answers in the current testlet. Submit Testlet takes you to the next testlet. After submitting your testlet, you will receive a prompt that allows for an optional break.
    - In the final testlet, you will be asked to select either Return to Testlet or Quit Exam. Choose Quit Exam if you wish to complete the exam. You will not be able to return to any testlet, and you will not receive credit for any unanswered questions. To prevent accidentally ending your exam, you will be asked to verify your selection, or you can choose Go Back. Upon verifying you wish to End Exam, you will be required to leave the test center with no re-admittance.

Navigation between simulations within a testlet is done using the number and arrow buttons directly beneath the toolbar or the arrow buttons at the bottom of the simulation. You can navigate between simulations within a testlet at any time before you submit the testlet.

Clicking on a number will take you to the corresponding simulation. Clicking on the bookmark icon beside the number on the left will flag the simulation to remind you to return to it before submitting the testlet.

Workspace: Task-Based Simulations have a designated workspace where all of the exam tools and exhibits open.

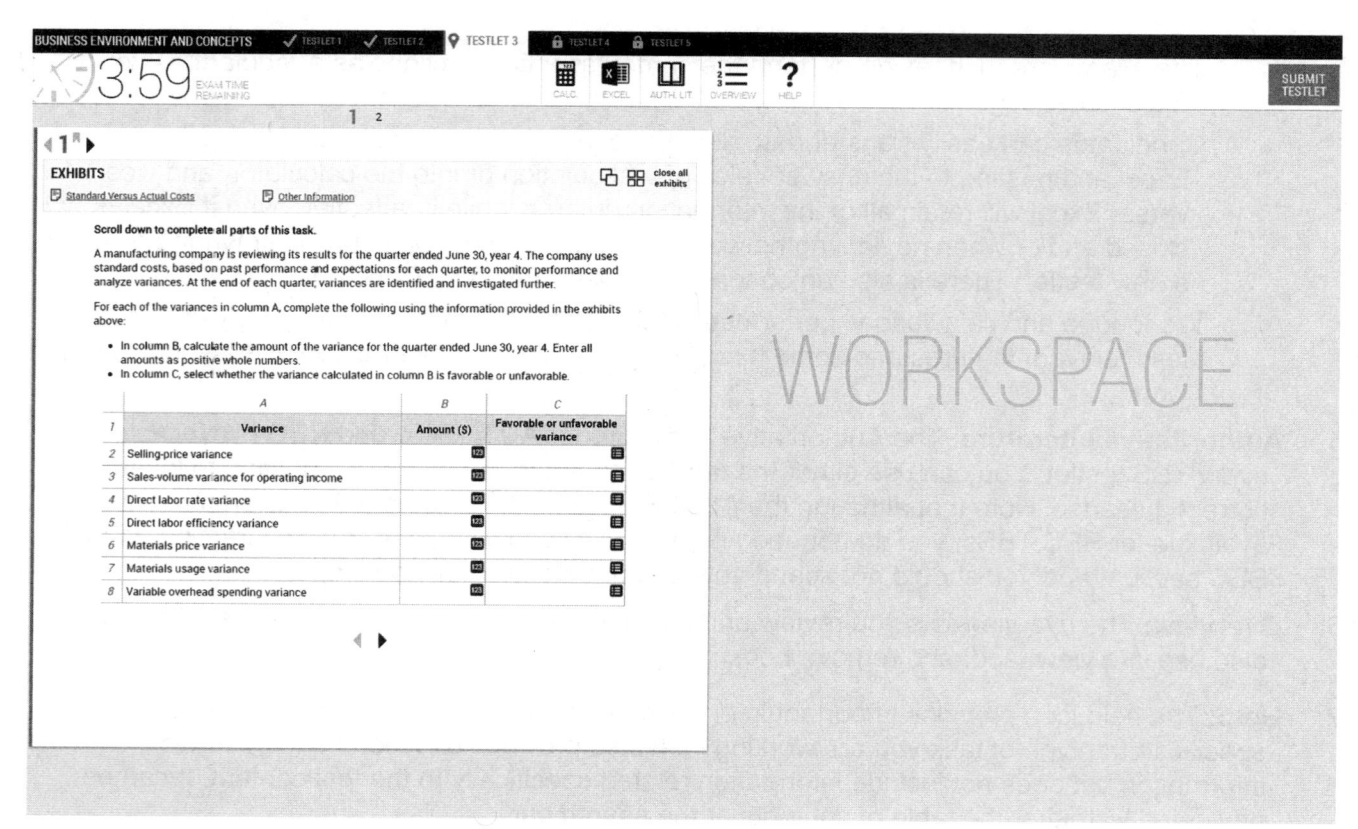

You can have multiple exam tools and exhibits open simultaneously, and you are able to freely resize and move each window.

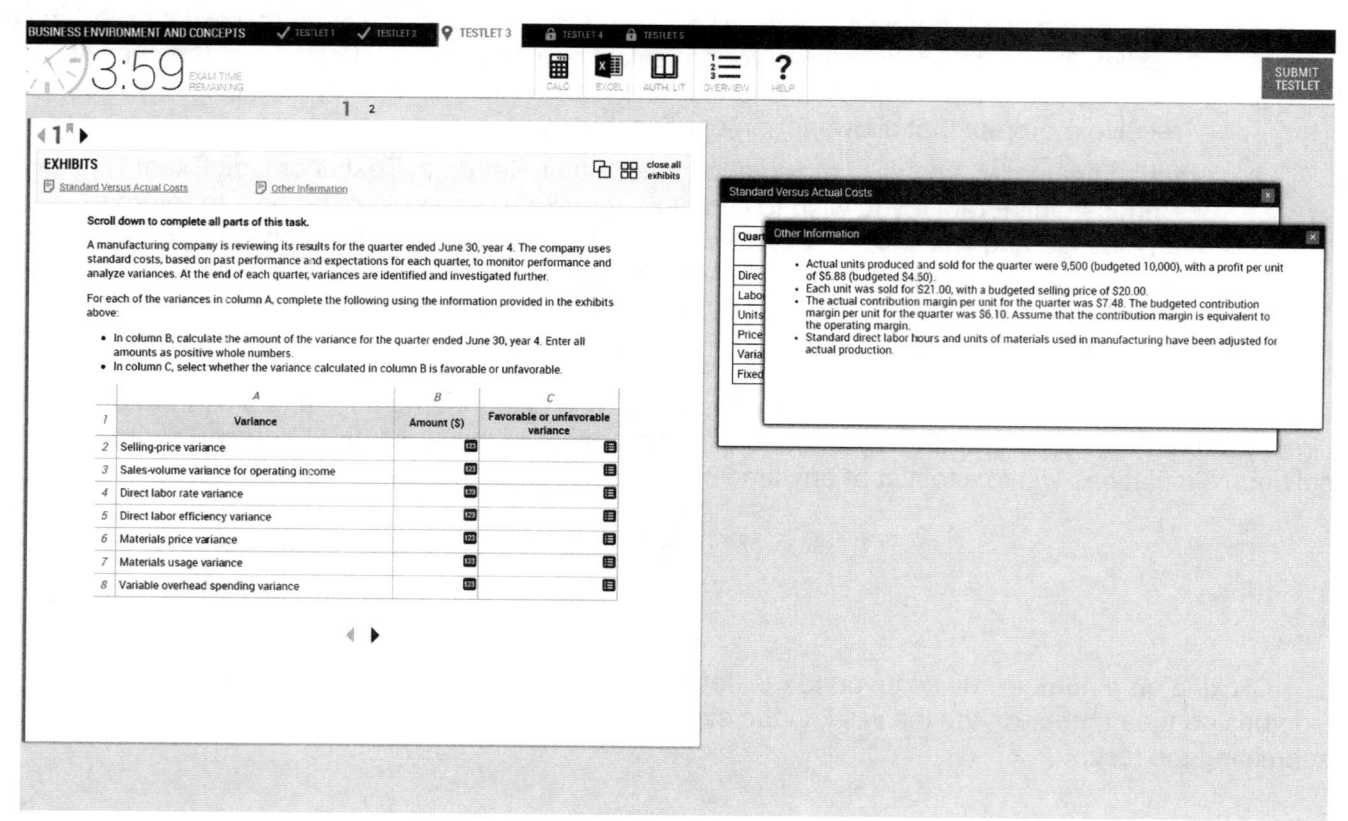

Answering Task-Based Simulations

Do not be intimidated by TBSs. Just learn the material and practice answering the different question types. Knowing **how** to work through the simulations is nearly as important as knowing what they test.

You can maximize your score on the TBS testlets of each exam section by following these suggested steps for completing Task-Based Simulations.

A. **Budget your time so you can finish before time expires.**
   1. Allot small segments of the total testing time to each specific task. We recommend you budget 18 minutes for each TBS.
   2. Track your progress to ensure you will have enough time to complete all the tasks.
   3. Use our Time Allocation Table to determine the time at which you need to start and finish each TBS testlet.

B. **Devote the first couple of minutes to scanning each TBS.**
   1. Spend no more than 2 minutes previewing the TBSs you received by clicking through the numbers beneath the toolbar at the top of the screen.
   2. You will be familiar with the layout of the TBSs if you have been practicing with Gleim TBSs under exam conditions.

C. **Answer all the tasks within the time limit for each testlet.**
   1. Read all of the exhibits (e.g., financial statements, memos, etc.) associated with the TBS you are working on before you attempt to answer the simulation.
      a. We have included detailed directions on using exhibits as source documents in the next section on Document Review Simulations. Much of those instructions can also be used when answering regular TBSs that contain exhibits.
   2. Do not skip any of the questions within a TBS. Make an educated guess if you are unsure of the answer and set a reminder for yourself by clicking the bookmark icon beside the TBS number at the top left of the simulation. There is no penalty for incorrect answers, so do not move on without at least selecting your best guess.

D. **Spend any remaining time wisely to maximize your points.**
   1. Ask yourself where you will earn the most points.
   2. Move from task to task systematically, reviewing and completing each one. Focus specifically on any TBS you flagged.
   3. Move on to the next TBS within the testlet or to the next testlet at the end of 18 minutes.

DOCUMENT REVIEW SIMULATIONS

Within the Task-Based Simulation testlets included in each CPA Exam section, you may find a Document Review Simulation (DRS). You are required to review various exhibits to determine the best phrasing of a particular document. The document will contain underlined words, phrases, sentences, or paragraphs that may or may not be correct. You then must select answer choices that indicate which (if any) changes you believe should be made in the underlined words, phrases, sentences, or paragraphs.

The DRSs always include the actual document you must review and correct and one or more exhibits. Exhibits vary from one DRS to the next because they contain the information to be used as sources for your conclusions. For example, these exhibits may be financial statements, emails, letters, invoices, memoranda, or minutes from meetings. You must read each DRS exhibit so that you are always aware of the resources available.

Answering Document Review Simulations

A. **Familiarize yourself with every part of the DRS.**

   Review each exhibit so you know what information is available. If your subject-matter preparation has been thorough, you should be able to identify quickly the most relevant information in each part of the DRS.

B. **Address every underlined portion of text in the DRS.**

   You must make an answer selection for every modifiable section of a DRS because each counts as a separate question. You will know an answer has been selected when you see that the white outline in the blue icon has changed to a white checkmark.

C. **Read the underlined section and answer choices carefully and completely.**

   Each underlined portion of text may have four to seven answer choices that may include the options to revise the text, retain the original text, or delete the text. Verify that each word or amount is correct in your choice before making your final selection.

D. **Clearly understand the information in the exhibits.**

   Quickly survey the various items; then analyze the most relevant facts specifically and refer to them to reduce the possible answer choices. Keep in mind that the relevant information may be presented or worded differently than the document you are revising.

E. **Double-check that you have officially responded to each underlined portion of text.**

   If you have time, go through the entire DRS once more to confirm that every underlined section has a white checkmark next to it.

Appendix B: Optimizing Your Score on the Task-Based Simulations (TBSs) and Written Communications (WCs)

WRITTEN COMMUNICATIONS (WCs)

Toolbar Icons and Operations

Each written communication contains a scenario that requires you to prepare a written memo or business letter in response. The following information and toolbar icons are located at the top of the testlet screen of each WC. The AICPA requires all candidates to review the Sample Test and Tutorials before sitting for the CPA Exam.

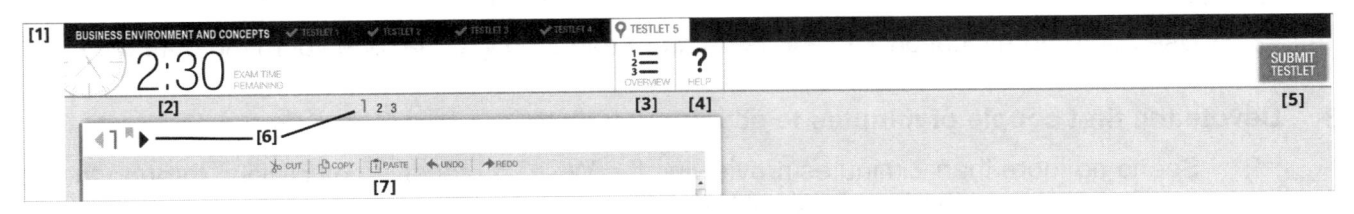

1. **Exam Section and Testlet Number:** The testlet number will always be 5 of 5 for the written communications in BEC.

2. **Time Remaining:** This information box displays how much time you have remaining in the entire exam. Consistently check the amount of time remaining in order to stay on schedule.

3. **Overview:** The overview lets you review and navigate the questions within a testlet. You can also use it to view, add, and review bookmarks.

4. **Help:** The help icon provides important information about certain functions and tool buttons specific to the type of task you are working in. It also provides directions and general information but does not include information related specifically to the test content. It can be navigated via either the table of contents or the search bar.

5. **Submit Testlet:** There are two options when you choose this icon from the toolbar.

    - In any of the first four testlets, you will be asked to select either Return to Testlet or Submit Testlet. Return to Testlet allows you to review and change your answers in the current testlet. Submit Testlet takes you to the next testlet. After submitting your testlet, you will receive a prompt that allows for an optional break.

    - In the final testlet, you will be asked to select either Return to Testlet or Quit Exam. Choose Quit Exam if you wish to complete the exam. You will not be able to return to any testlet, and you will not receive credit for any unanswered questions. To prevent accidentally ending your exam, you will be asked to verify your selection, or you can choose Go Back. Upon verifying you wish to End Exam, you will be required to leave the test center with no re-admittance.

6. **Navigation:** Navigation between simulations within a testlet is done using the number and arrow buttons directly beneath the toolbar or the arrow buttons at the bottom of the simulation. You can navigate between simulations within a testlet at any time before you submit the testlet. Clicking on a number will take you to the corresponding simulation. Clicking on the bookmark icon beside the number on the left will flag the simulation to remind you to return to it before submitting the testlet.

7. **Processor Tools:** You will be able to cut, copy, paste, undo, and redo by clicking on the appropriate icon above the response area.

Answering Written Communications

You can maximize your score on the written communications testlet by following these suggested steps for completing the WCs.

A. **Budget your time so you can finish before time expires.**
   1. Commit small segments of the total testing time to responding to each WC scenario.
   2. Track your progress so you have enough time to respond to all three scenarios.
   3. Use our Time Allocation Table to learn more about how to manage your time during the WCs.

B. **Devote the first couple of minutes to scanning each WC.**
   1. Spend no more than 2 minutes previewing the WCs you received by clicking through the navigation bar at the top of the screen.
   2. If you have been studying with the Gleim Premium CPA Review System, you will have used an exact emulation of the WCs on the CPA Exam and be comfortable with the layout already.

C. **Allocate 60 minutes to respond to the scenarios in the WC testlet.**
   1. Complete each response in no more than 20 minutes.
   2. Do NOT try to guess which is the ungraded pretest scenario. Respond to each scenario as though it counts!

D. **Now that you have spent most of your time responding to the scenarios, spend your remaining 15 minutes or so perfecting your responses for maximum points.**
   1. Edit your responses to ensure they meet the writing criteria of the AICPA and that you have effectively communicated your response.
   2. Move from scenario to scenario systematically, reviewing and completing each one.

Grading Written Communications

Your score on the WCs will make up 15% of your total score. The other 85% of your total score will be the sum of your scores on the multiple-choice testlets at 50% and the TBS testlets at 35%.

SUCCESS TIP

Your BEC Written Communications may cover topics outside the scope of the BEC Blueprint (i.e., they may relate to topics from the AUD, FAR, and/or REG Blueprints instead). Gleim includes written communication scenarios that cover all topics from all four sections of the exam in the Gleim system to ensure you are prepared. Also, while the graders are mainly evaluating your writing ability and will overlook minor technical mistakes, they will take content into account if your response contains egregious factual errors, off-topic information, or illegal advice. Therefore, you should (1) try to respond to each Written Communication as clearly as possible and (2) ensure that your response is free from off-topic or drastically incorrect information.

In the WCs, you will be graded on both technical content and writing skills. The AICPA's Sample Test states that the "technical content will be evaluated for information that is helpful to the intended reader and clearly relevant to the issue." It also states that writing skill scores will be based on three criteria from the AICPA: organization (structure, ordering of ideas, linking of ideas to one another), development (presentation of supporting evidence), and expression (use of standard business English). The AICPA advises that all responses "should provide the correct information in writing that is clear, complete, and professional. Only those writing samples that are generally responsive to the topic will be graded. If your response is off-topic, or offers advice that is clearly illegal, you will not receive any credit for the response."

Gleim has expanded the definitions of the AICPA's three writing skills criteria below. Note that the italics denote items taken from the AICPA; everything else is further clarification from Gleim.

Organization -- *the document's structure, ordering of ideas, and linking of one idea to another*

- *Overview/thesis statement*: Inform the reader of the overall purpose of the document; i.e., name the subject about which you are attempting to provide information.
- *Unified paragraphs (topic and supporting sentences)*: Make a statement, then use the remainder of the paragraph to back up that statement.
- *Transitions and connectives*: Words such as "because," "although," "however," and "moreover" allow you to connect related topics or shift the reader's attention to a new idea.

Development -- *the document's supporting evidence/information to clarify thoughts*

- *Details*: Simply asserting a fact, such as that debt on the balance sheet increases risk, is insufficient. The writer must describe the cause-and-effect relationship underlying this fact.
- *Definitions*: Accounting and finance terms, such as solvency and liquidity, may not be understood by the reader. The writer should explain them.
- *Examples*: The description of unfamiliar terms can be enhanced by the use of examples, such as the use of an expert system in the practice of distance medicine.
- *Rephrasing*: Stating an idea twice with different wording can also help the reader understand.

Expression -- *the document's use of conventional standards of business English*

- *Grammar (sentence construction, subject/verb agreement, pronouns, modifiers)*: Adherence to the basic rules of English grammar is essential.
- *Punctuation (final, comma)*: A period must be used to bring a complete sentence to a close. Commas should be used to separate items in lists as well as to separate clauses within a single sentence.
- *Word usage (incorrect, imprecise language)*: Business readers expect writers to avoid ambiguity and to choose the right word for the situation; for example, not to use the word "bond" where "note" is meant.
- *Capitalization*: The first word of a sentence and all proper names must be capitalized. Concepts and measures, such as liquidity and earnings per share, are not normally capitalized.
- *Spelling*: Business readers have an expectation that writers have a grasp of standard spelling conventions.

To help you gauge your proficiency in constructing a response that excels in all of the AICPA's criteria, the Gleim CPA Review Course allows you to assign a self-grade to your written communication responses. Self-grading your responses for practice written communication tasks will make you an expert on what the AICPA is looking for, and you will be able to quickly assess your response on the actual exam because you have practiced doing so during your studies.

You will grade yourself on technical content by noting (1) if your response is on-topic, (2) if you have any significant errors in the information you give, and (3) if you give any illegal advice. You will also grade yourself on a scale of 1 to 5 on each of the AICPA's writing skills criteria (organization, development, and expression). An average response is 3. Use 4 for better than average and 5 for outstanding. Use 2 for less than average and 1 for quite poor.

MANAGING TIME ON THE TBSs and WCs

Managing your time well during the CPA Exam is critical to success, so you must develop and practice your time management plan before your test date. The only help you will receive during your actual CPA Exam is a countdown of the hours and minutes remaining. When there are less than 2 minutes left in an exam section, the exam clock will begin to include the seconds and turn red, but you should be doing your final review by that point.

Each of the testlets on the exam is independent, and there are no time limits on individual testlets. Therefore, you must budget your time effectively to complete all five testlets in the allotted 4 hours.

The key to success is to become proficient in answering all types of questions in an average amount of time. When you follow our system, you'll have 2-17 minutes of total extra time (depending on the section) that you will be able to allocate as needed.

Each exam will begin with three introductory screens that you must complete in 10 minutes. Time spent in the introductory screens does not count against the 240 minutes you get for the exam itself. Then you will have two MCQ testlets. Each testlet contains half the total number of MCQs for that section (36/testlet for AUD, 31/testlet for BEC, 33/testlet for FAR, and 38/testlet for REG). Based on the total time of the exam and the amount of time needed for the other testlets, you should average 1.25 minutes per MCQ.

The final three testlets in AUD, FAR, and REG will have eight TBSs each: two in Testlet #3, three in Testlet #4, and three in Testlet #5. BEC will have four TBSs in two testlets, then a final testlet of three Written Communications (WCs). We suggest you allocate approximately 18 minutes to answering each TBS. On BEC, budget 25 minutes for each of the three WCs (20 minutes to answer, 5 minutes to review and perfect your response).**

To make the most of your testing time during the CPA Exam, you will need to develop a time management system and commit to spending a designated amount of time on each question. To assist you, please refer to the Gleim Time Management System.

**BEC candidates may prefer to allocate more time to the TBSs and reduce the 17 minutes of extra review time after the WCs. In this case, we suggest 20 minutes per TBS, for a total time of 40 minutes in Testlet 3 and 40 minutes in Testlet 4, leaving 9 minutes of final review after the WCs.

Appendix B: Optimizing Your Score on the Task-Based Simulations (TBSs) and Written Communications (WCs)   649

The table below shows how many minutes you should expect to spend on each testlet for each section. Remember, you cannot begin a new testlet until you have submitted a current testlet, and once you have submitted a testlet, you can no longer go back to it.

Time Allocation per Testlet (in minutes)

Testlet	Format	AUD	BEC**	FAR	REG
1	MCQ	45	38*	41*	47*
2	MCQ	45	38*	41*	47*
3	TBS	36	36	36	36
15-Minute Break					
4	TBS	54	36	54	54
5	TBS/WC	54	75	54	54
Total		234	223	226	238
Extra Time		6	17	14	2
Total Time Allowed		240	240	240	240

*Rounded down

The exam screen will show hours:minutes remaining. Focus on how much time you have, NOT the time on your watch. Using the times above, you would start each testlet with the following hours:minutes displayed on-screen:

Completion Times and Time Remaining

	AUD	BEC**	FAR	REG
Start	4 hours 0 minutes	4 hours 0 minutes	4 hours 0 minutes	4 hours 0 minutes
After Testlet 1	3 hours 15 minutes	3 hours 22 minutes	3 hours 19 minutes	3 hours 13 minutes
After Testlet 2	2 hours 30 minutes	2 hours 44 minutes	2 hours 38 minutes	2 hours 26 minutes
After Testlet 3	1 hour 54 minutes	2 hours 8 minutes	2 hours 2 minutes	1 hour 50 minutes
15-Minute Break				
After Testlet 4	1 hour 0 minutes	1 hour 32 minutes	1 hour 8 minutes	0 hours 56 minutes
After Testlet 5	0 hours 6 minutes	0 hours 17 minutes	0 hours 14 minutes	0 hours 2 minutes

Next, develop a shorthand for hours:minutes. This makes it easier to write down the times on the noteboard you will receive at the exam center.

	AUD	BEC**	FAR	REG
Start	4:00	4:00	4:00	4:00
After Testlet 1	3:15	3:22	3:19	3:13
After Testlet 2	2:30	2:44	2:38	2:26
After Testlet 3	1:54	2:08	2:02	1:50
15-Minute Break				
After Testlet 4	1:00	1:32	1:08	0:56
After Testlet 5	0:06	0:17	0:14	0:02

**BEC candidates may prefer to allocate more time to the TBSs and reduce the 17 minutes of extra review time after the WCs. In this case, we suggest 20 minutes per TBS, for a total time of 40 minutes in Testlet 3 and 40 minutes in Testlet 4, leaving 9 minutes of final review after the WCs.

The following pages of this appendix contain four example TBSs and three example WCs. We have included three written communication scenarios and a variety of TBS types, including Option List, Numeric Entry, Global Response Grid, and DRS, along with suggestions on how to approach each type. The answer key and our unique answer explanations for each TBS as well as an example response for each WC appear at the end of the appendix.

Again, do not substitute answering TBSs or WCs in your Gleim CPA Review Course with answering the ones presented here. Refer to these only for guidance on how to approach these difficult elements of the exam. It is vital that you practice answering TBSs and WCs in the digital environment of our online course so that you are comfortable with such an environment during your CPA Exam.

IT NETWORKS: OPTION LIST

The following TBS is an Option List, which is in essence multiple-choice questions. This type of task requires that you select a response from a list of choices. Some Option List TBSs may also require Numeric Entry type responses.

Select from the option list provided the term that best fits the network described in each item below. Each choice may be used once, more than once, or not at all.

Network	Term
1. An entity decentralizes the processing of tasks and data storage, as well as the assignment of these functions, to multiple computers in separate locations.	
2. A small company uses a network arrangement to make every device directly connected.	
3. An organization connects each office to a local Internet service provider and routes data through the shared, low-cost public Internet.	
4. A company uses the public Internet with password-required access to communicate with its customers.	
5. A company uses a link among devices in its headquarters building to enhance its productivity.	
6. An organization shares information within the organization by applying Internet connectivity standards and web software to its internal network.	
7. A company provides its customers with reliable, high-speed, and secure data transmission through a private network.	
8. A network of all networks all over the world.	
9. An organization is considering using a LAN arrangement utilizing various servers.	
10. The Internet and the public telephone system are typical examples of this kind of network.	

Option List

- Distributed processing
- Local area network (LAN)
- Wide area network (WAN)
- Client-server model
- Peer-to-peer arrangement
- Value-added network (VAN)
- Virtual private network (VPN)
- Intranet
- Extranet
- Internet

ABSORPTION VS. VARIABLE COSTING: NUMERIC ENTRY

This type of TBS requires that you calculate and then respond with some kind of number, e.g., an amount of currency, a ratio, etc. After clicking a cell, a field will appear that will automatically format your response. Be sure to review the formatted response before finalizing your answer. Some Numeric Entry TBSs may also require Option List type responses, which are in essence multiple-choice questions.

Galaxy Co. is a manufacturer of a single product. During January of Year 7, variable costs per unit and total fixed costs were constant, and the entity had no beginning or ending work-in-process or spoiled units.

After considering the exhibits, calculate the following amounts using absorption costing and variable costing. Enter those amounts in the shaded cells below. Enter all amounts as positive whole numbers.

	Absorption costing	Variable costing
1. January manufacturing cost per unit		
2. January 31 inventory		
3. January gross profit or contribution margin		

ABSORPTION VS. VARIABLE COSTING: EXHIBITS

Subject: January production
From: Ryan Jones, Production Manager
To: Ken Thomas, VP of Operations
Date: Year 7-02-10

Dear Ken:

January was a very good month in the production department. By producing 50,000 units, we surpassed the monthly goal by approximately 10%. We also achieved our other goals of matching actual unit costs with standard unit manufacturing costs of $6 for direct materials, $10 for direct labor, and $1 for variable overhead. Barring no breakdowns of equipment, we should be able to reach or surpass our goals for this month as well.

Best regards,

Ryan

Appendix B: Optimizing Your Score on the Task-Based Simulations (TBSs) and Written Communications (WCs)

Galaxy Co.
Trial Balance (partial)
January 31, Year 7

	Debit	Credit
Sales (51,000 units)		$1,530,000
Total manufacturing overhead	$150,000	
Variable selling and administrative costs	50,000	
Fixed selling and administrative costs	200,000	

Galaxy Co.
Balance Sheet*
December 31, Year 6

Assets
Current assets
   Cash $135,000
   Accounts receivable   19,000
   Inventory (5,000 units)   95,000
Total current assets $249,000
Noncurrent assets
   Equipment $76,000
   Accumulated depreciation   (24,000)
Total noncurrent assets   52,000
Total assets   **$301,000**

Liabilities
Current liabilities
   Accounts payable $ 34,000
   Accrued expenses   7,000
Total current liabilities $ 41,000
Noncurrent liabilities   26,000
Total liabilities   **$ 67,000**

Shareholders' Equity
Retained earnings $134,000
Common stock   100,000
Total shareholders' equity $234,000

Total liabilities and shareholders' equity   **$301,000**

*The applicable financial reporting framework is U.S. GAAP.

FINANCING POLICIES: GLOBAL RESPONSE GRID

> In Global Response Grid simulations, each distinct question has its own response table. This TBS is a type of Global Response Grid that uses both Numeric Entry and Option List questions.

Use the information provided in the exhibits to answer the following questions regarding Aaron, Inc.

For each option, select from the option list provided the correct type of policy. Each choice may be used once.

Option	Type of policy
1. Option 1	
2. Option 2	
3. Option 3	

Option List
Conservative policy
Moderate policy
Aggressive policy

For each type of capital, enter the appropriate amount in the designated cell to indicate the correct amount of capital in Year 8.

Capital type	Amount
4. Temporary Working Capital for Year 8	
5. Permanent Working Capital for Year 8	

For each fund type, select from the option list provided the correct financing type. Each choice may be used once, more than once, or not at all.

Fund	Type of financing
6. Mortgage bonds	
7. Debentures	
8. Preferred stock	
9. Term loan	
10. Common stock	
11. Commercial paper	
12. Retained earnings	
13. Trade credit	

Option List
Long-term financing
Spontaneous financing
Short-term financing

FINANCING POLICIES: EXHIBITS

Summary of Working Capital Structure

Aaron, Inc.

Year	Working Capital during Slack Season	Working Capital during Peak Season
Year 6	$55 million	$65 million
Year 7	$55 million	$72 million
Year 8	$55 million	$70 million

Appendix B: Optimizing Your Score on the Task-Based Simulations (TBSs) and Written Communications (WCs)

To: Gary Hayes, CEO
From: Juliana Hall, Controller
Date: October 6, Year 8
Subject: Financing options

Hi Gary,

I am emailing you per our previous correspondence regarding the financing options for our new project. My team has determined several possible levels of working capital that involve fundamental decisions regarding our firm's liquidity and the maturity composition of the debt portfolio.

I have listed the three financing options below. Each option has advantages and disadvantages. I will discuss further details at our next meeting.

- Option 1: $75 million equity and long-term debt against long-term assets, permanent working capital, and temporary working capital; $5 million short-term overdrafts and bank loans against temporary working capital.
- Option 2: $50 million equity and long-term debt against long-term assets and permanent working capital; $30 million short-term overdrafts and bank loans against permanent working capital and temporary working capital.
- Option 3: $65 million equity and long-term debt against long-term assets and permanent working capital; $15 million short-term overdrafts and bank loans against temporary working capital.

For your reference, I have attached a summary of our firm's working capital structure for the most recent 3 years.

Please let me know if you have any questions.

Regards,

Juliana

To: Juliana Hall, Controller
From: Frank Blake, Accounting Manager
Date: October 1, Year 8
Subject: Financing options

Hi Juliana,

As you requested, below are the current outstanding amounts of our capital funds.

Sources of funds	Dollar amount (in millions)
1. Mortgage bonds ($1,000 par, 7.5% due Year 26)	$105
2. Debentures ($1,000 par, 8% due Year 25)	215
3. Preferred stock ($100 par, 7.5%)	90
4. Term Loan (due in 11 months)	10
5. Common stock ($10 par)	100
6. Commercial paper	25
7. Retained earnings	325

Let me know if you need more information.

Frank

DOCUMENT REVIEW SIMULATION (DRS)

> This type of TBS requires that you analyze certain words or phrases in a document to decide whether to (1) keep the current text, (2) replace the current text with different text, or (3) delete the text. You must review various exhibits (e.g., financial statements, emails, invoices, etc.) presented with the original document in order to find the information necessary for each response.

EXHIBITS   close all exhibits

- Boat Gear Sales Order Form
- Email

You are an assistant treasurer who is required to send a memo to your supervisor regarding trade discounts. Assume a 360-day year. Use the information in the exhibits on the following pages to edit the memo.

To revise the document, click on each segment of underlined text below and select the needed correction, if any, from the list provided. If the underlined text is already correct in the context of the document, select *[Original Text]* from the list. If removal of the underlined text is the best revision to the document, select *[Delete Text]* from the list if available.

To: Donna Marie, Treasurer
From: Marco Henry, Assistant Treasurer
RE: Analyzing vendor discounts

As you requested, I investigated the credit terms of our current vendor, Boat Gear, Inc., and our possible future vendor, Boat King, Inc. Our current vendor offers us the following credit terms:

<u>We can save enough money from simply taking the discounts our current vendor offers by ordering more than 30 items</u> instead of waiting until the last day of the payment period.

- [A] *[Original Text]* We can save enough money from simply taking the discounts our current vendor offers by ordering more than 30 items
- [B] We can save enough money from simply taking the discounts our current vendor offers by paying by the 30th day after the invoice is received
- [C] We can save enough money from simply taking the discounts our current vendor offers by paying by the 15th day after we receive the goods
- [D] We can save enough money from simply taking the discounts our current vendor offers by paying by the 15th day after the invoice is received

<u>The vendor is offering a 3.5% discount.</u>

- [A] *[Original Text]* The vendor is offering a 3.5% discount.
- [B] The vendor is offering a 15% discount.
- [C] The vendor is offering a 30% discount.

Given our purchases of $475,000, we could offset many other expenses with this windfall. If we do not take the discount, we will need to <u>pay the entire balance by the 15th day.</u>

- [A] *[Original Text]* pay the entire balance by the 15th day.
- [B] pay the partial balance by the 60th day.
- [C] pay the entire balance by the 45th day.
- [D] pay the entire balance by the 30th day.
- [E] pay the partial balance by the 30th day.

-- Continued on next page --

Appendix B: Optimizing Your Score on the Task-Based Simulations (TBSs) and Written Communications (WCs)   657

-- Continued from previous page --

EXHIBITS   close all exhbits

📄 Boat Gear Sales Order Form   📄 Email

Based on my calculation, <u>the cost of not taking discounts offered by Boat King is 59% and is higher than the other option.</u>

- [A] *[Original Text]* the cost of not taking discounts offered by Boat King is 59% and is higher than the other option.
- [B] the cost of not taking discounts offered by Boat King is 74% and is lower than the other option.
- [C] the benefit from taking Boat King's discount is 74% and is higher than the other option.
- [D] the benefit from taking Boat Gear's discount is 87% and is lower than the other option.
- [E] the benefit from taking Boat Gear's discount is 72% and is higher than the other option.

Therefore, I concluded that the most attractive option for us is to <u>purchase from Boat King, pay in 45 days, and borrow from the bank.</u>

- [A] *[Original Text]* purchase from Boat King, pay in 45 days, and borrow from the bank.
- [B] purchase from Boat King, pay in 60 days, and do not borrow from the bank.
- [C] purchase from Boat Gear, pay in 15 days, and borrow from the bank.
- [D] purchase from Boat Gear, pay in 30 days, and do not borrow from the bank.
- [E] purchase from Boat Gear, pay in 15 days, and do not borrow from the bank.

I have attached a copy of my detailed calculation. Please let me know what you think.

Best,

Marco

DRS: EXHIBITS

To: Marco Henry, Assistant Treasurer
From: Donna Marie, Treasurer
Subject: Analyzing vendor discounts

Hello Marco,

Per our conversation, we did not take any vendor discount in the past as our company does not have enough cash on hand. I believe taking discounts can save us money even though we would have to borrow from a bank at an annual rate of 15% to take any cash discounts. Additionally, we are considering purchasing from a new vendor, Boat King, Inc., if they provide better credit terms than our current vendor. Boat King offers credit terms of 3/45, net 60.

Please compare the two vendors and let me know your thoughts.

Thanks,

Donna

Sales Order Form

Boat Gear, Inc.

327 S. Main Street
Seattle, WA 98101

Sold To: Sub Arctic Marine Supply, Inc.
1515 SW 9th Lane
Anchorage, AK 99507

Ship To: Sub Arctic Marine Supply, Inc.
1515 SW 9th Lane
Anchorage, AK 99507

Order Date	Shipped Via	Customer Purchase Order No.	Payment	Remarks
October 1, Year 8	Freight	A123	3.5/15 net 30	Purchase order received by phone

Item Code	Description	Qty	Unit Price	Amount
076X	Life Preserver	3	$25.00	$75.00
092B	Marine Oil	6	35.00	210.00
372N	Disinfectant Wipes	800	.05	40.00
259B	Band Aids	400	.10	40.00
172C	Antifreeze	1	45.00	45.00
	Subtotal			$410.00
	Other Charge			—
	Discount			—
	Sales Tax			—
	TOTAL			**$410.00**

Accepted By _Jason Humboldt, Sales Manager_ Date _October 2, Year 8_

Boat Gear, Inc., Sales Order Number _953288174_

Appendix B: Optimizing Your Score on the Task-Based Simulations (TBSs) and Written Communications (WCs) — 659

WRITTEN COMMUNICATION 1

> The following are three Written Communications. Respond to each scenario in a memo or other appropriate form of communication. Your response will be graded on your ability to logically organize and relay information.
>
> NOTE: Your Written Communications on the actual CPA Exam may cover topics outside the scope of the BEC Blueprint (i.e., they may relate to topics from the AUD, FAR, and/or REG Blueprints instead). Answer to the best of your ability, and remember that graders are mainly evaluating your writing ability and will overlook minor technical mistakes.

CUT   COPY   PASTE   UNDO   REDO

Pine Company has hired you to be its first Chief Risk Officer. As part of your job duties, you must explain the COSO Enterprise Risk Management (ERM) framework to executive management.

Prepare a memo to executive management summarizing the framework. In your summary, discuss the purpose of the framework, its components, and a principle related to each component.

Type your communication in the response area below.

REMINDER: Your response will be graded for technical content and writing skills. Technical content will be evaluated for information that is helpful to the intended audience and clearly relevant to the issue. Writing skills will be evaluated for development, organization, and the appropriate expression of ideas in professional correspondence. Use an appropriate business format with a clear introduction, body, and conclusion. Do not convey information in the form of a table, bullet-point list, or other abbreviated presentation.

Memorandum

To: Executive Management, Pine Company
Re: COSO Enterprise Risk Management (ERM) Framework

WRITTEN COMMUNICATION 2

The partners of Packitup Partnership are considering the decision to convert to the corporate form of business organization. During your discussions with them, you determine that they have only the vaguest ideas about the relationship between corporate debt and equity.

Prepare a memo to the partners of Packitup Partnership describing the concept of solvency, the two main components of corporate capital, and how capital structure decisions affect the risk profile of a firm.

Type your communication in the response area below.

REMINDER: Your response will be graded for technical content and writing skills. Technical content will be evaluated for information that is helpful to the intended audience and clearly relevant to the issue. Writing skills will be evaluated for development, organization, and the appropriate expression of ideas in professional correspondence. Use an appropriate business format with a clear introduction, body, and conclusion. Do not convey information in the form of a table, bullet-point list, or other abbreviated presentation.

Memorandum

To: Packitup Partnership
Re: Solvency and capital structure

WRITTEN COMMUNICATION 3

✂ CUT　📋 COPY　📥 PASTE　↶ UNDO　↷ REDO

Cyclone, Inc., has no chief information officer or information security officer. During your review of its operations, you discover that it decided to do business with its suppliers through electronic networking to take advantage of the cost savings without considering the security or infrastructure implications.

Prepare a memo to the CEO of Cyclone, Inc., distinguishing the Internet, an intranet, and an extranet, as well as a description of data encryption and the two principal types.

Type your communication in the response area below.

REMINDER: Your response will be graded for technical content and writing skills. Technical content will be evaluated for information that is helpful to the intended audience and clearly relevant to the issue. Writing skills will be evaluated for development, organization, and the appropriate expression of ideas in professional correspondence. Use an appropriate business format with a clear introduction, body, and conclusion. Do not convey information in the form of a table, bullet-point list, or other abbreviated presentation.

Memorandum

To: CEO, Cyclone, Inc.
Re: Electronic networking and encryption

TBS ANSWERS 1 OF 4

1. IT Networks (10 Gradable Items)

1. <u>Distributed processing.</u> Distributed processing involves the decentralization of processing tasks and data storage and assigning these functions to multiple computers, often in separate locations.

2. <u>Peer-to-peer arrangement.</u> Very small networks with few devices can be connected using a peer-to-peer arrangement, in which every device is directly connected.

3. <u>Virtual private network (VPN).</u> A VPN is a privately owned WAN and is a relatively inexpensive means to solve the problem of the high cost of leased lines. An entity can connect each office or LAN to a local Internet service provider and route data through the shared, low-cost public Internet.

4. <u>Extranet.</u> An extranet consists of the linked intranets of two or more organizations. It typically uses the public Internet as its transmission medium but requires a password for access.

5. <u>Local area network (LAN).</u> A LAN is any interconnection among devices in a single office or building. The development of the LAN resulted from the need to increase productivity.

6. <u>Intranet.</u> An intranet permits sharing of information throughout an organization by applying Internet connectivity standards and web software to the organization's internal network.

7. <u>Value-added network (VAN).</u> A VAN is a privately owned WAN that provides its customers with reliable, high-speed, and secure transmission of data.

8. <u>Internet.</u> The Internet is a network of networks all over the world.

9. <u>Client-server model.</u> In a client-server arrangement, servers are centrally located and devoted to the functions that are needed by all network users. The client-server model is the most cost-effective and easy-to-administer arrangement for LANs.

10. <u>Wide area network (WAN).</u> A WAN consists of a conglomerate of LANs over widely separated locations. It can be either publicly or privately owned. The Internet and the public telephone system are examples of publicly owned WANs.

TBS ANSWERS 2 OF 4

2. Absorption vs. Variable Costing (6 Gradable Items)

Absorption Costing

1. $19. (50,000 × $6) direct materials + (50,000 × $10) direct labor + (50,000 × $1) variable manufacturing overhead + [$150,000 − (50,000 × $1)] fixed manufacturing overhead = $950,000 total manufacturing cost

   $950,000 ÷ 50,000 units = $19 manufacturing cost per unit

2. $76,000. 5,000 units beginning inventory + 50,000 units manufactured − 51,000 units sold = 4,000 units ending inventory

   4,000 units ending inventory × $19 = $76,000 ending inventory

3. $561,000.

Sales (51,000 × $30)		$1,530,000
Cost of goods sold:		
Beginning inventory[1]	$ 95,000	
Cost of goods manufactured ($19 × 50,000)	950,000	
Minus: Ending inventory	(76,000)	(969,000)
Gross profit		$ 561,000

   [1] The applicable financial reporting framework is U.S. GAAP. This framework requires that inventories be measured at absorption cost. The January beginning inventory equals the December ending inventory.

Variable Costing

1. $17. (50,000 × $6) direct materials + (50,000 × $10) direct labor + (50,000 × $1) variable manufacturing overhead = $850,000 total manufacturing cost

   $850,000 ÷ 50,000 units = $17 manufacturing cost per unit

2. $68,000. 5,000 units beginning inventory + 50,000 units manufactured − 51,000 units sold = 4,000 units ending inventory

   4,000 units ending inventory × $17 = $68,000 ending inventory

3. $613,000.

Sales (51,000 × $30)		$1,530,000
Minus: Variable costs		
Manufacturing ($17 × 51,000)	$867,000	
Selling and administrative	50,000	(917,000)
Contribution margin		$ 613,000

TBS ANSWERS 3 OF 4

3. Financing Policies (13 Gradable Items)

1. <u>Conservative policy.</u> A conservative financing policy seeks to minimize liquidity risk by financing temporary working capital mostly with long-term debt and equity. Because Option 1 mainly uses long-term financing to finance long-term assets, permanent working capital, and temporary working capital, it is a conservative policy.

2. <u>Aggressive policy.</u> An aggressive financing policy reduces liquidity and accepts a higher risk of short-term cash shortages. Because Option 2 mainly uses short-term financing to finance temporary working capital and permanent working capital, it is an aggressive financing policy.

3. <u>Moderate policy.</u> Option 3 uses less long-term financing to finance temporary working capital than Option 1. But it uses more long-term financing to finance temporary working capital than Option 2. It is a moderate policy.

4. <u>$15,000,000.</u> As the firm's needs for working capital change on a seasonal basis, temporary working capital is increased or decreased. During the peak season, the firm requires more working capital to meet the needs of increasing sales. Temporary working capital in Year 8 is $15 million ($70 million – $55 million permanent working capital).

5. <u>$55,000,000.</u> Some liquid current assets must be maintained to meet the firm's long-term minimum needs regardless of the firm's level of activity or profitability. During the slack season in Year 6, Year 7, and Year 8, permanent working capital is $55 million.

Definitions

Spontaneous financing: Financing is spontaneous when current liabilities, such as trade payables and accruals, occur naturally in the ordinary course of business. Trade credit is created when suppliers offer the firm goods and services with payment delayed for a short time.

Short-term financing: Commercial paper consists of short-term notes payable issued in large denominations by corporations with high credit ratings to other corporations and institutional investors. Because the term loan is due in 11 months, it is short-term financing.

Long-term financing: Long-term financing includes long-term debt and equity financing. Mortgage bonds, debentures, preferred stock, common stock, and retained earnings are permanent financing.

6. <u>Long-term financing.</u>
7. <u>Long-term financing.</u>
8. <u>Long-term financing.</u>
9. <u>Short-term financing.</u>
10. <u>Long-term financing.</u>
11. <u>Short-term financing.</u>
12. <u>Long-term financing.</u>
13. <u>Spontaneous financing.</u>

Appendix B: Optimizing Your Score on the Task-Based Simulations (TBSs) and Written Communications (WCs)

TBS ANSWERS 4 OF 4

4. Document Review (5 Gradable Items)

1. <u>D) We can save enough money from simply taking the discounts our current vendor offers by paying by the 15th day after the invoice is received.</u> Payment term 3.5/15 net 30 means that if the customer pays the bill within 15 days of the invoice date, the customer can deduct 3.5% of the price. Otherwise the invoice amount is due in full 30 days from the invoice date. Thus, the company can save money by paying by the 15th day after the invoice date.

2. <u>A) *[Original Text]* The vendor is offering a 3.5% discount.</u> If the payment term is 3.5/15 net 30, the customer can pay the bill within 15 days of the invoice date at 96.5% (100% − 3.5%) of the price. Thus, 3.5% is the discount rate.

3. <u>D) pay the entire balance by the 30th day.</u> If the payment term is 3.5/15 net 30, the customer needs to pay the entire balance by the 30th day.

4. <u>E) the benefit from taking Boat Gear's discount is 72% and is higher than the other option.</u>

    Boat King:

    Cost of not taking discounts = [3% ÷ (100% − 3%)] × [360 days ÷ (60-day payment period − 45-day discount period)]
    = 3.0928% × 24
    = 74%

    Because the bank charges an annual interest rate of 15%, the benefit from (cost of not taking) Boat King's discount is 59% (74% − 15%) and is lower than the other option.

    Boat Gear:

    Cost of not taking discount = [3.5% ÷ (100% − 3.5%)] × [360 days ÷ (30-day payment period − 15-day discount period)]
    = 3.6269% × 24
    = 87%

    Because the bank charges an annual interest rate of 15%, the benefit from (cost of not taking) Boat Gear's discount is 72% (87% − 15%) and is higher than the other option.

5. <u>C) purchase from Boat Gear, pay in 15 days, and borrow from the bank.</u> Because the benefit from taking Boat Gear's discount is higher than the benefit from taking Boat King's discount, the company should purchase from Boat Gear, pay in 15 days, and borrow from the bank.

On the following pages you will find an example of responses at writing skill level 5 for each Written Communication. The Grading Written Communications section beginning on page 646 of this appendix has more information on what constitutes a level 5 response. These examples are intended to provide you with tips about how to structure sentences and state your ideas when completing Written Communications on the BEC portion. All other suggested responses provided by Gleim throughout your online courses are writing skill level 5 responses that are on-topic and contain no egregious errors or illegal advice.

WC ANSWERS 1 OF 3

Written Communication 1

To: Executive Management, Pine Company
Re: COSO Enterprise Risk Management (ERM) Framework

Presented below is a summary of the COSO ERM framework, including its purpose, components, and a principle related to each component.

The purpose of the COSO ERM framework is to provide guidance on managing the risks involved in creating, preserving, and realizing value. The framework consists of five interrelated components and twenty principles distributed among the components. Each component is classified as either a supporting aspect or common process. The two supporting aspect components are (1) governance and culture and (2) information, communication, and reporting. The three common process components are strategy and objective-setting, performance, and review and revision.

The governance and culture component relates to the organization's tone, lines of responsibilities, and risk culture. A principle related to this component is that the board of directors exercises risk oversight. By comparison, management has day-to-day responsibility for ERM, and the CEO is accountable for ERM and achieving strategy and business objectives.

The strategy and objective-setting component provides guidance on setting strategy and business objectives that align with the organization's mission, vision, core values, and risk appetite. A principle related to this component is that the organization defines its risk appetite.

The performance component provides guidance on identifying risks, assessing their severity, prioritizing risks, responding to them, and developing a portfolio view of risk. Performance in this context relates to risk management practice, not to operating performance. A principle related to this component is that the organization identifies risks that affect the achievement of strategy and business objectives.

The review and revision component provides guidance on reviewing and revising ERM capabilities and practices in response to performance results and changes in strategy and business objectives. A principle related to this component is that the organization reviews entity performance results and considers risk.

The information, communication, and reporting component relates to the organization's practices of capturing, processing, managing (organizing and storing), and communicating timely and relevant information to identify risks that could affect strategy and business objectives. A principle related to this component is that the organization leverages its information systems to support ERM.

Thus, the COSO ERM framework should provide criteria for assessing whether the organization's ERM culture, capabilities, and practices together effectively manage risks to strategy and business objectives. When the components, principles, and supporting controls are present and functioning, ERM is reasonably expected to manage risks effectively and to help create, preserve, and realize value.

The above depicts a level 5 answer. Consult the Grading Written Communications section of this appendix for a description of the three writing skills criteria.

Self-Grade

Below, grade your response on technical content and writing skills. Bubble in the circle next to the most appropriate score for your response based on the criteria given. Your **total** score is the sum of your scores on all six items. The maximum score is 19 points.

Technical Content Evaluation

Was your response on topic?	O No [0]	O Mostly [1]	O Yes [2]
Did your response have any *significant* errors?	O 0 errors [1]	O 1 major error [–1]	O 2 or more major errors [–2]
Did your response contain any illegal advice?	O No [1]	O Yes [0]	

Writing Skills Evaluation

	Poor	Below Average	Average	Above Average	Outstanding
Organization	O 1	O 2	O 3	O 4	O 5
Development	O 1	O 2	O 3	O 4	O 5
Expression	O 1	O 2	O 3	O 4	O 5

Disclaimer: This scoring schedule was developed by Gleim Publications as a guideline only. The AICPA has not released specific information on how the Written Communications are graded.

WC ANSWERS 2 OF 3

Written Communication 2

To: Packitup Partnership
Re: Solvency and capital structure

Solvency is a firm's ability to pay its noncurrent obligations as they come due and remain in business in the long run. It differs from liquidity, the ability to remain in business in the short run. The key ingredients of solvency are the firm's capital structure and degree of leverage. A firm's capital structure includes its sources of financing, both long- and short-term. These sources can be in the form of debt (external sources) or equity (internal sources).

Debt is the creditor interest in the firm. The firm is contractually obligated to repay debtholders. The terms of repayment (i.e., timing of interest and principal payments) are specified in the debt agreement. If the return on debt capital exceeds the amount of interest paid, debt financing is advantageous. The return is increased because interest payments on debt are tax-deductible. The tradeoff is that increased debt increases the firm's risk. Debt must be paid regardless of whether the firm is profitable. When risk reaches a certain level, either the firm will have to pay a higher interest rate than its return on debt, or creditors will refuse to lend any more money.

Equity is the ownership interest in the firm. Equity is the permanent capital of an entity, contributed by the firm's owners in expectation of a return. However, a return on equity is uncertain because equity is only a residual interest in the firm's assets. It is residual because it is the claim remaining after all debt has been satisfied. Periodic returns to owners of excess earnings are dividends. The firm may be contractually obligated to pay dividends to preferred shareholders but not to common shareholders.

Capital structure decisions affect the risk profile of a firm. For example, a firm with a higher percentage of debt capital will be riskier than a firm with a higher percentage of equity capital. Thus, when the relative amount of debt is high, equity investors will demand a higher rate of return on their investments to compensate for the greater risk. But a firm with a relatively larger proportion of equity capital will be able to borrow at lower rates because debt holders will accept lower interest in exchange for the lower risk.

The above depicts a level 5 answer. Consult the Grading Written Communications section of this appendix for a description of the three writing skills criteria.

Self-Grade

Below, grade your response on technical content and writing skills. Bubble in the circle next to the most appropriate score for your response based on the criteria given. Your **total** score is the sum of your scores on all six items. The maximum score is 19 points.

Technical Content Evaluation

Was your response on topic?	o No [0]	o Mostly [1]	o Yes [2]
Did your response have any *significant* errors?	o 0 errors [1]	o 1 major error [–1]	o 2 or more major errors [–2]
Did your response contain any illegal advice?	o No [1]	o Yes [0]	

Writing Skills Evaluation

	Poor	Below Average	Average	Above Average	Outstanding
Organization	o 1	o 2	o 3	o 4	o 5
Development	o 1	o 2	o 3	o 4	o 5
Expression	o 1	o 2	o 3	o 4	o 5

Disclaimer: This scoring schedule was developed by Gleim Publications as a guideline only. The AICPA has not released specific information on how the Written Communications are graded.

WC ANSWERS 3 OF 3

Written Communication 3

To: CEO, Cyclone, Inc.
Re: Electronic networking and encryption

The Internet is a network of networks all over the world. The Internet facilitates inexpensive communication and information transfer among computers, with gateways allowing servers to interface with personal computers. Very high-speed Internet connections (the Internet backbone) carry signals around the world and meet at network access points.

An intranet permits sharing of information throughout an organization by applying Internet connectivity standards and web software to the organization's internal network. An intranet addresses the connectivity problems of organizations that have many types of computers. Its use is restricted to those within the organization.

An extranet consists of the linked intranets of two or more organizations, for example, of a supplier and its customers. It typically uses the public Internet as its transmission medium but requires a password for access.

Encryption technology is vital for the security, and therefore the success, of electronic commerce, especially with regard to transactions carried out over public networks. The sender's encryption program encodes the data prior to transmission. The recipient's program decodes it at the other end. Unauthorized users may be able to intercept the data, but without the encryption key, they will be unable to decode it.

Private-key, or symmetric, encryption is the less secure of the two because it uses only one key. The single key must be revealed to both the sender and recipient. Public-key, or asymmetric, encryption is more secure. The public key used by the sender for encoding is widely known, but the related private key used by the recipient for decoding is known only to the recipient.

The above depicts a level 5 answer. Consult the Grading Written Communications section of this appendix for a description of the three writing skills criteria.

Self-Grade

Below, grade your response on technical content and writing skills. Bubble in the circle next to the most appropriate score for your response based on the criteria given. Your **total** score is the sum of your scores on all six items. The maximum score is 19 points.

Technical Content Evaluation

Was your response on topic?	O No [0]	O Mostly [1]	O Yes [2]
Did your response have any *significant* errors?	O 0 errors [1]	O 1 major error [–1]	O 2 or more major errors [–2]
Did your response contain any illegal advice?	O No [1]	O Yes [0]	

Writing Skills Evaluation

	Poor	Below Average	Average	Above Average	Outstanding
Organization	O 1	O 2	O 3	O 4	O 5
Development	O 1	O 2	O 3	O 4	O 5
Expression	O 1	O 2	O 3	O 4	O 5

Disclaimer: This scoring schedule was developed by Gleim Publications as a guideline only. The AICPA has not released specific information on how the Written Communications are graded.

APPENDIX C
AICPA UNIFORM CPA EXAMINATION
BEC BLUEPRINT WITH GLEIM CROSS-REFERENCES

The AICPA has indicated that the Blueprints have several purposes, including to

- *Document the minimum level of knowledge and skills necessary for initial licensure.*
- *Assist candidates in preparing for the Exam by outlining the knowledge and skills that may be tested.*
- *Apprise educators about the knowledge and skills candidates will need to function as newly licensed CPAs.*
- *Guide the development of Exam questions.*

For your convenience, we have reproduced the AICPA's BEC Blueprint. We also have provided cross-references to the study units in this book that correspond to the Blueprint's coverage.

Appendix C: AICPA Uniform CPA Examination BEC Blueprint with Gleim Cross-References

Area I – Enterprise Risk Management, Internal Controls and Business Processes (20–30%)

Gleim Study Unit	Content group/topic	Remembering and Understanding	Application	Analysis	Evaluation	
SU 3	**A. Enterprise risk management (ERM)**					
	1. Purpose and objectives	✓				Define ERM within the context of the COSO ERM framework, including the purpose and objectives of the framework.
	2. Components and principles	✓				Identify and define the components, principles and underlying structure of the COSO ERM framework.
		✓				Understand the relationship among risk, business strategy and performance within the context of the COSO ERM framework.
			✓			Apply the COSO ERM framework to identify risk/opportunity scenarios in an entity.
	B. Internal controls					
SU 1	1. Purpose and objectives	✓				Define internal control within the context of the COSO internal control framework, including the purpose, objectives and limitations of the framework.
SU 1	2. Components and principles	✓				Identify and define the components, principles and underlying structure of the COSO internal control framework.
			✓			Apply the COSO internal control framework to identify entity-level risks (inherent and residual) related to an organization's compliance, operations and reporting (internal and external, financial and non-financial) objectives.
			✓			Apply the COSO internal control framework to identify risks related to fraudulent financial and non-financial reporting, misappropriation of assets and illegal acts, including the risk of management override of controls.
			✓			Apply the COSO internal control framework to identify controls to meet an entity's compliance, operations and reporting (internal and external, financial and non-financial) objectives at the entity and sub-unit level.
			✓			Describe the corporate governance structure within an organization (e.g., tone at the top, policies, steering committees, oversight and ethics).

Appendix C: AICPA Uniform CPA Examination BEC Blueprint with Gleim Cross-References   671

Area I – Enterprise Risk Management, Internal Controls and Business Processes (20–30%) (continued)

Gleim Study Unit	Content group/topic	Skill: Remembering and Understanding	Skill: Application	Skill: Analysis	Skill: Evaluation	Representative task
	B. Internal controls (continued)					
SU 2	3. Sarbanes-Oxley Act of 2002	✓				Identify and define key corporate governance provisions of the Sarbanes-Oxley Act of 2002.
			✓			Identify regulatory deficiencies within an entity by using the requirements associated with the Sarbanes-Oxley Act of 2002.
	C. Business processes					
SU 1, SU 2, SU 20		✓				Describe the types and purposes of accounting and financial reporting systems along with the related tools and software, and the benefits they provide to an entity's business processes.
		✓				Distinguish business process controls by type (e.g., preventive vs. detective, automated vs. manual).
			✓			Identify the sequence of steps and the information, documents, tools and technology commonly used in key business processes (e.g., sales, cash collections, purchasing, disbursements, human resources, payroll, production, treasury, fixed assets, general ledger and reporting).
			✓			Identify the appropriate System and Organization Controls (SOC) for Service Organizations report to meet a user entity's needs and review the SOC report to obtain information such as the period covered, modifications and complementary user entity controls.
			✓			Identify an appropriate mix of business process controls (e.g., segregation of duties, input edit checks, authorization and approval, verifications, physical controls, controls over standing data, spreadsheet controls, reconciliations and supervisory controls) to prevent or detect errors in transactions.

Area I – Enterprise Risk Management, Internal Controls and Business Processes (20–30%) (continued)

C. Business processes (continued)

Gleim Study Unit	Content group/topic	Skill: Remembering and Understanding	Skill: Application	Skill: Analysis	Skill: Evaluation	Representative task
			✓			Identify the appropriate techniques, methods, systems or other tools that could improve the performance of a process.
				✓		Identify the structured and unstructured data needed to perform data analytics related to a key business process and identify the appropriate analytic technique for a given purpose.
				✓		Analyze the flow of transactions represented in a narrative, flowchart, data diagram and system interface diagram to identify the risks in key business processes related to the completeness, accuracy and continued processing integrity in input, storage, processing and output processes.

Appendix C: AICPA Uniform CPA Examination BEC Blueprint with Gleim Cross-References 673

Area II – Economics (15–25%)

Gleim Study Unit	Content group/topic	Remembering and Understanding	Application	Analysis	Evaluation	Representative task
	A. Economic and business cycles — measures and indicators					
SU 4, SU 5		✓				Understand the business cycle (trough, expansion, peak, recession) and leading, coincident and lagging indicators of economic activity (e.g., bond yields, new housing starts, personal income and unemployment).
SU 4, SU 5		✓				Recall the characteristics of market types (e.g., perfect competition, monopolistic competition, oligopoly, monopoly) as well as the common competitive strategies in each type.
			✓			Explain the impact on an entity's industry and operations due to changes in government fiscal policies, monetary policies, regulations and trade controls.
	B. Market influences on business					
SU 4, SU 5			✓			Use the laws of supply and demand and elasticity measures to explain the effect on a product.
			✓			Calculate the effect of inflation on a product's real price or an entity's investments, debt and future expenses.
			✓			Explain how changes in currency markets impact an entity.
			✓			Explain the opportunity cost of a business decision.
				✓		Determine the impact of market influences on an entity's business strategy, operations and risk (e.g., increasing investment and financial leverage, innovating to develop new product offerings, seeking new foreign and domestic markets and undertaking productivity or cost-cutting initiatives).
				✓		Determine the business reasons for, and explain the underlying economic substance of, significant transactions (e.g., business combinations and divestitures, product line diversification, production sourcing and public and private offerings of securities).

Area II – Economics (15–25%) (continued)

Gleim Study Unit	Content group/topic	Skill				Representative task
		Remembering and Understanding	Application	Analysis	Evaluation	
	C. Financial risk management					
SU 6, SU 7	1. Market, interest rate, currency, liquidity, credit, price and other risks		✓			Calculate and use ratios and measures to quantify risks associated with interest rates, currency exchange, liquidity, prices, etc. in a business entity.
	2. Means for mitigating/controlling financial risks		✓			Identify strategies to mitigate financial risks (e.g., market, interest rate, currency and liquidity) and quantify their impact on a business entity.

Appendix C: AICPA Uniform CPA Examination BEC Blueprint with Gleim Cross-References 675

Area III – Financial Management (10-20%)

Gleim Study Unit	Content group/topic	Remembering and Understanding	Application	Analysis	Evaluation	Representative task
SU 8	**A. Capital structure**					
			✓			Describe an organization's capital structure and related concepts, such as cost of capital, asset structure, loan covenants, growth rate, profitability, leverage and risk.
			✓			Calculate the cost of capital for a given financial scenario.
	B. Working capital					
SU 9, SU 10	1. Fundamentals and key metrics of working capital management		✓			Calculate the metrics associated with the working capital components, such as current ratio, quick ratio, cash conversion cycle, inventory turnover and receivables turnover.
				✓		Detect significant fluctuations or variances in the working capital cycle using working capital ratio analyses.
SU 7, SU 9, SU 10	2. Strategies for managing working capital			✓		Compare inventory management processes, including pricing and valuation methods, to determine the effects on the working capital of a given entity.
				✓		Compare accounts payable management techniques, including usage of discounts, factors affecting discount policy, uses of electronic funds transfer as a payment method and determination of an optimal vendor payment schedule in order to determine the effects on the working capital of a given entity.
				✓		Distinguish between corporate banking arrangements, including establishment of lines of credit, borrowing capacity and monitoring of compliance with debt covenants in order to determine the effects on the working capital of a given entity.
				✓		Interpret the differences between the business risks and the opportunities in an entity's credit management policies to determine the effects on the working capital of a given entity.
				✓		Analyze the effects on working capital caused by financing using long-term debt and/or short-term debt.

Area III – Financial Management (10–20%) (continued)

Gleim Study Unit	Content group/topic	Skill: Remembering and Understanding	Skill: Application	Skill: Analysis	Skill: Evaluation	Representative task
SU 6, SU 7, SU 8, SU 11	C. Financial valuation methods and decision models					
		✓				Identify and define the different financial valuation methods and their assumptions, including but not limited to fair value, Black-Scholes, Capital Asset Pricing Model and Dividend Discount Model.
		✓				Identify and define the different financial decision models and assumptions involved in making decisions relating to asset and investment management, debt, equity and leasing.
		✓				Identify the sources of data and factors that management considers in forming the assumptions used to prepare an accounting estimate.
		✓				Describe the process and framework within which management exercises its responsibilities over the review and approval of accounting estimates.
			✓			Calculate the value of an asset using commonly accepted financial valuation methods.
				✓		Compare investment alternatives using calculations of financial metrics (e.g., payback period, net-present value, economic value added, cash flow analysis and internal rate of return), financial modeling, forecasting, projection and analysis techniques.
				✓		Compare options in a lease vs. buy decision scenario.

Appendix C: AICPA Uniform CPA Examination BEC Blueprint with Gleim Cross-References 677

Area IV – Information Technology (15–25%)

Gleim Study Unit	Content group/topic	Remembering and Understanding	Application	Analysis	Evaluation	Representative task
	A. Understanding of information technology (IT)					
SU 2, SU 12, SU 14		✓				Explain the role that IT personnel, processes and strategies play in IT governance and in supporting an entity's overall vision, strategy and business objectives.
		✓				Define the basics of hardware, software, databases, networks, mobile technology, etc. used by an entity internally, externally and through outsourcing arrangements (e.g., application service providers and cloud computing).
		✓				Understand the advantages, disadvantages, risks and other considerations associated with cloud computing and IT outsourcing arrangements, including the use of System and Organization Controls (SOC) for Service Organizations reports from third parties.
			✓			Identify the role and benefits of information systems (e.g., enterprise resource planning, e-commerce and supply chain management systems).
	B. Risk associated with IT					
SU 15	1. Risk assessment		✓			Identify IT-related risks and describe mitigation strategies given risk severity, probability and costs.
SU 13	2. Change management	✓				Understand the risks associated with an inadequate change control and change management process for an entity's information systems and processes, including acquisition, integration and outsourcing.
SU 15	3. Security, availability, confidentiality and privacy		✓			Identify system access and segregation of duties risks.
			✓			Identify the risks (e.g., cybersecurity and internal) associated with protecting sensitive and critical information (e.g., proprietary and personal information) within information systems (including processing, storing and transmitting information internally and with external parties).
			✓			Perform threat identification to identify risks related to information confidentiality.
			✓			Perform threat identification to identify risks related to system availability.

678   *Appendix C: AICPA Uniform CPA Examination BEC Blueprint with Gleim Cross-References*

Area IV – Information Technology (15–25%) (continued)

Gleim Study Unit	Content group/topic	Skill: Remembering and Understanding	Skill: Application	Skill: Analysis	Skill: Evaluation	Representative task
	C. Controls that respond to risks associated with IT					
SU 15	1. General IT controls	✓				Understand the controls and testing strategies used in selecting, developing and implementing new information systems.
			✓			Identify effective IT control activities, including manual, IT dependent and automated controls, as well as preventive, detective and corrective controls.
SU 15	2. Logical and physical controls		✓			Identify logical and physical access controls (e.g., roles and rights and segregation of duties).
			✓			Identify the controls associated with protecting sensitive and critical information (e.g., proprietary and personal) within information systems.
			✓			Determine responses to information system confidentiality risks (e.g., incident response plan).
SU 13	3. Business resiliency	✓				Understand the importance of business resiliency for an entity and the key strategies, resources, business functions, employees and steps involved in planning for it.
	D. Data management and relationships					
SU 15	1. Governance		✓			Recognize the legal, ethical, business intellectual property and customer sensitivity considerations that should be included in a data governance program that covers what data is needed, the necessary practices throughout the data life cycle and assignment of responsibility for the governance program.
SU 13, SU 15, SU 20	2. Extract, transform and load data		✓			Understand the capabilities needed in data extraction tools and the important considerations in making a data extraction request such as the data source, format and integrity of the data.
			✓			Understand key characteristics of a relational database (e.g., data dictionary, data types, tables, records, fields, relationships, keys, views, queries and reports).

Appendix C: AICPA Uniform CPA Examination BEC Blueprint with Gleim Cross-References   679

Area IV – Information Technology (15–25%) *(continued)*

Gleim Study Unit	Content group/topic	Remembering and Understanding	Application	Analysis	Evaluation	Representative task
	D. Data management and relationships *(continued)*					
	2. Extract, transform and load data *(continued)*	✓				Understand considerations associated with loading data into the final target database (e.g., operational data store, data warehouse or data lake) including the constraints that apply (e.g., uniqueness, referential integrity, mandatory fields), the types of loading (initial, incremental, full refresh) and load verification.
			✓			Define the attributes of a data repository such as its relevance, elements to be included or excluded, relationships between those elements and characteristics used to determine its validity, completeness and accuracy.
			✓			Determine methods to transform raw data (structured and unstructured) to make it useful for decision-making by correcting or removing data in the dataset that is incorrect, inaccurate, incomplete, improperly formatted or duplicated and to convert, aggregate, merge, replace, validate, format and split data.
SU 20	3. Visualization	✓				Understand the capabilities needed in tools that support data modeling and analysis.
		✓				Understand the data visualization techniques used to make patterns, trends and correlations more easily detected in support of better decisions.

Area V – Operations Management (15–25%)

Gleim Study Unit	Content group/topic	Skill: Remembering and Understanding	Skill: Application	Skill: Analysis	Skill: Evaluation	Representative task
SU 16	**A. Financial and non-financial measures of performance management**					
			>			Calculate financial and non-financial measures appropriate to analyze specific aspects of an entity's performance (e.g., Economic Value Added, Costs of Quality-Prevention vs. Appraisal vs. Failure).
				>		Determine which financial and non-financial measures are appropriate to analyze specific aspects of an entity's performance and risk profile (e.g., Return on Equity, Return on Assets and Contribution Margin).
	B. Cost accounting					
SU 17, SU 18	1. Cost measurement concepts, methods and techniques		>			Apply cost accounting concepts, terminology, methods and measurement techniques within an entity.
			>			Differentiate the characteristics of fixed, variable and mixed costs within an entity.
			>			Compare and contrast the different costing methods such as absorption vs. variable and process vs. job order costing.
SU 19	2. Variance analysis			>		Determine the appropriate variance analysis method to measure the key cost drivers by analyzing business scenarios.

Appendix C: AICPA Uniform CPA Examination BEC Blueprint with Gleim Cross-References 681

Area V – Operations Management (15–25%) (continued)

Gleim Study Unit	Content group/topic	Skill: Remembering and Understanding	Skill: Application	Skill: Analysis	Skill: Evaluation	Representative task
	C. Process management					
SU 16	1. Approaches, techniques, measures, benefits to process-management driven businesses	✓				Identify commonly used operational management approaches, techniques and measures within the context of business process management.
	2. Management philosophies and techniques for performance improvement	✓				Identify commonly used management philosophies and techniques for performance and quality improvement within the context of business process management.
	D. Planning techniques					
SU 19	1. Budgeting and analysis		✓			Prepare a budget to guide business decisions.
				✓		Reconcile results against a budget or prior periods and perform analysis of variances as needed.
SU 7, SU 9, SU 10, SU 11, SU 16, SU 17, SU 18, SU 19	2. Forecasting and projection		✓			Use forecasting and projection techniques to model revenue growth, cost and expense characteristics, profitability, etc.
			✓			Prepare and calculate metrics to be utilized in the planning process, such as cost benefit analysis, sensitivity analysis, breakeven analysis, economic order quantity, etc.
				✓		Analyze results of forecasts and projections using ratio analysis and explanations of correlations to, or variations from, key financial indices.
				✓		Compare and contrast alternative approaches (such as system replacement, make vs. buy and cost/benefit) proposed to address business challenges or opportunities for a given entity.

INDEX

100% stacked bar graphs................ 614

ABC................................... 543
Absorption (full) costing................ 511
Access controls........................ 456
Accounting
    Costs............................... 119
    Cycles............................. 41, 42
    Information System (AIS)............. 362
    Profits............................. 120
    Rate of return...................... 318
Accounts
    Payable............................. 48
        Turnover....................... 299
    Receivable turnover ratio............ 280
Acid-test ratio......................... 276
Acquisition............................ 164
Activity
    Analysis........................ 545, 568
    -Based costing (ABC)................ 543
    Drivers............................ 546
    Level.............................. 12
    Log............................... 426
Ad hoc reports......................... 361
Administrative expenses................. 506
Aggressive policy...................... 274
AI.................................... 368
AICPA Blueprints....................... 669
AIS................................... 362
Alternate processing facility............ 404
Analysis, SWOT.................... 354, 481
Analyze data........................... 606
Annual profit plan..................... 569
Annuities............................. 321
Anomaly detection...................... 606
Antidumping........................... 168
Application
    Controls........................... 459
    Development....................... 393
    Processing phases................... 358
    Service provider (ASP).............. 419
    Software.......................... 382
        Controls....................... 455
Applications programmers................ 349
Appraisal costs........................ 492
Arc method............................ 113
Arithmetic controls.................... 461
Array................................. 359
Artificial intelligence (AI)............ 368
Assimilation........................... 166
AU-C 402............................ 65, 66
Audit
    Committee.......................... 61
    Trail............................. 361
        EDI............................ 426
Authentication......................... 457
Authorization.......................... 458
    Of transactions.................... 436
Availability of data................... 451

Average
    Collection period.................. 281
    Payables period.................... 299
    Total cost......................... 125
Avoidable costs........................ 553

Back
    -Office functions.................. 364
    Testing............................ 227
Backup................................ 402
Balanced scorecard..................... 481
Bar graphs............................ 612
Barriers, entry........................ 133
Batch
    Input controls..................... 460
    Processing......................... 356
Benchmarking.......................... 491
Best practices........................ 491
Beta.................................. 224
BI.................................... 369
Big data.............................. 600
Bill of lading......................... 45
Binary................................ 384
Biometric technologies................. 457
BIS................................... 351
Bit................................... 384
Bitcoin............................... 383
Block................................. 382
Blockchain............................ 382
Blueprints, AICPA..................... 669
Board of directors.............. 28, 57, 61
Bonds................................. 240
    Advantages........................ 240
    Bearer............................ 242
    Callable.......................... 241
    Commodity-backed.................. 241
    Convertible....................... 241
    Disadvantages..................... 241
    Income............................ 242
    Mortgage.......................... 242
    Ratings........................... 242
    Registered........................ 242
    Revenue........................... 242
    Serial............................ 241
    Term.............................. 241
    Valuation......................... 242
    Variable rate..................... 241
    Zero-coupon/deep-discount......... 241
Boolean............................... 359
Bottleneck operation................... 486
Bottom-up approach..................... 13
Boycott............................... 135
BPR................................... 485
Breakeven point....................... 548
Bubble charts......................... 621

Budget... 569
   Capital... 575
   Cash... 576
   Cost of goods sold... 574
   Cycle... 570
   Direct
      Labor... 572
      Materials... 572
   Financial... 569, 575
   Manufacturing overhead... 573
   Master (comprehensive)... 569
   Nonmanufacturing... 574
   Operating... 569, 571
   Production... 571
   Purchases... 571
   Sales... 571
Business
   Continuity... 402
      Management (BCM)... 405
   Cycles... 148
   -Enabling functions... 29
   Impact analysis... 406
   Information system (BIS)... 351
   Intelligence (BI)... 369
   Model... 12
   Process... 11
      Design... 393
      Outsourcing... 167
      Reengineering (BPR)... 485
   Processes... 11, 23
   Recovery... 406
   Resiliency... 402
   Risk... 15, 211
   -To-
      Administration (B2A) e-commerce... 421
      Business (B2B) e-commerce... 422
      Consumer (B2C) e-commerce... 422
By-products... 521
Byte... 384

Call option... 192
   Intrinsic value... 194
Callback... 456
Capital
   Asset pricing model (CAPM)... 224
   Budgeting... 313
   Cost of... 252
   Rationing... 331
   Structure... 250
Cardinality... 387
Carrying costs... 292
Cartel... 135
CASE... 400
Case-based reasoning systems... 368

Cash
   Budget... 576
   Collection... 279
      Schedule... 576
   Conversion cycle... 299
   Disbursements... 48, 53
      Flowchart... 51, 52
      Schedule... 577
   Flow
      At risk (CFAR)... 227
      Patterns... 333
   Flows... 314
   Payments... 298
   -Receipts flowchart... 46, 47
Cause-and-effect diagram... 490
Centralization... 357
Change
   Identification... 26
   Management... 26
Check digit verification... 460
Chief executive officer (CEO)... 57
Choropleth (filled map)... 623
Clean/normalize data... 605
Client... 416
   -Server... 416
Clock cards... 55
Cloud computing... 352
COBIT... 438
   5... 439
   2019... 442
   Performance Management (CPM)... 444
Code of ethics... 56
Coefficient of
   Correlation... 218, 223
   Variation... 222
Coincident indicator... 149
Cold site... 405
Collection float... 279
Combined visualization... 625
Common
   Costs... 474, 520
   Stock... 246
Company risk... 212
Compensating balance... 303
Complementary user entity controls... 66
Complements... 107
Completeness... 461
Compliance
   Objectives... 20
   Risks... 15
Component costs of capital... 253
Components of internal control... 20
Compound interest... 317
Computer
   -Aided software engineering (CASE)... 400
   Processing... 436
   Systems, access controls... 456
Concurrent update control (concurrency control)... 392
Confidentiality of data... 451
Conflicting-interest transactions... 58
Conformance costs... 492
Consensus mechanism... 383
Conservative policy... 273
Constant
   Growth model... 247
   Returns to scale... 126

Index

Constraint. 486
Consumer-to-
    Administration (C2A) e-commerce. 421
    Business (C2B) e-commerce. 421
    Consumer (C2C) e-commerce. 421
Contingency planning. 402
Contraction. 148
Contractionary monetary policy. 162
Contributors and reviewers. iv
Control
    Activities. 23, 31
    Baseline. 26
    Environment. 21, 31
    EUC. 400
    Objectives for Information and Related
        Technology (COBIT). 438
    Revalidation/update. 26
Controllability. 473
Controls. 42
    Fraud. 31
Conversion
    Cost. 506
    Cutover. 398
    Parallel. 398
    Phased. 398
    Pilot. 398
Corporate
    Governance. 41, 56
    Opportunity. 59
Corrective controls. 454
Correlation analysis. 218
COSO
    Framework. 18
        Enterprise risk management. 78
        Internal control. 18
    Objectives. 18
Cost
    Accounting. 53
    Avoidable. 553
    -Based transfer prices. 474
    Center. 472, 475
    Conversion. 506, 537
    Incremental. 508, 553
    Marginal. 123
    Of
        Capital. 252
        Goods
            Manufactured. 507
            Sold. 507, 574
            Not taking a discount. 301
    Opportunity. 119, 508
    Pool. 506
    Prime. 506
    -Push inflation. 152
    -Volume-profit (CVP)
        Analysis. 548
        Multiple products (or services). 551
Costing
    Absorption (full). 511
    Activity-based (ABC). 543
    Job-order. 532
    Variable (direct). 512

Costs
    Currently attainable (practical) standards. 568
    Direct. 506
    EDI. 425
    Factory operating. 573
    Fixed. 509
    Ideal (theoretical) standards. 568
    Indirect. 506
    Joint (common). 474, 520
    Manufacturing. 506
    Mixed (semivariable). 509
    Nonmanufacturing. 506
    Of quality. 492
    Period. 506
    Product. 506
    Relevant. 508
    Selling (marketing). 506
    Separable. 520
    Standard. 567
    Sunk. 508
    Value-adding. 508
    Variable. 508
Countervailing duties. 169
Country risk. 211
CPI. 150
Credit default risk. 211
Crisis management. 405
Critical success factors (CSFs). 481
Cross-subsidization. 543
Cryptocurrency. 382
CSF
    Functions. 447
    Implementation steps. 448
Culture. 78
Currency options. 200
Current
    Assets. 271
    Liabilities. 271
    Ratio. 276
Currently attainable (practical) standards. 568
Customer relationship management (CRM). 354
Cutover conversion. 398
CVP analysis. 548
Cyber risk. 94
    Management. 94
        Program. 95
        Team. 95
Cybersecurity. 435
    Framework (CSF). 447
Cyclical unemployment. 153

Data. 350
    Administrators (DAs). 348
    Analytics. 599
        Methods. 606
    Capture. 358
    Classification. 445
    Cleaning. 605
    Custodian. 445
    Definition language. 392
    Democratization. 446
    Dictionary. 348, 392
    Files. 359
    Fusion. 601
    Item. 384
    Lakes. 390
    Librarians. 349
    Management. 599
    Manipulation language. 392
    Mining. 367, 599
    Normalization. 605
    Owner. 445
    Quality criteria. 452
    Semi-structured. 601
    Steward. 445
    Structured. 601
    Taxonomy. 445
    Type. 359, 599
    Unstructured. 601
    Visualization. 608
    Vulnerability. 436
    Warehouse. 366, 390
Database. 386
    Administrators (DBAs). 348
    Management system (DBMS). 348, 391
    View. 391
Days' sales in
    Inventory. 297
    Receivables. 281
Debentures. 242
Debt. 250
    Covenants. 245
Decentralization of information processing. . . 357, 415
Decision support system (DSS). 367
Decisions, make-or-buy. 556
Deculturation. 166
Defense
    First line of. 29
    Second line of. 29
    Third line of. 29
Deficient-demand unemployment. 153
Deflation. 152
Delphi approach. 226
Demand. 105
    Elasticity of. 113
    Kinked. 134
    Law of. 106
    Market. 109
    Price elasticity of. 113
    -Pull inflation. 152
Deming, W. Edwards. 493
Denial of service (DoS) attack. 437
Deposit slip. 47
Depression. 148
Derivatives. 191
Derived demand. 163
Descriptive analysis. 606

Detective controls. 454
Determinants of
    Demand. 107
    Supply. 109
Device authorization table. 456
Diagnostic analysis. 606
Digital
    Certificates. 450
    Dashboard. 369
    Signatures. 451
Direct
    Costs. 506
    Labor. 505
    Materials. 505
Disaster recovery. 402
    Plan (DRP). 403
Discount
    Rate. 162, 319
    Trade. 301
Discounted
    Cash flow analysis. 319
    Loans. 302
    Payback method. 330
Diseconomies of scale. 126
Disintermediation. 393
Disinvestment. 554
Distributed
    Database. 392
    Processing. 357, 415
Diversifiable risk. 212
Diversification. 222
    Concentric. 165
    Conglomerate. 165
    Horizontal. 165
Divestiture. 164
Dividend
    Discount model. 247
    Payout
        Models. 247
        Ratio. 249
    Yield ratio. 249
Dividends in arrears. 248
Domestic content rules. 168
DoS attack. 437
Dot maps. 624
Drill-down analysis. 366
DSS. 367
Dumb terminals. 357, 415
Duties, segregation of. 455
Duty of
    Care. 58
    Loyalty. 58

E-
    Business. 420
    Commerce. 420
Earnings at risk (EAR). 227

Economic
　Costs. 119
　Exposure. 200
　Indicators. 148
　Order quantity (EOQ). 292
　Profit. 120, 480
　Rate of return on common stock. 479
　Value added (EVA). 480
Economies of scale. 126
EDI. 424
Effective rate. 302
EFT. 423
Elasticity of
　Demand. 113, 114
　Supply. 115
Electronic
　Commerce. 420
　Data interchange (EDI). 424
　Funds transfer (EFT). 423
　Money. 424
Embargo. 168
Employment, full. 154
Encryption. 450, 456
End user. 349
　Computing (EUC). 400
Enterprise
　Resource planning (ERP). 364
　Risk management (ERM). 78
　　Implementation steps. 92
　　Limitations. 90
Entity-level controls. 23
Environmental controls. 457
Equity. 246, 250
Equivalent units of production (EUP). 539
ERM limitations. 90
ERP. 364
Error listings. 361, 461
ESS. 369
Estimated net realizable value (NRV) method. . . . 523
EUP. 539
　FIFO. 541
　Weighted average. 541
Exception reports. 361
Excess reserves. 160
Exchange rate
　Fluctuations. 198
　Risk. 211
　Systems. 183
Executive support system (ESS). 369
Exercise price. 193
Expansion. 148
Expansionary monetary policy. 162
Expected
　Rate of return. 220
　Value. 255
Expert system. 369
Explicit costs. 119
Export subsidies. 169
eXtensible
　Business reporting language (XBRL). 418
　Markup language (XML). 418
External
　Auditors. 29
　Failure costs. 492
　Parties. 29

Extranet. 417

Factoring. 279
Fault-tolerant computer systems. 405
Federal
　Funds rate. 161
　Open Market Committee (FOMC). 159
　Reserve. 159
Fiduciary duty. 58
Field. 384
　Checks. 459
File. 385
Financial
　Budget. 569
　Factors. 185
　Leverage. 244
　Reporting. 60
Financing, short-term. 301
Firewall. 458
First line of defense. 29
Fiscal policy. 155
Fishbone diagram. 490
Fixed costs. 509
Flexible budget. 578
　Variance. 584
Float. 359
　Collection. 279
　Disbursement. 279
Flowcharts. 42
Focus area. 444
FOH
　Spending variance. 585
　Volume variance. 585
Forecasting. 226, 571
Foreign currency. 181
Forward
　Contracts. 196, 200
　Discount. 190
　Premium. 190
　Rate. 190
Fractional reserve banking. 160
Fraud
　Awareness. 32
　Controls. 31
　Management program. 31
　Preventing. 32
　Risk assessment. 31
　Types. 31
Frictional unemployment. 153
Front-office functions. 364
Full
　Disclosure. 58
　Employment. 154
Future value (FV) of an amount. 320
Futures contracts. 196

Game theory. 135
Gamification. 491
Gap
　Inflationary. 156
　Recessionary. 156

G

General
- Controls ... 455
- Ledger ... 53
  - /Financial reporting system (GL/FRS) ... 362
Gleim, Irvin N. ... iii
Globalization ... 147
Goal congruence ... 473
Governance ... 56
- Controls ... 23
Gross
- Margin ... 511
- Profit margin ... 475

H

Hacktivist ... 94
Hadoop ... 600
Hardware ... 350
- Controls ... 455
Hash totals ... 460
Heat maps ... 622
Hedging ... 192, 199
Help desk ... 349
Hierarchical database ... 386
High-low method ... 219
Histogram ... 490, 614
Hot site ... 404
Human
- Involvement ... 436
- Reasoning ... 368
- Resources ... 53
Hurdle rate ... 319
Hyperlink ... 418
Hypertext markup language (HTML) ... 418

I

Ideal (theoretical) standards ... 568
Idiosyncratic risk ... 212, 222
Illegal
- Acts ... 31
- Pricing ... 164
Implicit costs ... 119
Import quotas ... 168
In-memory analytics ... 600
Income
- Nominal ... 151
- Real ... 151
Incremental costs ... 508
Indenture ... 240
Index, consumer price (CPI) ... 150
Indirect
- Costs ... 506, 533, 543
- Labor ... 505, 533
- Materials ... 505, 533
Inelastic
- Demand ... 114
- Supply ... 115
Inferior good ... 107
Inflation ... 150
- Cost-push ... 152
- Demand-pull ... 152
- Rate of ... 150
- Risk ... 211
Inflationary gap ... 156

Information
- And communication ... 24
- Discovery ... 605
- Resources management (IRM) ... 365
- Security ... 451
- Technology (IT) ... 350
  - Infrastructure Library (ITIL) ... 355
  - Operations ... 348
Infrastructure-as-a-Service (IaaS) ... 419
Inherent
- Limitations ... 30
- Risk ... 79
Input ... 351
- Controls ... 459
Insiders ... 94
Integer ... 359
Integrated systems ... 362
Integration ... 166
- Horizontal ... 165
- Vertical ... 165
Integrity of data ... 451
Intelligent agents ... 369
Interactive processing ... 356
Interest
- Compound ... 317
- Rate
  - Nominal ... 157
  - Real ... 157
- Simple ... 317
Internal
- Audit function ... 59
- Auditors ... 29
- Control ... 11
  - Classification ... 454
  - Components ... 20
  - Definition ... 18
  - Responsible parties ... 28
- Failure costs ... 492
- Growth rate ... 478
- Rate of return (IRR) ... 327
Internet of Things (IoT) ... 600
In-the-money ... 193
Intranet ... 417
Intrinsic value
- Call option ... 194
- Put option ... 195
Inventory ... 292
- Costs ... 292
- Replenishment ... 292
- Turnover ... 295
Investment
- Center ... 472, 475
- -Grade bonds ... 242
- Risk ... 212
- Securities ... 214
Invoice ... 45
IRR ... 327
ISO 9000 ... 494
IT steering committee ... 394

J

Job
- -Order costing ... 532
- Time tickets ... 55

Index

Joint
    Products. 520
    Venture. 164
Junk bonds. 242
Just-in-time (JIT) inventory. 293

Key
    Integrity. 461
    Performance indicators (KPIs). 13
    Process. 12
Keynesian theory. 156
Kinked demand. 134

Labor
    Efficiency variance. 583
    Rate variance. 583
Lagging indicator. 149
LAN. 416, 417
Law of supply. 108
Lead time. 292
Leading economic indicator. 149
Lean operation. 486
Learning curve
    Analysis. 484
    Limitation. 484
Ledger. 382
Legislators and regulators. 29
Leverage. 244
Librarians, data. 349
Limit (reasonableness) and range checks. 459
Line
    Charts. 617
    Of credit. 301, 304
Liquidity
    Ratios. 275
    Risk. 211
Load verification. 390
Loan. 301
Local area network (LAN). 416, 417
Lockbox system. 279
Logical controls. 457
Long
    Position. 191
    -Run average total cost (LRATC) curve. 125
Lower control limit (LCL). 488

M1. 158
M2. 158
Mainframe. 415
Make-or-buy decisions. 556
Malware. 437
Managed float exchange rate system. 183
Management
    And support processes. 12
    By exception. 581
    Information System (MIS). 362
    Oversight controls. 23
    Processes tiers. 447
    Reporting system (MRS). 362
    Working group. 92

Manufacturing
    Costs. 506
    Overhead. 505
Margin
    Of safety. 550
    Requirements. 162, 197
Marginal
    Analysis. 121
    Cost. 123
    Product. 121
    Revenue. 123
Mark-to-market. 197
Market
    -Based transfer prices. 474
    Capitalization. 246
    -Clearing
        Price. 109
        Quantity. 109
    Demand. 109
    Equilibrium. 109
    Price. 109
    Risk. 212, 223
        Premium. 224
    Structures. 127, 131, 133, 134
    Supply. 109
    Value at risk (VAR). 227
Master file. 359
Materials
    Price variance. 582
    Quantity variance. 582
    Requirements planning (MRP). 294
Maturity
    Matching. 273
    Risk. 211
Medium of exchange. 157
Merger. 164
Midpoint method. 113
Miners. 383
Minimum wage. 118
Misappropriation of assets. 31
Mitigating factors. 32
Mixed (semivariable) costs. 509
Mobile technology. 420
Monetary
    Multiplier. 160
    Policy. 161
        Contractionary. 162
        Expansionary. 162
Money
    Creation. 159
    Market hedges. 200
    Supply. 158
Monitoring. 25
Monopolistic competition. 133
Monopoly. 131
Monte Carlo simulation. 226
MRP. 294
Multiplier effect. 155

Nation-states and spies. 94
Natural monopoly. 131
Negotiated transfer prices. 474

Net
- Present value (NPV) 322
    - Profile 334
    - Profit margin 475
    - Working capital 276

Network 350
- Administrator 348
- Analysis 606
- Client-server 416
- Technicians 348

Neural networks 368
Nominal
- Income 151
- Interest rate 157

Nonconformance costs 492
Nonfinancial performance measures 475
Nonmanufacturing costs 506
Nonparticipating preferred stock 248
Normal
- Goods 107
- Profit 120

Normalization 387

Object-oriented databases 390
Off-shore operations 485
OLAP 366
Oligopoly 134
Online
- Analytical processing (OLAP) 366
- Payment system 424
- Processing 356

Open-market operations 161
Operating
- Budget 569
- Cash flow ratio 277
- Cycle 298
- Leverage 244
- Processes 11
- Profit margin 475
- System 381

Operational
- Management 29
- Risks 15

Operations
- Objectives 19
- Risk 211

Operators 349
Opportunity 79
- Cost 119, 508

Option premium 193
Options 192
- Valuing 193

Ordering costs 292
Organizational needs assessment 393
Organized criminal 94
Output 351
- Controls 461

Outsourcing 485
- Arrangements 418

Overapplied overhead 536

Overhead
- Allocation rate 534
- Overapplied 536
- Underapplied 536
- Variance 536
    - Integrated 587

Packing slip 45
Parallel conversion 398
Pareto diagram 489
Passwords 456
Payables
- Deferral period 299
- Turnover in days 299

Payback 329
- Period 329

Payment voucher 52
Payoff table 255
Payroll 53
- Register 55
- System flowchart 54, 55

PCAOB 62
Peak 148
Peanut-butter costing 543
Peer-to-peer 416
Penalties 64
Perfectly
- Elastic
    - Demand 114
    - Supply 115
- Inelastic
    - Demand 114
    - Supply 116

Period costs 506
Phased conversion 398
Phillips curve 154
Phishing 437
Physical
- Controls 456
- -Quantity method 522

Pie charts 617
Pilot conversion 398
Platform-as-a-Service (PaaS) 419
Point-of-sale (POS) 426
Political
- Events 147
- Risk 211

Porter's five forces analysis 354
Portfolio risk 222
Power failures 404
Predictive analysis 606
Preemptive right 246
Preference decision 314
Preferred stock 248
Preformatting 459
Prescriptive analysis 606
Present value (PV) of an amount 320
Prevention costs 492
Preventive controls 454

Price
- Ceilings. 116
- Controls. 116
- Discrimination. 164
- Elasticity of
  - Demand. 113
  - Supply. 115
- Floors. 117
- Index. 150
- Maker. 131
- Searcher. 131
- Supports. 117
- Takers. 127

Pricing, illegal. 164
Prime cost. 506
Principal risk. 211
Private information systems. 401
Pro forma
- Balance sheet. 578
- Income statement. 574
- Statement of cash flows. 578

Probability. 220
- Distribution. 220

Process
- -Level controls. 24
- Costing. 537
- Mapping. 14
- Reengineering. 425

Processing. 351
- Controls. 461

Product
- -Cost cross-subsidization. 543
- (Inventoriable) costs. 506, 511

Production. 53
Profit
- Center. 472, 475
- Margin. 475
- Maximization. 124
- Plan, annual. 569

Profitability index. 331
Program
- Change control. 399
- Development. 400

Projects. 12
- Nonroutine. 12

Protectionism. 168
Prototyping. 400
Public
- Accounting firm. 62
- Company Accounting Oversight Board (PCAOB). 62
- -Key (asymmetric) encryption. 450
- -Switched networks. 417

Purchase
- Costs. 292
- Order. 50
- Requisition. 50

Purchases-payables
- -Cash disbursements. 48
- Flowchart. 49, 50

Purchasing. 48
- Power. 184

Pure
- Competition. 127
- Profit. 120

Put option. 192
- Intrinsic value. 195

Quality. 493
- Costs of. 492
- Management system (QMS). 494

Quantity
- Demanded. 105
- Supplied. 108

Quick (acid-test) ratio. 276

Rate
- Discount. 162
- Of return. 215
  - Expected. 220
  - Required. 213

Ratio
- Accounts receivable turnover. 280
- Current. 276
- Debt to
  - Equity. 252
  - Total assets. 251
- Long-term debt to equity capital. 252
- Operating cash flow. 277
- Quick (acid-test). 276
- Times-interest-earned. 251
- Total debt. 252
  - To
    - Equity capital. 252
    - Total capital. 251
- Working capital. 276

Rationing decision. 314
Ratios
- Capital structure. 251
- Inventory. 295
- Liquidity. 275

REA processing. 360
Real
- Income. 151
- Interest rate. 157
- -Time processing. 356

Receivables. 279
- Formulas. 280

Receiving report. 43, 48
Recession. 148
Recessionary gap. 156
Record. 385
- Count. 460, 461

Recovery. 148
- Center. 404

Redundant array of inexpensive discs (RAID). . . 405
Referential integrity. 387
Regression analysis. 216
Reintermediation. 393
Reinvestment rate. 335
Relational database. 387
Relevance. 474
Relevant
- Costs. 508
- Data. 605
- Range. 510
- Revenues and costs. 553

Reliance on others. 58

692   Index

Remittance
    Advice. 45
    Listing. 47
Reorder point, inventory. 292
Repatriation. 169
Reporting
    Objectives. 19
    Risks. 15
Required rate of return. 213
Reserve ratio. 160
Residual
    Income. 477
    Risk. 79
Resource
    Drivers. 546
    Markets. 163
Responsibility centers. 471
Retention. 478
Return. 215
    On
        Assets (ROA). 478
        Common equity (ROCE). 479
        Investment (ROI). 476
    Rate of. 215
Revenue
    Bonds. 242
    Center. 472, 475
    Effect on total. 115
    Marginal. 123
Reviewers and contributors. iv

Risk. 16, 79
    And return. 212, 215
    Appetite. 16, 79
    Assessment. 16, 21, 401, 403
        Tools. 227
    -Averse. 212
    Business
        Information system. 435
        Process. 11, 15
    Capacity. 79
    Company. 212
    Cyber. 94
    Diversifiable. 222
    -Free rate. 213, 224
    Identification. 16
    Idiosyncratic. 212, 222
    Inherent. 79
    Investment. 212
    Investor attitudes toward. 212
    Management. 16
        Enterprise. 78
        Leader. 92
        Processes. 16
    Monitoring. 16
    -Neutral. 213
    Portfolio. 222
    Premium. 213
    Profile. 15
    Residual. 79
    Responses. 16, 86
    Return principles. 211
    Security. 222
    -Seeking. 213
    Systematic. 212, 223
    Tolerances. 22
    Undiversifiable. 223
    Unsystematic. 212, 222
Robotic process automation (RPA). 368
Roles and responsibilities within the IT function. . . 348
RSS. 352
Rule-based expert systems. 369
Rules
    Antidumping. 168
    Domestic content. 168
Run-to-run control totals. 461

Safeguarding of assets. 19, 32
Safety stock. 292
Sales
    Forecast. 571
    Order. 45
    Price variance. 590
    -Receivables
        -Cash receipts. 43
        Flowchart. 44, 45
    -Value at split-off method. 522
    Variances. 590
    Volume variance. 590
Sarbanes-Oxley Act of 2002. 61
Scatter plots. 619
Schema. 392
Scrap. 510
Screening decision. 314

SDLC... 395
    Acceptance, installation, implementation... 398
    Build and development... 396
    Definition... 396
    Initiation, feasibility, planning... 396
    Operations and maintenance... 399
    System design... 396
    Testing and quality control... 396
Second line of defense... 29
Section 404... 63
Security risk... 222
Segregation of duties... 23, 43, 348, 436, 455
Self
    -Checking digits... 460
    -Dealing... 58
Sell or process further... 520
Selling (marketing) costs... 506
Semi-structured data... 601
Senior management... 28
Sensitivity analysis... 226
Separable costs... 520
Separation... 166
Sequence checks... 459, 461
Servers... 416
Service
    Auditor... 65
    Organizations... 65
    Providers... 29
Shared services... 485
Shareholder return... 249
Short
    Position... 191
    -Run average total cost (SRATC) curve... 125
Simple
    Interest... 317
        Loan... 302
        Regression... 216
Simulation... 226
Sinking fund... 240
Six Sigma... 487
Smart cards... 424
SmartAdapt... 2
Sniffing... 450
Social media... 423
Software... 350, 381
    -As-a-Service (SaaS)... 419
Solvency... 251
Special orders... 555
Split-off point... 520
Spoilage... 510
Spontaneous financing... 272
Spot rate... 190
SQL... 392
Stacked
    Area charts... 616
    Bar graphs... 614
Stakeholders... 56
    In business information systems... 351
Standard
    Costs... 567
    Currently attainable (practical)... 568
    Deviation... 221
    Ideal (theoretical)... 568

Statement
    Cash flow... 578
    Management... 63
    Pro forma income... 574
Static (master) budget... 578
Statistical
    Control charts... 488
    Process control (SPC)... 488
Stock
    Common... 246
    Preferred... 248
Stockout costs... 292
Storage... 351
Store of value... 157
Stovepipe systems... 362
Strategic
    Business units (SBUs)... 472
    Risks... 15
String... 359
Structural unemployment... 153
Structured
    Data... 601
    Query Language (SQL)... 392
Subservice organization... 65
Substitutes... 107
Substitution effect... 163
Sunk costs... 508
Supply... 108
    Chain... 365
    Of money... 158
    Shock... 152
Sustainability... 170
SWOT analysis... 354, 481
Symmetric encryption... 450
System
    Availability... 435
    Controls... 455
    Database management... 391
    Design, SDLC... 396
    Internal control... 63
    Operating... 381
Systematic risk... 212, 223
Systems
    Analyst... 349
    Control... 400
    Development life cycle... 395
    Information... 24
        Private... 401
    Programmers... 349
    Software... 381

Target
    Net income... 551
    Operating income... 550
Tariffs... 168
Term loan... 301
Terrorist... 94
Tests of controls... 66
Text
    Analysis... 606
    Mining... 600
Theory of constraints (TOC)... 486
Third line of defense... 29

Three-
- Tiered architecture. 416
- Way overhead variance analysis. 587

Time
- Series analysis. 226
- Value of money. 316

Timekeeping. 53
TOC. 486
Tone at the top. 28
Top-down approach. 12

Total
- Debt ratio. 251
- Product. 121
- Quality management (TQM). 493

Tracing. 426

Trade
- Barriers. 168
- Discount. 301
- Related factors. 185

Transaction
- Exposure. 199
- File. 360
- -Level controls. 24, 42
- Logs. 461
- Processing system (TPS). 356
- Trails. 435

Transfer
- Payments. 155
- Pricing. 473

Transformation. 351
Translation exposure. 201
Treadway Commission. 18
Treemap. 625
Trigger price mechanism. 168
Trojan horse. 437
Trough. 148
Two-way overhead variance analysis. 587

Unauthorized access. 436
Underapplied overhead. 536
Underlying. 192
Undiversifiable risk. 223
Unemployment. 153
- Cyclical. 153
- Deficient-demand. 153
- Frictional. 153
- Rate. 153
- Structural. 153

Uniform resource locator (URL). 418
Unique risk. 212
Unit of account. 157

Unitary elasticity of
- Demand. 114
- Supply. 115

Unstructured data. 601
Unsystematic risk. 212, 222
Upper control limit (UCL). 488
URL. 418

User
- Auditor. 65
- Entity. 65

Uses of money. 157
U.S. Treasury securities. 161
Usury laws. 116

Utility programs. 381

Validation. 461
Validity checks. 459

Value
- -Added networks (VANs). 417, 426
- Expected. 255

Variable
- Cost. 508
- (Direct) costing. 512

Variance
- Analysis. 579, 581
- Sales. 590

Variety. 602
- -Based value. 603

Velocity. 603
- -Based value. 603
- Of money. 158

Veracity. 603
- -Based value. 603

Virtual private networks (VPNs). 417
Virus. 404, 437

VOH
- Efficiency variance. 584
- Spending variance. 584

Volatility of data files. 359
Volume. 602
- -Based value. 603

Voucher. 53

Wage. 117
Warm site. 405
Webmaster. 349

Weighted-average
- Cost of capital (WACC). 257
- Method. 541

Wide area network (WAN). 417
Working capital. 271
- Net. 276
- Ratio. 276

World Wide Web. 418
Worm. 437

XBRL. 418
XML. 418

Yield curve. 240

Zero-balance
- Account. 298
- Checks. 460